Mixed Race America and the Law

CRITICAL AMERICA

General Editors: Richard Delgado and Jean Stefancic

White by Law: The Legal Construction of Race
Ian F. Haney López

Cultivating Intelligence: Power, Law, and the Politics of Teaching
Louise Harmon and Deborah W. Post

Privilege Revealed: How Invisible Preference Undermines America
Stephanie M. Wildmand with Margalynne Armstrong, Adrienne D. Davis, and Trina Grillo

Does the Law Morally Bind the Poor? or What Good's the Constitution When You Can't Afford a Loaf of Bread?
R. George Wright

Hybrid: Bisexuals, Multiracials, and Other Misfits under American Law
Ruth Colker

Critical Race Feminism: A Reader
Edited by Adrien Katherine Wing

Immigrants Out! The New Nativism and the Anti-Immigrant Impulse in the United States
Edited by Juan F. Perea

Taxing America
Edited by Karen B. Brown and Mary Louise Fellows

Notes of a Racial Caste Baby: Color Blindness and the End of Affirmative Action
Bryan K. Fair

Please Don't Wish Me a Merry Christmas: A Critical History of the Separation of Church and State
Stephen M. Feldman

To Be an American: Cultural Pluralism and the Rhetoric of Assimilation
Bill Ong Hing

Negrophobia and Reasonable Racism: The Hidden Costs of Being Black in America
Jody David Armour

Black and Brown in America: The Case for Cooperation
Bill Piatt

Black Rage Confronts the Law
Paul Harris

Selling Words: Free Speech in a Commercial Culture
R. George Wright

The Color of Crime: Racial Hoaxes, White Fear, Black Protectionism, Police Harassment, and Other Macroaggressions
Katheryn K. Russell

The Smart Culture: Society, Intelligence, and Law
Robert L. Hayman, Jr.

Was Blind, But Now I See: White Race Consciousness and the Law
Barbara J. Flagg

The Gender Line: Men, Women, and the Law
Nancy Levit

Heretics in the Temple: Americans Who Reject the Nation's Legal Faith
David Ray Papke

The Empire Strikes Back: Outsiders and the Struggle over Legal Education
Arthur Austin

Interracial Justice: Conflict and Reconciliation in Post–Civil Rights America
Eric K. Yamamoto

Black Men on Race, Gender, and Sexuality: A Critical Reader
Edited by Devon Carbado

When Sorry Isn't Enough: The Controversy over Apologies and Reparations for Human Injustice
Edited by Roy L. Brooks

Disoriented: Asian Americans, Law, and the Nation State
Robert S. Chang

Rape and the Culture of the Courtroom
Andrew E. Taslitz

The Passions of Law
Edited by Susan A. Bandes

Global Critical Race Feminism: An International Reader
Edited by Adrien Katherine Wing

Law and Religion: Critical Essays
Edited by Stephen M. Feldman

Changing Race: Latinos, the Census, and the History of Ethnicity
Clara E. Rodríguez

From the Ground Up: Environmental Racism and the Rise of the Environmental Justice Movement
Luke Cole and Sheila Foster

Nothing but the Truth: Why Trial Lawyers Don't, Can't, and Shouldn't Have to Tell the Whole Truth
Steven Lubet

Critical Race Theory: An Introduction
Richard Delgado and Jean Stefancic

Playing It Safe: How the Supreme Court Sidesteps Hard Cases
Lisa A. Kloppenberg

Why Lawsuits Are Good for America: Disciplined Democracy, Big Business, and the Common Law
Carl T. Bogus

How the Left Can Win Arguments and Influence People: A Tactical Manual for Pragmatic Progressives
John K. Wilson

Aftermath: The Clinton Impeachment and the Presidency in the Age of Political Spectacle
Edited by Leonard V. Kaplan and Beverly I. Moran

Getting over Equality: A Critical Diagnosis of Religious Freedom in America
Steven D. Smith

Critical Race Narratives: A Study of Race, Rhetoric, and Injury
Carl Gutiérrez-Jones

Social Scientists for Social Justice: Making the Case against Segregation
John P. Jackson, Jr.

Victims in the War on Crime: The Use and Abuse of Victims' Rights
Markus Dirk Dubber

Original Sin: Clarence Thomas and the Failure of the Constitutional Conservatives
Samuel A. Marcosson

Policing Hatred: Law Enforcement, Civil Rights, and Hate Crime
Jeannine Bell

Destructive Messages: How Hate Speech Paves the Way for Harmful Social Movements
Alexander Tsesis

Environmental Injustice in the Valley of Dreams: Immigrant Workers, Ecological Destruction, and the High-Tech Global Economy
David N. Pellow and Lisa Sun-Hee Park

Mixed Race America and the Law: A Reader
Edited by Kevin R. Johnson

Mixed Race America and the Law

A Reader

EDITED BY

Kevin R. Johnson

New York University Press

NEW YORK AND LONDON

NEW YORK UNIVERSITY PRESS
New York and London

Library of Congress Cataloging-in-Publication Data
Mixed race America and the law : a reader / edited by Kevin R. Johnson.
p. cm. — (Critical America series)
Includes bibliographical references and index.
ISBN 0-8147-4256-4 (cloth : alk. paper) —
ISBN 0-8147-4257-2 (pbk : alk. paper)
1. Racially mixed people—Legal status, laws, etc.—United States.
2. Mescegenation—United States. 3. Racially mixed people—
Government policy—United States.
I. Johnson, Kevin R. II. Critical America.
KF4755 .M59 2002
346.7301'3—dc21 2002011775

New York University Press books are printed on acid-free paper, and their
binding materials are chosen for strength and durability.

Manufactured in the United States of America
10 9 8 7 6 5 4 3 2 1

Contents

Acknowledgments

I am indebted to the editors of the Critical America series, Richard Delgado and Jean Stefancic, for suggesting the topic of this book to me and assisting me at every stage of the process, as well as providing moral support and intellectual guidance. Dean Rex Perschbacher of the University of California (UC), Davis School of Law offered leadership and extensive support that proved critical to completion of this project. The secretarial and editorial assistance of Glenda McGlashan, Kristi Case, Sue Williams, Paula Buchignani, Jeannie Camara, and Sara Buck, and especially Brigid Jimenez, made this book possible. Exceptional research assistants Fernando Aceves, Kristi Burrows, and Rosa Cabrera worked long and hard with deep commitment to research a diverse range of substantive bodies of law. Their efforts are most appreciated. Peg Durkin, Susan Llano, and Erin Murphy of the UC Davis law library responded promptly and politely to my many requests for obscure as well as routine materials.

My deepest debt is owed to my family, Virginia Salazar, Teresa, Tomás, and Elena. It is their unconditional support that makes all of my scholarly and other work possible. This book is about them and our future.

Mixed Race America and the Law

Introduction

Mixed Race America and the Law: A Reader focuses on the law concerning racial mixture in the United States. The book takes the reader on a journey through the legal intricacies posed by racial mixture and offers the historical, social, and political context surrounding the evolution of the law. Ironically, the general subject of this book—racial mixture—violates the law's monumental efforts to enforce racial separation during much of U.S. history. Until the United States Supreme Court intervened in 1967, laws in many states barred interracial marriage.

The mixed race literature has virtually exploded since the 1970s; for example, important books have been written on the mixed race experience. Many, such as James McBride, *The Color of Water: A Black Man's Tribute to His White Mother* (1996); Gregory Howard Williams, *Life on the Color Line: The True Story of a White Boy Who Discovered He Was Black* (1995); Judy Scales-Trent, *Notes of a White Black Woman: Race, Color, Community* (1995), focused on the experiences of people with African American and White parents. My own contribution to this genre, *How Did You Get to Be Mexican? A White/Brown Man's Search for Identity* (1999), sought to expand the dialogue to consider the mixed Anglo-Latino experience. Consistent with the goal of that book, this anthology studies the law's impact on a wide variety of mixed race peoples. This approach follows the general trajectory of civil rights scholarship, which over the 1990s expanded in scope to encompass the great diversity of racial minorities in the United States. Examples of this more extensive approach include Juan F. Perea, Richard Delgado, Angela P. Harris, and Stephanie M. Wildman, *Race and Races: Cases and Resources for a Diverse America* (2000), and Timothy Davis, Kevin R. Johnson, and George A. Martínez, *A Reader on Race, Civil Rights, and the Law: A Multiracial Approach* (2001). Racial mixture will undoubtedly shape the future study of race and civil rights in the United States. As minorities of many different types intermarry and rates of immigration of diverse peoples to this country remain high, more racial mixtures and mixed race peoples will emerge.

This anthology attempts specifically to bridge scholarship on the mixed race experience and the law. To this point, the legal relevance of racial mixture in the United States has received scant attention. A notable exception to this is Rachel F. Moran, *Interracial Intimacy* (2001), which provides an overview of the history of the law of racial mixture. By collecting foundational materials on the subject, I hope that this book will commence increased scholarly inquiry into this rich area.

Organized into twelve parts, each on a specific topic, this anthology includes excerpts of scholarly writings and then provides review questions for each part. The selection of scholarship for the anthology proved difficult. Space limitations made it impossible to include many excellent materials. To direct the reader to some of this important scholarship, a list of suggested readings concludes each section.

Part 1 outlines the history of the anti-miscegenation laws in the various states, which sought to limit interracial marriages between Blacks and Whites. Extralegal means, namely, "lynch law" and this nation's sordid history of lynching African American men accused (often wrongly) of crossing the color line, powerfully buttressed the legal prohibition. Anti-miscegenation laws in some states outlawed marriages between Whites and Asians and Native Americans. The readings document the slow demise of the anti-miscegenation laws in the courts. Interestingly, American Indian tribes have regulated marriages with nontribal members and continue to do so today.

Considering racial formation and mixed race identity, Part 2 outlines the legal definition of African American identity and the "one drop" rule, that is, the legal rule that one drop of Black blood made a person "African American." By operation of this rule of law, many mixed race people were classified as African American for discriminatory purposes. The readings also discuss the legal definitions and construction of Latina/os, Asians, and Native Americans and reveal how legal definitions often fail to comport with the complexities of race and racial mixture in the modern United States.

Part 3 discusses the phenomenon of mixed race people "passing" as White because of the benefits attached to Whiteness in our society. An individual's physical appearance, which varies dramatically among the mixed race population, affects the ability to assume a White identity. The readings focus on the legal ramifications of this passing, as well as efforts of Whites to "pass" as minorities to take advantage of affirmative action, employment, and public contracting programs.

Part 4 analyzes the heated controversy over the counting of multiracial people by the U.S. Bureau of the Census. The writings analyze the arguments for and against a proposed multiracial category, as well as the feared impacts of the change in classification. This part also discusses the legal impacts of the new method of counting multiracial people.

Part 5 considers the inheritance rights of the offspring of interracial relationships, as well as related issues. Historically, because interracial marriages violated the anti-miscegenation laws, mixed race children were deemed illegitimate and lost rights to inherit assets. African American women in marriage and other relationships with White men thus were denied the inheritance rights afforded legally recognized wives.

Part 6 focuses on discrimination against mixed race people. Whites at times have favored fairer-skinned African Americans over darker ones. Mixed race people can experience discrimination within minority communities because of their skin color, a practice sometimes referred to as "colorism." This part discusses the law's treatment of discrimination against mixed race people under the array of civil rights statutes designed to prohibit racial discrimination.

Part 7 reviews the difficult question of how mixed race people should classify themselves for purposes of affirmative action in higher education, public contracting, and employment. The difficulties of such classifications demonstrate the fault lines in defining race. Like the racial classifications discussed in connection with the 2000 Census, racial categorization for affirmative action necessarily reflects a certain arbitrariness.

In Part 8 we study the heated debate over the relevance of race to child custody and transracial adoption decisions. Should the race of a parent affect whether he or she should have custody of a mixed race child? Should a White couple be able to adopt an African American or Native American child, or one from a developing nation, and thus create an interracial family? These controversial questions pose conflicts between perceived individual and group rights.

Part 9 analyzes the treatment of mixed race people under the immigration and nationality laws, which have a long history of racial discrimination. Classified as racial minorities, mixed race persons were subject to racial exclusion from immigration and naturalization. Moreover, serving as a deterrent to interracial marriages, the nationality laws stripped female U.S. citizens of their citizenship if they married immigrants ineligible for citizenship, among whom were included non-Whites.

The United States is far from the first nation to encounter legal issues that arise from the emergence of a mixed race population. Part 10 offers a brief comparative look at the law's treatment of racial mixture in other countries. South Africa and Latin America have long histories of racial mixture that offer important insights for the U.S. experience.

Part 11 provides preliminary thoughts on the impact on the United States of an increasingly mixed race society. While some commentators predict that racism will evaporate with increasing intermarriage, others envision new, perhaps more virulent racisms flowing from the demographic changes.

Finally, Part 12 considers the future trajectory of mixed race legal studies.

Generally speaking, the early sections of the anthology focus on policing racial boundaries, the middle sections on racial classifications and their impact, and the conclusion on the legal impact of the growing mixed race population. Increasing racial mixture raises the question of the future of races and racism in the United States. Will mixed race people take us to a place of racial peace and tranquillity? Or will new racisms and social conflict emerge in the coming decades?

One important theme ties this anthology together. Modern commentators consider "race" to be a concept constructed by people—a so-called social construct—rather than something based in biological fact. (See, e.g., Michael Omi and Howard Winant, *Racial Formation in the United States: From the 1960s to the 1990s* [2d ed. 1994].) Biological rationales for racial difference popular in the scientific literature in the nineteenth and early twentieth century have waned, although they have not disappeared completely from the intellectual landscape. (See, e.g., Richard J. Hernnstein and Charles Murray, *The Bell Curve: Intelligence and Class Structure in American Life* [1994], offering race as possible explanation for intelligence differences among people.)

Mixed race people put the proverbial final nail in the coffin of the view that race is a biological reality. The changing, fluid boundaries exemplified by racial mixture demonstrate how society constructs people differently based on physical appearance and cultural, class, religious, and other traits. For example, even if the fundamental biological makeup of siblings is virtually identical, they may be treated as of different races in certain social contexts if they do not look alike physically. Society constructs each person in different ways. Moreover, different societies may construct the same person differently. The laws surrounding mixed race people—indeed, the "one drop" rule itself—demonstrate that race is a construction, something that people make up, a figment of the collective imagination. The law otherwise would be largely unnecessary to enforce racial boundaries. Nevertheless, the rigid racial classifications embedded in law often bear little resemblance to the real, fluid racial boundaries in everyday social life. As in other areas, the law finds it difficult to keep up with changing racial constructions and modern social realities.

Part I

Miscegenation, Intermarriage, and the Law

Part 1 considers the long history of the anti-miscegenation laws and the prohibition on interracial relationships in the United States. Originally directed at African American and White marriages, these laws sought to prevent the mixing of the races. The anti-miscegenation laws were buttressed by the disturbing history of lynching of African American men accused of, among other "crimes," crossing racial boundaries. (See generally James Allen, *Without Sanctuary: Lynching Photography in America* [2000]; 9 *Race, Law, and American History 1700–1990: Lynching, Racial Violence, and Law* [Paul Finkelman, ed., 1992].)

Both the laws and extralegal punishment demonstrate how White society considered interracial relationships to be a serious threat to the social order. As Gunnar Myrdal observed in his famous study of race relations in the United States:

> The ban on intermarriage has the highest place in the white man's rank order of social segregation and discrimination. Sexual segregation is the most pervasive form of segregation, and the concern about "race purity" is, in a sense, basic. No other way of crossing the color line is so attended by the emotion commonly associated with violating a social taboo as intermarriage and extra-marital relations between a Negro man and a white woman. No excuse for other forms of social segregation and discrimination is so potent as the one that sociable relations on an equal basis between members of the two races *may possibly* lead to intermarriage. (Gunnar Myrdal, *An American Dilemma: The Negro Problem and Modern Democracy* 606 [1944].)

In 1949, twenty-nine states had laws that prohibited racial intermarriage. (See Note, *Constitutionality of Anti-Miscegenation Statutes*, 58 Yale Law Journal 472, 472, 480–81 [1949].)

Beyond imposing criminal punishment on violators of the law, and a chill on the prospects of intermarriage, the anti-miscegenation laws had enduring impacts on African Americans. For example, "because the statutes made interracial marriages void, all offspring were considered illegitimate. Children and surviving spouses were denied the right to intestate inheritance, to take property under a will, to be granted letters of administration, and to receive worker's compensation benefits" (Jesse H. Choper, *Consequences of Supreme Court Decisions Upholding Individual Constitutional Rights*, 83 Michigan Law Review 1, 29 [1984]). Later chapters of this book discuss many of the impacts of the anti-miscegenation laws.

"Any history of antimiscegenation laws must begin with the regulation of black-white intimacy, but must not end there" (Rachel Moran, *Interracial Intimacy: The Regulation of Race and Romance* 17 [2001]). Importantly, the anti-miscegenation laws did not simply prohibit marriages between African Americans and Whites. Other racial mixtures also came within the purview of the laws, at times in surprising ways. (See, e.g., *Jones v. Lorenzen*, 441 P.2d 986 [Okla. 1965], applying law to prohibit marriage between persons of Mexican ancestry, classified as "White," and African Americans.) Indian-Anglo intermarriage was regulated for much of U.S. history. Arizona, California, Georgia, Idaho, Mississippi, Missouri, Montana, Nebraska, Nevada, Oregon, South Dakota, Utah, and Wyoming at one time or another all had laws forbidding marriages between Whites and Asian Americans. (See Pat K. Chew, *Asian Americans: The "Reticent" Minority and Their Paradoxes*, 36 William and Mary Law Review 1, 10 n.17 [1994].)

Interestingly, marriages of persons of Mexican ancestry and Anglos generally were not subject to the anti-miscegenation laws. Indeed, in nineteenth-century California, Anglo men married into wealthy ranchero families to gain political and economic opportunities as well as social status. (See Tomás Almaguer, *Racial Fault Lines: The Historical Origins of White Supremacy in California* 58–59 [1994].) At the same time, however, Anglo-Americans viewed Mexicans as racially inferior because they "had inherited the worst qualities of Spaniards and Indians to produce a 'race' still more despicable than that of either parent" *(Foreigners in Their Native Land: Historical Roots of the Mexican-Americans* 59–60 [David J. Weber, ed., 1973]).

The first modern judicial decision invalidating a state anti-miscegenation law apparently involved a Mexican American–African American marriage. (See *Perez v. Sharp*, 32 Cal. 3d 711, 198 P.2d 17 [1948].) Nearly twenty years later, building on the anti-caste principle of *Brown v. Board of Education*, 347 U.S. 483 (1954), the Supreme Court in *Loving v. Virginia*, 388 U.S. 1 (1967), held that Virginia's anti-miscegenation law violated the Equal Protection Clause of the Fourteenth Amendment of the U.S. Constitution. Randall Kennedy later observed that, "[u]nlike opponents of *Brown v. Board of Education*, antagonists of *Loving* were unable to mount anything like 'massive resistance.' They neither rioted, nor promulgated Congressional manifestoes condemning the Court, nor closed down marriage bureaus to prevent the desegregation of matrimony" (Randall Kennedy, *Marital Color Line*, The Nation, December 25, 2000, at 8).

Nevertheless, interracial romance continues to stir controversy in some quarters. Not until 2000 did Alabama voters, by a 60 to 40 percent margin, abolish the state's constitutional prohibition of interracial marriage. (See Alabama Statewide Amendment No. 2.) Forty percent of the voters *opposed* repeal of Alabama's patently unconstitutional anti-miscegenation law. In the early 1990s, a high school principal in Alabama garnered national attention when he threatened to cancel a prom upon learning that mixed couples planned to attend. (See Linda L. Ammons, *Mules, Madonnas, Babies, Bathwater, Racial Imagery and Stereotypes: The African-American Woman and the Battered Woman Syndrome*, 1995 Wisconsin Law Review 1003, 1027 n.106.) Until 2000, Bob Jones University, a private religious university in South Carolina, banned interracial dating, and it rescinded the ban only after a visit by presidential candidate

George W. Bush provoked national controversy. (See *Parents' Note Needed for Interracial Dates*, New York Times, March 8, 2000, at A20.) The attention paid to the O. J. Simpson case undoubtedly was influenced by the fact that he was accused of killing his White wife, Nicole Brown Simpson. Finally, occasional discrimination and violence against mixed race couples occur in daily life. (See *People Gather at Park to Show Support for Black Stabbing Victim*, Associated Press Newswire, July 30, 2001, reporting on a community rally supporting an African American man who was stabbed by White men in a restaurant while he was with his White girlfriend and another interracial couple; *Holley v. Crank*, 258 F.3d 1127 [9th Cir. 2001], holding that a brokerage office could be held liable for discrimination by one of its agents against an interracial couple whom he referred to as the "salt and pepper team.")

At the same time, some African Americans have opposed interracial relationships. (See Denise C. Morgan, *Jack Johnson: Reluctant Hero of the Black Community*, 32 Akron Law Review 529, 539–545 [1999], discussing the ambivalence of the African American community toward heavyweight boxing champion Jack Johnson because of his stated preference for White women.) "Marrying White" still stirs emotion among some African Americans.

Despite the legal prohibitions, interracial liaisons have long been commonplace in the United States, with the relationship between Sally Hemings and Thomas Jefferson being a most famous example. (See Annette Gordon-Reed, *Thomas Jefferson and Sally Hemings: An American Controversy* [1997].) Consequently, racial mixture long has been a part of the American mosaic.

Part 1 is divided into three sections: (1) an overview of the history of the anti-miscegenation laws; (2) the road to the U.S. Supreme Court's decision in *Loving v. Virginia* and its impact; and (3) analysis of the regulation of marriages other than those between African Americans and Whites.

A.

The History of the Anti-Miscegenation Laws

The anti-miscegenation laws have a long legal history in the United States. In this section, Eva Saks offers a brief historical overview of the laws. A. Leon Higginbotham and Barbara Kopytoff sketch the legal history of racial identification and the regulation of interracial relationships in antebellum Virginia, as well as the U.S. Supreme Court's sanctioning of such efforts. Peter Wallenstein focuses on the regulation of interracial marriage by the state of Alabama. Barbara Holden-Smith explains the rationale for lynching and the failure of the federal government to intervene. Emma Coleman Jordan further explores "lynch law" as enforcing the legal prohibition on race mixing.

1

Representing Miscegenation Law

Eva Saks

The word *miscegenation* was coined in 1864 by crusading *New York Daily Graphic* editor David Croly, in his political pamphlet *Miscegenation: The Theory of the Blending of the Races, Applied to the White Man and the Negro*. However, the criminalization of interracial relations, especially marriage, had begun in the colonial period. Maryland passed this country's first miscegenation statute in 1661. This statute criminalized marriage between white women and black men. Unlike most British colonial law, the miscegenation statute had no English statutory or common law precedents (although [one scholar] would analogize an 1841 Kentucky miscegenation decision to an English opinion nullifying the marriage of a countess and her footman). The statute's genealogy instead included moral and economic concerns: moral concerns of the parent country, England, which stemmed from the popular white mythology that blacks descended from Ham of Genesis and that their blackness was a punishment for sexual excess; economic concerns of Maryland and the Chesapeake Bay, where marriage between a white woman and a black slave would produce legally free children, thereby depriving the slave owner of potential slaves—a reduction in the stream of future earnings capitalized in the black body. Subsequent antebellum miscegenation statutes criminalized interracial sex and interracial marriage; such sex was, like all extramarital sex, prohibited as fornication but generally accepted (by the dominant culture) when occurring between white men and black women. Statutes prohibiting interracial marriage did not (arguably, nor were they meant to) deter white men from engaging in sex with black women, especially with their slaves; in fact, there were positive economic incentives for slave owners to do so, since the progeny of interracial intercourse with white fathers would become the white fathers' property. Yet all Southern states passed statutes criminalizing interracial marriage, as did many Northern states. . . . Miscegenation law, which during slavery kept interracial children slaves and after slavery bastardized them, originated as much in concerns about identifying the rights of (and in) future generations as in moral concerns. . . .

Miscegenation was a topic to which legislators paid increasing attention in the nineteenth century. This attention was heightened in mid-century, from 1840 through Reconstruction. (That legislators and judges paid increasing attention to the regulation and punishment of miscegenation at this time does not mean that interracial sex and marriage as social practices actually increased in frequency; the centrality of these practices to legal discourse was instead a sign that their relation to power was changing. The extent of uncoerced miscegenation before this period is a debated issue.) At the federal level, the framers of the Fourteenth Amendment endlessly discussed "miscegenation" and "amalgamation." . . . At the state level, there was an increase in the passage and enforcement of miscegenation laws. In substance, the federal government's Civil War amendments (1865–1870) and Civil Rights Acts (1866 and 1875) threatened the white South with the potential legal legitimation of interracial sex and intermarriage; in structure, these federal legal initiatives threatened the sovereignty of the individual Southern state courts that adjudicated miscegenation cases, since the empire of federal power was expanding through the U.S. Constitution, Congress, and judiciary. This put the state court judges of miscegenous bodies—white men charged with upholding state criminal law against federal constitutional challenges—on the defensive on many levels: sexual, economic, professional, and political. Six Southern states actually incorporated prohibitions of miscegenation into their post–Civil War constitutions.

However, in the post-Reconstruction period, even the U.S. Supreme Court was prepared to contract the federal government's power over race relations. They held in *Pace v. Alabama* (1882)[1] that the Alabama Code's punishment of interracial fornication more harshly than intraracial was constitutional under the Equal Protection Clause of the Fourteenth Amendment because it punished the black and white parts of the miscegenous body equally; the following year, they struck down the Civil Rights Acts. *Pace* was both a rehearsal and an important symbolic antecedent for the "separate but equal" rhetoric of the U.S. Supreme Court's decision upholding the constitutionality of segregated passenger trains, *Plessy v. Ferguson* (1896).[2] Thus did the crime of miscegenation play its symbolic part in maintaining the alienated status of American blacks.

Notes

Reprinted by permission from *Raritan: A Quarterly Review*, Vol. 8, No. 2 (Fall 1988). Copyright © 1988 by *Raritan*.

1. 106 U.S. 583 (1882).
2. 163 U.S. 537 (1896).

2

Racial Purity and Interracial Sex in the Law of Colonial and Antebellum Virginia

A. Leon Higginbotham Jr. and Barbara K. Kopytoff

I. Introduction

. . . [F]ew stress that colonial Virginia was . . . the "mother" of American slavery and a leader in the gradual debasement of blacks through its institution of slavery. Virginia was also one of the first colonies to formulate a legal definition of race and to enact prohibitions against interracial marriage and interracial sex. For more than three centuries, the Virginia courts and legislatures advocated and endorsed concepts of racial purity that we would call racist.

II. Definitions of Race and Racial Classifications

A. The Law of Slave Status

. . . In 1662 the House of Burgesses set down the law on the inheritance of slave status, and it remained virtually unchanged throughout the slave period in Virginia.[1] It was devised to settle the status of the mulatto children of free white fathers and slave Negro mothers. The act read:

> Whereas some doubts have arrisen whether children got by any Englishman upon a negro woman should be slave or free. Be it therefore enacted and declared by this present grand assembly, that all children borne in this country shalbe held bond or free only according to the condition of the mother. . . .[2]

There was a confounding of "negro" and "slave" in this early statute. It stated that the problem was the doubtful status of the mulatto children of "negro" women; yet "negro" must have meant "slave" or there would have been no question of the slave or free status of the children. In a world in which whites (here "Englishmen") were assumed to be free and Negroes were increasingly assumed to be slaves, a decision had to be made about the status of individuals who did not clearly belong to one race or the other: children whose parents represented two distinct races and two extreme statuses.

The statute did not say that all children of Negroes or of Negro women were to be slaves, probably because not all Negroes were then slaves. It would have seemed extreme, no doubt, even to white Virginians of that time, to enslave the child of two free people just because one or both of them were black. Some blacks were land owners and held slaves themselves. The statute said, rather, that all children would be "bond or free" according to the status of the mother. The rule embodied in the statute was thus phrased only in terms of status, not in terms of race.

A rough correspondence of race and status was assumed; however, they did not correspond entirely then and they diverged over time, partly as a result of the 1662 statute. They failed to correspond because of free Negroes. Some Negroes imported into Virginia before 1662 had never been slaves, and others who had been born slaves were later emancipated. The children of free black women were free under the statute, as were mulatto children born to white women. Free mulattoes were classified with free Negroes in terms of race and position in society. They also failed to correspond because, as white men mated with mulatto slave women, a class of very light-skinned slaves was produced. Some individuals, who were slaves because they were remotely descended in the maternal line from a Negro slave woman, had such a high proportion of European ancestry that they looked white. Some would even have qualified as legally white under eighteenth- and nineteenth-century Virginia statutes that defined race in terms of a specific proportion of white and nonwhite ancestry. Yet legally they were also slaves. Being legally white did not make one free if one's mother was a slave; being Negro or mulatto did not make one a slave if one's mother was free. The law of the inheritance of slave status was technically independent of race. This led to anomalies in the society, to people whose status was not considered appropriate to their race in the white Virginians' ideal conception of their slave society.

B. Statutory Definitions of Race in Virginia

When the three races first met in Virginia, there was no question or problem as to which race an individual belonged. It was evident at first glance. As Judge Roane observed in *Hudgins v. Wright:*

> The distinguishing characteristics of the different species of the human race are so visibly marked, that those species may be readily discriminated from each other by mere inspection only. This, at least, is emphatically true in relation to the negroes, to the Indians of North America, and the European white people.[3]

Initially, there was no need for statutory definitions of race, and there were no problems of racial identity to be solved by legislative fiat. However, as soon as the races began to mingle and reproduce, problems of racial identity arose. How should mixed race offspring be classified?

Strictly in terms of genetic contribution, the child of one white parent and one black parent had the same claim to being classified as white as he did to being classified as black. He was neither, or either, or both. One could decide to call such half-half mixtures mulattoes, but that merely raised the question of classification again in the next generation. Was the child of a mulatto and a white to be deemed a mulatto or a white? Or should another name, like quadroon, be devised for such a person?

Of course, the important point was not the name but the set of rights and privileges that accompanied the classification. In Virginia there were only three racial classifications of any legal significance, though there were far more combinations and permutations of racial mixture. Those three were "white," "Indian," and "Negro and mulatto." Mulattoes of mixed Negro and white ancestry had the same legal position as Negroes, although their social position may have been somewhat different. These legal classifications, then, gave rise to the need for a legal definition of race. As Winthrop Jordan notes, "[I]f mulattoes were to be considered Negroes, logic required some definition of mulattoes, some demarcation between them and white men."[4] Virginia was one of only two colonies to bow to the demands of logic by creating a precise statutory definition in the colonial period.

. . . Slaves who looked white had no special legal privileges until the nineteenth century, and then their only advantage was that they were relieved of the burden of proof in freedom suits. Race did, however, make a considerable difference for free people. Thus the first legal definition of mulatto appeared in a statute dealing with the rights of free persons.

In 1705 the Virginia legislature barred mulattoes, along with Negroes, Indians, and criminals, from holding "any office, ecclesiasticall, civill or military, or be[ing] in any place of public trust or power."[5] The mixed race individual defined as mulatto under the statute was "the child of an Indian, or the child, grandchild, or great grandchild of a Negro." Whites had distinct legal advantages, but mulattoes had no greater rights than Negroes. . . .

One notes in the statute's definition of mulatto the different treatment of those whose nonwhite ancestors were Indians as opposed to Negroes. A person with one Indian parent and one white parent was a mulatto. Someone with one Indian grandparent and three white grandparents was, by implication, legally white and not barred from public office under the statute. For Negro-white mixtures, it took two additional generations to "wash out the taint" of Negro blood to the point that it was legally insignificant. A person with a single Negro grandparent or even a single Negro great-grandparent was still considered a mulatto.

Why was there a difference in the legal treatment of white-Indian mixtures and white-Negro mixtures? Perhaps it was related to the degree to which a mixed race individual looked white to eighteenth-century white Virginians. Perhaps it was also because Europeans tended to see Indians as higher on the scale of creation than Negroes, though still lower than themselves.

Note that these definitions of race state the rule in theory; we do not suppose that they were rigidly followed in practice. We have found no case from this period in which a claim to being legally white was based on the exact proportion of white blood. At the time of the statute, in 1705, some eighty-five years after the first Negroes had arrived in Virginia, there would barely have been time for the four generations of offspring necessary to "dilute the taint" of Negro blood to the point that it did not count under law. Thus few, if any, white-Negro mixtures would have qualified as white, though there were likely some white-Indian mixtures who did.

The Virginia legislature, meeting in 1785, changed the legal definition of mulatto to those with "one-fourth part or more of negro blood."[6] Thus, by implication, those of one-eighth Negro ancestry (one Negro great-grandparent), who by the 1705 statute had been mulattoes, were now legally white. There is no mention in the statute of Indian ancestry. Interestingly, while the definition of mulatto in 1705 excluded from the category of white virtually all those with any Negro ancestry at the time, the 1785 definition, some four generations later, did not attempt to do the same. Instead, under the 1785 act a number of mixed race people who previously would have been classified as mulatto could be considered white. This was the only time Virginia law was changed to allow persons with a greater proportion of Negro ancestry to be deemed white. All subsequent changes were in the opposite direction—making a smaller proportion of Negro blood bar one from being considered white.

Objectively, the effect of statutes defining a mulatto as someone with a certain proportion of Negro or Indian ancestry, and implying that someone with a smaller proportion of nonwhite ancestry was legally white, was to make "white" into a mixed race category. By the early twentieth century, when those classified as white had to have "no trace whatsoever" of Negro "blood," there was indeed a great deal of untraced (and in some cases untraceable) Negro blood in the white population.

We see the notion that Negro ancestry can be gradually diluted into legal insignificance in the case of *Dean v. Commonwealth*.[7] There, a criminal defendant claimed that two witnesses were incompetent to testify against him because they were mulattoes, and mulattoes could not testify against whites. The court found the witnesses competent, since they had less than one-fourth Negro blood, the legal dividing line under the statute then in force. . . .

> . . . [F]rom the testimony it appeared certainly, that they had less than one fourth of negro blood. Their grandfather, David Ross, who was spoken of as a respectable man, though probably a mulatto, was a soldier in the revolution and died in the service. The evidence as to the grandmother was contradictory; though she was probably white, the mother was so certainly.[8]

The grandfather would have been incompetent to testify because he was a mulatto, but the grandchildren were not. The grandmother was probably white but the mother was certainly so. Thus, in mid-nineteenth-century Virginia, mulatto parents and grandparents could have children and grandchildren who were legally white. That became legally impossible only in the twentieth century, when any trace of Negro blood would disqualify a person from being considered white under the law. [See Part 2—Ed.]

D. Applications of Racial Classifications by Courts and by the Legislature in Private Acts

In drawing a racial line, the real concern of white Virginians seems to have been to maintain the purity of the white race and to preserve it from visible "darkening." There was no similar concern with preserving the Negro race from "lightening." While the statutes defined "mulatto" and, by implication, "white" in terms of the proportion of white and nonwhite ancestry rather than in terms of physical appearance, in practice distinctions were based on appearance. For most mixed race children there were no formal genealogies, no marriage records, no legal marriages. It would have been difficult to prove that one was one-sixteenth rather than one-eighth Negro, or one-eighth rather than one-fourth, and for the most part no one seemed to try. People did not base their legal claims on the exact proportion of white and nonwhite ancestry; when people claimed to be white, the matter was generally settled by appeal to their appearance.

. . . It was . . . important to know whether free persons were legally white or mulatto, for there were statutes imposing special burdens on free Negroes and mulattoes. Thus, Sylvia Jeffers and her children, emancipated in 1814 by the will of her deceased master, petitioned the Hustings Court of Petersburg, Virginia, in 1853 to be declared legally white.[9] The court granted their plea, and they were released from the civil and political disabilities from which they had suffered as free mulattoes. Sylvia Jeffers and her children were no more white, genetically or in appearance, after the court granted their petition than when they were slaves, but a declaration that they were legally white would have been of little use to them until they became free.

In a similar petition, this time before the Virginia Assembly in 1833, five members of the Wharton family asked after they were freed to be released from the operation of a statute requiring all slaves emancipated since 1806 to leave the commonwealth within twelve months. The assembly granted their petition, saying in the preamble to the act, "[I]t appears to the general assembly that [the petitioners] are not negroes or mulattoes, but white persons, although remotely descended from a colored woman."[10] In other petitions by "free persons of color" made at around the same time, the petitioners listed specific circumstances justifying their pleas, and the assembly usually granted only an extension of time beyond the twelve-month limit. In the Whartons' case, racial appearance was sufficient justification to exempt them entirely from the operation of the statute. Note here that even the legislature that had devised the statutory definition of mulatto and, by implication, of white seemed to be using a definition based not on proportion of ancestry as set out in the statute but rather on appearance. They were not declaring the Whartons white because of their exact proportion of white ancestry but because they had the appearance of white persons. If the applicants looked white, there was apparently little fear that they would darken and thus corrupt the white race.

The legal importance of racial appearance was set out formally in the 1806 case of *Hudgins v. Wright*. There, the court declared that racial appearance was to determine who bore the burden of proof in freedom suits. As Judge Roane said:

> In the case of a person visibly appearing to be a negro, the presumption is, in this country, that he is a slave, and it is incumbent on him to make out his right to freedom; but in the case of a person visibly appearing to be a white man, or an Indian, the presumption is that he is free, and it is necessary for his adversary to show that he is a slave.[11]

The presumption established in *Hudgins v. Wright* gave Nanny Pagee and her children their freedom in 1811. The Supreme Court of Virginia held in her case that the jury's finding, from visual inspection, that "Nanny Pagee, is a *white* woman . . . was quite sufficient; it being incumbent on the defendant to have proved, if he could, that the plaintiff was descended in the maternal line from a slave. Having not proved it, she and her children must be considered as free."

The statutes had imperfectly established the identity of black with slave and white with free. The judiciary stepped in with a modification in the form of a presumption setting the burden of proof differently in the case of those who appeared to be whites and Indians, on the one hand, and those who appeared to be Negroes, on the other. The judiciary was not unanimous in wanting to impose the extra burden on blacks seeking freedom. In the lower court in *Hudgins v. Wright,* Chancellor George Wythe had declared that when one person claimed to hold another in slavery, the burden of proof always lay on the claimant, "on the ground that freedom is the birth-right of every human being, which sentiment is strongly inculcated by the first article of our 'political catechism,' the bill of rights."[12] The Virginia Supreme Court refused to endorse this view, finding that it infringed too far on the property rights of white Virginians. . . .

If the individual claiming freedom was not, on inspection, unambiguously white, Indian, or Negro, the question of burdens, presumptions, and evidence became more complicated. One case contained an elaborate discussion of what evidence could be admitted to establish pedigree in the case of a mixed blood individual who claimed freedom based on descent in the maternal line from a free Indian. In *Gregory v. Baugh*[13] the plaintiff's maternal grandmother, Sybil, was "a copper-coloured woman, with long, straight, black hair, with the general appearance of an Indian, except that she was too dark to be of whole blood." The plaintiff himself was a "man of color." Among the questions that had to be decided was whether Sybil's dark color came from the maternal line, making her presumptively a slave, or from the paternal line, in which case she might be a free Indian. She might also have descended in the maternal line from an Indian who had been enslaved during a brief period when it was lawful to enslave some Indians. In that case, legally, she would be a slave. The question of what evidence could be introduced to establish her ancestry occupied much of the case. No simple presumption in the plaintiff's favor was made here as in *Hudgins v. Wright.*

In the case of light-skinned individuals of mixed ancestry, the question of whether the nonwhite blood came from the maternal or paternal line was of critical importance, as slave status was inherited only in the maternal line. Questions of evidence and proof became correspondingly more complicated. As Judge Roane noted in *Hudgins v. Wright:*

> When, however, these races become intermingled, it is difficult, if not impossible, to say from inspection only which race predominates in the offspring, and certainly impossible to determine whether the descent from a given race has been through the paternal or maternal line. In the case of *Propositus* of unmixed blood, therefore, I do not see but that the fact may be as well ascertained by the Jury or the Judge, upon view, as by the testimony of witnesses, who themselves have no other means of information: but where an intermixture has taken place in relation to the person in question, this criterion is not infallible; and testimony must be resorted to for the purpose of shewing through what line a descent from a given stock has been deduced; and also to ascertain, perhaps, whether the colouring of the complexion has been derived from a negro or an Indian ancestor.[14]

III. Voluntary Interracial Sex and Attempts to Discourage It

A. Concern over Interracial Sex

. . . The first clear legal pronouncement on interracial sex came in the 1662 statute on the inheritance of slave status. In Virginia before the 1660s, there was no unambiguous legal statement against interracial sex per se, as distinguished from illicit sex in general—that is, nonmarital sex. There were several instances of public condemnation of couples who engaged in interracial sex, but the importance of the race factor was unclear. The early cases are inconsistent in their treatment of blacks. When, in 1630, the council ordered "Hugh Davis to be soundly whipt before an assembly of negroes & others for abusing himself to the dishonr of God and shame of Christianity by defiling his body in lying with a negro," the Negro partner was not punished, and we cannot tell whether the sexual offense was made worse by the race of Davis's partner.[15] On the other hand, in 1640, when Robert Sweat had only to do public penance in church according to the law of England, for getting with child the Negro servant of another man, his Negro partner was to be "whipt at the whipping post."[16] In a case in 1649, penance in church was imposed on both the white man and his Negro partner. . . .

From Virginia's Eastern Shore counties, records of an unusual group of free black property owners have survived from the mid-seventeenth century. These records shed interesting light on the attitude of early Virginians toward race and interracial sex. In those counties during that brief era, free whites and blacks who committed sexual offenses were treated in a similar manner whether their partners were of their own race or not. In 1654 a black couple, "Richard Johnson, Negro and Negroe woman of the Family of Anthony Johnson, Negro," and a white couple, Abraham Morgan and Ann Shawe (who by the time the case was decided had become husband and wife), were reported by the churchwarden for fornication and adultery. The churchwarden was obliged to report them, so that "according to Lawe Such offenders maye receive punishment."[17] No difference in the treatment of the two couples was noted.

White men who fornicated with black or white women were charged a standard fine of five hundred pounds of tobacco. John Oever was fined that amount in 1663 for fornicating with Margaret Van Noss, a white woman, and Charles Cumnell had been given the same fine in 1658 for "Committinge . . . Ellicit Fornication with a Negro woman of Mr. Michael."[18] There is no mention of punishment for either of these women, but black women who can be identified from the record as being free blacks were called to stand trial for their actions, whether their partners were white or black. . . .

The punishments meted out to these free participants in illicit sexual unions seemed to depend more on their economic status and affluence than on their race. Regardless of the race of either party, men and women of property were fined; those who could not pay often were whipped; and men were required to pay damages and to support their free bastard children. Race did not make a noticeable difference when the offenders were known to be free.

There were other cases, however, in which the black partners went unnamed and unpunished. When Charles Cumnell was fined for fornicating with "a Negro woman of Mr. Michael," the fate of the woman was not mentioned. William Sriven was formally charged with "Committinge the sin of Fornication with a Negro woman," but his partner apparently was not charged. The Irishman John Dorman was convicted of getting a "Negro woman" with child and had to pay damages and costs. Again, the woman apparently was not charged. Furthermore, John Dorman was not specifically required to post security to ensure that the parish would not have to bear the cost of raising the child. The one unnamed Negro woman who appears to have been held accountable for her sexual behavior was attached to a black family. That was the "Negro woman of the Family of Anthony Johnson, Negro" with whom Richard Johnson, Negro, had committed fornication and adultery.

Who were the three nameless Negro women of whom no notice was taken except to say that white men had sinned with them? We suggest that they were slaves or servants for life if the slave status had not yet been fully formalized. There was no need to order the man to post bond ensuring support for the bastard children because the parish did not need to be concerned that these bastard children would become economic burdens. Rather, the children would become economic resources to the mothers' masters. There would have been no point in fining the women or ordering them to post bond, because they had no money. Their owners would not have posted bond to save them from whipping because they could not recover the money in the form of additional service. The women could, of course, have been whipped, but there is no record that they were.

Free blacks, on the other hand, were held to the same standard of sexual conduct as were whites. One might then be tempted to say that it was slave status rather than race that caused the difference in treatment in this early period, but that would be misleading. Race, after all, determined who could be enslaved. Thus a difference based on slave status was, in a sense, a difference based on race. A more accurate characterization might be to say that some free blacks could "rise above their race." These prosperous blacks of the Eastern Shore were not newly arrived Africans. They were highly acculturated men and women of African origin, property owners who were skilled at making a living in the new colony. Many of them were married and probably were Christians. The evidence from the Eastern Shore suggests that for a brief period they were treated as "black Virginians" rather than as members of an exotic and inferior race.

In any case, the specific significance of race in the early cases is uncertain, at least insofar as "race" meant purely physical characteristics. When there was a difference in the treatment of Negroes in the early cases, it might have been due to their "pagan" or Muslim religion as well as to their physical type. Yet these aspects of the Negro's separateness—physical type, religion, even language—tended to be parts of a parcel to early white Virginians. When there were exceptions, like the free blacks of the Eastern Shore who had mastered the language and culture of the whites, they were treated much as the whites were. That, however, was only in the early days of the Virginia colony, before ideas of race and social status had hardened. Later, when the parcel fell apart, the whites focused on physical type rather than on religion, language, or other aspects of culture, probably because it was the only aspect of difference that was immutable. Thus the role of race as physical type is unclear in the early cases. Negroes were sometimes, but not always, treated differently from whites. When they were, we attribute this difference in treatment to the fact that the whites saw them as fundamentally different sorts of human beings, not only because they had a different appearance but because they had a different culture as well. We cannot sort out the exact dimensions of the perceived difference in the minds of early white Virginians, and most likely they did not sort them out themselves at that time.

The early cases show that adultery and fornication were in themselves grounds for punishment, quite apart from the race of the participants. A number of early statutes explicitly condemned such actions. They were periodically reenacted, as in a 1691 law against a series of moral offenses, of which fornication and adultery were but two—the others being "swearing, curseing, prophaneing God's holy name, Sabbath abuseing, [and] drunkenness."[19]

By 1662, however, the Virginia legislators had singled out interracial sex for special and harsher treatment. They declared "that if any christian shall committ ffornication with a negro man or woman, hee or shee soe offending shall pay double the ffines imposed by the former act."[20] The former act to which this one referred set fines for fornication at five hundred pounds of tobacco. The "christian" to be fined double in the 1662 statute may be taken to mean any white person. Virginians tended to use the terms interchangeably at this early stage. Later, when called upon to distinguish them, they found race the more telling characteristic for legal discriminations.

The prescribed treatment of white men and white women who engaged in interracial sex was even-handed in the 1662 statute: both were to be fined. But what of their Negro partners? Why were they not punished under this statute? They were not even mentioned. This statute is the first in a long series of statutes, starting in 1662 and continuing over two hundred years until after the Civil War, that singled out whites for punishment in cases of voluntary interracial sex and marriage and ignored their nonwhite partners. While the records show that in a few early cases, as noted above, Negroes were punished along with their white partners under anti-fornication laws, the statutes specifically forbidding interracial sex and marriage were directed toward whites only.

B. Concern over the Production of Mulatto Children

While a number of statutes prescribed the same punishment for white men as for white women who engaged in interracial sex, it was the interracial sex of white women that seemed to concern the legislators most. That was evident from the wording of the early statutes. The 1662 statute noted in unemotional language that "some doubts have arrisen whether children got by any Englishman upon a Negro woman should be slave or free."[21] The statute set a fine for interracial sex double the normal one for fornication but omitted the adjective "filthy" that modified "fornication" in the earlier act. . . . The language suggests that the legislators were devising a practical solution to a practical problem. The act fined both white men and white women who engaged in interracial fornication, but it was the behavior of the men that prompted the law and set its tone.

In contrast, when the legislators were contemplating mulattoes produced by white women and nonwhite men, their revulsion is evident. A 1691 statute prohibiting interracial marriage stated:

> [F]or the prevention of that abominable mixture and spurious issue which hereafter may encrease in this dominion, as well by negroes, mulattoes, and Indians intermarrying with English, or other white women, as by their unlawfull accompanying with one another, Be it enacted by the authoritie aforesaid, and it is hereby enacted, that for the time to come, whatsoever English or other white man or woman being free shall intermarry with a negroe, mulatto, or Indian man or woman bond or free shall within three months after such marriage be banished and removed from this dominion forever. . . .[22]

A revision of this statute in 1705 adjusted the wording so that the interracial marriages of white men as well as white women were seen as leading to "that abominable mixture and spurious issue," and punishment for the white partner was changed to six months in prison, without bail, and a fine of ten pounds current money.[23] Indians were dropped from the statute. The minister who knowingly performed such a marriage was fined ten thousand pounds of tobacco, half to go to the informer. The provision was reenacted in 1753 and 1848.

It is significant that the prohibition on interracial marriage came in a statute that showed a growing concern over the presence of free Negroes and mulattoes in Virginia and enacted many measures designed to control their numbers. The act itself was entitled "An Act for Suppressing Outlying Slaves," and it noted the dangers in the possible alliances of free Negroes and mulattoes with slaves. One measure that the statute devised to reduce the danger was to require that an owner who set a slave free pay his transportation out of Virginia within six months. Another was . . . discouraging interracial marriages by prescribing banishment for the white partner. Yet another was a severe penalty on white women who had mulatto bastards. What the white Virginians seemed not to realize was that they had greatly increased the danger of alliance by classifying most mixed race individuals with blacks rather than with whites in terms of their legal rights.

While the increase in free mulattoes was one of the motivating factors behind the harsh treatment of white women who had mulatto bastards, it was not the only one. Free and indentured Negro and mulatto women also produced free mulatto children, and there were no comparable special punishments for these women. Nor were white men who sired free mulatto bastards subject to any punishment beyond the fine prescribed by statute for interracial fornication, and that was seldom applied. The legislators seemed to feel a particular distaste that white women, who could be producing white children, were producing mulattoes. Black women who produced mulatto children were not seen as making the same direct assault on white racial purity; they were unable to produce white children and thus did not affect the white race. There was no comparable concern over their "lightening" of the Negro race. In addition, . . . the legislators and their white male constituents may have wanted to save for themselves the white women, who were in short supply in the early years. . . .

C. Who Was Punished for Voluntary Interracial Sex and Why

We have noted that all of the statutes dealing specifically with voluntary interracial sex prescribe punishments for the white partners only. What were the reasons for such a glaring omission?

In the case of sexual relations between whites and their slaves, failure to punish the slave might have been a recognition that the slave had little choice in preventing the relationship, especially if the white were the owner. It might have been seen as bad policy or unreasonable to punish a slave for acquiescing to the demands of his or her master, even to demands for illicit behavior. In addition, many of the usual punishments were meaningless when imposed on slaves or would result in punishing their masters. Years could not be added to lifelong servitude; slaves could not be fined if they owned no property; and imprisonment would have deprived their masters of their work.

It is more puzzling why the penalties imposed on whites were not also meted out to free blacks and mulattoes. A likely explanation seems to be that whites, or "Christians"—with whom they were equated—were simply held to a higher moral standard than nonwhites in the eyes of the law, and that white racial purity, as well as sexual morality, was considered the special responsibility of the whites. Furthermore, voluntary interracial sex was probably considered the prerogative of whites, albeit an immoral one. The wishes and interests of whites were seen as determining relations between the races. Perhaps whites were so secure in their position of power and superiority that they assumed such relations would not occur unless initiated by whites. After the early years of the colony, as the lines of the racial caste system hardened, the freedom of choice of blacks was ignored in this as in so many other areas of life.

Under the statutes, whites were to be punished for these unions and their nonwhite partners were not. Also according to the statutes, white men and women were to be punished equally for such unions, at least when the unions did not produce children. In practice, however, we suspect that it worked differently. Black men may have been punished, either by their masters if they were slaves or by the law under the guise of punishment for other offenses. Although a review of county court cases would be needed to reveal the full dimensions of the gap between the law as written and as applied, we have a few cases that suggest how the law was applied. In one early case from lower Norfolk County, only the white woman was punished for fornication; her black partner was punished for something else. In two other cases, from the Virginia high court, the judges merely "winked" at the white men who kept black mistresses.

Cases in which white men were prosecuted for interracial sex rarely reached the highest courts of Virginia. We have found only two, despite the frequency with which mulatto children were born of black mothers. One reason lay in the rules of evidence: no black or mulatto could testify against a white at trial. Therefore, another white would have had to bring the complaint. Another reason was that society tended to wink at the casual liaisons of white men and black women. The two cases that reached the General Court of Virginia did not concern casual or clandestine sex; both involved cohabitation and open and stable relationships. In these cases, it seems that other whites did complain.

In *Commonwealth v. Jones,*[24] a case in the General Court of Virginia in 1845, a white man was prosecuted for "cohabiting with and keeping a female slave named Eveline." The fact that the court was in this case called upon to decide whether a white man could be prosecuted under the criminal code for fornication with a slave suggests that the issue had not been presented before. The court had decided in a prior case, *Commonwealth v. David Isaacs and Nancy West,*[25] that cohabitation of a white man and a free mulatto woman was not a common law crime but that the man might be prosecuted under a statute prohibiting fornication. In *Jones* the court held, similarly, that cohabitation of a white man with a slave was not a common law crime but was punishable under the criminal code.

Given all the thousands of such relationships between white men and slave women that must have occurred in Virginia before 1845, why did the question arise at this late date? Why did not everyone wink at this breach of the law as they had done countless times before? The unusual circumstance in this case was that Jones was cohabiting not with his own slave but with the slave of one Bennett M. Bagby, who presumably had not given his permission. Jones was interfering with Bagby's dominion over his property, Eveline, and it may be that Bagby's complaint brought about the criminal prosecution. Had Eveline been Jones's own slave, it is doubtful that the prosecution would have been initiated, for then the prosecution, rather than the cohabitation, would have been interfering with the property rights of a white Virginian. On appeal, the Virginia high court rejected the defendant's argument that since the statute prohibiting fornication did not apply to his slave partner, he should be exempt from prosecution too. It rejected his reasoning, holding "that a person who is not a servant or slave, having illicit intercourse with a slave, is as much within the operation of the statute as if both offending parties were free."

Although the question of statutory interpretation was resolved against the defendant, he received no punishment. The court set Jones free, declaring only that it did not have to declare its reasons for doing so:

> [A] majority of the Judges are of the opinion, that there are other errors disclosed by the record and proceeding of the cause, for which the judgment ought to be arrested; but there being a diversity of opinion among the Judges, as to the particular grounds upon which the judgment ought to be arrested, it becomes unnecessary to state them.
>
> It is therefore ordered, that it be certified to the Circuit Superior Court of Law and Chancery of the county of Powhatan, that the judgment on the verdict aforesaid ought to be arrested; and the defendant discharged and acquitted of the said prosecution.

. . . The disposition of the case . . . suggests more than anything else the great extent to which restrictions on the sexual behavior of white men with slave women were dismissed lightly.

D. Offspring of Interracial Unions

Virginians from an early date lashed out at interracial sex in language "dripping with distaste and indignation." The distaste turned to revulsion when they spoke of the resulting mulatto children, especially those with white mothers, as an "abominable mixture and spurious issue."

Mixed race offspring were disturbing to white Virginians for several reasons. First, they were anomalies. They simply did not fit into the whites' vision of the natural order of things: a great chain of Being comprised of fixed links, not of infinite gradations. Things that do not fit into the perceived natural order are seen as unnatural and often as dangerous and "abominable." The term *spurious,* used by the Virginia legislature for the children of marriages between whites and Negroes, shows a fundamental uneasiness and aversion to the idea of racial mixture, an aversion that is not entirely explainable by practical considerations. The aversion was greatest toward the mulatto children of white women. Since mulattoes were classified with blacks, the prospect of a mulatto child of a black mother was not as disturbing as that of a mulatto child of a white mother. It seemed less anomalous. Second, the idea of a racially based system of slavery depended on a clear separation of the races. Mulattoes challenged that idea. . . .

Third, mulattoes created a practical problem for a racially based system of slavery. They had to be classified in terms of status as well as in terms of race, and as we have discussed earlier, race did not automatically determine one's status as slave or free. The law of the inheritance of slave status was a response to the question of how to classify the children of white men and slave women, and the 1662 statute gave them the status of their mothers.

It has been suggested that, rather than having been dictated solely by racism, this policy might have reflected, among other things, the "prudential considerations of keeping a child with its mother and reimbursing the mother's master for its support."[26] But keeping a child with its slave mother hardly required such a drastic measure as making it a slave. Many free white children were raised from infancy by slave women. Had their mulatto children by white fathers been declared free, the slave mothers would probably have continued to raise them. Furthermore, masters could get reimbursement by making the child serve an indenture as well as by making it a slave. Whatever the precise combination of motives behind the rule of the inheritance of slave status, it had two notable practical effects: first, it separated the large majority of the children of interracial unions from whites by assigning them the status of slave; second, it provided slave owners with easy and cheap ways to increase the number of slaves they held. . . .

The rule that children were to take the status of their mothers meant that some mulattoes (the great majority) were slaves and some were free. Free mulattoes fell into two categories that were treated very differently. Under a 1691 statute, a mulatto bastard child *of a white woman* was to be bound out as a servant by the churchwardens until the age of thirty. The statute prescribed no similar fate for the legitimate mulatto children of white mothers or the legitimate or illegitimate mulatto children of free black mothers. The same statute prescribed banishment within three months for white women who married Negro, mulatto, or Indian men, so that the mother, and any legitimate mulatto children who went with her, were removed from local society anyway. When, however, in 1705, the penalty was changed to six months in prison and a fine, white women who served their time presumably were able to raise families of free legitimate mulatto children. These children were not to be sold into service for the benefit of the parish, for that provision applied only to bastard children, and while the products of the mixed marriages might have been spurious and abominable to the white Virginians, they were not illegitimate. The sacrament of marriage was effective even in the case of interracial marriage until 1849.

Just as the legislators were much harder on white women who produced free mulatto bastards than they were on free black women who also produced free mulatto bastards, the legislators were also much harder on the free mulatto bastards descended from white women than they were on other free mulattoes. What was the difference between the free mulattoes of white mothers and the others that the former should be treated more harshly? Perhaps it was an extension of the outrage the legislators felt toward the mothers of such children. Perhaps it was that they were evidence of the corruption of the white race in a way that the mulatto children of black mothers were not. Once Virginians had made the decision to classify mulattoes with blacks, the mulatto child of a white mother was an assault on racial purity. The mulatto child of a black mother merely exhibited a lighter shade within the range of skin color of the lower racial caste.

Notes

Published originally in 77 Georgetown Law Journal 1967 (1989).

1. See Act XII, 2 Laws of Va. 170, 170 (Hening 1823) (enacted 1662) (child to inherit mother's status); Act I, 3 Laws of Va. 137, 140 (Hening 1823) (enacted 1696) (same); Ch. XLIX, 3 Laws of Va. 447, 460 (Hening 1823) (enacted 1705) (same); Ch. XIV, 5 Laws of Va. 547, 548 (Hening 1819) (enacted 1748) (same); Ch. VII, 6 Laws of Va. 356, 357 (Hening 1819) (enacted 1753) (same).

2. Act XII, 2 Laws of Va. 170, 170 (Hening 1823) (enacted 1662) (emphasis omitted).

3. *Hudgins v. Wright,* 11 Va. . . . 71, 74 (1806) (Roane, J., concurring) (emphasis omitted).

4. Winthrop Jordan, *American Chiaroscuro: The Status and Definition of Mulattoes in the British Colonies* , 19 William and Mary Quarterly 183, 185 (1962).

5. Ch. IV, 3 Laws of Va. 250, 251 (Hening 1823) (enacted 1705). . . .

6. Ch. LXXVIII, 12 Laws of Va. 184, 184 (Hening 1823) (enacted 1785; effective 1787).

7. 45 Va. (4 Gratt.) 210 (1847).

8. *Id.* at 210 (emphasis omitted).

9. J. Johnston, Race Relations in Virginia and Miscegenation in the South, 1776–1860, at 206 (1970).

10. Ch. 243, 1832 Va. Acts 198, 198. . . .

11. *Hudgins v. Wright,* 11 Va. . . . 71, 74 (1806) (Roane, J., concurring). . . .

12. *Id.* at 71.

13. 25 Va. (4 Rand.) 246 (1827).

14. *Hudgins v. Wright,* 11 Va. at 73 (Roane, J., concurring).

15. Minutes of the Council and General Court of Colonial Virginia 479 (H. R. McIlwaine 1st ed. 1924). . . .

16. *Id.* at 477.

17. T. Breen and S. Innes, "Myne Owne Ground": Race and Freedom on Virginia's Eastern

Shore 1660–76, at 94–95 (1980). . . .

18. *Id.* at 95.

19. Act XI, 3 Laws of Va. 71, 71–72 (Hening 1823) (enacted 1691).

20. Act XII, 2 Laws of Va., 170, 170 (Hening 1823) (enacted 1662). . . .

21. *Id.*

22. Act XVI, 3 Laws of Va. 86, 86–87 (Hening 1823) (enacted 1691) (emphasis omitted).

23. Ch. XLIX, 3 Laws of Va. 447, 453 (Hening 1823) (enacted 1705). . . .

24. 43 Va. (2 Gratt.) 477 (1845).

25. 26 Va. (5 Rand.) 523 (1826).

26. Edmund Morgan, American Slavery, American Freedom: The Ordeal of Colonial Virginia 336 (1975).

3

Race, Marriage, and the Law of Freedom

Alabama and Virginia, 1860s–1960s

Peter Wallenstein

II. Power, Race, and Reconstruction: The Civil Rights Act of 1866 and the Fourteenth Amendment

In the first session after the Civil War, the Alabama legislature—like its counterparts in Virginia and the other southern states—enacted a new Black Code to accommodate the end of slavery. Among the new provisions, as instructed by the Constitutional Convention that met in late 1865, was a statute that outlawed interracial marriage. The Alabama Constitution of 1865 directed the legislature to make interracial marriages between whites and people of African ancestry "null and void *ab initio*, and mak[e] the parties to any such marriage subject to criminal prosecutions."[1] The legislature established a penalty of two to seven years imprisonment for both members of any interracial couple—a white and "any negro, or the descendant of any negro, to the third generation inclusive"—who "intermarry, or live in adultery or fornication with each other. . . ." The law also established penalties for any probate judge who knowingly issued a marriage license to an interracial couple and for any justice of the peace or minister of the gospel who performed a marriage ceremony for such a couple. Behavior that had been previously left up to individuals now became a question of criminal law. . . .

III. Race, Sex, and the Courts in Alabama, 1868–1877

[The article reviews the enforcement of Alabama's anti-miscegenation law. In a case that soon was overruled, the Alabama Supreme Court held that the law violated the U.S. Constitution. See *Burns v. State,* 48 Ala. 195 (1872).—Ed.]. The Lee County grand jury indicted Susan Bishop, a white woman, and Thornton Ellis, described as "descended of negro ancestors," for violating Alabama's laws governing sexual relations.[2] Under section 3598 of the Alabama Code of 1867, people convicted of living "together in adultery, or fornication" were "to be fined not less than one hundred dollars," and they could "also be imprisoned in the county jail, or sentenced to hard labor for the county, for not more than six months."[3] A second conviction "with the same person" subjected the offender to a minimum fine of $300 and a maximum imprisonment of twelve months; a third (or subsequent) conviction, again "with the same person," carried a mandatory sentence of two years either in the penitentiary or at hard labor for the county. Section 3598 covered same-race offenses. Section 3602 of the Code mandated imprisonment, for a term of two to seven years each, of a white person and a "descendant of any negro, to the third generation" if they were to "intermarry or live in adultery or fornication with each other."[4] A jury found Bishop and Ellis guilty of violating section 3602 and imposed a $100 fine on each of them, as though they had been convicted under section 3598.

They appealed their convictions. The Alabama Supreme Court upheld the conviction but reversed the penalty. The court expressed the notion that the trial judge had probably believed section 3602 violated the Civil Rights Act of 1866, and it rejected that premise. The federal law, Chief Justice A. J. Walker wrote, "does not prohibit the making of race and color a constituent of an offense, provided it does not lead to a discrimination in punishment."[5] As for section 3602, it "creates an offense, of which a participation by persons of different race is an element. To constitute the offense, there must be not only criminal intercourse, but it must be by persons of different races." Walker argued that because "[a]dultery between persons of different races is the same crime as to white persons and negroes, and subject to the same punishment," the Alabama statute did not contravene the Civil Rights Act.

IV. Tony Pace and the U.S. Supreme Court

It might appear that nothing more needed to be decided. Yet, among the cases appealed from trial courts in late-nineteenth century Alabama, one went on to the U.S. Supreme Court. The nation's high court demonstrated no difficulty in accepting the main lines of argument that supporters of the Alabama anti-miscegenation laws had developed. . . . Only the aberration of *Burns* remained as an exception and thus a reminder that the course of judicial history on miscegenation was not entirely inevitable.

In November 1881 a Clarke County jury convicted a black man, Tony Pace, and a white woman, Mary Jane Cox, under section 4189 on charges of "liv[ing] together in a state of adultery or fornication." Each received the shortest sentence that the law permitted, two years in the state penitentiary. When they appealed, the Alabama Supreme Court upheld the convictions. Each defendant's punishment, the court observed, "white and black," was "precisely the same." The differential punishment for interracial cohabitation was directed not "against the person of any particular color or race, but against the offense, the nature of which is determined by the opposite color of the cohabiting parties," an offense whose "evil tendency" was greater than if both parties were of the same race, as it might lead to "a mongrel population and a degraded civilization."

Pace appealed to the U.S. Supreme Court. Writing for a unanimous court, Justice Stephen J. Field rejected the argument that the Fourteenth Amendment's Equal Protection Clause offered a shield. Rather, he adopted the Alabama court's line of reasoning.

Viewing the two sections of the Alabama law, Justice Field found them "entirely consistent" and in no way racially discriminatory. Each, he insisted in all earnestness, dealt with a different offense. Section 4189, he wrote,

> prescribes a punishment for an offense which can only be committed where the two sexes are of different races. There is in neither section any discrimination against either race. Section 4184 equally includes the offense when the persons of the two sexes are both white and when they are both black. Section 4189 applies the same punishment to both offenders, the white and the black. Indeed, the offense against which this latter section is aimed cannot be committed without involving persons of both races in the same punishment. Whatever discrimination is made in the punishment prescribed in the two sections is directed against the offense designated and not against the person of any particular color or race.[6]

The decision was understood, from that time to the 1960s, as reflecting a validation of state anti-miscegenation laws. But the Supreme Court had not confronted the question of whether, given that Pace and Cox could not become husband and wife, they would inevitably be liable to prosecution for "adultery or fornication" if they lived as such. Only by implication had the ban against interracial marriage been addressed. Moreover, only by indirection did the Court address the question of whether, since it was a first offense, the sentence should have been for no more than six months. In any event, the Court had upheld the Alabama laws, and no southern state for the next eight decades displayed any inclination to repeal such laws. Certainly Alabama did not. The Supreme Court's decision in *Pace v. Alabama* would prove to have an even more durable career in the American law of interracial sex and, by extension, marriage than *Plessy v. Ferguson* would have on segregated transportation and, by extension, education.[7]

Notes

Published originally in 70 Chicago-Kent Law Review 371 (1994).

1. Alabama Constitution of 1865, art. IV, § 31.
2. *Ellis v. State,* 42 Ala. 525 (1868). . . .
3. Alabama Code § 3598 (1867).
4. Alabama Code § 3602 (1867).
5. *Ellis,* 42 Ala. at 526.
6. *Pace v. Alabama,* 106 U.S. 583, 585 (1883). . . .
7. *Plessy v. Ferguson,* 163 U.S. 537 (1896). . . .

4

Lynching, Federalism, and the Intersection of Race and Gender in the Progressive Era

Barbara Holden-Smith

II. The South's Strange Fruit

Southern trees bear a strange fruit,
Blood on the leaves and blood at the root;
Black body swinging in the Southern breeze,
Strange fruit hanging from the poplar trees.[1]

A. The Lynching Phenomenon

During and immediately after the Revolutionary War, lynching was practiced primarily in the East, where it was used as an extralegal means by which private citizens' groups carried out their own enforcement of the criminal law. As the nation's frontier expanded, however, the practice of lynching spread west and south and became a popular means of enforcing local mores as well as of punishing suspected law-breakers. So pervasive was the practice that by 1918 lynchings had occurred in all but six states. . . .

In the early 1880s, white victims outnumbered black victims, with most of the lynchings of whites occurring in the West. The white targets were often members of groups seen as outsiders by local citizens, such as Mormons in Indiana and Italian immigrants in the West and South. Native Americans, Chinese immigrant laborers, and Mexicans were also lynching victims. By the twentieth century, however, lynching had taken on a decidedly racial character and had become concentrated in the South. Thus, during the Progressive Era and afterward, lynching was inflicted almost exclusively by white Southerners upon black Southerners. Of the 4,742 reported lynchings that had taken place by 1968, 3,445 of the victims were black.

As lynchings became concentrated in the South, their brutality increased. The mass mob began to dominate lynchings in some Southern states, accounting, for example, for 35 percent of black lynchings in Georgia and 49 percent in Virginia from 1880 to 1930. These mass-mob lynchings were open affairs in which scores, and sometimes thousands, of whites participated. Members of the mob would often riddle the victim's body with thousands of bullets or burn him (or her) alive. Although whites were murdered as a form of summary justice, mass mobs confined their killings largely to blacks. Frequently, the leaders of the mob would sever the victim's body parts before his (or her) execution. These parts, along with what remained of the victim after death, were fought over by enthusiastic mob members, who had come from miles around to attend the lynching. Newspapers, after announcing the lynching in advance, sent reporters and photographers to capture the actions of the mob. Mob members could then enjoy seeing pictures of themselves beside the victim's charred remains as they read the newspapers' accounts of the incident.

Mass mobs acted with community approval and regularly included some of the community's leading citizens. Men constituted the majority of the actual lynchers, but women and children often attended. They took an active role in the murders by cheering on the lynchers, "providing fuel for the execution pyre, and scavenging for souvenirs after the lynchings."[2]

It is astonishing, given the barbarity of many Southern lynchings, just how commonplace and how acceptable they were, and how ordinary were the Americans who participated in such extreme violence. . . .

B. Reasons for Lynchings

. . . [T]he most persistent defense of lynching articulated by Southerners involved blacks' supposed inclination to commit one particular, serious violation of the criminal law: White men murdered black men by gun, rope, and burning, Southerners argued, because of the black man's propensity for raping white women. . . . [The author reviews the many alleged crimes for which whites lynched African Americans—Ed.]

III. The Systematic State Inaction

Whatever the cause of lynching's demise, the law had little or nothing to do with it. Throughout the Progressive Era, lynching remained a brutal crime that went largely uninvestigated, unprosecuted, unpunished, and undeterred by the agents of law at every level of government. State and local officials did not enforce existing law, and federal officials failed to enact any new legislation. Thus lynchers never faced any serious deterrent from the government and could murder black people openly, notoriously, and boldly, without fear of reprisal. . . . [T]he need for federal legislation [was] evidenced by the systematic failure of the Southern states—either from intention, indifference, or inability—to punish the crime of lynching. By the 1930s, most of the Southern states had specifically outlawed lynching. The first surge of such legislation occurred in the 1890s, partially in response to the threat of interracial unity posed by the Democratic Party. The second surge, in the 1920s, was probably prompted by the mass migration of African Americans from the South, as well as the increased militancy of African Americans after World War I. In addition, the 1920s legislation may partially have been a response to the near-passage of a federal anti-lynching statute in 1922, which generated fears among Southern whites that next time Congress might in fact succeed. Most of the statutes passed in the 1890s and the 1920s were weak. For example, none of them sought to prevent or punish the lynchings of persons who had not been accused of a crime. Instead, they sought only to deter or punish lynchings undertaken by mobs that seized prisoners from the custody of local sheriffs.

The near-total ineffectiveness of these laws during the Progressive Era requires no complex explanation: They were simply not enforced. . . .

IV. Congress Fails to Enact Anti-Lynching Legislation

[This section of the article discusses the history of anti-lynching proposals and the various arguments against a federal anti-lynching law—Ed.]

In the South, whites seemed obsessed with fears of interracial sex. Yet these fears were primarily masked by a rhetoric about the rape of white women by black men. As one writer to the editor of *The Nation* argued:

> You have never had to leave your home with a feeling that upon coming back you might find your wife or daughter outraged and probably dead. Well that is the condition that faces the Southern people day-to-day, and there is no law to stop it . . . until the negro comes to realize that it is sure death for him to commit this outrage.[3]

Several scholars have argued that lynching and its concomitant myth of rape were intimately connected with white male anxieties about sex in general, and particularly about interracial sex. For example, historian Joel Williamson contends that white men believed black men enjoyed a sexual freedom that the former wanted but could not achieve without great feelings of guilt.[4] In their sexual frustration, Williamson argues, white men projected onto black men the sexual thoughts they themselves dared not acknowledge and "symbolically killed those thoughts by lynching a hapless black man. . . . In effect, the black man lynched was the worst part of themselves. A function of lynching, if not indeed the primary function, was to offer up a sacrificial lamb for the sins of white men."

Hadley Cantril, on the other hand, contends that lynching reinforced a societal code in which white men alone possessed the "privilege" of interracial sex.[5] Southern culture strictly forbade interracial sex for white women, and indeed, the very notion was supposed to be morally and otherwise repugnant to them. Black women's views on interracial sex were seen as irrelevant, while black men were lynched to enforce the extreme taboo against interracial sex between black men and white women.

Thus lynching served, in part, as a sanction for voluntary sexual relations between white women and black men. Jacquelyn Dowd Hall, in her path-breaking work on rape and lynching, contends that in the South white women were viewed collectively as the keepers of white racial purity.[6] . . .

Beyond serving as a justification for lynching, the chimerical "beast-rapist" myth created an atmosphere of danger that kept the white Southern woman in a role of vulnerability and weakness. The use of black men as symbols of terror served in this way to keep Southern white women in their place: subservient, helpless, and dependent on men. . . .

[In opposing federal anti-lynching legislation], Representative James Buchanan of Texas set the tone for the Southern attack that was to come. In a long diatribe, Buchanan equated the Constitution with the natural order of the universe, extolled the virtues of the federal system, and ignored the possibility that the Reconstruction Amendments had changed the balance of federal and state power. Buchanan repeatedly asserted that lynching would cease once black men stopped the "diabolical crimes for which they are lynched." Voicing a theme to which the Democrats would return, Buchanan argued that the "Negro problem" was a peculiarly Southern predicament which would have been solved long ago "in the best interest of both races" if the Northern Republicans' political "machine" and the "so-called white uplift organizations of the North and East" had not been sending their "disturbing emissaries" to stir up trouble in the South. The result of such missions was clear to Buchanan:

> [In] the Southern States and in secret meetings of the Negro race [they] preach the damnable doctrine of social equality which excites the criminal sensualities of the criminal element of the Negro race and directly incites the diabolical crime of rape upon the white women. Lynching follows as swift as lightning, and all the statutes of State and Nation cannot stop it.[7]

In addition, Buchanan contended that whites of the South deplored lynching as much as anyone and that, while racial prejudice might to some degree provide the motive for lynching, the black race, the "race most addicted to the tragic infamy" of rape, "has long enjoyed its distinction as the most favored race protégé ever coddled and petted by the sentimental sacrifice of an indulgent people" and had brought lynchings upon itself by committing the "hellish outrage that fires the spirit of retaliation."

Continuing with Buchanan's themes of blacks as a uniquely Southern "problem" and rape as the cause of lynching, Representative [Thomas Upton] Sisson of Mississippi argued that

> as long as rape continues lynching will continue. For this crime, and this crime alone, the South has not hesitated to administer swift and certain punishment. . . . We are going to protect our girls and womenfolk from these black brutes. When these black fiends keep their hands off the throats of the women of the South then lynching will stop. . . .[8]

Furthermore, he argued, the Republicans would do the same thing if there were "Negroes in New England."[9] As another Southerner stated, removing controls on blacks would lead to a rampage of violence and rape, since the "Negro" exhibits "reckless indulgence of physical appetites and passions."[10] Indeed, argued Finis Garrett of Tennessee, the Dyer bill [the proposed federal anti-lynching law—Ed.] ought to be renamed "[a] bill to encourage rape."[11]

Notes

1. The lyrics are from the song "Strange Fruit," popularized by the jazz singer Billie Holiday, *quoted in* Jacquelyn Dowd Hall, Revolt against Chivalry: Jessie Daniel Ames and the Women's Campaign against Lynching 150 (1993).

2. W. Fitzhugh Brundage, Lynching in the New South: Georgia and Virginia, 1880–1930, at 37–38 (1993).

3. The Nation, July 6, 1916, at 11.

4. Joel Williamson, The Crucible of Race: Black-White Relations in the American South since Emancipation 308 (1984).

5. Robert L. Zangrando, The NAACP Crusade against Lynching, 1900–1950, at 10 (1980), *citing* Hadley Cantril, Psychology of Social Movements 93–122 (1941).

6. *See* Hall, *supra*, at 151–57.

7. 62 Congressional Record 468 (1921).

8. *Id.* at 1721.

9. *Id.*

10. *Id.* at 1713.

11. *Id.* at 548.

5

Crossing the River of Blood between Us

Lynching, Violence, Beauty, and the Paradox of Feminist History

Emma Coleman Jordan

IV. The Erasure of History

Contemporary histories of the South have focused on the primary targets of lynching: black men. These studies show that lynching became a central feature of the American imagination after the Civil War. As Mark Twain observed, lynching became a habit.[1] Systematic review of the conditions surrounding the most intense periods of lynching reveal that the practice thrived because there was a broad social consensus supporting it.

This social agreement was an indispensable common denominator of the widely varied circumstances surrounding 4,743 extralegal, violent, and public murders that took place between 1882 and 1968.[2] . . .

The quintessential lynching offense was social contact with a white woman by a black man, whether or not the contact had been mutually arranged.[3] Lynchings could be triggered by offenses as trivial as failure to observe the racial courtesy of moving aside to let a white woman pass, or as serious as rape or murder. The sanction for this bizarre spectrum of offenses was the same: spectacle lynching. These events were orchestrated to teach black people their proper place in society. To have the necessary terroristic effect of compelling compliance with the postslavery code of racial subordination, lynchings were usually held in public spaces and advertised in advance, oftentimes drawing festive crowds as large as ten thousand.

One of the myths about lynchings is that they occurred in the backwoods, organized by a few hooded Klansmen in the bayou, attended only by men, late at night or in the wee hours of the early morning, hidden by the cover of darkness. However, the facts reveal the participation of women and children in lynch mobs in what one scholar has described as "orgy-like atmospheres."[4] . . .

Thus the lynching experience became the defining experience of both whiteness and blackness. Through this gruesome social spectacle, repeated over and over in cities as widely dispersed as Elaine, Arkansas; Omaha, Nebraska; and Wilmington, Delaware, the code of behavior for "free" blacks was established. Lynchings became the preferred method of racial subordination because this ritualized form of violence served deeply shared norms of racial superiority. Lynchings were explicitly approved by large majorities in the South and were tacitly approved by large majorities in the North; thus they reflected not only the consensus of the communities in which these events occurred but the passive agreement of the entire nation. No one who participated in a lynching needed to fear criminal sanction. The rule of law became mob rule.

The phenomenon of mob rule reveals a further distortion of the history of lynching that became an accepted representation of fact over time. Lynching was not merely a hanging without a trial, a premature acceleration of an otherwise well-ordered judicial process. Despite the appearance of disorder, the repetitive structure of the lynching ritual reveals a practice that was as ritualized and detailed as the official ritual of the death sentence imposed after due process of law and carried out in state-sanctioned hanging. Lynch victims were frequently sexually mutilated, and spectators fought over souvenirs of the event. The souvenirs often included severed human body parts—ears, fingers, gonads, and toes of lynching victims placed in jars filled with alcohol and displayed in white homes and businesses as evidence of their participation in the ritual of lynch law.

W. E. B. Du Bois, responding to reports of a threatened lynching in Newman, Georgia, went to the town only to discover that Sam Holt, the victim, had already been lynched and that his fingers were on display.[5] Du Bois turned back, realizing that his mission was futile.

The actual events leading up to and immediately following a lynching were only the central core of concentric circles of terror radiating outward from the physical violence to its direct victim. The larger circle around a lynching created a complex process of incredible barbarity and inhumanity that established the dominance of the white majority and the subordination of blacks. The last circle is perhaps the cruelest of all. It consists of the creation of myths that falsely shrink the size of the mob, redraw the geography of culpability to include only the rural South, extract women and children from the mob, paint the victims as guilty without evidence, and focus on sexual predation, thereby eliminating the large number of lynchings that occurred for minor violations of the code of racial subordination. . . .

A. Repressed Memory as a Vivid Code of Racial Survival

. . . This memory has been processed in the form of healthy racial survival training given to virtually every black male child. The social code imposed by lynching extended well into the twentieth century. After the lynching of fourteen-year-old Emmett Till in Mississippi in 1955, a black man did not dare whistle at a white woman, nor did he dare indicate through his actions even the slightest interest in sex with white women.[6] No white woman could be trusted, even those who actively courted black men. They had the power to cry rape without accountability. They could launch a reign of terror upon an entire community of blacks with impunity.

During the O. J. Simpson trial, such "folk" knowledge became visible. For example, the belief that a jury would not render an impartial verdict if it was not a majority black jury was widely shared in the black community. Today we see it on display in the extremely disparate reaction of many blacks to the O. J. Simpson verdict, the Rodney King beating, and the shooting of Amadou Diallo by New York City policemen. The trial in each of these cases became a racial Rorschach test of lynching and associated attitudes about black male criminality. For example, a black man accused of murdering a white woman, his former wife, provided ample reinforcement of old stereotypes about black male criminality and, for blacks, fertile ground for reflection on the history of interracial sex. A black man's vicious beating by four white policemen, caught on videotape, served to reinforce either the brutality and lawlessness of policemen or the dangerous, criminal defiance of lawful authority by black men, depending on which history of lynching and lawlessness one had been exposed to. Needless to say, O. J. Simpson would have been lynched in Mississippi in 1955. Coming to terms with the current code of racial conduct reveals upon reflection that the attitudes of the past often prevail today. The question in the minds of black people was, is this trial in 1995 a fair trial? One can trace the responses of many to this trial to the lynching experience—to a memory of people being taken out of their homes without due process of law, mutilated, and tortured for doing less than O. J. Simpson was accused of doing. Black people know that O. J. could not expect, despite his celebrity, to be treated any differently than any other black man.

B. When Lynching Was the Law

Systems of law depend on the consensus of those governed. Therefore, social consensus permitted lynching to thrive with virtual impunity in the period from 1868 to 1955. The 1998 beheading and automobile lynching of a black man in Texas, although the product of two white criminals, revived the painful memories just under the surface of American life.[7] "Lynch law" is thus not an oxymoron. It was a fact of legal life that has implications for today, for the vestiges of this long-forgotten period of crude racial subordination remain. A legacy of the era of the act of lynching can be traced through folklore and modern popular culture to jury attitudes and presumptions about police decision making when interacting with black men. Whites have forgotten the legacy; blacks have not.

Notes

1. Mark Twain, *The United States of Lyncherdom, reprinted in* Mark Twain: Collected Tales, Sketches, Speeches and Essays 479, 480 (Louis J. Budd, ed., 1992). . . .

2. *See* Orlando Patterson, Rituals of Blood: Consequences of Slavery in Two American Centuries 179 (1998).

3. *See* Martha Hodes, White Women, Black Men: Illicit Sex in the Nineteenth Century South 176 (1997).

4. James P. Comer, Beyond Black and White 134 (1972).

5. *See* Hodes, *supra,* at 207–8. . . .

6. *See* Comer, *supra,* at 143. . . .

7. James Byrd Jr., forty-nine, was brutally beaten, chained to the back of a pickup truck, and dragged for more than two miles. *See* Clarence Waldron, *Three White Men Accused of Dragging Black Man to Death in Jasper, TX,* Jet, June 29, 1998, at 10. . . .

B.

The Road to Loving v. Virginia *and Its Impact*

The end of the anti-miscegenation laws came slowly. Famous for his visionary decisions, California Supreme Court Justice Roger Traynor wrote an opinion nearly two decades before the U.S. Supreme Court reached the same conclusion, finding that California's anti-miscegenation law violated the U.S. Constitution. The decision in *Perez v. Sharp* was the first in modern times to invalidate a state anti-miscegenation statute. Walter Wadlington puts *Loving v. Virginia*, 388 U.S. 1 (1967), into its proper legal context. Robert Pratt tells the real-life story of Richard Loving and Mildred Jeter. The Supreme Court's landmark decision is reprinted to offer the full flavor of this momentous decree. Randall Kennedy considers the social impacts of the decision and the fact that African American–White intermarriage rates lag far behind those of other groups.

6

Perez v. Sharp

California Supreme Court
32 Cal. 2d 711, 198 P.2d 17 (1948)

Justice Traynor:

[P]etitioners seek to compel the County Clerk of Los Angeles County to issue them a certificate of registry . . . and a license to marry. . . . In the application for a license, petitioner Andrea Perez states that she is a white person and petitioner Sylvester Davis that he is a Negro. Respondent refuses to issue the certificate and license, invoking Civil Code, section 69, which provides: ". . . no license may be issued authorizing the marriage of a white person with a Negro, mulatto, Mongolian or member of the Malay race."

Civil Code, section 69, implements Civil Code, section 60, which provides: "All marriages of white persons with negroes, Mongolians, members of the Malay race, or mulattoes are illegal and void." . . .

The right to marry is as fundamental as the right to send one's child to a particular school or the right to have offspring. . . . It must therefore be determined whether the state can restrict that right on the basis of race alone without violating the equal protection of the laws clause of the United States Constitution.

Distinctions between citizens solely because of their ancestry are by their very nature odious to a free people whose institutions are founded upon the doctrine of equality. For that reason, legislative classification or discrimination based on race alone has often been held to be a denial of equal protection. *Yick Wo v. Hopkins*, 118 U.S. 356 [1885]. . . .

In determining whether the public interest requires the prohibition of a marriage between two persons, the state may take into consideration matters of legitimate concern to the state. Thus, disease that might become a peril to the prospective spouse or to the offspring of the marriage could be made a disqualification for marriage. . . . Such legislation, however, must be based on tests of the individual, not on arbitrary classifications of groups or races, and must be administered without discrimination on the grounds of race. . . . It has been suggested that certain races are more prone than the Caucasian to diseases such as tuberculosis. If the state determines that certain diseases would endanger a marital partner or offspring, it may prohibit persons so diseased from marrying, but the statute must apply to all persons regardless of race. Sections 60 and 69 are not motivated by a concern to diminish the transmission of disease by marriage, for they make race and not disease the disqualification. Thus, a tubercular Negro or a tubercular Caucasian may marry subject to the race limitation, but a Negro and a Caucasian who are free from disease may not marry each other. If the purpose of these sections was to prevent marriages by persons who do not have the qualifications for marriage that the state may properly prescribe, they would make the possession of such qualifications the test for members of all races alike. By restricting the individual's right to marry on the basis of race alone, they violate the equal protection of the laws clause of the United States Constitution.

II

California's first miscegenation statute (Stats. 1850, ch. 140, p. 424) was enacted at the same time as two other statutes concerning race. . . . The two companion statutes provided: "No black or mulatto person, or Indian, shall be permitted to give evidence in favor of, or against, any white person. Every person who shall have one-eighth part or more of Negro blood shall be deemed a mulatto, and every person who shall have one half of Indian blood shall be deemed an Indian." (Stats. 1850, ch. 99, § 14, p. 230; repealed Code Civ. Proc., § 18, 1872.) "No black, or mulatto person, or Indian, shall be permitted to give evidence in any action to which a white person is a party, in any Court of this State. Every person who shall have one eighth part or more of negro blood, shall be deemed a mulatto; and every person who shall have one half Indian blood, shall be deemed an Indian." (Stats. 1850, ch. 142, § 306, p. 455; repealed Code Civ. Proc., § 18, 1872.)

In 1854, this court held that Chinese (and all others not white) were precluded from being witnesses against white persons on the basis of the statute quoted above. (*People v. Hall*, 4 Cal. 399, 404.) The considerations motivating the decision are candidly set forth: "The anomalous spectacle of a distinct people [Chinese], living in our community, recognizing no laws of this State except through necessity, bringing with them their prejudices and national feuds, in which they indulge in open violation of law; whose mendacity is proverbial; a race of people whom nature has marked as inferior, and who are incapable of progress or intellectual development beyond a certain point, as their history has shown; differing in language, opinions, color, and physical conformation; between whom and ourselves nature has placed an impassable difference, is now presented, and for them is claimed, not only the right to swear away the life of a citizen, but the further privilege of participating with us in administering the affairs of our Government." . . . For these reasons, therefore, "all races other than Caucasian" were held to be included in a statute referring only to a "black or mulatto person, or Indian."

California courts are not alone in such utterances. Many courts in this country have assumed that human beings can be judged by race and that other races are inferior to the Caucasian. Respondent's position is based upon those premises. He justifies the prohibition of miscegenation on grounds similar to those set forth in the frequently cited case of *Scott v. State* (1869), 39 Ga. 321, 324: "The amalgamation of the races is not only unnatural, but is always productive of deplorable results. Our daily observation shows us, that the offspring of these unnatural connections are generally sickly and effeminate, and that they are inferior in physical development and strength, to the full blood of either race." Modern experts are agreed that the progeny of marriages between persons of different races are not inferior to both parents. Nevertheless, even if we were to assume that interracial marriage results in inferior progeny, we are unable to find any clear policy in the statute against marriages on that ground.

Civil Code, section 60, like most miscegenation statutes . . . , prohibits marriages only between "white persons" and members of certain other so-called races. Although section 60 is more inclusive than most miscegenation statutes, it does not include "Indians" or "Hindus" . . . ; nor does it set up "Mexicans" as a separate category, although some authorities consider Mexico to be populated at least in part by persons who are a mixture of "white" and "Indian." . . . Thus, "white persons" may marry persons who would be considered other than white by respondent's authorities, and all other "races" may intermarry freely.

The [California] Legislature therefore permits the mixing of all races with the single exception that white persons may not marry Negroes, Mongolians, mulattoes, or Malays. It might be concluded therefrom that section 60 is based upon the theory that the progeny of a white person and a Mongolian or Negro or Malay are inferior or undesirable, while the progeny of members of other different races are not. Nevertheless, the section does not prevent the mixing of "white" and "colored" blood. It permits marriages not only between Caucasians and others of darker pigmentation, such as Indians, Hindus, and Mexicans, but between persons of mixed ancestry including white. If a person of partly Caucasian ancestry is yet classified as a Mongolian under section 60 because his ancestry is predominantly Mongolian, a considerable mixture of Caucasian and Mongolian blood is permissible. A person having five-eighths Mongolian blood and three-eighths white blood could properly marry another person of preponderantly Mongolian blood. Similarly, a mulatto can marry a Negro. . . . [A] person having seven-eighths white ancestry could marry a Negro. In fact two mulattoes, each of four-eighths white and four-eighths Negro blood, could marry under section 60, and their progeny, like them, would belong as much to one race as to the other. In effect, therefore, section 60 permits a substantial amount of intermarriage between persons of some Caucasian ancestry and members of other races. Furthermore, there is no ban on illicit sexual relations between Caucasians and members of the proscribed races. Indeed, it is covertly encouraged by the race restrictions on marriage.

Nevertheless, respondent has sought to justify the statute by contending that the prohibition of intermarriage between Caucasians and members of the specified races prevents the Caucasian race from being contaminated by races whose members are by nature physically and mentally inferior to Caucasians.

Respondent submits statistics relating to the physical inferiority of certain races. Most, if not all, of the ailments to which he refers are attributable largely to environmental factors. Moreover, one must take note of the statistics showing that there is a higher percentage of certain diseases among Caucasians than among non-Caucasians. The categorical statement that non-Caucasians are inherently physically inferior is without scientific proof. In recent years scientists have attached great weight to the fact that their segregation in a generally inferior environment greatly increases their liability to physical ailments. In any event, generalizations based on race are untrustworthy in view of the great variations among members of the same race. . . .

The Legislature is free to prohibit marriages that are socially dangerous because of the physical disabilities of the parties concerned. . . . The miscegenation statute, however, condemns certain races as unfit to marry with Caucasians on the premise of a hypothetical racial disability, regardless of the physical qualifications of the individuals concerned. If this premise were carried to its logical conclusion, non-Caucasians who are now precluded from marrying Caucasians on physical grounds would also be precluded from marrying among themselves on the same grounds. The concern to prevent marriages in the first category and the indifference about marriages in the second reveal the spuriousness of the contention that intermarriage between Caucasians and non-Caucasians is socially dangerous on physical grounds.

Respondent also contends that Negroes, and impliedly the other races specified in section 60, are inferior mentally to Caucasians. It is true that in the United States catalogues of distinguished people list more Caucasians than members of other races. It cannot be disregarded, however, that Caucasians are in the great majority and have generally had a more advantageous environment, and that the capacity of the members of any race to contribute to a nation's culture depends in large measure on how freely they may participate in that culture. There is no scientific proof that one race is superior to another in native ability. The data on which Caucasian superiority is based have undergone considerable reevaluation by social and physical scientists in the past two decades. Although scientists do not discount the influence of heredity on the ability to score highly on mental tests, there is no certain correlation between race and intelligence. There have been outstanding individuals in all races, and there has also been wide variation in the individuals of all races. In any event the Legislature has not made an intelligence test a prerequisite to marriage. If respondent's blanket condemnation of the mental ability of the proscribed races were accepted, there would be no limit to discriminations based upon the purported inferiority of certain races. It would then be logical to forbid Negroes to marry Negroes, or Mongolians to marry Mongolians, on the ground of mental inferiority, or by sterilization to decrease their numbers.

Respondent contends, however, that persons wishing to marry in contravention of race barriers come from the "dregs of society" and that their progeny will therefore be a burden on the community. There is no law forbidding marriage among the "dregs of society," assuming that this expression is capable of definition. If there were such a law, it could not be applied without a proper determination of the persons that fall within that category, a determination that could hardly be made on the basis of race alone.

Respondent contends that even if the races specified in the statute are not by nature inferior to the Caucasian race, the statute can be justified as a means of diminishing race tension and preventing the birth of children who might become social problems.

It is true that in some communities the marriage of persons of different races may result in tension. Similarly, race tension may result from the enforcement of the constitutional requirement that persons must not be excluded from juries solely on the ground of color, or segregated by law to certain districts within a city. In *Buchanan v. Warley*, 245 U.S. 60, 81 [1917], the Supreme Court of the United States declared unconstitutional a statute forbidding a "white person" to move into a block where the greater number of residences were occupied by "colored persons" and forbidding a "colored person" to move into a block where the greater number of residences were occupied by "white persons." The contention was made that the "proposed segregation will promote the public peace by preventing race conflicts." The court stated in its opinion that desirable "as this is, and important as is the preservation of the public peace, this aim cannot be accomplished by laws or ordinances which deny rights created or protected by the Federal Constitution." . . .

The effect of race prejudice upon any community is unquestionably detrimental both to the minority that is singled out for discrimination and to the dominant group that would perpetuate the prejudice. It is no answer to say that race tension can be eradicated through the perpetuation by law of the prejudices that give rise to the tension. Nor can any reliance be placed on the decisions of the United States Supreme Court upholding laws requiring segregation of races in facilities supplied by local common carriers and schools, for that court has made it clear that in those instances the state must secure equal facilities for all persons regardless of race in order that no substantive right be impaired. . . . In the present case, however, there is no redress for the serious restriction of the right of Negroes, mulattoes, Mongolians, and Malays to marry; certainly there is none in the corresponding restriction of the right of Caucasians to marry. A member of any of these races may find himself barred by law from marrying the person of his choice and that person to him may be irreplaceable. Human beings are bereft of worth and dignity by a doctrine that would make them as interchangeable as trains.

Respondent relies on *Pace v. Alabama*, 106 U.S. 583 [1882], in which the United States Supreme Court held constitutional an Alabama statute imposing more severe punishment for adultery or fornication between a white person and a Negro than for such acts between individuals belonging to the same race. [See Chapter 3—Ed.] The Alabama statute also referred to intermarriage but the court considered the case as one dealing solely with adultery and nonmarital intercourse. We are not required by the facts of this case to discuss the reasoning of *Pace v. Alabama* except to state that adultery and nonmarital intercourse are not, like marriage, a basic right, but are offenses subject to various degrees of punishment.

It is contended that interracial marriage has adverse effects not only upon the parties thereto but upon their progeny. Respondent relies on *Buck v. Bell*, 274 U.S. 200 [1927], for the proposition that the state "may properly protect itself as well as the children by taking steps which will prevent the birth of offspring who will constitute a serious social problem, even though such legislation must necessarily interfere with a natural right." That case, however, involved a statute authorizing sterilization of imbeciles following scientific verification and the observance of procedural guarantees. In *Buck v. Bell* the person sterilized was the feeble-minded child of a feeble-minded mother and was herself the mother of an illegitimate feeble-minded child. . . . The inheritability of mental defectiveness does not concern us here, for this case does not involve mentally defective persons. The Supreme Court of the United States later forbade the sterilization of criminals in *Skinner v. Oklahoma* [316 U.S. 535 (1942)], where the Legislature failed to provide a fair hearing and set up illogical and discriminatory categories. The racial categories in the miscegenation law are as illogical and discriminatory as those condemned by the Supreme Court in *Skinner v. Oklahoma*; and there is a corresponding lack of a fair hearing.

Respondent maintains that Negroes are socially inferior and have so been judicially recognized . . . , and that the progeny of a marriage between a Negro and a Caucasian suffer not only the stigma of such inferiority but the fear of rejection by members of both races. If they do, the fault lies not with their parents, but with the prejudices in the community and the laws that perpetuate those prejudices by giving legal force to the belief that certain races are inferior. If miscegenous marriages can be prohibited because of tensions suffered by the progeny, mixed religious unions could be prohibited on the same ground.

There are now so many persons in the United States of mixed ancestry, that the tensions upon them are already diminishing and are bound to diminish even more in time. Already many of the progeny of mixed marriages have made important contributions to the community. . . .

III

Even if a state could restrict the right to marry upon the basis of race alone, sections 60 and 69 of the Civil Code are nevertheless invalid because they are too vague and uncertain to constitute a valid regulation. A certain precision is essential in a statute regulating a fundamental right. "It is the duty of the lawmaking body in framing laws to express its intent in clear and plain language to the end that the people upon whom it is designed to operate may be able to understand the legislative will." . . . "It is a fundamental rule that no citizen should be deprived of his liberty for the violation of a law which is uncertain and ambiguous." . . .

Section 60 of the Civil Code declares void all marriages of white persons with Negroes, Mongolians, members of the Malay race or mulattoes. In this section, the Legislature has adopted one of the many systems classifying persons on the basis of race. Racial classifications that have been made in the past vary as to the number of divisions and the features regarded as distinguishing the members of each division. The number of races distinguished by systems of classification "varies from three or four to thirty-four." . . . The Legislature's classification in section 60 is based on [a classification] system suggested . . . early in the nineteenth century. . . . [One system] classified man into five races: Caucasian (white), Mongolian (yellow), Ethiopian (black), American Indian (red), and Malayan (brown). Even if that hard and fast classification be applied to persons all of whose ancestors belonged to one of these racial divisions, the Legislature has made no provision for applying the statute to persons of mixed ancestry. The fact is overwhelming that there has been a steady increase in the number of people in this country who belong to more than one race, and a growing number who have succeeded in identifying themselves with the Caucasian race even though they are not exclusively Caucasian. . . . The apparent purpose of the statute is to discourage the birth of children of mixed ancestry within this state. Such a purpose, however, cannot be accomplished without taking into consideration marriages of persons of mixed ancestry. A statute regulating fundamental rights is clearly unconstitutional if it cannot be reasonably applied to accomplish its purpose. . . .

The only reference made in the statute to persons of mixed ancestry is the prohibition of marriages between a "white person" and a "mulatto." Even the term "mulatto" is not defined. The lack of a definition of that term leads to a special problem of how the statute is to be applied to a person, some but not all of whose ancestors are Negroes. The only case in this state attempting to define the term "mulatto" in section 60 of the Civil Code leaves undecided whether a person with less than one-eighth Negro blood is a "mulatto" within the meaning of the statute. . . . Even more uncertainty surrounds the meaning of the terms "white persons," "Mongolians," and "members of the Malay race."

If the statute is to be applied generally to persons of mixed ancestry the question arises whether it is to be applied on the basis of the physical appearance of the individual or on the basis of a genealogical research as to his ancestry. If the physical appearance of the individual is to be the test, the statute would have to be applied on the basis of subjective impressions of various persons. Persons having the same parents and consequently the same hereditary background could be classified differently. On the other hand, if the application of the statute to persons of mixed ancestry is to be based on genealogical research, the question immediately arises what proportions of Caucasian, Mongolian, or Malayan ancestors govern the applicability of the statute. Is it any trace of Mongolian or Malayan ancestry, or is it some unspecified proportion of such ancestry that makes a person a Mongolian or Malayan within the meaning of section 60?

To determine that a person is a Mongolian or Malayan within the meaning of the statute because of any trace of such ancestry, however slight, would be absurd. If the classification of a person of mixed ancestry depends upon a given proportion of Mongolians or Malayans among his ancestors, how can this court, without clearly invading the province of the Legislature, determine what that decisive proportion is? . . . Nor can this court assume that a predominance in number of ancestors of one race makes a person a Caucasian, Mongolian, or Malayan within the meaning of the statute, for absurd results would follow from such an assumption. Thus, a person with three-sixteenths Malay ancestry might have many so-called Malay characteristics and yet be considered a white person in terms of his preponderantly white ancestry. Such a person might easily find himself in a dilemma, for if he were regarded as a white person under section 60, he would be forbidden to marry a Malay, and yet his Malay characteristics might effectively preclude his marriage to another white person. Similarly, a person having three-eighths Mongolian ancestry might legally be classed as a white person even though he possessed Mongolian characteristics. He might have little opportunity or inclination to marry any one other than a Mongolian, yet section 60 might forbid such a marriage. Moreover, if a person were of four-eighths Mongolian or Malayan ancestry and four-eighths white ancestry, a test based on predominance in number of ancestors could not be applied.

Section 69 of the Civil Code and section 60 on which it is based are therefore too vague and uncertain to be upheld as a valid regulation of the right to marry. . . . In summary, we hold that sections 60 and 69 are not only too vague and uncertain to be enforceable regulations of a fundamental right, but that they violate the equal protection of the laws clause of the United States Constitution by impairing the right of individuals to marry on the basis of race alone and by arbitrarily and unreasonably discriminating against certain racial groups.

Shenk, J. I dissent.

The power of a state to regulate and control the basic social relationship of marriage and its domiciliaries is here challenged and set at nought by a majority order of this court arrived at not by a concurrence of reasons but by the end result of four votes supported by divergent concepts not supported by authority and in fact contrary to the decisions in this state and elsewhere.

It will be shown that such laws have been in effect in this country since before our national independence and in this state since our first legislative session. They have never been declared unconstitutional by any court in the land although frequently they have been under attack. It is difficult to see why such laws, valid when enacted and constitutionally enforceable in this state for nearly 100 years and elsewhere for a much longer period of time, are now unconstitutional under the same Constitution and with no change in the factual situation. It will also be shown that they have a valid legislative purpose even though they may not conform to the sociogenetic views of some people. When that legislative purpose appears it is entirely beyond judicial power, properly exercised, to nullify them.

The prohibition of miscegenatic marriage is not a recent innovation in this state nor is such a law by any means unique among the states. A short history of miscegenatic marriage laws in this state and elsewhere will contribute to a better understanding of the problem at hand. A law declaring marriages between white persons and Negroes to be illegal and void was enacted at the first session of our Legislature. (Stats. 1850, ch. 140, p. 424.) Section 60 of the Civil Code declaring certain marriages invalid has existed since the advent of our codes in 1872, at which time it extended only to intermarriage between white persons and Negroes or mulattoes. It succeeded the prohibition against such marriages found in the above-mentioned statutes of 1850. Section 60 was amended in 1905 to include marriages between white persons and Mongolians (Stats. 1905, p. 554). The provisions of the law here attacked have remained unchallenged for nearly one hundred years and have been unchanged so far as the marriage of whites with Negroes is concerned. To indicate that the subject matter is not merely of ancient legislative consideration it should be noted that in 1933 the District Court of Appeal decided that sections 60 and 69 did not prohibit the marriage in this state of a white woman and a Filipino—a member of the Malay race (*Roldan v. Los Angeles County*, 129 Cal. App. 267 [18 P.2d 706]). That case was decided on January 27, 1933. Without delay the Legislature amended both sections to extend the prohibition to marriages also as between white persons and members of the

Malay race. The amendatory measures passed both houses of the Legislature and were signed by the governor on April 20th of the same year (Stats. 1993, p. 561) thus rendering nugatory the decision in the *Roldan* case—which was the obvious purpose of the legislation. As above indicated the present concern with the legislation is only as it affects marriages between white persons and Negroes.

Twenty-nine states in addition to California have similar laws. . . . Six of these states have regarded the matter to be of such importance that they have by constitutional enactments prohibited their legislatures from passing any law legalizing marriage between white persons and Negroes or mulattoes. Several states refuse to recognize such marriages even if performed where valid . . . particularly if an attempt has been made by residents of a state to evade the law. . . . The infrequency of such unions is perhaps the chief reason why prohibitive laws are not found in the remaining states. . . .

The ban on mixed marriages in this country is traceable from the early colonial period. For example, Maryland forbade the practice of marriage unions between Negroes or Indians and white persons as early as 1663. Laws forbidding marriages between Negroes and whites were passed in Massachusetts in 1705, in Delaware in 1721, in Virginia in 1726, and in North Carolina in 1741. In 1724, it was decreed in France that no Negro-white marriages were to take place in Louisiana. Most of the remaining states enacted similar legislation in the period between the formation of the United States and the Civil War.

Research has not disclosed a single case where a miscegenatic marriage law has been declared invalid. . . .

[The dissent reviews the authorities upholding anti-miscegenation laws—Ed.] The foregoing authorities form an unbroken line of judicial support, both state and federal, for the validity of our own legislation, and there is none to the contrary. . . .

Courts are neither peculiarly qualified nor organized to determine the underlying questions of fact with reference to which the validity of the legislation must be determined. Differing ideas of public policy do not properly concern them. The courts have no power to determine the merits of conflicting theories, to conduct an investigation of facts bearing upon questions of public policy or expediency, or to sustain or frustrate the legislation according to whether they happen to approve or disapprove the legislative determination of such questions of fact. . . . The fact that the finding of the Legislature is in favor of the truth of one side of a matter as to which there is still room for difference of opinion is not material. What the people's legislative representatives believe to be for the public good must be accepted as tending to promote the public welfare. It has been said that any other basis would conflict with the spirit of the Constitution and would sanction measures opposed to a republican form of government. . . .

Text and authorities which constitute the factual basis for the legislative finding involved in the statute here in question indicate only that there is a difference of opinion as to the wisdom of the policy underlying the enactments.

Some of the factual considerations which the Legislature could have taken into consideration are disclosed by an examination of the sources of information on the biological and sociological phases of the problem and which may be said to form a background for the legislation and support the reasoning found in the decisions of the courts upholding similar statutes. A reference to a few of those sources of information will suffice. . . . On the biological phase there is authority for the conclusion that the crossing of the primary races leads generally to retrogression and to eventual extinction of the resultant type unless it is fortified by reunion with the parent stock. . . .

The foregoing excerpts from scientific articles and legal authorities make it clear that there is not only some but a great deal of evidence to support the legislative determination . . . that intermarriage between Negroes and white persons is incompatible with the general welfare and therefore a proper subject for regulation under the police power. There may be some who maintain that there does not exist adequate data on a sufficiently large scale to enable a decision to be made as to the effects of the original admixture of white and Negro blood. However, legislators are not required to wait upon the completion of scientific research to determine whether the underlying facts carry sufficient weight to more fully sustain the regulation.

Those favoring present day amalgamation of these distinct races irrespective of scientific data of a cautionary nature based upon the experience of others, or who feel that a supposed infrequency of interracial unions will minimize undesirable consequences to the point that would justify lifting the prohibition upon such unions, should direct their efforts to the Legislature in order to effect the change in state policy which they espouse. . . .

7

The *Loving* Case

Virginia's Anti-Miscegenation Statute in Historical Perspective

Walter Wadlington

The Present Miscegenation Laws

Virginia's miscegenation laws were restructured and new limitations were imposed in 1924, when the General Assembly passed "An Act to Preserve Racial Integrity."[1] In some respects the new law repeated earlier proscriptions. Moreover, its sanctions were directed specifically at racial intermarriage, and it lacked special penalties for interracial fornication, such as a number of other jurisdictions adopted. However, a sweeping change in the scope of the law was effected by keying the miscegenation provisions to a new and very narrow definition of a "white person." The central features of the 1924 legislation [were] . . .

1. A provision forbidding any white person from marrying anyone other than a white person (or a person with no other admixture of blood than white and American Indian). For purposes of this limitation, a white person was redefined as one "who has no trace whatsoever of any blood other than Caucasian. . . ."

2. A prohibition against issuing a marriage license until the issuing official "has reasonable assurance that the statements as to color of both man and woman are correct." The act also empowered the state registrar of vital statistics to issue certificates of racial composition. The knowing or willful falsification of a racial registration certificate was made a felony.

3. All statutes relating to racial intermarriage which were then in effect were made applicable to marriages prohibited by new provisions. Thus the 1924 act carried forward from the Code of 1919 the provision rendering miscegenous marriages absolutely void, the civil and criminal applicability of the evasion provisions (dealing with domiciliaries who left the state to marry and then returned), and the criminal sanctions to be applied to both parties to a miscegenous marriage and to the person performing the ceremony.

The basic change embodied in the 1924 legislation was the shift of focus from the definition of a colored person to the definition of a white person. Without changing the definition of a colored person (one-sixteenth or more Negro blood) which had been adopted in 1910, it made it unlawful for a white person to marry anyone with any "trace whatsoever of any blood other than Caucasian." This made the prohibition against miscegenation broader than it had been in the past, since previously it had merely been unlawful for a white person to marry someone who met the statutory definition of "colored person." Thus for the first time following statehood the marriage of whites with Asiatics and other non-Negro races—and with persons possessing *some* Negro blood but less than one-sixteenth—was prohibited. And although the definition of "colored person" was changed in 1930 to include persons with any ascertainable Negro blood, the ban on miscegenous marriages remains broader than this definition would suggest.

The Pocahontas Exception

There was only one exception to the 1924 act's rule that a white person could not marry anyone with a trace of non-Caucasian blood. The act provided:

> It shall hereafter be unlawful for any white person in this State to marry any save a white person, or a person with no other admixture of blood than white and American Indian. For the purpose of this act, the term "white person" shall apply only to the person who has no trace whatsoever of any blood other than Caucasian; but persons who have one-sixteenth or less of blood of the American Indian and have no other non-Caucasic blood shall be deemed to be white persons.[2]

Constitutional Tests of the Present Miscegenation Laws

The Several Decisions of *Naim v. Naim*

Naim v. Naim, the first major test of the constitutionality of Virginia's miscegenation laws after their amendment in 1924, first reached the Supreme Court of Appeals in 1955.[3] The case was not a criminal prosecution but a suit for annulment. The plaintiff wife was white and her husband, according to the facts found by the court, was Chinese. The plaintiff was domiciled in Virginia when she and the defendant left the state to be married in North Carolina, which had no ban on such an interracial union. The parties returned to live in Virginia as husband and wife. Although the court found that the defendant was not a resident of Virginia at the time of the marriage, the defendant conceded that he and the plaintiff had left Virginia for the express purpose of evading its ban on interracial marriage.

In sustaining the lower court's annulment decree, the Supreme Court of Appeals specifically upheld the validity of the present miscegenation legislation. Replying to the key constitutional attacks based on the due process and equal protection clauses of the Fourteenth Amendment, the court said that regulation of marriage falls exclusively within the reserved powers of the states. Although the court did not indicate that an attack might successfully be made on a miscegenation statute if its classification was arbitrary, it pointed out that since no evidence of unreasonableness appeared in the record, the classification by the legislature would be accorded a strong presumption of validity once it was determined that the purpose of the law was within the purview of state regulation and that the statute bore a reasonable relation to that purpose.

An appeal was taken to the United States Supreme Court, which in a per curiam decision vacated the Virginia court's judgment and remanded the case because of the record's inadequacy "as to the relationship of the parties to the Commonwealth of Virginia at the time of the marriage in North Carolina and upon their return to Virginia."[4] . . . The Court justified its action on the ground that the constitutional issue was not presented "in clean-cut and concrete form, unclouded" by other problems not clearly appearing but possibly relevant to the disposition of the case. However, the Virginia Supreme Court of Appeals restated on remand what it considered to be the material facts and said that they were sufficient for the annulment ruling under Virginia law. The court then noted that not only was there no Virginia procedure under which the record could be sent back to the trial court for supplementation under the circumstances but that such a remand would in fact be contrary to existing practice and procedural rules. The court then reaffirmed its original decision upholding the annulment.[5]

When the case reached the United States Supreme Court for the second time, the Virginia court's decision in response to the first order was noted, and the case was dismissed as "devoid of a properly presented federal question."[6]

Notes

1. Virginia Acts of Assembly 1924, ch. 371.
2. Virginia Acts of Assembly 1924, ch. 371 § 5, at 535. . . .
3. 197 Va. 80, 87 S.E.2d 749 (1955), *vacated and remanded*, 350 U.S. 891 (1955), *aff'd*, 197 Va. 734, 90 S.E.2d 849, *appeal dismissed*, 350 U.S. 985 (1956).
4. 350 U.S. 891 (1955).
5. 197 Va. 734, 90 S.E.2d. 849 (1956).
6. 350 U.S. 985 (1956).

8

Crossing the Color Line

A Historical Assessment and Personal Narrative of Loving v. Virginia

Robert A. Pratt

On many evenings just before sunset, my grandmother and I would sit on our front porch. We lived in the rural black community of Battery, Virginia (approximately forty-five miles east of Richmond), which is located in Essex County. Suddenly, I would hear my grandmother remark: "Well, I see Richard's gone in for the night." I would then turn my head to follow the direction of her gaze, where I would see a white man driving his car down the dirt road leading to a house owned by my great-uncle. It was a two-story wood-frame house, which was one of the biggest in the neighborhood. Most of the rooms were usually rented out to various family friends, relatives, and occasionally to the families of those who worked at the sawmill—jointly operated by my great-uncle and his older brother, my grandfather.

Raymond and Garnet Hill, along with their two sons, lived there for a time in the early 1960s. Garnet's younger sister, Mildred, was a frequent visitor, especially on weekends. Mildred's three children usually accompanied her on these visits, but her husband never did—at least not during daylight hours. As my grandmother later explained, the white man who occasionally visited my great-uncle's house near nightfall was Richard Loving. The woman whom I knew as Mildred was his wife, and the three children with whom I occasionally played were their children.

If Richard Loving was to spend any time with his family in the state of Virginia, he had no choice other than to do so under the cover of darkness. He and his part-black, part-Cherokee wife had been banned from the state in 1959 for violating the state's miscegenation laws, which prohibited interracial marriage. Although Richard Loving and Mildred Jeter were legally married in Washington, D.C., in 1958, Virginia did not recognize the marriage and subsequently banned the couple from their native state. Not until 1967, when the United States Supreme Court declared Virginia's miscegenation statutes unconstitutional in *Loving v. Virginia*,[1] were Richard and Mildred Loving allowed to return to the state of their birth, having spent the first five years of their marriage in exile.

Richard Perry Loving and Mildred Delores Jeter had known each other practically all of their lives, as their families lived just up the road from each other in the rural community of Central Point, Virginia, located in Caroline County. Central Point had developed an interesting history of black-white sexual relationships over the years, which over time had produced a community in which a considerable number of the blacks were light-skinned. Some of the blacks in the area who were light enough to "pass" as white often did so, and some of those whose complexion was a little darker often claimed to be Native American, even though most of them were known to have black relatives. [See Part 3—Ed.] While there is undoubtedly a Native American presence in Caroline County, not everyone who claimed to be an "Indian" really was, but given the racial climate of the 1950s, some blacks thought it more socially acceptable to emphasize their Native American rather than their African ancestry.

Richard Loving spent most of his time in the company of these light-skinned blacks, who accepted him warmly, in part because his whiteness validated theirs but also because Richard's parents had lived among these people for most of their lives without asserting any of the prerogatives generally associated with white supremacy. For twenty-three years, Richard's father had defied the racial mores of southern white society by working for Boyd Byrd, one of the wealthiest black farmers in the community; and apparently, he never had any qualms about doing so. While the elder Lovings were not oblivious to racial differences, the close-knit nature of their community required a certain degree of interdependence which could sometimes lead to an acceptance of personal relationships in a particular setting that would have been anathema elsewhere. So when white Richard Loving, age seventeen, began courting "colored" Mildred Jeter, age eleven, their budding romance drew little attention from either the white or the black community.

Mildred (part black and part Cherokee) had a pretty light-brown complexion accentuated by her slim figure, which was why practically everyone who knew her called her "Stringbean," or "Bean" for short. Richard (part English and part Irish) was a bricklayer by trade but spent much of his spare time drag-racing a car that he co-owned with two black friends, Raymond Green (a mechanic) and Percy Fortune (a local merchant). Despite their natural shyness, both Richard and Mildred were well liked in the community, and the fact that they attended different churches and different schools did not hinder their courtship. When he was twenty-four and she was eighteen, Richard and Mildred decided to legalize their relationship by getting married.

Mildred did not know that interracial marriage was illegal in Virginia, but Richard did. This explains why, on June 2, 1958, he drove them across the Virginia state line to Washington, D.C., to be married. With their union legally validated by the District of Columbia, Mr. and Mrs. Loving returned to Central Point to live with Mildred's parents; however, their marital bliss was short-lived. Five weeks later, on July 11, their quiet life was shattered when they were awakened early in the morning as three law officers "acting on an anonymous tip" opened the unlocked door of their home, walked into their bedroom, and shined a flashlight in their faces. Caroline County Sheriff R. Garnett Brooks demanded to know what the two of them were doing in bed together. Mildred answered, "I'm his wife," while Richard pointed to the District of Columbia marriage certificate that hung on their bedroom wall. "That's no good here," Sheriff Brooks replied. He charged the couple with unlawful cohabitation, and then he and his two deputies hauled the Lovings off to a nearby jail in Bowling Green.

At its October term in 1958, a grand jury issued indictments against the couple for violating Virginia's ban on interracial marriages. Specifically, they were charged with violating Virginia's 1924 Racial Integrity Act. The act stipulated that all marriages between a white person and a colored person shall be absolutely void without any decree of divorce or other legal process, and it prohibited interracial couples from circumventing the law by having their marriages validated elsewhere and later return[ing] to Virginia. The Lovings waived their rights to a trial by jury and pled guilty to the charges. On January 6, 1959, Judge Leon M. Bazile sentenced each of them to one year in jail, but he suspended the sentences on the condition that they leave the state of Virginia and not return together or at the same time for a period of twenty-five years. The Lovings paid their court fees of $36.29 each and moved to Washington, D.C., where they would spend their next five years in exile.

During their years in the nation's capital, the Lovings lived with Mildred's cousin Alex Byrd and his wife, Laura, at 1151 Neal Street, Northeast. Their first child, Sidney, was born in 1958; Donald was born in 1959; and Peggy, the only girl, was born in 1960. The years in Washington were not happy ones for the couple. Richard struggled to maintain permanent employment while Mildred busied herself tending to the needs of their three children. During this time, they remained oblivious to the civil rights movement that was unfolding in their midst. "I just missed being at home," she told me years later. "I missed being with my family and friends, especially Garnet [her sister]. I wanted my children to grow up in the country, where they could run and play, and where I wouldn't worry about them so much. I never liked much about the city."

Virginia law would not allow Richard and Mildred Loving to live together as husband and wife in the state, nor would they be allowed to raise their mixed race children (considered illegitimate under state law) in Virginia. They could visit Virginia, but they could not do so together. They were not even allowed to be in the state at the same time; however, that did not stop them from trying or from succeeding on various occasions. Mildred and the children made frequent visits to Battery, Virginia, the rural black community where her sister and brother-in-law lived. When Mildred would arrive in Battery, some of the neighbors would begin to look at their watches to see how long it would be before Richard's car came cruising through the neighborhood. During those early years, Richard's visits to the "Big House" (the common nickname for my great-uncle's boarding house) occurred almost exclusively after dark; but after a time he became less cautious. Perhaps he was confident in the belief that our community would keep his secret, or he was convinced that the local authorities in Essex County (which was adjacent to Caroline County) were not that interested in monitoring his whereabouts. It was on those occasions that I played with the Loving children, especially Sidney, who was exactly my age.

The Lovings had not really been that interested in the civil rights movement, nor had they ever given much thought to challenging Virginia's law. But with a major civil rights bill being debated in Congress in 1963, Mildred decided to write to Robert Kennedy, the Attorney General of the United States. The Department of Justice referred the letter to the American Civil Liberties Union (ACLU). Bernard S. Cohen, a young lawyer doing pro bono work for the ACLU in Alexandria, Virginia, agreed to take the case. He would later be joined by another young attorney, Philip J. Hirschkop.

In October 1964, Cohen and Hirschkop filed a class action suit in the U.S. District Court for the Eastern District of Virginia. In January 1965, Judge Bazile presided over a hearing of the Lovings' petition to have his original decision set aside. In a written opinion, he rebutted each of the contentions made by Cohen and Hirschkop that might have resulted in a reconsideration of their clients' guilt. After citing several legal precedents he concluded: "Almighty God created the races white, black, yellow, malay and red, and he placed them on separate continents. And but for the interference with his arrangement, there would be no cause for such marriages. The fact that he separated the races shows that he did not intend for the races to mix."[2] The Lovings' attorneys appealed to the Virginia Supreme Court of Appeals, but their luck was no better there. On March 7, 1966, a unanimous court upheld Judge Bazile's decision. The convictions remained intact. Having exhausted their appeals in Virginia's courts, the Lovings proceeded to the U.S. Supreme Court.

On December 12, 1966, the U.S. Supreme Court agreed to hear the case. The [National Association for the Advancement of Colored People] (NAACP), the NAACP Legal Defense and Education Fund, the Japanese American Citizens League, and a coalition of Catholic bishops also submitted briefs on the couple's behalf. In preparing the brief for their clients, Cohen and Hirschkop reviewed the history of Virginia's miscegenation statutes dating back to the seventeenth century, referring to them as "relics of slavery" and "expressions of modern day racism." In concluding his oral argument on April 10, 1967, Cohen relayed a message to the justices from Richard Loving: "Tell the Court I love my wife, and it is just unfair that I can't live with her in Virginia."

Notes

Published originally in 41 Howard Law Journal 229 (1998).

1. 388 U.S. 1, 2 (1967).
2. *Id.* at 3. . . .

9

Loving v. Virginia

U.S. Supreme Court
388 U.S. 1 (1967)

Mr. Chief Justice Warren delivered the opinion of the Court.

This case presents a constitutional question never addressed by this Court: whether a statutory scheme adopted by the State of Virginia to prevent marriages between persons solely on the basis of racial classifications violates the Equal Protection and Due Process Clauses of the Fourteenth Amendment. For reasons which seem to us to reflect the central meaning of those constitutional commands, we conclude that these statutes cannot stand consistently with the Fourteenth Amendment.

In June 1958, two residents of Virginia, Mildred Jeter, a Negro woman, and Richard Loving, a white man, were married in the District of Columbia pursuant to its laws. Shortly after their marriage, the Lovings returned to Virginia and established their marital abode in Caroline County. [A] grand jury issued an indictment charging the Lovings with violating Virginia's ban on interracial marriages. On January 6, 1959, the Lovings pleaded guilty to the charge and were sentenced to one year in jail; however, the trial judge suspended the sentence for a period of 25 years on the condition that the Lovings leave the State and not return to Virginia together for 25 years. He stated in an opinion that:

> Almighty God created the races white, black, yellow, malay and red, and he placed them on separate continents. And but for the interference with his arrangement there would be no cause for such marriages. The fact that he separated the races shows that he did not intend for the races to mix.

After their convictions, the Lovings took up residence in the District of Columbia. . . .

The Supreme Court of Appeals upheld the constitutionality of the antimiscegenation statutes and, after modifying the sentence, affirmed the convictions. The Lovings appealed this decision, and we noted probable jurisdiction. . . .

The two statutes under which appellants were convicted and sentenced are part of a comprehensive statutory scheme aimed at prohibiting and punishing interracial marriages. The Lovings were convicted of violating § 20-58 of the Virginia Code:

> *Leaving State to evade law.*—If any white person and colored person shall go out of this State, for the purpose of being married, and with the intention of returning, and be married out of it, and afterwards return to and reside in it, cohabiting as man and wife, they shall be punished as provided in § 20-59, and the marriage shall be governed by the same law as if it had been solemnized in this State. The fact of their cohabitation here as man and wife shall be evidence of their marriage.

Section 20-59, which defines the penalty for miscegenation, provides:

> *Punishment for marriage.*—If any white person intermarry with a colored person, or any colored person intermarry with a white person, he shall be guilty of a felony and shall be punished by confinement in the penitentiary for not less than one nor more than five years.

Other central provisions in the Virginia statutory scheme are § 20-57, which automatically voids all marriages between "a white person and a colored person" without any judicial proceeding, and §§ 20-54 and 1-14 which, respectively, define "white persons" and "colored persons and Indians" for purposes of the statutory prohibitions. The Lovings have never disputed in the course of this litigation that Mrs. Loving is a "colored person" or that Mr. Loving is a "white person" within the meanings given those terms by the Virginia statutes.

Virginia is now one of 16 States which prohibit and punish marriages on the basis of racial classifications. Penalties for miscegenation arose as an incident to slavery and have been common in Virginia since the colonial period. The present statutory scheme dates from the adoption of the Racial Integrity Act of 1924, passed during the period of extreme nativism which followed the end of the First World War. The central features of this Act, and current Virginia law, are the absolute prohibition of a "white person" marrying other than another "white person," a prohibition against issuing marriage licenses until the issuing official is satisfied that the applicants' statements as to their race are correct, certificates of "racial composition" to be kept by both local and state registrars, and the carrying forward of earlier prohibitions against racial intermarriage.

I

In upholding the constitutionality of these provisions in the decision below, the Supreme Court of Appeals of Virginia referred to its 1955 decision in *Naim v. Naim*, 197 Va. 80, 87 S.E.2d 749, as stating the reasons supporting the validity of these laws. In *Naim*, the state court concluded that the State's legitimate purposes were "to preserve the racial integrity of its citizens," and to prevent "the corruption of blood," "a mongrel breed of citizens," and "the obliteration of racial pride," obviously an endorsement of the doctrine of White Supremacy. . . . The court also reasoned that marriage has traditionally been subject to state regulation without federal intervention, and, consequently, the regulation of marriage should be left to exclusive state control by the Tenth Amendment.

While the state court is no doubt correct in asserting that marriage is a social relation subject to the State's police power. . . . the State does not contend in its argument before this Court that its powers to regulate marriage are unlimited notwithstanding the commands of the Fourteenth Amendment. Nor could it . . . Instead, the State argues that the meaning of the Equal Protection Clause . . . is only that state penal laws containing an interracial element as part of the definition of the offense must apply equally to whites and Negroes in the sense that members of each race are punished to the same degree. Thus, the State contends that, because its miscegenation statutes punish equally both the white and the Negro participants in an interracial marriage, these statutes, despite their reliance on racial classifications, do not constitute an invidious discrimination based upon race. The second argument advanced by the State assumes the validity of its equal application theory. The argument is that, if the Equal Protection Clause does not outlaw miscegenation statutes because of their reliance on racial classifications, the question of constitutionality would thus become whether there was any rational basis for a State to treat interracial marriages differently from other marriages. On this question, the State argues, the scientific evidence is substantially in doubt and, consequently, this Court should defer to the wisdom of the state legislature in adopting its policy of discouraging interracial marriages.

Because we reject the notion that the mere "equal application" of a statute containing racial classifications is enough to remove the classifications from the Fourteenth Amendment's proscription of all invidious racial discriminations, we do not accept the State's contention that these statutes should be upheld if there is any possible basis for concluding that they serve a rational purpose. The mere fact of equal application does not mean that our analysis of these statutes should follow the approach we have taken in cases involving no racial discrimination. . . . In these cases, involving distinctions not drawn according to race, the Court has merely asked whether there is any rational foundation for the discriminations, and has deferred to the wisdom of the state legislatures. In the case at bar, however, we deal with statutes containing racial classifications, and the fact of equal application does not immunize the statute from the very heavy burden of justification which the Fourteenth Amendment has traditionally required of state statutes drawn according to race.

The State argues that statements in the Thirty-Ninth Congress about the time of the passage of the Fourteenth Amendment indicate that the Framers did not intend the Amendment to make unconstitutional state miscegenation laws. Many of the statements alluded to by the State concern the debates over the Freedmen's Bureau Bill, which President Johnson vetoed, and the Civil Rights Act of 1866, 14 Stat. 27, enacted over his veto. While these statements have some relevance to the intention of Congress in submitting the Fourteenth Amendment, it must be understood that they pertained to the passage of specific statutes and not to the broader, organic purpose of a constitutional amendment. As for the various statements directly concerning the Fourteenth Amendment, we have said in connection with a related problem, that although these historical sources "cast some light" they are not sufficient to resolve the problem; "[a]t best, they are inconclusive. The most avid proponents of the post-War Amendments undoubtedly intended them to remove all legal distinctions among 'all persons born or naturalized in the United States.' Their opponents, just as certainly, were antagonistic to both the letter and the spirit of the Amendments and wished them to have the most limited effect." *Brown v. Board of Education of Topeka*, 347 U.S. 483, 489 (1954). . . . We have rejected the proposition that the debates in the Thirty-Ninth Congress or in the state legislatures which ratified the Fourteenth Amendment supported the theory advanced by the State, that the requirement of equal protection of the laws is satisfied by penal laws defining offenses based on racial classifications so long as white and Negro participants in the offense were similarly punished. . . .

The State finds support for its "equal application" theory in the decision of the Court in *Pace v. Alabama*, 106 U.S. 583 (1883). In that case, the Court upheld a conviction under an Alabama statute forbidding adultery or fornication between a white person and a Negro which imposed a greater penalty than that of a statute proscribing similar conduct by members of the same race. The Court reasoned that the statute could not be said to discriminate against Negroes because the punishment for each participant in the offense was the same. However, . . . in rejecting the reasoning of that case, we stated "*Pace* represents a limited view of the Equal Protection Clause which has not withstood analysis in the subsequent decisions of this Court." *McLaughlin v. Florida* [379 U.S. 184, 188 (1964)]. As we there demonstrated, the Equal Protection Clause requires the consideration of whether the classifications drawn by any statute constitute an arbitrary and invidious discrimination. The clear and central purpose of the Fourteenth Amendment was to eliminate all official state sources of invidious racial discrimination in the States. . . .

There can be no question but that Virginia's miscegenation statutes rest solely upon distinctions drawn according to race. The statutes proscribe generally accepted conduct if engaged in by members of different races. Over the years, this Court has consistently repudiated "[d]istinctions between citizens solely because of their ancestry" as being "odious to a free people whose institutions are founded upon the doctrine of equality." *Hirabayashi v. United States*, 320 U.S. 81, 100 (1943). At the very least, the Equal Protection Clause demands that racial classifications, especially suspect in criminal statutes, be subjected to the "most rigid scrutiny," *Korematsu v. United States*, 323 U.S. 214, 216 (1944), and, if they are ever to be upheld, they must be shown to be necessary to the accomplishment of some permissible state objective, independent of the racial discrimination which it was the object of the Fourteenth Amendment to eliminate. Indeed, two members of this Court have already stated that they "cannot conceive of a valid legislative purpose . . . which makes the color of a person's skin the test of whether his conduct is a criminal offense." *McLaughlin v. Florida* [379 U.S.] at 198 (Stewart, J., joined by Douglas, J., concurring).

There is patently no legitimate overriding purpose independent of invidious racial discrimination which justifies this classification. The fact that Virginia prohibits only interracial marriages involving white persons demonstrates that the racial classifications must stand on their own justification, as measures designed to maintain White Supremacy. We have consistently denied the constitutionality of measures which restrict the rights of citizens on account of race. There can be no doubt that restricting the freedom to marry solely because of racial classifications violates the central meaning of the Equal Protection Clause.

These convictions must be reversed. *It is so ordered.*

10

How Are We Doing with *Loving*?

Race, Law, and Intermarriage

Randall Kennedy

The Supreme Court issued its ruling [in *Loving v. Virginia*] on June 12, 1967. Given that thirty years have elapsed since that landmark decision, it seems appropriate to ask: "How are we doing with *Loving*?"

The answer to that question depends on one's goals. A person committed to the idea that the United States should be governed as a pigmentocracy, by and on behalf of white people, cannot be pleased that *Loving* occupies a totally secure niche in American constitutional jurisprudence; that its ethos is sufficiently vibrant to have caused a principal to lose his job in Wedowee, Alabama, for voicing opposition to interracial dating and marriage [see introduction to Part 1—Ed.]; and that the very conduct that the *Loving* decision helped legitimate has become sufficiently acceptable that, by 1991, Senator Strom Thurmond—once a fire-eating segregationist—could find himself fighting unreservedly on behalf of the imperiled Supreme Court nomination of Clarence Thomas, a black man who resided in Virginia and lived in married bliss with a white woman named Virginia.

By contrast, *Loving* is a story of unambiguous triumph for those who march under the banner of Freedom to Choose, who believe that—except in narrow circumstances irrelevant to this discussion—government should play no part in regulating the contractual decisions of private parties, and who grant a virtually indefeasible presumption of authenticity and voluntariness to the actual choices that people make. Milton Friedman and Richard Epstein have been intensely critical of various aspects of post-*Brown* race relations law, arguing that anti-discrimination provisions have been both wastefully inefficient and intolerably oppressive.[1] I would suppose, though, that they and other libertarian-minded critics of anti-discrimination laws in the private sector would applaud *Loving* insofar as it racially deregulates the marriage market without imposing any burdens on private decision making. In the post-*Loving* regime, at least in terms of race—sexual preference is a different matter—no one has to worry about governments either thwarting desires to marry or prohibiting decisions to avoid certain associations, even if the avoidance is racially discriminatory. Furthermore, in the post-*Loving* era, and again I would suppose to the delight of the Friedmans and Epsteins of the country—and many others as well—there have been no public efforts aimed at affirmative action in the marriage marketplace—no quotas, set-asides, or goals and timetables. In sum, the post-*Loving* era can be viewed as a sort of laboratory in which, at least in terms of race relations, the legal regime that some libertarians espouse has been allowed to operate.

The answer to the question "How are we doing with *Loving*?" is considerably more ambiguous for those who believe, as I do, that the polity is under an obligation to stop, if not reverse, the train of dismal consequences unleashed by white supremacist practices in the past; that one such consequence is the social ostracism that continues to afflict African Americans; and that one reflection of and contribution to that ostracism is the extent to which the marriage market remains racially segmented. According to the calculations of Douglas Besharov and Timothy Sullivan, in 1960 about 1.7 percent of married blacks had a white spouse.[2] In 1990 the percentage had risen to about 5.9 percent.[3] Moreover, the pace of increase in marriage across the black-white racial frontier is quickening, especially in terms of white men and black women.

Besharov and Sullivan contend approvingly that the realities reflected by these numbers show "a strong, unambiguous trend toward integration within American families." I share their approval for reasons I will make clear in a moment. I am considerably more troubled than they are, however, about what their statistics reveal about the present state of race relations. They note that "African Americans are substantially less likely to marry whites than are Hispanics, Asians, or native Americans." But that rather bland formulation obscures the fact that, in Nathan Glazer's words, "Blacks stand out uniquely among the array of American ethnic and racial groups in the degree to which marriages remain within the group."[4] Other peoples of color have followed a pattern pursuant to which intermarriage with whites increased over time. Of marriages in which a person of Japanese ancestry participated in the 1940s, for example, about 10 to 15 percent involved intermarriages with whites; by the 1960s, nearly half of the marriages in which a person of Japanese ancestry participated involved intermarriages with whites. There has been a lesser degree of intermarriage [of Whites] with other groups, such as people of Chinese and Korean ancestry. But the rates at which individuals in these groups intermarry with whites have always been greater than black-white rates of intermarriage.

There is considerable reluctance to view the relatively low rates of black-white intermarriage as a problem. One source of reluctance is a desire to avoid nourishing an already swollen racial egotism that afflicts many whites; some people understandably fear that positing intimate association with whites as a valuable commodity will only exacerbate the vice of white racial pride. Another source of reluctance is that portraying low rates of black-white intermarriage as a problem will reinforce long-standing beliefs that blacks lack a decent sense of racial self-respect and want nothing more than to become intimate, especially sexually intimate, with whites. A third source of reluctance stems from the sense that marriage cannot or should not be thought of in distributive terms because, based on tender feelings of love, it occupies a wholly different plane than jobs, housing, schooling, or any of the other institutions, goods, or services that are the typical subjects of debate in discussions over race relations policy.

Each of these concerns points toward political and analytical difficulties that make the subject of black-white intermarriage treacherous terrain. In my view, however, the relative paucity of black-white intermarriages is an important problem that warrants attention and discussion. That blacks intermarry with whites at strikingly lower rates than others is yet another sign of the uniquely encumbered and peculiarly isolated status of African Americans. It is also an impediment to the development of attitudes and connections that will be necessary to improve the position of black Americans and, beyond that, to address the racial divisions that continue to hobble our nation. Marriage matters. That is why white supremacists invested so much time, thought, and energy into prohibiting marriage across racial lines. Marriage plays a large role in governing the intergenerational transfer of wealth. It also is central to maintaining a stable race line. After all, when people intermarry and produce children of mixed race, racial identifications, racial loyalties, and racial kinships blur.

Granted the social significance of intermarriage, what should one's stance toward it be? In my view, black-white intermarriage is not simply something that should be tolerated—it is a mode of partnership that should be applauded and encouraged. Intermarriage is good because it signals that newcomers or outsiders are gaining acceptance in the eyes of those in the dominant population and are perceived by them as persons of value on whom it is worth risking one's future. Intermarriage is also good because it breaks down the psychological boundaries that separate and distance people on racial grounds, opening up new expectations and experiences that would otherwise remain hidden. Intermarriage encourages the inculcation of transracial empathy that is crucial for enabling people to place themselves in the shoes of others racially different from themselves. Few situations are more likely to mobilize the racially privileged individual to move against racial wrongs than witnessing such wrongs inflicted on one's mother-in-law, father-in-law, spouse, or child. Fortified by such lessons and animated by a newly drawn map of racial self-interest, participants in interracial marriage are likely to fight against the racial wrongs that menace loved ones.

There are, of course, powerful forces arrayed against increased rates of black-white intermarriage. One impediment is the residual influence of white opposition. Some polls suggest that as much as 20 percent of the white population continues to believe that interracial marriage should be illegal. Some of these people express their disapproval in ways that go beyond answering the questions of pollsters. Through stares, catcalls, and even . . . violence, they put a pall over interracial intimacy, driving up its costs and frightening off some who might otherwise explore its possibilities. It is a terrible fact that in many locales, mixed couples face a substantial risk that they will be subjected to abuse by those who feel affronted by a form of loving that they perceive as "unnatural."

A second impediment is the centrifugal force of black solidarity. . . .

Blacks who intermarry with whites can expect to be viewed with skepticism, if not hostility, by many other blacks who will consider them to be racial defectors. It does not matter that there are many examples of blacks who, though intermarried with whites, have consistently and militantly fought to improve the fortunes of African Americans. I think, for example, of Frederick Douglass, Walter White, Richard Wright, James Farmer, and Marian Wright Edelman. For one thing, despite their actions these figures will receive a certain amount of derision from blacks who will complain that they "talked black but slept white," thereby limiting their potential overall contribution to the African American community.

A third impediment has to do with the brutal consequences of deprivation: the fact that, because of historical and ongoing oppression, many blacks will simply have less to offer in the marriage market. Black people live shorter lives, typically have less education, are objects of discrimination, and face all manner of racial obstacles in the struggle for upward mobility. The extent to which this is true is the extent to which blacks will seem less of a "good catch" to many people, particularly whites, in the marriage market. I don't suggest for a moment that marriage is reducible to a commercial transaction. Obviously marriage often involves an entire array of delicate and mysterious feelings and motivations—lust, love, and the deepest springs of self-identity. Marriage, however, also triggers concerns about dollars and cents, social advancement, finding a good catch. As long as black people are kept in a state of relative social, political, and economic deprivation, others will be less inclined to want to marry them. . . .

Notes

1. *See generally* Richard A. Epstein, Forbidden Grounds: The Case against Employment Discrimination Laws (1992), arguing that employment markets are largely competitive and therefore regulation cannot be justified; Milton Friedman, Capitalism and Freedom 108–15 (1962), arguing in favor of the free market approach for solving such problems.

2. *See* Douglas J. Besharov and Timothy S. Sullivan, *One Flesh,* New Democrat, July–August 1996, at 19.

3. *See id.* at 21.

4. Nathan Glazer, *Black and White after Thirty Years,* Public Interest, Fall 1995, at 67.

C.

Beyond Black and White

As alluded to earlier in this part, state laws regulated Indian-White intermarriage differently than White marriages with African Americans. The differential treatment reflected the place of Indians relative to African Americans in the racial hierarchy, as well as gender inequalities. Bethany Berger considers the history of legal and social regulation of Indian-White marriages. Karen Woods analyzes anti-miscegenation laws by Indian tribes.

Some states, particularly in the West, which experienced significant immigration from Asia, prohibited Asian-White marriages. The California anti-miscegenation law, for example, made unlawful marriages between whites and "Mongolians" or "members of the Malay race." Leti Volpp considers the evolution of the legal regulation of Asian-Anglo marriages in California.

11

After Pocahontas

Indian Women and the Law, 1830–1934

Bethany Ruth Berger

III. Federal and State Governments and Indian Women: As Themselves, as Mothers, and as Wives

B. Indian Women as Wives and Mothers: Intermarriage and Beyond

1. A Not-So-Brief Note on Intermarriage

Marriages between white men and Indian women dominate the non-Indian popular and historical consciousness. In his sardonic debunking of popular perceptions of the American Indians, *Custer Died for Your Sins*, Vine Deloria writes that as an official with the National Congress of American Indians, although "it was a rare day when some white didn't visit my office and proudly proclaim that he or she was of Indian descent," all but one of these claimed Indian ancestors were women.[1] He explains this "Indian grandmother complex" as a product of the different racial connotations of marriage to a man as opposed to a woman of a different race: "A male ancestor has too much of the aura of the savage warrior, the unknown primitive, the instinctive animal, to make him a respectable member of the family tree. But a young Indian princess? Ah, there was royalty for the taking."

Not all intermarriages were between Indian women and white men. A census taken in 1825 of the Alabama Cherokee, for example, found that fully one-third of white people married into the tribe were women. Among the members of the Iroquois Confederacy in New York as well, several cases throughout the late nineteenth and early twentieth centuries concern white women marrying tribal men.

There is, however, probably some factual basis for the perception that most of those Indians who intermarried were women. Both the Alabama Cherokee and the New York Iroquois had remained well established and relatively prosperous on their land after significant white settlement had taken place. Due to federal removal of Indians from their lands and later facilitation of the transfer of land to non-Indians under the General Allotment Act, few Indian societies could claim these conditions. The single whites in Indian country were typically men, including soldiers, traders, and missionaries. By the time unmarried white women began to arrive, the Indian men of that area had probably been killed, removed, or so impoverished that they hardly made attractive prospective mates.

But military force and Indian impoverishment were not the only forces behind Indian-white marriages. Equally important, particularly in the earlier years, seems to have been a practice of various Indian tribes of marrying into an extratribal group to establish ties to that group. Jacqueline Peterson, in her excellent dissertation on women in the fur trade, writes that many of the Siouan and Algonquin-speaking tribes of the Great Lakes region used intermarriage to form and stabilize commercial and political alliances.[2] Those tribes, she found, perceived "intermarriage as a means of entangling strangers in a series of kinship obligations. Relatives by marriage were expected not only to deal fairly, but to provide protection, hospitality, and sustenance in time of famine."

While Europeans might be compelled to intermarry for commercial reasons, Indian women were also an independent source of attraction for the untamed country. Reports of their beauty returned to the Old World, such as the following by John Lawson:

> As for the Indian Women which now happen in my Way, when young, and at Maturity, they are as fine shaped Creatures . . . as any in the Universe. They are of a tawny complexion, their Eyes very brisk and amorous, their Smiles afford the finest Composure a Face can possess, their Hands are of the finest Make, with small, long Fingers, and as soft as their Cheeks, and their whole Bodies of a smooth Nature. They are not so uncouth or unlikely as we suppose them, nor are they Strangers or not Proficients in the soft Passion.[3]

Such reports were accompanied by tales that Indian women were not only easy to love but easy to leave. "They never love beyond Retrieving their first Indifferency," the same author wrote, "and when slighted, are as ready to untie the Knot at one end, as you are at the other."[4] Despite this encouragement of easy mating and leaving, stable relationships seem to have been the rule rather than the exception. . . .

For the women, intermarriage might have been a source of increased power as broker between both worlds. The lovely but passive Indian woman, loved and then easily discarded, was certainly not the only existing model. Indian wives among the fur traders of the North American Northwest in particular gained prestige and acclaim from both Indians and whites and often "exert[ed] as much influence within the fur trade household as their 'civilized' White spouses."[5]

The records of Colonial Virginia, for another example, present a Pamunkey woman whose relationship to her white lover was very different from that of Pocahontas and [John] Rolfe. Thirty-five years after Pocahontas died in England, a woman, probably a relative, ascended the Pamunkey throne. Queen Cockacoeske was chief of the Pamunkeys between 1656 and 1686 and worked within the Virginian colonial system to recapture some of the power her people had lost since Powhatan's chiefdom. During this time she had a son by English captain John West, whose first wife was rumored to have left him over the affair. Although her half-white son attended the Queen in meetings with the colonial government and seems to have been expected by the English to succeed her, upon her death the Pamunkey placed her niece on the throne.

Neither the powerful Indian woman nor the Indianized white man, however, was a comfortable figure for the lawmakers of the dominant society in its quest to eliminate the Indian problem by either removing or absorbing the Indians. Cockacoeske is an obscure figure of colonial history, and the white descendants of her son have never fought to prove their lineage. American history and culture celebrate Pocahontas's spirit because it benefited and was ultimately contained by the white race. . . .

Prominent figures among assimilationist "Friends of the Indians" even advocated intermarriage as a way both to assimilate the Indians and to improve the white race:

> Some prejudice, it is true, appears against the idea of admixture or mingling. . . . But . . . while ten grains of Indian to one hundred of white man might be injurious to the quality of the white race, half a grain to one hundred might supply exactly the element needed to improve it. . . . What happy result can there be to the lamb, but in absorption, digestion, assimilation in the substance of the lion. After this process he will be useful—as part of the lion.[6]

Both quotes reveal the duality of the white perceptions of the Indians. Unassimilated, they were "injurious," "defiled," and treated as such—denied citizenship, herded to reservations, and subject to miscegenation laws. Absorbed to the point of invisibility, on the other hand, they were beneficial and even celebrated.

A primary site for this absorption was the women. Legal decisions and legislative enactments reinforced this bivalent view. Both judges and lawmakers encouraged white men to marry Indian women without assimilating into their tribes, interpreted Indian marital customs to permit their husbands to abandon them without legal obligation, and discouraged ties between mother and child as long as those ties included affiliation with tribal relations.

2. Indian Women as Wives

a. Federal Cases: Status of the Non-Indian Husband

The unique legal status of Indians as members of "dependent sovereign nations" attached a peculiar mix of privileges and liabilities to Indian status. Indians throughout the nineteenth century found their rights to independence on their own land repeatedly abrogated and were persecuted when they refused to remain on the ever-smaller pieces of land they were allotted. With the resulting constant upheaval and diminution of hunting lands, the Indian people were not only legally and militarily beset but economically impoverished. On the other hand, they were also immune from criminal prosecution for crimes against Indians committed on Indian land. In addition, as various treaties and then the Dawes Allotment Act divided and parceled out tribal lands in efforts to "civilize" the Indians through ownership of private property, Indian status also equaled entitlement to often valuable property. In the century before the Indian New Deal, the federal courts considered a series of cases regarding which of the legal attributes of "Indian-ness" the white husbands of Indian women would hold.

... [T]he Supreme Court ... held in *United States v. Rogers*[7] that a white man who had intermarried and been adopted into the Cherokee Nation was not exempt from federal criminal jurisdiction. It appeared from the pleadings that Rogers had fully assimilated with the Nation:

> [Rogers] voluntarily and of his free will removed to the portion of the country west of the state of Arkansas, assigned and belonging to the Cherokee tribe of Indians and did incorporate himself with said tribe, and from that time forward became and continued to be one of them, and made the same his home, without any intention of returning to the said United States. . . . [A]fterwards [in the same month] he intermarried with a Cherokee Indian woman, according to the[ir] forms of marriage, and ... continued to live with said Cherokee woman, as his wife, until September, 1843, when she died, and by her had several children, now living in the Cherokee nation, which is his and their home.

The decision was not necessary to prevent lawlessness in white communities; the crime occurred on tribal lands in the Indian Territory west of Arkansas, and the victim was another "white" man who had similarly joined the Cherokee Nation. Nor was it necessary to protect the Cherokee community: Rogers had, through his adoption, subjected himself to the jurisdiction of Cherokee laws. Rather, the decision was an exercise in line-drawing, prohibiting intermarriage from becoming a method through which a white man could renounce his allegiance to the United States and join an Indian nation.

The decision is cited as the beginning of the end of jurisprudence treating Indians as foreign sovereigns. Justice [Roger] Taney stated that the Cherokee Nation was not

> a separate and distinct government or nation, possessing political rights and powers such as authorize them to receive and adopt, as members of their state, the subjects or citizens of other states or governments ... and thereby to sever their allegiance and citizenship from the states or governments to which they previously appertained....

But while this decision had obvious implications for Indian sovereignty, it affected the wives of intermarried white men as well. Their husbands could no longer fully assimilate themselves with their people but remained subject to the authority of the white government, unable to regard an Indian nation as sovereign in the way that their wives could. Following *Rogers*, legal shifts in allegiance would occur only from the Indian, and almost always female, side.

... [In 1888] Congress passed a statute declaring that Indian women who married white men would thereby become American citizens.[8]

The law was ostensibly designed to protect Indian women from unscrupulous white men who would marry them only to gain rights to Indian land. Although the statute responded to a real problem, it equally addressed the fear raised by *Rogers* that white men would assimilate with their wives' tribes. The amendment was intended to ... "mak[e] citizens of the United States instead of making Indians of our citizens." ... In gaining United States citizenship, intermarried Indian women were to lose their bonds with their tribes.

In 1894 the Senate established the Dawes Commission to investigate and report on the best means to extinguish tribal titles and divide the land among individual Indians of those tribes. The main problem addressed by the Commission was the status of the many whites claiming Indian citizenship among them. The Commission condemned the efforts of the tribes to ensure that such whites would not be allotted tribal lands. . . .

In light of this history and the condition of the tribal court systems, the Commission recommended that non-Indian tribunals determine who was eligible for tribal citizenship. Upon their recommendation the Commission was empowered to review applications to tribal citizenship and prepare the rolls that would alone constitute the membership of the tribes they represented.

In *Stephens v. Cherokee Nation*, the Supreme Court considered appeals of numerous decisions of the Commission, with 166 presented in printed briefs. . . .

The first case concerned a William Stephens, who was born in Ohio to a mixed blood woman and white man and had moved back to Cherokee country with his mother to seek readmission for both of them in 1873. The Chief of the Cherokees said he was convinced of the honesty and genuineness of Stephens's claim and wished the tribal council to pass a motion for his readmittance. The Commission, however, denied Stephens's application because the Cherokee Council had not yet memorialized his readmission. The court of appeals for the Indian territory upheld the denial.

The second appeal described was that of F. R. Robinson, a white man who applied to be enrolled on the basis of his marriage to a woman of Choctaw and Chickasaw blood in 1873. She had since died, and Robinson had remarried, to a white woman, in 1884. The Choctaw Nation opposed his enrollment on the grounds that he had "forfeited his rights as such citizen by abandonment or remarriage." The Dawes Commission, however, granted his application for citizenship, which was upheld in court.

The final case described concerned the application of Richard Wiggs, another white man, and his family for enrollment in the Chickasaw Nation. Wiggs had married Chickasaw woman Georgia Allen in 1875. Allen died in 1876, and in 1886, Wiggs married Josie Lawson, a white woman, with whom he had a daughter. The Commission held that Wiggs should be enrolled. The appellate court directed that his wife and daughter were to be enrolled as well.

In his opinion for the Court, Justice [Melville] Fuller did not touch on the justice or wisdom of these federal decisions of citizenship but simply reiterated that the government had the power to make them. Given paramount authority over Indian tribes, he wrote, Congress had the power to empower the Dawes Commission to determine who was entitled to citizenship and to make out correct rolls of citizens, "an essential preliminary to effective action in promotion of the best interests of the tribes."[9] In the single recognition of what this grant of power would mean for the Indian people, he noted that the legislation made a distinction between admission to citizenship and allotment of property, as if "there might be circumstances under which the right to a share in the latter would not necessarily follow from the concession of the former."

Justice Fuller returned to this distinction seven years later in the *Cherokee Intermarriage Cases*.[10] The Cherokee Code stated that the "rights and privileges herein conferred through intermarriage shall not extend to a right of soil or interest in the vested funds of this Nation," unless such intermarried persons contributed a specified sum to the general treasury. The Court affirmed the appellate court's ruling that the law was valid, but only for those who had intermarried after the law's enactment in 1875.

Justice Fuller's opinion in the *Intermarriage Cases* is perhaps most interesting for its presentation of the ways in which Cherokee laws regarding intermarriage developed reactively, responding to federal laws and decisions of federal courts. For example, although the Cherokees had always had a treaty right to permit white persons to reside in the Nation subject to Cherokee laws, immediately after *United States v. Rogers* the Cherokee Council passed an act stating that the Cherokees would exercise jurisdiction over all those entering Cherokee lands. The Court noted that the act was aimed at regulating intermarriage with white men. Further, the Cherokee Council adopted the law at issue in the *Intermarriage Cases* in 1874, when the "rapidly growing value of Cherokee lands" and the imminence of legislation making the land available to individual citizens was perceptible. Moreover, although the code had been enacted over twenty-five years before, the question of its enforcement was not brought to the courts until 1903, a few years after the *Stephens* decision. Then, faced with massive loss of Cherokee lands to those who had once been married to blood Cherokees, a large number of citizens by blood filed a protest with the Department of the Interior against the participation of intermarried persons in the distribution of the 4,420,406 acres then held communally by the Cherokee Nation.

The opinion in the *Intermarriage Cases* is sensitive to the significance of various Cherokee declarations of membership. It distinguishes laws such as the 1855 law regarding jurisdiction over non-Cherokees and that permitting Cherokees by marriage to vote in tribal elections on the grounds that "[u]nder the polity of the Cherokees citizenship and communal ownership were distinct things." Despite this perceptiveness, however, the Court held that until the Cherokees codified this distinction in 1875, those who intermarried into the Nation gained a right to communal tribal property. No less than the other major federal decisions of the period, therefore, the decision helped facilitate the loss of tribal lands to non-Indians and the disappearance of the tribal unit in favor of the male-headed nuclear family.

b. States: Status of the Indian Wife

As the federal courts were effectively declaring that white husbands of Indian women could gain their wives' rights to tribal property but not their national identity, state courts were creating a body of jurisprudence under which men, Indian or white, had almost no legal obligation to their Indian wives. The dominant view of judicial treatment of Indian marriage and divorce is that stated by Felix Cohen, that "Indian tribes have been accorded the widest possible latitude in regulating the domestic relations of their members."[11] This established doctrine, and the extension of the general rule that marriages would be upheld if valid where contracted, disguised the extent to which assumptions regarding the dissolute nature of sexual relations with Indian women often led courts to assume Indian marriages invalid without question. In 1832, for example, Circuit Judge James Duane Doty ended an era in the established Indian-white community of Green Bay, Wisconsin, by indicting thirty-six of its principal male inhabitants for fornication with their Indian and mixed blood wives.[12] In 1917, moreover, only one year after the Supreme Court announced that Indians cohabiting without the benefit of marriage according to state law could not be prosecuted for adultery, the Minnesota Supreme Court confidently declared that a majority of mixed blood Indians were not the issue of lawful wedlock.[13]

But more important, the dominant view disguises both the extent to which nontribal courts read and interpreted sex-neutral tribal customs as existing for the benefit of men at the expense of women and the extent to which recognition of Indian customs was reserved for those the courts labeled uncivilized and thus undeserving of the protection of law. This view also does not acknowledge that the judicial interpretations of Indian customs damaged women both by stigmatizing them as participants in what courts saw as illicit intercourse and by leaving them economically insecure due to easy abandonment. More objective descriptions of marriage among Indian tribes reveal that marriages were neither so easily entered nor so frequently ended as the courts present them. Nor was the judicial vision that emerged during the nineteenth century inevitable even from the limited evidence of tribal customs that American courts had to work with. . . .

The earliest cases presenting the doctrine of divorce by abandonment were . . . Alabama cases dealing with women remaining in the East after Indian removal. Throughout the next century, judges cited these cases as precedent in determining the effect of Indian marriages. Two of these opinions concerned the validity of promissory notes made by Delilah Wall, a Choctaw woman, in light of the common law rule against a married woman's ability to contract. Delilah and David Wall had been married by a justice of the peace in 1831 and had lived together until 1839, when David left for the Choctaw country west of the Mississippi.[14] . . . [T]he court treated both [notes] as valid on the ground [that] the husband took no part of the wife's property under Choctaw law. As a consequence of this "peculiarity," the court held, the wife must have the capacity to contract to protect her property.

The gravamen of the opinions, however, is whether abandonment of an Indian woman would dissolve a marriage. After stating that "[a]ll the testimony in relation to rights of husband and wife, under Choctaw law, may have been of a disputable or doubtful nature," Justice [Henry] Goldthwaite proceeded to make law on that same doubtful testimony. The court immediately cast the custom of relatively easy dissolution of marriage as one designed for the convenience of the husband: "By [Choctaw] law, it appears that the husband may at pleasure dissolve the relation. His abandonment is evidence that he has done so." The court harks [back] to various classical sources to justify the decision, stating that "[h]owever strange it may appear, at this day, that a marriage may thus easily be dissolved, the Choctaws are scarcely worse than the Romans, who permitted a husband to dismiss his wife for the most frivolous causes," and that "[m]arriages among the Indian tribes must be regarded as taking place in a state of nature. . . ."

The court's recognition of the custom, however, seems to stem from a disdain for the perceived barbarism of the Indians, and it is grouped together with various other privileges of state law also denied to them:

> Do our laws allow Indians to participate equally with us in our civil and political privileges? Do they vote at our elections, or are they represented in our legislature, or have

> they any concern as jurors or magistrates, in the administration of justice? Are they subject to our laws of marriage and divorce, and would we sustain a criminal prosecution for bigamy, if they should change their wives and husbands at pleasure, and according to their own customs, and contract new matrimonial alliances? I apprehend that every one of these questions must be answered in the negative. . . .[15]

. . . Because the tribe that Delilah Wall was part of had, in the eyes of the court, insufficiently renounced their Indian allegiance, her abandonment was equal to a divorce, dissolving any legal relation to her husband.

Alabama's judicial "recognition" of Indian divorce in the *Wall* cases prevented Delilah Wall from defending herself as a *femme couvert*. Ironically, within this same period the Tennessee Supreme Court used its recognition of Cherokee marriage customs to declare that a separated woman *was* a *femme couvert* and as such could not bring an action to recover her property.[16] Margaret Morgan had married Gideon Morgan in 1813 according to the customs of the Cherokee tribe and had several children by him, but they were living apart at the time of the suit. The "property" at issue was several slaves Margaret's mother had given Margaret in 1828, who were sold to cover Gideon Morgan's debts. Here, where an Indian woman was trying to assert her property rights independent from those of her husband, the court did not treat the separation as a "divorce by abandonment."

The *Morgan* court claimed that in recognizing the Cherokee marriage as the equivalent of a state marriage, it was upholding the right of the tribe to regulate marriage within its jurisdiction. This claim is patently hollow. One of the few tribes to have written laws at this period, Cherokee law had long established that "the property of Cherokee women after their marriage cannot be disposed of by their husbands, or levied upon by an officer to satisfy a debt of the husband's contracting, contrary to her will and consent, and disposable only at her option. . . ."[17] This was particularly true for Cherokee women marrying white men. A law enacted in 1819 declared that the property of any Cherokee woman who married a white man was not "subject to the disposal of her husband, contrary to her consent."

Moreover, while courts framed their recognition of abandonment of an Indian woman as a divorce as an acknowledgment of tribal sovereignty over domestic relations, they also tended to imply that because informal dissolution was available, the prior "connexion" was not a marriage at all. Regarding the ten-year cohabitation and parenting of three children by Colonel Johnson, a government agent in Indian country, with Tapissee, the daughter of a chief, a Missouri court declared:

> [I]t is clear that all such connexions, which have taken place among the various tribes of North American Indians, either between persons of pure Indian blood, or between half breeds, or between the white and Indian races, must be regarded as a mere illicit intercourse, and the offspring be considered as illegitimate. . . .[18]

In addition, because a majority of these cases involved white men leaving Indian women when the possibility of return to civilization came along, judges often framed divorce by abandonment as a male privilege. See, for example, the language of the *Johnson* court: "[T]he understanding of the parties is that the *husband* may dissolve the contract at his pleasure." The Alabama court described Indian marriage customs with an even greater gender slant: "When a *man* found a *woman* he wished to marry, he made her a present of a blanket and she became his wife—when he wished to dissolve the marriage, he abandoned her."[19]

The women, moreover, were presented as degraded by their acquiescence to this practice: they were concubines or "article[s] of trade"; they were "bought" and "abandoned." The reservation of Indian divorce for uncivilized Indian women was made clear after, in a widely reported case, the Oklahoma Supreme Court seemed to suggest that a man could divorce a white woman by abandoning her and removing to Indian land.[20] Despite the limiting nature of the facts of that case, the courts soon modified the doctrine to suggest that Indian divorces would not be available if the court deemed the parties to be insufficiently Indian. As the Minnesota Supreme Court clarified in *La Framboise v. Day*,[21] a man might be the son of a white man, might speak English, might work as a clerk in a general store, yet still divorce his Indian wife by leaving her if he observed Indian customs, "particularly in the matter of buying and abandoning their women."

Perhaps more important, husbands retained no legal obligations to their Indian wives if they decided to move on: "It is plain that among the savage tribes on this continent, marriage is merely a natural contract, and that neither law, custom or religion has affixed to it any conditions or limitations or forms other than what nature has itself proscribed."[22] Or, in the words of the North Carolina Supreme Court, "[I]t can never be held that mere cohabitation, with an understanding that it may cease at pleasure, can constitute a marriage, or carry with it the rights and disabilities of that relation."[23]

Revealingly, the one case in which a court held that an Indian divorce was invalid involved an Indian woman trying to abandon a white man. In *Wells and Wells v. Thompson*,[24] Creek woman Mary Wells took her children and moved to her father's home in Creek land after her white husband, William, took up with another woman. Mary was later allotted land under the Treaty of Dancing Rabbit Creek. After Mary's death in 1836, William sold her allotted land. Their children challenged his claim to ownership and his right to sell the land. The Alabama court held that William had inherited and lawfully conveyed the land; because the separation did not occur on Indian land, the marriage could not be dissolved by Creek custom. . . .

Notes

Published originally in 21 American Indian Law Review 1 (1997).

1. Vine Deloria Jr., Custer Died for Your Sins 3 (1969).

2. Jacqueline Louise Peterson, The People in Between: Indian-White Marriage and the Genesis of a Metis Society and Culture in the Great Lakes Region, 1680–1830, at 87–88 (1981).

3. John Lawson, History of North Carolina: Containing the Exact Description and Natural History of That Country, Together with the Present State Thereof and a Journal of a Thousand Miles Traveled through Several Nations of Indians, Giving a Particular Account of Their Customs, Manners, Etc. 194 (Frances L. Harriss, ed., 2d ed. 1952). . . .

4. *Id.* at 199. . . .

5. Peterson, *supra*, at 87. . . .

6. Philip C. Garrett, Indian Citizenship: Proceedings of the Fourth Annual Lake Mohonk Conference 8–11 (1886). . . .

7. 45 U.S. (4 How.) 567 (1845). . . .

8. Ch. 818, 25 Stat. 392 (1888). . . .

9. *Stephens v. Cherokee Nation,* 174 U.S. 445, 488 (1899).

10. 203 U.S. 76 (1906).

11. Felix S. Cohen's Handbook of Federal Indian Law 137 . . . (1942).

12. Peterson, *supra*, at 1.

13. *In re* Liquor Election in Beltrami County, 163 N.W. 988, 989 (Minn. 1917).

14. *Wall v. Williamson,* 8 Ala. 48, 48 (1845) (*Wall I*). . . .

15. *Wall v. Williams,* 11 Ala. 826, 837–38 (1847) (*Wall II*).

16. *Morgan v. McGhee,* 24 Tenn. (5 Humph.) 13 (1844).

17. Act of Nov. 2, 1829, Laws of the Cherokee Nation: Adopted by the Council at Various Periods 142–43 . . . (1852).

18. *Johnson v. Johnson's Administrator,* 30 Mo. 72 (1860).

19. *Wall II,* 11 Ala. at 828–29 (emphasis added). . . .

20. *Cyr v. Walker,* 116 P. 931 (Okla. 1911). . . .

21. 161 N.W. 529 (Minn. 1917).

22. *Johnson,* 30 Mo. at 88.

23. *State v. Ta-cha-na-tah,* 64 N.C. 521, 523 (1870).

24. 13 Ala. 793 (1848).

12

A "Wicked and Mischievous Connection"

The Origins of Indian-White Miscegenation Law

Karen M. Woods

The Anglo-American antipathy toward Indian-white marriages is common knowledge. For the earliest settlers, religious injunctions and fears of the "other" were at the heart of miscegenation bans; by the nineteenth century, ideas about the relationship among religion, biology, and culture reinforced the legalized racial divide. What is less well known is that some Indian nations responded to Anglo-American laws with miscegenation laws of their own. In a world where racial identity determined citizenship and land rights, these Indian nations refused to give Anglo-Americans the sole power of definition.

Cherokee Law of Intermarriage: Citizenship, Sovereignty, and Land Rights

Intermarriage was a controversial issue among native peoples as well, even among the Cherokees, who are said to have intermarried with whites more than any other native tribe. Like the U.S. government, the Cherokees used race as a measure of citizenship. As Fergus M. Bordewich reminds us, "The concept of 'Indianness' has long been rooted at least partly in the belief that blood is fundamental to identity."[1] The control of citizenship was also a sovereignty issue. In order to have treaty rights upheld in the U.S. courts, the Cherokees could not afford—as no tribal nation could afford—to have questions raised about the Nation's status as a sovereign political entity. Any incursion onto that sense of separate "Indianness" was diplomatically perilous. In part, this was a defensive reaction to what Maureen Konkle defines as white "logic of identity-thinking," which "*always* has as its ultimate objective the destruction of Native political organization for the purpose of gaining Native land."[2] At the same time, Cherokee miscegenation law rejected white definitions of "Indianness" and claimed the right of self-definition.

The Cherokee regulation of intermarriage is of particular interest because the Cherokees had the first written code of native law, and because their resistence to removal gave New England intellectuals a rallying cry and represented "a laboratory for the civilization dreams of nineteenth-century policymakers."[3] Other southeastern tribes followed the Cherokee model and incorporated the regulation of intermarriage into their code of law.

The regulation of marriages between Cherokee women and white men was one of the earliest concerns of the new Cherokee legal system. Unlike the states, where Indian-white marriages were banned or otherwise frowned upon, white spouses were accepted in the Cherokee Nation and granted the privileges of citizenship. These laws were chiefly designed to maintain Cherokee lands and to regulate citizenship. The Cherokees wanted to protect Cherokee women and the Nation from white fortune hunters. In November 1819, [Cherokee Nation] President John Ross signed into a law a measure that required white men who marry Cherokee women to do so according to white laws (with a minister or judge and a license), limited them to one wife, prohibited white husbands from disposing of their wives' property, and imposed the payment of damages and forfeit of Cherokee citizenship should they leave their wives. The Choctaw Nation passed a similar law in 1840.

The regulation of these marriages and the citizenship status of the parties involved, including that of the mixed blood children, remained a concern of the Cherokee until the end of the nineteenth century, when the Cherokee court system was dismantled by the U.S. government. White citizens were a small but growing minority in the Cherokee Nation. According to the 1825 Cherokee census, there were 13,563 native citizens and 147 white men and 73 white women married into the Nation. An 1825 Cherokee law clarified a disputed point: that the children of a married white man and Cherokee woman were citizens of the Cherokee Nation, just as mixed descendants of Cherokee women were. In 1829 the National Council addressed the citizenship status of a white citizen after the death of a Cherokee spouse: the law said that if the marriage had produced children, then the white widow or widower could remain a Cherokee citizen as long as he or she remained single or remarried a Cherokee. If the marriage was childless, then the widow or widower was "deprived of citizenship." This was one of the rare regulations that applied to white men and women equally. Its harsher elements were repealed by an 1843 act which said that white childless widows or widowers could remain citizens as long as they did not marry a white spouse.

Despite this regulation of Indian-white marriages, there was still concern that it was too easy for white men of low character to marry Cherokee women. An 1828 article signed "Socrates" in the *Cherokee Phoenix* argued that a stricter law was needed "to exclude the thief, the robber, the vagabond and the tipler and adulterer, from the privilege of intermarrying with Cherokee women." "Socrates" suggested that an office be established in which white men would bring recommendations testifying to their good character and would post bond for their honorable behavior; if they did not live up to their testimonials, the marriage would be nullified and they would be expelled from the Nation.[4]

Over the years, the Cherokee government adopted the "Socrates" plan. The 1839 "Act to Legalize Intermarriage with White Men" reiterates the provisions of the 1819 law and adds that if "the fact should afterwards be established that he left a wife elsewhere, he shall be subject to removal as an intruder." A revised version of this act in 1843 made the provisions even stricter: instead of getting a license from the clerk of a district court, the prospective husband had to apply to the National Council. He also had to take an oath of allegiance to the Cherokee Nation and "freely alienate himself from the protection of all other governments." In like manner, the Choctaw Nation was increasingly concerned with white exploitation of native women. In 1849 the Choctaw Nation passed "AN ACT compelling a white man living with an Indian woman to marry her lawfully" or leave the Nation for good. (The man must be of good character in order for marriage to be allowed.)[5] The Cherokee laws became progressively more strict. In addition to the license and loyalty oath, by 1855 a white groom had to have a certificate of "good moral character" from seven Cherokee citizens. By 1866 the law referred to the "intermarriage of white men and foreigners" and required the signature of ten Cherokees "by blood" who had known the groom for six months. (This is one of the rare mentions of "blood" in Cherokee intermarriage law. White Cherokee citizens who had married into the nation were not acceptable witnesses. Only Cherokees by birth were permitted to vouch for a white hopeful husband.) Similar versions of these laws were passed in 1880 and 1890, and the Choctaws used these as models for their 1888 law. While the marriages of white men to Cherokee women were strictly regulated, there seems to have been no similar procedure for the marriage of white women to Cherokee men.

At the same time that it became more difficult for white men to marry into the Cherokee Nation, the law codified the customary practice of accepting marriages between Cherokees and other Indians. An act entitled "Intermarriage of Cherokees with Other Indians" reaffirmed that Indians from the tribes in Indian Territory who married into the Cherokee Nation were Cherokee citizens.[6] This law affirmed "Indianness" as a unique identity, a gesture of cultural and political solidarity.

While Cherokee intermarriage laws regulated Cherokee-white marriages, another strain of Cherokee miscegenation law banned Cherokee-black marriages. In these laws, the influence of white racial thought is evident. This ban on Cherokee-black marriages emerged within the context of a developing slave code. As the Cherokee elite took up white farming methods, the need for labor led to the adaptation of plantation-style slavery. Traditionally, Cherokee "slaves" were other Indians taken captive in war, their "slave" status marked by their lack of kinship ties. By the 1820s, however, Cherokee slavery resembled Southern white slavery. The Cherokees viewed themselves as radically different from Africans, now viewed as suitable slaves by virtue of their skin color. According to the 1825 census, there were 1,277 African slaves in the Cherokee Nation. . . . While many Cherokees did adopt the white system of African slavery, it is important to realize the preremoval Cherokee slave codes, unlike the antebellum white slave codes, say little about the behavior of masters and slaves. Most notably, "the hysteria which usually accompanied any suggestion of sexual relationships between white women and blacks is missing."[7]

Five years after the 1819 law regulating marriages with white men, the National Council resolved "[t]hat intermarriages between negro slaves and indians, or whites, shall not be lawful." Slaveowners who permitted their slaves to intermarry with "Indians or whites" would be fined $50. Male Indians and whites who married a "negro woman slave" would be punished with fifty-nine stripes [lashes with a whip—Ed.], while female Indians and whites who married a "negro man slave" would receive twenty-five stripes. Note that the law bans marriage only to "negro slaves"—free blacks are not mentioned. While the law regulating Cherokee-white marriages focused mainly on the actions of white men and seemed unconcerned with white women who married into the Nation, this ban affected all white and Cherokee men and women who crossed the black color line. (The women did get a slightly more lenient punishment.) The available records show that in 1888 the Choctaws similarly banned intermarriage between "Choctaws" and "negroes."

The 1827 New Echota Constitution addressed the citizenship status of mixed race descendants of intermarriage. The constitution said that "the [descendants] of Cherokee men by all free women, except the African race" and "the posterity of Cherokee women by all free men" are citizens. The use of the term *all free men* allows for the citizenship of children of a Cherokee mother and a free black father. (It is not clear whether this was a holdover from the traditional matrilineal society or the adoption of the Southern white policy of the child following the "condition of the mother.") The male descendants of a Cherokee mother and a free black father were allowed to vote, a right extended to "all free male citizens, (excepting negroes and descendants of white and Indian men by negro women who may have been set free)." These descendants, however, were ineligible for public office: "No person who is of negro or mulatlo [*sic*] parentage, either by the father or the mother side, shall be able to hold any office of profit, honor, or trust under this Government." The children of Cherokee mothers and free black fathers were thus eligible for a form of second-class citizenship (they could vote but not hold office), while the children of black mothers had none of the rights of citizenship.

Following removal to Indian Territory (now Oklahoma), the laws became increasingly severe, and the status of the slaves and free blacks in Cherokee law consequently declined. In the 1840s and 1850s it became illegal for slaves and free blacks "not of Cherokee blood" to own property, sell liquor, and carry a weapon; it was also illegal for Cherokee citizens to teach them to read or write. Fears of revolt and collusion between free blacks and slaves led to slave patrols and a crackdown on free blacks who aided in escapes. After an 1842 revolt, all free blacks (except those freed by Cherokee citizens) were ordered to leave the Nation by January 1, 1843.

The 1839 Tahlequah Constitution repeated the provisions of the first constitution, providing that mixed blood descendants were citizens (but ineligible to hold public office), except if their mothers were African.[8] In the same year the National Council passed "An Act to Prevent Amalgamation with Colored Persons." This law echoed the earlier 1824 ban, but it moved closer to the language of white racism, especially in its use of the term *amalgamation,* which was the term used to describe "[r]ace-mixing" during the antebellum period. The law banned intermarriage between "a free male or female citizen with any slave or person of color not entitled to the rights of citizenship." This confusing law expanded the terms of the 1824 ban on marriage with slaves to include free "colored persons." In effect, a free citizen (who had to be Cherokee, white, Cherokee-white, or Cherokee-black with black inheritance on the paternal side) could marry someone of African descent under one condition only: that the intended spouse was a Cherokee-black citizen whose African inheritance came from his or her father. The penalty for most participants in Cherokee-black marriages was not to exceed fifty lashes, but the penalty for "any colored male who may be convicted under this act" was one hundred lashes. It is clear that black male transgressions were feared the most; the hysteria about black male sexuality . . . is clearly visible in this new ban.

So what impact did Cherokee miscegenation laws actually have? [Rennard] Strickland argues that the laws banning intermarriages were generally followed but not enforced, and that there was little Cherokee-black intermarriage. Cherokee David Brown reassured his white audience in 1825 that "there is hardly any intermixture of Cherokee and African blood."[9] . . .

The regulation of "tribal blood" through miscegenation laws was part of a policy to keep Cherokee property in the hands of Cherokee citizens and to protect sovereignty through the preservation of "Indianness." For example, while Cherokee-white marriages were allowed, a white man could not inherit property from a deceased Cherokee wife unless they had living children. The ban on Cherokee-black marriages was meant to preserve "tribal blood" and to limit the inheritance of property by mixed blood children. Like white officials, Cherokee officials struggled with the measurement of blood quantum as the definition of citizenship became increasingly complicated.

Notes

Published originally in 23 Legal Studies Forum 37 (1999).

1. Fergus M. Bordewich, Killing the White Man's Indian: Reinventing Native Americans at the End of the Twentieth Century 73 (. . . 1996).
2. Maureen Ann Konkle, *Writing the Indian Nation: U.S. Colonialism, Native Intellectuals, and the Struggle over Indian Identity,* doctoral dissertation, University of Minnesota (1997), at 86.
3. Rennard Strickland, Fire and the Spirits: Cherokee Law from Clan to Court xiii (. . . 1975).
4. *Intermarriages,* Cherokee Phoenix, April 3, 1828, at 4.
5. Constitution and Laws of the Choctaw Nation 106 . . . (1869) (Vol. 11 Constitution and Laws of the American Indian Tribes).
6. Laws of the Cherokee Nation: Adopted by the Council at Various Periods 274–78 (. . . 1852).
7. Theda Perdue, Slavery and the Evolution of Cherokee Society, 1540–1866, at 50, 57 (. . . 1979). . . .
8. Laws of the Cherokee Nation, *supra,* at 7 (part 2).
9. David Brown, *Letter,* Religious Intelligencer, October 15, 1825, at 311.

13

American Mestizo
Filipinos and Anti-Miscegenation Laws in California

Leti Volpp

. . . By the time the Supreme Court finally declared anti-miscegenation laws unconstitutional in *Loving v. Virginia,* thirty-nine states had enacted anti-miscegenation laws; in sixteen of these states, such laws were still in force at the time of the decision. While the original focus of these laws was primarily on relationships between blacks and whites, also prohibited were marriages between whites and "Indians" (meaning Native Americans), "Hindus" (South Asians), "Mongolians" (into which were generally lumped Chinese, Japanese, and Koreans), and "Malays" (Filipinos). Nine states—Arizona, California, Georgia, Maryland, Nevada, South Dakota, Utah, Virginia, and Wyoming—passed laws that prohibited whites from marrying Malays. The statutes varied in their enforcement mechanisms: some simply declared miscegenous marriages void; others punished them as felonies.

I. California: Asian Invasions

In 1850, California enacted a law prohibiting marriages between "white persons" and "negroes or mulattoes." Twenty-eight years later, a referendum was proposed at the California Constitutional Convention to amend the statute to prohibit marriages between Chinese and whites. While the so-called "Chinese problem" was initially conceptualized as one of economic competition, created by the importation of exploitable laborers without political rights, the issue of sexual relationships between whites and Chinese also functioned as a prime site of hysteria.

Invoked were fears of hybridity. John Miller, a state delegate, speculated that the "lowest most vile and degraded" of the white race were most likely to amalgamate with the Chinese, resulting in a "hybrid of the most despicable, a mongrel of the most detestable that has ever afflicted the earth."[1] Miscegenation was presented as a public health concern, for Chinese were assumed by most of the delegates to be full of "filth and disease." Some argued that American institutions and culture would be overwhelmed by the habits of people thought to be sexually promiscuous, perverse, lascivious, and immoral. For example, in 1876 various papers stated that Chinese men attended Sunday school in order to debauch their white, female teachers. In response to the articulation of these fears, in 1880 the legislature prohibited the licensing of marriages between "Mongolians" and "white persons."[2]

The next large group of Asian immigrants—those from Japan—was also the subject of antagonism, leading to further amendment of the anti-miscegenation laws. While the impetus for tension was, again, economic, two prime sites of expressed anxiety were school segregation and intermarriage. Those who sought school segregation depicted the Japanese as an immoral and sexually aggressive group of people and disseminated propaganda that warned that Japanese students would defile their white classmates. The *Fresno Republican* described miscegenation between whites and the Japanese as a form of "international adultery," in a conflation of race, gender, and nation. In 1905, at the height of the anti-Japanese movement, the state legislature sealed the breach between the license and marriage laws and invalidated all marriages between "Mongolian" and white spouses.[3]

II. "Little Brown Men"

Tension over the presence of Chinese and Japanese had led to immigration exclusion of Chinese and Japanese laborers through a succession of acts dating between 1882 and 1924. Because industrialists and growers faced a resulting labor shortage, they began to import Filipinos to Hawaii and the mainland United States. Classified as "American nationals" because the United States had annexed the Philippines following the Filipino-American War, Filipinos were allowed entry into the country. On the mainland, a majority of Filipinos resided in California, with sizable numbers also in Washington and Alaska. By 1930 the number of Filipinos on the mainland reached over forty-five thousand. During the winter they stayed in the cities—working as domestics and gardeners, washing dishes in restaurants, and doing menial tasks others refused. In the summer they moved back to the fields and harvested potatoes, strawberries, lettuce, sugar beets, and fruits. . . .

On the mainland, 93 percent of all who emigrated from the Philippines were males, the vast majority between sixteen and thirty years of age. While some scholars have focused on patriarchal Asian values as the reason for early Asian migration being an almost exclusively male phenomenon, others have pointed to labor recruiting patterns and the specifics of immigration laws themselves as restricting the immigration of Asian women. United States capital interests wanted Asian male workers but not their families, because detaching the male worker from a heterosexual family structure meant he would be cheaper labor.

The Filipinos lived in barracks, isolated from other groups, allowed only dance halls, gambling resorts, and pool rooms of Chinatown as social outlets. They led ostracized lives punctuated by the terror of racist violence. Many restaurants and stores hung signs stating, "Filipinos and dogs not allowed."[4] Anxiety about what was called the "Third Asian Invasion" was expressed primarily around three sites: first, the idea that Filipinos were destroying the wage scale for white workers; second, the idea that they were disease carriers—specifically of meningitis; and, third, the idea that they were sexually exploiting "American and Mexican" girls.

The dance halls where Filipinos could pay ten cents to dance for one minute with hired dancers—usually white women—were the one location where Filipinos could mingle socially with white women. Filipinos were conceptualized as sexually attractive to vulnerable girls, due to their willingness to spend their wages on their natty appearance. One active member of the movement to exclude Filipinos from the United States described them as "little brown men attired like 'Solomon in all his glory,' strutting like peacocks and endeavoring to attract the eyes of young American and Mexican girls."[5] In response to the dance halls, white male violence erupted in several locations. The most publicized of these riots took place in Watsonville, California, where a mob of five hundred white men raided nearby farms, killing one Filipino and beating several.

The tenor of the times is made apparent in the report of a trial of a Filipino man, Terry Santiago, who had stabbed Norma Kompisch, a white dance hall girl, twenty-two times. The judge hearing the case, Judge Lazarus, hurled "a vehement condemnation of dance hall operators who make white girls dance with Filipinos." Judge Lazarus referred to his desire to "bring to public attention this very real evil. I once referred to Filipinos as savages. There was never a more typical case than this to justify my statement."[6]

Police conducted raids on parties at which white women and Filipino men intermingled. . . .

Anti-Filipino spokesmen also raged about the evils of intermarriage. The Northern Monterey Chamber of Commerce charged, "If the present state of affairs continues there will be 40,000 half-breed[s] in California before ten years have passed."[7] Two representatives from the Commonwealth Club and the president of the Immigrant Study Commission warned of "race mingling" which would create a "new type of mulatto," an "American Mestizo."[8]

There appears to have been a greater level of tension felt about Filipino male sexuality than for Chinese and Japanese. The president of the University of California testified before the House Committee on Immigration and Naturalization in 1930 that Filipino problems were "almost entirely based upon sexual passion."[9] While Chinese and Japanese were also considered sexually depraved—and perhaps more sexually perverse—Filipinos appeared to be specifically characterized as having an enormous sexual appetite, as more savage, as more primitive, as "one jump from the jungle." Their sexual desires were thought to focus on white women.

A possible reason for any sexual differentiation of Filipino men from Chinese or Japanese men was the link to Spanish colonialism. One contemporary writer referred to "the Latin attitude of Filipinos toward the opposite sex: he is assertive and possessive; she is his and his alone."[10] E. San Juan Jr. has also argued that the myth of Filipino sexuality was a departure from the "Anglo Saxon conception of the Oriental male," which he links to the media and popular identification of Filipinos with blacks during the Filipino-American War of 1898–1903.[11] Yet it is important to point out here that, as Ronald Takaki has documented, in the late 1800s, Chinese were also ascribed both physical attributes and "racial qualities" that had been assigned to blacks.[12] Further complicating this analogy is the fact that one contemporary observer argued that blacks, unlike Filipinos, caused less tension because they knew they were not supposed to intermarry with whites.

III. Legal Challenges

The right of Filipinos to intermarry was not seriously challenged in California until the early 1920s. . . .

[T]ension over relationships between Filipinos and white women was heightened due to the *Yatko* case, which took place in 1925 in Los Angeles.[13] Timothy Yatko, a Filipino waiter, had married Lola Butler, a white woman, in San Diego. The couple had met at a dance hall in Los Angeles and lived together after their marriage until Butler left Yatko. She worked as a singer and a dancer in a girl show where Harry Kidder, who was white, also worked as a substitute piano player. Yatko spotted the two together, and when he saw Kidder kissing his wife in Kidder's apartment, he stabbed Kidder, who died. In the murder trial, the state collaterally attacked the legality of the marriage in order to permit Lola Butler to testify against Yatko. Counsel for the state contended that the marriage was void because Yatko was Filipino and therefore "Mongolian." The court was asked to rule on the racial classification of Filipinos because there was no earlier decision on the subject. Contemporary accounts referred to the anti-miscegenation statute as what was, at that point in time, "an old and almost forgotten State law."

In arguing the point of whether or not Yatko should be considered a "Mongolian," counsel cited ethnologists, the encyclopedia, and various federal decisions in naturalization cases. Counsel for the state discussed the evil effects of miscegenation generally and pointed to Mexico as a specific example of the effects of race mixture. "We see the result that the Mexican nation had not had the standing, had not the citizens as it would otherwise if it had remained pure." This reference to purity, not surprisingly, was intended to describe the Spanish colonizers, not indigenous people, for counsel went on to state that "when the white people, or the Caucasians, came to the United States they did not intermarry with the Indians, they kept themselves pure."

The judge agreed. He stated:

> [T]he dominant race of the country has a perfect right to exclude all other races from equal rights with its own people and to prescribe such rights as they may possess. . . . Our government is in control of a large body of people of the insular possessions, for whom it is acting as a sort of guardian and it has extended certain rights and privileges to them. . . . Here we see a large body of young men, ever-increasing, working amongst us, associating with our citizens, all of whom are under the guardianship and to some extent the tutelage of our national government, and for whom we feel the deepest interest, of course, naturally. . . . The question ought to be determined whether or not they can come into this country and intermarry with our American girls or bring their Filipino girls here to intermarry with our American men, if that situation should arise.

The judge alluded several times to his long residence in the South and shared his "full conviction" that

> [the] Negro race will become highly civilized and become one of the great races only if it proceeds within its own lines marked out by Nature and keeps its blood pure. And I have the same feeling with respect to other races. . . . I am quite satisfied in my own mind . . . that the Filipino is a Malay and that the Malay is a Mongolian, just as much as the white American is of the Teutonic race, the Teutonic family, or of the Nordic family, carrying it back to the Aryan family. Hence, it is my view that under the code of California as it now exists, intermarriage between a Filipino and a Caucasian would be void.

Accordingly, the court allowed Lola Butler to testify. She represented Yatko "as the aggressor and Kidder as her chivalric defender." Yatko was convicted and sentenced to serve a life sentence in San Quentin.

The opinion of the judge in the *Yatko* case, that Filipinos, or Malays, were Mongolian, was shared by the attorney general of the State of California, U. S. Webb. In 1926, Webb authored an opinion letter stating that "Malays belong to the Mongoloid race." The letter was in response to an inquiry from the District Attorney of San Diego County, who wondered whether the San Diego County clerk should issue marriage liscenses to "Hindus and white persons and to Filipinos and white persons." Webb called this "more a question of fact than one of law," noted that he was unable to find any judicial determination of these questions, and proceeded to share the prevailing ethnology of the day. While "the Hindu," reported Webb, generally did not appear ethnologically to be a member of the Mongolian race, "Malays" were indeed so classified. While the first "great ethnologist" . . . had divided the human race into five classes (the white, black, yellow, brown, and red), the "most recent and best recognized variation" reduced the classification to three divisions by combining brown and red with the Mongolian in a division generally referred to as "Mongolian-Malay or yellow-brown." While Webb's letter was written to influence the action of counties, it was not binding, and the reaction of county clerks appears to have been mixed.

The analysis in Webb's letter was embraced by a Los Angeles superior court judge who issued the first of five decisions on this question. These five cases appear to be the only litigation—other than as collaterally raised in *Yatko*—on this issue in the State of California. In this first case, a white woman, Ruby F. Robinson, sought to wed a Filipino named Tony V. Moreno. Robinson's mother filed a suit against Los Angeles County and secured first a temporary and later a permanent injunction against [Los Angeles] County Clerk [L. E.] Lampton to restrain him from issuing a marriage license. Evidence as to Moreno's race adduced by the county's counsel and by the attorneys representing the mother "ranged over the whole of anthropological literature, from Linnaeus and Cuvier in the eighteenth century down to recognized textbook writers of today." The county argued that according to the best authorities, Filipinos are Malays and Malays are not Mongolians; the mother's counsel, assisted by expert testimony, argued that all the brown races are Mongolian. Judge Smith ruled in favor of Robinson's mother, that Filipinos were Mongolians. The decision was followed by protest in the Filipino community.

Following the *Robinson* case, L.A. County Clerk Lampton appeared to begin to deny marriage licenses to Filipinos seeking to marry white women. In 1931, Gavino C. Visco petitioned to marry Ruth M. Salas. Lampton denied this petition on the grounds that Visco was a Mongolian and that Salas was white. The couple appealed, and Superior Court Judge Guerin ordered Lampton to issue a license. But the case did not turn on Visco's Filipino identity, rather on the identity of Salas. The court held that Salas was "not a person of the Caucasian race." Salas, born in Mexico, had a mother born in Los Angeles and a father born in Mexico. As a nonwhite, Salas was not barred from marrying a Filipino, no matter whether Visco was classified as Mongolian or otherwise nonwhite. Nellie Foster, a contemporary writer, reported that the judge asserted that he would have granted the marriage license even if Salas had been white, which suggests that Judge Guerin did not think that Filipinos should be classified as "Mongolians."

The third and fourth cases in which this issue surfaced involved attempts at annulments of marriage. Estanislao P. Laddaran sought an annulment of his marriage to Emma F. Laddaran on the basis that the marriage had been in violation of the law, because he was "of the Filipino race" and his wife was "of the Caucasian race." The court refused. Shortly thereafter, in the *Murillo* case, Judge Gould also refused to annul a marriage, this time on the wife's petition that her Filipino husband was a member of the Mongolian race.

In *Murillo,* Judge Gould noted that while it was true that modern ethnologists had limited the number of racial groups to the white, the black, and the yellow, "these writers warn us that there is no fixed line of demarcation, that these classifications are simply loose fitting generalizations, that the races are still differentiating, and that the race divisions are simply convenient terms as an aid in classification." The judge rejected the modern-day scientific definition of Mongolian in favor of what the state legislature had in mind when it enacted the law. He asserted that if the legislators had anticipated modern scientific classifications, not only would whites be prohibited from marrying "Chinese, Japanese and Koreans (who are popularly regarded as Mongolians)," and "not only with Filipinos and Malays," but also "Laplanders, Hawaiians, Esthonians, [*sic*] Huns, Finns, Turks, Eskimos, American Indians, native Peruvians, native Mexicans and many other peoples, all of whom are included within the present day scientist's classification of 'Mongolian.'"

The fifth case before the Superior Court was *Roldan v. Los Angeles County.* Roldan, an "Illocano in whose blood was co-mingled a strain of Spanish," sought to marry Marjorie Rogers, a "Caucasian" from England. Los Angeles County Clerk Lampton refused. Ruling that neither Rogers nor Roldan was Mongolian, Judge Gates approved the marriage petition. The state appealed the case to the California Appellate Court, which in a divided opinion upheld the Superior Court decision, holding that there was no legislative intent to apply the name Mongolian to Malays when the statute had been enacted and amended. As in the *Murillo* case, the opinion, written by Judge Archbald, expressly followed not the scientific but the common understanding of what Mongolian meant at the enactment of the anti-miscegenation statute. The opinion noted that the classification of races into the five grand subdivisions of white, black, yellow, red, and brown was commonly used in 1880 and 1905, the dates when the statute was amended to cover "Mongolians." Because Salvador Roldan was a Malay and not a Mongolian, the L.A. County clerk was forced to issue him a marriage license.

In most of these opinions, the judges were careful to note that they were not addressing the "social question" of these marriages and suggested that if the "common thought" of today required, the legislature should address the issue. The legislature complied.

Nine days before the Roldan decision was issued, State Senator Herbert Jones, an exclusionist, introduced senate bills to amend the anti-miscegenation statute to include "Malays." On the same day, the secretary of the California Joint Immigration Committee requested its sponsoring organizations, the American Legion, the Native Sons and Daughters of the Golden West, and the California State Federation of Labor, to ask members to urge adoption of the bills. Two months later, both bills passed the Senate unanimously. The only dissenting voice in the Assembly was a Los Angeles County representative whose district included a large Filipino community. In April, Governor James Rolph, a prominent member of the Native Sons, signed the bills into law, effectively retroactively voiding and making illegitimate all previous Filipino-white marriages by defining any marriage of Caucasians with "negroes, Mongolians, members of the Malay race, or mulattoes to be illegal and void."

The 1934 passage of the Tydings-McDuffie Act promising eventual independence to the Philippines effectively halted Filipino immigration and, indeed, was successfully enacted because of the efforts of those seeking to exclude Filipinos from the United States. Exclusion led to the dissipation of obsessive anxiety over Filipino sexuality. While California subsequently became the first and only state after Reconstruction to rule that its anti-miscegenation laws were unconstitutional, in the 1948 case of *Perez v. Sharp*, the legislature refused to expunge the invalidated laws from the California Civil Code until 1959.

Notes

1. Megumi Dick Osumi, *Asians and California's Anti-Miscegenation Laws, in* Asian and Pacific American Experience: Women's Perspectives 6 (Nobuya Tsuchida, ed., 1982). . . .

2. *See* 1880 Cal. Stat. Ch. 41, Sec. 1, p. 3. . . .

3. *See* Cal. Civ. Code § 60 (1906): "All marriages of white persons with negroes, Mongolians, or mulattoes are illegal and void."

4. *See* Luciano Mangiafico, Contemporary American Immigrants: Patterns of Filipino, Korean, and Chinese Settlement in the United States 35 (1988).

5. This quote was attributed to Justice of the Peace D. W. Rohrback, a leader of the Northern Monterey County Chamber of Commerce. *See* H. Brett Melendy, Asians in America: Filipinos, Koreans and East Indians 55 (1977).

6. Yet he "did not blame" the Filipinos. "They are vainly attempting to adjust themselves to civilization, but haven't the training or education. They are only one jump from the jungle. It is

our fault for bringing them here." *Dance Halls Hit: White Girl Tells of Filipino Attack*, San Francisco Chronicle, May 17, 1936, at 3. . . .

7. *See* The Philippines Reader: A History of Colonialism, Neocolonialism, Dictatorship, and Resistance 59–60 (Daniel B. Schirmer and Stephen Rosskamm Shalom, eds., 1987).

8. *See* Osumi, *supra*, at 18. . . .

9. *Hearings before the Commission on Immigration and Naturalization*, 71st Cong. 35 (1930), statement of Dr. David Barrows of the University of California. . . .

10. Melendy, *supra*, at 69.

11. *See* E. San Juan Jr., *Configuring the Filipino Diaspora in the United States*, 3 Diaspora 117, 120 (1994). . . .

12. *See* Ronald Takaki, Iron Cages: Race and Culture in Nineteenth Century America 217–19 (2d. ed. 1990). . . .

13. *See* Nellie Foster, *Legal Status of Filipino Intermarriage in California*, 16 Sociology and Social Research 441, 444–45 (1932). . . .

Review Questions

1. How did the anti-miscegenation laws evolve with changing notions of race and class in the United States?
2. In light of Justice Traynor's national reputation for his innovative torts, contracts, and other decisions, why has his path-breaking opinion in *Perez v. Sharp* (1948), invalidating California's anti-miscegenation law, received so little attention?
3. Was the Supreme Court's decision in *Loving v. Virginia* (1967) inevitable in light of *Brown v. Board of Education* (1954)? (See Anders Walker, *Legislating Virtue: How Segregationists Disguised Racial Discrimination as Moral Reform following* Brown v. Board of Education, 47 Duke Law Journal 399 [1997].)
4. Did *Loving* have much of an impact? Why are African American–White intermarriage rates so low compared to other racial groups? Why do many personal ads in newspapers include statements such as "single white male seeks white female"? (See Note, *Racial Steering in the Romantic Marketplace*, 107 Harvard Law Review 877 [1994].)
5. What lessons can we learn from the legal history concerning regulation of Indian-White intermarriage and the Asian experience with anti-miscegenation laws? Are all racial minorities the subject of negative stereotypes about their sexuality?
6. If you are unmarried, would you consider marrying a person of another race? If you are married, did your spouse's race play any role in your decision to marry? Consider the following:

> One is left to wonder how an individual's choice of a spouse—particularly one of a different race—in fact is influenced by society, race, politics, and personal sensibilities, as well as by mere chance and the amorphous emotion known as love. Interracial relationships in the United States historically have been viewed as political statements, whether it be slaveholders' exerting horribly abusive power over Black women or Eldridge Cleaver's controversial views about the dominance of white women through violence. Many informed observers agree that racial identity entails at least some personal choice. One wonders how one of the most important choices in many of our lives could be made independent of the identity formation process. (Kevin R. Johnson, *Racial Mixture, Identity Choice, and Civil Rights*, Civil Rights Journal [Fall 1998], at 44–45.)

Suggested Readings

Harvey M. Applebaum, *Miscegenation Statutes: A Constitutional and Social Problem,* 53 Georgetown Law Journal 49 (1964).

Steven A. Bank, *Anti-Miscegenation Laws and the Dilemma of Symmetry: The Understanding of Equality in the Civil Rights Act of 1875,* 2 University of Chicago Law School Roundtable 303 (1995).

Amii Larkin Barnard, *The Application of Critical Race Feminism to the Anti-Lynching Movement: Black Women's Fight against Race and Gender Ideology, 1892–1920,* 3 UCLA Women's Law Journal 1 (1993).

Derrick Bell, *The Last Black Hero: A Chronicle of Interracial Love and Sacrifice,* 8 Harvard BlackLetter Journal 275 (1991).

Theodore G. Bilbo, Take Your Choice: Separation or Mongrelization (1947).

Margaret F. Brinig, *The Supreme Court's Impact on Marriage, 1967–1990,* 41 Howard Law Journal 271 (1998).

Under Sentence of Death: Lynching in the South (W. Fitzhugh Brundage, ed., 1997).

Stephen L. Carter, *"Defending" Marriage: A Modest Proposal,* 41 Howard Law Journal 215 (1998).

James Harmon Chadbourn, Lynching and the Law (1993).

Intermarriage in the United States (Gary A. Cretser and Joseph J. Leon, eds., 1982).

David G. Croly, Miscegenation: The Theory of the Blending of the Races Applied to the American White Man and Negro (1864).

James Elbert Cutler, Lynch-Law: An Investigation into the History of Lynching in the United States (1969).

David Brion Davis, The Problem of Slavery in Western Culture (1966).

Arthur H. Estabrook and Ivan E. McDougle, Mongrel Virginians (1926).

Race, Law, and American History 1700–1990: Lynching, Racial Violence, and Law (Paul Finkelman, ed., 1992).

Nellie Foster, *Legal Status of Filipino Intermarriage in California,* 16 Sociology and Social Research 441 (1932).

Madison Grant, The Passing of the Great Race (1916).

Ariela J. Gross, *Litigating Whiteness: Trials of Racial Determination in the Nineteenth-Century South,* 108 Yale Law Journal 109 (1998).

Cheryl I. Harris, *Finding Sojourner's Truth: Race, Gender, and the Institution of Property,* 18 Cardozo Law Review 309 (1996).

A. Leon Higginbotham, In the Matter of Color: Race and the American Legal Process (1978).

Martha Hodes, White Women, Black Men: Illicit Sex in the Nineteenth Century South (1997).

John James Holm, Race Assimilation or the Fading Leopard's Spots (1910).

Hrishi Karthikeyan and Gabriel J. Chin, *Preserving Racial Identity: Population Patterns and the Application of Anti-Miscegenation Statutes to Asian Americans, 1910–1950,* Asian Law Journal (forthcoming 2002).

Karen Isaksen Leonard, Making Ethnic Choices: California's Punjabi Mexican Americans (1992).

Samuel Marcosson, *Colorizing the Constitution of Originalism: Clarence Thomas at the Rubicon,* 16 Law and Inequality Journal 429 (1998).

Rachel F. Moran, Interracial Intimacy: The Regulation of Race and Romance (2001).

Edward Murguía, Chicano Intermarriage: A Theoretical and Empirical Study (1982).

Laurence C. Nolan, *The Meaning of* Loving*: Marriage, Due Process and Equal Protection (1967–1990) as Equality and Marriage, from* Loving *to* Zablocki, 41 Howard Law Journal 245 (1998).

Note, *Constitutionality of Anti-Miscegenation Statutes*, 58 Yale Law Journal 472 (1949).

Note, *Racial Steering in the Romantic Marketplace,* 107 Harvard Law Review 877 (1994).

Megumi Dick Osumi, *Asians and California's Anti-Miscegenation Laws, in* Asian and Pacific American Experiences: Women's Perspectives (Nobuya Tsuchida ed., 1982).

Peggy Pascoe, *Miscegenation Law, Court Cases, and Ideologies of "Race" in Twentieth-Century America*, 83 Journal of American History 44 (1996).

———, *Race, Gender, and Intercultural Relations: The Case of Interracial Marriage,* 12 Frontiers 5 (1991).

Orlando Patterson, Rituals of Blood: Consequences of Slavery in Two American Centuries (1998).

Jacqueline Louise Peterson, The People in Between: Indian-White Marriage and the Genesis of a Metis Society and Culture in the Great Lakes Region, 1680–1830 (1981).

Maria P. P. Root, Love's Revolution: Interracial Marriage (2001).

Paul Rosenblatt, Terri A. Karis, and Richard D. Powell, Multiracial Couples: Black and White Voices (1995).

Judy Scales-Trent, *Racial Purity Laws in the United States and Nazi Germany: The Targeting Process,* 23 Human Rights Quarterly 259 (2001).

Keith E. Sealing, *Blood Will Tell: Scientific Racism and the Legal Prohibitions against Miscegenation,* 5 Michigan Journal of Race and Law 559 (2000).

Reva Siegel, *Why Equal Protection No Longer Protects: The Evolving Forms of Status-Enforcing State Action,* 49 Stanford Law Review 1111 (1997).

David D. Smits, *"Squaw Men," "Half-Breeds," and Amalgamators: Late Nineteenth-Century Anglo-American Attitudes towards Indian-White Race-Mixing,* 15 American Indian Culture and Research Journal 29 (1991).

Paul R. Spickard, Mixed Blood: Intermarriage and Ethnic Identity in Twentieth-Century America (1989).

Lenore A. Stiffarm, with Phil Lane Jr., *The Demography of Native North America: A Question of American Indian Survival, in* The State of Native America: Genocide, Colonization, and Resistance (M. Annette Jaimes, ed., 1992).

Mark Strasser, Loving *in the New Millennium: On Equal Protection and the Right to Marry,* 7 University of Chicago Law School Roundtable 61 (2000).

Stewart E. Tolnay and E. M. Beck, A Festival of Violence: An Analysis of Southern Lynchings, 1882–1930 (1995).

Emily Field Van Tassel, *"Only the Law Would Rule between Us": Antimiscegenation, the Moral Economy of Dependency, and the Debate over Rights after the Civil War,* 70 Chicago-Kent Law Review 873 (1995).

Anders Walker, *Legislating Virtue: How Segregationists Disguised Racial Discrimination as Moral Reform following* Brown v. Board of Education, 47 Duke Law Journal 399 (1997).

Lynn D. Wardle, Loving v. Virginia *and the Constitutional Right to Marry, 1790–1990,* 41 Howard Law Journal 289 (1998).

Karen Woods Weierman, *"For the Better Government of Servants and Slaves": The Law of Slavery and Miscegenation,* 24 Legal Studies Forum 133 (2000).

Joel Williamson, New People: Miscegenation and Mulattoes in the United States (1980).

Part II

Racial Identity

Part 2 focuses on the legal aspects of racial formation and mixed race identity. The most famous legal definition of *African American*—the "one drop" rule—classifies a person as African American if he or she has a single drop of Black blood in his or her ancestry. Some observers contend that the rule had positive as well as negative impacts. Christine Hickman, for example, argues that the broad definition of *African American* built solidarity among Blacks and effectively defined the African American community as we know it today.

As a legal matter, racial identification was central to slavery, as only Blacks could be enslaved. The "one drop" rule, an expansive, rigid definition of African American, crystallized with the rise of Jim Crow and allowed for the efficient segregation of the races.

The legal simplicity of the "one drop" rule runs head on into the complexities of racial identity for mixed race people in modern social life. The complexities increase exponentially once one looks beyond Black-White mixture. "Mexicans commonly consider themselves a 'mestizo' or mixed race, acknowledging their Indian, European and (sometimes) their African heritage. In contrast, in the United States Whites have clung to the belief that their racial heritage is 'pure'" (Juan F. Perea, Richard Delgado, Angela P. Harris, and Stephanie M. Wildman, *Race and Races: Cases and Resources for a Diverse America* 870 [2000]). Asian and African American intermarriage also has increased significantly in recent years, with a corresponding rise in the number of African-Asian people. According to current estimates, nearly 15 percent of the total births in California are multiracial/multiethnic. (See Sonya M. Tafoya, *Check One or More . . . : Mixed Race and Ethnicity in California* [Public Policy Institute of California Report, 2000].)

At the individual level, multiracial people may feel torn between two (or more) ancestries. W. E. B. Du Bois famously described the analogous struggle among African Americans, specifically "the double consciousness" and "two-ness" of being "American" and "Black." (See W. E. B. Du Bois, *The Souls of Black Folk* 2 [Longmans 1965 ed.; 1st ed. 1903]. Similar struggles occur among and within mixed race people.

In certain circumstances, some mixed race individuals, depending in large part on physical appearance, may voluntarily assume a racial identity. What factors influence that choice? Consider the following:

> Candace Mills, the black editor of *Interrace* magazine (who is married to a white man), . . . says that it is far more gratifying for mixed-race blacks to identify with the oppressed

> group since championing the causes of the underdog allows them to feel that they are "black and proud" revolutionaries. To the contrary, the gratifying feeling of being a revolutionary is not necessarily the main reason for mixed-race people choosing to identify with the minority side of their ancestry. That decision most likely has to do with the typical openness of the black community in contrast to the white community. (Jon Michael Spencer, *The New Colored People: The Mixed Race Movement in America* 54 [1997].)

U.S. law has responded to racial mixture in circumstances other than slavery and segregation. For example, indigenous peoples in territories that later became part of the United States have intermarried with Anglos for centuries. Despite the lengthy history of intermarriage, federal Indian law and tribal law continue to struggle to define who is an "Indian" for purposes of various Indian programs. Similarly, racial identity of mixed race persons is of modern importance for purposes of the U.S. Census and affirmative action. (See Parts 4 and 7.)

Part 2 analyzes (1) the ostensible simplicity of the "one drop" rule and racial classification; (2) the real-life complexities of identity for mixed race peoples; (3) *mestizaje*, that is, racial mixture among Latinas/os and how that mixture is viewed by Latinas/os and Anglos; and (4) the legal definition of Indians by the federal government and Indian tribes.

A.

Legal Simplicity: The "One Drop" Rule

In this section, Ian Haney López considers judicial determination of a person's race and how it illustrates the social construction of races and racial identity. Christine Hickman's influential analysis of the "one drop" rule provides insights into its pros and cons. Ariela Gross analyzes litigation over "Whiteness" and its significance to the institution of slavery. Michael Elliott considers racial classifications in the nineteenth century, specifically the landmark case of *Plessy v. Ferguson*, 163 U.S. 537 (1896).

14

The Social Construction of Race

Some Observations on Illusion, Fabrication, and Choice

Ian F. Haney López

Under the jurisprudence of slavery as it stood in 1806, one's status followed the maternal line. A person born to a slave woman was a slave, and a person born to a free woman was free. In that year, three generations of enslaved women sued for freedom in Virginia on the ground that they descended from a free maternal ancestor. Yet, on the all-important issue of their descent, their faces and bodies provided the only evidence they or the owner who resisted their claims could bring before the court.

> The appellees . . . asserted this right [to be free] as having been descended, in the maternal line, from a free Indian woman; but their genealogy was very imperfectly stated. . . . [T]he youngest . . . [had] the characteristic features, the complexion, the hair and eyes . . . the same with those of whites. . . . Hannah [the mother] had long black hair, was of the right Indian copper colour, and was generally called an Indian by the neighbours. . . .[1]

Because grandmother, mother, and daughter could not prove they had a free maternal ancestor, nor could Hudgins show their descent from a female slave, the side charged with the burden of proof would lose. Allocating that burden required the court to assign the plaintiffs a race. Under Virginia law, Blacks were presumably slaves and thus bore the burden of proving a free ancestor; Whites and Indians were presumably free, and thus the burden of proving their descent fell on those alleging slave status. In order to determine whether the Wrights were Black and presumptively slaves or Indian and presumptively free, the court, in the person of Judge [St. George] Tucker, devised a racial test:

> Nature has stampt upon the African and his descendants two characteristic marks, besides the difference of complexion, which often remain visible long after the characteristic distinction of colour either disappears or becomes doubtful; a flat nose and woolly head of hair. The latter of these disappears the last of all; and so strong an ingredient in the African constitution is this latter character, that it predominates uniformly where the party is in equal degree descended from parents of different complexions, whether white or Indians. . . . So pointed is this distinction between the natives of Africa and the aborigines of America, that a man might as easily mistake the glossy, jetty clothing of an American bear for the wool of a black sheep, as the hair of an American Indian for that of an African, or the descendant of an African. Upon these distinctions as connected with our laws, the burden of proof depends.[2]

The fate of the women rode upon the complexion of their faces, the texture of their hair, and the width of their noses. Each of these characteristics served to mark their race, and their race in the end determined whether they were free or enslaved. The court decided for freedom:

> [T]he witnesses concur in assigning to the hair of Hannah . . . the long, straight, black hair of the native aborigines of this country. . . .
>
> [Verdict] pronouncing the appellees absolutely free. . . .

After unknown lives lost in slavery, Judge Tucker freed three generations of women because Hannah's hair was long and straight.

III. Social Race and Racial Formation

C. Racial Formation

Race must be viewed as a social construction. That is, human interaction rather than natural differentiation must be seen as the source and continued basis for racial categorization. The process by which racial meanings arise has been labeled racial formation. In this formulation, race is not a determinant or a residue of some other social phenomenon but rather stands on its own as an amalgamation of competing societal forces. Racial formation includes both the rise of racial groups and their constant reification in social thought. [There are] four important facets of the social construction of race. First, humans rather than abstract social forces produce races. Second, as human constructs, races constitute an integral part of a whole social fabric that includes gender and class relations. Third, the meaning-systems surrounding race change quickly rather than slowly. Finally, races are constructed relationally, against one another, rather than in isolation. . . .

In the early 1800s, people in the United States ascribed to Latin Americans nationalities and, separate from these, races. Thus a Mexican might also be White, Indian, Black, or Asian. By the 1840s and 1850s, however, U.S. Anglos looked with distaste upon Mexicans in terms that conflated and stigmatized their race and nationality. This animus had its source in the Anglo-Mexican conflicts in the Southwest, particularly in Texas and California. In the newly independent Texas, war propaganda from the 1830s and 1840s purporting to chronicle Mexican "atrocities" relied on racial disparagements. Little time elapsed following the U.S. annexation of Mexican territory in 1848 before laws began to reflect and reify Anglo racial prejudices. Social prejudices quickly became legal ones, highlighting the close ties between race and law. In 1855, for example, the California Legislature targeted Mexicans as a racial group with the so-called "Greaser Act." Ostensibly designed to discourage vagrancy, the law specifically applied to "all persons who are commonly known as 'Greasers' or the issue of Spanish and Indian blood . . . and who go armed and are not peaceable and quiet persons."[3]

Typifying the arrogant belligerence of the times are the writings of T. J. Farnham:

> No one acquainted with the indolent, mixed race of California, will ever believe that they will populate, much less, for any length of time, govern the country. The law of Nature which curses the mulatto here with a constitution less robust than that of either race from which he sprang, lays a similar penalty upon the mingling of the Indian and white races in California and Mexico. They must fade away; while the mixing of different branches of the Caucasian family in the states will continue to produce a race of men, who will enlarge from period to period the field of their industry and civil domination, until not only the Northern States of Mexico, but the Californias also, will open their glebe to the pressure of its unconquered arm. The old Saxon blood must stride the continent, must command all its northern shores, must here press the grape and the olive, here eat the orange and the fig, and in their own unaided might, erect the altar of civil and religious freedom on the plains of the Californias.[4]

Immune to the bitter irony of his own words regarding unaided might and the altar of freedom, Farnham called for the conquest of California on the grounds that "the Californians are an imbecile, pusillanimous race of men, and unfit to control the destinies for that beautiful country."[5]

Notes

Published originally in 29 Harvard Civil Rights–Civil Liberties Law Review 1 (1994).

1. *Hudgins v. Wright*, 11 Va. . . . 134, 134 (Sup. Ct. App. 1806).
2. *Id.* at 139–40.
3. Cal. Stat. 175 (1855). . . .
4. T. J. Farnham, Life, Adventures, and Travel in California 413 (1840). . . .
5. *Id.*

15

The Devil and the "One Drop" Rule

Christine B. Hickman

Introduction

For generations, the boundaries of the African American race have been formed by a rule, informally known as the "one drop" rule, which, in its colloquial definition, provides that one drop of Black blood makes a person Black. In more formal, sociological circles the rule is known as a form of "hypodescent," and its meaning remains basically the same: anyone with a known Black ancestor is considered Black. Over the generations this rule has not only shaped countless lives, it has created the African American race as we know it today, and it has defined not just the history of this race but a large part of the history of America.

. . . [M]any scholars have misunderstood the way that [the "one drop"] rule has shaped the Black experience in America. . . . The Devil fashioned [the rule] out of racism, malice, greed, lust, and ignorance, but in so doing he also accomplished good: His rule created the African American race as we know it today, and while this race has its origins in the peoples of three continents and its members can look very different from one another, over the centuries the Devil's "one drop" rule united this race as one people in the fight against slavery, segregation, and racial injustice.

I. Treatment of Mixed Race People: The Early Legal Record

Race mixing between Whites and Blacks in America is not new. Rather, it began almost immediately after the first Africans arrived in the United States. . . .

The unique American definition of "Black" has roots that are almost as old as race mixing on this continent. . . .

A. The First African Americans and the First Race Mixing

[This section summarizes the early history of African American–White "mixing" in the United States, which is reviewed in Part 1—Ed.]

B. Mulattoes: Black by Law

The legal treatment of mulattoes as Blacks, with all of the attached legal disabilities, may have begun as early as the seventeenth century. One of the earliest judicial uses of the term *mulatto* to describe a person of mixed Black-White descent appears in the Virginia case of *In Re Mulatto.*[1] The opinion was issued in 1656, just as race-based slavery was taking a firm hold. Although the opinion consists of a single sentence, and we know of no supporting record to illuminate the facts of the case, its logic constructs the American view of racial mixture between Black and White that has endured for over three hundred years. *In Re Mulatto* in its entirety states: "Mulatto held to be a slave and appeal taken."

Without discussion or debate, the court thus apparently articulated the first judicial expression of the rule of hypodescent. Implicit in its opinion is the finding that the litigant was of both African and European descent, but the court found that the European ancestry made no legally significant difference at all, and the holding is likely to have severed whatever ties this racial hybrid had with his European ancestry. In fact, it was the African ancestry that both defined his status and determined his fate.

A statute passed by the Virginia legislature in 1662, less than a decade after *In Re Mulatto* and forty-three years after the first Africans arrived, shows the early importance of drawing broad boundaries around the Negro race. Undoubtedly in recognition of the fact that most interracial fornication occurred between White men and Black women, the law provided: "[C]hildren got by an Englishman upon a negro woman . . . shall be held bond or free only according to the condition of the mother. . . ."[2] Significantly, this law broke with the traditional English common law rule that the children follow the status of the father. Instead it provided that children born of a Black mother and a White father would follow the common law applicable to farm animals—the child would follow the status of the mother.

Keeping "mulattoes" on the Black side of the color line was both psychologically and economically important. Its psychological importance arose because, as Winthrop Jordan writes, "[t]he social identification of children requires self-identification in the fathers."[3] White fathers were thus excused from social responsibility for their children and in this way benefited from the classification of their illegitimate children as "Black." They escaped responsibility not only for including these children in their families but also for including them in their larger family of the White race. "If [the White father] could not restrain his sexual nature, he could at least reject its fruits and thus solace himself that he had done no harm. . . . By classifying the mulatto as Negro he was in effect denying that intermixture had occurred at all."[4]

This classification scheme had several economic benefits for White settlers. It insulated White males from any responsibility for supporting their offspring by Black women slaves; these offspring became the property, and the responsibility, of the woman's master. Thus the birth of mulattoes provided an economic advantage to both the father, in the form of freedom from parental responsibility, and the mother's slaveholder, in the form of a new slave. This latter factor perhaps added another perverse incentive for the sexual abuse of slave women: The birth of mulatto children to a Black mother increased the plantation's inventory, as though the child were a lamb or a bale of cotton. The economic advantages of rearranging the lines of descent were thus significant.

In addition to providing that biracial children took the status of their racially enslaved mothers, early statutes reinforced the point that mulattoes were not considered desirable offspring in any event. A 1691 statute, which provided for the banishment of Whites who intermarried with a Negro or mulatto, was enacted for the express purpose of thwarting the births of that "abominable mixture and spurious issue"—mulattoes.[5] . . .

While the majority of mulatto children were born to Black mothers and inherited their slave status, legislation was passed to ensure that the mulatto offspring of free White women did not go unpunished. The 1691 Virginia law mentioned above imposed a fine on a White woman who had a "bastard child by a Negro," added five years to her term if she were an indentured servant, and committed the mulatto child to slavery until the age of thirty, regardless of the status of the White mother. This type of punishment was not unusual. For a time, Maryland took even a stronger stand, enslaving White women who, "to the disgrace of our nation," married Negroes, as well as enslaving their children.

In many of the colonies, then, interracial marriage was formally prohibited. . . . [See Part 1—Ed.]

II. Proposals for a Multiracial Category: Critiquing the Discourse

A. The "One Drop" Rule: The Misapprehension of the Historical Context

. . . . [H]istorian Paul Spickard, who has written the definitive history of twentieth-century mixed race Americans, is sometimes too quick to denounce the work of the "one drop" rule. Spickard, for example, argues:

> The function of the one-drop rule was to solidify the barrier between Black and White, to make sure that no one who might possibly be identified as Black also became identified as White. For a mixed person, then, acceptance of the one-drop rule means internalizing the oppression of the dominant group, buying into the system of racial domination.[6]

I agree that for a biracial person—a person who feels loyalty to parents of two different races—accepting the "one drop" rule will in some (but certainly not all) cases lead to the painful internalization of societal racism. However, I do not agree that accepting this rule constitutes "buying into the system of racial domination." History, in fact, shows us that the opposite is true: Often, those who fought the "one drop" rule were the ones who "bought into" the system of racial domination, and those who accepted this rule fought racial domination. . . .

B. Rebiologizing Race

6. Race, Biology, and the Law: The Racial Credential Cases

As racial mixing continued largely unchecked by the laws that purported to prohibit it, the result was children. As intermixture continued through the generations, many children became light-skinned, even White-skinned. While in most statutes mulattoes were classified with Blacks, "logic required . . . some demarcation between [mulattoes] and white men"[7] in order to establish a clear way of distinguishing someone White from someone who would not be considered White.

Without a bright line to distinguish White from mulatto, the efficient administration of American society, in which substantial legal rights were based on being White, would have been impossible. Guarding the port of entry to White status was essential to the protection of the delicate social order of a racial caste system, and the persistence and extent of illegitimate race mixing made this an issue of both importance and some delicacy. On the one hand, families considered White for generations had to be protected from the social consequences of an unknown dalliance by a distant ancestor. "To have pushed the definition [of black] any further would have embarrassed too many prominent 'white' families."[8] As the court noted in *State v. Davis*, "It would be dangerous and cruel to subject to this disqualification [being regarded as someone in the degraded class] persons bearing all the feature[s] of a white on account of some remote admixture of negro blood."[9] On the other hand, steps had to be taken to curb "[t]he constant tendency of this [mixed race] class to assimilate to the white, and the desire of elevation, [that] present frequent cases of embarrassment and difficulty."[10] Finally, maintaining the color line, however ethereal, was important as a matter of social etiquette. As Chief Justice [Joseph Henry] Lumpkin lamented in *Bryan v. Walton*: "Which one of us has not narrowly escaped petting one of the pretty little mulattoes belonging to our neighbors as one of the family?"[11]

a. Adjudicating Fractions of Blood. . . . [M]any states had laws that specifically set forth the fraction of Negro blood necessary to make a person Black. Over the years, this fraction ranged from one-quarter to one drop.

The concept of "pure blood," based as it was on pure conjecture, proved difficult both to litigate and to adjudicate. Even though fractional definitions of race gave the appearance of judicial objectivity, fairness, and consistency, the rationale for the decisions switched fairly quickly from a pseudo-scientific basis to the common social meaning of race. . . .

b. Racial Adjudication prior to Fractional Statutes. We begin our analysis of these cases with *State v. Thurman*,[12] an Alabama case in which the stakes based on racial classification were highest—life or death—and in which there was not a statute defining White, Negro, or mulatto. The question presented to the court was whether the defendant Thurman, who was convicted of rape or attempted rape of a White woman, would be executed or imprisoned. If he were a Negro or mulatto the law provided for his execution. If he were neither Negro nor mulatto, he would not be executed. . . .

While the court noted that the fact the defendant had "kinky hair and yellow skin" would "tend to prove that he was a mulatto," it was not conclusive enough to prove that he was mulatto rather than someone closer to a White person. The court's anguish was over the lack of "clear language" from the legislature in defining who was mulatto. "If the statute against mulattoes is by construction to include quadroons, then where are we to stop? . . . This discretion belongs to the Legislature." Uncomfortable with having Thurman's fate rest on such an imprecise standard, the court spared Thurman's life due to the inability of the prosecution to sustain its burden of proving that the defendant was a mulatto. Thereafter, the Alabama legislature passed a definition of race, which, like so many other states, defined race using racial fractions.

c. Counting by Fractions. The apparent mathematical clarity of the fractional statutes gave the appearance of objectivity and rationality, and while a few cases attempted to apply this fractional approach, it too proved difficult to litigate for the party who bore the burden of proof. Thus, in criminal cases, when race was an element of the offense, convictions were difficult to obtain when the physical appearance of the defendant made him appear racially ambiguous. The party bearing the burden of proof had to undertake a kind of human title search, by either tracing the defendant's ancestors for several generations and proving *their* race or relying on physical characteristics as a precise indicator of the fraction of Black ancestry.

In such cases, the prosecution often lost for failure to sustain a difficult burden of proving the fractions. For example, in the 1885 Virginia case of *Jones v. Commonwealth,*[13] Isaac Jones appealed his two-year-and-nine-month sentence imposed for the felony of marrying a White woman "against the peace and dignity of the commonwealth" in the face of a statute that defined a Negro as "a person who had one-fourth or more negro blood in him." Jones's defense was that his blood was not one-quarter Black within the meaning of the statute. Although the court found that Jones was a "mulatto of brown skin" and that his mother was a "yellow woman," the conviction failed due to the prosecution's failure to sustain their burden of proving that "the *quantum* of negro blood in his veins" exceeded one-fourth.

The difficulty of this human title search is further illustrated by the case of *Ferrall v. Ferrall,*[14] in which the petitioner-husband wished to have his marriage declared void on the grounds that his wife "was and is of negro descent within the third generation." The issue in the divorce case, which would determine the husband's responsibility for spousal and child support, was whether his wife's great-grandfather was a "real negro," that is, one who did not have any White blood in him, so that the fractional requirement could be met. In rejecting the notion that the racial origin of the great-grandparent should be ascertained by the general consensus of the community, the court strictly construed the statute and found that since the husband could not prove that the great-grandfather was a real Negro of unmixed blood, his wife could not be shown to be one-eighth Negro as required by statute.

Where the fractions could be "objectively" substantiated, however, the fractional requirements were strictly construed. For example, in *Peavey v. Robbins,*[15] plaintiff sued the voting inspectors for not allowing him to vote. He testified that both his mother and grandmother were White and that his father was a "dark colored man with straight hair" and that his grandfather was a "dark red-faced mulatto, with dark straight hair." The court simply did the ancestral mathematics and concluded that if the plaintiff's grandfather were a mulatto, that is, half White and half Black, "the plaintiff would be within the fourth degree" and therefore ineligible to vote.

d. Expert Testimony. When the difficulty of the ancestral title search became apparent, the court sometimes resorted to the use of "scientific experts" who could divine quantum of blood by visual inspection. . . .

In *Gary v. Stevenson*,[16] another suit for freedom, the "expert" witnesses disagreed. One testified that, upon visual inspection, "he could discover no trace of the negro blood in [the plaintiff's] eyes, nose, mouth or jaws—his hair is smooth and of the sandy complexion, perfectly straight and flat, with no indication of the crisp or negro curl; his eyes blue, his jaws thin, his nose slim and long." The "expert" concluded that it would take "at least twenty generations from the black blood to be as white as complainant." A second expert disagreed, judging the complainant as having "a small amount of negro blood; not more than a sixteenth, perhaps not so much . . . [his] upper lip rather thicker than in the white race—temperament sanguine." The thick lip and pleasant temperament were "scientific" evidence of the Black blood.

Sometimes the certified "experts" allowed to testify before the jury did not pretend to have scientific training at all. In *State v. Jacobs*,[17] the court's expert was certified on the grounds that "he was a planter, an owner and manager of slaves . . . more than twelve years, that he . . . had had much observation of the effects of the intermixture of the negro . . . blood." The court affirmed both his expertise and his opinion, stating:

> [I]t would often require an eye rendered keen, by observation and practice, to detect, with any approach to certainty, the existence of any thing less than one-fourth of African blood. . . . A free negro . . . may . . . be a person who . . . has only a sixteenth. The ability to discover the infusion of so small a quantity of negro blood . . . must be a matter of science . . . admitting of the testimony of an expert [such as] Pritchett.

With experts of this caliber, it was not a quantum leap for the court to allow such "scientific" expertise to give way to lay opinion of the witnesses on the theory that racial identification was a matter of common knowledge. Thus, in an 1892 North Carolina case, lay testimony was competent to show that a litigant was of "mixed blood": "It was not necessary that the witness should be an expert to testify to a matter which is simply one of common observation."[18] Similarly, in an 1829 case a jury awarded freedom to a litigant, announcing, "We of the jury . . . find, from inspection, that the said plaintiff . . . is a white woman." Finally, in *State v. Hayes*, a criminal defendant urged that she was White because her mother was White. In rejecting her contention, the court stated, "I was satisfied from inspection that she was a mulatto. . . . The African taint reduced her to the same degraded state, as if she were a free negro."[19]

Notes

1. McIlwaine 504 (1656), *reported in* 1 Helen Catterall, Judicial Cases concerning American Slavery and the Negro 78 (1926).
2. 1662 Act XII, II Hening 170 (1662), *quoted in* Paul Finkelman, The Law of Freedom and Bondage: A Casebook 16 (1986).
3. Winthrop D. Jordan, White over Black 167 (1968).
4. *Id.* at 178. . . .
5. Virginia, Act XVI, *quoted in* A. Leon Higginbotham Jr., In the Matter of Color, Race and the American Legal Process: The Colonial Period 44 (1978). . . .
6. Paul R. Spickard, *The Illogic of American Racial Categories, in* Racially Mixed People in America 19 (Maria P. P. Root, ed., 1992). . . .
7. *See* Jordan, *supra*, at 168.
8. *See* Eugene D. Genovese, Roll, Jordan, Roll, 420 (1974).
9. *State v. Davis,* 18 S.C.L. (2 Bail.) 558, 559 (1831). . . .
10. *White v. Tax Collector of Kershaw District,* 31 S.C.L. (2 Rich.) 136, 139 (1846).
11. *See Bryan v. Walton,* Suppl. to 33 Ga. 11, 24 (1864). . . .
12. 18 Ala. 276 (1850).
13. 80 Va. 18 (1885).
14. 69 S.E. 60 (N.C. 1910).
15. 48 N.C. (3 Jones Law) 339 (1856). . . .
16. 19 Ark. 580 (1858).
17. 51 N.C. (6 Jones) 284 (1859). . . .
18. *Hopkins v. Bowers* 111 N.C. 175, 178 (1892).
19. 2 Helen Catterall, Judicial Cases concerning American Slavery and the Negro 339 (1929), quoting *State v. Hayes,* 17 S.C.L. (1 Bail.) 275 (1829).

16

Litigating Whiteness

Trials of Racial Determination in the Nineteenth-Century South

Ariela J. Gross

II. The Shifting Essences of Race in the Nineteenth-Century South

A. Racial Knowledge

Until 1854, Abby Guy and her four children lived on the Bayou Bartholomew, bordering Louisiana, while William Daniel and his family lived in the hills. Tennessee-born Daniel, having come from Alabama in 1844 with his large family, was one of the earliest settlers in sparsely populated, rural Ashley County. He was a town father who served as justice of the peace, postmaster, and the first notary public in the area. In 1850, Daniel owned fifteen slaves and 240 acres of land, one of only four men in the county with more than ten slaves of taxable age. In his only brush with the wrong side of the law, Daniel was cited in court in 1849 for giving his slaves too much freedom, "to the annoyance of the neighborhood." Although the citation was dismissed, it may have been the occasion for Daniel's decision to begin treating Abby Guy and her children as his slaves, a shift in their circumstances that led Guy to bring suit in the circuit court.

Just one year later, Guy and her children were listed in the 1850 census as the only free negroes among the 269 households of Ashley County. . . .

We know from the work of social historians that there was a substantial number of free blacks in the South in the 1850s and that they were concentrated in two areas: a band along the Upper South and a few cities of the Deep South with long histories of free mulatto elites (New Orleans, Louisiana, and Charleston, South Carolina, in particular). Yet even in Ashley County, Arkansas, a frontier area with no established free black community, the match between black identity and slave status was not perfect. Perhaps being on the "frontier" worked to Abby Guy's benefit. People on the move had more opportunity to reshape their identities and reinvent themselves racially; new communities were more likely to allow people to live on the margins of social orders that were still emerging. Furthermore, the number of people of mixed race, both slave and free, had grown over the course of the antebellum period, blurring the color line and increasing the number of people who lived on a "middle ground." These people caused ideological discomfort to Southerners in the 1850s, and legislatures passed laws making it increasingly difficult for slaveholders to free their slaves and for freed slaves either to stay in their home state or to live unfettered lives. Although this was not an easy time in which to live on the middle ground, such a ground did exist.

People on the middle ground made it difficult to argue that race was self-evident and commonsensical. Just as federal courts in the early twentieth century fell back on a "common knowledge" test for white citizenship [see Part 9—Ed.], judges in the nineteenth-century South repeatedly held that the determination of an individual's race was "a question very proper for a jury," because the jury represented the sense of the community; race was something commonsensical—something we *know when we see it*. Witnesses in the courtroom reinforced the notion of race as common sense by invoking the idea that there was an ineffable quality making someone white that any Southerner could discern—and, likewise, that a drop of African blood would make itself known, and a Southerner could sense it "as the alligator . . . knows three days in advance that a storm is brewing." It was not unusual for witnesses to explain that they did not need to know the finer points of physiology or craniology to know "the distinction between the caucasian and african races"—they just knew. Yet at the same time, trials that involved the determination of someone's race demonstrated not consensus around a single, commonsense definition but disagreement, conflict, and concern for the consequences of being wrong.

Abby Guy embodied racial unknowability in one of its most tantalizing forms: the light-skinned young woman. She and her lawyers played on fears of hidden essences by telling a tale of white slavery. In her complaint, Guy claimed that her mother had been "a poor destitute orphan child in the state of Virginia, without any friend or home and living from place to place," sold by slave traders into slavery in Alabama, to William Daniel's father. Guy explained in her complaint that Daniel's father had treated her family well, and because their condition was "more favored than that of an ordinary slave," Guy's mother and Guy herself "submitted during his life, to that condition." Guy claimed that William Daniel's father had willed her manumission, although this was only an "admission of that previous Right," but that William Daniel, after his father's death, "tore them from their home and . . . reduced them . . . to a state of slavery."

White slavery stories like that of Abby Guy reverberated through both Northern and Southern culture via journalistic and literary accounts. Abolitionists and fugitive slaves writing from the North used cases like Abby Guy's to illustrate to their Northern readers the ultimate horror of slaveholders' evil: the possibility of *white slavery*. . . . Lawyers for women seeking their freedom on the grounds of whiteness encouraged jurors to do exactly the same: They conjured the horror of the wrongful enslavement of pure white womanhood.

White Southerners' fear of people of African descent lurking unknown in their midst provided a courtroom narrative that inverted the "white slavery" story. While racial unknowability might mean the unjust enslavement of white women, it seemed more likely that those of "negro blood" were passing as white [see Part 3—Ed.], making fools of those who accepted them. . . . [W]hites' fear of being tricked by slaves animated much of the litigation in Southern courts, and the greatest blow to a white man's honor would be to be deceived into bestowing the honors of whiteness on a "negro." . . . Like the white slave, the passing black threatened white men's sense of themselves and their families, lending urgency to the question of racial knowability.

B. *Evidence and Essences*

1. Abby Guy

In the trial of *Guy v. Daniel*, a variety of criteria were discussed on both sides to prove Guy's race. Along with the evidence of inspection and medical experts, the jurors heard from a large number of neighbors of Guy and Daniel. Guy's lay witnesses focused on her social identity, her associations with white people, and her having performed tasks that white people quintessentially performed. Richard Stanley testified that she "visited among white folks, and went to church, parties, etc." Keightly Saunders, a fifty-seven-year-old farmer who owned four slaves, one a mulatto, in 1850, testified that Guy "visited among the whites as an equal." Saunders was "locally known as quite a character," a drinker and storyteller, free with "curse words which flowed in his conversation like water from a spring." Nevertheless, he commanded respect in the neighborhood and was a friend of Judge Hawkins, who was considered the leader of the bar in the region. Saunders's testimony for Guy must have carried considerable weight. Jeremiah Oats, a farm laborer with no slaves or land of his own in 1850, had done work for Guy, and he testified that she had been competent to contract and pay her bills herself. William M. Drucker, Sheriff of Ashley County, himself a slaveholder, explained that he did not tax Guy because she was a widow, whatever her racial status.

William Daniel emphasized documentary evidence of Abby Guy's slave origins. He produced his father's will, which did not free Guy but devised her to James Condra, Daniel's brother-in-law, as well as Daniel's receipt for Guy from Condra. Daniel admitted that Guy had been of little value to him as a slave and so he had "permitted her to go when and where she pleased, for several years past," but when she left the State of Arkansas for Louisiana, he brought her and her children home and asserted his right of ownership over them. He argued, in effect, that as a slave she must be black, because only blacks are slaves. There was another dimension to his argument: He should not have to prove her racial identity because status was enough. If he could prove that she was rightly his slave, she should not be free, whatever her degree of blood, whatever her racial identity. Abby Guy, on the other hand, having no credible evidence of a right to freedom in previous free status, no documentation of "that previous Right," had to make her case in her own person. Her right to freedom inhered in her whiteness. Her success at trial rested on her ability to shift the ground of argument to that question.

On behalf of William Daniel, Thomas S. Thompson, a relatively wealthy farmer with six slaves, told the jury that he had known both Guy and her mother, Polly, as slaves, although they were both "bright mulatto." Thompson betrayed some confusion over the exact determination of their racial status—Polly "was a yellow woman, darker than white. . . . Could not say whether Polly was of African or Indian extraction. I have seen some only of half blood who would provably be as white as Polly was." But he was much more confident about their slave status. Polly "always held herself as a slave and acted as such. She and Guy always labored and conducted themselves as slaves in the family, with the exception that they took more care of themselves perhaps than others."

On cross-examination, Thompson admitted that he was Daniel's brother-in-law and that he "had never studied Physiology nor the distinction of races." He also admitted that he had seen white persons who worked in the fields become as dark as Guy and her mother, and he had seen white persons with hair as curly as theirs. Several other farm laborers testified about Guy and Polly's slave status, but they acknowledged the difficulty of determining their racial status. As James Barnett noted, he "had seen persons *recognized as white*, who were as dark as Polly."

William Daniel's witnesses made no strong claims about Guy's racial identity. Indeed, implicit in their acknowledgment that people of ambiguous appearance fell on both sides of the line between white and "negro" was a claim that status should decide race, or at least that race could not decide status; what mattered was how people *recognized* Guy and her mother, which depended on whether they were slaves or free. Abby Guy, on the other hand, made a strong claim to a whiteness that should overwhelm all evidence of slave status or ancestry in slavery. She asked the jury to consider her white because she acted white, because she looked white, and because doctors found her to be white.

After the testimony closed, the lawyers for both Guy and Daniel proposed instructions for Judge [Theodoric F.] Sorrels to give the jury. The judge gave all of the instructions drafted by Abby Guy's lawyers, which charged the jury to follow a "one-fourth rule" with one wrinkle: Guy and her children could only be proved slaves if they had more than one-fourth "negro blood" *or* if they were descended in the maternal line from a slave who was one-fourth negro or more. Furthermore, "every presumption, consistent with reason, should be indulged in favor of freedom." The judge refused to give most of William Daniel's proposed instructions, including an instruction to ignore "all evidence on Physiology, [which] is irrelevant," and several to the effect that evidence that Guy had been held in slavery should be evidence of her status as a slave.

The Ashley County jury gave a verdict for Abby Guy and her children in favor of freedom. The jury list for *Daniel v. Guy* no longer exists, save for the name of the foreman, Ambrose Bull, a forty-nine-year-old farmer who owned six slaves and property worth $1,000 in 1850. William Daniel won his appeal to the Arkansas Supreme Court, which rejected the one-fourth rule propounded by the trial court in favor of a rule of maternal descent (implicitly, a one-drop-of-blood rule, as one could be held "negro" with only a tiny fraction of African ancestry as long as it passed through the maternal line).[1] Daniel succeeded in having the case retried in neighboring Drew County, where he thought he would find a more sympathetic jury. That case also ended in a verdict for Guy.

This time, Daniel appealed on the ground that the jury had based their verdict on an improper exhibition of Guy's feet, for which she had been required to remove her shoes and stockings in court, as well as the more general ground that "there was a total want of evidence to support the verdict." The Arkansas Supreme Court, however, thought it quite appropriate to inspect a person's feet in order to detect "negro blood," and it refused to disturb the jury verdict.[2] Chief Justice English, who had also delivered the opinion establishing the "one drop" rule, nevertheless expressed his own skepticism about the jury's decision, remarking in dictum that "it is possible that the jury found against the preponderance of evidence, through reluctance to sanction the enslaving of persons, who, to all appearance, were of the white race, and, for many years before suit, had acted as free persons and been treated as such." So, in 1861, it affirmed the verdict in *Daniel v. Guy*, setting Guy and her children free on the eve of the Civil War.

Notes

Reprinted by permission of the Yale Law Journal Company and William S. Hein Company from the Yale Law Journal, vol. 105, pp. 109–188 (1998).

1. *See Daniel v. Guy,* 19 Ark. 121, 131–32 (1857).
2. *See Daniel v. Guy,* 23 Ark. 50, 52, 55 (1861). . . .

17

Telling the Difference

Nineteenth-Century Legal Narratives of Racial Taxonomy

Michael A. Elliott

I. Blood Rhetoric and Beyond

The best-known narrative of racial taxonomy is the "one drop" rule, which marks a person as racially "other" no matter how small the fraction of "blood" he or she has inherited from a nonwhite group. The rule has long been the target of those—white and black—seeking to illuminate the illogic of race. . . . Yet the "one drop" rule does not have the transhistorical, universal legal tradition in the United States that some contemporary race theorists presume. Rather, laws that defined race through biological ancestry became more common only after Reconstruction, and the fraction of "blood" requisite for African American identity most often decreased after the turn of the twentieth century. While the "one drop" rule may have been a custom, especially in some Southern communities, Tennessee was the only state to have codified it into law as of 1910; Virginia did not adopt its more famous "one drop" law until the 1920s. . . .

Throughout the nineteenth century, state courts drew the boundaries of racial classification—defining "white," "black," and even "mulatto"—in ways that stopped short of the "one drop" rule. Because laws that discriminated against African Americans on the basis of race, with the exception of those that pertained to U.S. citizenship, were state rather than federal statutes, federal courts were usually able to avoid the issue altogether. Confronted with the question of racial taxonomy in the infamous *Plessy v. Ferguson* . . . decision,[1] the U.S. Supreme Court continued this tradition as it simultaneously proclaimed the "separate but equal" doctrine to be acceptable. Writing for the majority, Justice Henry Billings Brown held that although some states had ruled that "any visible admixture of black blood stamps the person as belonging to the colored race; others that it depends upon the preponderance of blood; and still others that the predominance of white blood must only be in the proportion of three fourths," the federal government was under no obligation to establish a single standard of racial classification. In other words, laws may force people to become "separate," even if the same people are not separated the same way across the country.

At this moment in *Plessy*, which occurs at the very conclusion of the majority opinion, Brown voices his odium for engaging in the project of racial taxonomy, in spite of the fact that the entire force of his decision authorizes precisely such a project.

Throughout his opinion, for example, Brown had based the Court's approval of racial segregation on the premise that such distinctions are "founded in the color of the two races," that they are "the result of natural affinities" and "racial instincts." Such descriptions of race and racial difference presume the kind of biological distinction that was (and is) most often articulated through the metaphor of blood and blood fractions. When, however, Brown concludes by deliberately eschewing a single standard of ancestry by which to divide races, he puts forward another version of racial identity altogether. In order for such widely varying racial standards to prevail, race must be a product of local, not universal, standards; it must be a product of social construction. This *Plessy* opinion does not go so far as to consider race to be the arbitrary instrument of power that we now think it to be, but Justice Brown hints at an awareness that the law does not simply reflect an order of racial difference prior to and outside of it. By letting this patchwork of conflicting state standards prevail, the Court shows that the law is complicit in the creation of race.

Plessy refuses to offer its own narrative of racial taxonomy, but it shows what is at stake when courts do. In drawing the boundary lines of racial division, nineteenth-century courts were forced to find the rhetorical and narrative means of bridging two versions of race: race as a socially determined category that required the intervention of the courts themselves, and race as the product of underlying principles of natural history and biology. While it seems obvious to us today (and indeed may have been obvious to many of these judges themselves) that race-as-social contradicts race-as-natural, this contradiction was not a debilitating liability to legal cases of racial taxonomy. Instead, these two ideas about race were more often considered to be complementary determining forces that could and should be reconciled by moving racial taxonomy cases onto the dockets of the highest courts of the states.

NOTE

1. 163 U.S. 537 (1896).

B.

Real Complexity

Mixed race identity proves a good deal more complicated than the "one drop" rule and other classification schemes suggest. In this section, college president Greg Williams offers his experiences as a mixed African American–White man. The late Trina Grillo discusses life as the daughter of Afro-Cuban–Italian parents. The changing racial identity of Richard Delgado's fictional character Rodrigo, of the influential *Rodrigo Chronicles*, reveals a few of the complexities of racial identity. Carrie Okizaki offers the perspective of a "*hapa* daughter of a Japanese father and a [European] mother." The identity choices of mixed race people prove particularly important to systems of racial classification, which in modern times generally rely on self-identification. (See Parts 4 and 7.)

18

Life on the Color Line

The True Story of a White Boy Who Discovered He Was Black

Gregory Howard Williams

That first Friday, Uncle Jim picked me up at lunchtime. We stopped at every small-town diner between Muncie and Albany dumping rotten meat, fruit, potato rinds, and all types of stinking garbage into large oil drums lashed on the back of his truck. I tried to brace the cans as we raced over the country roads. It all went smoothly until Uncle Jim plunged pell-mell down a dip, sending me a foot in the air. I managed to keep the drums in place, but was drenched with slimy garbage.

Uncle Jim had an extra work shirt in the cab, but by late afternoon when we arrived at a small-town café, I was reeking of garbage. While I wrestled a can to the alley, a middle-aged white man appeared at the rear door. From his long, casual chat with Uncle Jim I guessed he was the owner. My body tensed when I heard the man ask: "Who's that white boy?"

Uncle Jim said I was his nephew.

"He's the whitest colored boy I ever seen. Are you sure he wasn't just caught in the wrong net?" The owner chuckled.

I wanted to smash his face with the can when I lugged it back to the diner, and caught him gaping at me. His sharply pressed long white apron reminded me of the Ku Klux Klan leader I saw on Uncle Osco's new television following the 1954 Supreme Court decision outlawing segregated schools. [*Brown v. Board of Education*, 347 U.S. 483 (1954)—Ed.] That beefy-faced, white-robed Klansman stood in front of a burning cross, railing against black and white children learning together. He claimed that the Supreme Court was encouraging "race-mixing" and the only result would be the "bestial mongrel mulatto, the dreg of human society." In the refuge of Uncle Osco's sitting room, I had laughed at the pale, jowly southerner. In a white sheet and pointed hat, he looked more like the "dreg of society" than anybody I knew. Yet his nasal repetition of "mongrel mulatto" finally hit like a thunderbolt. He was talking about me. I was the Klan's worst nightmare. I was what the violence directed against integration was all about. I was what they hated and wanted to destroy. And that was the biggest puzzle in the world to me because I had absolutely nothing.

The café owner had a different idea. He didn't want to destroy me, he wanted to exhibit me. While I lugged garbage from his rear door, he hovered there beckoning me inside. There were people he wanted me to meet, he coaxed. He tried to engage me in conversation. "Gonna be a pig farmer like your uncle?" he asked with a chuckle.

"I'm gonna be a lawyer," I quipped.

His face reddened with laughter. "You gonna have to shovel a lot of shit to make that happen. Come on, these folks really want to see you. We all wanna see Muncie's first colored lawyer. I even got a piece of pie for you."

I knew he was insulting me, but I was tempted by the pie. When I noticed Uncle Jim frowning, I mumbled "No thanks." Soon the café owner was miles behind, and I was overcome by feelings of self-pity, confusion, and anger. As Uncle Jim turned down a gravel lane, I concentrated more on keeping the garbage off me than on fantasizing about dumping it on the man who had ridiculed my dream.

As the truck slowed, a strange form sprouted on the horizon. Uncle Jim pulled to a stop, and I realized it was the unfinished foundation of a house protruding three feet above the ground. The black tar paper sides and top gave it a sinister aura. It was Uncle Jim's home.

"Boy, I'm sorry about that ol' white man," he said as we carried groceries to the house. "He don't know shit. I learned a long time ago that you just have to laugh at white folks or they'll drive you crazy. Forgit 'bout him. We gonna have us a helluva dinner."

19

Anti-Essentialism and Intersectionality
Tools to Dismantle the Master's House

Trina Grillo

My father was born in Tampa, Florida, of Cuban Black parents. Much of his life was spent firmly claiming his place among American Blacks. My mother was the daughter of Italian immigrants. I was born in 1948 and soon thereafter moved to the San Francisco Bay Area. There were four children in my family. At times it seemed to me that we were half the biracial population of the Bay Area. We were stared at wherever we went, although it took me a while, probably until I was five, to realize that the stares were not always ones of admiration. Of course, we did not define ourselves as biracial then. Instead, we were considered, and considered ourselves, Black, or Negro as we then said. Still, our skin color and our parents' interracial marriage were always causes for comment. My race and my skin color have been issues that have preoccupied me for a good part of my life, and I see little prospect of this changing anytime soon.

When I began teaching at Hastings Law School in 1977, I knew that I wanted to write about multiraciality. I did a little research and proceeded to write—nothing. At that time there was little interest in the popular culture in that subject, and virtually nothing in the legal literature, so it is easy to see why I gave up on my project. Multiraciality did not seem to matter to anyone but me.

But now I cannot turn on *Oprah* without seeing a segment on multiraciality, right in between the shows on incest and the shows on weight loss. . . . We are everywhere, in numbers hard to ignore. But one thing has not changed. No one knows how to talk about us.

I looked at two newspapers yesterday and saw the racial descriptions of the jurors in the O. J. Simpson trial. One paper said there were "eight Blacks, one Anglo, one Hispanic and two persons of mixed race." The other paper said there were eight Blacks, two Hispanics, one Anglo, and one person who identified himself as half white and half American Indian. There were four items about each juror described in the paper: gender, age, occupation, and racial background. From a more complete description of the racial backgrounds of the jurors, I found out that one of the Hispanics was a Hispanic/Black, classified as mixed race by one paper and as Hispanic by another. Interestingly, neither paper classified this juror as Black, although that would be my "first" classification of myself.

So we have no stable conventions for describing multiracial persons, at least none that match what we perceive to be reality. . . .

[W]e must fully understand that race is not a biological concept but a social and historical construct. The reason that I grew up considering myself, as we then said, Negro, is that a racist system described me in that way. Most Blacks in the Untied States are persons of "mixed blood," if such a thing can be said to exist, and have both white and Black ancestors. If there were such [a] thing as a biological white, I would be at least half that, and so would many other Blacks. However, the fact that race is a historical and social construct certainly does not mean that it does not exist. Experiences, histories, and communities have all developed around this concept; so if we abandon race, we abandon communities that may have been initially formed as a result of racism but have become something else entirely.

All the scientific literature says that biological races do not exist. Instead, races were created as a mechanism for the oppression of certain groups of people. But once created, they remain. We are then left with these questions: How should we regard people of mixed race? How is it possible to take our experiences seriously without having them turned into a means of separating ourselves from other Blacks or into a means of ranking people of color, with those of mixed race given more power than other Blacks? (I should say that my focus is on mixtures that include Black, because that is the experience with which I am familiar; because the history is different, the issues are surely different for persons of mixed race who are, for example, Asian and white).

If we accept the definition of Black that we have been given—a definition that historically defined anyone with "one drop of Black blood" as Black—we ignore the existence of multiracial people. We ignore people whose experiences may be different from those experiences that have been defined as constituting the Black experience—that is, the "essentialized" Black experience. By so essentializing, we assume that the taxonomy of race proposed by nineteenth-century white supremacists—that human beings can be classified into four races and everyone fits neatly into one slot—is a valid one. On the other hand, if we do classify multiracial people as Black, the potential for group solidarity is much greater. "We are all Black," we say. "You cannot divide us."

. . . Is it possible to create a Black-identified biracial identity? Can one be biracial or multiracial and also be Black? Or is the historical freight still too great for that to be possible? One thing I am sure of: The fact that a person is biracial is an important piece of who she is. It is something I would find of interest if I were reading her work or listening to her speak. We need a way to say that, a way that does not compromise the community of Black people.

Rodrigo's Twelfth Chronicle

The Problem of the Shanty

Richard Delgado

["Rodrigo" is a fictional character in a series of famous chronicles by Professor Richard Delgado that analyze important legal and social issues of our times.—Ed.]

The half-brother of famed American civil rights lawyer and activist Geneva Crenshaw . . . Rodrigo was born in the United States but moved to Italy when his father, an African American serviceman, was assigned to a U.S. outpost there. Rodrigo completed high school on the base, then attended an Italian university on government scholarships, graduating near the top of his law school class. In [the first installment of the series], . . . Rodrigo looks up the Professor while on a return trip to the United States to investigate graduate law study. After discussing various LL.M. programs, the two engage in a spirited discussion of race, affirmative action, the decline of the West, and other topics.

Despite their age differences, the two become good friends, discussing law and economics, . . . love, . . . Redemptive Tragedy of Race, . . . legal rules, . . . the critique of normativity, . . . relations between men and women, . . . Enlightenment political theory, . . . black crime, . . . racial discrimination and the rule of law, . . . the role of merit, . . . clinical practice, . . . the legal profession and its discontents, . . . and America's racial future. . . . During this time, Rodrigo progresses from the status of law student to professor at a public law school in the Midwest. He and the Professor continue their relationship, seeing each other at meetings, conferences, and airports.

"Rodrigo, we've never discussed your Latin side," I said. "Mostly we've talked about African Americans or people of color in general. I gather you're taking a greater interest in your roots these days?"

"I am. My dad's African American, as you know, and my mom is Italian. But some of my ancestors lived in the Caribbean and my dad still speaks Spanish fluently. Did I tell you that Giannina and I are talking about applying for a Fulbright in Mexico sometime?"

"You keep talking about it," Giannina said. "You sometimes forget that I'm in the middle of a certain educational program. I'm not as free to pick up and leave as you professors, although it's something I'd love to do with you someday."

Rodrigo blushed. "I sometimes get carried away. Sorry, Giannina. Maybe we'll content ourselves with a quick trip down to see the Professor, at least until you graduate. Where were we?"

21

"What Are You?"
Hapa-*Girl and Multiracial Identity*

Carrie Lynn H. Okizaki

Introduction

"What are you?" As the *hapa* daughter of a Japanese father and a half-German, half-English mother, people have often asked me this question. I have had total strangers ask me, "Where were you born?" After my response of "Colorado," I usually get a reply like: "Oh, I thought maybe you were from Hawaii—has anyone ever told you that you look Hawaiian?" As a child, I was never quite sure what to make of such questions. Before I actually visited Hawaii, I had always pictured an island where everyone looked like me. The truth is, I do not really know "what I am."

II. Multiracial Identification

William Wei, author of *The Asian American Movement*, identifies the importance of racial identification in the context of the Asian experience, in order to establish a voice in society:

> Without a self-defined identity . . . they were vulnerable psychologically and politically. They therefore consciously set out to develop "a new identity by integrating [their] past experiences with [their] present conditions" and to raise "group esteem and pride, for it [was] only through collective action that society's perception of the Asian-American [could] be efficiently altered."[1]

Many multiracial individuals lack sufficient categories with which to racially identify themselves.

Almost all Americans, by definition, are of mixed race heritage; it is estimated that most African Americans, Latinos, American Indians, and even a large number of people who consider themselves to be White are multiracial. Despite these numbers, those who genuinely view themselves as biracial or multiracial are not permitted to "race" themselves as such. Social and legal constraints do not allow acceptance of multiraciality. As one commentator stated:

> [A]s long as it is assumed that each person will fall into one and only one category, people of mixed race will frustrate the system. The system is supposed to enable its users to

> pigeonhole people, to have a handy set of categories (and perhaps stereotypes) to relate them to. Mixed-race people will cause anxiety among those for whom it is important to establish a one-category classification for everyone.[2]

It is not only White individuals who take comfort in racial boundaries, but "all racial and ethnic groups."[3]

Historically, multiracial children who were the products of "sexual taboos" or whose existence could result in criminal punishment represented a violation of the ideal of racial purity and a stain on the concept of whiteness. . . .

. . . The issue of nonexistent societal recognition and participation in the political discourse is only one part of the problem faced by biracial or multiracial individuals. Another part stems from issues of self-identification. A significant portion of the United States considers itself biracial or multiracial. . . .

One example of this phenomenon is Tiger Woods, who has single-handedly managed to bring golf into America's pop culture. While age is one factor contributing to America's fascination with Tiger, race is another. On the day Tiger won the Masters, many reporters asked Tiger how he felt to be the first African American to win the prestigious tournament. Tiger, however, is one-quarter Thai, one-quarter Chinese, one-quarter African American, one-eighth Native American, and one-eighth White. It is clear that Tiger is uncomfortable being cast as a role model for other African American golfers and pigeonholed into a monoracial Black race categorization. Tiger, however, may not have much choice in the matter. Tiger looks like an African American—according to societal perceptions and conceptions of race—and multiracial individuals are classified into one racial category, usually based on how they are perceived.

A. Who Am I? Rejection by Both Cultures

Many cultures—the Japanese, Koreans, and Vietnamese—have historically believed in a racial purity so extreme that half-breeds literally are "cast out."[4] Often, "multiracial people who are part Caucasian are seen as inherently 'whitewashed,'" and loyalty to both cultures is constantly questioned. An example of minorities not accepting multiracial individuals as part of their community can be seen at the annual Japanese Cherry Blossom Festival. The festival prohibits anyone who is less than one-half Japanese or does not "look Japanese" from participating.[5]

One Asian American college student named Song Richardson explained the internal conflict such alienation causes:

> I can see them look at me and some don't think I can understand Korean. I hear them making derogatory remarks about the fact that I'm mixed. . . . I'll walk into a market and see someone behind the counter who looks like my Mom, and I'll feel a certain affection. But then she'll treat me with complete lack of respect and cordiality. Differently than she would treat a white person who comes into the market.[6]

White society also refuses to accept multiracial people as "one of their own"—especially in light of the narrow definition afforded to the meaning of whiteness. Furthermore, racial stereotypes associated with physical appearance continue to pervade American culture.

Notes

Published originally in 71 University of Colorado Law Review 463 (2000).

1. William Wei, The Asian American Movement 46 (1993). . . .
2. Stephen Satris, *What Are They, in* American Mixed Race 54–55 (Naomi Zack, ed., 1995).
3. *See* Cynthia L. Nakashima, *An Invisible Monster: The Creation and Denial of Mixed-Race People in America, in* Racially Mixed People in America 162, 175 (Maria P. P. Root, ed., 1992). . . .
4. This is seen by the many numbers of women and their biracial children who were ostracized from their native countries after having sexual relations with American soldiers stationed in those counties during World War II, the Korean conflict, and Vietnam. [See Part 9—Ed.]
5. *See* Timothy P. Fong, The Contemporary Asian American Experience: Beyond the Model Minority 234–35 (1998).
6. *Id.* at 235. . . .

C.

Mestizaje *and* La Raza Cósmica

Racial mixture is openly acknowledged in Latin America. (See Part 10.) Latinas/os in the United States also appreciate the racial mixture within the community. In this section, George Martínez discusses from a philosophical perspective racial mixture among Latinas/os, known as *mestizaje*, as well as Anglo denigration of that mixture. Athena Mutua considers the impacts of hybridity among Latinas/os.

22

Latinos, Assimilation, and the Law

A Philosophical Perspective

George A. Martínez

. . . [The famous Mexican philosopher José Vasconcelos] argues that a "cosmic race," or *raza cósmica,* will arise in order to accomplish the "divine mission of America."[1] The *raza cósmica* will be formed by the "synthesis" of the existing races. Since, in his view, North America operates on the basis of "racial segregation," whereas Latin America operates on the basis of *mestizaje,* or racial mixing, he contends that the cosmic race will arise from Latinos.

As for the providential "mission of America," Vasconcelos says that society goes through three distinct stages. He describes them as "the material, the political and the aesthetic." The mission of America is to produce an aesthetic society. Such a society can only be achieved by an "emotional race" who are able to appreciate beauty. Because hybrid Latinos have a great sense of beauty, they have a duty to help bring about the aesthetic state. . . .

Border theorist Gloria Anzaldúa has recently developed a similar view that suggests that Latinos are called to live in a uniquely important way. Anzaldúa argues that borders can generate new types of human knowledge.[2] Latinos represent the new mestizo, or person of mixed race. By virtue of their mixed ancestry, such persons exist in the borderlands and learn to understand and appreciate contradictions and ambiguity. They are able to move between cultures. According to Anzaldúa, Latinos, by virtue of their existence in the borderlands, have long been involved in cultural mixing. Given this, Latinos are uniquely positioned to help generate new types of cultural knowledge.

. . . [Contrary to the positive concept of *mestizaje,* the] dominant group has inculcated an image of inferiority in Latinos. For example, the Anglo colonizers in the American southwest produced disparaging discourses regarding Mexican Americans. For instance, the historian David Weber writes:

> Anglo Americans found an additional element to despise in Mexicans: racial mixture. American visitors to the Mexican frontier were nearly unanimous in commenting on the dark skin of Mexican mestizos, who, it was generally agreed had inherited the worst

qualities of Spaniards and Indians to produce a "race" still more despicable than that of either parent.[3]

Similarly, the dean of Texas historians, Walter Prescott Webb, wrote:

Without disparagement it may be said that there is a cruel streak in the Mexican nature, or so the history of Texas would lead one to believe. This cruelty may be a heritage from the Spanish of the Inquisition; it may, and doubtless should, be attributed partly to the Indian blood.[4]

Notes

Published originally in 20 UCLA Chicano-Latino Law Review 1 (1999).

1. Patrick Romanell, Making of the Mexican Mind: A Study in Recent Mexican Thought 133 (1952).
2. *See* Gloria Anzaldúa, Borderlands/La Frontera: The New Mestiza (1987); Renato Rosaldo, Culture and Truth: The Remaking of Cultural Analysis 216 (1989).
3. Foreigners in Their Native Land: Historical Roots of the Mexican-Americans 59–60 (David J. Weber, ed., 1973).
4. Walter Prescott Webb, The Texas Rangers: A Century of Frontier Defense 14 (1965).

23

Shifting Bottoms and Rotating Centers

Reflections on LatCrit III and the Black/White Paradigm

Athena D. Mutua

[T]he Spanish language marks or is perhaps part and parcel of a racial system characterized by a notion of "hybridity." This racial system combines culture, national origin, lineage, and color (and perhaps "alienage," which refers to citizenship) differences, the oppression of which presents a case of seeming permanence crucial to the "bottom" metaphor, where Latinos/as are often vanquished. Conceptualizing the notion of a "hybridized" racial system would draw on several traits and ideas.

Generally the idea is, as blacks are "raced" as colored and Asians "raced" as foreign, Latinos/as when they are not raced as black or white are "raced" as hybrid (being "raced" both as partially foreign and partially colored in a way that racializes their ethnicity and many of its components). . . .

Here the standard is a facetious notion of white purity, with Latinos being considered something less than pure white due to their lineage. In addition, having black and Native American ancestry results in Latinos being seen as potentially colored. . . . Elizabeth Martinez captures these first two points in discussing the devils of dualism in the lengthy passage quoted below.

> The issue of color, and the entire Black/White definition, feed on a dualism that shaped the U.S. value system as it developed from the time of this nation's birth. The dread of "race-mixing" as a threat to White supremacy enshrined dualism. Today we see that a disdain for mixture haunts and inhibits U.S. culture. Because it does not recognize hybridism, this country's racial framework emphasizes separateness and offers no ground for mutual inclusion. I, for one, remember growing up haunted by that crushing word "half-breed" meaning me. It was years before Mestizaje-mixing began to suggest to me a cultural wealth rather than a polluted bloodline. U.S. society, the Dean of Denial, still has no use for that idea, still scorns the hybrid as mysteriously "un-American."[1]

Such disdain helps explain why the nature of Latino/a identity seems to baffle and frustrate so many in this country. The dominant culture doesn't easily accept complex ideas or people, or dialectics of any sort, and the Latino/a must be among the most complex creatures walking this earth, biologically as well as culturally. . . .

Martinez captures the essential components of a racial system of hybridity. Although she states that hybridity is not recognized in the U.S. culture, it seems more accurate to say it is not valued. The foreign and colorized aspects of a hybridized system are the basis for exclusion and oppression within the U.S. context and form the categor[ies] of a hybridized racial system. These categories are present simultaneously in Latinos/as, but one aspect may be the focused site of oppression at one time and a different aspect at another time. Further, individual Latinos/as may experience different combinations of these categories of oppression depending on how the individual looks, behaves, dresses, or speaks. Speaking [S]panish may be one mark of this hybridized racial system.

Note

Published originally in 53 University of Miami Law Review 1177 (1999).

1. Elizabeth Martinez, *Beyond Black/White: The Racisms of Our Time,* 20 Social Justice 22 (1994), reprinted in The Latino/a Condition: A Critical Reader 455 (Richard Delgado and Jean Stefancic, eds., 1998).

D.

Indians, Intermarriage, and the Law of Indian Identity

Indian identity has important legal consequences, particularly in recent years with the increasing number of disputes over tribal assets. For example, in distributing $56 million allocated by Congress to the Seminole tribe for the taking of much of Florida in the early nineteenth century, a heated controversy arose concerning whether Black Seminoles—descendants of slaves—were members of the Seminole tribe. (See William Glaberson, *Who Is a Seminole, and Who Gets to Decide?* New York Times, January 29, 2001, at A1.)

Federal law generally permits Indian tribes to define tribal members. Tribes employ a variety of definitions. (See, e.g., Revised Constitution of the Jicarilla Apache Tribe, Article III [1987], defining membership as including the person on tribal rolls as of a specific date and a person of at least three-eighths Jicarilla blood born after that date whose mother or father was a member or is granted membership by three-fourths' majority of the tribal council.) Major definitional difficulties result from the existence of persons of mixed Indian ancestry. In this section, William Hagan offers a historical perspective on the problem of defining who is an Indian. Christopher Ford discusses the definition of *Indian* under federal Indian law. Finally, Judith Resnik offers an example of efforts by an Indian tribe to discourage marriage of nontribal members by limiting tribal membership of children.

24

Full Blood, Mixed Blood, Generic, and Ersatz

The Problem of Indian Identity

William T. Hagan

One of the most perplexing problems confronting American Indians today is that of identity. Who is an American Indian? The question is raised in a bewildering variety of situations. Contingent on its resolution can be the recognition of a group by the federal government, voting rights in a multimillion-dollar Alaskan corporation, or acceptance of an individual as a member of a pueblo's tightly knit society. Nor is this a question that has arisen only recently. It has been a problem for individuals, tribes, and government administrators since the birth of this nation.

Four centuries to the year after Christopher Columbus began the semantic confusion over how to label the original inhabitants of this hemisphere, Commissioner of Indian Affairs Thomas Jefferson Morgan spoke to a more important issue. He devoted six pages of his 1892 annual report to the question: What is an Indian? "One would have supposed," observed Morgan, "that this question would have been considered a hundred years ago and had been adjudicated long before this." "Singularly enough, however," he continued, "it has remained in abeyance, and the Government has gone on legislating and administering law without carefully discriminating as to those over whom it has a right to exercise such control."[1]

Nearly a century after Commissioner Morgan expressed surprise at this state of affairs, the Department of Education (1980) spent $90,000 to try to establish a useful definition of the term *Indian*. Another government agency, the Branch of Federal Acknowledgment, plans to spend millions to try to determine which of nearly a hundred tribes applying for federal recognition should merit it.

The founding fathers provided little guidance in the Constitution on matters relating to Indians. They included no legal definition of the term *Indian* and in fact mentioned the word only twice. The federal agencies responsible for the conduct of Indian affairs, first the War Department and then the Interior Department, failed to fill the gap, and it was left to the courts to grapple with the problem of Indian identity.

Note

Published originally in 27 Arizona and the West, A Quarterly Journal of History 309 (1985).

1. *Report of the Commissioner of Indian Affairs, August 27, 1892, in* Sixty-first Annual Report of the Commissioner of Indian Affairs . . . (. . . 1892), 31.

25

Administering Identity

The Determination of "Race" in Race-Conscious Law

Christopher A. Ford

Most "Indian law" in the United States focuses on tribes rather than on individuals, but there are enough exceptions to muddy the waters. Traditionally, the term *Indian* was conceived in classically racial terms. In 1846, for example, the Supreme Court ruled that a White person adopted by an Indian tribe was not Indian for federal jurisdictional purposes.[1] Indians under United States law have seldom been regarded as an undifferentiated group, however, and jurisdictional statutes governing tribal courts and other measures have usually held "Indian" status to obtain primarily through specific tribal affiliation. The Indian Reorganization Act of 1934, for example, defined "Indian" to include

> all persons of Indian descent who are members of any recognized Indian tribe now under Federal jurisdiction, and all persons who are descendants of such members who were, on June 1, 1934, residing within the present boundaries of any Indian reservation, and shall further include all other persons of one-half or more Indian blood.[2]

This classification system made Indian categorization largely a function of recognition by the tribe itself, combined with the delineation of a specific population base group of tribal affiliates and direct descendants. This essentially tribe-by-tribe approach has been an enduring tradition of U.S. "Indian" law. Even where statutes defined the scope of government aid programs as applying to "Indians throughout the United States," administrative policy has often attempted to limit programs to Indians living on reservations or having particularly close tribal ties.

In the area of tribal court jurisdiction, the Supreme Court in *Oliphant v. Suquamish Indian Tribe*[3] ruled that tribal courts had no jurisdiction over non-Indians. Shortly thereafter, in *United States v. Wheeler*,[4] the Court interpreted *Oliphant* as holding that the jurisdiction of each tribal court system was limited specifically to tribe members. Perhaps to avoid the strict scrutiny standard applied to "racial" classifications, federal case law on tribal court jurisdiction has emphasized that . . . "Indian" is not a "race" category but is rather a designation "based on a totality of circumstances, including genealogy, group identification, and lifestyle, in which no one factor is dispositive."[5]

Although not wholly consistent with traditional U.S. practice, perhaps the most ingenious approach to classification was taken by the Supreme Court in *Morton v. Mancari.*[6] In that case, non-Indian employees of the Bureau of Indian Affairs (BIA) brought suit to challenge a BIA preference program for Indians. Justice [Harry] Blackmun, writing for the Court, held that this pro-Indian BIA preference was not actionable invidious discrimination. Blackmun reasoned that, under the legislative scheme of the Indian Reorganization Act of 1934, Congress had the permissible goal of ending the situation "whereby the primarily non-Indian-staffed BIA had plenary control, for all practical purposes, over the lives and destinies of the federally recognized Indian tribes."

Significantly, the *Morton* Court expressly declared the designation "Indian" to be a predominantly *political* one:

> The preference is not directed towards a "racial" group consisting of "Indians"; instead, it applies only to members of "federally recognized" tribes. This operates to exclude many individuals who are racially to be classified as "Indians." In this sense, the preference is political rather than racial in nature.

The BIA Indian preference, therefore, was in keeping with the expressed legislative intent of Congress "to promote economic and political self-determination for the Indian." Because the preference was "reasonable and rationally designed to further Indian self-government," the program did not constitute a violation of plaintiffs' due process rights.

The *Morton* concept has, at least, the virtue of formal consistency. Indian tribes occupy a peculiar niche within the United States constitutional system as "domestic dependent nations,"[7] retaining some of a prior independent sovereignty enjoyed before the coming of Whites to the Americas and preserved by treaty negotiations with the U.S. government. The "domestic" part of the "domestic dependent nations" formulation ensures that Indian tribes are no longer sovereign enough to make alliances with or alienate land to foreign nations. Being deemed sovereign powers that have negotiated their attachment to the United States, however, Indian tribes may define the limits of their jurisdiction and the contents of their membership rolls vis-à-vis the federal system with a great deal of freedom—as, by analogy, delineations of citizenship by foreign states are given deference by U.S. authorities. The status of Indian tribes as quasi-independent entities more sovereign (in some sense) than the constituent states of the Union themselves has allowed Indian case law to escape both constitutional "strict scrutiny" and many of the conceptual ambiguities . . . seen in [other racial classification schemes]. . . .

The designation of "Indian" is, to be sure, not quite as conceptually crisp as . . . *Morton* . . . would suggest. The actual eligibility criteria for the BIA program, for example, stipulated that "[t]o be eligible for preference in appointment, promotion, and training, an individual must be *one-fourth* or more degree Indian blood and be a member of a federally-recognized tribe." In practice, the process of adjudicating "blood" content may sometimes turn out to be a "political" one undertaken by the "recognized" tribes themselves, but it is perhaps significant that the Court was still unable to steer Native American classification entirely away from the dangerous shoals of pseudo-biological "race."

. . . The "political" approach of U.S. "Indian" law is a creature of the peculiar history of Native Americans as peoples with a recognized sovereignty antecedent to their incorporation in the U.S. legal system, and who can thus be said to have some legitimate right to participate in defining their own membership. . . .

Notes

1. *United States v. Rogers*, 45 U.S. (4 How.) 567, 572–73 (1846).
2. 25 U.S.C. § 479 (1988).
3. 435 U.S. 191 (1978).
4. 435 U.S. 313 (1978).
5. *Duro v. Reina*, 821 F.2d 1358, 1363 (9th Cir. 1987) [*reversed on other grounds*, 495 U.S. 676 (1990)—Ed.].
6. 417 U.S. 535 (1974).
7. *Cherokee Nation v. Georgia*, 30 U.S. (5 Pet.) 1, 17 (1831).

26

Dependent Sovereigns

Indian Tribes, States, and the Federal Courts

Judith Resnik

Introduction

In 1941, Julia Martinez, a member of the Santa Clara Pueblo, and Myles Martinez, a Navajo, were married. The couple resided on the Santa Clara Pueblo; they had several children. In 1939 the Santa Clara Pueblo promulgated an ordinance detailing its membership rules. The ordinance provided that children of *female* members who married outside the Pueblo would not be Santa Clarans, while children of *male* members who married outside the Pueblo would be members. In the early 1970s, Julia Martinez and her daughter Audrey filed a lawsuit under Title I of the Indian Civil Rights Act (ICRA) of 1968.[1] Having been unsuccessful in their efforts to persuade the Pueblo to change its membership rules, Julia and Audrey Martinez asked the federal court for declaratory and injunctive relief—to invalidate the Santa Clara Pueblo's ordinance and to require that the Pueblo count the Martinez children as members.

In 1978 the United States Supreme Court decided the case of *Santa Clara Pueblo v. Martinez.*[2] Justice Thurgood Marshall, writing for the majority, interpreted Title I of the ICRA to impose "certain restrictions upon tribal governments similar, but not identical, to those contained in the Bill of Rights and the Fourteenth Amendment." However, the only express jurisdictional and remedial provision of the statute was habeas corpus. *Santa Clara Pueblo v. Martinez* thus raised the question of whether the federal court should imply a right of action and federal court jurisdiction to hear the alleged violation of the Indian Civil Rights Act. According to the Court, implication of a right of action and federal court review for claims such as those raised by Julia and Audrey Martinez would undermine the congressional purpose of preserving "tribal sovereignty" and "self-government." Therefore, no implied cause of action existed, and the federal courts could not hear the discrimination charge.

Santa Clara Pueblo is a major case in federal Indian law. *Santa Clara Pueblo* also offers a fascinating illustration of how the United States government conceives of its citizens as holding simultaneous membership in two political entities. According to the Indian Citizenship Act of 1924, all Indians are United States citizens, but that citizenship cannot "impair or otherwise affect" their rights to tribal property.[3] The 1968 Indian Civil Rights Act provides that "[n]o Indian tribe in exercising powers of self-government shall . . . deny to any person within its jurisdiction the equal protection of its laws." Julia and Audrey Martinez represented a group of Santa Claran women who had married non–Santa Clarans and the children of such marriages. The Martinez women came to federal court to obtain "equal protection." The obvious problem with this claim was the tension arising from being a member of two governments, the Santa Clara Pueblo and the United States.

In *Santa Clara Pueblo,* Justice Marshall described the extent of federal control over Indian tribes: All "aspect[s] of tribal sovereignty . . . [are] subject to the superior and plenary control of Congress." But, Justice Marshall explained, Indian tribes retain a substantial measure of sovereignty; they "remain a 'separate people, with the power of regulating their internal and social relations.'" Thus, according to the Court, if federal courts were to imply a power to "intervene" in tribal decisions, the courts would undermine the authority of a group whose powers have already been limited. "A fortiori, a resolution in a foreign forum of intra-tribal disputes of a more public character, such as the one in this case, cannot help but unsettle a tribal government's ability to maintain authority." Congress intended to protect the tribes from "undue interference." Hence the federal courts should not imply jurisdiction and remedies beyond the one (habeas corpus) specified in the legislation. Julia and Audrey Martinez were sent back to the tribal forum, which had already refused their requests for reconsideration of the tribal ordinance.

III. Reasons to Give Voice

A. The Interdependencies of Norms

4. The Need for Membership

The Santa Clara Pueblo has a long history. Anthropologists and ethnographers trace its roots to the fifteenth century. A substantial amount of information is available about the Pueblo's history, including its religious, social, and political organization. During the period prior to the codification of membership rules in the 1930s, scholars of the Santa Clara Pueblo did not discuss "membership" as an organizing feature of the society. Further, if the Martinez family is illustrative, "membership" as defined in the 1939 Ordinance may still not be a central factor in some important aspects of the community's life. The lower courts stated that the children of the Martinez family spoke Tewa, the language of the Pueblo, and participated in its religious and cultural life.

"Membership" itself is a category created by the Santa Clara Pueblo in the context of its interaction with the United States. Membership is a category imposed by the United States, which has "counted" Indians for a variety of purposes since the cavalry went around naming and numbering Indians in the nineteenth century. Indian "membership" is relevant to a myriad of federal jurisdictional rules. United States rules also provide the basis for the generation of restrictive "membership" practices, for the United States offers a limited pool of resources to those who are "members" of Indian tribes. The laws of the United States use lineage as one of the indications of whether an individual is an Indian.

Moreover, assimilationist policies of the United States attempted to weaken individuals' tribal identification based on shared work, shared culture, and shared language, thereby encouraging tribal identification based on lineage ties. It has been the policy of the United States to encourage Indian children to live away from their homes, to go to boarding schools, and to meet individuals other than those from their tribe. As anthropologists of the Santa Clara Pueblo have noted, in the twentieth century intermarriages between Santa Clarans and non–Santa Clarans began to increase, as mobility and larger cultural pressures affected the previously agrarian and self-contained society.

5. The Benefits of Membership

Federal involvement is not limited to the process by which "membership" rules are defined and codified, nor to creating the cultural backdrop that made "membership" an issue. Federal benefits (some might call them "reparations") flow directly to those who are counted as "members." While the federal government can define Indian status differently than a tribe might, the federal government also relies on tribal definitions as a basis for the distribution of benefits.

The availability of federal benefits is central to understanding why the Martinez family tried to obtain recognition of its children as members of the Pueblo. According to the trial court opinion, the "most important of the material benefits [that Ms. Martinez's children sought] is that referred to as land use rights." The United States government holds the Pueblo land in trust for the Pueblo as a whole. The Santa Clara Council has authority to specify individual use of land. The United States government, through the Department of Housing and Urban Development, gives monetary assistance to member Indians who build homes on Pueblo land. Federal policy looked to tribal decisions; the Martinez family argued that, without the Pueblo's recognition of them as members, the Martinez children could not receive federal health and housing assistance. Thus being a "member" of the Santa Clara Pueblo was not simply an event of moment for purposes of that community.

Exactly how the lack of Santa Claran membership affected the Martinez family was a matter of dispute between the parties. Julia Martinez's lawyers argued in their Supreme Court brief: "Denial of membership has caused hardship to the Martinez family, especially in obtaining federal medical care available to Indians. In 1968 Julia Martinez's now-deceased daughter Natalie, suffering from strokes associated with her terminal illness, was refused emergency medical treatment by the [federally funded and run] Indian Health Service. This was solely because her mother had previously been unable to obtain tribal recognition for her."[4] The Pueblo responded that it was not at fault, that it "had no control over whether or not the Martinez children would obtain medical care. This was a matter solely within the province of the Bureau of Indian Affairs."[5]

The Supreme Court did not probe the effects of Santa Claran recognition of the Martinez children on federal benefits. Moreover, while the Court assumed the primacy of membership for tribal sovereignty, the Court did not discuss how often federal law has exercised control over Indian tribal membership or how federal benefits are linked to tribal membership. . . .

6. Membership and Gender

The Santa Clara Pueblo chose to link membership with gender and to limit membership to those who could claim that their fathers were Santa Claran. I do not know the genesis of this rule. Some suggest that the rule reflects the gendered hierarchy of the Pueblo, that the male members of the Pueblo wanted to deter women from marrying non–Santa Claran men. But questions need to be asked about how the Pueblo's gendered hierarchy came into being; the United States often singled out men to be designated as leaders of Indian tribes. Santa Claran men might have held the power to make rules at least in part because the United States assumed men and only men could be rulemakers.

The 1939 Santa Clara membership rules are also congruent with United States traditions of subordination of women. United States common law rules were that the husband conferred status on the wife and the father conferred status on the child. . . . In contrast, some nineteenth-century writers described the interests of Indian women in tribal property to be great, and sometimes greater than, the interests of men. The writers also stated that such treatment of women was further proof of Indian tribes' lack of "civilized" ways.

When considering the genesis of the Santa Clara membership rules, I wonder whether federal statutes existing since the late 1880s and linking gender, lineage, and property rights played any role. In 1888, Congress enacted a statute (still on the books) that provided that an "Indian woman" who married a citizen of the United States gained United States citizenship but retained her interest in tribal property.[6] In 1897, Congress legislated that the children of an "Indian woman" and a "white man" married prior to the enactment of that legislation would have the same rights and privileges as did other members of the mother's tribe.[7] This legislation altered the United States common law rule that the "condition of the father prevails in determining the status of the offspring." Some federal officials explained the 1888 legislation as aimed at encouraging assimilation of Indians. The thesis was that women would follow men and that male heads of households would provide the cultural framework for the household. It was hoped and assumed that if "white men" could not by virtue of marriage assert title over tribal property, white men would not live with the Indian women to whom they were married on the reservation. When the women followed the men, they would then live and raise their children in a white culture. Federal administrative regulations have also distinguished between "Indian men" and "Indian women"; for example, the BIA provided families of Indian men married to non-Indian women with general assistance more readily than when Indian women married non-Indian men.[8]

The 1939 codification of female subordination seems to have been supported, if not influenced and encouraged, by the traditions of the United States, a country in which women have long been expected to "follow their men"; a country in which home, name, income, and status are for many women defined by the home, name, income, and status of the men to whom they are related as wives and daughters.

Notes

1. 25 U.S.C. §§ 1301-3 (1982). . . .
2. 436 U.S. 49 (1978).
3. Pub. L. No. 175, 43 Stat. 253 (1924). . . .
4. Supreme Court Brief of the Respondents, *Santa Clara Pueblo v. Martinez*, No. 76-682, at 33 (Oct. Term, 1976). . . .
5. Supreme Court Reply Brief of the Petitioners, *Santa Clara v. Martinez*, No. 76-682, at 13 (Oct Term 1976). . . .
6. An Act in Relation to Marriage between White Men and Indian Women, ch. 818, 25 Stat. 392 (codified at 25 U.S.C. § 182 [1982]). . . .
7. 25 U.S.C. § 184 (1982). . . .
8. Shirley R. Bysiewisz and Ruth E. Van de Mark, *The Legal Status of the Dakota Indian Woman,* 3 American Indian Law Review 255, 276–77 (1975).

Review Questions

1. Are all racial classifications just as arbitrary as the "one drop" rule? If so, should we ever consider race in any program requiring racial classifications, such as affirmative action, employment discrimination remedies, and legislative redistricting decisions?
2. Are the experiences of biracial and multiracial people specific and dependent on physical appearance, socioeconomic class, and other factors?
3. Is *la raza cósmica* a myth? Is it the same as claiming racial superiority over other groups?
4. Do the various legal definitions of *Indian* make sense? Are classifications of *Indian* necessary to ensure tribal sovereignty and to allow the U.S. government to administer programs that attempt to remedy the serious injustices done to Indians in the past?
5. How do you identify racially? Has your racial identity changed over the course of your life?

Suggested Readings

Russel Lawrence Barsh and James Younglood Henderson, The Road: Indian Tribes and Political Liberty (1980).

Margo S. Brownell, *Who Is an Indian?: Searching for an Answer to the Question at the Core of Federal Indian Law,* 34 University of Michigan Journal of Law Reform 275 (2001).

John O. Calmore, *Exploring Michael Omi's "Messy" Real World of Race: An Essay for "Naked People Longing to Swim Free,"* 15 Law and Inequality Journal 25 (1997).

Miscegenation Blues: Voices of Mixed Race Women (Carol Camper, ed., 1994).

Jo Carrillo, *Identity as Idiom:* Mashpee *Reconsidered,* 28 Indiana Law Review 511 (1995).

Felix S. Cohen's Handbook of Federal Indian Law (Rennard Strickland et al., eds., 1982).

F. James Davis, *The Hawaiian Alternative to the One-Drop Rule, in* American Mixed Race: The Culture of Microdiversity 115 (Naomi Zack, ed., 1995).

———, Who Is Black? One Nation's Definition (1991).

Kenneth A. Davis, *Racial Designation in Louisiana: One Drop of Black Blood Makes a Negro!* 3 Hastings Constitutional Law Quarterly 199 (1976).

Marisol de la Cadena, *Reconstructing Race: Racism, Culture and Mestizaje in Latin America,* NACLA: Report on the Americas, May–June 2001, at 16.

Richard Delgado, *Rodrigo's Fifteenth Chronicle: Racial Mixture, Latino-Critical Scholarship, and the Black-White Binary,* 75 Texas Law Review 1181 (1997).

Alfreda A. Sellers Diamond, *Becoming Black in America: A Book Review Essay of* Life on the Color Line *by Gregory Howard Williams,* 67 Mississippi Law Journal 427 (1997).

Raymond T. Diamond and Robert J. Cottrol, *Codifying Caste: Louisiana's Racial Classification Scheme and the Fourteenth Amendment,* 29 Loyola Law Review 255 (1983).

Allison M. Dussias, *Geographically-Based and Membership-Based Views of Indian Tribal Sovereignty: The Supreme Court's Changing Vision,* 55 University of Pittsburgh Law Review 1 (1993).

Carlos A. Fernández, *La Raza and the Melting Pot: A Comparative Look at Multiethnicity, in* Racially Mixed People in America 126 (Maria P. P. Root, ed., 1992).

Jack D. Forbes, Africans and Native Americans: The Language of Race and the Evolution of Red-Black Peoples (2d ed. 1993).

———, *The Manipulation of Race, Caste and Identity: Classifying AfroAmericans, Native Americans and Red-Black People,* 17 Journal of Ethnic Studies 1 (1990).

Lise Funderburg, Black, White, Other: Biracial Americans Talk about Race and Identity (1994).

Bijan Gilanshah, *Multiracial Minorities: Erasing the Color Line,* 12 Law and Inequality Journal 183 (1993).

Carole Goldberg-Ambrose, *Not "Strictly" Racial: A Response to "Indians as Peoples,"* 39 UCLA Law Review 169 (1991).

Neil Gotanda, *A Critique of "Our Constitution Is Color-Blind,"* 44 Stanford Law Review 1 (1991).

Sandy Marie Anglás Grande, *American Indian Geographies of Identity and Power: At the Crossroads of Indígena and Mestizaje,* 70 Harvard Educational Review 467 (2000).

Eric Henderson, *Ancestry and Casino Dollars in the Formation of Tribal Identity,* 4 Race and Ethnic Ancestry Law Journal 7 (1998).

Berta Esperanza Hernández-Truyol, *The LatIndia and Mestizajes: Of Cultures, Conquests, and Latcritical Feminism,* 3 Journal of Gender, Race and Justice 63 (1999).

The State of Native America: Genocide, Colonization, and Resistance (M. Annette Jaimes, ed., 1992).

Alex M. Johnson Jr., *Destabilizing Racial Classifications Based on Insights Gleaned from Trademark Law,* 84 California Law Review 887 (1996).

Kevin R. Johnson, How Did You Get to Be Mexican? A White/Brown Man's Search for Identity (1999).

Jayne Chong-Soon Lee, *Navigating the Topology of Race,* 46 Stanford Law Review 747 (1994).

Fred Lomayesva, *Indian Identity—Post Indian Reflections,* 35 Tulsa Law Journal 63 (1999).

Patrick Macklem, *Distributing Sovereignty: Indian Nations and Equality of Peoples,* 45 Stanford Law Review 1311 (1993).

Scott L. Malcomson, One Drop of Blood: The American Misadventure of Race (2000).

James McBride, The Color of Water: A Black Man's Tribute to His White Mother (1996).

Martha Menchaca, *Chicano-Mexican Cultural Assimilation and Anglo-Saxon Cultural Dominance,* 11 Hispanic Journal of Behavioral Sciences 203 (1989).

Eric Miller, *Signifyin' Nothing? Conversations on Race, Color, and Community,* 13 Harvard BlackLetter Law Journal 241 (1997).

Margaret E. Montoya, *Academic Mestizaje: Reproducing Clinical Teaching and Re/framing Wills as Latina Praxis,* 2 Harvard Latino Law Review 349 (1997).

Rachel F. Moran, *Full Circle, in* Critical Race Feminism: A Reader 113 (Adrien Katherine Wing, ed., 1997).

Edward Murguía, Chicano Intermarriage: A Theoretical and Empirical Study (1982).

Michael Omi, *Racial Identity and the State: The Dilemmas of Classification,* 15 Law and Inequality Journal 7 (1997).

Michael Omi and Howard Winant, Racial Formation in the United States: From the 1960s to the 1990s (2d ed. 1994).

Angel R. Oquendo, *Re-Imagining the Latino/a Race,* 12 Harvard BlackLetter Law Journal 93 (1995).

Cindy D. Padget, *The Lost Indians of the Lost Colony: A Critical Legal Study of the Lumbee Indians of North Carolina,* 21 American Indian Law Review 391 (1997).

Kathryn R. L. Rand and Steven A. Light, *Virtue or Vice? How IGRA Shapes the Politics of Native American Gaming, Sovereignty, and Identity,* 4 Virginia Journal of Social Policy and the Law 381 (1997).

Edward Byron Reuter, The Mulatto in the United States (1918).

G. William Rice, *There and Back Again—An Indian Hobbit's Holiday: "Indians Teaching Indian Law,"* 26 New Mexico Law Review 169 (1996).

Richard Rodriguez, Brown (2002).

Natsu Taylor Saito, *From Slavery and Seminoles to AIDS in South Africa: An Essay on Race and Property in International Law,* 45 Villanova Law Review 1135 (2000).

Judy Scales-Trent, Notes of a White Black Woman: Race, Color, Community (1995).

Jon Michael Spencer, The New Colored People: The Mixed-Race Movement in America (1997).

Paul R. Spickard, Mixed Blood: Intermarriage and Ethnic Identity in Twentieth-Century America (1989).

Rennard Strickland, *The Genocidal Premise in Native American Law and Policy: Exorcizing Aboriginal Ghosts,* 1 Journal of Gender, Race and Justice 325 (1998).

Pauline Turner Strong and Barrik Van Winkle, *"Indian Blood": Reflections on the Reckoning and Refiguring of Native North American Identity,* 11 Cultural Anthropology 547 (1996).
Gerald Torres and Kathryn Milun, *Translating* Yonnondio *by Precedent and Evidence: The Mashpee Indian Case,* 1990 Duke Law Journal 625 (1990).
Enid Trucios-Haynes, *The Legacy of Racially Restrictive Immigration Laws and Policies and the Construction of the American National Identity,* 76 Oregon Law Review 369 (1997).
Alan R. Velie, *Indian Identity in the Nineties,* 23 Oklahoma City University Law Review 189 (1998).
Rebecca Walker, Black, White, and Jewish: Autobiography of a Shifting Self (2001).
David C. Williams, *The Borders of the Equal Protection Clause: Indians as Peoples,* 38 UCLA Law Review 759 (1991).
Lawrence Wright, *One Drop of Blood,* New Yorker, July 25, 1994, at 46.
Naomi Zack, Race and Mixed Race (1993).

Part III

"Passing"

Part 3 considers the legal and personal impacts of "passing," or efforts by African Americans—many of mixed ancestry—and other racial minorities to "pass" as White. This practice arose as a response to the negative consequences (e.g., slavery, segregation, discrimination) associated with being classified as a racial minority in the United States. For example, to avoid segregation, some African Americans assumed a White identity for access to jobs and economic opportunity. Passing thus represented resistance to the segregation enforced by law and social custom.

Because legal and social privilege attach to Whiteness (see generally Stephanie Wildman, *Privilege Revealed: How Invisible Privilege Undermines America* [1996]), attempts to "pass" should not be surprising. However, such conduct can have damaging psychological consequences on those who deny their Black, Latina/o, Asian American, or Native American ancestries. In addition, African Americans who pass as White may face hostility from other African Americans who consider it a betrayal of their race.

The ability to pass in large part is a function of an individual's personal appearance. Certain phenotypes make it possible to be perceived as White, whatever one's actual ancestry, which in turn often correlates with mixed ancestry. Social settings may influence the perception of one's race as well. A person may seem "less" White when surrounded by African Americans in a particular place or "more" White in a group of White people. This, of course, supports the notion that race is a social construction.

In Part III, Cheryl Harris offers a story of her grandmother's struggles passing to work "White" jobs in Chicago. Randall Kennedy critically analyzes the history of passing by African Americans and whether the practice is morally justifiable in certain circumstances. Alex Johnson discusses how segregated housing effectively prevents passing. Robert Chang discusses racial fluidity by looking at the cultural mystique surrounding golfing sensation Tiger Woods. Adrienne Davis offers insights on racial fluidity based on her experiences in Nicaragua. Kevin Johnson discusses passing as "Spanish" by Mexican Americans. Mary Coombs compares racial passing to that done by lesbians and gay men "in the closet." Finally, Luther Wright Jr. discusses Whites fraudulently seeking to adopt a Black identity—to pass as African American in order to secure affirmative action and related benefits.

27

Whiteness as Property

Cheryl I. Harris

In the 1930s, some years after my mother's family became part of the great river of Black migration that flowed north, my Mississippi-born grandmother was confronted with the harsh matter of economic survival for herself and her two daughters. Having separated from my grandfather, who himself was trapped on the fringes of economic marginality, she took one long hard look at her choices and presented herself for employment at a major retail store in Chicago's central business district. This decision would have been unremarkable for a white woman in similar circumstances, but for my grandmother, it was an act of both great daring and self-denial, for in so doing she was presenting herself as a white woman. In the parlance of racist America, she was "passing."

Her fair skin, straight hair, and aquiline features had not spared her from the life of sharecropping into which she had been born in anywhere/nowhere, Mississippi—the outskirts of Yazoo City. But in the burgeoning landscape of urban America, anonymity was possible for a Black person with "white" features. She was transgressing boundaries, crossing borders, spinning on margins, traveling between dualities of Manichaean space, rigidly bifurcated into light/dark, good/bad, white/Black. No longer immediately identifiable as "Lula's daughter," she could thus enter the white world, albeit on a false passport, not merely passing but *tres*passing.

Every day my grandmother rose from her bed in her house in a Black enclave on the south side of Chicago, sent her children off to a Black school, boarded a bus full of Black passengers, and rode to work. No one at her job ever asked if she was Black; the question was unthinkable. By virtue of the employment practices of the "fine establishment" in which she worked, she could not have been. Catering to the upper middle class, understated tastes required that Blacks not be allowed.

She quietly went about her clerical tasks, not once revealing her true identity. She listened to the women with whom she worked discuss their worries—their children's illnesses, their husbands' disappointments, their boyfriends' infidelities—all of the mundane yet critical things that made up their lives. She came to know them but they did not know her, for my grandmother occupied a completely different place. That place—where white supremacy and economic domination meet—was unknown turf to her white co-workers. They remained oblivious to the worlds within worlds that existed just beyond the edge of their awareness and yet were present in their very midst.

Each evening my grandmother, tired and worn, retraced her steps home, laid aside her mask, and reentered herself. Day in and day out, she made herself invisible, then visible again, for a price too inconsequential to do more than barely sustain her family, and at a cost too precious to conceive. She left the job some years later, finding the strain too much to bear.

From time to time, as I later sat with her, she would recollect that period, and the cloud of some painful memory would pass across her face. Her voice would remain subdued, as if to contain the still-remembered tension. On rare occasions she would wince, recalling some particularly racist comment made in her presence because of her presumed shared group affiliation. Whatever retort might have been called for had been suppressed long before it reached her lips, for the price of her family's well-being was her silence. Accepting the risk of self-annihilation was the only way to survive.

Although she never would have stated it this way, the clear and ringing denunciations of racism she delivered from her chair when advanced arthritis had rendered her unable to work were informed by those experiences. The fact that self-denial had been a logical choice and had made her complicit in her own oppression at times fed the fire in her eyes when she confronted some daily outrage inflicted on Black people. Later, these painful memories forged her total identification with the civil rights movement. Learning about the world at her knee as I did, these experiences also came to inform my outlook and my understanding of the world.

My grandmother's story is far from unique. Indeed, there are many who crossed the color line never to return. Passing is well known among Black people in the United States and is a feature of race subordination in all societies structured on white supremacy. Notwithstanding the purported benefits of Black heritage in an era of affirmative action, passing is not an obsolete phenomenon that has slipped into history.

The persistence of passing is related to the historical and continuing pattern of white racial domination and economic exploitation that has given passing a certain economic logic. It was a given to my grandmother that being white automatically ensured higher economic returns in the short term, as well as greater economic, political, and social security in the long run. Becoming white meant gaining access to a whole set of public and private privileges that materially and permanently guaranteed basic subsistence needs and, therefore, survival. Becoming white increased the possibility of controlling critical aspects of one's life rather than being the object of others' domination.

My grandmother's story illustrates the valorization of whiteness as treasured property in a society structured on racial caste. In ways so embedded that they are rarely apparent, the set of assumptions, privileges, and benefits that accompany the status of being white has become a valuable asset that whites sought to protect and that those who passed sought to attain—by fraud if necessary. Whites have come to expect and rely on these benefits, and over time these expectations have been affirmed, legitimated, and protected by the law. . . .

28

Racial Passing

Randall Kennedy

I. Passing: A Definition

Passing is a deception that enables a person to adopt certain roles or identities from which he would be barred by prevailing social standards in the absence of his misleading conduct. The classic racial passer in the United States has been the "white Negro": the individual whose physical appearance allows him to present himself as "white" but whose "black" lineage (typically only a very partial black lineage) makes him a Negro according to dominant racial rules. A passer is distinguishable from the person who is merely mistaken—the person who, having been told that he is white, thinks of himself as white and holds himself out to be white (though he and everyone else in the locale would deem him to be "black" were the facts of his ancestry known). . . .

Estimates regarding the incidence of passing have varied greatly. Walter White claimed that annually "approximately 12,000 white-skinned Negroes disappear" into white society.[1] Roi Ottley asserted that there were 5 million "white Negroes" in the United States and that forty to fifty thousand passed annually.[2] Professor John H. Burma's estimates were considerably lower. He posited that some 110,000 blacks lived on the white side of the color line and that between 2,500 and 2,750 passed annually.[3] Given its secretive nature, no one knows for sure the incidence of passing. It is clear, however, that at the middle of the twentieth century, large numbers of African Americans claimed to know people engaged in passing.

II. Passing Stories

"Blacks" have passed for "white" in a wide variety of circumstances. One extraordinary instance occurred in 1848 when Ellen Craft—the daughter of a master and his slave mistress—escaped from bondage by train, boat, and carriage on a four-day journey from Macon, Georgia, to Philadelphia, Pennsylvania. Ellen Craft pretended to be white. Her slave husband was part of her disguise; he pretended to be her servant. And there was one more twist: Ellen Craft traveled not as a white woman but as a white man. To obtain freedom for herself and her husband, she temporarily traversed gender as well as racial lines.

In contrast to the Crafts, who passed for whites to journey north to escape slavery, Walter White passed for white to journey south to investigate lynchings. White was fair-skinned, blue-eyed, and blond-haired, the son of light-complexioned Negroes who were stalwarts of the black middle class in Atlanta, Georgia. His mother worked at home while his father was a mail carrier. Because of their coloring, the Whites sometimes found themselves in the middle of racial misunderstandings. When Walter White's mother and sisters boarded segregated streetcars, for example, Caucasian men who believed the women to be white often jeered at them when they sat in the Negro section. A much more serious racial misunderstanding occurred in 1931 when Walter White's father was struck by an automobile driven by a white physician who practiced at Atlanta's Grady Hospital. At that time, the hospital was divided into two sections. The white section was clean and renovated; the black section, dirty and dilapidated. The physician took White's father to the white section of the hospital. Before long, though, a visit by a son-in-law apprised the hospital staff of their "error." Recounting the episode in his autobiography, Walter White wrote that his father "was snatched from the examination table lest he contaminate the 'white' air, and taken hurriedly across the street in a driving downpour . . . to the 'Negro' ward," where he died sixteen days later.[4]

Although Walter White could have passed, he recalls deciding at an early age to associate himself with the African American community. The formative event that molded his sense of communal attachment stemmed from the Atlanta riot of 1906. Goaded by false stories of Negro men raping white women, a white mob terrorized blacks in Georgia's capital in an awful explosion of racial hatred. Caught in town amid marauding whites, young Walter and his father escaped serious injury only because of the camouflage given them by their light complexions. They witnessed, however, terrible crimes committed against other Negroes:

> We saw a lame Negro bootblack . . . pathetically try to outrun a mob of whites. Less than a hundred yards from us the chase ended. We saw clubs and fists descending to the accompaniment of savage shouting and cursing. Suddenly a voice cried, "There goes another nigger!" Its work done, the mob went after new prey. The body with the withered foot lay dead in a pool of blood in the street.

At one point, a mob menacingly approached White's home, a participant in it yelling: "That's where the nigger mail carrier lives! Let's burn it down! It's too nice for a nigger to live in!" White's father determined that he and his son would defend the family homestead with firearms if necessary. White recalls that his father said to him "[i]n a voice as quiet as though he were asking me to pass him sugar at the breakfast table . . . 'Son, don't shoot until the first man puts his foot on the lawn and then—don't you miss.'" "In that instant," White relates,

> there opened up within me a great awareness; I knew who I was. I was a Negro, a human being with an invisible pigmentation which marked me as a person to be hunted, hanged, abused, discriminated against, kept in poverty, and ignorance, in order that those whose skin was white would have readily at hand a proof of their superiority [so

> that] [n]o matter how low a white man fell, he could always hold fast to the smug conviction that he was superior to two-thirds of the world's population.

It so happened that the mob never attacked the Whites' house. It quickly retreated when fired upon by White's black neighbors.

Years later, White devoted much of his attention to defending African Americans against racially motivated violence. His principal means of struggle was exposure. Working on behalf of the NAACP [National Association for the Advancement of Colored People], he gathered facts about lynchings and other atrocities and carefully publicized them in an effort to arouse American public opinion. However, the daring way in which he pursued this task brought him close to danger. In 1919 he traveled to Phillips County, Arkansas, to investigate the deaths of some 250 blacks killed in an effort to discourage collective organization by African American cotton farmers. When whites in Phillips County became aware of White's purpose, he was forced to escape hurriedly. "You're leaving mister, just when the fun is going to start," White recalls being told by the conductor of the train on which he made his getaway. "A damned yellow nigger is down here passing for white and the boys are going to get him." "No matter what the distance," White later observed, "I shall never take as long a train ride as that one seemed to be."

Other blacks have passed as white in order to shop, sleep, or eat meals at racially exclusive establishments. St. Clair Drake and Horace R. Cayton report that some light-skinned Negroes in Chicago whom they interviewed in the forties spoke of going to white establishments "just to see what they are like and to get a thrill."[5]

The most sensational case arising from an alleged effort to pass was the lawsuit that pitted Alice Jones against Leonard Kip Rhinelander.[6] Jones was the daughter of a white mother and a black father, a couple of modest means. The Rhinelanders, by contrast, traveled in the highest circles of white, wealthy New York Society; Kip stood to inherit millions from his parents' estate. When they learned that their son had married a colored waitress, they insisted that he put an end to the relationship. Buckling to their demands six weeks into his marriage, he sought an annulment on November 27, 1924, claiming that Alice had deceived him about her race. Initially he alleged that she had tricked him by stating falsely that she was white. Later he alleged that she had tricked him not by outright falsehood but more subtly, by silently but knowingly taking advantage of his mistaken belief that she was white.

Alice Jones's defense put the legal proceedings on the front pages of the New York dailies for weeks. Her defense was that he could not have been ignorant about her racial identity because, in terms of her physiognomy, he knew *everything* there was to know about her. She argued that he could not rightly claim to have been hoodwinked because he had, so to speak, been under the hood. To support this argument, Alice's attorneys put into evidence two dramatic items. The first was correspondence that clearly indicated that she and Kip had had extensive sexual relations prior to their marriage. The other was Alice herself: her attorney obtained permission for Alice to disrobe and show herself behind closed doors to the all-male, all-white jury. The purpose in doing so was to show the jurors that there were aspects of her physiognomy, including her nipples, that would have put Rhinelander on notice about her race. In his summation to the jury, Jones's attorney stressed that Rhinelander had had "unlimited opportunities to look [at her body]." The lawyer went on to say:

> I let you gentlemen look at a portion of what he saw. You saw Alice's back above the bust. You saw her breast. You saw a portion of her upper leg. He saw all of her body. And you are going to tell me that he never suspected that she had colored blood! . . . You saw that with your own eyes . . . that colored blood was coursing through her veins.

The attorney for Rhinelander made an all-out plea for the jury simply to register its disgust with interracial marriage. "There isn't a father among you," he declared, "who would not rather see his son in his casket than to see him wedded to a mulatto woman." The jury found in Jones's favor.

III. Judging Passers

Passing has generated a wide range of responses. Many have been negative. Aggrieved slave owners viewed as treacherous thieves runaway slaves who passed in order to gain freedom. Segregationists condemned white Negro passers as an insidious danger that threatened the very foundations of the nation. Such people, it was feared, might contaminate white bloodlines by marrying unsuspecting Caucasians. According to Professor Joel Williamson, "Southern whites in the early twentieth century became paranoid about invisible blackness."[7]

The most thoroughgoing effort in American history to prevent and punish passing emerged in Virginia in the 1920s with the birth of the Anglo Saxon Clubs of America. Fear of interracial intimacy and passing prompted club activists to lobby in favor of extending Jim Crow segregation and ferreting out passers, especially those with children who attended white public schools. It also prompted them to lobby in favor of narrowing the state's definition of who counted as a white person and the state's regulations governing matrimony. . . . The Anglo Saxon Clubs wanted Virginia to take additional steps to purify its white population but were thwarted finally by opponents who maintained that, unless restrained, the club's exacting racialism would lead to a situation in which some of the leading white families of the state would have to be reclassified as colored—indeed, a situation in which few "real" white people would be left.

White supremacists are not the only ones who have condemned black passers. Opponents of white supremacy have also objected. They have done so on two main grounds. The first is that passing constitutes a betrayal of African Americans. The second is that the costs of passing outweigh its benefits.

The relationship of passing to racial loyalty was central to Frances Ellen Watkins Harper (1825–1911), an extraordinary black woman who distinguished herself as a journalist, political activist, poet, and novelist. Her best-known exploration of passing is found in her novel *Iola Leroy*, which chronicles the life of a light-skinned Negro woman who refuses to pass. The daughter of a master and a slave whom he freed and married, Iola Leroy looks like a white woman, as did her mother. Indeed, throughout her childhood Iola Leroy believed herself to be white because her parents shielded her from knowledge about her black ancestry. During the Civil War, Dr. Gresham, a white physician in the Union Army, proposes to her. He tells Iola Leroy that he knows of her racial background but wants to marry her anyway. "Love, like faith," he observes, "laughs at impossibilities. I can conceive of no barrier too high for my love to surmount."[8]

Attracted to Dr. Gresham, Iola Leroy nonetheless rejects his offer because of her determination "to cast [her] lot with the freed people as a helper, teacher, and friend." In her view, Gresham's proposal creates a stark choice. She could marry him, which would ultimately entail, she believes, becoming white. Or she could reject him and stand with her people, a course that entails remaining black. She chooses the latter.

To make sure that readers get the message that Iola Leroy made the correct choice, Harper reiterates the necessity of choosing racial sides throughout her novel. Years after Iola Leroy refuses Gresham the first time, Harper creates a scene in which her heroine refuses him again: "I don't think that I could best serve my race by forsaking them and marrying you. . . . I must serve the race which needs me most."

A second anti-passing theme is that benefits derived from passing are not worth its costs. In the 1990s, Ronald E. Hall maintained that "[p]assing for white inflicts psychological trauma on those who try it, because it requires them to erect a wall between who they are or could be as persons and who they are or try to be amid white society."[9] In 1950 the Negro actress Janice Kingslow reached the same conclusion despite the offer of a lucrative contract from a Hollywood studio in return for her agreement to change her name and racial identity. In *I Refuse to Pass*, Kingslow explained why she rejected this deal: "What good was fame or money if I lost myself? This wasn't just a question of choosing a pleasant-sounding false name to fit on a theatre marquee. [Passing] meant stripping my life clear of everything I was. Everything that had ever happened to me."[10]

In nonfiction, Reba Lee's *I Passed for White* is a memorable illustration of the idea that passing can be a spurious remedy, even worse than the predicament that the passer attempts to flee.[11] This fascinating memoir tells the story of a woman whose biological father was white and whose biological mother was a light-skinned Negro. Lee grew up in Chicago with her maternal relatives. She never knew her father. He was a student at the University of Chicago who quickly dropped Lee's mother, a waitress, when she became pregnant. Before Reba was born, her mother married a Negro man who conscientiously raised her as his own child.

From an early age, Lee sought to escape being identified as black. She preferred friendships with whites, even when they expressed dislike for Negroes, and even though her relationships with them were contingent on her ability to hide her racial background. Her conduct was shaped in part by the influence of a grandmother, who constantly praised the extent to which her relatives had been whitened by slavemasters in the antebellum period. "Our family," the grandmother proudly proclaimed, "has some of the best blood of the old South in it." Lee's conduct was also shaped by deep ambivalence about both blacks and whites. She resented whites who felt themselves to be superior to Negroes but simultaneously felt herself to be superior to Negroes—or at least the "niggery" ones.

> I felt bitter when I saw a cheap, flashy white girl walking along as if she owned the earth, but I felt worse when I saw a fat, sloppy Negro girl or a smart-alecky dressed-up one. I

> was on edge about the Negroes coming up from the South, the ignorant, dirty ones. . . . I didn't like them and it gave me a sick, distasteful feeling to have them called "my" race.

Finally, Lee was prompted to pass because she yearned to be free of the limitations imposed by the race line. She wanted "to work without any colored label" prejudicing whites against her from the outset, without regard to her individual talents.

So Reba Lee passed. Without telling any of her relatives where she was going, she fled her home in Chicago, left behind a brief goodbye letter, took an airplane to New York City, renamed herself, and became a white woman. Racially privileged now, she obtained a clerical job and social connections that would probably have been denied to her in her old incarnation as a Negro. Through her new friends, she met a rich, young, white man who married her.

At first she was happy with her new station—"as thrilled as an actress who sees her name in lights for the first time." Passing, however, became increasingly burdensome. She repeatedly found herself in situations in which whites, thinking that she was one of "them," freely damned "the niggers"—verbal aggressions that bothered her despite her own alienation from Negroes. Hearing a man proudly assert at a dinner party that he would not amorously touch a nigger with a ten-foot pole, Reba said to herself: "I'd have to get used to it. It shouldn't be any worse than for my white blood to hear talk against the whites. But it was worse. I had been brought up colored." Still more trying was the strain of hiding her past. At the same time that Reba deceptively told her in-laws that her parents were dead, she sent herself letters and gifts that she showed to her in-laws from fictitious friends and relatives. Being on guard all the time against a slip that might unravel her tale of lies imposed a terrible burden that she eventually decided was too heavy to bear. "I had entered the Promised land," she mused, "[b]ut now that I was there . . . I did not want to go on with it. I was sick to the bone of lying and pretending. I was sick of the fear of being found out."

The fear is realistic. For all of Reba's adeptness at constructing a new identity, the stickiness of her past confounds her. One evening she goes with her husband and some friends to a jazz club in Greenwich Village. There she is noticed by a black musician who knew her from Chicago. When he approaches her familiarly, she succeeds in preventing him from blowing her cover altogether. But the obvious connection that they share bothers her husband. She tells him that in Chicago she briefly attended a multiracial public school. But he is reluctant to believe her—a reluctance that grows because of a second incident. Reba becomes pregnant, a development that terrifies her because of the prospect that she may give birth to a baby whose colored skin or kinky hair will reveal her racial secret. As it turns out, she encounters real difficulties with her pregnancy. She goes into labor prematurely and produces a stillborn child. In her terror, exhaustion, and agony she asks a nurse: "Is it black?"—a question that irredeemably poisons her relationship with her husband, who now suspects that she had an affair with the black musician at the jazz club.

Even more important to Reba than the shadow of exposure, however, is her discovery that, in the end, she did not really like living with whites—at least the ones she was around. Far from being a better class of individuals,

> [t]hese people were no better, no, not as good, as the colored people I had known. More mannerly, yes, more knowledgeable and cultivated, acquainted with all the good things of life, but for all their background and opportunities they were less genuine, less understanding, less tolerant in their relations to each other. And less happy. The joy of living was not in them. . . . Oh, I liked the charming homes . . . the feeling of privilege. The rich white feeling. I liked what the whites *did* but not what they *were*. . . . I realized now that I had never been truly happy among them.

So Reba Lee crosses the race line once again. She divorces her husband and returns to her black relatives and friends in Chicago who, as she portrays it, accept her back without recrimination.

The risk of being unmasked—outed—is only one of many costs to be considered by individuals contemplating passing. Another, ironically, is loss of status; a well-educated black man who might be outstanding in Negro circles, might only be moderately successful or even mediocre in the white world. Relating the testimony of a black man who rejoined the Negro fold, Gunnar Myrdal reports that among the reasons the man gave for rejecting passing was that while "he [was] 'tops' in the Negro community" for doing a certain job, among whites he would be among many and "far from the social ceiling." Moreover, "[b]ecause his profession was one in which there [were] few qualified Negro workers, he got his position more easily as a Negro than he would have as a white man."[12]

Although condemnation of passing is the dominant motif in the fictional and nonfictional literature of racial subterfuge, other responses are also discernible. As one of Nella Larsen's passers observes regarding the ambivalence with which many blacks react to passing: "We disapprove of it and at the same time condone it. It excites our contempt and yet we rather admire it. We shy away from it with an odd kind of revulsion, but we protect it."[13] For some observers, condoning passing stems from a perception that racial masquerade can constitute an unpleasant but acceptable adaptation to racist mistreatment. In *Plum Bun*, Jessie Redmon Fauset describes a Negro woman who passes occasionally in order to enjoy restaurants and orchestra seats that are customarily reserved for whites. Fauset comments tenderly that the woman "employed her colour very much as she practiced certain winning usages of smile and voice to obtain indulgences which meant much to her and which took nothing from anyone else."[14] "It was with no idea of disclaiming her own that [this woman] sat in orchestra seats . . . denied to coloured patrons," Fauset continued. Rather, the woman's passing stemmed from "a mischievous determination to flout a silly and unjust law."

The nonfiction literature by and about passers is also full of references to passing as a mode of resistance or subversion. Ray Stannard Baker noted that passing awakened glee among many Negroes because they viewed it as a way of "getting even with the dominant white man."[15] Langston Hughes repeatedly defended passing as a joke on racism.[16] . . .

Two of the most important challenges to racial oppression in twentieth-century American constitutional law involve episodes of passing. On May 30, 1942, police in San Leandro, California, questioned a young man who was walking down the street with a young woman, his date, because of suspicion that he was violating Military Exclusion Order No. 34, which directed all persons of Japanese ancestry in California to report to United States military authorities in order to prepare for evacuation and internment. When confronted by the police, the man claimed to be "Clyde Sarah," a person of Spanish-Hawaiian ancestry. In fact, the man's name was Fred Toyosaburo Korematsu, a son of Japanese parents. In addition to producing a fake name and altering his draft card, Korematsu had subjected himself to plastic surgery. In 1944 the United States Supreme Court upheld the constitutionality of the provisions under which Korematsu was punished, in a ruling that has been widely condemned.[17]

A second case involved a black man, James Hurd, who challenged the constitutionality of a court order evicting him from his home.[18] He was evicted at the behest of white neighbors who complained that he had breached a restrictive covenant under which promises had been made that his home would never be sold to or occupied by a Negro. At trial, Hurd raised broad legal issues but also a narrow factual objection. He asserted that the eviction would be improper because he was a Mohawk Indian and not a Negro. Voicing this defense was none other than Charles Hamilton Houston, the great mentor of the African American civil rights bar in the years prior to *Brown v. Board of Education*[19] and a lawyer keenly attentive to the ramifications of tactical choices he made as a litigator. Houston lost on the issue of racial classification (though he ultimately won on the federal constitutional issue). The important point here, though, is that Houston attempted to use passing—this time passing for Indian—as a vehicle for advancing not only his client's cause but the broader cause of racial justice.

True, in some—maybe all—instances, passing entrenches racial lines of exclusion by reinforcing the norm that certain sectors of society are open only to those who are white or are at least perceived as white. Passing, moreover, has been seen as constituting such a trivial challenge to racial restrictions that some arbiters of the color bar permit masquerades to go forward as long as passers outwardly obey the rules of white supremacy—that is, pretend actually to be white in return for receiving the privileges that white skin obtains. . . .

Passing, however, does pose at least some challenge to racist regimes. That is why they typically try to prevent it. Fleeing bondage by passing may have been an individualistic response to the tyranny of slavery, but it did free human beings and helped belie the canard that slaves were actually content with their lot. The successful performance of "white man's work" by a passing Negro upset racist claims that blacks were categorically incapable of doing such work. The extent of the disturbance is severely limited by the practical necessity of keeping the passing secret. But under some circumstances a limited disturbance is about all that can be accomplished.

Some critics accuse passers of being complicit in the regimes that they attempt to escape. Sometimes they are. They may even become loud and fervent bigots. But doing so has not typically been a necessary entailment of passing. And it is at least plausible that some passers have attempted to challenge racist practices from their newly acquired positions of racial privilege. It is true that, when accomplished successfully, passing divorces its practitioners from others in the subordinated group. But the same can be said about other strategies that escape the contempt that is routinely heaped upon passing. The millions of blacks who fled segregationist oppression in the Jim Crow Era could be said to have adopted an "escapist" solution to their plight, which distanced them from those they left behind. But few commentators malign participants in the Great Migrations on this account. Immigrants who leave the land of their birth are often lionized in American popular culture. Passers, though, are similar to immigrants in important respects. . . . Just as immigrants leave their homelands for what they perceive as better opportunities abroad, sometimes casting away names and languages in the process, so, too, do passers leave their racial homeland for what they perceive as better opportunities elsewhere. While the immigrant is widely hailed for his initiative, however, the passer is widely cursed as a self-seeking opportunist.

In the litany of charges arrayed against passing, none is more prevalent than the complaint that passers are "living a lie." This indictment warrants attention that can usefully be divided into two parts: one that considers complexities regarding forms of deception and a second that considers the conditions under which deceptiveness may be deemed morally and legally permissible.

There are many ways to be deceived. At one end of the spectrum, a person can attempt to mislead by telling a clear falsehood—stating that a light was green when one knows, in fact, that the light was red. At the other end, one can attempt to mislead by declining to disclose information that would prompt observers to think or act in ways that one wants to avoid. This latter scenario has often framed the modus operandi of the passer. . . .

When Adam Clayton Powell Jr. passed for white during his first years at Colgate College, he did not tell his classmates that he was white. He simply declined to correct their mistaken impression that was based on his appearance.

The real issue, though, is not whether a passer deceives; as I have defined passing, deception is an essential part of the enterprise. The issue is how to assess the deception. Deceptions are by no means equal. Some are morally allowable, while others are not. It is one thing to lie to a murderer to protect a prospective victim. It is another to lie to a judge simply to injure a more accomplished rival. Many observers who would generally condemn passing would nonetheless excuse it in the case of a person seeking to escape death or enslavement. . . . If one accepts this proposition, however, what counts as exceptional? If deception to flee slavery is morally permissible, what about deception to flee the other caste-like limitations that have burdened most blacks? In my own view, passing to escape these stultifications was and remains morally permissible as long as it can be accomplished by means that do not impose morally prohibitive costs on innocent parties. Honesty and candor are surely presumptive virtues. But only that. For purposes of escaping immoral oppression, the presumption against dishonesty is overcome.

. . . Consider the case of Anna D. Van Houten. In Massachusetts in the early 1890s, Asa P. Morse proposed marriage to Van Houten. She accepted. But he subsequently withdrew his offer upon learning that she had Negro antecedents. She sued him for breach of promise to marry. His defense was that she had obtained his promise by fraudulently concealing her racial lineage.[20]

At trial, the presiding judge instructed the jury that, as a matter of law, Van Houten had a duty to answer truthfully any inquiries Morse made of her but had no duty to communicate all of the previous circumstances of her life. Clearly, Morse never questioned Van Houten about her racial lineage. Van Houten won a jury verdict. On appeal, however, her victory was overturned on the grounds that the trial judge's instructions to the jury were faulty. According to the Supreme Judicial Court of Massachusetts, the trial judge erred by failing to instruct the jury that fraud could be perpetrated through omission—the assertion of a half-truth. . . . [T]he court declared, if the plaintiff made favorable statements about her family, she was obligated to reveal everything material about it. She did not have to say anything about her family. But if she did talk about it, "she was bound not only to state truly the facts which she narrated, but [to refrain from suppressing or concealing] any facts which were necessary to a correct understanding on the part of the defendant of the facts which she stated."

What the justices seem to have suspected is that Van Houten had painted a portrait of her Charleston, South Carolina, family that led her fiancé to have a certain impression of it, without telling him certain other facts that would probably have led him to a very different impression. Likely to be established as facts, for instance, were suggestions at trial that the second husband of Anna Van Houten's mother was a colored barber, who was also reputed to be Anna's father, and that her mother, too, was about one-eighth black. Such omissions, the court concluded, would amount to fraud and permit any promises based on them to be withdrawn without liability. The court therefore voided Van Houten's jury verdict and ordered a retrial.

[I]t might be asked why people in Van Houten's position should be prompted by law or moral sentiments to propitiate the racial biases that Morse harbored or to which he was reacting. For law or public morality to require Van Houten to tell Morse of her colored lineage because she knew that it would matter to him is perhaps to give undue deference to destructive prejudice. The case is close; the competing arguments, strong. Ultimately I believe that Van Houten committed no legal or moral wrong but confess to feeling troubled and equivocal about this conclusion.

IV. Passing Today

Passing of various sorts remains controversial. Heated debate surrounded Secretary of State Madeleine Albright when journalists reported that some of her ancestors were Jews who had perished in the Holocaust, and some charged that she, a practicing Episcopalian, had misleadingly denied knowledge of those facts to maintain distance from her Jewish roots. And of course, passing with respect to sexual orientation has sparked several debates central to recent struggles for gay and lesbian liberation. Examples include disputes over the morality of outing and the federal government's "don't ask, don't tell" policy, which effectively demands passing as a requirement for military service by lesbians and gays.

One might have thought that racial passing and anxieties about it would have been rendered marginal by now, given substantial declines in the intensity and power of anti-black feelings and practices. Simply being perceived as black no longer bars one absolutely from most of society's attractive opportunities. But for some observers, the specter of racial disunity, racial disloyalty, and even racial dissolution looms larger now because African Americans have more choice now than ever before regarding whom to date, where to live, or what school to attend. With more choices, larger numbers of blacks have more opportunity to distance themselves physically, socially, and psychologically from other blacks. The prospect of new modes of passing in which, regardless of hue, Negroes become so-called "oreos"—black on the outside but white on the inside—has played a role in prompting some African Americans to pursue a renewed commitment to group solidarity. Some who are inspired by black nationalist aspirations would like to impose a black communitarianism that would instill a heightened sense of racial obligation into African Americans. People with this view . . . consider it urgent that blacks eschew assimilation into "mainstream" (i.e., "white") society. Many of them also assert unapologetically that blacks ought to prefer one another over nonblacks. A broad array of African Americans—including many who pursue their schooling and professional activities in racially integrated settings—have adopted these ideological premises. They disparage blacks marrying whites, oppose interracial adoptions involving black children, and resist changes in verbal formulations or census classifications that would enable those now deemed to be "black" to identify themselves differently (e.g., as a "multiracial" person). [See Part 4—Ed.] They see these activities as kindred to passing and condemn them as "escapist," "inauthentic," even "fraudulent" efforts that will lead to a debilitating "whitening" of what should be an authentically "black" African American community.

Who is right in the debate over racial passing? Is it a self-defeating betrayal of one's race? Or is it a defensible assertion of individual autonomy? Satisfactory answers cannot be determined in the abstract. They depend on the surrounding circumstances. What are the consequences for declining to pass? What are the alternatives for seeking one's goals? To whom must one lie in order to pass? To which groups, if any, does one feel a sense of affiliation? To what extent does passing entrench or subvert a given social order? Answers depend, moreover, on the judge's baseline values.

Notes

Originally published in 62 Ohio State Law Journal 1145 (2001).

1. Walter White, *Why I Remain a Negro*, Saturday Evening Post, October 11, 1947.
2. Roi Ottley, *Five Million U.S. White Negroes*, Ebony, March 1948. . . .
3. John H. Burma, *The Measurement of Negro "Passing,"* 52 American Journal of Sociology 18, 20–21 (1946). . . .
4. Walter White, A Man Called White: The Autobiography of Walter White 136 (1948).
5. St. Clair Drake and Horace R. Cayton, Black Metropolis: A Study of Negro Life in a Northern City 162 . . . (1945). . . .
6. *In re* Rhinelander's Will, 36 N.Y.S. 2d 105 (1942). . . .
7. Joel Williamson, New People: Miscegenation and Mulattos in the United States 103 (1995).
8. Frances E. W. Harper, *Iola Leroy, in* The African-American Novel in the Age of Reaction: Three Classics 86 (William L. Andrews, ed., 1992).

9. Ronald E. Hall, *Blacks Who Pass, in* Brotherman: The Odyssey of Black Men in America—An Anthology 474 (Herb Boyd and Robert L. Allen, eds., 1995).

10. Janice Kingslow, *I Refuse to Pass*, 8 Negro Digest, May 1950, at 30.

11. Reba Lee, I Passed for White (1955). . . .

12. Gunnar Myrdal, An American Dilemma: The Negro Problem and Modern Democracy 686 (1962).

13. Nella Larsen, Passing 56 . . . (1929). . . .

14. Jessie Redmond Fauset, Plum Bun: A Novel without a Moral 15 . . . (1928). . . .

15. Ray Stannard Baker, Following the Color Line: American Negro Citizenship in the Progressive Era 163 . . . (1908).

16. *See, e.g., Jokes on Our White Folks, in* Langston Hughes and the Chicago Defender: Essays on Race, Politics, and Culture, 1942–62 (Christopher C. DeSantis, ed., 1995); *Fooling Our White Folks*, Negro Digest, April 1950; *Why Not Fool Our White Folks*, Chicago Defender, January 5, 1958.

17. *Korematsu v. United States,* 323 U.S. 214, 223–24 (1944).

18. *Hurd v. Hodge,* 334 U.S. 24, 28 (1948).

19. 347 U.S. 483 (1954).

20. *See Van Houten v. Morse,* 162 Mass. 414 (1894).

How Race and Poverty Intersect to Prevent Integration

Destabilizing Race as a Vehicle to Integrate Neighborhoods

Alex M. Johnson Jr.

Race—that is, whiteness—is the vehicle through which social status or esteem is achieved. In order to maintain its value it must be protected. One vehicle for maintenance is the use of segregated neighborhoods, in which members contribute materially to intragroup status by refusing to sell or live in proximity to Blacks and, to a lesser degree, other minorities. Moreover, segregated neighborhoods enhance the property right in whiteness because the very exclusivity of the neighborhood (the fact that no blacks live there) raises the intergroup status of whites, thereby lowering the intergroup status of Blacks, who are excluded because of their perceived inferior racial status.

Segregated neighborhoods . . . enhance or reinforce the way that racial categorization establishes the intragroup's shared trait of whiteness. As long as racial classification remains dichotomous, dividing people into whites and others, some way of defining the shared trait that characterizes the white intragroup is necessary. Within the wide variety of skin tones or phenotypes, there are individuals who visually are "racially indeterminate." I contend that in a world without fixed racial classifications, defining who is white and, conversely, who is other or nonwhite is not as easy as it might seem. Consider the phenomenon of "passing," in which individuals who would be classified as Black pursuant to the one-drop-of-blood rule [see Part 2—Ed.] pass as whites based on their phenotype. Racially segregated neighborhoods, however, provide and reinforce racial definitions or categorizations that, to an extent, preclude passing. An individual from an inner-city ghetto is presumed to be Black irrespective of phenotype. Similarly, one residing in an all-white suburb is presumed to be white based on residence. Thus the instability of racial definitions based on phenotype, which in turn destabilizes the one-drop-of-blood rule, leads quite naturally to the use of proxies to determine who is authentically white and who is not. Because phenotype alone does not automatically consign individuals into one group or the other, the desire to make sure that individuals are assigned to certain groups creates policing problems. Residence in certain neighborhoods serves as an easy vehicle with which to police racial boundaries.

My contention might seem improbable at first glance, but a lengthy quote, worthy of repeating, captures the essence of my claim:

> Though [Woody] often proclaimed his blackness, and though he had a Negro grandparent on each side of his family, he nevertheless looked to all the world like your typical white boy. Everyone, on first meeting him, assumed as much. I did, too, when we began to play together nearly a decade earlier, just after I had moved into the middle-class neighborhood called Park Manor, where Woody's family had been living for some time.
>
> There were a number of white families on our block when we first arrived; within a couple of years they had all been replaced by aspiring black families like our own. I often wondered why Woody's parents never moved. Then I overheard his mother declare to one of her new neighbors, "We just wouldn't run from our own kind," a comment that befuddled me at the time. Somewhat later . . . my mother explained how someone could be black though he or she looked white. She told me about people like that in our own family—second cousins living in a fashionable suburb on whom one would never dare simply to drop in, because they were "passing for white." . . . It dawned on me after this conversation with my mother that Woody's parents must have been passing for white in preintegration Park Manor. The neighborhood's changing racial composition had confronted them with a moment of truth.[1]

[P]reserving racial identity in a world in which passing becomes possible—a world in which phenotype does not correlate with the "one drop" rule—creates error costs in maintaining and assigning racial classifications. When some are defined as Black by the one-drop-of-blood rule but are visibly white, problems arise. From the other perspective, when millions of people who perceive themselves as whites have more than one drop of Black blood because of their remote Black ancestry, strict adherence to the "one drop" rule becomes problematic because it threatens the maintenance of white racial identity. One way to alleviate the problem is through the use of other symbols that correlate with racial identification, which has the effect of sending visible signals of racial identity irrespective of phenotype. The transaction costs of racial classification can thereby be reduced if geographic location correlates with racial identity.

Racial categories become more fixed and absolute, and transaction costs in maintaining these fixed categories decrease, in an environment in which the person's address or neighborhood membership becomes a proxy for race. Not only does neighborhood become a proxy for race, but it also has an internalizing effect on its inhabitants. If inhabitants of different racial categories reside in different neighborhoods, these inhabitants can learn very early what race they are supposed to identify with and what norms and values are associated with that race. They learn to accept and value the extent of the differences because of the absence of the other.

Thus one of the functions of segregated neighborhoods is educative, but not educative in ways that are explicitly racist. An example will perhaps clarify my thesis. Think of two cities, one racially integrated and one segregated. In a world without explicit racism, a world in which there are no theories that one race is intellectually or in any other way inferior to another race (race being based on skin color or phenotype), it seems quite plausible to assume that in the integrated neighborhood different skin colors would seem largely irrelevant. I find it hard to believe that one would think differently of other people in the integrated neighborhood because of their skin color. It is extremely likely that skin color in that neighborhood would be largely irrelevant, treated like eye color, a trait upon which no entitlement or anything else important would turn.

Compare that neighborhood with the two separate neighborhoods in which an equal number of whites and Blacks reside. Even in the absence of overt racism, I find it just as hard to believe that the inhabitants of the two neighborhoods would not notice difference, that everyone else in their neighborhood is like them (thereby creating "us") and that everyone else in the other neighborhood is different (thereby creating "them").

NOTE

1. Glenn C. Loury, *Free at Last? A Personal Perspective on Race and Identity in America, in* Lure and Loathing: Essays on Race, Identity, and the Ambivalence of Assimilation 1, 2–3 (Gerald Early, ed., 1993).

30

Who's Afraid of Tiger Woods?

Robert S. Chang

[S]ports, at least on the playing field and with the exception of ice hockey, represents one of our most highly integrated institutions. As an aside, I might ask why sports and the military are two of the most highly integrated institutions in this country. Of course, there are some pockets of resistance—golf comes to mind. But even there we have the nice coincidence of Tiger Woods's spectacular victory at the Masters, celebrated as another breach of the color barrier. We see then that even in the highly discriminatory world of golf, hard work and merit are the keys to success. Tiger Woods, like Jackie Robinson [the first African American permitted to play major league baseball—Ed.], didn't engage in the discourse of victimhood; they didn't ask for affirmative action. Instead, through their exceptionalism they overcame. So when Jackie Robinson and Tiger Woods are held up as role models, what exactly are we being told? I am reminded of the way Asian Americans and Cuban Americans have been constructed as model minorities. And so other minorities and poor Whites are told to be like us—if they don't succeed, it's their fault. They should stop engaging in the discourse of victimhood. . . .

Although I am not much into spectator sports, I am fascinated by the way sports is represented as a democratic institution where you are limited only by the extent of your abilities (read: content of your character). Sports represents a key component in our nation's narrative of racial progress. Sports becomes a model of how racial progress has been achieved through a system of merit.

So when I see mainstream media celebrations of Jackie Robinson and Tiger Woods, I worry about how this affects other discourses, other institutions. How does this affect our efforts to preserve affirmative action? Why isn't education like sports? How do we resist the nation's false narrative of racial progress that makes our efforts to overcome racial subordination more difficult?

Instead, we see different communities struggling over the body of Tiger Woods. Is he African American? Asian American? Thai? Chinese? Native American? [Woods has claimed all these ancestries. See also Chapter 31.—Ed.] Why have certain communities become so invested in his racial affiliation or identity? What is to be gained? Should we let him "just be who he is," as he has requested? As a multiracial figure, does he represent the deracinated national body? Is the multiracial Tiger Woods the anti-racist hero of the next millennium?

Tiger Woods forces us to ask the "race" question. . . . The fear is that multiracial figures like Tiger Woods . . . are complicating the already-overburdened racial taxonomy in the United States. This fear may account for the apparent conflict between "[t]hose advocating . . . [for official recognition of a multiracial category in the 2000 Census, who] are largely multiracial persons, parents in interracial unions who advocate on behalf of their mixed race children, and multiracial advocacy organizations" [see Part 4—Ed.] whereas "[t]hose opposed to such changes are largely representatives of traditional civil rights groups."[1] How are we to negotiate this tension? Are we ready to have such a discussion?

But ready or not, multiracial persons . . . are here (and have actually been here for a long time). Fear about the complexity of the discussion should not make us shy away from the tough questions. As we explore the tough questions, we should get a few things straight. It would be naive to believe that multiracialism operates solely in the realm of the descriptive. Like any other racial "descriptor," it is always already political. By this I mean no more and no less than that there are no literal White, Black, etc., persons. If our racial categories are not naturally existing phenomena, then these categories have been created or constructed by human agents and human institutions through specific and diffuse enactments of power. I suppose that it is possible to imagine a world where "race" might simply be a descriptor without having the sort of political and material effects that it has in our world. However, this would require a different history, one that has yet to be written or lived.

Note

1. Kenneth E. Payson, *Check One Box: Reconsidering Directive No. 15 and the Classification of Mixed-Race People*, 84 California Law Review 1233, 1235–36 (1996).

31

Identity Notes Part One
Playing in the Light

Adrienne D. Davis

I. Dreaming in Black and White in Nicaragua

During the summer of 1992, I participated in a property-rights conference in Nicaragua. In my free time, I wandered the streets of León with old and new colleagues, looking for leather goods and dreaming of the heroes honored in the murals. As I met more Nicaraguans, I realized that my prior forays outside the United States to France and the Bahamas had not prepared me for a country where race was not governed by the politics and economics of black and white. I found myself negotiating not merely the politics of Coca-Cola-roofed houses but also a foreign structure of race into which I (alarmingly) seemed to fit nowhere and everywhere.

Until then, I had always been Black in the American imaginary. My skin tone is coffee with cream or double latte, depending on your coffee aesthetic. With big lips (now considered "full," I suppose) and curly hair, my phenotype guaranteed my racial designation through most of my life. With this phenotype, born in 1965, I have been "black" in both capital and lowercase, Afro-American, African American. When I was fifteen I was even called a "colored girl" by an older white man, who I do not think meant offense, as he said it in the process of giving me a scholarship. The names may have changed to protect the innocent, but the significance of being the opposite of white never did. Although now I am an academic who studies race as a social construct, my own appearance had always warranted racial certainty. In America, I could never "pass."

Upon arriving in Managua, however, the racial certainty I brought with me from the States evaporated. The features that locate me as Black in America do not map onto the unfamiliar turns and curves of the Nicaraguan structure of race. In León, I learned that my brown skin and pouting lips might make me Miskito-Spanish, Caribbean-Spanish, African-Spanish, perhaps even pure Miskito. My brown skin was only the beginning of the interrogation rather than the end, an initial descriptor rather than a final conclusion. I slipped through the cracks of the Nicaraguan racial regime. I began to feel somewhat of a spectacle as children pointed and were scolded for doing so by adults who were trying to hide their own stares. I still remember with vivid affection one little girl selling candy at a concert we attended. She alternated between charming my group into giving her precious American dollars and returning to my side to interrogate me about my looks, which she could not fathom.

My intention is not to romanticize the seeming racial fluidity I encountered in Nicaragua while condemning racial practices in the United States. Even during my short stay in Nicaragua, it became clear that race was controversial and politically salient there: historically determined and heavily regulated. During the course of the international conference, titled "Revolution, Participatory Democracy, and Property: Nicaraguan Property Regime after Sandinistan Land Reform," speakers and audience members made repeated reference to the marginalization of Miskito Indians within both the national politics and the academic discourse of property rights. The texture of the debate and arguments demonstrated to me that this marginalization was also contested in other areas of rights and participation.

My own racial anxiety increased when, after three days in the conference room of three hundred, I concluded that while my own racial appearance may have been contested, that of the Nicaraguans was not. The conference participants readily marked and distinguished the Miskito Indians as well as their privileged counterparts, the Spanish. Nicaragua indeed had its own complex map of racial relations and domination. The only trouble was that they could not map me.

II. The Tyranny of Categories

My Nicaraguan experience impressed on me the contingency of systems of racial classification. Despite sometimes dramatic efforts to fix it through complex systems of racial tracking and surveillance, "race" itself remains a concept that we continually invent and construct. Yet, as the recent debates over the verdict in the O. J. Simpson trial demonstrate, most Americans, of all races, do not view race as indeterminate but rather as physically cognizable, stable, and culturally significant. Moreover, as a culture we locate race primarily in black and white. My story about traveling in Nicaragua suggests that racial taxonomies are local and political, rather than universal and scientific. I cannot be located on the Nicaraguan racial map. . . . Thus far, only in the United States is my race determined and determinate.

32

"Melting Pot" or "Ring of Fire"?
Assimilation and the Mexican American Experience

Kevin R. Johnson

I. The Myth of Spain and Assimilation through Denial

Approaching sixty years, my mother, born Angela Gallardo, has lived a difficult life. Although nobody would or could ever fill me in on all the details, according to family lore my grandmother was born in El Paso, Texas, though instincts tell me she was born in Mexico. Her mother, my great-grandmother (Josephine Gonzales), was a Mexican citizen who lived in Mexico most of her life. My mother was born in 1938 in Brawley, California, a small agricultural town in the Imperial Valley, about an hour's drive from San Diego. About all my family told me about my mother's father, my maternal grandfather (Charles Daniel Swalez), is that he was killed in an automobile accident when my mother was a child. A sprinkling of distant family still lives in the Imperial Valley area, though my mother lost touch with them long ago, something not that uncommon for Latinos in rural communities.

My mother grew up in downtown Los Angeles. With olive-colored skin and gray hair that once was black (she always emphasized that it was "dark brown"), she stands just under five feet tall. In her younger adult years, and intermittently now, she talked incessantly. Her preferred nickname, "Angie," reflects the assimilationist tendencies she shared with my grandmother. . . .

Despite their Mexican roots, my mother and grandmother were ardently assimilationist in outlook. Marrying Anglo men was part of the grand assimilationist strategy. Another aspect of the plan was for my mother and grandmother to claim that they were not of *Mexican* but *Spanish* ancestry. Always the storyteller, one of my grandmother's favorite tales concerned her mixed Spanish-French background, with particular emphasis on the Spanish. This theme, in fact, found itself in many of her stories. My mother also claimed a "Spanish" ancestry.

Over the years, I realized this elusive Spanish heritage was very much an exaggeration. My grandmother, with her indigenous phenotype, and my mother, with her olive-colored skin, seemed no different from the other Mexican Americans in the San Gabriel Valley [east of East Los Angeles, where we lived—Ed.]. My great-grandmother, who never mentioned her Spanish background in my presence, was a Mexican citizen who lived in Mexico. All of our relatives in the Imperial Valley, only a few miles from the U.S.–Mexico border, were Mexican American. "Where are all the Spaniards?" I could only wonder.

A "Spanish" heritage is not an uncommon myth and indeed is one embraced by some Latinos today. Many understand at least implicitly that being classified as Mexican is disfavored in the United States, especially in the Southwest before the development of the civil rights consciousness of the 1960s. The phenomenon of Latinos attempting to "pass" as Spanish, and therefore as White, is a variation of the "passing" of other minorities as White. To many Anglos, being "Spanish" is more European, and therefore more acceptable to Whites, than being of Latin American ancestry. My mother and grandmother knew the southern Californian world in which they lived and the racial hierarchy that existed, even if they recognized it in simple terms (i.e., that many people did not like Mexicans and that they had better convince them they were not Mexicans).

This Spanish mythology was fully consonant with my mother's assimilationist leanings. To this day, rather than pronounce her maiden name (Gallardo) in proper Spanish, which requires a special "ll" sound similar to "y," she says it as it would be said in English, as in the word "fallen." Consequently, the word "lard," and all of the images that the word connotes, sticks out right in the middle. My wife, Virginia, and I laugh about it today. But those efforts served a critical function for my mother and many others of her generation. The Anglicizing, thereby "Whitening," of their Spanish last names was an important step for a Mexican American attempting to pass as White.

In no small part because of her assimilationist nature, my mother consciously avoided teaching her children Spanish. She spoke Spanish, though losing some of it over the years. As for many in her generation, Spanish was considered an educational impediment. The theory was that we needed to master English (which would not be possible if we learned Spanish) so that we could succeed in school, a view held to this day by some Latinos. In my mother's generation, it was not unheard of for public school teachers to punish students for speaking Spanish. When I was growing up, my mother and grandmother spoke Spanish only when they wanted to have a private conversation in our presence. My mother would become irritable—rare for her—when my brother and I teased her for speaking "Mexican." "It is *Spanish*," she would emphasize. "There is no *Mexican* language."

While my mother and grandmother lived in a state of denial, the Anglo men in the family often emphasized their Mexican ancestry, though in dramatically different ways. When my grandmother talked about her Spanish background, my step-grandfather would sarcastically respond: "Get off it. You're a Mexican like the rest of them." Weakly saying that he did not know anything and laughing uncomfortably, my grandmother was visibly wounded. Similar exchanges occurred regularly. In a much more constructive way, my father would emphasize the positive side of my mother's Mexican background to me. He told me as a child that the mixture of his "Swedish" (an exaggeration) and my mother's Mexican bloodlines was good, and that I would be strong.

II. Race, Ethnicity, and Nationhood for Latinos: Some Assimilation Lessons

Some Latinos, like my mother and grandmother, attempt to "pass" as Spanish in the United States. In the Southwest, to be stigmatized by Anglos as "Mexican" places one at a distinct disadvantage in certain circumstances. A Latino who attempts to live as Anglo suffers in other ways, however. My mother's assimilation ordeals reveal the psychological and related costs. My experiences, though far less severe, reveal the pain suffered by mixed race persons thought to be White.

In essence, the capability of "passing" is a double-edged sword. Adrian Piper eloquently captures the pain she suffered as an African American who might have been able but declined to "pass" as White.[1] Some Blacks demanded proof of her Blackness; others subjected her to White slurs. At the same time, some Whites in academia have suggested that she declared a Black identity to reap affirmative action benefits. [See Part 7—Ed.] This Catch-22 greatly affects the shaping of one's identity as well as life experiences. Over my lifetime, I have experienced both sorts of challenges to my identity. Some Latinos express curiosity about my background, where I come from, my commitment to Latino issues, and Spanish-speaking skills, probing whether I am only a "check-the-box" Latino in pursuit of the benefits of affirmative action. Whites with similar concerns scrutinize my identity as a Latino. Life under a microscope at times is disorienting, uncomfortable, and burdensome.

Piper also offers insights into another layer of complexity. She resented some family members with fair complexions who sealed themselves off from the rest of the family as part of their attempt to pass as White. Although able to achieve higher status, they left their Black family behind, with all the emotional turmoil and sadness that resulted. As has been my experience . . . , minorities who "look White" hear some horrible things about what Whites think about their kinship group. Moreover, attempts to "pass," as my mother and grandmother harshly learned, are not always successful. Not all persons recover from the pain of rejection and sting of defeat. Like Piper, I at times resent yet understand efforts to appear White (and gain its privileges) through adoption of a phantom "Spanish" identity.

Note

1. *See* Adrian Piper, *Passing for White, Passing for Black*, 58 Transition 4 (1992).

33

Interrogating Identity

Mary Coombs

The phenomenon of passing demonstrates vividly the impact of racial classification. A person who passes can obtain many of the benefits whiteness provides in this society. People who understand themselves as black may seek those benefits by passing either permanently and totally or intermittently and strategically. [Judy] Scales-Trent [in her book *Notes of a White Black Woman: Race, Color, Community* (1995)] uses the analogy of immigration for the first sort of passing. One might draw a similar analogy between temporary, strategic passing, such as some blacks passing as white in the workforce while returning regularly to their African American home communities, and the actions of Mexican or Palestinian laborers who cross the border every day to work in a wealthier neighboring land.

An individual need not choose to pass to be seen and treated as if she were white. Scales-Trent notes that she obtains the benefits of passing unwillingly; she is treated better because of white strangers' assumptions about her. "There is no way around it. I am passing all the time as I walk through the world. . . . And I feel like a fraud. And I hate it." Scales-Trent's reaction is parallel to that of Queer Nation activists and suggests she might want a button that says: "How dare you assume that I'm white?"

Passing also has costs. As a black woman, Scales-Trent wishes to date black men and finds herself preferring men who are not similarly fair-skinned. Yet, when she does so, she puts the man in danger from whites who disapprove of black men dating white women. There are other costs as well—white strangers may assume it is safe to be racist in front of her. After describing a casually racist comment made by a cabdriver who did not hesitate to pick her up, she concludes, "I'm always waiting, waiting for them to say it. Please don't say it. . . . Jesus God, cabbie, can't I even go across town in a cab without having my whole identity called into question?" The more permanent passing that Scales-Trent analogizes to immigration has its own enormous costs. A person who seeks to live her life passing must give up much of what she is, be ever alert not to say or do anything that would expose her immigrant status. She is cut off from the family she left behind. There are no cards or letters or visits back home, as immigrants might share. The passing person and the blacks who once claimed her as family all live with the emotional turmoil of what might occur if the pretense is revealed.

The problem of passing or avoiding passing is one that has been particularly salient for gays and lesbians. The analogies between racial passing and sexual orientation passing, noted by Scales-Trent and others, are revealing though imperfect. Passing is an intergenerational phenomenon for African Americans. The children of one who passes will be seen as white and the connection with the African American community erodes through the generations. At some point the progeny "are" white, subject only to the possible risks of someone else tracing the buried connection or a toss of the genetic dice that produces a child whose appearance recapitulates that of a black ancestor. For gays and lesbians, the familial issues of passing are distinct. One's sexual orientation does not seem to depend on one's parents' sexual orientations and certainly not on their public presentation as gay or straight. Nonetheless, with that caveat, I believe we can learn something about the impetus for and effects of passing by examining it within both the racial and sexual orientation categories.

As gays and lesbians, many of us pass, willingly or unwillingly, every day. Coming out, the flip side of passing, is a never-ending process for the individual and the community. The gay and lesbian community faces a particular problem in its invisibility. A large proportion of those who identify themselves as black and are considered as such by the African American community carry visible markers of their racial identity in skin and hair sufficient for whites to see them as black. Even if those who are visibly black are not a random sample, because of the continuing linkages of color and status, most whites will know or at least know of blacks in positions across the socioeconomic spectrum. Those people whom the heterosexual community is most certain to know as gay or lesbian, however, are a highly atypical group by demeanor and by presumed socioeconomic markers. For too many straight people, the only gays they think they know or know of are the drag queens and dykes on bikes who comprise the sensationalized pictures of gay pride parades. The response of many people to claims of gay rights might well be different if they knew that their dentists, the construction worker on the corner, the accountant across the street, and, yes, even their sister are gay or lesbian. Passing has severe community costs. Collective efforts to define and publicize the extent of our community may protect us by countering the efforts of the right to define the meaning and scope of queerness.

Both the costs and benefits of passing are rooted in the significance of these identity categories. Gays and lesbians pass because of the hegemonic assumptions of compulsory heterosexuality. Racial passing is a phenomenon of blacks passing as white and not the reverse, because of the rules of hypodescent [see Part 2—Ed.] and because in our society whites claim and receive a property value in their whiteness. . . .

Who's Black, Who's White, and Who Cares

Reconceptualizing the United States' Definition of Race and Racial Classifications

Luther Wright Jr.

I. Introduction

Philip and Paul Malone, twin brothers from Boston, applied to be firefighters in 1975 but were not hired because of low civil service test scores. The brothers reapplied in 1977, changing their racial classifications from "white" to "black." Due to a court mandate requiring Boston to hire more minority firefighters and police, the Malones were hired in 1978, even though their civil service test scores remained the same. Had the Malones listed their race as white in 1977, they most likely would have been denied employment a second time. In 1988, ten years after being hired, the Malone brothers' racial classifications were questioned by a Boston Fire Commissioner when the twins applied for promotion to lieutenant. The commissioner, who knew the twins personally, was puzzled when he saw that they listed their race as black. After a state hearing, Philip and Paul Malone were fired for committing "racial fraud."[1]

Hispanic and black organizations in Boston criticized the city government for allowing the Malones to work for ten years before questioning their racial identity. These organizations called for a full investigation of the Malones' case and for prompt investigation of other allegations of racial fraud. One Boston official claimed that as many as sixty other firefighters had engaged in racial fraud to obtain jobs, but other officials estimated that the actual number was closer to ten. Shortly after the Malones' hearing, eleven Boston firefighters classifying themselves as Hispanic were investigated; two resigned.

In the mid-1980s, allegations of racial fraud also surfaced in the political arena. In 1984, Stockton, California, city councilman Mark Stebbins survived a recall election organized by a black councilman he defeated in November 1983. Stebbins, described as a man with a "broad nose, light complexion, blue eyes and curly brown hair . . . [worn] in a short Afro style," had run as a black candidate in the Stockton, California, City Council election. While the birth certificates of Stebbins's parents and grandparents listed their race as white, and Stebbins acknowledged that his siblings were white, he contended that he was black. At the time of the election, Stebbins's council district was 46 percent Latino and 37 percent black. Accused of lying about his race to get votes, Stebbins argued that he first *believed* he was black when he was growing up and other children referred to him as "niggerhead." Stebbins also hinted that his claim was premised on the belief that he had a black ancestor who had passed as white. Despite this somewhat tenuous assertion, many of the black leaders in the community accepted him as black, apparently to gain more minority influence on the council.

American society has long differentiated among individuals on the basis of race. Yet, as Professor Paul Finkelman recently noted, "[t]he word 'race' defies precise definition in American Law."[2] No physical attribute or collection of physical attributes adequately defines "race." It was this lack of a precise definition of race that led to accusations of racial fraud in the Malones and Stebbins cases. The makeshift definition of race used during the Malones' hearing encompassed appearance, self-identification of the family in the community, and ancestry. In the Stebbins election, California voters and leaders created a definition of race premised on physical features and personal self-identification but paid absolutely no attention to Stebbins's obviously white ancestry. Finkelman argues, and the Malones and Stebbins cases support the assertion, that the American definition of race is much like Justice Potter Stewart's definition of obscenity—"I know it when I see it."[3] The problem with race, as with pornography, is that people "see it" differently.

III. The Need to Define Race Today

D. *The Problem of . . . "Soulmaning"*

2. "Soulmaning"

From slavery to the present, some black individuals have passed for white. In recent years, however, incidents of whites claiming to be black have become more and more frequent. . . . "[S]oulmaning" . . . describe[s] whites passing for black to gain employment, education, and political opportunities. The Malones and Stebbins incidents illustrate the soulmaning phenomenon. [In a footnote, the author explains that

> *Soul Man* was a 1986 movie starring C. Thomas Howe, Rae Dawn Chong, and James Earl Jones. In the movie, Howe plays Mark Watson, a wealthy California student who is admitted to Harvard Law School, but whose father refuses to pay the tuition. Unable to qualify for student aid and loans because of his father's wealthy status, Watson takes tanning pills and puts on makeup to make himself appear black, so that he can win a minority scholarship for which no minority has applied.]

a. Using Race as a Political Tool.

While the case of Mark Stebbins may seem unbelievable, his case is probably more common than unusual. In many instances, the "Black Pride" movement of the 1960s encouraged people to take pride in and embrace their fractional black heritage. Mark Stebbins could very well have been one of these individuals, but that seems very unlikely. The political benefit that he received by identifying himself as black in a district composed of 37 percent blacks and 83 percent minorities is a classic example of soulmaning. Running as a white candidate in this district against a black incumbent would have resulted in defeat if the voters voted along racial lines. It is not unreasonable to argue that Stebbins declared himself black in order to win the race.

Regardless of his motivations, blacks in the district were willing to embrace Stebbins because of the much-needed black political power he could generate as a black council member. In a society so heavily reliant on race, it is advantageous for all minority groups to accept those who self-identify with the group in order to inflate their numbers and political entitlements. Consequently, minority groups may welcome those who are soulmaning when it is beneficial to the group at large. When, however, the benefit is incurred only by the individual, the attitude of the minority group is usually more hostile.

b. Using Race to Obtain Job Opportunities.

The case of the Malone twins demonstrates soulmaning in the context of employment. The Malones were found guilty of committing racial fraud to obtain a job. The Malones apparently believed that there was some benefit to be gained by classifying themselves as blacks. Soulmaning in the job context does not elicit the open-armed response that Stebbins received in the political arena. As Massachusetts Department of Personnel Administration [official] David Hayley pointed out at the time of the Malone incident, the reaction of minorities in this instance was much different. Hayley argued that because the Malones denied two minorities the opportunity to serve as Boston firefighters, no one would ever know what those two minority firefighters might have accomplished. This type of sentiment seems to be common among minorities in this context. The Malones took advantage of a hiring policy designed to remedy past and present discrimination in city government. In this remedial context, a standardless definition of race will allow racial fraud to continue, and there will be no remedy for past discrimination. The reality of affirmative action, calls for diversity, and even political campaigns may make soulmaning a recurring phenomenon. Failure to develop intelligent rules in this arena could lead to strained racial tensions and the blatant abuse of policies designed to bring about social justice.

Notes

1. Peggy Hernandez and John Ellement, *Two Fight Firing over Disputed Claim That They Are Black,* Boston Globe, September 29, 1988, at 32. . . .

2. Paul Finkelman, *The Color of Law,* 87 Northwestern University Law Review 937, 937 n.3 (1993) (book review).

3. *See Jacobellis v. Ohio,* 378 U.S. 184, 197 (1964) (Stewart, J., concurring). . . .

Review Questions

1. Comment on the following:

   The concept of passing embodies a notion of multiple possible identities, and privileges the *self-experienced* identity as true, while the beliefs of others are the result of the person's successful deception. Can someone whose self-identity is consistent with the perceptions of others, then, ever be said to be passing? [Judy] Scales-Trent writes that "I also know black people who did not know they were black until they found out by accident in their later years. And I know of black people whose parents have decided to never tell them they are black." Is this last person "black" on any criteria but the racist concept of hypodescent? (Mary Coombs, *Interrogating Identity*, 11 Berkeley Women's Law Journal 222, 237 [1996].)

2. Should we condemn "passing" by fair-skinned African Americans and Latinas/os in the modern United States? Is passing a betrayal of your race?
3. Is Tiger Woods African American?
4. What lessons can be drawn from the fact that the same person may be treated as being of different "races" in different countries?
5. Is the "passing" of whites as racial minorities a significant problem?
6. Classroom Exercise: Half of the class should defend racial passing in certain circumstances, while the other half should condemn it.

Suggested Readings

Devon W. Carbado and Mitu Gulati, *Working Identity*, 85 Cornell Law Review 1259 (2000).

Janet E. Halley, *The Politics of the Closet: Towards Equal Protection for Gay, Lesbian, and Bisexual Identity*, 36 UCLA Law Review 915 (1989).

Kevin R. Johnson, How Did You Get to Be Mexican? A White/Brown Man's Search for Identity (1999).

Kenneth L. Karst, *Myths of Identity: Individual and Group Portraits of Race and Sexual Orientation*, 43 UCLA Law Review 263 (1995).

Earl Lewis and Heidi Ardizonne, Love on Trial: An American Scandal in Black and White (2001).

Adrian Piper, *Passing for White, Passing for Black*, 58 Transition 4 (1992).

Sharon Elizabeth Rush, *Equal Protection Analogies—Identity and "Passing": Race and Sexual Orientation*, 13 Harvard BlackLetter Law Journal 65 (1997).

Judy Scales-Trent, Notes of a White Black Woman: Race, Color, Community (1995).

Gregory Howard Williams, Life on the Color Line: The True Story of a White Boy Who Discovered He Was Black (1995).

Kenji Yoshino, *Assimilationist Bias in Equal Protection: The Visibility Presumption and the Case of "Don't Ask, Don't Tell,"* 108 Yale Law Journal 485 (1998).

Part IV

The Census

Part 4 analyzes the racial and ethnic classifications employed by the U.S. Bureau of the Census for mixed race people. The racial and ethnic classification scheme employed by the Census has evolved considerably over the last century:

> . . . In the 1890 Census, eight separate racial classifications were recognized: white, Black, Mulatto, Quadroon, Octoroon, Chinese, Japanese and Indian. The classification of Black was reserved for those persons having three-fourths or more "black" blood; Mulatto described persons having from three-eighths to five-eighths black blood; Quadroon referred to those having one-fourth black blood; and Octoroon meant those persons having one-eighth or any trace of black blood. The 1900 Census dropped Mulatto, Quadroon and Octoroon from the list, reducing the number of racial classifications to five. "Mulatto" reappeared in the 1910 and 1920 Census, along with the possibility of a person being classified as "Other." "Mulatto" disappeared, apparently for good, with the 1930 Census, which also added Mexican, Filipino, Hindu and Korean to the list of available racial classifications. "Mexican" was deleted for the 1940 Census, and Hindu and Korean were removed for the 1950 Census, which also reclassified "Indian" as "American Indian." The 1960 Census added Hawaiian, Part Hawaiian, Aleut and Eskimo. In 1970, the categories of Part Hawaiian, Aleut and Eskimo were deleted and "Negro" became "Negro or Black." In 1980 and 1990, a number of additional categories (including Guamanian, Samoan, Korean and Vietnamese) were added, and Eskimo and Aleut were reinstated as possible racial classifications. In fact, in the 1980 and 1990 Census, there were fifteen options for determining the race of a respondent, although nine of those classifications were grouped under the heading of "Asian or Pacific Islander." (Carol R. Goforth, *"What Is She?" How Race Matters and Why It Shouldn't,* 46 DePaul Law Review 1, 14–15 [1996].)

As the many changes suggest, racial classifications used by the Bureau of the Census are by necessity arbitrary. For example, *Hispanics,* a term the U.S. government coined, today are classified as an ethnic, not a racial, group, even though Anglos in the United States historically have treated Latinas/os, particularly those of Mexican ancestry, as a separate and distinct race in parts of the United States. (See generally Rodolfo F. Acuña, *Occupied America: A History of Chicanos* [4th ed. 2000]; and Tomás Almaguer, *Racial Fault Lines: The Historical Origins of White Supremacy in California* [1994], both analyzing the history of racialization of Chicanos/as in United States.) In the past, the Bureau of the Census classified persons of Mexican ancestry as a "race" but changed this classification after receiving objections from the Mexican government and the U.S. Department of State. (See George A. Martínez, *The Legal Construction of Race: Mexican-Americans and Whiteness,* 2 Harvard Latino Law Review 321, 329 [1997].)

The inaccuracies of the Census classification system increase when one accounts for racial mixture and intermarriage in the United States. Mixed race people by definition do not fall neatly into any single racial or ethnic category. In the 1990s a movement emerged and demanded that the Bureau of the Census include a new "multiracial" category in the 2000 Census that more accurately reflects the racial origins of mixed race people.

Controversy resulted from the feared impacts of the change. Affirmative action programs, enforcement of the anti-discrimination laws, budget allocations for federal programs, and legislative redistricting stood to be affected by the new method of counting racial minorities. (See Deborah Ramirez, *Multicultural Empowerment: It's Not Just Black and White Anymore,* 47 Stanford Law Review 957, 968–69 [1995].) African American advocacy groups feared that a change in Census categorization might result in the perceived reduction in the Black population, which could reduce resources for social programs designed to remedy discrimination against African Americans. (See Lisa K. Pomeroy, *Restructuring Statistical Policy Directive No. 15: Controversy over Race Categorization and the 2000 Census*, 32 University of Toledo Review 67, 73 [2000].) Some feared the creation of a formal racial hierarchy, reminiscent of the one that existed in apartheid South Africa, with "coloreds" long serving as a buffer between Whites and Blacks. (See Part 10.)

The Census Bureau ultimately decided to allow the checking of more than one box to reflect one's racial ancestry. For the 2000 Census, the race and ethnicity questions read as follows:

7. Is [the person] Spanish/Hispanic/Latino?

   ❑ No, not Spanish/Hispanic/Latino
   ❑ Yes, Puerto Rican
   ❑ Yes, Mexican, Mexican American, Chicano
   ❑ Yes, Cuban
   ❑ Yes, other Spanish/Hispanic/Latino

8. What is [the person's] race? Mark . . . one or more races to indicate what this person considers himself/herself to be.

   ❑ White
   ❑ Black, African American, or Negro
   ❑ American Indian or Alaska Native
   ❑ Asian Indian
   ❑ Japanese
   ❑ Native Hawaiian
   ❑ Chinese
   ❑ Korean
   ❑ Guamanian or Chamorro
   ❑ Filipino
   ❑ VietnameseSamoan
   ❑ Other Asian
   ❑ Other Pacific Islander
   ❑ Some other race. . . .

The ultimate impact of the change allowing multiple racial identities remains unclear. However, preliminary results of the new multiracial system in the 2000 Census were that over seven million people claimed to be of more than one race, which was smaller than many expected. The Bureau of Census reported:

> . . . *Less than 3 percent of the total population reported more than one race.* Of the 6.8 million respondents who reported two or more races, 93 percent reported exactly two. The most common combination was "White *and* Some other race," representing 32 percent of the two or more races population. This was followed by "White *and* American Indian and Alaska Native," representing 16 percent, "White *and* Asian," representing 13 percent, and "White *and* Black or African American," representing 11 percent. . . . (U.S. Bureau of the Census, Overview of Race and Hispanic Origin, Census 2000 Brief 5 [March 2001]; emphasis added.)

A major shortcoming of the 2000 Census mixed race population data is that, because "Hispanics" are classified as an ethnic rather than a racial group, the mixed Latino/a population is not measured.

In Part 4, Kenneth Payson summarizes the history of racial classification schemes used by the Bureau of the Census, their importance in the enforcement of the antidiscrimination laws, and their inability to deal with changing racial demographics. Deborah Ramirez summarizes the legal impacts of the Census's racial classifications. A multiracial advocate as well as a White mother of mixed Black-White children, Susan Graham passionately argues for a separate multiracial category. Tanya Hernández criticizes the Census proposal (which eventually went into effect) of permitting multiple racial identifications and offers an alternative proposal. Reginald Leamon Robinson supports the Census approach as a step toward racial justice. Nathaniel Persily discusses the potential legal impacts of the new Census approach to racial categorization. Gloria Sandrino-Glasser and Luis Toro explore the Census's treatment of "Hispanics," many of whom are of mixed racial and ethnic ancestry. Finally, Jack Forbes, a prominent Native American Studies scholar, concludes Part 4 by advocating that Latinas/os identify as indigenous peoples for Census purposes.

Check One Box

Reconsidering Directive No. 15 and the Classification of Mixed Race People

Kenneth E. Payson

III. Why Race Data Are Collected and How They Are Used to Track and Remedy Race-Based Discrimination

Since the first census in 1790, the race question has appeared on every census. The primary reason for establishing the census was to collect information on electoral representation. From 1790 to 1840, the census distinguished only White and Negro. In 1850, Negro was divided into Mulatto and Black. In 1860, Indian and Chinese categories were added, with Japanese added in 1870.

Although racial and ethnic information is still collected, the data have acquired new importance with the advent of the civil rights movement. Race information has become essential in implementing court decisions involving civil rights as well as in allocating government resources to meet the needs of various racial groups that have suffered discrimination.

The decennial census, in which a wide variety of information in addition to race is collected, is the most comprehensive accounting of the United States population. The Census Bureau itself, as well as public and private organizations, make use of the data by studying the relationships among various component items of information. Not surprisingly, the analysis is often directed along racial lines, studying the relationship between race and correlates such as health, education, income, housing, and employment.

The racial data collected by the Census Bureau also support many legislative efforts to end discrimination. The Civil Rights Act of 1964,[1] the Voting Rights Act of 1965,[2] and the Equal Employment Opportunity Act of 1972[3] all depend on census data for compliance and enforcement efforts. Not only are relationships among the collected census data studied, but the census data serve a vital role in illuminating other race data collected by federal agencies charged with implementing anti-discrimination legislation and affirmative action laws in areas such as labor, housing, and education.

Typically, federal agencies compare their own data, collected in a specific context, to more general demographic data derived from the census. If resource allocation among the agency-collected racial data does not comport with expectations based on the census data, inferences of discrimination can arise. For example, the Equal Employment Opportunities Commission (EEOC) was created to enforce laws prohibiting employment discrimination based on race, color, religion, sex, national origin, age, and disability. EEOC's enforcement responsibilities include affirmative employment planning for agencies of the federal government and oversight of federal agency discrimination complaint processing.

Since 1966 the EEOC has collected, maintained, and analyzed employment data on groups protected under anti-discrimination and affirmative action statutes to assist in administration and compliance activities in both the private and federal sectors. Moreover, the EEOC has a fifteen-year series of employment data specifically based on the categories defined in Directive No. 15.

In order to carry out its mission, the EEOC requires that employers submit information on the racial makeup of their workforces. While employer-reported race data alone can indicate discriminatory patterns of job assignments or promotions within an organization, proving discriminatory hiring practices requires information about the demographics of the available labor pool and/or the general population. For this comparison, census data are often used to define the demographics of the control population.

For example, if employment race data are compared with the demographics of the available labor pool and the comparison indicates that persons of certain racial groups are underrepresented among the employed, inferences of discrimination can arise. Unless employer-reported data are compared with census data of the larger labor pool, discriminatory hiring practices cannot be discerned. In order to derive meaningful information, however, the data from both agencies must represent information on the same racial groups. Therefore, it is crucial that the same race categories are used or that the race categories that are chosen can be reaggregated into standardized categories in a consistent manner. Moreover, since the EEOC uses these data to analyze employment trends over time (for example, to measure employer compliance), data comparability over time is also critical. This need for standardized racial categories and definitions led to the promulgation of Directive No. 15 in 1978.

IV. Directive No. 15

The categories [before the 2000 Census—Ed.] are largely the result of the activities of the Federal Interagency Committee on Education (FICE). Finding a lack of useful data on racial and ethnic groups, in June 1974 the FICE created the Ad Hoc Committee on Racial and Ethnic Definitions to develop common categories and definitions of racial and ethnic groups in order to facilitate federal collection of racial and ethnic enrollment and other educational data on a compatible and nonduplicative basis. . . .

In April 1975 the FICE proposed five categories: American Indian or Alaskan Native, Asian or Pacific Islander, Black/Negro, Caucasian/White, and Hispanic. The Ad Hoc Committee considered creating a category of "Other" to account for mixed race people or for people who wanted to state a unique racial background. However, most committee members opposed the inclusion of an "Other" category, fearing that it would complicate results, add to costs, and legitimately apply only to a small number of people.

. . . [The Office of Management and Budget (OMB)] promulgated Directive No. 15—the standards for racial and ethnic classification for use by all federal agencies.[4] For the first time, standardized categories and definitions were to be used for all reporting on racial and ethnic groups at the federal level.

Directive No. 15 "provides standard classifications for recordkeeping, collection, and presentation of data on race and ethnicity in Federal program administrative reporting and statistical activities." Notably, the directive specifically disclaims any scientific or anthropological bases for the classifications, suggesting that government collection of racial data be viewed as an instrument of social policy rather than an instrument of anthropological or biological research. . . .

V. Evaluation of Directive No. 15's Current Utility

. . . . With respect to persons of mixed racial and/or ethnic origins, Directive No. 15 [before revisions that went into effect for the 2000 Census—Ed.] provides that "[t]he category which most closely reflects the individual's recognition in his community should be used." This "community recognition" test is understandable, and it probably adequately reclassified most mixed race persons in light of social conditions extant at the time of Directive No. 15's promulgation. However, changed social conditions and conceptions of race and racial identity render this test unworkable today.

Specifically, an increasing number of mixed race persons not of African ancestry and an emerging group of mixed race Black persons who identify as mixed race reveal the flaws of the "community recognition" test and its implicit reliance on the "one drop" rule. [See Part 2 for discussion of the "one drop" rule—Ed.] It is not clear that the "one drop" rule is applicable to non-Black mixed race persons. Moreover, many mixed race persons, including mixed Black-White persons, are asserting their mixed race identities and resisting monoracial classification. Consequently, mixed race persons are often inconsistently and arbitrarily reclassified under the current scheme, which renders race data used to track and remedy race-based discrimination unreliable.

In contrast to the 1960s, Blacks today make up only about half of the non-White population of the United States. Just since 1980, the Asian and Hispanic populations have nearly doubled. This growth in the non-Black minority population is even more striking when viewed in the context of the few states that account for most of such growth. For example, in 1993, Blacks made up only 16 percent of California's non-White population, with Asians accounting for 24 percent and Hispanics accounting for 58 percent.

Today, over a quarter of the United States population is non-White. The Census Bureau projects that by the middle of the next century, the proportion of non-White persons will account for half of the United States population. Of the non-White population, it is estimated that the proportion of Blacks will drop to roughly one-third, Asians will account for 21 percent, and Hispanics will account for nearly half. This increase in the number of non-Black minorities is tied to an increase in the number of non-Black mixed race persons. Moreover, after nearly a century of minimal Black-White mixing, there is an emerging generation of "new mulattoes" among whom are not only individuals with one Black and one White parent but individuals with one Black and one non-Black, non-White parent as well (e.g., Black-Asian).

This broad range of race mixing is occurring in a social climate different from that which characterized earlier mixing, one that reflects both increased opportunity and inclination to cross racial boundaries. These conditions both help explain why intermarriage has increased significantly since the 1960s and predict its continued increase. Moreover, they help us understand why the socialization of the resulting mixed race offspring is being transformed.

American society has become increasingly accepting of racial and cultural heterogeneity, particularly since the 1960s. [*See* Part 1 for discussion of *Loving v. Virginia*, in which the Supreme Court invalidated Virginia's anti-miscegenation law—Ed.]. . . .

One indicator of the growing number of mixed race people is the growing number of mixed race marriages. According to the Census Bureau, the number of interracial married couples involving either a White or a Black spouse has grown from 310,000 in 1970 to 1,161,000 in 1992, and their proportion of all married couples has increased from 0.6 percent in 1970 to 2.2 percent in 1992. Yet these data represent only intermarriages where Blacks or Whites marry someone of a different race. Therefore, marriages between Asians and Native Americans, for example, would not be included in the data. Moreover, since the Census Bureau does not consider Hispanics to be a racial group, Latino, Chicano, and other persons classified as Hispanic are currently included mostly within the White population data. Therefore, a marriage between a Latino spouse and a White spouse would not be considered a mixed marriage. When the number of marriages between Hispanics and non-Hispanics is included, the number of intermarried couples has grown from 894,000 in 1970 to 2,316,000 in 1992. This represents an increase in the proportion of intermarried couples from 1.9 percent of all married couples in 1970 to 4.4 percent in 1992.

Intermarriage between Whites and those of Asian descent accounts for most interracial unions. The frequency of these unions is attributable both to the increasing desirability of Asians as sexual partners among non-Asians and to the tendency for resistance to intermarriage among first-generation Asian immigrants to abate in succeeding generations. For example, in 1970, 42 percent of Sansei (third-generation) Japanese American men and 46 percent of Sansei women were married to non-Japanese. Chinese American outmarriage rates have also steadily increased, from about 10 percent in the 1950s, to 13 percent in the 1960s, to 18 percent in the 1970s. Filipino American outmarriage rates in the 1970s were 38 percent for women and 19 percent for men. These factors are especially salient given that the Asian population has grown at a faster rate than any other racial group. If similar increases in intermarriage rates occur among succeeding generations of Asians, the number of mixed race persons of Asian descent will likewise represent much of the growth in the mixed race population.

Other groups exhibit similar outmarriage trends. By the third generation, the outmarriage rate for Latinos approaches 30 percent. Native Americans have always had high outmarriage rates of about 50 percent. Black-White marriages, while accounting for the fewest mixed marriages, are also increasing. The number of Black-White married couples in the United States increased almost 300 percent from 1970 (65,000) to 1992 (246,000).

Because the Census Bureau does not collect multiracial data, we can only infer that most of the children of interracial marriages are mixed race. As of the 1980 census, there were approximately 2 million children living in multiracial households. Moreover, any estimates of multiracial children based on interracial marriage data do not include mixed race children born out of wedlock, nor do such estimates include adult mixed race persons. . . .

In the 1990 census, almost 10 million persons used the "Other" race category. Of the 8 million write-in responses to the race question, 253,000 indicated mixed racial parentage such as "Black-White," "White-Chinese," "Multiracial," or "Interracial." This 253,000 figure is not an estimate of the multiracial population but only represents that number of respondents who indicated that they were mixed race in the write-in box. Some mixed race persons attempted to identify as mixed race by eschewing the instructions and marking more than one box. Since the census scanners are designed to read only one marked box, such a person was monoracially classified based on whichever box was marked more darkly. Moreover, many more mixed race persons may have followed the instructions to choose only one box. Census Bureau demographers therefore acknowledge that "many more would identify with mixed-race if the option were provided."

Not only is the number of mixed race persons growing, but mixed race persons today, both those who have Black ancestry and those who do not, are growing up in a very different social climate than that which characterized the development of the "one drop" rule. We have seen that race mixing between Black and White occurred frequently early in United States history. Recall that for most of the past one hundred years, persons of mixed African and European ancestry conceived of themselves and were perceived by others as being Black. Moreover, while such persons had White ancestry, it was often generations removed. They were raised in households and communities that were Black and that did not have direct contact with White family members or communities. Black-White inter*marriage*, however, is a more recent phenomenon. Today, mixed race children are being raised in households with racially different parents. They therefore have the opportunity to interact with racially different parents, extended families, and communities. Consequently, increasing numbers of such persons, including mixed race Blacks, are choosing to identify multiracially.

On the whole, we see fundamental differences in race mixing today. First, many mixed race persons today are race mixtures that were neither contemplated nor experienced before in U.S. history. Second, mixed race persons, including a new generation of mixed Black-White persons, are socialized in both non-White and White worlds, unlike mixed Black-White persons of earlier generations. Third, the result is an increasing number of persons who conceive of themselves as multiracial and who therefore actively resist monoracial classification efforts.

Notes

Published originally in 84 California Law Review 1233 (1996).

1. Pub. L. No. 88-352, 78 Stat. 241 (codified as amended in scattered sections of 42 U.S.C.).
2. Pub. L. No. 89-110, 79 Stat. 437 (codified as amended in scattered sections of 42 U.S.C.).
3. Pub. L. No. 92-261, 86 Stat. 103 (codified as amended in scattered sections of 5 U.S.C. and 42 U.S.C.).
4. [*Office of Management and Budget, Directive No. 15, Race and Ethnic Standards for Federal Statistics and Administrative Reporting*, 43 Federal Regulations 19, 260 (1978)—Ed.].

36

Multicultural Empowerment

It's Not Just Black and White Anymore

Deborah Ramirez

II. Demographic Changes

C. Multiracial Minorities: Erasing the Premise of a Single Racial Identity

[Before the 2000 Census,] federal and state data collection agencies, including the United States Census Bureau, compile[d] racial and ethnic statistics on the premise that individuals identify with a single racial and ethnic group. This notion of monoracial identity is reinforced by the decennial census, which requires individuals to categorize themselves as a single race.

Self-identification enables the census to avoid categorizing a person of multiracial ancestry as white, black, Asian, or other. If a woman's parents consider themselves white but she thinks of herself as Asian because her great-great-great-grandmother was Chinese, the Census Bureau will not challenge her if she checks "Asian" on the form. The Office of Management and Budget's 1980 Statistical Policy Directive No. 15 also relies on self-identification, advising people to designate the racial and ethnic group with which they most identify.[1] However, by failing to provide categories for those who identify themselves as multiracial, the census ignores mixed race individuals who may have been consciously raised in two or more distinctive cultural traditions. If these individuals choose to identify themselves in multiracial terms, attempts to impose a single racial classification upon them would relegate their multiracial identities to second-class status. Multiracial people view identity as multidimensional and deserve acknowledgment and appreciation of all their heritages. . . .

The size of the multiracial population is difficult to estimate because of the lack of a multiracial census category. However, indirect data suggest tremendous growth. For example, one study of mixed marriages indicates that

> [t]he number of children living in families where one parent is white and the other is black, Asian, or American Indian . . . has tripled from fewer than four hundred thousand in 1970 to one and a half million in 1990 and this doesn't count the children of single parents or children whose parents are divorced.[2]

As the multiracial population grows, existing racial classification schemes become increasingly inadequate. As more children are born to parents from difference racial groups, two problems emerge. First, the existing racial classification scheme's reliance on self-identification creates opportunities for individuals to strategically streamline their identity in order to qualify for certain admissions programs or government benefits. For instance, consider admission standards that require Asians to score ninety on a test but admit blacks with an eighty-four. An Asian-black applicant scoring eighty-six will be admitted only if he identifies himself as black rather than Asian. We could solve this problem by defining individuals' race and ethnicity for them, but this approach invites an inquiry we surely would like to avoid. Alternatively, we could create identical racial remedies for all people of color. However, under this approach, is a multiracial person of partial white ancestry to be deemed white or a person of color? Even if such determinations are possible, uniform remedies for all people of color threaten to dilute benefits historically intended for black Americans: Affirmative action programs may fill their ranks with Asians and Latinos, leaving blacks once again out in the cold.

Second, if growth in the multiracial population prompts federal and state data-gathering agencies to create a multiracial category, individuals who currently identify themselves as black, Asian, or Native American may instead identify themselves as multiracial. Given the large number of multiracial individuals, a multiracial census category could generate a staggering statistical shift in population. Maria P. P. Root notes:

> Currently, it is estimated that 30–70% of African Americans by multigenerational history are multiracial; virtually all Latinos and Filipinos are multiracial, as are the majority of American Indians and Native Hawaiians. Even a significant proportion of White-identified persons are of multiracial origins. The way in which the Census Bureau records data on race makes it very difficult to estimate the number of biracial people, let alone multiracial persons, in the United States. Any estimates that have been made are conservative.[3]

Creating a multiracial category would dilute the statistical strength of established minority groups. As the number of people claiming multiracial identity increases, membership in existing minority groups would necessarily decrease. This statistical change would have an enormous impact on matters immensely important to minority communities: electoral representation, the allocation of government benefits, affirmative action, and federal contracting rules. Certain districts created under the Voting Rights Act of 1965 to encourage minority representation might have to be redrawn as minority group numbers decrease. This statistical shift would also affect local school boards and civil rights agencies that utilize traditional minority categories. The federal government relies on monoracial categories to monitor a wide array of programs and entitlements, including: minority access to home mortgage loans under the Home Mortgage Disclosure Act, enforcement of the Equal Credit Opportunity Act, public school desegregation plans, minority business development programs, and enforcement of the Fair Housing Act. Creation of a multiracial category also has the potential to disrupt equal employment opportunity recordkeeping and affirmative action planning on the part of employers who are required to collect ethnic data under Title VII of the Civil Rights Act of 1964.

Notes

1. Office of Management and Budget, Directive No. 15, Race and Ethnic Standards for Federal Statistics and Administrative Reporting § 2(b) (May 12, 1977). . . .

2. Lawrence Wright, *One Drop of Blood*, New Yorker, July 25, 1994, at 49.

3. Maria P. P. Root, *Within, Between, and Beyond Race, in* Racially Mixed People in America 9 (Maria P. P. Root, ed., 1992) (footnotes omitted).

37

The Real World

Susan R. Graham

Data Needs in Education

Parents are instilling new pride in our multiracial children. We are sending them to school with the knowledge that they can be proud of all of their heritage. What happens then? In North Carolina, a teacher asked a multiracial teenager in front of the class, "You're so light, are you sure your mother knows who your father is?" In Georgia, a teacher said to a child, "You should go home and figure out what you are—you can't be both." In Maryland, a school secretary came into a kindergarten class and announced she was there to decide a child's race.

Schools are fighting back. The National PTA [Parent-Teacher Association] has endorsed a multiracial classification, which is very important to our success in the educational system. Progressive administrators are saying, "We don't care what the federal government says, we will let our multiracial children be multiracial. It's the right thing to do." Progressive schools are not waiting for [OMB, or Office of Management and Budget] Directive No. 15 to catch up with reality. Progressive schools recognize that "valuing diversity" is more than just a fashionable phrase. Progressive schools want the multiracial classification, and they want it now because of the following examples:

1. What happened in Wedowee, Alabama, is an example of overt racial discrimination against a multiracial student, Revonda Bowen. Hulond Humphries, principal at Randolph County High School, stated in an open assembly that Revonda Bowen's parents had made a "mistake" (referring to her parents' marriage and her birth). Is Revonda Bowen, a biracial student, entitled to be free from racial discrimination as "guaranteed" by Title VI of the Civil Rights Act of 1964?

2. A fourth-grade student takes a national test with his peers. The first question he is asked is his race. He is multiracial, and his race is not listed on the test, although his peers see their races. He feels singled out and becomes upset. His emotional state affects his test scores. Should a multiracial child be subjected to lower performance and achievement scores because OMB Directive No. 15 does not reflect his race?

3. Federal officials accused five Georgia school districts of unfairly steering blacks into special education, remedial classes, and other low-level programs. U.S. Secretary of Education Richard Riley expressed concern about racially biased tracking in schools. Multiracial students are also subjected to racial tracking biases. How can you accurately know if there is racially biased tracking against multiracial students in our country if you do not collect accurate racial data on them?

4. The National Research Council sent out a survey for recent graduates of doctoral programs with instructions to "check only one box" on the question of racial identity. Multiracial respondents were not satisfied with the choices, because there was no multiracial category. The surveys were returned to those persons who chose more than one box. One would assume a person who earned a doctorate degree would know how to classify him- or herself racially. Why would the National Research Council collect inaccurate data?

Data Needs in Employment

The first case I heard of regarding employment problems was from an engineer who worked for a government contractor. He had requested a multiracial classification on his employment records. The employer refused, giving "government requirements" as the reason. The company solved its problem: They hired him as black and fired him as white. We can all understand that the company got its affirmative action number—erroneously. This is neither fair nor accurate.

The human resources director of one of the largest corporations in Georgia voiced a legitimate concern. Race is an item on the job application form. In 1992, 6 percent of job applicants refused to answer the race question. In 1993, 20 percent of job applicants refused to answer the race question. I asked the director why she thought such a high percentage refused to fill out race information. She told me the majority of people who refused indicated there was not an appropriate category for them.

Other examples of discrimination in employment:

1. A multiracial job applicant filled in "White" when made to choose one race classification. The personnel director, who knew her family, called and asked why she chose not to help the company fill its affirmative action requirements (by choosing the majority race instead of the minority race). Should discrimination occur because accurate data for multiracial employees do not exist?

2. More and more universities are actively recruiting faculty that can serve as role models for their student population, including Blacks, Asians, Hispanics, Native Americans, veterans, women, physically challenged people, gays, and lesbians. Multiracial students need multiracial role models too. How will a university know if a prospective employee is multiracial if its data entries do not include the category and its hiring practices discriminate?

Let's be realistic. Multiracial children grow up to be multiracial adults, who join our workforce. We need to face this and remedy the situation now.

Legislative Update

The states had to do what the federal government would not do. Ohio was the first state to mandate the multiracial classification on school forms in the state, effective July 31, 1992. Illinois was the second state. The state of Georgia passed the most progressive legislation for multiracial people in the country in February 1994. Senator Ralph David Abernathy sponsored the legislation. . . . Senate passage was unanimous; House passage was overwhelming. (Senate Bill 149 has since been signed into law and became effective July 1, 1994.)

This legislation mandates that all school forms, state agency forms, and employment forms and applications include the classification *multiracial.* It further mandates that no written document or computer software in the state of Georgia shall bear the designation of *other* as a racial or ethnic classification. In July 1995, Indiana and Michigan became the fourth and fifth states to enact legislation.

Ohio, Illinois, Georgia, Indiana, and Michigan. Five states, 10 percent of all states. Is that a significant percentage for demographers? I do not know. What I do know is that more states will follow. Texas and Maryland have also introduced legislation. What I do know is that in each state, legislators and interracial families are fed up with the lack of progress on the federal level for the rights of multiracial people.

The Catch-22 of Directive No. 15

The PROJECT RACE proposal for a revised directive differs from that of some other organizations. We propose the addition of the classification *multiracial* to the five basic racial and ethnic categories without further breakdown. In other words, multiracial children would only check *multiracial* and not be forced to list the race and ethnicity of their mothers and fathers.

Our motives are threefold. First, to demand that multiracial children explain their heritage is unnecessary in most instances. Schools, employers, lenders, and others do not care about the breakdown. It is unnecessary for compliance purposes and only serves to satisfy curiosity. Second, if multiracial children are told they must further qualify themselves on forms, it says two things to them: You must do something your peers do not have to do; and we are not finished with your identification yet. Some government entities have actually argued that to list the races of the parents would require too much print on a form. Third, adopted people have told us that they may be uncomfortable with the mother's race/father's race format, because the races of their biological parents may be different from that of their adoptive parents.

Using the terminology of "multiracial identification," as opposed to mother's race/father's race, makes a subtle but critical distinction. One of the main points we are articulating to the government is the absolute necessity of self-identification. For example, Directive No. 15 now states: "The category which most clearly reflects the individual's recognition in his community should be used for purposes of reporting on persons who are of mixed racial and/or ethnic origins." A change in this method of identification is crucial. "Eyeballing" by a teacher, employer, census enumerator, or anyone is subjective, highly inaccurate, and probably a violation of civil rights. No one should be allowed to "guess" a person's race based on the perceived color of his or her skin, on the person's surname, or on any other criteria.

We have replaced this antiquated method in Directive No. 15 with:

> Self-identification must be utilized for all persons. If self-identification is attempted and refused, the data shall default to one of the six categories, or be allocated to the six categories on a proportionate basis, as long as the method for category assignment is consistent for the reporting agency or group.

Current Statistical Issues

A concern that has been voiced to us, largely by demographers, is that of a loss of numbers to certain racial communities if a multiracial classification is implemented. I am personally offended at statements by these same people that entire groups of people are against the multiracial category.

Some have said, "Blacks are against this." Senator Abernathy of Georgia, who championed our legislation, is a black leader. In fact, not one black legislator in Georgia voted against our bill. Incidentally, Georgia has the fourth-highest percentage of black legislators in the country. Majority Leader William Mallory of Ohio, the first state legislator to sponsor our legislation, is black. Many, many black educators, civil rights leaders, psychologists, educators, and others support the multiracial classification.

PROJECT RACE is not an organization made up only of partners in black-white marriages. We have Hispanic, Asian, and Native American members and advocates in all combinations. To trivialize their needs is unacceptable. But for the sake of argument, let's explore the perceived "loss of numbers" problem.

First, I would like to stress that the multiracial category enables multiracial people to have the choice of an accurate designation. It is an important option for any person with parents of different races. This does not mean that this choice is appropriate for everyone. Some multiracial people choose to identify with one race only. They have every right and every opportunity to do so in our society.

Now the census numbers. Example: I am white, my husband is black. My children are white by default on the census figures (whereby the children take the race of the mother). Minority groups have lost two numbers. Because in the majority of white-black interracial marriages the mother is white, the federal government, by its "mother calculation," arbitrarily takes away minority numbers—exactly what we have been accused of doing.

Will millions of people "jump ship" from another classification into the multiracial classification? No. In the 1991–1992 school year, before a multiracial category was added to forms, 489 students in the Cincinnati Public Schools chose the classification of *other.* In the 1992–1993 school year, the first year of the multiracial category, 527 students chose *multiracial.* The category of *other* was eliminated beginning with the 1992–1993 school year. In the 1993–1994 school year, 629 students chose *multiracial.* Every racial and ethnic minority increased as well during those years. Did students in Cincinnati jump ship into the multiracial classification? No. We have similar results in the data from the Fulton County, Georgia, schools.

Fear is irrational by its very nature. The fear of a loss of numbers is irrational. The fear that multiracial children will undermine the racial balance of this country is irrational and racist. The fear that a multiracial category will ruin affirmative action and entitlements for minorities is unproved and unfounded.

38

"Multiracial" Discourse

Racial Classifications in an Era of Color-Blind Jurisprudence

Tanya Katerí Hernández

For the past several years, there has been a Multiracial Category Movement (MCM) promoted by some biracial persons and their parents for the addition of a "multiracial" race category on the decennial census. The stated aim of such a new category is to obtain a more specific count of the number of mixed race persons in the United States and to have that tallying of mixed race persons act as a barometer and promoter of racial harmony. As proposed, a respondent could choose the "multiracial" box in lieu of the presently listed racial classifications of American Indian or Alaskan Native, Asian or Pacific Islander, Black, White, or Other. . . . On October 29, 1997, the U.S. Office of Management and Budget (OMB) adopted a federal Interagency Committee recommendation to reject the multiracial category in favor of allowing individuals to check more than one racial category. Some MCM proponents are not satisfied with the OMB's decision, because multiple box checking does not directly promote a distinct multiracial identity. . . .

Multiracial discourse contends that a mixed race census count is necessary because race has become too fluid to monitor. The theory posits that the inability to identify psychologically with just one racial category is inherent to mixed race persons alone and that the growing number of mixed race persons demonstrates the futility of racial categorization as a practice. For instance, MCM proponents often refer to the growing numbers of persons who choose the "Other Race" category to support the premise that the racial categories are inadequate for mixed race persons. . . .

I. The Background and Motivation of the Multiracial Category Movement

The MCM has been described as "a movement that is not entirely based upon the question of racial mixture *per se*" in that its focus is on the presumed classification needs of Black biracial persons. In fact, the principal proponents of the multiracial category are "monoracial" Black and White parents of biracial children.

The initial impetus for the MCM was the discomfort many White-Black interracial couples felt when choosing racial classifications for their mixed race children on educational data collection forms. Yet the MCM demand for a multiracial category is usually presented in terms of its disapproval of all forms of racial classification. For example, Susan Graham—a White mother of two Black-White biracial children, the executive director of Project RACE (a national organization advocating on behalf of multiracial children), and one of the principal advocates for the availability of a multiracial category—states that true progress would be the eradication of all racial classifications.[1] Similarly, Carlos Fernández, former president of the Association of Multiethnic Americans, has also argued that his preference is that "racial and ethnic classifications should be done away with entirely."[2] These statements reflect the general view among multiracial-category proponents that the use of current or any racial classifications is a form of discrimination in that the focus it places on race diminishes the humanity of the individuals it purports to represent. The MCM advocates describe their movement as an instrumental step toward the "dream of racial harmony," as opposed to the creation of "one more divisive category." The MCM frequently posits that multiracial persons are a "unifying force" on the theory that multiracial persons "as a group may be the embodiment of America's best chance to clean up race relations." Thus proponents value a multiracial category for its perceived shift away from the rigidity of racial classifications, which some perceive as a cause of racial hostility. The hope is that the multiracial category will act as an acknowledgment of the fluid and nebulous character of race and hence its meaninglessness as a grouping of persons. In effect, MCM proponents implicitly wish to use the multiracial category as a mechanism for moving toward a color-blind society that will effectuate racial equality. . . .

The implicit color-blind vision of the MCM is also reflected in what I term the "symmetrical identity demands" of the White parents who predominate among the MCM's spokespersons. The "symmetrical identity demand" is the appeal for all racial aspects of a child to be acknowledged in that child's public assertion of racial identity: "I'm part of this kid, too, no matter who he looks like." As one parent of multiracial children testified in a recent congressional hearing, without a multiracial category, biracial children are forced to "choose one parent over the other." One can empathize with the parental impulse to have their familial connection to their children publicly reflected in the collection of racial data. However, claims to different racial ancestries are not socially symmetrical in effect. That is to say, what the parents of biracial children may fail to perceive is that while the political acknowledgment of White racial ancestry can be beneficial to the individual child, it also unfortunately reinforces societal White supremacy when society places greater value on White ancestral connections than on non-White connections. "Whiteness is an aspect of racial identity surely, but it is much more; it remains a concept based on relations of power, a social construct predicated on white dominance and Black subordination."[3] Thus the symmetrical identity demand can also function as a claim to having biracial children inherit all of the privileges of White status, which White parents logically would like to extend to their children as protection from racism against non-Whites. In short, the insistence on symmetry in racial categorization is color-blind in its refusal to acknowledge the sociopolitical nature of race.

In demanding a separate mixed race category, the MCM misconstrues race as solely a cultural identification. Specifically, such a demand presupposes that there are "pure Black" experiences that make a person authentically Black and, inversely, that the lack of such authenticating cultural experiences makes a person "less Black." Part of what drives the push for a separate racial category is the desire to reflect more accurately the cultural experiences of biracial Blacks living in an interracial context. Although there may be a cultural component to the identification of persons who have been socially segregated into insular communities and who have a history of varied cultural ties to different African countries and tribes, such cultural manifestations are not uniform across the African diaspora. For instance, the cultural attributes of the insular Black community in New York are not equivalent to the cultural attributes of insular Black communities in Oaxaca, Mexico, or in Loíza, Puerto Rico. The uniformity of Black social identification throughout the Black diaspora is by virtue of the fact that a Black person is viewed as distinct because of appearance, ancestry, or both, and not because of any commonality in culture. The OMB's recent decision allowing mixed race persons to be counted with a "check-all-that-apply" system of racial classification also mistakenly construes race as cultural identification. If race were primarily a form of cultural identification, then an option to check more than one box would be appropriate for those persons reared within a mixed cultural context. But race is a group-based experience of social differentiation that is not diminished by a diverse ancestral heritage. Further, the OMB decision may result in the division of a multiple-race response into shares; therefore, it is ill-suited to a collection of race data for measuring social differentiation.

The . . . concern with racial-cultural authenticity is not necessarily shared by all mixed race persons. Contrary to the MCM posture, the community of biracial persons is not a monolith. There are a great number of biracial persons whose racial identity is rooted in blackness because of the political meaning of race in this society. The perspective of biracial persons with respect to issues of racial identification in general and the presumed need for a multiracial category in particular can vary greatly from the perspective of monoracial parents. For example, when interviewed, one biracial person noted, "It took until I was twenty for my mother to understand that I identified black. That was very hard for her. She looked at it as these were her *kids*, and so we were Jewish and we were black. . . . It was very hard for her to understand that."[4] Although their number is overstated by the MCM, there are biracial persons who favor a multiracial category to alleviate the psychological pressure of living in a racially stratified society. Notwithstanding the well-meaning desire to mitigate the pain of racial bias, it should be noted that "monoracial" non-Whites share the same desire to escape the burdens of being socially differentiated by virtue of their race. The anguish experienced by targets of racial bias is not a dynamic peculiar to the "culture" of mixed race persons. The view of race as culturally based, like the MCM's inadvertent reification of race as a biological construct, mistakenly essentializes the concept of race, thereby precluding honest assessments of the social and political meanings of race that are significant in shaping racial identity. This nation's history of racial oppression has particular salience in an analysis of the MCM, especially given its dominance by Black-White mixed race persons and their parents. . . .

II. The Adverse Consequences of Multiracial Discourse

A. The Reaffirmation of the Value of Whiteness in Racial Hierarchy

[T]he demand for statistical recognition of mixed race persons—and acknowledgment of all aspects of an individual's racial identity—is occurring within a sociopolitical context that values White ancestry and denigrates non-White ancestry. In such a racial caste system, it is impossible to acknowledge mixed race persons officially without actually elevating the status of those who can claim to be other than "pure" Black, no matter how egalitarian the intent of the MCM. This same elevation of mixed race classes is evident in various Latin American countries and in apartheid South Africa, in ways that powerfully illuminate the implications of furthering multiracial discourse in the United States. [See Part 10—Ed.].

B. The Dissociation of a Racially Subordinated Buffer Class from Equality Efforts

In the 1980s, when discussion of the multiracial category first arose in the United States, the public began to draw its attention to the concern that White men would soon be "the new minority." By the 1990s, the media frequently informed the public that the decline in the White population had reached "dramatic" proportions. In 1990, *Time* magazine reported that "[s]omeday soon, surely much sooner than most people who filled out their Census forms last week realize, white Americans will become a minority group."[5] Whites' alarm about becoming a minority has also expressed itself in polling data indicating skewed perceptions of the nation's current demographics and job opportunities.

The concern with the "browning of America" has accompanied increasing consternation with the continued existence of racial reparation programs and fears of race wars akin to White-minority antebellum fears of slave revolts. Thus the desire of some mixed race persons to be recognized as members of a distinct racial group coalesces with the systemic motivation to defuse demands for racial justice and maintain a structure of White supremacy. . . .

Appropriation of the MCM by disaffected Whites is also a concern, because, as is widely known, subordinated group members will eventually flee from such classifications when given the choice. While the United States has generally taken a binary White/non-White approach to racial stratification, given its current concern with the decreasing number of Whites and the consistent White preference for persons of color who more closely approximate a White appearance, the United States is still susceptible to acknowledging a Latin American–type mixed race buffer class. In addition, the long-standing U.S. habit of utilizing a system of exceptionalism, whereby an individual Black person may be deemed socially acceptable "because you are not like the rest of them," demonstrates the ability of White North Americans to make distinctions among subordinated group members even within a bipolar hypodescent framework. Societal willingness to make distinctions within a subordinated class is integral to the construction of privileged middle-tier communities. There is also some MCM willingness for social distinction of biracial persons, as revealed by some proponents' opposition to a mixed race census count that omits an actual multiracial category: "We need the terminology of 'multiracial' in there. . . . As it is, my children cannot be multiracial children. My children can be 'check-all-that-apply' children, and I do not consider that fair."[6]

. . . [T]he inclusion of parental racial-component information or an ability to check more than one racial category could very well replicate the antebellum fractional approach to race, which is epitomized by the categories of octoroon, quadroon, and Mulatto—social groups systemically encouraged to dissociate from subordinated Blacks.

Apart from the concern with the advisability of recognizing a mixed race buffer community throughout the United States, the MCM must be wary of advancing its proposal under the banner of color-blindness, which has served as a veil for the maintenance of race-based privilege in recent United States case law. . . .

In fact, the simultaneous growth of multiracial discourse and civil rights retrenchment should alert the MCM to the appropriation of its identity movement by others more concerned with dismantling social-justice programs. This phenomenon is particularly well highlighted in the development of color-blind jurisprudence. When Justice [Antonin] Scalia declares that "[i]n the eyes of government, we are just one race here[; i]t is American,"[7] it is in the context of a case that hinders the federal government's ability to institute affirmative action programs.

D. Measurement of Racial Progress Hindered

In analyzing the advisability of a mixed race census count, it is particularly important to examine the uses of census racial data. Census racial data are principally used to enforce the civil rights mandates against discrimination in employment, in the selling and renting of homes, and in the allocation of mortgages. . . .

The important political implications of racial classifications make the OMB's recent "check-all-that-apply" option as hazardous as the multiracial category itself. . . . When a person of color experiences discrimination, that experience of racism is not cut in half because the person is only "one-half Black" or "one-half Asian." Because the census's race question is a mechanism for monitoring the extent to which socioeconomic opportunities are stratified by race, it is nonsensical to divvy up the racial classification response into shares (like the long-since-repudiated categories of octoroon, quadroon, and Mulatto) when the social experience of race is not perceived in shares. Furthermore, the comprehensive scope of the OMB "check-all-that-apply" decision inflates the race-as-culture fractioning of race's political meaning. The OMB decision is comprehensive in that any individual can check as many boxes as reflect her racial heritage without viewing herself as a mixed race person because both parents are of the same race. This fractured mechanism for monitoring patterns of racial difference will underappreciate the extent to which socioeconomic opportunities are structured by race and therefore function as a color-blind racial classification system.

III. A Race-Conscious Racial Classification Proposal

A race-conscious racial classification system is an instrumental mechanism for monitoring racial discrimination. . . . The compilation of statistical data can act as a social-systems monitor when individuals utilize the data to call society to account for the entrenched benefits of race-based privilege. Even if the current scheme of civil rights laws were dismantled, it would still be important to measure the extent of race discrimination consistently over time, thereby developing other mechanisms for addressing such racism. . . .

Given the significant uses of the census racial data and the persistence of racial discrimination, it is important to utilize a classification scheme built around the political meaning of race and make that focus a prominent feature of the census form's instructions.

I propose a Race-Conscious Racial Classification System that modifies government data collection forms by dispensing with such vacuous pseudoscientific racial definitions and, instead, employs an approach rooted in the sociopolitical meanings of race. This proposal is asserted not as the definitive classification scheme but merely as an invitation for developing a classification system organized around the political meaning of race for more effective use of racial data. By focusing on the political meaning of race, a race-conscious classification system can avoid the distortions of a race-as-culture focus. The race-as-culture focus invites responses about personal identity rather than monitoring social differentiation based on racial ancestry. The following proposal is set forth primarily as a vehicle for initiating the discussion of the importance of race-conscious racial classifications, rather than being a concrete model for statistical data collection. The current list of racial classifications should be accompanied by the following explanation (exclusive of footnotes):

> Recognizing that there are no such things as scientifically pure races or ethnicities, and that a person's individual identity can never be reduced to a single box, this form requests that you indicate which single race and/or ethnicity you find most politically and socially meaningful. Because the collection of racial and ethnic data is utilized and compiled for the specific purpose of monitoring discrimination in society (see attached list of civil rights statutes which rely upon the Census Bureau collection of racial data), this classification system focuses upon the ways in which your appearance and assertion of race affect your treatment by others in society.
>
> In order to assess the political role of your racial background you may reflect upon the following questions. When first interacting with others, in what ways does your appearance affect the interaction? For instance, an individual who in his or her daily interactions in society finds that others consistently react to him or her as White or Black, and modify their behavior based upon that physical assessment, can conclude that his or her White or Black phenotype determines the sociopolitical role of his or her racial background, regardless of how diverse that particular individual's ancestry actually is. Alternatively, when you share the details of your racial ancestry, how does that revelation affect your treatment by others? For instance, where an individual may phenotypically appear White, but when sharing his or her background with others discloses that his or

> her ancestry also includes Blacks and then finds that the listener is fixated only on the person's Black ancestry, then it would be appropriate for such an individual who personally identifies as White and Black to conclude that the "Black" racial classification reflects the sociopolitical role of his or her diverse racial background.

The goal of the proposed Race-Conscious Classification System is to cultivate a more precise understanding of the ways in which race is socially and politically significant, apart from its role as one of many factors in personal identity formation. By designing a classification system that interrogates the political content of race, the collection of racial data can more closely correspond with the social dynamic such data seek to measure. Furthermore, the proposal's disjunction of the political meaning of race from the cultural approach to race also preserves an individual's ability to assert a varied personal identity. Specifically, the frank explanation of the reasons for a public inquiry into political race may assure the respondent that the complex and varied ways individuals construct and restructure their personal identities are not being called into question or challenged by the Census Bureau.

Notes

Published originally in 57 Maryland Law Review 97 (1998). Copyright © 1998 by Maryland Law Review. Reprinted with permission.

1. *Review of Federal Measurements of Race and Ethnicity: Hearings before the Subcommittee on Census, Statistics and Postal Personnel of the House Committee on Post Office and Civil Service*, 103d Cong. (1993), at 120 (written testimony of Susan Graham, executive director of Project RACE).
2. *Id.* at 127 (testimony of Carlos Fernández, president, Association of Multiethnic Americans).
3. Cheryl I. Harris, *Whiteness as Property*, 106 Harvard Law Review 1709, 1761 (1993).
4. Lise Funderburg, Black, White, Other: Biracial Americans Talk about Race and Identity 112 (1994), interviewing René-Marlene Rambo.
5. William A. Henry III, *Beyond the Melting Pot*, Time, April 9, 1990, at 28, 28. . . .
6. Elizabeth Shogren, *Panel Rejects "Mixed-Race" Census Category*, Los Angeles Times, July 9, 1997, at Al . . . (quoting Susan Graham, national MCM leader and president of Project RACE). . . .
7. *Adarand Constructors, Inc. v. Peña*, 515 U.S. 200, 239 (1995) (Scalia, J., concurring in part and concurring in the judgment).

39

The Shifting Race-Consciousness Matrix and the Multiracial Category Movement

A Critical Reply to Professor Hernández

Reginald Leamon Robinson

II. Shifting Race-Consciousness Matrix to Human Equality: Critiquing Hernández's Race-Oriented Proposal

A. *A Race-Conscious Approach—The Sole Solution*

. . . . [Professor Tanya] Hernández advances a race-consciousness approach as an alternative to the MCM [Multiracial Category Movement], and in so doing she argues two vital points. [See Chapter 38—Ed.] First, she critiques how this MCM negatively impacts federal civil rights laws. For Hernández, if Congress adopts multiracial categories, whites will perniciously use these categories to destroy nondiscrimination principles. According to Hernández, these whites will also become ever more emboldened in their push for color-blind laws so that they effectively promote a white supremacy agenda. . . . Second, she questions whether the MCM's goals will eliminate racial categories and promote racial justice.

It is my view, however, that we cannot end a race-consciousness matrix through laws that have racial constructs as their central feature. If whites commit themselves immorally to racist practices and if blacks internalize these practices and refuse to imagine themselves beyond their race, we cannot legislate morality. And especially when society deeply connects itself to a racist Manifest Destiny, "moral" laws do not change our immoral hearts, and morality has nothing to do with whiteness, blackness, and otherness. Rather, we must "raise" or alter our consciousness, and . . . we must develop an integrated community in which citizens express publicly an inner faith in an ethical life. . . . Since the Civil War Amendments, the federal government has used a race-conscious approach, and this approach has not ended race, racism, and white supremacy. As such, Justice [Henry Billings] Brown in *Plessy v. Ferguson* aptly noted that racial superiority and inferiority turn on how we think (e.g., our consciousness).[1] For example, our most progressive statutes, often born out of necessity, like the Civil Rights Act of 1991, have not ended racial discrimination and sexual harassment in the workplace. . . .

B. *The Multiracial Category Movement: The Advent of an Unimagined Social Reality*

The MCM asks us to shift our race-consciousness matrix, and in so doing we can create space for human equality. This shift evidences itself because open-minded people, perhaps people who have talked about why "Auntie Ethel" has fair or brown skin, support the MCM. Within the MCM, blacks, whites, Latinos and others wish to destroy all racial classes, and what remains will perhaps be a variety of ethnicity or culture which . . . any person can practice. Although I argue for ethnicity over race as we move toward a nonracial identity, I am aware that "ethnicity" as a socially constructed category must be thoroughly interrogated by critical theorists, so that we can publicly note how dominant social institutions have used "ethnicity" to shield darker Europeans from the stigma of "blackness." By labeling darker Europeans as "white," dominant social institutions prevented similarly situated citizens from recognizing common interests, thus undermining coalition politics or class solidarity. Although ethnicity has a checkered history and dubious origins, I think that, unlike race, ethnicity can be successfully co-opted, principally because many different kinds of people with different racial heritages have already been included within its cultural boundaries. Regardless of its political origins, I think (perhaps wrongly) that ethnicity centers itself on cultural practices, especially because culture excuses phenotypical differences and racial pedigrees. It would appear that ethnicity then does not depend on apparent (racial) distinctions. Rather, ethnicity proffers the promised inclusion that we all ultimately seek.

Unlike broadly inclusive nonracial cultural practices, unitary race-thinking and racial classes wound a person's spirit and humanity. Racial classes reduce a person simply to a racial caste, and they lock her in. How can we break this racial caste, a prison that prevents free, unbordered thinking about ourselves and others? First, we ought to recognize publicly that blacks and other so-called racial groups, such as Native Americans and Chicanos, have different "racial" heritages, and second, if we have biracial parents, we—offspring of the love—acknowledge both parents, not because we approve the racial group to which they claim membership but because love truly knows no such limitation, *viz.*, race. . . . If I can acknowledge my heritage on a census report, then the society learns how widespread biracial and multiracial identities are. This acknowledgment gradually undermines unitary racial thinking, and it weakens, and eventually ends, our historical and political commitment to a race-consciousness matrix. With the end of racial, and ultimately ethnic, categories, the MCM represents that "instrumental step toward the 'dream of racial harmony,' as opposed to the creation of 'one more divisive category.'"[2]

If the MCM constitutes a radical shift in our racial consciousness, does it quite frankly matter that white mothers, for example, are key proponents of the MCM? Does it also matter that these white mothers might be motivated by a desire to be validated in their children's identity? Does it matter to the MCM that these white mothers find traditional racial categories too constraining, too marginalizing? Basically, does it matter that the white mothers are narrowly driven by selfish motives?

Hernández answers in the affirmative. For her, such motives more than suggest that the MCM uses new racial rhetoric to advance an old racist consciousness. I disagree. . . .

Specifically, Hernández asserts that the legal recognition of multiracial categories resonates with a color-blind society and its Supreme Court jurisprudence, and this approach prefers whites over blacks. Hernández thus suggests that white parents in their blind, narrowly rational, self-interested approach to self-validation advocate for symmetrical identity. As such, biracial children will not have to choose one parent over another. However, Hernández argues quite rightly that historical whiteness has always been the preferred racial category. Thus, if symmetrical racial identity means that white and black genotypes attain legal recognition, then the white identity prevails over the black identity. Explicitly, then, symmetrical racial identity cannot succeed because such symmetry belies the realpolitik of racism and white supremacy. Hernández further suggests that the white mothers either know of this nation's preference for whiteness or prefer ignorance, and in this way they simply achieve through the MCM what the hypodescent rule prohibits. That is, under the "one drop" rule, which is for practical purposes still viable today, our society constructs a person as "black" if either parent passes a certain percentage of "black" blood to the child. [See Part 2—Ed.] Equally important, if the child looks black, society forces her into the "Nigger" category, and most important, if the child does not look black but in fact has received "black" blood, then society has an especially keen interest in determining that child's race, so that she does not blur the all-important racial divide and so that she does not attain social benefits to which whites are deemed specific heirs. In short, these white mothers are using the MCM not only to vitiate niggerization of their biracial children but also to confer upon them their birthright—the invisibility of white social privileges.

Let's assume that Hernández correctly captures the core factor behind the white mothers' impassioned pleas for a multiracial category. How does this assumption undermine the powerful shift in the race-consciousness matrix that we have used to create and maintain space between people of apparently different racial groups? For me, this assumption is not fatal to my argument. What Hernández has missed in her argument is the historical irony that now plagues these white mothers who have not recognized the inherent injustice of the hypodescent rule—the "one drop" rule. [See Part 2—Ed.] Historically, during the Antebellum era, the child inherited the mother's legal status. It mattered not if she were light, bright, and damn near white; if she had the proverbial one drop of black blood, the child was socially doomed and spiritually pilloried. This rule served several purposes. First, the rule ensured the relative stability of the racial color line. Second, this rule ensured that black slave females would not use their sexual appetites to corrupt free-born, white Christian males into siring black babies in the far-flung hope that the mulatto child would be birthed into a free legal status. And equally important, if a child were enslaved illegally, she could point to the free mother, and on that basis she could attain her freedom. This cause was more likely advanced by black men and women who sought their freedom in a legal venue. Yet, in any venue, racial pedigree stood centerstage. Unless one is totally blind, the MCM is irony writ large.

Notes

Published originally in 20 Boston College Third World Law Journal 231 (2000).

1. 163 U.S. 537, 551 (1896)....

2. Tanya Katerí Hernández, *"Multiracial" Discourse: Racial Classification in an Era of Color-Blind Jurisprudence*, 57 Maryland Law Review 97, 108 (1998)....

Color by Numbers
Race, Redistricting, and the 2000 Census

Nathaniel Persily

II. The Multiracial Checkoff

. . . . Pursuant to Office of Management and Budget (OMB) directives, the Census Bureau [for the 2000 Census allowed] individuals for the first time to check more than one race. This decision, which effectively creates sixty-three possible combinations of racial categories, promises to bend the minds and challenge the computation capabilities of courts, lawyers, and state redistricting authorities in the coming years. Contrary to the view expressed by many social scientists, however, the actual political and legal effects of this change will be minimal, at least in the short term. . . .

[As mentioned in the introduction to Part 4, a small percentage of persons in the 2000 Census checked more than one box.—Ed.]

B. How to Tabulate Multiracial Respondents: The New OMB Directive and the "One Drop" Rule

Because enforcement of civil rights laws depends on accurate evaluations of changed circumstances over time, comparisons between racial data in the 2000 Census and previous censuses are necessary to evaluate compliance with those laws. Therefore, enforcement agencies need to be able either to recode earlier data into the sixty-three categories of the 2000 Census data or to convert the new data into the old format. Even beyond drawing comparisons with earlier data, moreover, those charged with enforcing the relevant laws will need to decide whether each of the sixty-three categories of racial data is *relevant* to fulfill the various purposes of the civil rights statutes. And if sixty-three categories should be collapsed into a more manageable set, what rules of "reassignment" of multiracial individuals can make the data more usable while not torturing the data in a way contrary to the purposes of the civil rights laws?

Recognizing the importance of accurate and usable racial data in the context of civil rights enforcement, the Office of Management and Budget (OMB) sought to establish consistent rules for tabulating this new form of data. The OMB issued Bulletin No. 00-02,[1] which provides the following rules of aggregation:

Federal agencies will use the following rules to allocate multiple race responses for use in civil rights monitoring and enforcement.

1. Responses in the five single race categories are not allocated.
2. Responses that combine one minority race and white are allocated to the minority race.
3. Responses that include two or more minority races are allocated as follows:
   a. If the enforcement action is in response to a complaint, allocate to the race that the complainant alleges the discrimination was based on.
   b. If the enforcement action requires assessing disparate impact or discriminatory patterns, analyze the patterns based on alternative allocations to each of the minority groups.

By redesignating multiracial respondents as some category other than white, the OMB approach thus creates a presumption—at least in the enforcement of civil rights laws—that the complainant should not be disadvantaged by the new census format. In other words, by recategorizing mixed race respondents as members of the protected group under the civil rights laws, the data will be tabulated in a light most favorable to the alleged victim of a civil rights violation.

C. The Legal Questions Posed by the Multiple Race Checkoff Option

Critics of the OMB guidelines have described them as a modern version of the "One Drop Rule"—the Jim Crow–era law where one drop of black blood, or one iota of black ancestry, made someone black. [See Part 2—Ed.] They maintain that OMB "assigns" a race to an unwilling respondent—reducing a black-white respondent to "black" and ignoring the more complex self-identity expressed on the census form. The guidelines not only contradict the purpose of the multiracial checkoff option (i.e., to avoid forcing multiracial individuals to choose among alternative, single identities), the argument goes, but they misallocate people who would otherwise not want to group themselves with members of a certain single-race category.

This concentration on individual identity misses the point of the OMB guidelines and misunderstands the statutory purposes for which the census race data are used, at least in the redistricting context. The overarching question in challenges to redistricting plans (or to changes of them) is whether the racial composition of an area operates alongside trends in race-based voting behavior to decrease or deprive a minority of the opportunity to compete equally in elections. The size and homogeneity of the minority population seeking redress are only two pieces to the puzzle of a voting rights claim.

Of course, should courts or claimants reject the OMB guidelines, then some rare claims of minority groups may be dismissed because the group would be too small to elect its candidate of choice even should they prove their vote was otherwise diluted. In other words, if the minority group's only chance at a successful voting rights claim is through a coalition with a multiracial group, the aggregation rules may make a difference. As the data above suggested, however, such phenomena will be largely nonexistent for the 2000 round.

1. Implications for Section 5 Preclearance and Retrogression

For purposes of Section 5 [of the Voting Rights Act],[2] the relevant issue is whether the new form of the data will make it easier or more difficult to prove "retrogression in the position of racial minorities with respect to their effective exercise of the electoral franchise." To evaluate retrogression in minority voting power using the new multiracial data, the [Department of Justice] DOJ must decide (1) what constitutes a diminution in that minority group's voting power and (2) who should be included in the definition of the group whose voting power will be affected by the new plan. Although it has nothing, per se, to do with multiraciality and the census, the first question will have deeper consequences than the second.

As the 2000 round of redistricting approaches, the criteria for judging retrogression are in flux. During the last round, it was quite clear that any reduction in the number of majority-minority districts was likely to constitute retrogression under Section 5. In other words, while a state with two majority-minority districts in 1990 could redraw its district lines however it wanted, whatever plan it produced for the 1992 election had to maintain two majority-minority districts.

Then came *Shaw v. Reno*.[3] In *Shaw* and its progeny, the Supreme Court began striking down majority-minority districts as unconstitutional because race constituted the predominant factor in their creation. Although later cases established that compliance with the Voting Rights Act could constitute a compelling state interest justifying the use of race as a predominant factor, the trail of decisions in the 1990s suggests that the current Court may be more likely to strike down a majority-minority district than one with a minority population under 50 percent. How the DOJ will respond to the Supreme Court's greater scrutiny for majority-minority districts, while fulfilling its obligation to prevent retrogression, is a mystery. Some DOJ lawyers have suggested they will adopt a more flexible and functionally based approach to determine retrogression—wherein the number of majority-minority districts is neither a safe harbor nor a floor for purposes of retrogression. The inquiry for preclearance may look more like a Section 2 analysis this time around, with the DOJ basing its decisions on the interplay of political and demographic factors to determine whether a new set of district lines diminishes the minority's voting power. In some regions, only maintenance of the majority-minority district could avoid retrogression. In others, where voting is less polarized, for example, a lower percentage of minority voters may be needed to maintain the same level of minority voting power, and thus the DOJ would clear a less-than-majority-minority district. The threshold question is really whether the Bush Justice Department will enforce the Voting Rights Act. [Attorney General] John Ashcroft . . . will have great power and discretion to object to redistricting plans that turn back the clock on minority representation. How he will exercise that discretion will be much more important than how multiracial data will be tabulated.

Were the DOJ to keep the "no-reduction-in-majority-minority-districts" baseline (which is, of course, current law) or to establish another objective test for retrogression (e.g., a 40 percent rule), then the unique character of the multiracial census could come into play. The issue, as stated above, is whether the relevant "minority" for judging retrogression includes only the uniracial group or a combination of that group with the multiracial group. By adding the multiracial population to the uniracial population, a district then may appear to be majority-minority, and thus retrogression could be avoided.

Consider a (very) hypothetical jurisdiction in which the plan currently in effect has a district with a black majority, but the new, proposed plan has a district that splits the black community captured by the old district and joins part of it with a large black-white community. If the size of the biracial community is equal in size to the portion of the black community now sliced off from that district, is there retrogression? The aggregation rules may make a difference in that the biracial community would be recoded as "black" under the OMB guidelines and thus the district would retain a majority-minority district. Were each category to remain disaggregated or treated by the DOJ as an independent racial group, then perhaps the new districting plan would appear retrogressive for the black population.

2. Vote Dilution under Section 2

A similar set of issues arises under Section 2 of the Voting Rights Act.[4] In order to prove vote dilution, the voter must show that the minority group of which he or she is a member is large and compact, votes cohesively, and cannot elect its candidate of choice because of racial bloc voting. In order to fulfill each one of these *Gingles*[5] prongs, a voter must employ census race data along with election returns to establish how the districting system operates in a given political-racial context to prevent minorities from exercising an equally effective vote.

The new racial categories, if they rise to significant levels and are left unaggregated, may complicate bloc voting analysis at every stage. First, as in the example described above in the context of Section 5, a decisive number of multiracial respondents could decrease the size of a minority community to the point that it would not form a majority in a compact single-member district. In that event, a minority group would be left without a Section 2 claim unless the court agrees that the minority plus the multiracial group should be the relevant "racial group" for bloc voting purposes (which would be the natural consequence of following the OMB guidelines). Of course, if courts entertain "influence district" claims, under which a minority with no chance of reconstituting itself as a majority can claim vote dilution, or interracial coalition-based claims between two different racial groups that together but not individually form a majority, then the size and effect of the multiracial population is inconsequential.

Second, as the number of distinct racial groups per precinct increases, the ability of any individual group to prove racially polarized voting patterns, though feasible, would become more difficult. What were racially "homogeneous precincts" would appear less homogeneous. In other words, certain precincts will now appear more diverse (e.g., fewer 100 percent white or 100 percent black precincts), and consequently, one's inferences as to the preferred candidate of any racially defined community could be less reliable. . . .

This problem in particular should not be overblown, though. Racially polarized voting—where it exists—usually jumps at the observer from the graph that tries to capture it. The statistical "noise" generated by the new multiracial checkoff option will not likely be a problem for the 2000 Census, and sophisticated statistical tools will likely ensure that it is not a problem in the near future.

D. Summary

The overwhelming majority of Voting Rights Act cases have been litigated on behalf of blacks and Hispanics. Neither of these groups will be affected by the new multiracial checkoff option. As the data show, very few blacks . . . also check another race. Such small percentages . . . are insignificant in proving a Voting Rights Act claim. And Hispanics are completely unchanged by the initiation of the multiracial checkoff opportunity: vote dilution for Hispanics remains decided by the Hispanic origin question, not the race question. In a certain respect, the existence of the Hispanic origin question in addition to the race question on the previous two censuses presented a logistical and legal challenge identical to those presented with the new multiracial checkoff opportunity. Because Hispanics could be of any race, anyone who checked Hispanic at least once (i.e., just as under the OMB guidelines) was called Hispanic. Similarly, whites were then separated based on Hispanic origin, such that non-Hispanic whites became the uniracial group "opposing" the multiracial community that also checked Hispanic. This disaggregation and reaggregation never presented a problem for litigating voting rights claims for Hispanics.

For American Indians, some unique problems might arise because of the multiracial question. Although the data presented in the dress rehearsal and American Community survey did not signify any danger posed by the multiracial question, other scholars analyzing the 1990 Census question on ancestry have suggested that in some areas of the country, such as Oklahoma, whites will be eager to identify themselves as part American Indian and could drive up the multiracial percentages to levels above 10 percent. At the same time, a large percentage of American Indians will also choose white as a second race on the census form. A similar phenomenon appears to occur in Hawaii with regard to Asians. Although vote dilution or retrogression claims concerning American Indians and Asians have been relatively rare, legal problems involved with the multiracial checkoff opportunity—should they arise anywhere—would most likely arise in the context of such claims.

Notes

Published originally in 85 Minnesota Law Review 899 (2001). Copyright © 2001 by Nathaniel Persily. Reprinted with permission.

1. Office of Management and Budget, Bulletin No. 00-02, Guidance on Aggregation and Allocation of Data on Race for Use in Civil Rights Monitoring and Enforcement (March 9, 2000). . . .
2. 42 U.S.C. § 1973c (1994).
3. 509 U.S. 630 (1993).
4. 42 U.S.C. § 1973 (2000).
5. *See Thornburg v. Gingles,* 478 U.S. 30, 50–51 (1986).

41

Los Confundidos
De-Conflating Latinos'/as' Race and Ethnicity

Gloria Sandrino-Glasser

B. The Conflation in the Twentieth Century: Formal Confusion of Race and Nationality

2. The National Census

The confusion of race for nationality was formalized by the United States Bureau of the Census. The deliberate mixing by the Census Bureau of the concepts of race, nationality, and country of origin placed the confusion on a national scale. . . . The growth of the Mexican population after 1910 led to a new category being added to the race/color question in the 1930 census. The coding instructions for the race/color entry stipulated that "all persons born in Mexico, or having parents born in Mexico, who are definitely not White, Negro, Indian, Chinese or Japanese, should be returned as Mexican." This entry in the 1930 census was the first time that a nationality was formally recognized as a race.

a. The Censuses: 1940, 1950, 1960, and 1970—Conflation by Another Race

The Censuses of 1940, 1950, 1960, and 1970 illustrate a change in the conflation; first Mexicans, then other Latin American origin populations ceased to be a separate race and were declared to be "White." The conflation of Mexican nationality and the "White" category started with the 1940 census. The coding instructions in 1940 stipulated that "Mexicans were to be listed as White, unless they were definitely Indian or some other race other than White." The census of 1950 reported that there were three major races: White, Negro, and Other. The coding instructions in 1950 stated that "[p]ersons of Mexican birth or ancestry who are not definitely Indian or other non-white race, were classified as white."

The coding instructions in both the 1940 and 1950 censuses, instructing the persons to choose White unless they were "definitely Indian or some other race other than White," transformed the conflationary images of Mexicans from one race to another. The significance of this change is twofold. First, the conflation is still of nationality with race, although instead of with "another" race it is with the white race. Thus the change of the conflation illustrated in these two censuses demonstrates a conflation in transition, constructed by the ideas about race. Second, the new conflation effectively obliterates the "Indians" of the Mexican populations. As Jack Forbes argues, "With any mixture of bloods the 'Indian' is supposed to disappear, that is, to be 'blanched' out, becoming white."[1]

The increase in the 1950s of the Puerto Rican population living in the mainland mandated more information about Puerto Ricans. Thus the 1960 census stated that "Puerto Ricans, Mexicans or other persons of Latin descent would be classified as 'White' unless they were definitely Negro, Indian, or some other race." In addition, the Spanish surname criterion was used to approximate the Mexican origin population in the five southwestern states. In New York State only, a question was asked about birthplace, with three possible answers: United States, Puerto Rico, Elsewhere.

As a result of the political pressure by Latino groups in the 1960s, the 1970 census adopted the category "Spanish heritage population."

In 1969 the Bureau of the Census began attempting to create a new, fictitious group of people called "Spanish," "Spanish Origin," "Spanish Heritage," or other forms of the specific national designation "Spanish." It should be stressed that "Spanish" refers directly to Spain as a country and to a European, White nationality. Contrary to popular usage, "Spanish" does not refer to a specified language, since Castilian, Gallego, Catalán, and Basque are all equally "Spanish" languages. In choosing to create a "Spanish Origin" group, the Census Bureau consciously conceived of this population as overwhelmingly "White" and "Indo-European." The Spanish Heritage population was defined as (1) having a Spanish surname or Spanish language in the five southwestern states; (2) of Puerto Rican birth or parentage in the three Middle Atlantic states; and (3) of Spanish language in the remaining forty-two states.

B. The 1980 Census

For both political and statistical reasons, efforts to improve the coverage of the Latin American origin population led to the use of several items designating Latin American national origin or ancestry in the 1980 census. . . . The 1980 census included an item on the 100 percent enumeration schedule that required all households to indicate whether their members were of Spanish/Hispanic origin or descent. Those responding affirmatively were asked to indicate whether their origin was Mexican, Puerto Rican, Cuban, or other Spanish/Hispanic Origin. The accompanying instructions for this question read as follows:

> A person is of Spanish/Hispanic origin or descent if the person identifies his or her ancestry with one of the listed groups, that is, Mexican, Puerto Rican, etc. Origin or descent (ancestry) may be viewed as the nationality group, the lineage, or country in which the person or person's parents or ancestors were born.

Although the "Spanish/Hispanic" choice in the 1980 census was intended as a mixture of a culturally derived term that was partially operationalized by nationality and partially by culture, the result was the expansion of the conflation. First, the instructions for the "origin or descent" question failed to provide a workable definition for the

"Spanish/Hispanic" choice. The instructions failed to differentiate between the Spanish/Hispanic as a national origin and as a race.

According to demographers analyzing the 1980 census responses, 40 percent of those classified as "Hispanics" using secondary identifiers gave a negative answer to the Spanish/Hispanic origin census question. Instead, they wrote their country of origin in the space left for "Other" in the question designed to establish race. Those in the Latin American origin population, which exhibited the greatest "consistency," self-identifying as "Spanish/Hispanic" in addition to secondary "Hispanic" identifiers, were primarily of Mexican and Puerto Rican origins. In addition, this group had considerably lower socioeconomic status (in terms of income, occupation, and education) than the "inconsistent" 40 percent mentioned above. "Inconsistent" respondents were primarily Central and South Americans; a small percentage were Puerto Ricans and Cubans.

The 1980 census analysis illustrates the institutionalized conflation of Latinos' race and nationality. The question intended to elicit the "race" of the respondent is poorly constructed; it cues people for racial categories and national origin. . . .

Note

Published originally in 19 UCLA Chicano-Latino Law Review 69 (1998).

1. *See* Jack D. Forbes, *The Hispanic Spin: Party Politics and Governmental Manipulation of Ethnic Identity*, 19 Latin American Perspective 59, 59 (1992).

42

"A People Distinct from Others"

Race and Identity in Federal Indian Law and the Hispanic Classification in OMB Directive No. 15

Luis Angel Toro

III. Biological Race, Directive No. 15, and the Immigrant Analogy

Hispanics are defined in Directive No. 15 as the ethnic group whose "culture or origin" is Spanish, "regardless of race," and Mexican Americans are specifically described as a "Spanish cultur[al]" subgroup.[1] . . . [I]t is clear that Directive No. 15 perceives Mexican Americans as a white ethnic group. This perception is at odds with Chicano identity and the Chicano people's historical experience of racial oppression, as well as the present, ongoing racial discrimination against Mexican Americans.[2] The perception also differs from the determinations Congress made when it decided that Mexican Americans needed to be covered under laws addressing racial discrimination. . . .

Directive No. 15 describes Chicano difference from the white majority as an "ethnic" difference rather than a racial one. In other words, it describes Chicanos as part of the "white" race, but a part that has yet to fully assimilate into the mainstream status enjoyed by members of that group. This construct, sometimes described as the "immigrant analogy," holds that minorities in American society will all progress down the path of assimilation taken by such white ethnic groups as the Irish, the Jews, and the Italians, at least to the extent that minorities work as hard as members of those groups worked to gain acceptance as deserving of white status. . . .

The differences between the ethnic experiences of a member of a racially subordinated minority group and a member of the white majority are profound. . . .

. . . Racialized minority groups are those defined as inherently inferior, whether because of genetic differences or because members of these groups are the products of backward, deficient cultures. Racialized minority groups are, by definition, not eligible for assimilation into the Anglo majority. Indeed, since the very process of assimilating into white society involves defining oneself as not part of any racialized minority group, most members of racialized minorities cannot "pass" as white. [See Part 3—Ed.] The ethnic experience of an American not eligible for assimilation is very different from that of a white American, because the fact of ethnic difference is used to justify second-class treatment for the racially subordinated minority group member.

VIII. Directive No. 15 as a Barrier to Chicano Progress

. . . [T]he conceptualization of the "Hispanic" classification as an "ethnic" rather than a "racial" group (the only "ethnic" group the federal government recognizes) reduces the usefulness of much federal data, along with data generated to conform to Directive No. 15. This occurs because many people who are actually members of racially subordinated minorities are labeled as "White, Hispanic." This affects data concerning both "Hispanics" and African Americans. When data comparing "Whites" and "Blacks" are compiled, the presence of Mexican Americans and others misidentified as "White Hispanics" in the "White" sample will create an illusion that the disparity in income and other measures of community vitality between the majority population and the African American community is smaller than it is in reality, because the presence of persons in the "White" sample who do not in reality enjoy the societal benefits of "White" status will skew the results. Similarly, the presence of African Americans in the "non-Hispanic" sample will skew the results. . . .

IX. Directive No. 15 and Self-Identification

A. Two Chicano Examples

A Mexican couple immigrates to the United States and has children. They receive a Census form in the mail and set about determining their own and their children's racial identity. Looking at the racial categories, the couple sees none that describe them. They do not view themselves as American Indians but as *mestizos*, persons of mixed European and indigenous heritage. They are not enrolled members of a recognized tribe, nor are they identified as Indians in the community in which they live. By the same token, neither are they identified as whites. In the "Hispanic origin" question, the couple sees "Mexican, Mexican American, or Chicano" specifically listed as a "Hispanic" group. They identify themselves as part of that group and as being of "Other" race on the race question.

This couple might identify their children in the same manner. Alternatively, they might believe that a "Mexican or Mexican American" is only someone who was born in Mexico. As immigrants, they may not be familiar with the north-of-the-border term *Chicano*. Since their children were born in the United States, they answer the "Hispanic origin" question in the negative. Knowing that there are millions of people like their children in this country and believing that there must be some place on the Census form for them, they think again about the race question. Obviously, their children are not white: Every day they face the avoidance behaviors and "microaggressions" exhibited by whites, designed to remind them that they are not part of that group. They do not believe that their children are part of the "Black" or "Asian/Pacific Islander" groups, so they think again about the American Indian category. Perhaps aware of the "one drop" rule that, at least culturally, defines as Black any person with any known African ancestor or trace of apparent African ancestry, they conclude that "community recognition" as Indian means being treated as nonwhite on the basis of apparent indigenous ancestry. Therefore they mark their children as members of the "American Indian or Alaskan Native" race.

Now, suppose that a fourth-generation Chicano is filling out a Census form. Spiritually uplifted by the cultural pride inherent in the concept of Aztlán, he identifies himself racially as "American Indian" but answers yes to the "Hispanic origin" question, marking the "Mexican, Mexican American, or Chicano" box. To the respondent, this seems like a decent reflection of his *mestizo* identity. To the Census Bureau, it is a wrong answer.

Suppose now that this same fourth-generation Chicano is responding to a question under the combined race/ethnic short format permitted under Directive No. 15. Choosing between the selections "White, Hispanic" and "American Indian" is easy. The respondent selects "American Indian" as the response, because he has never been treated as a white person in his community; because "Hispanic" seems an inaccurate description of a Chicano culture that has a strong indigenous influence; and because in physical appearance, that is, "racially," the respondent is far closer to being a Native American than a European.

B. Two Filipino Examples

Now, let us imagine that a Filipina with a Spanish surname is filling out the Census form. She was born to parents who moved to the United States shortly after World War II. She is aware that "Spanish surname" used to be the name of today's "Hispanic" classification, and the Philippines were a Spanish colony for centuries before becoming a U.S. dependency after the Spanish-American War in 1898. She is a Catholic, but neither she nor any member of her family speaks Spanish. She knows some Chicanos at work, but her close friends are all Filipino.

Examining the "race" question, she faces little difficulty. The Philippines are Pacific islands, and "Filipino" is specifically listed as a subgroup of the designation "Asian/Pacific Islander." She identifies herself "racially" as "Filipino." The next question asks her if she is of "other Spanish origin or culture." She seems to fit under this broad categorization. Her name, like that of many Filipinos, is Spanish, and the Roman Catholic religion was brought to the Philippine Islands by Spanish conquistadors. She feels that this satisfies the "other Spanish culture or origin" criterion, so she indicates that she is also of "Hispanic origin," selecting the "Other Hispanic" box.

Her brother lives nearby and receives a Census form. He works at a place with many Chicanos and spends a great deal of time socializing with them. Like his sister, he identifies himself as "racially" Filipino. Turning to the "Hispanic origin" question, he perceives that this question is designed to capture persons like his coworkers who identify as Mexican American, and not persons from the Philippines. He therefore answers no to the "Hispanic origin" question.

This hypothetical is not offered to imply that Filipinos are responsible for the gap between "Hispanic" and Chicano achievement. Certainly, Filipinos are a racialized minority group in the United States with a long history of oppression. This hypothetical does reveal, however, that the decision whether to answer the "Hispanic origin" question affirmatively may not relate at all to the question of whether the person is a member of one of the groups the classification is meant to capture. For both Chicanos and Filipinos, responding to Directive No. 15 requires guessing how a white person would classify them rather than exercising the power of self-definition.

Even for a Filipino, however, the decision whether or not to claim "Hispanic origin" might be tactical under the combined format. If the person feels that being identified as "Hispanic" might be more advantageous than being identified as an "Asian/Pacific Islander," for example, because affirmative action is being used as an excuse to cap Asian/Pacific Islander admissions to a university, the decision to claim "Hispanic origin" might allow the person a competitive advantage, secured, of course, at the expense of the Chicano community. At least in this instance, the person could claim that switching categories did not detract from the overall goal of affirmative action—to assist racially subordinated minorities in a racist society. The same cannot be said of whites who employ the same device to help their careers and defeat the goals of affirmative action as they relate to the Chicano community.

Notes

Published originally in 26 Texas Tech Law Review 1219 (1995).

1. *Directive No. 15, Race and Ethnic Standards for Federal Statistics and Administrative Reporting,* 43 Federal Regulations 19,260, 19,269 (Office of Management and Budget 1978).
2. *See* Derrick Bell, Faces at the Bottom of the Well 199–200 (1992).

43

Native Intelligence

New Census Rules Affect All Persons of Pre-Columbian American Ancestry

Jack D. Forbes

All persons who are descended from the original inhabitants of North, Central, and South America are now required to mark the "American Indian" question on the United States Census for 2000 or on any other government forms designed to communicate with the federal government if they maintain affiliation or "community attachment" to their indigenous nationality or identity.

The 2000 Census will have a section on "race" that will allow persons to check off "American Indian or Alaska Native" if they are "a person having origins in any of the original peoples of North and South America (including Central America), and who maintains tribal affiliation or community attachment." This is the new definition of "American Indian and Alaska Native" recently adopted by the Office of Management and Budget.

This means that all persons whose ancestry goes back to the Americans who were living in the Americas before the arrival of the Europeans now have a chance to respond. Still further, they will be asked to give the name of their principal native community or tribe, such as Maya, Garifuna, Mixtec, Yaqui, Aztec, Cree, or Apache. Or they can name a more specific community, such as Kanjobal, Yucatec, Chiricahua Apache, Tohono O'odham, Quiche, and so on. Or they can even name a specific pueblo or reservation, such as Acoma, Hotevila, Pine Ridge, or Tepoztlan.

This is new. Previously, indigenous heritage from south of the U.S.–Mexican boundary was ignored. That led to our schools failing to teach about the heritages of the Toltecs, Olmecs, Purepechas, Mapuche-Araucanians, Tainos, other Arawaks, Caribs, and many other great American peoples. And many schools also overlooked the Aztecs, Mayas, and Incas and all of the Andean peoples who lived before the Incas. And, of course, many social service agencies ignored the existence of indigenous peoples from south of the border and Canada, failing to hire translators or offering other needed services.

Now, under the new rules, persons who come from Spanish-speaking countries or have a Spanish-language heritage can mark two places on the census. They can mark the "Hispanic/Spanish Origin/Latino" question (in the "ethnicity" section) if they wish. And then they also must answer the "American Indian" question in the "race" section if they have an attachment to their Original American (Indigenous) background.

If persons do not wish to recognize their Indigenous ancestry or if it is not important to them, then they can ignore "American Indian" by selecting "White" (which will identify them as "a person having origins in any of the original peoples of Europe, the Middle East, or North Africa"). That way they can repudiate America in favor of Europe.

In the same manner, a person who does not want to be counted as "Hispanic," "Latino," or "Spanish Origin" does not have to mark that question. Some persons may be of pure American Indigenous ancestry and they may not want to be counted as "Hispanic." Others may not speak Spanish even if they are from a Latin American country. Still others may not like the terms used (Hispanic, Spanish, Latino).

On the new census a person who has more than one racial background can mark more than one place within the "race" question. A Puerto Rican, Dominican, or Cuban, for example, who is of mixed African and American (Indigenous) races may want to mark both the African and American Indian boxes, writing in Taino, Boricua, or Ciboney for one's tribe. Some may wish to mark White also, if they have European ancestry. Some persons of Mexican origin might wish to check both the White and American Indian boxes. Other Mexican Americans may want to check only the American Indian box, since the Mexican people have so much more Indigenous ancestry than they have of the European. It depends on which "attachment" is most important, to the heritage of the Spaniards or that of Cuauhtémoc (or both).

The 2000 Census gives us all a chance to identify ourselves in the manner in which we wish to be known. Under the "race" question, for example, we do not have to mark all of our ancestry but only "American Indian" if that is the most important part of our identity.

It is very important that we identify ourselves with our Indigenous communities, such as Mixtec, Zapotec, or Apache, so that public agencies will know that we exist and that we have a right to proper services in our languages, to proper schooling for our children, and to representation in the opportunities which the society has to offer. We cannot persuade educators to include us in the textbooks unless they know that we exist. So it is for our children, also, that we must reverse the conquest and recover our heritage as the FIRST AND ORIGINAL AMERICANS!

Review Questions

1. What lessons can be gathered from the U.S. Bureau of the Census's history of racial classifications?
2. Should the U.S. Bureau of the Census abandon all efforts to categorize people on the basis of race? If not, how should mixed race people be counted?
3. If we continue racial categorizations in the Census, what changes should be made? Should the "race" and "Hispanic" categories be merged? Is a separate "multiracial" category necessary? In reality, aren't most people in the United States multiracial?
4. What ethnic and racial box(es) did you check in Census 2000? Why?

Suggested Readings

Nancy A. Denton, *Racial Identity and Census Categories: Can Incorrect Categories Yield Correct Information?* 15 Law and Inequality Journal 83 (1997).

Richard T. Ford, *Race as Culture? Why Not?* 47 UCLA Law Review 1803 (2000).

Carol R. Goforth, *"What Is She?" How Race Matters and Why It Shouldn't,* 46 DePaul Law Review 1 (1996).

L. Scott Gould, *Mixing Bodies and Beliefs: The Predicament of Tribes,* 101 Columbia Law Review 1702 (2001).

Tanya Katerí Hernández, *The Interests and Rights of the Interracial Family in a "Multiracial" Racial Classification,* 36 Brandeis Journal of Family Law 29 (1997–1998).

Christine B. Hickman, *The Devil and the One Drop Rule: Racial Categories, African Americans, and the U.S. Census,* 95 Michigan Law Review 1161 (1997).

A. Leon Higginbotham Jr. and Barbara K. Kopytoff, *Racial Purity and Interracial Sex in the Law of Colonial and Antebellum Virginia,* 77 Georgetown Law Journal 1967 (1989).

Alex M. Johnson Jr., *Rethinking the Process of Classification and Evaluation: Destabilizing Racial Classifications Based on Insights Gleaned from Trademark Law,* 84 California Law Review 887 (1996).

Sharon M. Lee, *Racial Classifications in the U.S. Census: 1890–1990,* 16 Ethnic and Racial Studies 75 (1993).

Patrick F. Linehan, *Thinking Outside of the Box: The Multiracial Category and Its Implications for Race Identity Development,* 44 Howard Law Journal 43 (2000).

George A. Martínez, *The Legal Construction of Race: Mexican-Americans and Whiteness,* 2 Harvard Latino Law Review 321 (1997).

Carrie Lynn H. Okizaki, *"What Are You?" Hapa-Girl and Multiracial Identity,* 71 University of Colorado Law Review 463 (2000).

Lisa K. Pomeroy, *Restructuring Statistical Policy Directive No. 15: Controversy over Race Categorization and the 2000 Census,* 32 University of Toledo Law Review 67 (2000).

Julissa Reynoso, *Race, Censuses, and Attempts at Racial Democracy,* 39 Columbia Journal of Transnational Law 533 (2001).

Clara E. Rodríguez, Changing Race: Latinos, the Census, and the History of Ethnicity in the United States (2000).

Victor C. Romero, *"Aren't You Latino?" Building Bridges upon Common Misperceptions,* 33 University of California Davis Law Review 837 (2000).

Gabrielle Sándor, *"Other" Americans,* American Demographics, June 1994, at 36.

Jon Michael Spencer, The New Colored People: The Mixed-Race Movement in America (1997).

Symposium, *Border People and Antidiscrimination Law,* 17 Harvard BlackLetter Law Journal 23 (2001).

Enid Trucios-Haynes, *Why "Race Matters": LatCrit Theory and Latina/o Racial Identity,* 12 La Raza Law Journal 1 (2000–2001).

Part V

Inheritance Rights

Part 5 focuses on the inheritance rights of mixed race people. As we saw in Part 1, before 1967 the laws of many states prohibited marriages between African Americans and Whites. The law often classified children of interracial relationships as "illegitimate," possessing the diminished inheritance rights held by all illegitimate children. Consequently, the anti-miscegenation laws in operation limited the ability of Black women and mixed race children to accumulate assets, which resulted in long-term impacts on the distribution of wealth. By all accounts, African Americans lag significantly behind Whites in accumulated assets, much more so than with respect to income.

Patricia Collins discusses the general impacts of the anti-miscegenation laws on inheritance rights. Cheryl Harris outlines the legal history surrounding interracial families' lack of inheritance rights and compares the limited property rights available to African American women to those of White women. Adrienne Davis surveys the legal decisions in this area, including limitations on slaveholders' ability to free slaves by will. Joan Tarpley considers how stereotypes of Black women influenced the development of inheritance law after emancipation. Finally, Helen Jenkins raises the issue of how new scientific methods may allow for the vindication of inheritance rights.

44

Gender, Black Feminism, and Black Political Economy

Patricia Hill Collins

. . . . Laws against interracial marriage were only abolished in the 1960s. [See Part 1—Ed.] One objective of these laws was to deter African American men from marrying White women. The increasing number of U.S. Black men who now date and marry White women reinforces notions that these two groups did in fact have a long-standing sexual attraction. However, another interpretation of anti-miscegenation laws examines their effect on African American women. Such laws regulated property relations and thus regulated the intergenerational accumulation of wealth. Historically, White women's property was intertwined with that of their fathers and spouses, and Black men remained poor. Thus neither White women nor Black men could bring substantial property to marriages. For Black men, such laws regulated sexuality. In contrast, if African American women were allowed to marry White men—propertied White men who ran things or working-class White men who claimed the family wage as their birthright—African American women theoretically gained access to White male property. More important, their mixed race but legally Black children did too. Within prevailing gender hierarchies, for Black women such laws regulated wealth.

The second set of laws concerns the intergenerational inheritance of property. . . . U.S. Black and White families, [as well as] facilitat[ing] the intergenerational transfer of cultural capital, . . . can also be seen as sites where property or material capital is accumulated, invested, and transferred from one generation to the next. In a similar fashion, debt and poverty can also be inherited. Rules that rendered the biologically White children of legal marriages legitimate and thus entitled to the property of their White fathers also worked to deny Black and/or mixed race children access to the property of their White fathers. In a context of anti-miscegenation laws that rendered mixed race children with White fathers born to nonmarried Black mothers illegitimate, claims on their fathers' property had little meaning. Instead, African American social institutions—primarily African American extended families—were forced to bear the cost of raising not just the children fathered by Black men but those fathered by White men as well.

Overall, wealth differences between races as well as gender distinctions within races that originated under slavery have meshed with an intergenerational class disadvantage organized through and passed on via Black women's placement in a distinctive work-family nexus. Until the 1970s, the combination of legal restrictions against interracial marriage and Black men's lower income meant that the majority of Black women could not marry wealth, nor could their mixed race children inherit it. Moreover, in a context where the presence or absence of state-sanctioned marriage conferred differential political rights on women and men based on their marital status, racial classification, and assets, Black women remained severely disadvantaged.

Finding Sojourner's Truth
Race, Gender, and the Institution of Property

Cheryl I. Harris

I. The Narrative: Property as Law, Property as Metaphor

B. Slavery as a Racially Gendered Narrative

The maintenance of racial boundaries was of critical significance and was inextricably tied to the notion of legacy. Under racial ideology in the United States, race is inherited biological status. This ideology dictates that for the subordinated, it is in the blood, like an inherited disease; for the racially privileged, it is in the blood, like a birthright, and is treated and regarded as protected property. Where race is defined as a genetic marker, then, like all aspects of biological transmission, policing race requires tracking and circumscribing reproduction. . . .

Under slavery, defining who was property and who owned property—who was Black and who was white—then became a matter of regulating reproduction and subordinating women on the basis of a racially stratified construction of gender. Slavery was a "race [and gender] making situation."[1]

This regime had several complex features involving both social sanctions and legal rules. Some were rules of property law governing inheritance and legacy. Others came in the form of contract rules and criminal sanctions. All sought to regulate human beings through racial hierarchy in ways that valued white over Black bodies and asserted control over all women's reproduction as an aspect of white male procreative power.

Rules of inheritance were interrelated and functioned in particularly cruel and efficient ways. In general, while the rules of inheritance determined that status and property passed through the father, the status of being a slave was inherited from the mother. The rule had compelling economic logic: If a child of a slave woman inherited the status of the mother, regardless of whether the father was slave or free, Black or white, then the supply of slaves could be continually replenished through the use of a Black woman's body. Complementing this rule of inheritance was a companion rule of noninheritance that erased any claim of legacy between a slave child and her white father. This was derivative of the rule that barred illegitimate children from claiming their father's property. These rules inscribed the procreative power of ruling-class white men, allowing them to determine the parameters of heirship and ensure that the category of legal heirs remained white.

Rules of contract, particularly the marriage contract, and the social regulation of white female monogamy worked in tandem with inheritance rules to enhance the protection of property. Generally, the common law proscribed the legal recognition of slave marriages through the application of the rule that slaves could not contract.

However, property was secured through the adoption of contradictory social and legal sanctions on marriage for Black and white women: Black women were excluded from legal marriages with either Black or white men, while white women were socially coerced to marry white men and legally barred from marrying Black men. As Eva Saks explains, because the concept of "white blood" created among whites an identity as members of a common family that "shared 'race-as-property,'" then "the role of marriage is to keep property 'in the white family.'"[2] The bar on interracial relationships and marriage, so-called anti-miscegenation laws, [See Part 1—Ed.], were criminal sanctions designed to protect the ideology of racial purity and whiteness. As it pertained to relationships between Black women and white men, then, the legal sanction of marriage was withheld so that such a union could not produce legal Black heirs. This foreclosed the possibility that any nonwhite offspring of a white father could claim inheritance or property.

Similarly, the legal nonrecognition of marriages between Black men and women protected property in several ways. It first ensured that there were no competing claims by Black men to Black women or children based on the marriage contract, thereby reducing legal impediments to their commercial alienation and reproduction. Moreover, as Black children were the product of unions that were not legal marriages, they were legally fatherless and could thus assert no claims to parental property, even assuming that the prohibition on property ownership by Blacks had somehow been averted. The complex matrix of rights and duties inhering in the marriage contract contradicted central premises of slave law and would have accorded slaves an aspect of personhood that conflicted with their masters' property interests.

Unlike Black women, who were excluded from legal marriages, white women were both excluded from and coerced toward marriage. White women were barred from marrying Black men to ensure the protection of property at both the symbolic and material levels. The bar on interracial marriage between Black men and white women not only sought to guarantee that the property in whiteness remained "pure" and inviolate; since the legal status of the child as slave or free was inherited from the mother, the prohibition sought to prevent the birth of legally free nonwhite children—children who would "deprive the slaveowner of potential slaves [and cause] a reduction in the stream of future earnings capitalized in the black body."[3] At the same time, white women's marriage with white men was defined as an essential requirement of womanhood. Indeed, a woman achieved recognition as "woman" through marriage and the production of heirs, through which property could be secured.

Further, while miscegenous sex between white men and Black women was ubiquitous and, for white men, an expected right of ownership coercively enforced, the sexual behavior of white women and Black men was regulated through the "violent enforcement of the social taboo" against sexual relations between them. This rule was key: While a white man could father either a white or a Black child, a white woman could give birth only to a white child. Through social and criminal sanctions prohibiting sexual contact between white women and Black men, the dominant class sought to guarantee that the boundaries of white lineage were not transgressed and that white bloodlines remained "pure."

To be sure, as has often been noted, white female monogamy and the restriction of female sexuality is of critical importance in a system of private property as "[i]t is the only means by which a man can assure himself that his wealth will be inherited by his offspring."[4] But in a system in which white racial identity is heritable property (as, conversely, is Black racial identity) and is perhaps the most significant and valuable form of property, this prohibition took on heightened importance.

In contrast, while sexual contact between Black men and white women was rigorously policed, the sexual abuse and rape of Black women was decriminalized. This allowed for the full sexual exploitation of Black women's bodies and systematic sexual abuse without social consequences or legal sanction.

These differentiated rules for Black and white women governing the marriage contract and sexual access facilitated the establishment of manhood and womanhood as racialized constructs. Moreover, the presumed innate and subordinate status of women was not only a part of societal norms but was upheld as a principle of law. This provided the legal legitimation of a "natural" hierarchy. As Margaret Burnham points out, just as many believed that natural law and the divine order dictated the inferior position of slaves of both sexes, so too did natural law dictate the inferiority of white women. Thus, she states, "slaves were the moral inferiors of white men. White women were white men's moral superiors, but their physical and intellectual inferiors."[5]

C. Property as the Framework of Difference and Similarity

Property was a critical dimension of liberty; thus the lack of it was an important feature in justifying and reinscribing the subjugated position of women and slaves. Liberty was predicated on independence, which in turn was predicated on property ownership. Neither white women nor slaves had access to property or to power on terms equal to white men. Fundamental civil liberties such as owning property as well as political rights such as the franchise were reserved for those who owned or at least could own themselves and thus, by extension of their labor, acquire property. This was related to the idea that those who lacked a stake in society were a dependent class and thus were not socially responsible, as they were unable to exercise free will. Initially, the new American order, animated by the influence of social contract theory, derived the liberal rules of the polity from man's consent. But these were rules that were reserved in both racial and gender terms.

For slaves, who stood outside civil society altogether, the legal dominion of the master was nearly total. For (white) women, who were outside the public sphere, male power was qualified and not absolute but nevertheless determinative of the scope and dimensions of their rights to property and access to power. Yet all these limitations were not deemed inconsistent with the norms of equality. Indeed, republicanism and values of equality flourished along with the institution of slavery and the subordination of women. Rights discourse was inherently linked with systemic exclusion that was purportedly mandated by "natural" differences.

These presumed natural differences between white and Black men and women had both similar and dissimilar consequences for Black and white people generally and for Black and white women in particular. Ideologically and materially, white women, like slaves, remained subordinate to white men in part through their general exclusion from owning and controlling property, while at the same time white women's potential resistance to patriarchal oppression was co-opted through granting them interests in property that included slaves.

While both Black and white women were excluded from owning property, the reasons for and consequences of that exclusion were distinct. Black women as slaves were outside civil society. This rendered them incapable of owning property and legally subject to the absolute dominion of their masters. Those who were unable to claim self-ownership by reason of their inferior status as slaves—a position dictated by their natural essential inferiority—were simply not part of the calculus and were outside the polity. The rules that constrained power thus applied to those within society. Under slavery, not everyone's labor was recognized as a source of property. The labor of the slave gave rise to no rights to property, and indeed, the laborers became the object of property itself. The valuation of labor was racially determined: The conception of race as binary opposites of white and Black hierarchically ordered was inscribed by and within the system of slavery. Under this dualistic philosophy, which embraced freedom and domination simultaneously, "men" were naturally born to freedom just as "slaves" were naturally consigned to subordination. The American political regime not only assumed an economic actor motivated by self-interest; it further assumed that actor to be white or one who was within the symbolic system of "white."

White women's exclusion from property and other rights was ideologically grounded on the separation of the public and private spheres, the latter being the domain to which women were consigned. They were not outside civil society and were in fact a part of the community; however, they were not autonomous individuals but a subordinate part of the male-headed family. Property, which was the impetus to enter the social contract, was not then a right attained and controlled by individuals; it was a right accrued by males as actual or potential heads of families. This means that a married woman had no individual right to property or to her labor, as she was naturally under the authority of the male who headed her household. What rights white women acquired were those that were conceded to them or that devolved to them as a part of the family.

Under these conditions, since property was essential to full participation in the polity, white women were without equal power. . . .

White women were not treated as a species of legal property in the way that slaves of both sexes were treated, nor were they required to serve as sexual property, as were Black women. But married white women were prohibited from controlling property, precluded by the principle of "unity of the person" and the doctrine of coverture, which governed the legal status of married women. Under this doctrine, husband and wife were said to be one. Indeed, it is more accurate to say that "man and wife are one—but the man is the one."[6] This made marriage a form of civil death for women—a way in which white women legally disappeared. Despite the diversity of rules governing property among the colonies and later the states, none permitted any married woman to act independently with regard to property, even with respect to property that she might have contributed to the marriage. Thus, alone, married women had no right to contract, to convey property, or to act as executors of an estate.

While taking a different form from chattel slavery, this was the property dimension of patriarchal control and a central feature of domination. Male dominance came in the guise of protection. Indeed, women's rights were defined as no more than the right to rely on male protection. To the extent that such protection might fail, white women were given access to property, but at the price of their acceptance of a completely derivative and ultimately co-opted role. Only with and through their husbands, in cooperation with white male power, could white women achieve agency and the ability to act. These male-defined rules governing property severely constrained the behavior and power of white women both inside and outside the household. As Marylynn Salmon notes, the actual relationship circumscribed by the regime of property was one of women's "enforced dependence."[7]

In significant measure, by the nineteenth century property law governing married women was concerned with articulating the exceptional circumstances under which white women were allowed limited control over the family estate or the maintenance of separate estates. Where male abuse of power undermined or directly contradicted the governing presumption of the marriage contract—that a wife and children required no autonomy because they could rely on the male for support—these reforms or exceptions from the doctrine of spousal unity were born of necessity. The great irony is that to the extent that white women were permitted control over property as part of the campaign to abolish the structure of coverture, reforms for white women were achieved by accepting the rules of existing property regimes including slavery. The improvement of white women's legal status through the recognition of white women's capacity to contract, to attain a divorce and secure marriage settlements, and to convey and inherit property was linked to recognizing white women's contractual and property rights in slaves.

For example, in Maryland rules governing dower, a woman's share in her deceased husband's estate, were expanded to allow her a more equitable share by defining slaves as personal property included within the family estate. [Marylynn] Salmon, with no hint of irony, notes that the benefits to (white) women were considerable as Maryland women "retained absolute control over a certain portion of the personal wealth of their families [and] [t]heir ability to bequeath it gave to a certain class of Maryland matrons significant power within the family."[8] Although rules in other jurisdictions varied with regard to whether slaves were personal or real property, through the dower system the economic protection of white women was secured by extending them rights in slaves. In this way, white women achieved greater autonomy with respect to property and thus benefited through acquiring a material stake in slavery.

Perhaps what this reveals is that, in significant measure, white women's relation to property cannot be captured by the dichotomy of having property or being property, because in some dimensions both can be said to be true. Under certain limited conditions white women were allowed to have property, or perhaps more accurately, to have access to property on male-defined terms. This accorded them a certain derivative power and supplied a material incentive to co-optation that was embedded in the ideological stakes over womanhood. At the same time, white women were also occupied and controlled in a manner not unlike other property, although they were not subject to legal rules that allowed them to be bought and sold in the market.

White women were in some measure "propertized," though they were not property itself; they were treated in a manner *like* property but were not treated *as* property as a matter of law, as were slaves. In critical ways, the subordination of white women—their purported natural status as inferiors—affirmed the moral validity of slavery and white male power. Slavery assigned a particularly subordinated position to Black women and was also highly influential in shaping an ideology of white womanhood that conformed to the demands of that regime. Interrogating the content of womanhood through the construction of property under racial patriarchy reveals that white women were both subjects and perpetrators, both victims and victimizers.

Notes

Published originally in 18 Cardozo Law Review 309 (1996).

1. John O. Calmore, *Racialized Space and the Culture of Segregation: "Hewing a Stone of Hope from a Mountain of Despair,"* 143 University of Pennsylvania Law Review 1233, 1241 (1995)....
2. Eva Saks, *Representing Miscegenation Law*, Raritan (Fall 1988), at 39, 52, 55.
3. *Id.* at 43.
4. Mary Louise Fellows, *The Law of Legitimacy: An Instrument of Procreative Power*, 3 Columbia Journal of Gender and the Law 495, 495 (1993)....
5. Margaret A. Burnham, *An Impossible Marriage: Slave Law and Family Law*, 5 Law and Inequality Journal 187, 195 (1987).
6. Glanville Williams, *The Legal Unity of Husband and Wife*, 10 Modern Law Review 16, 18 (1947).
7. Marylynn Salmon, Women and the Law of Property in Early America, at xv (1986).
8. *Id.* at 150.

The Private Law of Race and Sex
An Antebellum Perspective

Adrienne D. Davis

I. The Racial Economics of Sex

B. The Southern Dimension of Inheritance

In 1808, the estate of Charles F. Bates, an attorney and planter in Virginia, became the subject of a complicated probate. The conflict arose from the existence of two testamentary documents, one dated 1799 and the other dated 1803. Both of these documents had been executed prior to Bates's marriage to Mary Heath Bates in 1806. There was no question that Bates had revoked the second will by cutting his name out of it. But Bates's widow argued that because the second will included a general clause with an intact signature revoking all prior wills, her husband had destroyed both wills and hence had died intestate. As the couple had no surviving children, Bates's widow would have been his principal heir under Virginia succession law. In contrast, Bates's mother argued that his cancellation of the second will also canceled his revocation of the first will, leaving that document intact and dispositive. His mother was the primary beneficiary of the first will.

In an *en banc* rehearing, the Supreme Court of Appeals of Virginia concluded that both wills had been canceled. Thus, Bates was declared an intestate, entitling his widow to the majority of his estate. As is typical in probates and challenges to wills, the holding of the court turned on its assessment of Bates's intent. They determined that he had planned to author a third will to govern the disposition of his estate and in the interim had revoked both of the previous documents.

There was an intriguing revelation in Bates's second will of a daughter born prior to his marriage to Mary Heath Bates. Bates had written:

> I have a daughter called *Clemensa*, at *Walter Keeble's*, in Cumberland, I declare her to be free to every right and privilege which she can enjoy by the laws of *Virginia*. I most particularly direct, that she be educated in the best manner that ladies are educated in *Virginia*. I give her my lot in the town of *Cartersville*, and three hundred dollars, to be laid out at interest, renewed yearly, and paid when she marry or come of age.[1]

Bates introduced his only child into antebellum Virginia society as illegitimate, black, and enslaved. Her presence in certain aspects of the case and her marked absence in others illustrate how slavery added a racial dimension to postmortem wealth transfers.

C. Sexual Relationships and Material Commitments

Bates's mother and widow, the parties to the case, struggled over whether Bates's probate would be governed by a will or the law of intestacy. Testamentary transfer and intestate succession are the two mechanisms through which Anglo-American law disposes of estates. Testamentary transfers are essentially wealth transactions after death, which are not enforceable until death, while intestate succession governs the default, dictating distribution of the estate in the absence of a will. Wills might then be thought of as privately directed transfers, which probate courts must decide whether to implement or invalidate. In the absence of a will or in the case of its invalidation, intestate succession emerges as the state's fixed preference for the descent of estates. Thus the conflict in *Bates v. Holman* implicated both of the doctrinal mechanisms that govern postmortem wealth transfers.

Per succession law, neither widows nor parents were entitled to full inheritance. Intestacy law directed the lineal transmission of estates, with a life interest in a conjugal partner. Why then was Bates's daughter, Clemensa, not permitted to revel in "lineal glory"?

None of the several opinions issued by the court noted where Clemensa stood within the line of intestate succession. Her potential status as an "heir," who might exercise her own claim to the estate, thereby altering the distribution of the estate between Bates's widow and mother, was completely overlooked. In fact, one of the opinions says, "[T]he law makes ample provision for the widow: but far different is the case respecting his natural daughter, who, together with her future offspring, the law has doomed to perpetual slavery, to her nearest blood relations, unless emancipated by their clemency. . . ." A similar expression of sentiments is as follows:

> As to *Clemensa*, it is, *perhaps*, her misfortune that the testator died intestate: I say, *perhaps*, for circumstances might have happened to change his opinion on that subject. Her's [*sic*] is, at most, the common case of a party's failing to provide by will for those who have strong claims upon him.

It appears clear that any rights, whether to emancipation or wealth, inuring to Clemensa would stem from Bates's own testamentary authority and not from her own rights of inheritance. Hers is a missing link in the chain of estate succession for reasons the court does not feel compelled to explain, but only to lament.

I turn then to the will. In it, Bates recorded his intent to disinherit his white heirs from a portion of his estate and leave it to his emancipated black daughter. Such a testamentary transfer clearly deviated from the distribution that succession law would have ordered, and it appears to transgress southern norms of propriety.

Yet the court gives very strong indication that it would have upheld the interracial transfer of freedom and wealth contemplated in the will had Bates not revoked it. In addition to the paragraph quoted above, one of the opinions proclaimed that "it is much to be lamented, that he was, by the hand of providence, prevented from making a suitable provision for the two worthy objects of his filial and paternal regard and affection; and for whose welfare and happiness he had uniformly shewn the most laudable solicitude." Moreover, the court's holding that Bates had intended to revoke both wills was based in large part on its conclusion that he must have planned to create a *third* will, providing for both his wife and Clemensa. One judge wrote:

> [The testator] then had a young wife, in the seventh or eighth month of her pregnancy, with the prospect of a numerous progeny before him; besides the moral, as well as natural obligations he was under, to make ample provision for his illegitimate daughter, already recognised and emancipated, and for whose welfare and happiness he had shewn very great anxiety and solicitude. To me it is inconceivable that any rational man, with the common feelings of humanity, thus circumstanced, could suffer such a will to exist for a single moment: but we have already seen that it had been deliberately and solemnly revoked.

Even as one member of the court, Judge [William] Fleming, expressed his own displeasure at Clemensa's existence and condemned Bates's "having formed an imprudent (though not uncommon) temporary connection," he applauded Bates's motives:

> [Bates] recognised the *fruit* of his unhappy amour, called her his daughter *Clemensa*, declared her to be *free*, gave particular directions respecting her education, and made a handsome permanent provision for her, manifesting thereby a laudable instance of natural affection, and making the best atonement in his power, for his former indiscretion.

The strong rhetoric of the opinion is worthy of some consideration. On the one hand, the judges reaffirm the immorality of Bates's sexual liaison, suggesting that such liaisons were unusual and reprehensible rather than fundamental to the political economy of the system of slavery. On the other hand, they present Bates's attempts to provide for Clemensa as laudable, a combination of "natural affection" and sin-offering. As a doctrinal matter, Clemensa's status in the chain of intestacy is not given any legitimacy. Instead, the possibility of her participation in her father's estate is coded through *his* obligation. The court represents Bates as a sovereign property holder motivated by laudable goals. Thus the ironically named Clemensa's claim on her father is merely one of "natural affection," a presocial set of animal sympathies, rather than the claims of natural justice, still less legal justice. Apart from affirming that natural affection for their illegitimate miscegenistic offspring could still thrive in the hearts of the white elite, the case also offers another role to Clemensa, as an object of penance or atonement, rather than as a subject holding independent legal rights. The case ends by upholding the sovereign power of Bates's intentions (in this case, by declaring that no validly formalized intentions actually existed) and by trumpeting the charity that motivated both Bates's and the judges' own words, even as it puts both that charity and its object firmly outside the ken of the law.

. . . . The *Bates* decision suggests that the tensions between intestate succession and testamentary freedom . . . were complicated by the sexual and racial dynamics and norms of slavery. Understanding Clemensa's exclusion from the chain of succession to her father's estate entails a consideration of how antebellum law assigned status-based abilities and disabilities to sexual relationships. Intestate succession doctrine excluded from intestacy rights black children like Clemensa, thereby protecting the white lineal family. But Bates's testamentary freedom then permitted him to alter that order, thereby apparently transgressing the norms of race, sex, and property established by intestate succession doctrine.

II. Intestate Succession: The Tale of Three Charities

In *Malinda and Sarah v. Gardner*,[2] the disposition of the estate of a manumitted slave named Tom turned on a legal search among his survivors for what the Supreme Court of Alabama termed "inheritable blood." The court was called to answer two questions. First, would antebellum law accord companionate slave relationships any legal abilities, such as property rights of inheritance? Second, could the court articulate a rationale that would support the legal rule? In a crude sense, the first question might be thought of as distributional, the second as ideological, though in practice, of course, the issues were considerably less clear-cut.

A. "Inheritable Blood"

Tom was enslaved until 1828, when his owner's will directed his manumission. The same will also emancipated Tom's companion, a woman named Charity. As legislative authorization of testamentary manumissions was required in Alabama, later that year the legislature gave effect to the testator's wishes, passing an act that emancipated Tom and Charity, as well as their two children, Malinda and Sarah.

Prior to their manumission by the legislature, Tom and Charity had ceased their relationship. By the time he gained his freedom, Tom had "taken up" with another woman, also enslaved. Coincidentally, this second companion was also named Charity. Tom purchased her, and although they shared a public companionate relationship until Tom's death, because he never emancipated her they were also bound by the legal relationship of master and enslaved. In addition, the rigidity of the doctrine of *partus sequitur ventrem* dictated that their children, Organ, Miles, and Rebecca, were the slaves of their father.

During the probate of Tom's estate, the court determined that he had died without a will (intestate), not an uncommon occurrence in that culture, particularly for free people of color. Therefore, the court proceeded to dispose of his estate according to principles of intestate succession.

The probate court concluded that none of the relationships that any of the parties shared with Tom rose to the level of a legal entitlement to his estate. Since he died without legal heirs, the law dictated that his estate would escheat to the ownership of the state of Alabama. The factual intricacies of the case become essential to understanding the parties' claims and the results.

Because Tom held them as his slaves, the second Charity and their three children were included in his estate that escheated to the state. Case law was well settled that a decedent's estate could and did include his own family, even in the case of blacks who publicly held themselves out as family. The state legislature subsequently passed an act emancipating all of Tom's slaves that had escheated (his family) and relinquishing the state's claim to the remainder of the estate. The act directed that the rest of the property be distributed among the second Charity and all five of Tom's children "in such portions as it would descend to them by the statute of distributions." Paradoxically, having concluded under the classificatory system of intestate succession that Tom died without legal heirs, the probate court was now directed to return to this same scheme to determine the legitimacy and priority of claims. The probate court concluded that all of the five children were entitled to share equally in Tom's escheated, now relinquished estate.

Malinda and Sarah, daughters of the first Charity, appealed the probate court's decision to the Supreme Court of Alabama. They argued that the probate court erred in concluding that Tom had died without heirs, and that because Tom's relationship to their mother had been tantamount to a marriage, they should have been declared the sole heirs of their father's estate at his death. They therefore challenged as wrongful the escheat to Alabama and the subsequent relinquishment and redistribution of the estate to all of the children and the second Charity. Following this logic to its disturbing conclusion, they also argued that the state did not have the authority to manumit the second Charity or her children, Organ, Miles, and Rebecca. Thus Malinda and Sarah not only sought to exclude appellees from Tom's estate but to enslave their half-siblings and father's widow.

The appellees responded that the legislative act of 1852 remained dispositive of Tom's estate because the probate court's findings regarding Tom's failure of legal heirs were correct. They argued that the legislative authorization of their manumission was valid, as was the probate court's subsequent determination that all of Tom's children would share the estate equally with the second Charity.

In the very first line of the opinion, the court states the holding and reveals its underlying logic: "Malinda and Sarah could not claim as heirs proper of their father, for the reason that both the father and mother were slaves, and persons in that condition are incapable of contracting marriage. . . ." The author of the opinion, Justice [Henry] Goldthwaite, relied on standard antebellum doctrine that did not accord the companionate relationships of the enslaved any of the legal rights of marriage. However, if slave unions survived emancipation, then civil rights would inure to them, even without formal state licensing. The disability of rights suppressed by enslavement could come to fruition at emancipation. One might think of this as a "dormancy" theory of rights allocation.

In *Gardner*, though, the court determined that Tom and the first Charity had not remained engaged in a companionate relationship legally sufficient to "earn" the rights that a dormancy rule might command to blossom. Likewise, Tom never emancipated the second Charity; therefore, her rights remained "suppressed" at his death. Accordingly, the court affirmed the probate court's findings and upheld the escheat to the state, the legislative manumissions, and the equal distribution of the estate among appellants and appellees.

The distributive effects of the decision are immediately apparent: it disabled the succession of estates among the enslaved. Also, the parties to the suit were *free blacks* who were seeking to terminate the ongoing effects of the disability of slavery. . . .

III. Testamentary Transfers and the Rhetorical Structure of Honor

When Elijah Willis died in 1855, he left a will executed in 1854, devising his entire estate to his executors with instructions to emancipate his concubine, Amy, and his children by her in Ohio and to liquidate the remainder of his estate to purchase land and homes for them in a free state. In *Jolliffe v. Fanning and Phillips*,[3] Willis's brothers-in-law, who had been appointed executors in an earlier will dated 1846, sought a decree to prevent the admission of the second will into probate. They contended that its postmortem transfer of freedom and a substantial amount of wealth violated two provisions of a state statute, and that therefore the entire will was void. In 1841, South Carolina had passed legislation that prohibited testamentary emancipations and devises or bequests to slaves, including those made through trusts. The probate court refused to admit the will, and Jolliffe, the executor of the second will, appealed.

A. Testamentary Freedom and Southern Hierarchy

As the appellate court characterized it, "[Appellees] say that the paper in question is void in all its parts, because, first, its provisions show it to be at war with the settled policy of this State as to slavery and emancipation; and, second, those provisions make it void in whole, by virtue of the words of the fourth section of the Act of Assembly." The South Carolina legislature was soon joined by other southern states in prohibiting testamentary manumissions, the socially preferred form of emancipation, thereby strengthening the state's assertion of slavery as a public institution.

Manumission not only terminated the *property* relationship between master and slave but imbued the freed person with legal personality, thereby altering his or her relationships with the state and other members of southern society. In some ways, then, it amounted to a privately ordered conferral of legal subjectivity that reordered the legal relationships of the manumitted not just with the former master but with everyone else in society. Intermittently, the southern states asserted the creation of a whole legal personality via manumission as the province of the legislature. . . .

Manumission also posed a threat to the connection between race and status. Despite the complex genealogies and scopic identities of many slaves and free persons, "Southern law was under great pressure to recognize only two statuses and to identify them with race."[4] As the Supreme Court of North Carolina declared: "It was, indeed, early found in this State, as in most of the others . . . that the third class of free negros was burdensome as a charge on the community, and, from its general characteristics of idleness and dishonesty, a common nuisance."[5] Legally, whiteness was a defense to being enslaved; not surprisingly, the pure converse that blackness would amount to a presumption of enslavement was a rule operative in every state except Delaware. The presence and growth of a free black population threatened the equation of blackness with enslavement. Southern whites also feared that a free community of color might lead to collaboration and insurrection or foment dissatisfaction among slaves, who could see that blackness need not be equated with an existence of degraded servitude. The prohibitions of testamentary manumissions represented one of several devices that states used to minimize the growth of the free colored population.

Southern legislatures also prohibited testamentary transfers of property to slaves either directly or via the creation of a trust. Such postmortem gifts to slaves threatened property and status norms of southern culture. . . .

Other scholars have written excellent accounts of how courts tried to negotiate testamentary manumissions, but they largely have neglected transfers such as Willis's. Postmortem emancipations to concubines and offspring by them complicated the more general social threats posed by testamentary emancipation. While all postmortem conveyances of emancipations and wealth to the enslaved affected the racial distribution of individual wealth, wills such as Willis's purported to disinherit white heirs at law in favor of blacks acknowledged as *sexual family*. One might expect that such transfers to a testator's concubine and children by her would pose unique, perhaps heightened threats to the southern social order.

First, such wills deviated from the social norms of those manumissions that were permitted. Overwhelmingly, slaveholders who emancipated slaves did not free their entire workforce. Most manumissions were of a select few for loyalty or heroic acts. Far from representing ideological condemnations of slavery, such "affectionate" or "heroic" manumissions supported the rhetoric of slavery as a benign institution. Transfers to concubines did not endorse the rhetoric of benevolence. . . .

Second, these wills transferred wealth to enslaved women who had been the testators' companions. While the receipt of property is no doubt of secondary importance compared to the receipt of freedom and legal personality, by these actions the slaveholders altered the cultural order that did not distribute a decedent's wealth to his family if his companion suffered from the disability of enslaved status. And because the amounts of the postmortem gifts were often quite significant, the family might gain not only freedom but social status, particularly if they left the community.

Finally, in their public acknowledgment of a slaveholder's sexual, compassionate, and filial bonds with the enslaved class, the wills document the testators' deviations from the code of acceptable sexual behavior. Miscegenistic relations largely were tolerated if conducted under an aura of secrecy. While many of the testators adhered to this norm of discretion during their lives, their wills represented postmortem defiance of the racial sexual order.

IV. The Postbellum World

A. Intestate Succession and Legitimacy

In *Butler v. Butler*,[6] the validity of a lease and mortgages turned on the determination of black inheritance rights. The intestate, Allen Butler, had fathered two families. While enslaved, he formed a union with Mary Ann, which lasted ten years. However, the union, being terminated by his sale, did not survive his emancipation. Subsequently, Butler married Mariah Conway, with whom he lived for forty years until his death. Each of the surviving families (Mary Ann and Mariah and her children) claimed succession rights and, thereby, the ability to enforce conveyances they had made. Similarly, in *Lewis v. King*[7] an intestate's second companion, Mary Baker, claimed that she was entitled to the entirety of his estate, which she had encumbered by lease and conveyance. She argued that intestate's children and grandchildren from a previous relationship had no inheritance rights, by virtue of being born while the intestate remained enslaved.

A second, related question pertained to the state's liability for children whom it defined as illegitimate and hence unable to make claims upon the estates of their fathers. The legitimacy of enslaved children had not affected the state, as their sole legally recognized relationship was with the master who enslaved them. But free black children, born out of wedlock, were able to make claims upon the public for support. While such claims were minimal, in the aggregate the southern states confronted assuming financial responsibility for the overwhelming majority of black children.

Thus the question of "inheritable blood" took on new significance in the postbellum period. Pure antebellum doctrine, which had maintained the hierarchies of slavery, now threatened the integrity of property titles in the southern states. Revisiting the impact of enslavement on "inheritable blood" placed considerable pressure on the old rules and doctrinal axes, identifying various points of vulnerability of the private law framework. For instance, Laura Edwards emphasizes the impact on marriage:

> Before the Civil War, both marriage and slavery created the boundaries that separated the household from the state and located people on either side of that divide as dependents or household heads. With the abolition of slavery, marriage acquired even greater importance in structuring southern society because it was now the only institution that legally constituted households.[8]

2. Interracial Marriages

Immediately following the end of the war, all of the southern states passed anti-miscegenation legislation. Those states that had not explicitly prohibited interracial marriages in the antebellum period now did so; those that had previously done so strengthened their statutes, enhancing penalties and broadening the scope of prosecution. [See Part 1—Ed.].

4. Summary

The threat of interracial marriage pressed contract doctrine from a different angle. Southern courts uniformly rejected the contract rationale for prohibiting enslaved marriages and embraced a definition of marriage as a social and public, not private, institution, thereby placing it beyond the scope of federal regulation. This had the effect of maintaining sexual relationships between blacks and whites in the nonobligatory sphere, segregated still from economic entitlements and property rights then accruing to black relationships recognized as "marriages." Recognizing the economic effects of this, black legislators in the Reconstruction Congress pushed to eliminate anti-miscegenation laws, arguing that they maintained black concubinage. Of course, such legislation did not, could not, succeed. As Mary Frances Berry notes: "The white men had not flouted the interracial marriage taboo. Instead, they reinforced the subordination of blacks by arranging their sexual relationships with African-American women in whatever fashion they desired."[9] In the postbellum era, black men would have material obligations stemming from sexual relationships with black women; white men still would not.

B. Testamentary Transfers

One of the wealthiest and most influential planters in post–Civil War Georgia, David Dickson, died in 1885. Dickson's will sparked controversy over his long-term sexual liaison with a black woman, casting the Supreme Court of Georgia, in *Smith v. DuBose*,[10] into the middle of an immense scandal. Like so many men of his class, Dickson had enslaved a black concubine and fathered a child by her. At his death, their daughter, Amanda, and her mother, Julia, were Dickson's only family, apart from his collateral heirs. While Dickson's lifetime sexual habits were not in themselves transgressive, his postmortem disposition of his estate was. Dickson's will provided that his very large estate would go almost entirely to his daughter and her children, also fathered by a white man. Amanda Dickson—a former slave, black and illegitimate—stood poised to take control of one of the most valuable estates in Georgia, worth half a million dollars.

Neither Amanda nor her mother would have been entitled to Dickson's estate in the absence of a will, as the laws of illegitimacy remained in effect. Accordingly, Dickson's collateral heirs challenged the validity of the will on several counts. They alleged that the devises and bequests had been obtained through the undue influence and improper control of Amanda and her mother, Dickson's concubine; that mother and daughter were guilty of fraud in inducing Dickson to believe he was Amanda's father; that Dickson lacked capacity to make a will; that the jury ought to be instructed that they were authorized to discount the women's credibility as witnesses if the women exhibited moral turpitude; that Julia's conduct toward Dickson during their life together was "overbearing rather than submissive"; and finally, that the postmortem transfers contemplated by Dickson violated public policy. Thus, Dickson's collateral heirs demanded that the will be declared void. In short, they drew on the same bank of stereotypes and charges characteristic of the antebellum challenges to wills of this type.

The Supreme Court of Georgia upheld the trial court's admission of the will into probate, which the intermediate appellate court had affirmed as well. Core passages from Justice [Samuel] Hall's defense of the validity of the will illustrate how little had changed from the antebellum to the postbellum sexual economies.

First, the opinion stressed the primacy of the testamentary power:

> Among the rights of citizens of this State . . . are the right to the acquisition and enjoyment of private property and the disposition thereof, the right to vote, hold office, etc. It is unquestionably true that a testator, by his will, may make any disposition of his property, not inconsistent with the laws or contrary to the policy of the State.

Representing the testamentary transfer as a core component of citizenship, analogous to the exercise of fundamental political rights, mirrors the antebellum rhetoric of testamentary freedom. Thus, even with increasing pressures put on the legal system by the possibility of individual deviance without the policing of racial relations offered by slavery, the court upheld the primacy of the will.

Next, the court discussed the heirs' contentions that enforcement of the will would amount to putting judicial force behind Dickson's breach of racial and sexual norms. Justice Hall's opinion dispensed with these arguments . . . :

> We know of no constitutional provision or statute or any decision of our courts, nor are we aware of any principle of the common law, which holds it to be immoral or wrong for the putative father to make provision for his illegitimate child, whether that child be white or colored; or for the illegitimate offspring of such child, whatever the complexion of such offspring may be. . . .

Hall's opinion then elaborated the legal protection of Julia's and Amanda's rights as Dickson's sexual family:

> [W]hatever rights and privileges belong to a white concubine, or to a bastard white woman and her children, under the laws of Georgia, belong also to a colored woman and her children, and that the rights of each race are controlled and governed by the same enactments or principles of law.

Thus the language of affective obligation and family appeared to have ongoing resonance, suggesting that the code of honor remained somewhat intact. The opinion combined these ideas with a new rhetoric of racially neutral protection of rights. The court's assertions of lack of racial bias in the assignment of rights to sexual relationships preserved the appearance of the legitimacy and fairness of the legal system. Appeals to color-blind norms would of course prove crucial in the jurisprudence of race and segregation that governed until *Brown v. Board of Education*.[11]

Beyond the protection of family and rights, the court conducted a detailed consideration of the public policy challenges to enforcement of the will, examining how other courts had dealt with them. Justice Hall quoted at length decisions upholding contracts against public policy challenges. This turn, from a discussion of testamentary transfers as core property rights to a precedential analysis centered on the integrity of contracts, is a fascinating one. Georgia had followed the rest of the southern states in concluding that the Civil Rights Act, giving blacks the same rights to make and enforce contracts as whites, did not apply to contracts between members of the groups for marriage. In the wake of upholding the prohibition on David Dickson's and Julia's entry into a marital contract as against public policy, the Supreme Court of Georgia evoked the primacy of contract to uphold Dickson's testamentary transfer to that same sexual family.

This then demonstrates the final point to be made about the private law framework that governed the postbellum sexual economy. . . . Courts continued to enforce testamentary transfers from white men to enslaved women. In the postbellum world, they escaped servitude but remained concubines.

Notes

Published originally in 51 Stanford Law Review 221 (1999).

1. *Bates v. Holman,* 13 Va. . . . 502, 504–5 (1809).
2. 24 Ala. 719, 724 (1854).
3. 44 S.C.L. (10 Rich.) 186 (1856).
4. Mark V. Tushnet, The American Law of Slavery 1810–1860: Considerations of Humanity and Interest 203 (1981).
5. Cox v. Williams, 39 N.C. (4 Ired. Eq.) 15, 17 (1845). . . .
6. 44 N.E. 203 (Ill. 1896).
7. 54 N.E. 330 (Ill. 1899).
8. Laura F. Edwards, *"The Marriage Covenant Is at the Foundation of All Our Rights": The Politics of Slave Marriages in North Carolina after Emancipation,* 14 Law and History Review 81, 85 (1996). . . .
9. Mary Frances Berry, *Judging Morality: Sexual Behavior and Legal Consequences in the Late Nineteenth-Century South,* 78 Journal of American History 835, 854 (1991).
10. 78 Ga. 413 (1887).
11. 347 U.S. 483 (1954).

47

Blackwomen, Sexual Myth, and Jurisprudence

Joan R. Tarpley

The language of the Supreme Court of Alabama in *Dees v. Metts*,[1] a 1944 decision, is quintessential for its description of both the cultural belief of immorality in interracial sexual relations and the policy claim of the social importance of racial purity. The Alabama Supreme Court justices told a story of sex and the evil seduction of a white man, Ben Watts, by a Blackwoman mistress. It seems that only because the issue before the court was the validity of a gift deed did the majority ultimately decide not to engage in "jezebel" jurisprudence. The dissenting justice was smitten with the power he perceived the mistress to have and made it clear that he believed lust had besotted Ben Watts, possibly beyond sound mind.

Ben Watts was a white man who bequeathed his entire estate to Nazarine Parker, a Blackwoman with whom he had lived for many years without a ceremonial marriage. He had also given her the entire estate by gift deed five months before he died, reserving unto himself a life estate. Finally, he had built himself a smaller house adjacent to the larger one in which she lived in his later years. It is clear that with each step he took, Watts was intent on protecting the woman and himself from the miscegenation code and on giving her all that he possessed. Relatives of Watts contested the will and brought an action to have the deed set aside. White businessman after businessman testified as witnesses in the case that Watts was of sound mind, an astute businessman and a man of strong will, determined and not easily persuaded. In having the will drawn, Watts had requested the local banker to be executor, saying:

> I want you to draw up a will and I want to fix it up this morning. . . . I want to leave what I have for this Negro woman that has been taking care of me all the time. You know how white people are about Negroes, and I want to be sure this thing is handled right because I want her to have what I've got. All my own people have ever done for me was to borrow money and never pay it back. I want to see that she gets it, and I want to see that some white man sees that she does get it.

The Alabama court strongly disavowed the relationship:

> It is reprehensible enough for a white man to live in adultery with a white woman, thus defying the laws of both God and man, but it is more so, and a much lower grade of de-

> pravity for a white man to live in adultery with a Negro woman. . . . "Reclamation may be made of the one; but, for the other, there is little, if any, hope." . . . Fortunately, the cases of such depravity are very rare.

The court then discussed a case where a white man lived with a Blackwoman to whom five children were born. The man willed all of his property to the children. The *Watts* court declared that this case furnished a disgraceful example of other such rare depravity. The court also noted that the public policy of the state was intended "to prevent race amalgamation and to safeguard the racial integrity of white peoples as well as the racial integrity of Negro peoples." The court finally concluded, however, that while Watts chose the evil way of life, and no matter how sinful he may have been and however disgraceful his conduct, he was of sound mind and not unduly influenced.

The dissent strongly argued otherwise. Willing to create a special undue-influence law for illicit relationships between white men and Blackwomen, the dissent argued that:

> We are not here concerned with the question of the invalidity of transactions because in contravention of public policy, as for example, a conveyance of property in consideration of entering into or continuance of illicit sexual relations between the parties. We are concerned with whether a will or gift of his estate by a white man to a negro woman with whom he is living in a state of adultery carries implications peculiar to such situation, which may, in connection with other facts, support a finding of undue influence.

The dissent insisted that a "reasonable inference [can be drawn] that the man has become so infatuated with his Negro mistress as to render her the dominant party in matters of special interest to her."

Clearly, there she is—"jezebel"—with all of her seductive power. In fact, the dissent wrote: "Her alleged declarations above quoted carry reasonable implication of her activity in procuring the will and deed, *and also of her sense of power to get what she wanted; the role of a mistress, rather than that of acquiescence or servile submission to the dominant will of the man*." Thus, amazingly, the white man Watts, reputed to be an astute businessman and of strong will, had become the victim in the dissent's story.

In *Dees v. Metts*, the court made it very clear that the basic physical sexual involvement of the parties, he a white man and she a Blackwoman, carried fundamental illicitness to a new level. The deed and the will were the doctrinal issues. The opinion, however, leaves no doubt that without the testimony of the many white businessmen on behalf of the white banker who did become the proponent of the will, the deed and will were likely to have been set aside. Watts had his way in the end, but it did require having a white man handle the matter so that the Blackwoman's deed could be held valid. "Jezebel" is starkly vivid in this decision. . . .

[The article proceeds to analyze how stereotypes of African American women informed the development of inheritance law.—Ed.]

Note

1. 17 So. 2d 137 (Ala. 1944).

48

DNA and the Slave-Descendant Nexus

A Theoretical Challenge to Traditional Notions of Heirship Jurisprudence

Helen Bishop Jenkins

For about two hundred years, the tenacious tradition of African American oral family history kept alive a persistent story told by the descendants of a mulatto slave. The crux of that story was that America's third president, Thomas Jefferson, fathered a child by his slave Sally Hemings.

The nagging issue of this paternity debate, which has raged for decades, reached a conclusion with the deoxyribonucleic acid (DNA) testing conducted by British and Dutch geneticists at Oxford, Leicester, and Leiden universities. By mapping the DNA of the descendants of Eston Hemings, Sally Hemings's son, and the descendants of Field Jefferson, Thomas Jefferson's son, scientists concluded that Thomas Jefferson was most likely the biological father of Eston Hemings Jefferson, although the debate continues that other explanations cannot be ruled out.

In 1996 a short article appeared in several newspapers describing the mission of two African American sisters and their curious and persistent investigation to establish their lineage as the slave descendants of George Washington.[1] Apart from the usual curiosities regarding their purported birthright, the relationship between these sisters and their alleged ancestor also raises legal issues—should such a connection be concretely established.

For descendants of slaves in America, establishing these blood ties is important for claims of birthright and family. [T]he proof provided by genetic testing in such cases should also have ramifications for property law.

With the proliferation of the use of DNA testing in the last few years to establish paternity, grand-paternity, and great-grand-paternity, evidence of paternity through DNA testing is "virtually foolproof" and "perhaps the most persuasive that a claimant can present." . . .

II. Potential Claimants: Historical Overview

In addition to the severe and degrading life conditions of plantation existence, slave women often had to endure relentless sexual abuse at the hands of their plantation masters. Slave women could not refuse or defend themselves against being "raped with abandon by their masters and their masters' sons," for fear of being beaten. As Neal Katyal recounts:

> The absolute control possessed by the master gave him the power to exploit a slave's sexuality. Southerner Fanny Kemble exclaimed that "it is notorious, that almost every Southern planter has a family more or less numerous of illegitimate colored children." Abolitionists also referred to the incestuous relationship between masters and slaves, intimating that slave owners raped their own daughters. . . . Sara Remond exclaimed that the 800,000 mulattoes living in the United States [in 1859] were all the result of rape.[2]

Although slave offspring produced from a master were mulattos, they were considered black according to the "one drop" rule. [See Part 2—Ed.] Actual numbers of children by white owners would be higher than the numbers of recognizable mulatto offspring due to the fact that there would be significant numbers of such mixed race offspring who would bear few white characteristics.

Rape of female slaves that created offspring was also economically motivated, particularly after Congress abolished slave importation in 1808. A slave owner could force his slaves to have sex with him, "his family, friends or other slaves, and then profit from the intercourse by selling or enslaving the baby." Given the opportunity for master-slave sexual contact, the social and legal framework that fostered its existence, and the reality that racially mixed children were born of these unions, there is evidence that the interest in DNA testing to establish family ties today might well be expected to increase.

Scientific literature on genetics provides stark examples of the legal complications involved when using DNA testing to determine heirship many decades after the death of the alleged father. [The article proceeds to analyze the issues.—Ed.]

Notes

1. *See* Robert Jackson, *George Washington in Family Apple Tree, Sisters Say*, Rocky Mountain News, November 4, 1996, at 24A; Anita Szoke, *Former Peoria Sisters Claim Famous Roots: George Washington a Branch on Family Tree, according to Pair*, Peoria Journal Star, November 22, 1996, at A9.

2. Neal Kumar Katyal, Note, *Men Who Own Women: A Thirteenth Amendment Critique of Forced Prostitution*, 103 Yale Law Journal 791, 799–802 (1993) (footnotes omitted).

Review Questions

1. What can be done to remedy the harm done to African Americans by the enforcement of the inheritance laws?
2. Are reparations necessary to compensate African Americans in interracial relationships for the systematic—and legal—denial of rights to inherit property?
3. Why have the inheritance consequences of the anti-miscegenation laws been so little studied?
4. Have you personally been affected by the inheritance laws? Have you benefited or lost out?

Suggested Readings

Mary Frances Berry, *Judging Morality: Sexual Behavior and Legal Consequences in the Late Nineteenth-Century South*, 78 Journal of American History 835 (1991).

Margaret A. Burnham, *An Impossible Marriage: Slave Law and Family Law*, 5 Law and Inequality Journal 187 (1987).

Laura F. Edwards, *"The Marriage Covenant Is at the Foundation of All Our Rights": The Politics of Slave Marriages in North Carolina after Emancipation*, 14 Law and History Review 81 (1996).

Mary Louise Fellows, *The Law of Legitimacy: An Instrument of Procreative Power*, 3 Columbia Journal of Gender and Law 495 (1993).

Annette Gordon-Reed, Thomas Jefferson and Sally Hemings: An American Controversy (1997).

Ariela J. Gross, *Litigating Whiteness: Trials of Racial Determination in the Nineteenth-Century South*, 108 Yale Law Journal 109 (1998).

A. Leon Higginbotham Jr. and Barbara K. Kopytoff, *Racial Purity and Interracial Sex in the Law of Colonial and Antebellum Virginia*, 77 Georgetown Law Journal 1967 (1989).

Eva Saks, *Representing Miscegenation Law*, Raritan (Fall 1988), at 39.

Marylynn Salmon, Women and the Law of Property in Early America (1986).

Mark V. Tushnet, The American Law of Slavery 1810–1860: Considerations of Humanity and Interest 203 (1981).

Emily Field Van Tassel, *"Only the Law Would Rule between Us": Antimiscegenation, the Moral Economy of Dependency, and the Debate over Rights after the Civil War*, 70 Chicago-Kent Law Review 873 (1995).

Part VI

Discrimination and "Colorism"

Discrimination against mixed race peoples differs in some respects from that directed at other racial minorities. For example, discrimination by Indians and Whites against mixed race Indians, known disparagingly as "half breeds," has a long history. (See David D. Smits, *"Squaw Men," "Half-Breeds," and Amalgamators: Late Nineteenth-Century Anglo-American Attitudes toward Indian-White Race-Mixing,* 15 American Indian Culture and Research Journal 29 [1991].) Part 6 analyzes the legal history of discrimination against mixed race people.

There are many complex dimensions to discrimination against mixed race people. Whites discriminated against Blacks of mixed ancestry just as they discriminated against all African Americans. As a historical matter, persons of mixed African American ancestry were classified under the "one drop" rule and discriminated against as Black. (See Part 2.) For example, in *Plessy v. Ferguson*, 163 U.S. 537, 538 (1896), the Supreme Court upheld a segregation law challenged by a person "of mixed descent, in the proportion of seven eighths Caucasian and one eighth African blood [although] the mixture of colored blood was not discernible in him. . . ."

At the same time, however, whites in employment and social life have generally preferred lighter- over darker-complected Blacks, with skin color often a function of racial mixture. As discussed in Part 3, some light-skinned African Americans were able to avoid classification as Black, and the discrimination that it would entail, by "passing" as white.

"Colorism," discrimination based on skin color, has emerged as a legal issue. Studies show that dark-skinned African Americans suffer greater discrimination than other Blacks. In contrast, some lighter-skinned African Americans are viewed as not "Black enough" (see Leonard M. Baynes, *Blinded by the Light; but Now I See*, 20 Western New England Law Review 491, 492 [1998].) The law is beginning to respond to color discrimination.

Similar issues arise among Latinas/os. Fair complexion may be valued as a "positive" trait. *Güero,* Spanish slang for "white one," is a term of endearment frequently used to refer to a fair-complected Latina/o. (See Kevin R. Johnson, *How Did You Get to Be Mexican? A White/Brown Man's Search for Identity* 7 [1999].)

In Part 6, Leonard Baynes offers thoughts about discrimination against darker-skinned African Americans and Latinas/os. Trina Jones considers the application of the federal anti-discrimination laws to colorism claims. Identifying analytical deficiencies in the judicial treatment of colorism among African Americans, Tauyna Lovell Banks predicts an increase in skin-color discrimination claims—with growing complexity—

in the future. Leonard Baynes discusses the complexity of color in a specific controversy over the hiring of a faculty member at an elite U.S. law school. Laura Padilla studies color consciousness among Latinas/os. Kevin Johnson analyzes schisms among Mexican Americans and recent Mexican immigrants, which take on a racial dimension because many recent immigrants are more indigenous-appearing (and less "mixed") than the established Mexican American community in the United States.

If It's Not Just Black and White Anymore, Why Does Darkness Cast a Longer Discriminatory Shadow Than Lightness?

An Investigation and Analysis of the Color Hierarchy

Leonard M. Baynes

I. Introduction

In the United States, a color hierarchy exists between and among people of color, which spans different racial and ethnic groups. The premise is very simple and very clear: Lighter is better and darker is worse. . . . A dark-skinned person of color is likely to encounter more discrimination than his/her light-skinned counterpart. In fact, one survey of African Americans showed that darker-skinned African Americans are twice as likely to report that they have been victims of discrimination than those with lighter-skinned complexions.[1] Like darker-skinned Blacks, darker, more Indian-looking Mexican Americans also reported a significantly greater amount of discrimination than the lighter, more European-looking Mexican Americans.[2] . . .

III. African American and Latino Colorism

A. African American Colorism

African American society has its own discrimination, often light against dark, which sadly was modeled on the White-against-Black paradigm. It was not uncommon for very light-skinned Blacks (sometimes nicknamed the "blue vein society" because you could see their veins through their skin) to exclude dark-skinned Blacks from their clubs and activities based on skin color. Other organizations would discriminate based on whether a person's skin color was lighter than a brown paper bag. Many of these organizations have changed and now include African Americans of a wide rainbow of colors. . . .

Much of this intrarace discrimination stems from internalized White discrimination and the fact that who was Black was defined by the law of hypodescent. [See Part 2 for a discussion of the "one drop" rule.—Ed.] . . .

African American society reproduced the same type of discrimination that White society spawned, that is, light over dark. Some of the discrimination is also based on the maximization of advantage by some light-skinned Blacks. They might have felt that they did not want to share the little that they had with anyone else, including darker-skinned peers. There also may be some resentment by the darker-skinned Blacks toward the lighter-skinned Blacks. The lighter-skinned Blacks were descended from the slave master. As a result, they may have some historic advantages. They worked in the master's house as opposed to the field. The house slave presumably had a more [cushy] job than the field hand. By being in the house, the house slave was more likely to learn the master's ways. In addition, by being the master's offspring, the house slave was more likely to be educated and might even be emancipated by the master.

In fact, "historical evidence indicates that Whites placed greater economic value on slaves of mixed parentage and used skin tone or degree of visible white ancestry" as a means to determine the kind of treatment the slave would receive.[3] Biracial slaves "brought the highest prices on the slave market, and the white aristocracy preferred light-skinned Blacks for personal service. . . . White males were more likely to select light-skinned female slaves over darker ones for sexual unions." Whites believed that "[B]lacks with white ancestry were intellectually superior to those of pure African ancestry."

The lighter-skinned Blacks "were conscious of the distinctions between themselves and darker slaves" and may have indeed believed that their lighter skin (and white ancestry) made them superior.[4] Others may not have bought into this White ideology but must have realized that they had certain advantages over the darker-skinned Blacks.

Some of the tensions between the two groups stem from this historical advantage and the desire by some of the lighter ones to preserve this advantage. Biracial Blacks were "over represented in the free Black population and under represented among slaves."[5] By 1850 biracial Blacks "made up 10-15% of the total Black population, 37% of all free Blacks and 8% of slaves." The majority of prominent Blacks were at one time biracial; they often married biracial spouses and as a result passed their light-complected advantage on to their light children. "Research conducted before and during the Civil Rights Movement suggested a continuing relationship between variations in skin tone and life chances . . . of [African] Americans. [Light]-skinned Blacks had higher levels of attainment than darker Blacks on virtually every dimension of stratification." In the twentieth century, more darker-skinned Blacks moved into the upper rungs of Black society. This can be attributed to the increased education as well as the intermarriage of some darker-skinned Blacks into old-line biracial families. It also resulted from increased expansion of the black middle class during the 1960s. In addition, there was the development of social pride in being Black, namely, "Black Is Beautiful!" and the distinctive contributions of black music, literature, and history to the American society. But studies show that light skin still has certain advantages.

These days, the discrimination in the African American community is often dual-sided: light versus dark and dark versus light. In the film *School Daze,* which takes place on an all-Black college campus, Spike Lee underscores this duality and divides the students into two groups: the wannabees (more often light-skinned and middle class), who are members of fraternities and sororities, and the jigaboos (more often dark-skinned and from lower economic background), who are often members of Black militant groups. In the film, it is evident that the two groups despise and intimidate each other.[6]

B. Latino Colorism

In Mexico, a great deal of mixing occurred between the Spaniards and Native American populations and some African Blacks. "The term 'Mestizo' meant half-Spanish and half-Indian."[7] It eventually "came to refer to the entire mixed population regardless [of] the degree of mixture." Colonial Mexico under the Spaniards had a fixed caste system with a detailed ranking of racial categories. [See Part 10—Ed.]

> During . . . Spanish rule, the Mestizos occupied a middle status position while the Indians were on the bottom of the ethnic status ladder. . . . The lighter Mestizos were given preference by the Spanish, and there developed a structure of status . . . based on skin color and the degree of Spanish ancestry. . . . The Mestizos took pride in their Hispanic ancestry and tried to deny their Indian backgrounds.

The Mestizos now govern Mexico, and the pure Indian people have remained on the bottom of society.

In most Latin American societies, unmixed Africans are considered Blacks and are accorded less favorable treatment than mixed people. In some Latin American countries, light mixed race people and Mestizos are considered White and will be referred to euphemistically as "brunette" or "little mulatto." In Puerto Rico, unmixed Africans and the darkest biracial persons are at the bottom of society. Black skin color is not preferred. "The terms for racial identities indicate gradations of color and have varied meanings [such as] *blanco* (white), *negro* (African black), *mulata* (mulatto), *trigueno* (wheat-colored, olive-skinned), and *moreno* (brunette, attractively dark)."[8] *Grifa* is someone with light skin but tightly curled hair, and *jaba* is someone with light skin but African facial features. These categories vary from place to place and are very fluid. It seems most people prefer to be designated as a *trigueno*, and no one wants to be a *negro*. It seems at least in some places that *trigueno* is a fairly broad category covering many people whose skin coloration ranges from light olive to medium brown. The problem, however, exists that when some of these *triguenos* who are darker in complexion move to the United States, they are more easily racialized as nonwhite. Becoming Black must be a real shock for their identity when they were raised to think of themselves as White, even though some of them must know that Grandma or Grandpa was Black.

About 10 percent of the Puerto Ricans who relocated to the mainland are of unmixed African ancestry, and half or more have some African ancestry. So 60 percent of these migrants will be perceived in the United States as being Black, "while in Puerto Rico most were known as whites or by [some other] designation other than Black."[9] In fact, during World War II, Puerto Ricans were treated similarly to African Americans. All "Puerto Ricans in the U.S. Army were in segregated camps, even in Puerto Rico, and the United States Navy refused to accept any Puerto Ricans."

V. Does This Preference for Light and Abhorrence of Dark Exist Today?

C. Light-Skinned Blacks Have Higher Incomes and More Professional Positions Than Darker-Skinned Blacks

Professors [Michael] Hughes and [Bradley R.] Hertel, using data from the 1980 National Survey of Black Americans, conducted by the Institute for Social Research at the University of Michigan, and 1983 census data, found that Blacks with lighter skin have higher socioeconomic status, have spouses higher in socioeconomic status, and have lower Black consciousness than those with dark skin.[10] Dark-skinned Blacks earned only seventy cents for every dollar a light-skinned Black earned. Of professional and managerial occupations—those with high status—light-skinned Blacks held 27 percent of them, as compared to 15 percent of dark-skinned Blacks who were employed in those positions. Professors Hughes and Hertel believe that "skin color . . . operates as a diffuse status characteristic." They said that they "focused on [W]hites because they are the ones who are generally responsible for making upper-level management and personnel decisions. They are more likely to decide whether people get through educational institutions." And when Whites see a darker-complected Black person, Hughes and Hertel state that the white person thinks he or she is seeing someone "less competent"—someone less like them than a light-complected Black person. This view of the White perspective is subject to disagreement.

D. Light-Skinned Latinos Have Higher Incomes and More Professional Positions Than Darker-Skinned Latinos

. . . Mexican Americans with a more "European . . . appearance have more enhanced life chances as measured by higher socioeconomic status than Mexican Americans with indigenous Native American" features.[11]

"The greatest number of years of formal education was reported for fathers and mothers of respondents in the [l]ight/European category while the lowest socioeconomic levels are found in the [d]ark/Indian group."[12] A similar relationship between color and features relates to the fathers' occupation—those who were light/European held more prestigious jobs than those who were dark/Indian. For the respondents of the survey, although they had achieved higher socioeconomic status than their fathers, "it remained the case in the later generation that the lighter the skin color and the more the European the features, the higher the socioeconomic status." Mexican Americans who were lighter/more European had attained 9.5 mean years of education, while darker/more Indian Mexican Americans had completed only 7.8 years on the average. Investigations of levels of income revealed the same pattern, with light/European [Mexican Americans] earning $12,721 while the dark/Indian group earned only $10,480.

Darker-skinned Latinos are also likely to encounter discrimination in the sale and rental of homes. In fact, like African Americans and unlike other Latinos, Puerto Ricans live in highly segregated areas and have developed underclass communities. This difference between Puerto Ricans and other Latinos is perceived to be because of their more pronounced African ancestry. In addition, darker-skinned Latinos are more likely to be questioned by Border Patrol officers in and about the border. . . .

VII. Conclusion

In the United States there is a color hierarchy between and among people of color that spans different racial and ethnic groups. The premise is very simple and very clear: It is that lighter is better and darker is worse. So even if we all agree that race itself no longer matters, color will still be a problem because darkness casts a longer discriminatory shadow than lightness. A dark-skinned person of color, whether Black or Latino, is likely to encounter more discrimination than his or her light-skinned counterpart.

Notes

Published originally in 75 Denver University Law Review 131 (1997). Copyright © 1997 by Denver University Law Review. Reprinted with permission.

1. *See* Verna M. Keith and Cedric Herring, *Skin Tone and Stratification in the Black Community,* 97 American Journal of Sociology 760, 755 (1991).

2. *See* Carlos H. Arce et al., *Phenotype and Life Chances among Chicanos,* 9 Hispanic Journal of Behavioral Science 19, 29 (1987); Edward E. Telles and Edward Murguia, *Phenotypic Discrimination and Income Differences among Mexican Americans,* 71 Social Science Quarterly 682 (1990).

3. Keith and Herring, *supra,* at 761–62.

4. *Id.* at 762.

5. *Id.* at 753.

6. School Daze (Forty Acres and a Mule Filmworks, 1988).

7. F. James Davis, Who Is Black? 88 (1991).

8. *Id.* at 103. ("*Trigueño* connotes a status almost equal to that of *blanco,* and even some unmixed Whites [as well as Blacks] prefer to be identified by this favorable term.")

9. *Id.* at 104.

10. Michael Hughes and Bradley R. Hertel, *The Significance of Color Remains: A Study of Life Chances, Mate Selection, and Ethnic Consciousness among Black Americans,* 68 Social Forces 1105 (1990).

11. Arce et al., *supra,* at 19.

12. *Id.* . . .

50

Shades of Brown
The Law of Skin Color

Trina Jones

II. Color Distinctions through the Lens of Time

B. After the Civil War: 1865–2000

1. Colorism within the White Community. . . .

. . . [Historically,] when forced to deal with Blacks, Whites preferred Blacks with lighter skin tones. . . . Colorism was . . . apparent in employment practices. From Reconstruction to well into the twentieth century, desired positions regularly went to lighter-skinned Blacks over equally qualified darker-skinned Blacks.

Many of these trends continue today. As contact between the races has increased (especially in the aftermath of the civil rights movement), Whites still seem to prefer and to find less threatening persons who look more like themselves. These preferred individuals tend to be lighter-skinned and economically better off. Black women who play romantic leads in major Hollywood films tend to have lighter skin and longer hair. Lighter-skinned women with European features predominate among successful Black contestants in beauty pageants and in music videos. They are also more likely than darker Blacks to be selected to endorse mainstream commercial products. In other employment settings, sociologists have found that even when researchers control for socioeconomic background, lighter-skinned Blacks fare better educationally and occupationally than their darker peers.[1]

2. Colorism within the Black Community.

In the post–Civil War era, skin color differences continued to play an important role within the Black community, as elite mulattoes sought to maintain the privileged status they had acquired during slavery. In order to distinguish themselves from the darker-skinned masses, these mulattoes established separate communities in which skin color served as the key to access. Mulattoes formed exclusive social clubs, like the Blue Vein Society of Nashville, and created separate churches. In the former, admission was based on whether an applicant's skin color was light enough for the veins in the wrist to be visible. In the latter, the paper bag test was sometimes employed to determine admissibility. Under that test, a person seeking to join a color-conscious congregation was required to place his or her arm inside of a brown paper bag and could attend church services only if the skin on the arm was lighter than the color of the bag. Mulattoes also lived in separate residential communities, such as the Chatham and East Hyde Park sections of Chicago and the Striver's Row and Sugar Hill areas of New York, which were known to be populated by light-skinned professionals. In addition, mulattoes formed separate professional and business associations. One of the most important areas in which mulattoes received superior treatment to darker-skinned Blacks was in education. Mulattoes formed preparatory schools and colleges that denied access to persons who were too dark. Many historically Black colleges and universities established in the nineteenth century also discriminated on the basis of color in their admissions process. Not only were educational institutions segregated by color, but their curricula differed as well. In schools attended by mulattoes, students received a liberal arts education. By contrast, darker-skinned Blacks were taught in schools and programs that focused primarily on vocational learning. This focus on training in practical skills reinforced the placement of darker-skinned Blacks into lower-paying, less-skilled positions.

Thus, at the turn of the century, the class of successful Blacks was largely comprised of the visibly mixed population. These differences were reflected in the leadership of the Black community, where mulatto elites also dominated the intellectual and political life. Indeed, of the twenty-one men and two women among W. E. B. Du Bois's Talented Tenth, all were mulatto save one.[2]

Although the mulatto elite were generally in a higher socioeconomic class than unmixed Blacks due to their historically favored status, they were nonetheless rejected by the White community because of their Black blood. In addition, their lighter skin and better socioeconomic status spawned resentment within the Black community. Some of this resentment may have been fueled by the practice of passing, whereby light-skinned Blacks who looked sufficiently White would conceal their Black ancestry and pretend to be White. [See Part 3—Ed.] For the most part, however, the mulatto elite was admired by Blacks, and throughout the early part of the twentieth century the bond among Blacks of all skin tones grew.

The alliance between mixed and unmixed Blacks was further strengthened during the Black Power movement of the 1960s. That movement revived the affirmation of Blackness that had characterized the Harlem Renaissance. The celebration of all things Black (e.g., "black pride, black beauty, black achievement, black history, and the use of the term 'black' rather than 'Negro'") comprised a major portion of the agenda of the Black Power movement. On the surface, skin color differences seemed less important as light- to medium-skinned Blacks such as Andrew Young, Jesse Jackson, Julian Bond, Adam Clayton Powell Jr., and Angela Davis joined forces with darker-skinned leaders such as Eldridge Cleaver, Stokely Carmichael, and Huey Newton. Still, at the same time that "Black unity" was the rallying cry of the movement, lighter-skinned Blacks were sometimes ostracized and made to feel as if they had to prove their Blackness. The perceived demand for lighter-skinned Blacks to prove their loyalty was due to a learned mistrust, which may have been fueled by the fact that some lighter-complected persons had historically rejected their status as members of the

Black race because of feelings of superiority or out of an effort to improve their socioeconomic standing in society.

Throughout the 1970s, some members of the Black community continued to view disfavorably lighter-toned Blacks. These individuals were stereotyped as morally weak and mentally unstable because of their mixed racial heritage. They were also accused of thinking that they were more intelligent and attractive than unmixed Blacks. Despite these negative critiques, if a lighter-toned person exhibited allegiance to Black causes and embraced her Black heritage, darker Blacks usually accepted her into their extended family.

The above history has affected contemporary relations within the Black community. . . . When their guards are down, many Blacks will readily share stories involving intraracial colorism. As is the case within the White community, the dominant preference operates in favor of lighter skin tones. Researchers have found that when asked to choose from a selection of White and Black dolls, Black children tend to select White dolls.[3] Black men tend to prefer lighter-skinned women as intimate companions. Blacks with lighter skin tones also fare better educationally and economically than darker Blacks.[4] Indeed, since the 1960s, most Blacks elected or appointed to prominent governmental positions have had light skin.

[In a footnote, the article states:

[One authority notes] the success of light-skinned Black leaders, including:

> Robert Weaver, secretary of the Department of Housing and Urban Development, and the first Black U.S. cabinet member (1966); Edward W. Brooke, the first Black senator since Reconstruction (1966); Thurgood Marshall, the first Black Supreme Court justice (1967); Maynard Jackson, the first Black mayor of Atlanta (1974); Andrew Young, the first Black U.S. ambassador to the United Nations (1976); Patricia R. Harris, the first Black woman cabinet member (1976); Ernest Morial . . . the first Black mayor of New Orleans (1977); David Dinkins, the first Black mayor of New York (1989); Douglas Wilder of Virginia, the first Black governor (1989); General Colin L. Powell, the first Black chairman of the Joint Chiefs of Staff (1989) [and later Secretary of State]; Ron Brown, the first Black to chair the Democratic National Committee (1989); Sharon Pratt (Dixon) Kelly, the first Black female mayor of a major city, Washington, D.C. (1990). . . .]

Colorism among Blacks does not operate uniformly in favor of persons with lighter skins. Indeed, some Blacks with darker skin pigmentation distrust and have expressed hostility toward Blacks with lighter skin tones. For example, when Sharon Pratt Dixon ran for mayor of Washington, D.C., some Blacks questioned whether this light-skinned Black woman could understand the issues that affected them. Similarly, when Vanessa Williams was crowned as the first Black Miss America, some Blacks criticized the pageant for selecting someone who was not "Black enough."

C. The Social Psychology of Contemporary Black-White Colorism

[S]kin color still matters in the United States. For many persons within both White and Black communities, light- to medium-brown skin is associated with intelligence, refinement, prosperity, and femininity. Darkness is associated with toughness, meanness, indigence, criminality, and masculinity. These meanings are historically based.

The association between skin color and class can be traced back to the early division between house slaves and field slaves and the fact that, due to the status of their White fathers, some light-skinned slaves were granted greater educational and professional opportunities. The higher socioeconomic class of lighter-skinned Blacks may have made them appear less foreign and therefore less threatening to Whites. Their elevated status also may have rendered them more attractive to darker-skinned Blacks. To some extent, class-based distinctions are self-perpetuating because socioeconomic advantages are passed down from one generation to another—with classism intensifying the effects of colorism. Skin color, however, functions as more than an indicator of class: a person's relative lightness or darkness determines whether she can access the benefits associated with a particular class. This phenomenon occurred in the post–Civil War era when elite mulattoes created social and political organizations into which access was granted or denied based on one's skin color, regardless of one's actual socioeconomic class. Thus persons whose skin was light enough were allowed entry even if they were poor. Conversely, wealthy persons were denied access if their skin was too dark. In these circumstances, skin color itself served as the determinant of status, regardless of a person's actual socioeconomic class.

The meaning attributed to skin color today does not rest merely on historical class-based differences between light-skinned Blacks and darker-skinned Blacks—as the darkening of O. J. Simpson's photo illustrates. [In connection with a story about the criminal prosecution of Simpson for allegedly murdering his White wife, one national magazine published a darkened picture of him.—Ed.] Although it is hard to prove, contemporary colorism also appears to draw upon concepts of good and evil that predate European colonization of North America. In the European tradition, "whiteness" or "fairness" is associated with purity and innocence, and "blackness" is associated with dirt, evil, and death. Contemporary beliefs that lighter-skinned persons are more attractive than darker-skinned individuals, or that darker-skinned persons are more evil or criminal than their lighter counterparts, may relate to these traditions.

Finally, because skin color is often an indicator of mixed racial heritage, contemporary colorism may draw upon racism and nineteenth-century ideologies of race. Here the argument is that Blacks with lighter skin tones are superior to Blacks with darker skin tones because of the former's White ancestry; lighter-skinned Blacks, however, are nonetheless inferior to Whites because their heritage is not completely White. Thus a White person might view a lighter-skinned Black as preferable to a darker-skinned Black because of her allegedly closer connection to Whiteness. The infusion of White blood may lead Whites to conclude that lighter-skinned Blacks are more intelligent and capable than darker Blacks. To the extent that people of color have been socialized to accept these racist norms, they may also unconsciously view lighter-skinned Blacks as being racially superior. This argument also works in the reverse. A Black person might view a light-skinned person as inferior to darker Blacks because of her mixed ancestry. Thus, instead of elevating her worth, her White ancestry would diminish her value within the Black community. This response may be a defense against the dominant tendency to prize White racial heritage; that is, it may be an effort to counter the stigma of not being White enough. It also may be a form of reverse racism, that is, a manifestation of the belief that visibly unmixed Blacks are culturally and intellectually superior.

III. Color in Contemporary Law

A. Statutory Support for Color Claims

Courts have examined the question of color most extensively in the area of employment discrimination law. Title VII of the Civil Rights Act of 1964 and 42 U.S.C. § 1981 of the Civil Rights Act of 1866 are of particular relevance.[5] Title VII prohibits discrimination in employment on the basis of race, color, religion, sex, and national origin. Section 1981 provides, in part, that "[a]ll persons . . . shall have the same right . . . to make and enforce contracts . . . as is enjoyed by white citizens." Section 1981 contains neither the word "race" nor the word "color." The Supreme Court has held, however, that § 1981 affords a remedy against discrimination on the basis of race in both private and public employment.[6]

Courts should readily recognize color claims under Title VII given that the statute expressly includes color as a protected category. Absent strong evidence to negate this statutory language, a textual approach to statutory interpretation favors recognition of these claims. This conclusion is buttressed by evidence in Title VII's legislative history suggesting that Congress intended to provide protection against "shade" discrimination.

Although § 1981 does not use the word "color," the 1866 act does reference "white citizens." Use of this color-coded terminology implies that the statute extends to color claims. . . .

The Supreme Court has stated that the phrase "as enjoyed by white citizens" clarifies Congress's concern with the racial character of the rights protected under § 1981, but it has never directly addressed the issue of color. . . .

B. Substantive Content of Color Claims

. . . [L]itigants and the courts have often treated color synonymously with race without attempting to determine if and where these claims differ. *Porter v. Illinois Department of Children and Family Services*[7] illustrates this point. The plaintiff, a light-skinned Black male, filed a claim under Title VII alleging discrimination on the basis of both race and color. Neither the plaintiff nor the court made any attempt to distinguish between the two forms of discrimination. Rather, they both used the terms interchangeably.

. . . Analysis of the case law reveals that although courts have considered whether color claims are separately cognizable under Title VII and § 1981, few have afforded this question much attention in their written opinions. Most courts merely state that color claims either are or are not permitted, without offering any explanation for their conclusions and without delving too deeply into what makes a color claim analytically distinct.

Walker v. Internal Revenue Service[8] is a notable exception. In *Walker*, the United States District Court for the Northern District of Georgia held that an allegation of discrimination based on skin color states a cognizable claim under Title VII. There, a light-skinned Black employee alleged that her supervisor, a dark-skinned Black, discriminated against her because of her lighter skin tone. The court concluded that the plaintiff's claim was not barred because the plaintiff and her supervisor were of the same race. The court observed that, after the United States Supreme Court's 1987 decision in *Saint Francis College v. Al-Khazraji*,[9] "it is not even required that a victim of discrimination be of a distinctive physiognomical sub-grouping [from the perpetrator of the discrimination]." Thus the court was willing to recognize a color discrimination claim under Title VII when the plaintiff and the defendant were of the same race.

In allowing the action to proceed, the court also rejected the defendant's assertion that "color" has generally been interpreted to mean the same thing as "race." The court stated that both the statute and case law "repeatedly and distinctly refer to *race and color*." In attempting to distinguish color claims from race claims, the court explained that, in some situations, the most practical way to bring a Title VII suit may be on the basis of color as opposed to race. . . .

Walker is critically important because it is the first case in which a court recognized that Title VII provides a remedy for intraracial color discrimination. In addition, the opinion offers the most detailed judicial analysis of skin color discrimination to date. Indeed, other courts have shown a greater willingness to recognize color discrimination claims under Title VII after *Walker*. . . .

As an initial matter, the court in *Walker* is correct in concluding that the mere fact that a plaintiff and defendant are of the same race should not *legally* bar the bringing of an intraracial color claim. [I]t is not legally impossible for a Black plaintiff to prove that she was the victim of discrimination by a Black defendant.

The more subtle question raised by *Walker* concerns whether there should be a *factual* presumption that a Black defendant did not discriminate because the plaintiff is also Black. Such a presumption is insupportable. It is well documented that individuals within protected classifications are not immune from the forces of socialization at work in the larger society. These persons may incorporate the dominant society's views and may very well unconsciously act upon those views in ways that are harmful to members of their own groups. Thus women discriminate against women (e.g., on the basis of race). Men also discriminate against men (e.g., on the basis of masculinity or femininity). And . . . Blacks discriminate against Blacks (e.g., on the basis of skin color). As we know, some free mulattoes owned slaves; some light-skinned slaves believed they were intellectually and socially superior to darker slaves; and some light-skinned persons, favored by the White majority, expressed hostility toward their darker-skinned Black brethren and sought to disassociate themselves from darker Blacks in order to protect their favored status. Although conventional analysis relying on cases in other factual contexts could have been employed in *Walker* to destroy any factual presumption that discrimination does not occur between individuals of the same race, an understanding of colorism assists in this effort by explaining how such discrimination may occur between Blacks of varying skin tones. In short, it encourages courts to look beyond the broad category of race and to investigate the ways in which more subtle forms of discrimination occur.

Unfortunately for analytical purposes, the *Walker* opinion dealt only with intraracial color discrimination. The case involved a member of one race discriminating against a member of the same race on the basis of skin color. Because of this factual context, the court had no cause to examine the question of interracial color discrimination (a case where members of one race distinguish between members of a different race on the basis of skin color). Yet . . . interracial color discrimination exists. The question thus arises: Should courts treat interracial claims differently than intraracial claims? Should the fact that a White person awards benefits to a light-skinned Black individual create a factual presumption that she has not discriminated against a darker-skinned Black person? [T]he answer is no.

Fundamentally, interracial claims are no different from intraracial claims. As with intraracial claims, courts must not overlook interracial discrimination by proceeding blithely on the assumption that a White person cannot be racist if she awards benefits to someone within the same race as the plaintiff. We can readily comprehend the fallacy of this assumption when we acknowledge that a White person might distinguish between a Black person who has recently emigrated from Haiti and harbors an accompanying accent and a Black person who was born in the United States. In that situation, national origin supplies the basis for the intragroup comparison. Color operates in a similar fashion: lighter skin color, like the absence of a foreign accent, brings the person receiving favorable treatment closer to the preferred ideal—with skin color, that ideal is whiteness. Again, the central point is that one cannot allow a focus on broad racial categories to obscure the fact that racial groups are not monolithic and that nuanced forms of intragroup discrimination, like colorism, exist.

Finally, *Walker* fails to articulate clearly the essence of a color claim and how it differs from a race claim. The key point that needs to be understood is that colorism and racism are distinct phenomena that sometime[s] overlap. At times, racism will occur regardless of a person's color. Thus a person whose skin is White, but whose ancestors are known to be Black, may be classified as Black and subject to racist acts on that basis. At times, colorism will operate independently of race. Thus two individuals within the same racial classification may be subject to different treatment because of their varying skin tones. In that situation, the basis for distinction is not their placement in a particular racial category but rather their color within that category. Of course, the meaning afforded color may result from racist beliefs; that is to say, being light or dark may have meaning because being light or dark is associated with being of or closer to a certain racial ideal (i.e., White). However, the meaning afforded color may result from factors unrelated to racist beliefs. Colorism may stem from historically based assumptions about the correlation between color and socioeconomic class, color and beauty, color and intellect, or color and criminality, among other things. Finally, at times colorism and racism will overlap; that is, a person will be treated differently because of assumptions about both her race and her color. Thus a Black woman with chocolate brown skin may be subject to both racism and colorism simultaneously.

In sum, although they sometimes overlap, color claims are analytically different from race claims. The separation of individuals into racial categories and subsequent discrimination on that basis is, in essence, racism. The negative treatment of individuals on the basis of skin color is colorism. The danger is that if courts focus solely on race, they may overlook discrimination based on skin color because it may be difficult to believe that a person who hires Blacks will engage in discrimination against other Blacks, or that a person who is Black would discriminate against another Black person. If, however, courts understand colorism, then they are more likely to perceive the intricate ways in which people discriminate even within racial categories.

Notes

Published originally in 49 Duke Law Journal 1487 (2000).

1. *See* Michael G. Hughes and Bradley R. Hertel, *The Significance of Color Remains: A Study of Life Chances, Mate Selection, and Ethnic Consciousness among Black Americans,* 68 Social Forces 1105, 1116–17 (1990).
2. *See* Kathy Russell et al., The Color Complex: The Politics of Skin Color among African Americans 31–32 (1992).
3. *See* Kenneth B. Clark and Mamie P. Clark, *Racial Identification and Preference in Negro Children, in* Readings in Social Psychology (Eleanor E. Maccoby et al., eds., 1947). . . .
4. Numerous sociological studies have documented that lighter-skinned Blacks tend to fare better socially, educationally, economically, and politically than darker-skinned Blacks. *See, e.g.,* Hughes and Hertel, *supra,* at 1116–17 . . . ; Verna M. Keith and Cedric Herring, *Skin Tone and Stratification in the Black Community,* 97 American Journal of Sociology 760, 777 (1991) . . . ; Nayda Terkilsden, *When White Voters Evaluate Black Candidates: The Processing Implications of Candidate Skin Color, Prejudice, and Self-Monitoring,* 37 American Journal of Political Science 1032 *passim* (1993). . . .
5. 42 U.S.C. § 2000e (1994) ("Title VII"); 42 U.S.C. § 1981 (1994).
6. *See Johnson v. Railway Express Agency,* 421 U.S. 454, 459–60 (1975). . . .
7. No. 98-1158, 1998 Westlaw 847099 (7th Cir. Oct. 29, 1998).
8. 713 F. Supp. 403 (N.D. Ga. 1989).
9. 481 U.S. 604 (1987). . . .

51

Colorism
A Darker Shade of Pale

Taunya Lovell Banks

I. Introduction

. . . [T]he traditionally paradigmatic instance of race discrimination in America is discrimination by a member of one racialized group against a person from a different racialized group (interracial discrimination). The traditional paradigm operates even when the alleged basis for discrimination is not race but rather ethnicity, nationality, or color. Courts typically treat these latter categories as proxies for race.

More recently, the traditional American race discrimination paradigm has come under sustained challenge in cases brought by white ethnics and Latinas/os against members of their own race. In these cases, courts sometimes view ethnicity or color as a proxy for race. These same courts have been more reluctant to dissociate color from race in the context of cases brought by blacks. . . . U.S. courts rigidly adhere to the commonly accepted notion that a person with *any known* African ancestry is raced as black. [See Part 2—Ed.] An overwhelming majority of people raced as black in the United States, however, have mixed ancestry and vary widely both in skin tone and phenotypical characteristics. . . . African ancestry trumps all other racial markers.

In practice, . . . differences in skin tone and phenotype among black people do have meaning in the United States, especially for blacks with the darkest skin tones and the least European phenotypes. Social science studies indicate that blacks and whites, and perhaps other nonwhites, distinguish among blacks based on skin tone. Yet the government's definition of the racial category "black" impedes recognition by courts that black people can be differentially racialized. To the extent that discrimination laws seek to address impermissible treatment based on membership in a different racialized group, the reluctance of courts to view shades of color as a relevant criterion in discrimination claims by and against blacks is ill founded.

The need for courts to pay attention to discrimination based on skin tone and phenotype is heightened by the changing demographics of American society. In the twenty-first century, discrimination cases are less likely to be of the traditional transracial type and more likely to be about gradations in physical characteristics among members of ostensibly the same racialized group. . . .

In this article, I suggest that colorism, skin tone discrimination against dark-skinned but not light-skinned blacks, constitutes a form of race-based discrimination.

Skin tone discrimination coexists with more traditional forms of race discrimination that affect all blacks without regard to skin tone and phenotype. I use employment discrimination cases to illustrate the willingness of the courts to acknowledge more subtle forms of race-based discrimination for white ethnics and Latinas/os, and the inability of the courts to fashion a coherent approach to colorism claims involving black claimants.

II. Colorism and the Courts

Litigants usually rely on two statutes to advance colorism discrimination claims: Title VII of the Civil Rights Act of 1964[1] and 42 U.S.C. section 1981.[2] . . .

A. Section 1981 Cases

1. Early Colorism Cases

Latinas/os do not fit neatly within America's traditional rigid racial categories. . . . Because section 1981 does not cover discrimination based on national origin, courts often struggle to fit discrimination claims by Latina/o plaintiffs into the section 1981 framework.

In some early section 1981 colorism cases involving Latina/o plaintiffs, courts used ethnicity as a synonym for race if the plaintiff's racial identity was unclear. These courts linked skin tone with ethnicity in recognizing a race claim. For example, in 1977, when the Mexican American plaintiff in *Vigil v. City of Denver*[3] sued his public employer under section 1981, alleging discrimination based on race, color, and national origin, the court allowed the color claim, reasoning that Mexican Americans often are identified on the basis of their skin tone, and thus a claim of discrimination based on color may be a basis for discrimination against Mexican Americans. Even though Mexican Americans were classified by the government in the 1970s as white for census purposes [see Part 4—Ed.], the court said:

> Although skin color may vary significantly among individuals who are considered Mexican-Americans, skin color may be a basis for discrimination against them. We note that skin color may vary significantly among individuals who are considered "blacks" or "whites"; both these groups are protected by § 1981, and § 1981 is properly asserted where discrimination on the basis of color is alleged. Indeed, the Supreme Court has concluded that in the Denver area, Mexican-Americans are victims of the same type of discriminatory treatment as blacks: ["]Negroes and Hispanoes in Denver suffer identical discrimination in treatment when compared with the treatment afforded Anglo students.["]

The court linked ethnicity and discrimination based on dark skin tone with discrimination against blacks, suggesting that dark skin tone is a negative racial marker.

Courts' willingness to draw connections between race and the ethnicity and skin tone of Latinas/os is a thread running through the section 1981 cases involving Latina/o litigants. . . .

Courts seem less willing to make this connection when the race of the Latina/o litigant is clearly identified. In *O'Loughlin v. Procon, Inc.*,[4] a section 1981 race claim, the plaintiff, described as "a black male citizen of Cuba," lost in part because the court concluded that the absence of claims by other blacks about racial slurs was proof that the plaintiff's claims were groundless. The court failed to consider that because the plaintiff, Hugh O'Loughlin, was black *and* Cuban, he might have been differentially racialized from black Americans due to his ethnicity.[5]

Thus, if a plaintiff's race is unclear, . . . the courts use ethnicity and skin tone as surrogates for race. As one court said in allowing a claim by a Mexican American under section 1981, race encompasses "some non-racial . . . ethnic groups." When, however, the plaintiff's race is clearly identified, as in *O'Loughlin*, courts tend to ignore the impact of skin tone and ethnicity. This tendency has a disproportionate impact on litigants with apparent African ancestry.

Courts' refusal to consider the impact of ethnicity in race claims involving black litigants is even more apparent in disputes between two black litigants. In *Sere v. Board of Trustees*,[6] the plaintiff, a black Nigerian, sued his light-skinned black American supervisor, alleging discrimination based on race and national origin. The federal district court dismissed Sere's discrimination claim, treating his case as a national origin claim and thus not cognizable under section 1981. The court labeled both Sere and his light-skinned black American supervisor as black, and it noted that Sere's replacement was a light-skinned black American. In dismissing Sere's colorism claim, the trial judge acknowledged that discrimination based on skin tone can occur among members of the same racialized group but concluded that the plaintiff failed to establish that a colorism claim was actionable under section 1981. The court opined that recognition of colorism claims would force courts to engage "in the unsavory business of measuring skin color and determining whether the skin pigmentation of the parties is sufficiently different to form the basis of a lawsuit." Yet, in other cases involving Latinas/os, courts seem more willing to engage in just this sort of inquiry.

In both *O'Loughlin* and *Sere*, the courts view race discrimination very narrowly. This narrow construction of race for parties with any African ancestry ignores ethnic or color differences between the parties that result in different racial statuses. . . . Any *remote* African ancestry makes one indistinguishably black and blinds courts to the racial meanings conveyed by ethnicity and skin color. The preference by some white and black employers for light-skinned black employees is grounded in the stigma attached to African slavery. Thus skin tone bias, rather than traditional racial animus, can be an alternative basis of discrimination against a dark-skinned person of African descent.

2. Saint Francis College v. Al-Khazraji

As the preceding discussion suggests, courts in the early section 1981 colorism cases failed consistently to recognize ethnic or color differences when analyzing race-based discrimination claims. Any uncertainty in this area should have been resolved when the U.S. Supreme Court in *Saint Francis College v. Al-Khazraji*[7] recognized that a section 1981 race claim can lie between parties of different ethnicities who are members of the same race. The plaintiff, Majid Ghaidan Al-Khazraji, a man of Iraqi descent, claimed that he has denied tenure in violation of section 1981 because he was of the Arabian race. Iraqis are classified as white under United States law. Saint Francis College argued unsuccessfully that Al-Khazraji, a white person, could not sue another white person alleging racial discrimination under section 1981.

Pointing out that racial categories in this country have changed since the nineteenth century when section 1981 was enacted, the Court cited examples of European ethnic groups that were considered separate races in the 1860s and 1870s. It acknowledged that "[c]lear-cut [racial] categories do not exist . . . [and] some, but not all, scientists . . . conclude that racial classifications are for the most part sociopolitical, rather than biological, in nature." Thus the Court concluded that Congress intended section 1981 to protect "identifiable classes of persons who are subjected to intentional discrimination solely because of their ancestry or ethnic characteristics," whether or not the discrimination would be classified as racial in terms of modern scientific theory.

3. Later Colorism Cases

The court in *Saint Francis College* arguably permitted interethnic discrimination claims to be brought in American courts. The post–*Saint Francis College* cases have tended to recognize interethnic claims between members of the same racial group—unless the parties are black. The First Circuit, for example, suggested in *Sinai v. New England Telephone & Telegraph Co.*[8] that an Israeli of Jewish/Hebrew ancestry could establish a race-based discrimination claim against a white person (presumably not of Jewish/Hebrew ancestry) under section 1981 by stating that "the jury could find that Israel is one of those countries in which the populace is composed primarily of a particular race." The Third Circuit has also treated discrimination claims between ethnic whites as interracial claims.

Yet a black litigant who brought a post–*Saint Francis College* interethnic claim fared no better than the pre–*Saint Francis College* litigant in *Sere*. In *Ohemeng v. Delaware State College*,[9] a black Ghanaian college professor asserted a race-based discrimination claim under both section 1981 and Title VII. The employer, Delaware State College, a historically black college, discharged Ohemeng rather than considering him for two positions for which he qualified. Instead, the college hired two Americans, a black and a white. Relying, no doubt, on the rationale in *Saint Francis College*, Ohemeng initially argued that "he belonged to a subset of the Negroid race having a distinct ancestry or distinct ethnic characteristics" from black Americans. Professor Ohemeng stated a claim similar to that of the plaintiff in *Saint Francis College*, but the district court in a footnote responded that the "plaintiff [had] not factually developed that claim." One wonders what more Professor Ohemeng needed to prove. In a footnote, the court said that Ohemeng had failed to establish a race discrimination claim under either section 1981 or Title VII because he was replaced by a black American.

B. Title VII Colorism Cases

Unlike section 1981, Title VII specifically mentions "color" as a protected category. . . .

Given the anecdotal and social scientific evidence regarding colorism discussed earlier, one would assume that the most common colorism case would involve a dark-skinned claimant suing to address the inequity resulting from the social capital possessed by light-skinned members of the same racialized group. Yet two of the earliest Title VII in-group colorism cases, *Ali v. National Bank of Pakistan*[10] and *Walker* [see Chapter 50—Ed.], involved light-skinned claimants. In *Ali*, a light-skinned Pakistani from the Punjab province accused his supervisor, a dark-skinned Pakistan citizen from the Sind province, of discrimination based on skin tone variation among Pakistanis. The federal district court dismissed the Title VII claim, saying that Ali failed to establish that his treatment was based on skin color. The court suggested, however, that colorism claims arising from discriminatory practices not linked to racial subordination in the United States are actionable under federal law.

A similar conclusion by the trial judge in *Felix v. Marquez*[11] seems crucial to recognition of the colorism claim in that case. Carmen Felix, a Puerto Rican native, sued another Puerto Rican native, claiming that she was discriminated against because of her race. The judge concluded that a discrimination claim by one Puerto Rican "with a mixed racial ancestry" against another Puerto Rican presumably of "unmixed" racial ancestry represented one of those rare colorism cases. After a detailed discussion of Felix's genealogy and phenotypical characteristics, the trial judge noted that Felix's maternal grandfather was black and that her father "had the physical characteristics of a person with a partial African ancestry." His comments on the appearance of a witness in the case reaffirmed the importance, in his mind, of skin tone as a racial marker. He wrote: "[W]ith due respect for his emphatic testimony that [the witness] considers his race to be Puerto Rican, his color would cause him to be identified in the continental United States as Black." In *Felix*, the plaintiff's skin tone and phenotype used in tandem with genealogy operated as racial markers.

The decision in *Felix* also suggests that race is a separate and distinct category from ethnicity. Sidestepping the fact that both parties were Puerto Ricans and the legal meaning attaching to this fact, the judge explained that a pure colorism claim was rare "because color is usually mixed or subordinated to claims of race discrimination."

The court sees color claims as being subsumed by race, obscuring the way in which skin tone within a racialized group can mediate racial discrimination. As a result, what on its face appears to be an intragroup colorism claim becomes an interracial colorism claim. This result is possible because the court treats Puerto Ricans as an ethnic group composed of many races.

III. A Preview of Future Colorism Claims?

One . . . case, *Rodriguez v. Gattuso*,[12] looks more like the interracial colorism claims I anticipate in the future. Robert Rodriguez, described by the court as "a United States citizen of black Latino ancestry," spoke by telephone with Biagio Gattuso about renting one of his apartments. When Rodriguez, who is dark-skinned, met with Gattuso, he was told that the apartment was no longer available. The next day, when Rodriguez's wife, Carol, characterized by the court as "a United States citizen of white Latino ancestry," telephoned to confirm that the apartment was not available, Gattuso told her that the apartment was vacant, and she agreed to meet with him. After meeting with Carol Rodriguez, Gattuso wanted to meet her husband before finalizing the deal. A few days later, when both Roberto and Carol arrived to finalize the agreement, Gattuso "reacted in an excited and nervous manner, offering several excuses." Gattuso claimed that there were two couples ahead of Roberto and Carol Rodriguez, that the apartment would not be ready for another few weeks, and that he did not know whether Roberto and Carol Rodriguez were capable of paying the rent.

The court permitted the colorism claim under [the applicable housing discrimination laws], saying that

> [m]ost often "race" and "color" discrimination are viewed as synonymous, just as the term "white citizens" is most often contrasted with "black citizens"—a racial distinction. But the very inclusion of "color" as a separate term in addition to "race" in [the housing laws] implies strongly that someone who is of the same race ("race" used in the ethnic sense, not the broader sense announced in *St. Francis College v. Al-Khazraji* as the 19th century understanding of that term) but who is treated differently because of his dark skin has been discriminated against because of his *color*—something expressly forbidden by [the law].

Thus the federal district court in *Rodriguez* does a better job of seeing the differences and connections among race, ethnicity, and skin color. Ironically, *Rodriguez* was decided by the same district court that denied the colorism claim in *Sere* six years earlier.

IV. Implications and Reflections

The confusion of courts regarding the complexities of racialization will become even more apparent when the increasing number of people who classify themselves as bi- and multiracial or as white nevertheless encounter discrimination because others identify them as black or nonwhite. Ironically, those features most often associated with black people—dark skin color, a broad nose, woolly hair, large buttocks, and thick lips—and most easily used as racial markers will have less evidentiary weight in establishing discrimination without recognition of colorism claims.

Despite the need to recognize and address discrimination based on skin tone, caution about colorism claims is warranted. One lesson the Title VII and section 1981 cases teach us is that colorism claims between black litigants are difficult to sustain and to distinguish from claims based on personal antagonism unrelated to skin color. Further complicating matters is the question of whether color preference and the resulting discrimination may be something practiced by all cultures as a result of politically and socially motivated bias, an issue raised by the *Ali* case.

In addition, any recognition of colorism claims also must address the difficulty with using the courts to make skin tone distinctions with significant legal implications. The federal district judge in *Felix*, for example, had great difficulty making legally significant color distinctions. The subjective character of color distinctions is illustrated by the way the judge describes Carmen Felix, as of a medium shade, and the way she describes herself, as dark olive. Arguably these terms carry different implications. The judge's characterization of Felix as of a medium shade suggests that her complexion is medium brown, and brown skin tone has a distinct racial connotation in the United States: It means *nonwhite*. However, the term "olive," used by *Felix*, is often used to describe Southern Europeans such as Italians or other European ethnic groups considered white in the United States. Descriptions of skin tone in this country invariably convey race. Thus solutions are understandably elusive.

Notes

Originally published in 47 UCLA Law Review 1705 (2000).

1. Pub. L. No. 88-352, § 703, 78 Stat. 255 (1964). Title VII provides in relevant part:

> It shall be an unlawful employment practice for an employer— (1) to fail or refuse to hire or to discharge any individual, or otherwise to discriminate against any individual with respect to his compensation, terms, conditions, or privileges of employment, because of such individual's race, color, religion, sex, or national origin.

42 U.S.C. § 2000e-2(a)(1) (1994).

2. 42 U.S.C. § 1981 (1994). Section 1981(a) provides:

> All persons within the jurisdiction of the United States shall have the same right in every State and Territory to make and enforce contracts, to sue, be parties, give evidence, and to the full and equal benefit of all laws and proceedings for the security of persons and property as is enjoyed by white citizens, and shall be subject to likc punishment, pains, penalties, taxes, licenses, and exactions of every kind, and to no other....

3. No. 77-F-197, 1977 WestLaw 41 (D. Colo. May 23, 1977).

4. 627 F. Supp. 675 (E.D. Tex. 1986).

5. Ethnicity often is confused with national origin. National origin usually refers to the country of *recent* origin, whereas ethnicity is often used to denote ancestry, the cultural identity or origin of one's ancestors. In fact, from a legal perspective, there may be little real difference between race and ethnicity in the United States....

6. 628 F. Supp. 1543 (N.D. Ill. 1986), *aff'd*, 852 F.2d 285 (8th Cir. 1988).

7. 481 U.S. 604 (1987).

8. 3 F.3d 471 (1st Cir. 1993).

9. 676 F. Supp. 65 (D. Del. 1988).

10. 508 F. Supp. 611 (S.D.N.Y. 1981).

11. No. 78-2314, 1981 WestLaw 271 (D.D.C. March 26, 1981).

12. 795 F. Supp. 860 (N.D. Ill. 1992).

52

Who Is Black Enough for You?

An Analysis of Northwestern University Law School's Struggle over Minority Faculty Hiring

Leonard M. Baynes

I. The O'Brien Hylton Hiring Controversy at Northwestern

. . . Professor [Maria] O'Brien Hylton was a tenured member of the DePaul University Law Faculty. Her husband, Dr. Keith Hylton, was an untenured member of the Northwestern University Law Faculty. In the summer and fall of 1994, Boston University Law School heavily recruited and offered immediate tenure to both [Maria] O'Brien Hylton and Keith Hylton.

In an effort to retain Keith Hylton, Northwestern considered O'Brien Hylton for a teaching position. According to its then-dean Robert L. Bennett, Northwestern considered O'Brien Hylton for a teaching position because "we wanted to retain her husband, who is a valued member of the faculty." Dean Bennett further stated that "[w]e would have wanted to retain him regardless of his color." Despite a hiring freeze at Northwestern, Professor O'Brien Hylton was interviewed. Dean Bennett reported that the faculty appointments committee reviewed Professor Maria O'Brien Hylton's "scholarly writings, looked at her teaching experience and weighed such things as academic interest, collegiality and quality and style of scholarship."

Professor Keith Hylton is of the opinion that his wife's candidacy lost support because of a concerted campaign against O'Brien Hylton's candidacy by students. Student groups in the Northwestern community were not sanguine to O'Brien Hylton's candidacy. The chair of the Black student group believed that O'Brien Hylton should not be counted as Black. Meanwhile, the co-chair of the Latino student group said that O'Brien Hylton should not be counted as Hispanic either, because she "seems to identify more as a Black." Some female students objected to O'Brien Hylton's candidacy because they believed she was being considered solely because of her husband. As a result, both Hyltons lost interest in going to Northwestern and were contemplating going to Boston University.

The racial and ethnic identity of Professor O'Brien Hylton also became an issue when, according to O'Brien Hylton, Professor Joyce Hughes [of Northwestern] personally called O'Brien Hylton. Hughes was not a member of the faculty appointments committee. According to O'Brien Hylton, Hughes asked O'Brien Hylton whether she should be considered "a minority candidate." O'Brien Hylton said that the "gist of Professor Hughes's questioning was, 'How black are you?'"

In late October, an informal faculty meeting was held to discuss O'Brien Hylton's candidacy. At the meeting, Professor Joyce Hughes allegedly argued that O'Brien Hylton should not be considered "a minority candidate."

Subsequently two members of the faculty appointments committee met with O'Brien Hylton alone and stated that they were not going to recommend a tenured offer to the faculty, but that they were willing to go forward with offering her a visiting or untenured position. When asked why, O'Brien Hylton was told that, although the appointments committee was "unanimous on the merits," among the faculty there were "enough votes in opposition to kill the offer, and that in light of this and the controversy, it would be 'too divisive' to put the recommendation before the faculty." O'Brien Hylton rejected the offer. After O'Brien Hylton rejected the offer, the appointments committee decided not to go forward with a recommendation of any sort. As a result of the controversy, both Hyltons accepted the tenured positions at Boston University.

O'Brien Hylton did not help clarify these concerns about her racial and/or ethnic identification when she told the *New York Times* that she did not define herself in "racial terms" and that "I really don't spend a lot of time defining myself; other people do."[1] However, in a *Boston Globe* interview, O'Brien Hylton reported that she identified herself as "Black" on a form she completed as a clerk for a federal judge.[2] She also stated that she had been a member of Black organizations in college, in law school, and while practicing [law]. . . .

II. Black as Defined by Social Construct

So many times in the African American community, a person is ostracized for not being "Black" enough. Much of this self-definition may be an effort by the African American community to control the definition of who is Black. People cannot be "Black" if they are too light-skinned, if they are too middle-class, if they are too ambitious, if they are too refined, if they work too hard, if they are married to (or otherwise affiliated with) a White person, if they never lived in the ghetto or now do not live in the ghetto, if they have too many White friends, if they speak and write in standard English, if they are too well educated, or if they are not born in the United States. The list of characteristics excludes so many people that I sometimes wonder how many people are really "Black."

This type of comment happens often in the African American community. The recipients of these comments are not even necessarily of any particular economic class or complexion. It sometimes happens when students are succeeding academically in school and someone says that "they are acting White." This situation is exemplified by the Spike Lee film *School Daze,* which takes place at an all-Black college. [See Chapter 49—Ed.]

This process of definition by exclusion seems to be a contest as to who is the most victimized—and probably disguises a fear by those doing the excluding that they are being left behind and rejected. In doing so, it fails to appreciate that anyone of African ancestry in the United States, regardless of skin color, economic status, affiliation with White people, educational level, or national origin, is subject to some form of racial discrimination by some White Americans.

Maria O'Brien Hylton is a classic New York ethnic combination. Her mother is an African Cuban and her father is a White Australian of Irish ancestry. In her response to the *New York Times* interviewer, Maria O'Brien Hylton said that she did not think of herself in racial terms. Yet in an interview with the *Boston Globe*, Maria O'Brien Hylton seemed to give an inconsistent response when she told the interviewer that she always considered herself Black. Of course, these two statements may not necessarily be inconsistent. First, many people who feel comfortable with their Blackness do not feel it is necessary to define themselves in racial terms. Given that the African American community defines "Black" by means of exclusion, this desire not to define oneself by using racial constructions will pose problems with some members of that community. Second, Maria O'Brien Hylton is of a multiracial background; she is both Black and White. Her responses to these questions are congruent with her mixed race ethnic background. . . .

III. Analysis

A. Race in Faculty Hiring

In Maria O'Brien Hylton's case, Northwestern had a rare opportunity to meet several potential affirmative action needs in one faculty hire, namely, to employ a woman who happened to be Black and a Latina. However, Professor Maria O'Brien Hylton's candidacy was opposed by the student groups one would expect to be her natural constituents—women, African Americans, and Latinos/Latinas. Enthusiastic support by these groups for Maria O'Brien Hylton's candidacy may have moved the school to offer her a tenured position. Maria O'Brien Hylton's race and gender may not have been the pivotal factors in Northwestern's decision, but given the discussion about race and gender concerning her candidacy, these had to be major factors in her being considered for the position in the first place.

B. Scrutiny of Faculty Candidates of Color by Faculty of Color in the Hiring Process

Many observers were outraged by the Northwestern hiring debate. Many Whites use the Northwestern hiring debate as an example of the intraracial prejudice that exists in the African American community. They did not understand "what not being Black enough was." The news media worsened the situation by failing to clarify the issues and instead sensationalizing them. Many people of color were also outraged by the Northwestern hiring debate. The newspaper accounts trivialized an important discussion of a complex issue. In the process, several members of our community—Joyce Hughes, Maria O'Brien Hylton, and Keith Hylton—were scapegoated. Furthermore, the issue was raised at the wrong time and in the wrong way—in the midst of a hiring decision. The hiring struggle also had the potential to drive a rift between and among African Americans and Latinos/Latinas.

Notes

Published originally in 2 Michigan Journal of Race and Law 205 (1997). Copyright © 1997 by Michigan Journal of Race and Law. Reprinted with permission.

1. Rohan Preston, *Battle to Keep a Black Professor Leaves Bruised Egos and Reputations*, New York Times, March 8, 1995, at B8.

2. Irene Sege, *Not Black Enough? Law Professor Heads to BU after Furor at Northwestern over Her Racial Identity*, Boston Globe, February 9, 1995, Living section, at 63.

53

Social and Legal Repercussions of Latinos' Colonized Mentality

Laura M. Padilla

II. Internalized Oppression and Racism

Internalized racism has been the primary means by which we have been forced to perpetuate and "agree" to our own oppression.[1]

A. Working Definitions of Internalized Oppression and Racism

When a victim experiences a hurt that is not healed, distress patterns emerge whereby the victim engages in harmful behavior. Internalized oppression has been described as the process in which these distress patterns reveal themselves:

> [T]hese distress patterns, *created by oppression and racism from the outside*, have been played out in the only two places it has seemed "safe" to do so. First, upon members of our own group—particularly upon those over whom we have some degree of power or control. . . . Second, upon ourselves through all manner[s] of self-invalidation, self-doubt, isolation, fear, feelings of powerlessness and despair. . . .[2]

Thus internalized oppression commences externally; that is, dominant players start the chain of behavior through racist and discriminatory behavior. This could range from exclusion because of race (e.g., from a job or a store), to negative generalizations about a race (e.g., "We don't need any more wetbacks—they just take away our jobs") and capitalization on the fears created by those generalizations, to derogatory comments about a particular individual on racial grounds (e.g., "We shouldn't give her the job—she'll miss too much work because Mexican women are always pregnant").

Those at the receiving end of the prejudicial behavior then internalize negative perceptions about themselves and other members of their own group and act accordingly. When this internalization process occurs within a particular racial or ethnic group, it manifests itself at [different] levels.

B. Internalized Racism in the Latino Community

Internalized oppression operates rather uniformly, regardless of ethnicity or sexual orientation, through some common patterns of behavior, yet it also manifests itself uniquely depending on the negative stereotypes it causes a particular group to internalize. Internalized racism has its roots in internalized oppression; that is, there is always some triggering oppressive behavior. For Latinos, we "share a unique experience of oppression and survival in the United States. Mexicans and Puerto Ricans, who constitute the largest and oldest Latino/a communities within the official borders of the United States, were attacked, invaded, colonized, annexed, and exploited by the United States."[3] Racist and discriminatory behavior toward Latinos is clearly deep-rooted. After the Mexican American War ended in 1848, people of Mexican origin faced lynchings, land theft, and virulent racism. Later, in times of economic depression, people of Mexican origin—citizens and noncitizens alike—were deported en masse. . . . As a result, many Mexican-origin people internalized the racism and learned to despise all things Mexican.

It is our unique history that we have internalized that gives rise to our particular brand of internalized racism. Latinos, for example, may be conditioned to believe that other Latinos, particularly recent immigrants, are unfairly taking advantage of U.S. social services, or we may refrain from using Spanish in professional settings because it will betray our heritage, or we may believe that whiter is better. "From the Latina/o viewpoint, the desirability of whiteness represents the internalization by the colonized of the colonizers' predilections."[4] . . .

At the corporate level, internalized racism involves harmful or destructive conduct by members of a group toward other members of the group. "[Internalized racism] has been a major ingredient in the distressful and unworkable relationships which we so often have with each other. It has proved to be the fatal stumbling block of every promising and potentially powerful . . . liberation effort that has failed in the past."[5] Internalized racism at the corporate level can thus thwart Latinos' empowerment efforts. For example, Latino groups often wither when leadership issues revolve around how "ethnic" one is. To wit, at California Western School of Law, one year a majority of the La Raza law students refused to elect a blonde student to a board position because she was not perceived to be "Mexican" enough, even though she was born in Mexico and was a committed activist. Politics of race impeded her advancement and prevented her from performing work beneficial to the Latino community. The same politics of race exists among the La Raza Lawyers Association of San Diego, where members' credibility is sometimes based on whether they are perceived as "too dark" or "too light," depending on the issue.

Internalized racism in the Latino community also reveals itself at the individual level. For example, members of my family, as well as their friends, have attempted to one-up each other about how *guero* [fair, light-skinned, or "White"; see Chapter 32—Ed.] their children or grandchildren are. My mother's best friend once bragged about how *guera* her first granddaughter was as she pulled out a photograph of a . . . dark baby with thick black hair. Rather than question why her friend felt compelled to assert her granddaughter's "*guera*-ness," my mother and I instead later compared the granddaughter's "*guera*-ness" to the "*guera/o*-ness" of our own family members. We succumbed to the conditioning that white is better. Latinos also use this grading process to rank the acceptability of boyfriends, girlfriends, spouses, and partners. Lighter is preferred; darker is acceptable as long as that person is Latino. To go any darker may put you at risk of family alienation. As one Latino expressed:

> The unpleasant truth is that whether or not Mexican-Americans consider interracial relationships to be acceptable has everything to do with the specific race involved. The clearest analogy: a ladder. The social ladder, if you will. At the top of the ladder is the color white, owing to generational assumptions that the fair-skinned shall inherit the earth. At the bottom is the color black, the color of subjugation. Inferiority. In the middle, nesting precariously between the extremes, is the color brown.[6]

I married a Caucasian and in reflecting on why, I realize that the reasons are many, complex, and positive, and that I never consciously chose to not marry a Latino. However, it is not as clear to me whether I subconsciously chose to not marry a Latino. While I spent much time with my Latino classmates, especially in connection with the Stanford Latino Law Students' Association (SLLSA), I did not date them. One reason, at least in law school, was that there were not many Latinos to choose from and many of them had girlfriends. Another reason was that I saw too many marriages in my family break up because of the man's infidelity. Of course, I did not then assume that all Latino males were unfaithful, but it made me nervous. That nervousness was compounded when I became active with the La Raza Lawyers Association of San Diego. At parties and out-of-town conferences, I noticed that a significant number of men suddenly lost their wedding rings and seemed to spend too much time with women who were not their wives. So I remind myself that this behavior is characteristic of many men, not just Latinos. Am I succumbing to internalized racism by believing negative stereotypes about Latino men, or am I being practical? That is one of the dangers of internalized oppression; we frequently do not realize when or how we are prejudiced against ourselves.

Notes

Published originally in 53 University of Miami Law Review 769 (1999).

1. Suzanne Lipskey, Internalized Racism 1 (1987).
2. Lipskey, *supra*, at 3–4.
3. Angel R. Oquendo, *Re-Imagining the Latina/o Race,* 12 Harvard BlackLetter Law Journal 93, 120 (1995).
4. Berta Esperanza Hernández-Truyol, *Borders (En)Gendered: Normativities, Latinas, and a LatCrit Paradigm,* 72 New York University Law Review 882, 900 (1997).
5. Lipskey, *supra*, at 1. . . .
6. Ruben Navarrette Jr., A Darker Shade of Crimson: Odyssey of a Harvard Chicano 107 (1993).

54

Immigration and Latino Identity

Kevin R. Johnson

I. Immigration and Intra-Latino Conflict

Immigration occasionally has contributed to *inter*group and *intra*group conflict. Conflict between Latinos and African Americans has been studied and at various times has been sensationalized by the media. For example, in a well-known *Atlantic Monthly* article, Jack Miles contends that employers in Los Angeles prefer docile Mexican immigrants over African Americans.[1] Similarly, heavy press coverage has focused on Cuban–African American conflict in Miami and African American–Central American tensions in the Washington, D.C., metropolitan area.[2]

While *inter*group hostility receives attention, *intra*group conflict between immigrants from Mexico and the established Mexican American community in the United States is generally ignored. Such tension, however, is almost inevitable in light of the immigration and the ongoing diversification of the Latino community. [Importantly, many Mexican immigrants today are darker and more indigenous-appearing than the more assimilated and fairer, established Mexican Americans in the United States.—Ed.] Moreover, the unequal distribution of legal rights among Latinos contributes to the tensions. Many laws, for example, distinguish between Latinos based on immigration status. Latino noncitizens can be deported while Latino citizens cannot. . . .

The Supreme Court has sanctioned legal distinctions made between Latino immigrants and citizens. In *Espinoza v. Farah Manufacturing Co.*,[3] the Supreme Court held that Title VII of the Civil Rights Act of 1964 did not prohibit discrimination on the basis of alienage status, even though it barred discrimination based on race and national origin. In so doing, the Court affirmed dismissal of the claim of Cecilia Espinoza, a lawful permanent resident from Mexico married to a U.S. citizen. Similarly, in *Mathews v. Diaz,*[4] a case brought by Cuban noncitizens lawfully in this country, the Supreme Court rejected an equal protection challenge to a federal law denying federal medical benefits to certain legal immigrants. . . .

A. Intra-Latino Conflict in Los Angeles

1. Hostility between Mexican Americans and Mexican Immigrants

Divisions exist in the Mexican American community on the issue of immigration. To state the obvious, not all (and perhaps not many) Mexican Americans favor open borders with Mexico. Indeed, about 25 percent of Latino voters, all citizens who are more or less integrated into the political community, supported California's now infamous Proposition 187, which bars undocumented persons from receiving public benefits. Such restrictionist sentiments make it uncertain where undocumented Mexican immigrants fit into the broader Latino community. This uncertainty has historically been a difficult issue for Chicano activists. For example, in attempting to organize farmworkers, César Chávez and the United Farm Workers struggled to establish a principled position on undocumented Mexican immigrants because, while agricultural growers hired them to break strikes, undocumented Mexican immigrants formed the core of the union's membership.

Many Mexican Americans, who as a group are racialized by Anglo society, desire to restrict immigration because of the distinctions that they make between themselves and Mexican immigrants. A prominent example of this phenomenon can be seen in East Los Angeles, a well-established Mexican American community that was the site of Chicano activism in the 1960s, which has experienced a steady stream of Mexican immigrants during the last part of this century. This immigration has been accompanied by the growth of anti-immigrant sentiment among Mexican Americans in the area. Some have claimed Mexican immigrants are too poor, that too many live in the same home (causing property values to decline), and that the increase in Spanish-speaking children in the schools impedes the education of non-Spanish-speaking children. Some Mexican Americans whose parents were barred from speaking Spanish when they were in school have changed Catholic churches so that they can attend masses conducted in English, not Spanish. One young Mexican American's explanation of the differences between Mexican Americans and Mexican immigrants in another southwestern city sheds some light on the tensions in East Los Angeles: "[I]t's not that we hate them or anything. . . . It's just that we don't have anything in common with them. I don't speak Spanish. I don't listen to their music. *We just come from different worlds.*"[5]

Sentiments like these have had a palpable impact on Latino lives. Mexican Americans reportedly have threatened to call the Immigration and Naturalization Service on Mexican immigrants, whom they at times refer to as "wetbacks." Mike Contreras, a second-generation Mexican American, admits to yelling "Turn down that wetback music" to any newcomer blaring *ranchera* (Mexican country) music.[6] Some Mexican Americans speak of Mexican immigrants overconsuming public benefits and express fear about losing jobs to cheap immigrant labor. At the same time that dominant society accuses Mexican Americans of not assimilating into the mainstream, some Mexican Americans claim that the new Mexican immigrants fail to assimilate.

Mexican immigrants, not surprisingly, tell very different stories. The immigrants say, "Mexican Americans think they are 'superior' to us. We are willing to work hard while 'Americans' are not." The immigrants criticize Mexican Americans for speaking poor Spanish, for being traitors to their heritage, and having coddled childhoods; in effect, they are *pochos*.[7] One Mexican immigrant in Los Angeles claimed to have developed friendships with Anglos and African Americans rather then Mexican Americans who denigrated Mexican immigrants as "wetbacks" and "beaners."

As this demonstrates, Mexican Americans and Mexican immigrants at some level have different group identities and speak with different "voices." This comes as no surprise considering the two groups' different experiences and social positions in the United States. Besides differences in class and immigration status, many new Mexican immigrants in the 1990s have more indigenous features and dark complexions that render them less able to assimilate than fair-complexioned Latinos.

2. Causes of the Conflict

Tensions between Mexican Americans and Mexican immigrants are rooted in class and social status. Class differences between the established Mexican American and Mexican immigrant communities are exacerbated by the poor rural roots of many Mexican immigrants.

Moreover, the tension in part reflects Mexican American adoption of dominant society's racial attitudes and values. Despite claims to the contrary, all immigrant groups assimilate to some degree, even if dominant society refuses to extend them full membership in society. Some assimilation inevitably results from extended immersion in a different culture. Part of immigrant efforts to assimilate may include the adoption of the dominant society's racism. Unfortunately, this is the case for some Latinos.

As one observer noted, "Discrimination and racist behavior generally are [processes] by which one racial group seeks to produce esteem for itself by lowering the status of the other group. . . . Status comes about by disparaging others, by asserting and reinforcing a claim to superior social rank."[8] This sort of status-seeking is particularly acute for immigrants:

> [N]ewly arrived immigrants unable to speak the dominant language have often lost whatever status they enjoyed in their homeland, while their reason for having left is often to gain a higher status than was possible in their homeland. During this time of high status mobility, many immigrants engage in high levels of discrimination. Status competition explains the tension that often exists between different minority groups as each new group seeks to establish its place in the social hierarchy.[9]

Hostility between Mexican immigrants and Mexican Americans reflects competition for the scarce resource of social status. As one political scientist explained, "What happens is the assimilated people feel embarrassed by the poverty and rural ways of the immigrants. Mexican-Americans want to fit into the American culture and do not want to be associated with immigrants."[10] Mexican Americans in essence seek placement at a higher rung of the social ladder than Mexican immigrants. In attempting to attain that goal, they distinguish between themselves and Mexican immigrants in ways remarkably similar to how Anglos distinguish between themselves and Mexican Americans. This suggests that in certain circumstances Mexican Americans may side with dominant society, not other racially subordinated peoples.

Notes

1. Jack Miles, *Blacks vs. Browns*, Atlantic Monthly, October 1992, at 41. . . .

2. *See* James N. Baker with Clara Bingham, *Minority against Minority*, Newsweek, May 20, 1991, at 28.

3. 414 U.S. 86 (1973).

4. 426 U.S. 67 (1976).

5. Julie Amparano and Mark Shaffer, *When Cultures Collide*, Arizona Republic, April 13, 1997, at A1 (emphasis added), quoting a Mexican American high school student in Phoenix, Arizona.

6. Sonia Nazario, *Natives, Newcomers at Odds in East L.A.*, Los Angeles Times, March 4, 1996, at A1. . . .

7. *See* Richard Delgado, *Rodrigo's Fourteenth Chronicle: American Apocalypse*, 32 Harvard Civil Rights–Civil Liberties Law Review 275, 299 and n.115 (1997), mentioning that *pocho* is slang for a person of Mexican ancestry "who does not speak Spanish and has lost touch with his or her roots."

8. Richard H. McAdams, *Cooperation and Conflict: The Economics of Group Status Production and Race Discrimination*, 108 Harvard Law Review 1003, 1044 (1995).

9. *Id.* at 1055–56 (footnotes omitted).

10. Amparano and Shaffer, *supra*, at A1, quoting Louis DeSipio, political science professor at University of Illinois.

Review Questions

1. Should there be legal remedies for discrimination on the basis of skin color? Should it matter whether the claim is against a White person or a minority group member discriminating against another minority group member on the basis of color?
2. Colorism affects Latinas/os, Asian Americans, and Native Americans as well as African Americans. The phenomenon also can be observed in many different countries. (See Part 10). Is colorism—and racism generally—a part of human nature?
3. Have you ever seen a family member make reference to the skin color of another family member in a derogatory or positive way? How did you react?

Suggested Readings

Carlos H. Arce, Edward Murguia, and W. Parker Frisbie, *Phenotype and Life Chances among Chicanos*, 9 Hispanic Journal of Behavioral Sciences 19 (1987).

Taunya Lovell Banks, *Both Edges of the Margin: Blacks and Asians in* Mississippi Masala, *Barriers to Coalition Building*, 5 Asian Law Journal 7 (1998).

F. James Davis, Who Is Black? (1991).

Verna M. Keith and Cedric Herring, *Skin Tone and Stratification in the Black Community*, 97 American Journal of Sociology 760 (1991).

Kathy Russell, Midge Wilson, and Ronald Hall, The Color Complex: The Politics of Skin Color among African Americans (1992).

Alex M. Saragoza, Concepción R. Juarez, Abel Valenzuela Jr., and Oscar Gonzalez, *History and Public Policy: Title VII and the Use of the Hispanic Classification*, 5 La Raza Law Journal 1 (1992).

William C. Smith, *The Hybrid in Hawaii as a Marginal Man*, 39 American Journal of Sociology 459 (1934).

Edward E. Telles and Edward Murguia, *Phenotypic Discrimination and Income Differences among Mexican Americans*, 71 Social Science Quarterly 682 (1990).

Part VII

Affirmative Action

"Box Checking" and Advantage-Taking

Part 7 focuses on the classification of mixed race peoples in higher education and employment affirmative action programs, perhaps the most well known and controversial examples of racial classifications in U.S. law. Importantly, the appropriate racial or ethnic "box" for mixed race peoples to check for affirmative action purposes is far from self-evident.

Some commentators contend that mixed race people manipulate the system to maximize the possibility of receiving positive affirmative action benefits. Instances of fraud by Anglos claiming to be Black (see Chapter 34, discussing the Malone brothers) or having a distant Indian relative have been reported. Some abuse is more subtle. As Richard Delgado has stated, "Box-checking . . . enables those of white or near-white appearance to benefit from affirmative action without suffering the worst forms of social stigma and exclusion" (Richard Delgado, *Derrick Bell's Toolkit—Fit to Dismantle that Famous House?* 75 New York University Law Review 283, 296 [2000]).

Even with the attacks on affirmative action in the 1990s, some ameliorative programs are likely to remain in the future, especially in the private sector. Conservative commentators have attacked affirmative action programs for, among other reasons, the arbitrariness of racial classifications, including the difficulties in fitting mixed race people into a category. They claim that, like the elaborate racial classification scheme in apartheid South Africa (see Part 10), racial classifications for affirmative action programs are so arbitrary that they should be abolished. In turn, affirmative action supporters argue for the maintenance of racial categorization to aid in efforts to remedy past discrimination. Fraud by certain persons attempting to "game" the system, in their view, is a limited problem, considering that the minority population in higher education and in most high-paying jobs, even if arguably inflated, is quite low.

Ruth Colker discusses some of the problems with racial classifications in affirmative action programs in employment, public contracting, and university admissions. John Martinez analyzes the specific problem of "overinclusion," the classification of persons of mixed ancestry who do not, in fact, identify with a minority community as minorities in order to inflate the numbers of "underrepresented minorities" in the student body. Kenneth Payson considers the hiring of mixed race people by law firms. Luis Toro focuses attention on "box checking" by minorities and nonminorities. P. S. Deloria and Robert Laurence analyze the difficult question "Who is an Indian?" for purposes of law school admissions. Christopher Ford raises the possibility of fraud in affirmative action programs. Finally, Kevin Johnson studies racial classifications concerning Latinas/os.

55

Bi
Race, Sexual Orientation, Gender, and Disability

Ruth Colker

In 1977 the federal government issued Statistical Policy Directive No. 15 to standardize the definition of race used by the public and private sectors. [See Part 4—Ed.] ...

The problems with this Directive can be seen in an early affirmative action controversy from New York City. After New York City instituted an affirmative action program for promotion from police officer to sergeant, six officers came forward and asked to be reclassified from white to black or Hispanic. One officer indicated that he had originally checked both "black" and "white" on the application form but that the department computer had arbitrarily classified him as white. A similar problem occurred in Boston when two firefighters, the Malones, claimed they were black because their maternal great-grandmother was black.[1] The assertion about being black was brought into question because they did not make that assertion until after they had taken the first exam for the position. Moreover, there was some question as to whether they held themselves out in the community as black. At a hearing, however, two co-workers testified that they knew the firefighters had been hired as blacks, so the perception within the firefighting community was that they were black.

The New York and Boston cases show the awkwardness of racial classification systems, even for benign purposes. In both cases the question was whether the public safety employees could be considered black. There was no discussion of the need for a "mixed race" category and whether the "mixed race" category should be treated differently than the "black" category.

In another context, Randall Kennedy has challenged what he calls the "racial distinctiveness" thesis—an argument that race or minority status imbues an individual with a distinctive contribution to a field or life experience.[2] The shortcomings of the racial distinctiveness thesis can be seen especially in the New York and Boston cases. Nowhere in the classification problem that was considered did anyone ask whether these individuals had a special reason to be deserving of affirmative action protection. Had they experienced educational or economic deprivation because of their racial status? Did they have a special interest in assisting with public safety problems in minority communities? Kennedy encourages us to ask these kinds of questions closely in specific contexts and not to assume that all people of color are alike. Boston and New York felt more comfortable developing and enforcing clumsy categories of "black" and "white," with all blacks benefiting from affirmative action and no whites benefiting, than asking these more probing questions. As a result of such policies, the Malones of this society will have an incentive in the future, when seeking the benefits of affirmative action, to check the box "black" at the earliest possible stages of the application process and not to acknowledge their mixed race background. Such actions will perpetuate the "one drop of blood" rule, under which a person with a known trace of African ancestry is considered to be black. [See Part 2—Ed.]

Although the federal government has been slow to recognize the "mixed race" category, some private institutions have begun to try to change this practice of insisting that people classify themselves into rigid categories. Columbia Law School, for example, asks student applicants for admission who wish to have their ethnic background taken into account to submit ethnic statements. In addition, the application invites students to check off more than one racial or ethnic category if appropriate. . . .

The Columbia Law School policy, however, of seeking personal narratives is not without its problems. First, it seems to presume that the only purpose of affirmative action is to assist individuals in overcoming historical disadvantage. Affirmative action for African Americans in law school admissions, however, serves other purposes, such as diversifying a student body, educating African Americans who can serve as role models for the next generation, and increasing the quantity and quality of legal services available to the black community. There is no reason to place the burden of explaining those benefits on the individual candidate; Columbia Law School is as capable of describing those benefits as the candidate.

Second, the Columbia model seems to presume only racial minorities have a significant ethnic or racial story to reveal. Too often we think of whites as not having a race (hence the label "white," which stands for an absence of color). To move fully toward a multiracial jurisprudence, however, I would argue that we need whites as well as others to contemplate the significance of race in their lives. For many whites it may be a story of race privilege, but it is still a story about how race has mattered in their lives. The Columbia model seems to suggest that not all candidates will comment on their race or ethnicity; if everyone were expected to comment, then there would be no need to offer an optional question. And certainly, if the point of the question is to allow candidates to ask for special treatment so that they may overcome obstacles they have faced in life, then one might well imagine that many whites would not be able to offer any evidence of special obstacles due to their race. On the other hand, I believe it would be good for us to have institutions or individuals encourage us to consider how our race has mattered in our personal history and to understand our race as part of a spectrum rather than part of bipolar categories.

If we collected more histories of how race has mattered in people's lives, we might be able to determine if darker-skinned blacks are the victims of more discrimination in our society than lighter-skinned blacks. If so, we might want to create legal or political structures to break down that color consciousness. The Columbia Law School model might enable us to more specifically determine who is deserving of affirmative treatment because of prior social or economic disadvantage, although these disadvantages should not be the only factors in determining who is worthy of affirmative treatment. An example may illuminate my argument. Two black individuals may be applying for admission to Columbia Law School. Candidate number one comes from a middle-class background. Her parents were university professors, and she went to schools in middle-class neighborhoods as well as to a private Ivy League college. Candidate number two comes from a working-class background. His parents had only a high school education and worked in menial jobs such as janitorial work and housecleaning. He went to a historically segregated black college in the South. Assuming that both applicants have equivalent grades and test scores, I would suggest that candidate number two is more deserving of affirmative action in admissions. Both of them will help diversify the classroom and serve as role models for blacks in our society, but candidate number two has experienced a more racially constructed and thereby disadvantaged educational background than candidate number one. Ideally, we would have space in our law schools for both candidates, but realistically, we often have to make difficult choices. I am simply suggesting that a history of disadvantage may be relevant to making these tough choices.

Notes

1. Steven Marantz and Peggy Hernandez, *Defining Race a Sensitive, Elusive Task,* Boston Globe, October 23, 1988, at 33, 40.

2. Randall L. Kennedy, *Racial Critiques of Legal Academia*, 102 Harvard Law Review 1745, 1778 (1989).

56

Trivializing Diversity

The Problem of Overinclusion in Affirmative Action Programs

John Martinez

"We noticed you checked off the box for 'Hispanic' in your law school application," said the law school professor to the applicant, "but you didn't say anything in your personal statement, nor is there anything in the rest of your admissions file about your ethnic status. The faculty admissions committee asked me to call you to follow up on that. Could you tell me a little about yourself in that regard?"

"My ex-husband was Hispanic, and I had a baby by him," she responded.

"We do not view a woman who has had a baby by a Hispanic father as having acquired the father's ethnic status," said the professor. "Unless you can provide us with information that qualifies you for diversity status, we will go ahead and handle your application under our non-diversity applications process."

III. The Problem of Overinclusion

The problem of overinclusion has usually been voiced by opponents of affirmative action who were themselves participants in such programs. Richard Rodriguez was an early critic, complaining that he should not have been admitted to Stanford under affirmative action.[1] Similarly, Stephen Carter complained bitterly about being admitted to Yale under an affirmative action program.[2]

There are various other settings, however, that seem to have gone unnoticed but where the problem of overinclusion is nevertheless present. For example, we seldom hear about people, like the law school applicant described at the outset of this essay, who have attempted unsuccessfully to pass as Hispanic for the purposes of being included in an affirmative action program. [See Part 3—Ed.] Similarly, we rarely hear about people who have "passed" unnoticed through an affirmative action program and who have assimilated into a particular institution either undiscovered or unreported. Why are such situations rarely discussed in the debate or viewed as areas of concern?

One of the possible reasons for the lack of inquiry into such situations is that it is to the advantage of institutions such as law schools to forgo critical examination of applicants' minority status and simply have the applicants self-designate. Since the American Bar Association, through its accreditation standards, examines each school's progress toward achieving diversity, schools are encouraged to pad their numbers. It is thus in the schools' interests not to look too closely at students or faculty candidates who self-designate as people of color. The schools may rationalize their failure to inquire further in such circumstances as advancing the interests of the law school applicants' or faculty candidates' individual self-definition, autonomy, or freedom of association.

Another possible reason we do not hear more complaints about overinclusion is because there are no generally accepted standards to determine whether any particular individual meets the affirmative action criteria of a given plan. The absence of such standards is both a cause and effect of the overinclusion phenomenon. Since there are no such standards, candidates are almost routinely included in affirmative action programs unless they fail the "laugh test," as in the case of the "Hispanic" woman described in the beginning of this essay. Furthermore, the lack of standards encourages people to include themselves in such programs if they have even a minimal claim for inclusion, because any attempt by an institution to exclude them will immediately focus attention on all aspects of the affirmative action program involved. In light of the rather tentative endorsement of affirmative action plans by courts, no program administrator or institution is eager to invite or undergo such an inquiry.

C. Avoiding Overinclusion

1. Sensitivity for the Enrichment Difference

The utilitarian objective of affirmative action is to enrich society by including people with diverse backgrounds and life experiences in its major institutions. Thus, there is surely some diversity value in having a neoclassical economist on any law school faculty. Similarly, there is a general diversity value in having people on the faculty of different ages, races, cultures, and graduate schools. Thus an African American from a well-to-do family could serve as a role model for other African Americans, even if the person's role is only a passive and unassuming one.

Problem cases arise when ethnic diversity is the value claimed by a candidate for an affirmative action program and the candidate has little or no prior association with the claimed group or characteristic. Such "born again" ethnic or racial affiliations should not be difficult to ascertain from a person's resumé, letters of recommendation, or personal statements, as illustrated by the telephone conversation described at the outset of this essay. The key task for evaluators of such candidates is to take the time to thoroughly review an applicant's background, activities, and associations instead of accepting a self-designation at face value. If such an approach is followed, the enrichment dimension will have more meaning, as those who claim an ethnic affiliation only for their convenience or only when they will receive a benefit will be excluded from affirmative action programs.

2. Sensitivity for the Deprivation Difference

There are two ways to identify the deprivation difference among prospective affirmative action program participants. First, a candidate can be differentiated according to whether she meets the remedial/compensatory criterion by asking questions such as: What are the factual indicators of underprivileged status that you claim? To what extent were such circumstances of your own making? Have you been the victim of discrimination because of the racial, ethnic, or other minority group with which you identify?

A second way to identify the deprivation difference is through proxies. Candidates can be asked to self-designate according to racial or ethnic criteria. These proxies are useful in light of the close correlation between race and ethnic status and socioeconomic deprivation. Proxies, however, are neither perfectly reliable nor easy to administer, and they leave many questions unanswered. For example, does a Spaniard who wishes to practice law in the United States qualify? Does a Hispanic from New York who is fluent in Japanese and expects to work in Tokyo for a Japanese law firm qualify?

To help resolve these questions, an additional guiding principle should be the applicant's desire to benefit those from discrete groups *in this country* and who will work to provide services to such groups or serve as a role model *in this country*. We may refer to this as the "Help Our Own—For Our Own" criterion. Under this principle, neither of the previously described applicants would qualify: the Spaniard is not from this country, and the Hispanic will not benefit her community in this country.

Of course, any of these people might initially qualify for consideration under affirmative action programs under the enrichment dimension discussed above. Once that *prima facie* stage is reached, however, the task becomes one of balancing the enrichment and social justice dimensions. Since some of the potential beneficiaries of affirmative action qualify for reasons of enrichment, social justice, or both, how will the institution that is administering the program assure that each is given its proper weight? This consideration is discussed next.

3. Balancing Enrichment and Social Justice Diversity

Life is a constant process of balancing. We cannot allow either the enrichment factor or the social justice factor to override the other. Thus, for example, we should not unthinkingly select a neoclassical economist or a white Harvard *magna* ahead of an otherwise equally qualified person of color. Similarly, we should not automatically select a woman of color who had to work throughout college to support her children, if her undergraduate record consists entirely of failing grades.

Decision makers in institutions who take the task of affirmative action seriously must engage in deep self-reflection about the definition and weight of the factors used to evaluate candidates for affirmative action programs. Failure to attribute positive weight to underprivileged status and demonstrated ability to overcome such obstacles—as well as racial, ethnic, or other differences—dismisses something of value. Just as significantly, however, the failure to examine the genuineness of such claims constitutes the equally serious offense of trivializing diversity.

Notes

Published originally in 12 Harvard BlackLetter Law Journal 49 (1995).

1. *See* Richard Rodriguez, Hunger of Memory: The Education of Richard Rodriguez (1982); *see also* Linda Chavez, Out of the Barrio: Toward a New Politic of Hispanic Assimilation (1991). . . .
2. *See* Stephen Carter, Reflections of an Affirmative Action Baby (1991). . . .

57

Check One Box

Reconsidering Directive No. 15 and the Classification of Mixed Race People

Kenneth E. Payson

[Some] mixed race persons . . . are counted as minorities but treated as though they were White. This phenomenon should cause us to question the wisdom of the current classification scheme, for to classify as minorities persons who are socially regarded as White not only understates the discrimination rates against minorities, but in a time when minority group membership can result in entitlements (due to affirmative action), this phenomenon finds such minority-group-based allotments distributed to persons who may be functionally White.

Take, for example, law firm hiring. Law firms are not immune to the increasing social pressure to diversify their workforces. Indeed, those who fill out National Association of Law Placement (NALP) forms for law school placement offices are expected to give figures on attorney hiring by race. Thirty years after [the passage of the Civil Rights Act of 1964], there are still comparatively few minority lawyers in the more prominent American law firms, and those few minority lawyers are largely among the associate ranks. Therefore, there is continued pressure for law firms to hire minority lawyers.

Inroads are being made by minority lawyers, but what do we know about the nature of those hires? Are the minority attorneys hired representative of the minority law students on the job market? Or, as I will suggest, are those persons counted as minority hires disproportionately part-White? Since there are no data, I can offer only my own observations.

When I was interviewing with law firms during my second year of law school, I did not openly identify my race, yet my work with the Asian Law Journal and with the Asian Pacific American Law Students Association probably resolved any questions potential employers may have had about my racial background. Perhaps this explains why I was so often interviewed by minority lawyers in firms that were predominantly White. I immediately noticed a striking tendency among those lawyers of color: the surprising lack of color.

In response to my questions about minority representation among the attorney ranks, one attorney—a blonde-haired, blue-eyed woman—began counting off minority lawyers, beginning with herself as African American. In another firm, the lone minority lawyer was of partial Mexican descent. Understandably, as the market opens up to persons of color, law firms apparently will seek minorities who are more palatable to themselves and to their predominantly White clients. To the extent possible, they would likely hire minorities who do not look or act too different from Whites. A mixed race person who has been raised by a White parent will not only probably physically look more White but be able socially to act more White as well.

I wish to stress that I do not challenge these persons' self-identity as persons of color; I am glad to see their presence, as they do represent inroads in minority hiring. And, I must admit, I have likely benefited from employers' ability to claim me, in good faith, as a minority hire. Yet, if part-White persons represent a disproportionate number of minority hires, then how much more dismal is the picture of minority hiring with respect to the majority of minority persons who are not mixed race? Has a person who has a White parent suffered the kind of disadvantage that we presume monoracial minorities have suffered? Or is a part-White person not only visually and behaviorally more palatable but also privy to the social ties and important networks via her White parent?

"A People Distinct from Others"

Race and Identity in Federal Indian Law and the Hispanic Classification in OMB Directive No. 15

Luis Angel Toro

VIII. Directive No. 15 as a Barrier to Chicano Progress

"[B]ox checking" occurs when a person who is identified in the community as being part of the white or Anglo majority claims to be a member of a racially subordinated minority group and uses that status to reap benefits meant to address the problems that group faces.[1] Since an extremely limited amount of aid is reserved for affirmative action programs, box checking severely decreases the amount of assistance a targeted racially subordinated group receives and necessarily postpones the date when the affirmative action program can dissolve, having achieved its goals. In the meantime, the problems affirmative action programs are meant to address remain and may even worsen. . . .

Suppose, for example, that an Anglo seeks admission to law school. Bombarded by news reports that claim that less-qualified minorities are being let into law school ahead of their (allegedly) superior Anglo counterparts, she might decide to make admission more likely by claiming to be a member of an underrepresented minority group. But which one? Assuming that this person is culturally identified as part of the white American mainstream, her choices are limited. Passing as an Asian or African American would be relatively difficult. If the institution follows the federal practice of requiring proof of tribal affiliation to be considered an American Indian, that route would be closed as well.

The best choice for the would-be box checker would be to claim that she is of "Hispanic origin." After all, Directive No. 15 says that one can be both Hispanic and white, and the test for being "Hispanic" is merely having some "Spanish culture or origin." The box checker might apply a "one drop" rule to herself, claiming "Hispanic origin" on the basis of a single known Spanish ancestor. A bolder box checker might fabricate a tale of Spanish ancestry or might even claim that the ability to speak Spanish or play some Spanish-style guitar music qualifies her as having "Spanish culture" without any Spanish ancestry.

The case of Robert E. Lee illustrates the ease with which whites can manipulate the "Hispanic" classification so as to qualify themselves for benefits intended to reach racially subordinated Latino groups such as Chicanos or Puerto Ricans. Lee, a retired naval officer known to his friends as "Bob Lee," changed his name to "Roberto Eduardo Leon," announced that his grandfather was Spanish, and petitioned his employer, a county agency, to change his racial/ethnic designation from white to Hispanic. In newspaper interviews, he peppered his speech with Spanish phrases; his supportive boss was quoted as saying, "Bob, I mean Roberto, is a highly regarded professional. . . . It's nice to have a Hispanic on our staff."[2] Lee's request was initially approved by the county director of employee relations, but the decision was overturned by the county executive, who went on to place heavy administrative burdens (most significantly, proof that the applicant was regarded in the community as a member of the group he or she wished to transfer into) on anyone wishing to change his or her designation in the future. A disappointed Lee fumed, "It appears that there are no objective methods for making a decision. . . . [T]he hard evidence is that I have a Spanish grandfather."[3]

"Roberto" Lee's case created a furor because it was obvious that a white person was taking advantage of a loophole to claim benefits meant to address racial discrimination. The tragedy of Directive No. 15 for Chicanos is that Lee should have been considered "Hispanic" under the terms of that directive. A single Spanish grandparent is more than enough to satisfy the "other Spanish origin" prong of the "Hispanic" test, especially when the directive makes it clear that biological ancestry is the way cultural identity is measured. Lee's ruse failed because he initially identified himself as white, then made an obvious attempt to use a loophole by changing his name.

In the years since Lee's well-publicized attempt to take advantage of programs aimed at "Hispanics," several other stories involving white persons attempting similar maneuvers have been reported. Often this has been coupled with editorializing against affirmative action, at least for "Hispanics." Today, a box checker may escape detection by claiming Hispanic origin at the outset of a hiring, contracting, or admissions process. Would-be box checkers realize that having a Spanish surname is not a necessary condition of being "Hispanic," so they need not call attention to themselves by changing their name. Box checking works because most, if not all, agencies, like the county agency that employed Lee, are not equipped to check into claims that a person has a Spanish ancestor and simply take such assertions as true. Indeed, discomfort over "checking blood lines" makes many who run affirmative action programs shy away from any attempt to rein in box checking even when it is known to be taking place. . .

The extent of box checking is unknown. A rough estimate will become possible only when Chicanos note a disparity between the number of "Hispanics" claimed by an employer or a school and the number of persons identified as racialized minority group members lumped together under that label, or when recordkeepers keep track of the numbers of members of specific communities, such as the Chicano community. One such set of data, examining "Hispanic" admissions to law school, revealed that the number of Chicano and Puerto Ricans declined, both in relative and absolute terms, during a period covering most of the 1980s when "Hispanic" [as defined by the Bureau of the Census—Ed.] admissions rose.[4] . . . It seems extremely likely that programs intended to benefit Chicanos and other racialized minorities have been hijacked by white box checkers and Spanish Americans for whom the "immigrant analogy" can be thought to hold, because there is little to differentiate Spanish Americans from other European immigrant groups, such as Irish or Greek Americans.

If extensive box checking in government programs is taking place, one would expect the beneficiaries to promote the idea that there is a unified Hispanic community. . . . One need look no further than the pages of *Hispanic* magazine to find exactly that sort of promotion. In its December 1993 issue, the magazine included a number of Hispanic "Bests and Worsts" and its "Top Ten Reasons to Be Hispanic."[5] The class orientation of the magazine is revealed by its advertisements for luxury items and by "Reason Number 8 to Be Hispanic": "You can order water from busboys in restaurants." After a page advertising tickets to the 1994 World Cup of soccer, the magazine goes on to its "Closet Hispanic Award," given each year to people who are not identified as members of a racialized minority group but who meet Directive No. 15's "Hispanic" definition.[6] "Previous winners of this secret award are Vanna White, Raquel Welch, and Linda Carter, who are all Hispanic," the magazine asserts. "This year's recipients are baseball great Ted Williams (Mexican mother) and Walt Disney (born in Spain)." The fact that neither Williams nor Disney was culturally identified as Chicano or even Latin American has no bearing on their Hispanic identity, according to the authors of this magazine. Indeed, right next to the "Closet Hispanic Award" is the "Most Ridiculous Issue," which, not surprisingly, is "Are we Hispanics, Latinos, Chicanos, Spanish, Mexican Americans, Cuban Americans, Puerto Ricans, etc., etc.? Who cares? Let's move on!"

Obviously, if box checkers are becoming successful by marketing themselves as (often quite unthreateningly white) substitutes for Chicano progress, it is in their interest to declare the substantial differences among Chicanos, Puerto Ricans, Cubans, and Spaniards "ridiculous" and something that progressive members of these communities should not address. If someone actually examined the differences among these groups, those currently benefiting from the "Hispanic" classification might lose their ability to order around busboys in restaurants; indeed, their Chicano busboy might start up a business and compete with them. One can expect that any revision of Directive No. 15 to measure more accurately the progress of Chicanos will be strongly resisted by those who wish to promote the view that being born in Spain or having a Mexican ancestor, even if one has passed out of the Chicano community, makes one Hispanic. . . .

Notes

1. Directive No. 15, Race and Ethnic Standards for Federal Statistics and Administrative Reporting, 43 Fed. Reg. 19,260, 19,629 (Office of Management and Budget 1978). . . .

2. *See* Stephanie Mansfield, *Roberto Leon, Instant Hispanic: Eligible for Job Preference,* Washington Post, March 11, 1979, at A1.

3. *See Gilchrist Ruling Costs Leon-Lee Minority Status,* Washington Post, April 27, 1979, at B5. . . .

4. Michael A. Olivas, *Legal Norms in Law School Admissions: An Essay on Parallel Universes*, 42 Journal of Legal Education 103, 113 n.56 (1992). . . .

5. *The Best and Worst of 1993*, Hispanic, December 1993, at 20.

6. *Id.* at 22.

59

What's an Indian?

A Conversation about Law School Admissions, Indian Tribal Sovereignty, and Affirmative Action

P. S. Deloria and Robert Laurence

LAURENCE: . . . Let's let them debate the wisdom or not of the various rationales for affirmative action. Can't we just accept that any number of institutions—governmental and private, voluntarily or under compulsion—are engaged in affirmative action programs these days? Given such a program that strives to reach Indians, how is it done? Or, as our title says, "What's an Indian?"

DELORIA: It won't work, but go ahead.

LAURENCE: O.K., here's the hypothetical; not so hypothetical, really. A colleague on the Admissions Committee stops by my office and says that the law school has received an application from someone claiming to be an Indian. How, she wants to know, does the Committee react, and, in particular, What's an Indian?

DELORIA: That question gets asked a lot and people are surprised to hear that our answer is not always to check for enrollment in a federally recognized Indian tribe.

LAURENCE: "Not always." The answer is sometimes "Yes"?

DELORIA: Sure. Various federal entitlements are based on enrollment. If the school is looking for [Bureau of Indian Affairs (BIA)] support—well, actually the BIA generally supports *students*, not schools—if the law school wants to tap into BIA support for its students, then the BIA's criterion—generally 1/4 blood in a recognized tribe[1]—must be used. But if there is no connection between the question asked and a particular federal requirement, then there is no easy answer.

LAURENCE: Why not?

DELORIA: Because the answer to your question requires that one define exactly why the institution wants to have an Indian around.

LAURENCE: Which is to ask why the institution has an affirmative action policy at all, right?

DELORIA: Right. As I said earlier.

LAURENCE: Well, imagine a spectrum of "Indianness." On one end you have enrollment in a federally recognized Indian tribe. On the other end is anyone who self-identifies as an Indian.

DELORIA: That strikes me as less a spectrum of "Indianness" and more a classification of identifiers. In one case, it's a government who is doing the identification and in the other it's the individual. There is no reason to expect that those persons identified as "Indians" by a government—federal or tribal—will be more "Indian" than those who only identify themselves as "Indians." There may be some sort of attenuated correlation, but nothing one can count on. Think of Audrey Martinez.

[Interlude with *Santa Clara Pueblo V. Martinez.*[2]]

LAURENCE: Start here: The U.S. Constitution does not bind the activities of Indian tribes.[3] No state action; no federal action; Indian tribal governments predate that of our own by many generations,[4] and they didn't ratify our Constitution. In 1968 Congress passed the Indian Civil Rights Act (ICRA),[5] which gave constitution-like protections to persons—Indians and non-Indians alike—who are subject to tribal authority. That statute has been before the United States Supreme Court directly only once, in the *Martinez* case.

The Santa Clara Pueblo, a small tribe in New Mexico, has a membership rule that discriminates on the basis of sex. [See Chapter 26—Ed.]

DELORIA: Make that "distinguishes on the basis of sex."

LAURENCE: Agreed. The children of women who marry outside the tribe are not members, while the children of women who marry inside the tribe (and children born out of wedlock) *are* members. The children of all Santa Claran men are members. In the famous case, Julia Martinez, a Santa Claran, . . . and her daughter, Audrey, sued the Pueblo in federal court alleging discrimination in violation of the Indian Civil Rights Act. They lost at the district court,[6] won at the Tenth Circuit,[7] but lost again before the Supreme Court.[8] The Supreme Court held that the ICRA was a legitimate infringement of tribal sovereignty (not all agree), but that it created no civil cause of action that could be sued over in federal court. . . . [C]ivil enforcement is only in tribal court. Since the tribe granted no relief, the outcome was that Audrey Martinez, while a full-blooded Indian, is the member of *no* Indian tribe.

[End of Interlude]

So, where were we? Audrey Martinez, while unenrolled is *surely* an Indian for some purposes. Like affirmative action?

DELORIA: As I said: that depends on exactly why the institution wants to have an Indian around.

LAURENCE: It's hard to imagine a reason for affirmative action that would not be satisfied by Audrey's presence: she speaks an Indian language, practices an Indian religion, has Indian parents and children, *looks* like an Indian, if that's important to you.

DELORIA: It's not hard to imagine an affirmative action program in which she would not be considered an Indian. *Morton v. Mancari*[9] dealt with such a program.

LAURENCE: For our readers, *Mancari* was the Supreme Court's first affirmative action case, several years before *Bakke*,[10] and held that the BIA's hiring preference for Indians was constitutional.

DELORIA: You have to be more careful in your observation about Audrey Martinez's eligibility: it may be hard for you to imagine a *reason* for having affirmative action that would exclude her, but it's not hard to imagine the *existence* of an affirmative action program, like *Mancari*'s, based on membership. Besides, a program that uses an objective criterion like membership will be easier to administer.

LAURENCE: Granted, and I guess I'd expect the government to use its own definition of Indian when administering its own affirmative action plans.

DELORIA: Ah ha! It's for that reason that we are not, in this conversation, going to be able to finesse the underlying rationales for affirmative action, as you will soon see. I assume, though, that no one would suggest that administrative convenience is, in and of itself, an underlying rationale.

LAURENCE: O.K. Suppose the law school asks your difficult "why-do-you-want-an-Indian" question and decides that it is to diversify the student body, to make it less white, less wealthy, less homogeneous. "Cultural pluralism" is the going phrase. Would that be appropriate?

DELORIA: Look. There are two basic reasons for affirmative action. One: a mostly white institution wishes to diversify itself. Two: pay-backs. The first is essentially for the benefit of the white institution; it is saying, in essence, that it would be for the benefit of its present, mostly white, students that they be educated in the presence of non-whites. The second *may* be for the benefit of the mostly white institution—to assuage well-known white liberal guilt—but mostly it is reparations for past wrongs. Now here is what is, for me, a nearly fundamental principle: to the degree than an institution is taking affirmative action steps to service itself, *its* definition of "Indian" might control, but to the extent that it's trying to pay-back the Indians for past wrongs, then to that same extent the Indians have an important say in how the program is structured and whom it serves.

LAURENCE: O.K. Then . . .

DELORIA: . . . back to Audrey Martinez. She is not an Indian under every possible definition, but if the school's interest is in cultural pluralism, it would be crazy to exclude her because she isn't enrolled.

LAURENCE: . . . [D]omestically, I'm bothered by self-identification.

DELORIA: Why?

LAURENCE: Because you can't get fifteen white guys in the same room together without one of them claiming some Indian blood in his family tree. Why is it, do you suppose, that white people are so inclined to claim Indian blood and so disinclined to claim African or Asian blood?

DELORIA: The noble savage myth. It's good in white eyes to be just a little savage, especially if the ancestor is, as is almost always claimed to be the case, on one's grandmother's side.

LAURENCE: And usually an Indian princess.

DELORIA: Yes; though it's important to claim little enough Indian blood so as not to be subject to any real prejudice. Many are they who claim to be Indian, but few are they who are putting their land into trust, to be held for their benefit by the government.

LAURENCE: What about this myth, though? Indians, of course, were no more "savage" than Africans or Asians.

DELORIA: Or Europeans.

LAURENCE: Touché.

DELORIA: We're not talking reality, but myth. The Africans' myth is subjugation and Uncle Tom; the Indians' is being environmentally conscious and "in touch with the Earth." "One-with-nature-hood."

LAURENCE: Maybe that's the myth in a 1990s-New-Age-Costnerian sense, embodied most graphically by the remarkably tidy Indian village in "Dances with Wolves." [This was a popular 1990 film—Ed.] But the myth that I grew up with, as a midwestern white kid in the '50s and '60s, was less Sierra Club than Outward Bound: buffalo hunting and counting coup.

DELORIA: Right. The image changes. Perhaps the most glorious part of the image is that we stood up to you, although outnumbered and outarmed. A little Indian blood is the picante sauce of the white man.

LAURENCE: But that's my point exactly. Take the case of William Trogdon, who writes under the name William Least Heat-Moon. He was recently described this way in *The Atlantic:* "Heat-Moon is in a sense two people, and he writes about our continent. . . . With both the canny wordliness of his Irish and English background and the mystical time sense of his Osage ancestors."[11] How can one resist a claim to a little "mystical time sense?" I have no idea how Osage Dr. Trogdon is and do not accuse him of creating his own ancestry, but it is not hard to imagine *some* white man claiming Osage kin just in order to get a little "mystical time sense." Who's to challenge?

In fact, the 1990 census seems to indicate that more and more people are claiming to be Indian on the census forms. The *New York Times* had a front page article in March on this phenomenon.[12] Many of these "new" Indians may be people with substantial Indian blood who are only now feeling comfortable saying that publicly. But, apropos of our discussion, the *Times* article said:

> Since the Census Bureau does not require proof of heritage, it is impossible to know how many people falsely assert an Indian background. In a few well-publicized cases, people with only a tiny percentage of Indian blood have been able to take an advantage. For example, a California contractor, who is one-sixty-fourth American Indian, obtained $19 million in contracts set aside for minority-owned companies on the rapid transit system in Los Angeles, more than any other "disadvantaged" company.
>
> In addition, some whites who believe it is fashionable to be Indian no doubt stretch the truth about ancestry. Indians call such people "wanna-bees."
>
> "The usual story from these people is, 'My grandmother was a Cherokee princess,'" said Sue Bad Moccasin, a Choctaw in Lincoln, Nebraska, who helps people trace their Indian roots. "And we just smile and say, 'Oh, that's very interesting.'"

How can we go to Indian self-identification without opening the law school up to these charlatans?

DELORIA: I think that the applicant, especially if unenrolled, but maybe in any case, should be put to the proof of having been an Indian at some important time in the past.

LAURENCE: "Been an Indian" or "held oneself out as an Indian"?

DELORIA: "*Been.*" One does not become an Indian just by declaring oneself an Indian.

LAURENCE: Again, because it's too easy?

DELORIA: Not only that, but even where one is put at risk by declaring himself an Indian. Surely holding oneself out at some hippie rock concert or crystal-throbbing New Age convergence doesn't count, but neither does putting one's money or even freedom on the line at, say, Alcatraz in the '70s. I think we're talking here about some connection with Indian family or community.

LAURENCE: You mean *reservation* community, or would hanging around the Indian Center in downtown Cleveland do?

DELORIA: In theory, Cleveland will do, but given the last spot to fill and an applicant from Pine Ridge, South Dakota and one from Cleveland, I'd probably take the Pine Ridge resident, because I think that is what your institution is looking for.

LAURENCE: Does it matter what you or I think the institution is looking for?

DELORIA: Here we go again. If the institution is trying to make reparations for past wrongs, then *yes*, it matters what Indians and their friends think. If the institution is only trying to improve itself, then our input is less necessary, though, under your original hypothetical, they asked.

LAURENCE: You know, I've been reading that the same problem occurs with respect to "Hispanics." It is often pointed out—usually by conservative opponents of affirmative action—that Europeans from Spain do not fit the affirmative action goals of many institutions. [See Chapter 58—Ed.] Is there any difference between restricting one's "Hispanicness" to the New World and restricting one's "Indianness" to reservation life?

DELORIA: No, that is to say I think both restrictions may make sense. New World Hispanics began their divergence from Spaniards a very long time ago. It may be—probably is—the case that an institution intent on diversity needs little more European diversity and is seeking the New Worlders' perspective. An affirmative action program that is surprised by this distinction or unable to explain it strikes me as a poorly defined one. Ditto the case of the reservation/non-reservation distinction.

LAURENCE: I've got a problem: if the goal of the affirmative action program is diversity in the student body, then does the admittee have an obligation to *be an Indian* during his tenure?

DELORIA: Like requiring him to wear his hair in braids?

LAURENCE: Yeah, or, you know, listen to Indian music, join NALSA [the Native American Law Students Association], *not* blend in?

DELORIA: Can the answer be anything but "no"? How could there be such an obligation? . . .

LAURENCE: But doesn't that, then, strike at the heart of diversity-based affirmative action? I took a swipe at William Trogdon earlier, or rather at *The Atlantic*'s stereotyping of his "mystical time sense." But diversity-based affirmative action assumes, doesn't it, that Indians are *somehow* different from whites, else why bother to diversify? It seems like my choice is either to advance stereotypes or forget diversity, not an attractive array of options. Doesn't this potential stereotyping kill the theory behind diversity-based affirmative action?

DELORIA: No, though it may be a minor wound. Being a member of an ethnic group does not *guarantee* anything one way or another about one's politics, ethics, beliefs. Since neither of us in fact knows Audrey Martinez we were making a great leap of faith earlier in assuming that she would actually diversify a law school student body. But there is a good chance that she would, certainly a better chance than choosing to fill a seat randomly from society at large. Still, the institution may lose the gamble because of who she, in fact, is, or who she decides to be upon admission.

LAURENCE: You once told me that it is legitimate for an Indian to choose to "act white" during law school. I guess what you told me is that criticism that an Indian student "passed" during law school is a cheap criticism. Law school is hard enough without additional requirements. . . .

DELORIA: . . . "Politically correct" requirements would be the current term. If I said that, I was right, with the caveat that one was an Indian before entry. A person who was never an Indian before law school, nor in law school, but gets in as an Indian and emerges into the race only upon graduation, is not "passing." That person is an opportunist and does not get my respect. On the other hand, the Indian who plays white is much more admirable than a white who plays Indian, at least when he or she does it for survival in that most Anglo-American of all Anglo-American institutions, the law school. I think that there's a time—and an obligation—to go home and serve one's community, but that's another issue. All I'm saying now is that it shouldn't be permissible in the usual case for the first Indian-related activity in one's life to be the application to a white institution under the institution's affirmative action program.

LAURENCE: But doesn't that, again, mean that the diversity goal of affirmative action is meaningless? How does a school diversify if it can't be sure if its admittees will ever be seen again, as Indians?

DELORIA: It's just a gamble, like I said. Is it any different from admitting the privileged child of a rich potential donor? Suppose the child has taken to the street and become a Marxist hippie. So, you admit him or not based on the gamble that he'll end up a rich donor.

LAURENCE: Scratch a hippie and you'll find a three-piece suit.

DELORIA: Right. So, if you want to diversify, you decide in what direction diversity is important, and roll your dice toward that end. It seems to me that for most purposes, the policy is better advanced by the unenrolled Audrey Martinez than by a card-carrying Cherokee member, 1/256th, from Orange County. An urban Indian from Chicago would almost certainly diversify the student body, though whether in the direction that the faculty seeks is unclear. So again the question is stated: why have affirmative action? Are you trying to diversify the law school for the good of the majority's education or to diversify the legal profession because the Indians out there need more Indian lawyers? [Discussion of a Supreme Court decision touching on related issues is deleted—Ed.]

DELORIA: This question of the institution's control over the Indian groups that it has admitted is the other side of the "passing" coin, isn't it?

LAURENCE: Yes, it would appear that the institution's desires, in a diversity-based affirmative action plan, are that the Indian be an Indian, but not *too* Indian. That the Indian bring to the community *some* diversity, but not the aspects of her culture that we whites may find repugnant. And *Martinez* always reminds us that it is romantic to think that the latter aspects never exist. [Additional explanation of *Martinez* is deleted—Ed.]

LAURENCE: . . . I'd like to go all the way back to the beginning, now, and to consider the alternative answer to your question, "Why do you want Indians around, anyway?" Instead of diversity, how are the problems different when affirmative action is designed to right past wrongs?

DELORIA: There is a good deal that is sensible about that justification. It's the "Track Shoe" situation: For years races have been run with the Indians required to wear hip boots. It's not exactly right for the whites to change the rules, remove the restriction, and expect everything to be automatically equal.

LAURENCE: "Thenextracewillberunfairly.OnyourmarkgetsetBANG."

DELORIA: Right. Not only don't the Indians have track shoes, they don't even know when the gun is going off.

LAURENCE: Do we agree that, if reparations are going to be made, it makes sense to do it based on membership in a group, rather than on an individualized inspection of merit? Advocates of tribal sovereignty have to be a little leery, don't we, of the recognition of group rights beyond Indian tribes?

DELORIA: Yes. Every self-identified minority group which claims, and is granted, a right of self-determination dilutes a bit the notion of *tribal* sovereignty. It is that sovereignty, of course, rooted in history made long before Columbus arrived, that makes American Indian law unique.

LAURENCE: So, in the end, we have this: Pluralistic driven affirmative action is sensible; just as surely, it is difficult to administer when it comes to Indians. "Indian" should not be defined for these purposes as based only on enrollment. Rather, both in addition to and instead of enrollment, some past identification with the American Indian community should be demonstrated. While the university may entertain some hope that the students admitted will wear their "Indianness" in the open, there should be no requirement, nor even personalized expectation, that they do so. On the other hand, the institution may express disapproval of those customs that run decidedly against the grain of institutional norms.

With respect to reparations-based affirmative action, the institution is on solid historical grounds because of wide-spread abrogations of treaty provisions promising education to the Indians. This could, perhaps, lead to a narrower definition of "Indian" than used above for the pluralism-based affirmative action. On the other hand, the definition above is broadly consistent with the treaty-based theory. Certainly, for an institution with both kinds of affirmative action in mind, our broad definition is appropriate. . . .

NOTES

Published originally in 44 Arkansas Law Review 1107 (1991).

1. *See, e.g., Morton v. Mancari,* 417 U.S. 535, 553 n.24 (1974) (blood quantum requirements for Bureau of Indian Affairs Indian hiring preference).
2. 436 U.S. 49 (1978).
3. *Talton v. Mayes,* 163 U.S. 376 (1896).
4. *McClanahan v. Arizona State Tax Comm'n,* 411 U.S. 164, 172 (1973).
5. 25 U.S.C. §§ 1301–3 (1983).
6. 402 F. Supp. 5 (D.N.M. 1975).
7. 540 F.2d 1039 (10th Cir. 1976).
8. 436 U.S. 49 (1978).
9. 417 U.S. 535 (1974).
10. *Regents of the University of California v. Bakke,* 438 U.S. 265 (1978).
11. *745 Boylston Street,* 268 The Atlantic 4 (No. 3, September 1991).
12. *Census Finds Many Claiming New Identity: Indian,* New York Times, March 5, 1991, at A1, col. 2 .

60

Administering Identity

The Determination of "Race" in Race-Conscious Law

Christopher A. Ford

I. Administering Identity

A. *Malone v. Haley*—Pressure on the System

[This case was discussed briefly in Chapter 34—Ed.]

The case of *Malone v. Haley,*[1] an unreported single-justice opinion of the Supreme Judicial Court of Massachusetts, illustrates some . . . conundrums [in racial classification schemes]. Paul and Philip Malone, twin brothers who lived in Milton, Massachusetts, took part in 1975 in a city civil service competition for jobs with the Boston Fire Department. They scored poorly and were not accepted. The twins, who were fair-haired and light-skinned, had identified themselves as White in the 1975 test application. In 1977 they tried again, this time identifying themselves as Black. The Boston Fire Department had by that time become subject to a court-ordered affirmative action program, under which the city maintained separate minority candidate lists for firefighter vacancies. The twins' 1977 test scores of 57 and 69, respectively, would not have qualified them for the job as White candidates, but based on their self-identification as Black they were hired and served on the force for ten years. The Malones' troubles began in 1987 when they sought promotion to lieutenant, and the fire commissioner noticed that the twins were classified as being "Black." A hearing officer declared that the Malones were not Black and had therefore falsified their 1977 application and examination materials, in violation of state Personnel Administration Rule 3(4)(c). The state's personnel administrator promptly fired the brothers. Noting that the department had required only racial "self-identification" in 1977, the Malones appealed, arguing that they should still be considered Black by the department.

Deferring to the "particular domain of the factfinder who had an opportunity to observe the witnesses and to judge their credibility," Judge Herbert Wilkins of the Supreme Judicial Court for Suffolk County, Massachusetts, followed the hearing officer's three-part test for adjudicating claims to racial identity.

> [T]he Malones might have supported their claim to be Black[:] (1) by visual observation of their features; (2) by appropriate documentary evidence, such as birth certificates, establishing Black ancestry; or (3) by evidence that they or their families hold themselves out to be Black and are considered to be Black in the community.

Neither Malone brother, Wilkins wrote, met any of these three criteria. To begin with, both had "fair skin, fair hair coloring, and Caucasian facial features." The personnel administrator had concluded that "they do not appear to be Black." The birth certificates of the Malone brothers and of their parents also showed the Malone family to have been "reported consistently to be White" for three generations. "Finally, there was no evidence that the Malones identified themselves personally or socially as Blacks," except for the narrow purpose of claiming jobs and promotion in the Fire Department. Judge Wilkins also found substantial evidence that they "did not claim Black status honestly or in good faith" but did so only to take advantage of the department's minority hiring program.

The Malones' case created a stir in Boston. Fearing an epidemic of false racial claims, one city councillor asked the state attorney general to begin an investigation of the Fire Department. Mayor Raymond Flynn ordered an investigation into the fire, police, and school departments, and by the time Judge Wilkins's opinion came down, eleven firefighters were under investigation on similar grounds.

B. Bright Lines and Fuzzy Concepts

The case of the "Mixed-Up Malones" illustrates some of the minefields that may develop where resources are allocated to people on the basis of their membership in a particular group. Judges and administrators are less fortunate than social scientists: they must at some point draw lines between rival claimants, rewarding one and sending the other home empty-handed. However analytically "soft" a particular classification may be, making it a centerpiece of governmental resource-allocation will require that it be "hardened" dramatically. . . .

"[F]igures speak and when they do, Courts listen." Modern anti-discrimination law depends fundamentally upon statistical showings of minority group underrepresentation. Federal courts have for years used statistics as a means of judging discrimination, but in recent years the volume and complexity of statistically grounded litigation have increased enormously. The Supreme Court has recognized that "'[s]tatistical analyses have served and will continue to serve an important role' in cases in which the existence of discrimination is a disputed issue."[2] The Supreme Court today generally requires plaintiffs to show a "factual predicate" of considerable detail to substantiate a charge of discrimination. In the statutory context of Title VII litigation, for example, the courts since *Griggs v. Duke Power Co.*[3] have permitted prima facie cases of employment discrimination to be shown by statistical evidence that an employment practice has a disproportionately adverse impact on some protected class, irrespective of discriminatory intent. "Disparate impact" cases under Title VII have therefore invariably revolved around statistical showings of varying detail—either comparisons of minority representation in the workforce to that in the general population or, in more recent years, to that in increasingly narrow population subsamples. Whatever the relevant population sample, however, employment discrimination is often provable only through statistics. . . .

The law thus requires we make very "hard" variables indeed of the comparatively "soft" notions of race and ethnicity. Similarly detailed factual predicates are required in voting rights cases as well. *City of Mobile v. Bolden*[4] required that a demonstrable discriminatory "purpose" be shown in cases arising under the Voting Rights Act of 1965. Congress, fearing that this new rule might miss discrimination that was "masked and concealed," amended section 2 of the Act in 1982 to make it clear that a finding of discriminatory purpose was no longer required. Since this amendment, findings of discrimination in voting rights cases have revolved almost exclusively around statistical evidence. . . . The post-1982 "results" standard of Voting Rights Act litigation thus also places a great burden on classificatory procedures.

Assuming that identifying discrimination is unproblematic, what happens once discrimination has been found? Whatever the specific remedies adopted, we still require some coherent understanding of who precisely is to be helped, and why. If, as with so-called victim-identification orders in Title VII enforcement, particular victims of discrimination can be identified, the remedy-directing answer may be straightforward. Harder questions arise with "indirect victim," "procedure-neutralization," and "compliance" orders and in any other circumstances in which there is no close correlation between personal disadvantage at the hands of a particular defendant and gaining advancement through a legal remedy directing that defendant to undertake particular employment practices. In such cases, group-specific targeting might be felt to be an appropriate proxy for "real" disadvantage or might be adopted on the strength of an assumed connection between group membership and other social wrongs of the general sort in question. In either case, a clear and coherent idea of "group" is necessary—particularly when even "benign" race-based classifications are subject to the exacting equal protection requirements of "strict scrutiny."

D. The Muddiness of Race

This is precisely the difficulty with the categories of "race" and "ethnicity." While sex is (arguably) a dichotomous variable, race is nothing of the sort. "[B]iologically it is a continuous variable, or, to be precise, a series of variables, most of which are continuous. A person's racial identity is largely a social phenomenon, rather than a biological one."[5]

If the various human "races" were different *species*, their differentiation and classification would be much more manageable. While different species cannot breed with each other, humans invariably do—and the phenotypical characteristics we traditionally associate with particular "races" are not quanta of racial identity but infinitely modulated characteristics that further shade into each other with each successive union. Indeed, the criteria for "racial" differentiation themselves are but socially conditioned ones: in biological terms can we say with certainty that George Wallace is more "different" from Stokely Carmichael than Carmichael himself is from Siad Barre? And if "racial" differentiation seems problematic, what are we to make of "ethnic" identity, in which a host of indefinable cultural, educational, and environmental factors complicate these already-muddy waters? As one scholar provocatively put it, "[M]ost native-born U.S. Negroes far from being nonwhite, are in fact part white. They are also by any meaningful definition of culture, part Anglo-Saxon, and they are overwhelmingly Protestant."[6] However strongly racial and ethnic differences may be perceived, and however "real" they may be insofar as they powerfully affect the lives people lead, can they be pinned down with the conceptual coherence and replicability that group-oriented benefit allocation requires?

There exist two basic approaches to this classificatory task:

1. *Self-reported identity*—individuals are asked to assign themselves a racial identity based upon the particular group with which they most closely identify or of which they otherwise feel a part; and
2. *"Other-ascribed" identity*—individuals are placed into categories according to the perceptions of their racial or ethnic identity held by a designated decision-making third party. An individual's membership in a particular group might thus be determined according either to
   (a) *Member reference*—whether or not members of that group (however defined) consider her to be a fellow member, or
   (b) *Nonmember reference*—whether or not nonmembers of that group consider her to be a member of that group.

It seems to be taken for granted in modern American racial jurisprudence that these categories are coterminous. For gender-based classification, this may be true: one would not, in most cases, expect divergence between someone's self-perceived identity as a male, on the one hand, and the agreement of either men or women about this fact of biological identity, on the other. With respect to racial and ethnic characterizations, however, this cannot so easily be said to be true. Therefore, these classification schemes may produce different results. If racial and ethnic identity is to remain a salient factor in the allocation of social benefits, we must be aware of how various procedural systems may differ; we must be willing to examine the degree to which the policy interests served by each such classification scheme map the contours of sociological identity. The proper procedure for "administering race" is the core dilemma of modern race-conscious law.

II. Administering Benefits

A. Employment: The EEOC and Affirmative Action

The first modern "affirmative action" program was established in 1969, when the U.S. Department of Labor issued the "Philadelphia Plan" to set up racial hiring goals and timetables for contractors involved in federally assisted construction projects in that city. Since then, a network of federal regulations has been put in place requiring federal contractors, private employers, public school systems, institutions of higher education, the armed forces, and various organs of local, state, and federal government to implement anti-discrimination measures of various sorts. An important part of such regulation has been to require racial and ethnic group–based preferences in hiring and promotion decisions, in an effort to make up for past discrimination suffered and to overcome disadvantages "built in" to American society by a legacy of historical and ongoing wrong. The success of this remedial effort relies on the existence of the discrete and definable classification categories that are its stock in trade. If benefits are to be provided to people "on the basis of . . . their membership in a specified group or groups," the law must have some clear and coherent way of identifying groups and group members. Whenever there are "Malones" willing to challenge their allocated position in a benefit-distribution scheme, the system must be willing to examine its foundations.

Preferential programs rely for their coherence on making hard numbers out of the conceptually muddy—that is, "soft"—variable of racial identity. Given that the pervasive ethno-racial cost-accounting of government policy relies inescapably on detailed statistical data, where does this information come from? In the employment context, the group-keyed allocation of benefits for purposes of "affirmative action" is derived from two very different sources of information. The first of these is the U.S. Census and the various population projections derived from it. The second is the information provided by employers through their Equal Employment Opportunity filings as mandated by federal law. . . .

[The article discusses the U.S. Census racial classifications, which were discussed in Part 4—Ed.]

2. Employer EEO Filings

Of all classification systems in the United States, race classification carried out through Equal Employment Opportunity (EEO) regulations and the group-preferential hiring and promotion policies of affirmative action programs has perhaps the most immediate impact on American lives. The government has been unable to provide much definitional help to the administrators of such programs, however. The Department of Labor's EEO rules for federal contractors, for example, included "Standard Federal Equal Employment Opportunity Construction Contract Specifications," which defined "minority" by describing various racial groups merely as "having origins in" or as the "original peoples" of various continents (Africa, Europe, Asia, the Americas). Despite the indeterminacy of these definitions, the failure of federal contractors to apply specified minority hiring goals may result in the termination of an employer's federal contracts and debarment from future contracts. Under Title VII of the Civil Rights Act of 1964,

> every employer, employment agency, and labor organization subject to this title shall (1) make and keep such records relevant to the determinations of whether unlawful employment practices have been or are being committed, (2) preserve such records for such periods, and (3) make such reports therefrom, as the Commission shall prescribe by regulation or order.[7] . . .

Federal district courts are given jurisdiction to enforce compliance upon the application of the Equal Employment Opportunity Commission (EEOC) or the U.S. Attorney General. EEO record-keeping requirements expressly

> supersede any provision of State or local law which may conflict with them. Any State or local laws prohibiting inquiries and record-keeping with respect to race, color, national origin, or sex do not apply to inquiries required to be made under these regulations and under the instructions accompanying [EEO] Reports.[8] . . .

The Bureau of the Census compiles [Metropolitan Statistical Area (MSA)] breakdowns of local occupational categories by sex, Hispanic origin, and race for federal EEO officials from the self-reported sex, race, and ethnicity responses of the "short form" questionnaire and the detailed education and occupational breakdowns of the "long form." The classification procedures for judging employer compliance, however, are quite different. The group definitions suggested to employers generally follow the "original peoples" formulation found in federal regulations. These definitions are not entirely consistent with the Census definitions. While the Census statistics treat Hispanic origin as a category independent of race, the employer guidelines themselves expressly define the "Black" and "White" groups to *exclude* persons of *Hispanic origin*. The Census Bureau tries to resolve this tension between the census and EEO classification by re-counting "Hispanic" as an exclusive category as it compiles MSA statistics from raw census data.

More fundamentally, however, there is a tension between the methods of the Census/MSA systems and employer EEO systems of classification. Census-derived data are ultimately self-reported. Racial and ethnic classifications of employees are seldom so. To begin with, federal EEO compliance officials apparently have no way of "verifying" the figures employers submit in their EEO filings. The law prohibits the use of Census data to connect employer responses to individual names, so EEO filing and MSA data cannot be directly linked. EEO regulations also actively discourage asking employees to classify themselves, and federal compliance officials apparently feel that employee-by-employee self-identification surveys are beyond their capacity. Compliance audits may check employer EEO reports against the group-classified personnel records employers are required to keep but cannot systematically "verify" individual classifications. [Office of Federal Contract Compliance Programs (OFCCP)] audits of employers suspected of "underutilizing" women or minority groups can include an on-site investigation by an "Equal Opportunity Specialist" (EOS), but if any takes place at all, EOS "verification" of employer-submitted hiring figures is only of the most informal sort, based on stereotyped group categories and a cursory "visual survey" of employees encountered. That such impressionistic "verification" may sometimes occur is indicated by the care with which employers often seek to stage-manage EOS on-site visits to show off "units which are fully utilized with women and minorities . . . [and] areas of affirmative action accomplishments." As a rule, however, federal auditors rely exclusively on employer-submitted figures. Compliance is thus evaluated by comparing *individually* self-reported "availability" data with *employer*-reported group hiring and promotion figures.

Employer data are usually the product of what might be called "intuitive-appraisal tests." If, to the recording official, a person "seems" to be Black (or Hispanic, Asian, etc.) she is classed as so being. The use of employee self-identification for EEO record-keeping (which would be more consistent with MSA data) is permitted but is strongly discouraged given the "sensitivity" of such inquiries. As an alternative, federal regulators encourage simply making a "visual survey" of the workforce.

Notes

1. No. 88-339 (Sup. Jud. Ct. Suffolk County, Mass., July 25, 1989).

2. *International Brotherhood of Teamsters v. United States,* 431 U.S. 324, 339 (1977) (modification in original), quoting *Mayor of Philadelphia v. Educational Equality League,* 415 U.S. 605, 620 (1974).

3. 401 U.S. 424 (1971).

4. 446 U.S. 55, 66–68 (1980).

5. Kingsley R. Browne, *Biology, Equality, and the Law: The Legal Significance of Biological Sex Differences,* 38 Southwestern Law Journal 617, 666–67 (1984) (footnote omitted).

6. Yehudi O. Webster, *The Racialization of America* 144 (1992), quoting Albert Murray, The Omni Americans: New Perspectives on Black Experiences and American Culture 79–80 (1970).

7. Title VII, Civil Rights Act of 1964, Pub. L. No. 88-352, § 709(c), 78 Stat. 241, 262 (codified as amended at 42 U.S.C. § 2000e-8(c) [1988]).

8. 29 C.F.R. § 1602.29 (1993). . . .

61

"Melting Pot" or "Ring of Fire"?

Assimilation and the Mexican American Experience

Kevin R. Johnson

Latino diversity causes practical problems regarding affirmative action and related programs that must be addressed. As one Supreme Court justice recognized, one federal agency was required "to trace an applicant's family history to 1492 to conclude that the applicant was 'Hispanic' for purposes of a minority tax certificate policy."[1] Assuming race may be considered as a factor in future governmental programs, other questions are posed. For example, should differences in the Latino community affect eligibility for affirmative action programs? Specifically, should immigrants from Latin America—as opposed to Latino citizens—be eligible for affirmative action? These and related questions raise potentially explosive issues within the Latino community. However, the remedial arguments for affirmative action for Mexican Americans whose families have lived in this country for generations at first glance may appear stronger than for recent immigrants from Latin America. In a similar vein, inequities arguably result when Latino immigrants are eligible for affirmative action programs designed to remedy pervasive systemic discrimination against African Americans. Although increasing diversity, immigrant eligibility may not provide relief for past discrimination. Immigrants, even if racial minorities, have not descended from persons subject to centuries of racial subordination in the United States. Whether that fact should be determinative or whether other factors militate in favor of inclusion of immigrants in affirmative action programs is an open question. The issue becomes even more difficult, however, because immigrants of color may be subject to discrimination once in this country.

Due to Latino diversity, some, most prominently Peter Brimelow in the much-publicized anti-immigrant polemic *Alien Nation*, claim that community leaders have constructed a fake identity for purposes of securing affirmative action and other benefits. This characterization misses the point that Latinos share common interests, political and otherwise, that deserve group treatment. These critics ignore the fact that Latinos as a group, even though diverse, are not integrated into the political and economic mainstream. Put differently, dominant society classifies Latinos as a distinct group of foreigners. Affirmative action is designed to remedy the negative group treatment of Latinos by facilitating economic integration and assimilation.

After several years of practicing law, I applied for a law teaching job. The American Association of Law Schools provides a standardized form résumé that makes it easier for law schools to quickly screen large volumes of faculty candidates. Along with an assortment of biographical information, such as where you attended law school, whether you were a member of your school's law review, whether you clerked for a judge, and where you have been employed, the form asks you to classify your background. As I always had done as far back as I can recall, I classified myself as Chicano. Before doing so, I wondered whether I should continue this practice. In discussing the matter with my wife, she asked me if I had grown ashamed of my background. That not being the case, I self-identified, though I worried that I might be viewed as an impostor by law schools in search of a bona fide Latino.

In one of my first interviews for a teaching position, I stepped into a senior professor's office. After the ordinary pleasantries, the question came—a question never posed to me in private law practice but apparently one on the minds of members of many faculty appointment committees: "How did you get to be Mexican?" [This pointed question became the title of a book—Ed.] That at least is how I translated the question. Although asked numerous times in my life, the question generally has been presented in a more roundabout, diplomatic way.

Sentiments like these have not been limited to my initial hiring. Shortly after I had earned tenure at [University of California] Davis, a friend on the faculty appointments committee at another law school, which according to one ranking is a "Top 20" school, asked if I was interested in interviewing for a job. I later flew out to interview. The day, at least from my end of the table, went extraordinarily well. Indeed, I made a presentation to the faculty that may have been my best ever. Many complimented me and I felt positive about the experience. The next day began with breakfast with the dean of the law school. We talked for a bit about the school before he moved to the important issues. The dean bluntly told me that, although the school did not have any "regular" faculty positions open, the central administration might give the law school an additional slot for a "minority hire." This all was news to me. The dean continued. "Before we can even think about offering you a job, we will have to check to see if you qualify as a minority." These few words quickly brought me down to earth. Maybe the previous day had not gone so well. Maybe they just wanted a Latino for political reasons. The school at the time was on the Hispanic National Bar Association's "Dirty Dozen" list of law schools, a select group of schools with no Latino faculty members.

Note

1. *Metro Broad., Inc. v. Federal Communications Comm'n*, 497 U.S. 547, 633 n.1 (1990) (Kennedy, J., dissenting) (citation omitted).

Review Questions

1. Should children of mixed marriages be ineligible for affirmative action and related programs?
2. Should law schools and employers, like the U.S. Bureau of the Census, simply rely on a person's self-identification with a racial group? Are the alternatives too costly and intrusive?
3. Is "box checking" a significant problem in law schools and the job market? If so, what should be done?
4. Have you ever "checked the box" for an educational or employment advantage? Have you known anybody who has? How did it make you feel?

Suggested Readings

Chris Ballentine, *"Who Is a Negro?" Revisited: Determining Individual Racial Status for Purposes of Affirmative Action*, 35 University of Florida Law Review 683 (1983).

Paul Brest and Miranda Oshige, *Affirmative Action for Whom?* 47 Stanford Law Review 855 (1995).

Krista L. Cosner, *Affirmative Action in Higher Education: Lessons and Directions from the Supreme Court*, 71 Indiana Law Journal (1996).

Richard Delgado, *Derrick Bell's Toolkit—Fit to Dismantle That Famous House?*, 75 New York University Law Review 283 (2000).

Harry J. Holzer and David Neumark, *What Does Affirmative Action Do?* 53 Industrial and Labor Relations Review 240 (2000).

Kevin R. Johnson, How Did You Get to Be Mexican? A White/Brown Man's Search for Identity (1999).

Part VIII

Race, Child Custody, and Transracial Adoption

Part 8 offers perspectives on the legal relevance of race in child custody decisions and transracial adoptions. Such decisions involve mixed race children or the creation of mixed race families.

With increasing intermarriage in the United States, the parent's race has become an issue in child custody disputes. In the past, parents have claimed that because the other parent had an interracial relationship, he or she was the superior custodial parent. Use of race in this fashion is inconsistent with modern notions of civil rights and equality. Race, however, still may enter the child custody analysis in more benign and difficult ways. For example, an African American parent of a mixed race child who physically appears Black may claim that he or she is the best custodial parent because of his or her ability to help the child develop a healthy racial identity and to address the racism that the child will likely confront in U.S. social life.

Part 8 also discusses the formation of mixed race families through transracial adoption, which has proven to be particularly controversial. Should it matter that a White family seeks to adopt an African American, Asian American, or Native American child? Some contest transracial adoption on the ground that removing children from the birth community threatens the continued existence of minority communities. In this vein, the Indian Child Welfare Act recognizes the Indian tribe's interest in the adoption of an Indian child and establishes procedures before such an adoption can be finalized. Within the African American community, some fear that African American children will be harmed—culturally and otherwise—if raised by White parents. Law has intervened to resolve the disputes over transracial adoption. To this point, the law has tended to side with those fearing the destruction of minority communities.

International adoption, particularly of children from Asia and Latin America, has been on the rise. Such adoptions, often by White families, have raised a variety of concerns. Besides concern with taking a child from his or her native society, the fact that African American children wait for adoption in the United States while international adoption thrives suggests that Black children are less desirable than those from Asia and Latin America. (See Elizabeth Bartholet, Family Bonds: Adoption and the Politics of Parenting 142-43 [1993].)

Importantly, controversies of this nature are of relatively recent origin. Custody issues in a mixed race marriage did not arise frequently when such marriages were unlawful in many states. (See Part 1.) Significant numbers of transracial adoptions were virtually nonexistent before the 1960s. Only with the civil rights movement and the open embrace of the anti-discrimination principle has the issue even been recognized as one worthy of attention.

The subsections consider (1) the role of race in child custody decisions; (2) transracial adoption, including international adoption; and (3) the Indian Child Welfare Act.

A.

Child Custody

Gayle Pollack studies the case law in the area before the U.S. Supreme Court decision of *Palmore v. Sidoti* (1984), which addressed a child custody dispute that emerged when the child's mother began a relationship with an African American man. Twila Perry analyzes the problems of using race as a factor in the child custody determinations after *Palmore.*

62

Palmore v. Sidoti

U.S. Supreme Court
466 U.S. 429 (1984)

Chief Justice Burger delivered the opinion of the Court.

We granted certiorari to review a judgment of a state court divesting a natural mother of the custody of her infant child because of her remarriage to a person of a different race.

I

When petitioner Linda Sidoti Palmore and respondent Anthony J. Sidoti, both Caucasians, were divorced in May 1980 in Florida, the mother was awarded custody of their 3-year-old daughter.

In September 1981 the father sought custody of the child by filing a petition to modify the prior judgment because of changed conditions. The change was that the child's mother was then cohabiting with a Negro, Clarence Palmore, Jr., whom she married two months later. Additionally, the father made several allegations of instances in which the mother had not properly cared for the child.

After hearing testimony from both parties and considering a court counselor's investigative report, the court noted that the father had made allegations about the child's care, but the court made no findings with respect to these allegations. On the contrary, the court made a finding that "there is no issue as to either party's devotion to the child, adequacy of housing facilities, or respectability of the new spouse of either parent." . . .

The court then addressed the recommendations of the court counselor, who had made an earlier report "in [another] case coming out of this circuit also involving the social consequences of an interracial marriage." . . . From this vague reference to that earlier case, the court turned to the present case and noted the counselor's recommendation for a change in custody because "[t]he wife [petitioner] has chosen for herself and for her child, a life-style unacceptable to the father *and to society*. . . . The child . . . is, or at school age will be, subject to environmental pressures not of choice." . . .

The court then concluded that the best interests of the child would be served by awarding custody to the father. The court's rationale is contained in the following:

> The father's evident resentment of the mother's choice of a black partner is not sufficient to wrest custody from the mother. It is of some significance, however, that the mother did see fit to bring a man into her home and carry on a sexual relationship with him without being married to him. Such action tended to place gratification of her own desires ahead of her concern for the child's future welfare. *This Court feels that despite the strides that have been made in bettering relations between the races in this country, it is inevitable that Melanie will, if allowed to remain in her present situation and attains school age and thus more vulnerable to peer pressures, suffer from the social stigmatization that is sure to come. . . .*

The Second District Court of Appeal affirmed without opinion, . . . thus denying the Florida Supreme Court jurisdiction to review the case. . . . We granted certiorari, . . . and we reverse.

II

The judgment of a state court determining or reviewing a child custody decision is not ordinarily a likely candidate for review by this Court. However, the court's opinion, after stating that the "father's evident resentment of the mother's choice of a black partner is not sufficient" to deprive her of custody, then turns to what it regarded as the damaging impact on the child from remaining in a racially mixed household. . . . This raises important federal concerns arising from the Constitution's commitment to eradicating discrimination based on race.

The Florida court did not focus directly on the parental qualifications of the natural mother or her present husband, or indeed on the father's qualifications to have custody of the child. The court found that "there is no issue as to either party's devotion to the child, adequacy of housing facilities, or respectability of the new spouse of either parent." . . . This, taken with the absence of any negative finding as to the quality of the care provided by the mother, constitutes a rejection of any claim of petitioner's unfitness to continue the custody of her child.

The court correctly stated that the child's welfare was the controlling factor. But that court was entirely candid and made no effort to place its holding on any ground other than race. Taking the court's findings and rationale at face value, it is clear that the outcome would have been different had petitioner married a Caucasian male of similar respectability.

A core purpose of the Fourteenth Amendment was to do away with all governmentally imposed discrimination based on race. . . . Classifying persons according to their race is more likely to reflect racial prejudice than legitimate public concerns; the race, not the person, dictates the category. . . . Such classifications are subject to the most exacting scrutiny; to pass constitutional muster, they must be justified by a compelling governmental interest and must be "necessary . . . to the accomplishment" of their legitimate purpose. . . .

The State, of course, has a duty of the highest order to protect the interests of minor children, particularly those of tender years. In common with most states, Florida law mandates that custody determinations be made in the best interests of the children involved. Fla. Stat. § 61.13(2)(b)(1) (1983). The goal of granting custody based on the best interests of the child is indisputably a substantial governmental interest for purposes of the Equal Protection Clause.

It would ignore reality to suggest that racial and ethnic prejudices do not exist or that all manifestations of those prejudices have been eliminated. There is a risk that a child living with a stepparent of a different race may be subject to a variety of pressures and stresses not present if the child were living with parents of the same racial or ethnic origin.

The question, however, is whether the reality of private biases and the possible injury they might inflict are permissible considerations for removal of an infant child from the custody of its natural mother. We have little difficulty concluding that they are not. The Constitution cannot control such prejudices but neither can it tolerate them. Private biases may be outside the reach of the law, but the law cannot, directly or indirectly, give them effect. "Public officials sworn to uphold the Constitution may not avoid a constitutional duty by bowing to the hypothetical effects of private racial prejudice that they assume to be both widely and deeply held." . . .

. . . Whatever problems racially mixed households may pose for children in 1984 can no more support a denial of constitutional rights than could the stresses that residential integration was thought to entail in 1917. The effects of racial prejudice, however real, cannot justify a racial classification removing an infant child from the custody of its natural mother found to be an appropriate person to have such custody.

The judgment of the District Court of Appeal is reversed.

It is so ordered.

63

The Role of Race in Child Custody Decisions between Natural Parents over Biracial Children

Gayle Pollack

II. Discussion of Custody Decisions

A. Child Custody Decisions—The "Best Interests of the Child" Test

The current standard for most custody decisions is the "best interests of the child" test. It is mandated by statute in a number of states and is the generally accepted test in child custody proceedings, although it is implemented in varying ways. Some states leave a broad statutory statement for the judiciary to interpret, while others carefully set out factors for the courts to consider.

The best interests of the child test itself is highly discretionary and places the child at the center of the decision, while parental interests are peripheral. Unfortunately, under this test it is difficult to identify specific judicial motives for placement unless judges record all of their considerations in their opinions. In particular, the best interests test does not specify the relevance of race. Thus judges have ample opportunity to overlook, underconsider, or affirmatively hide the role of race in their custody decisions.

B. Race in Child Custody Decisions—Case Law up to *Palmore v. Sidoti*

The lack of structure over the judicial consideration of race in custody cases allows for judges' personal or unconscious biases to play a role in their decision making. Even a well-meaning judge may make a decision that inappropriately incorporates race without explicitly examining how the issue should be considered in child custody decisions, and thus may not fully consider the best interests of the child. A brief overview of custody and adoption case law will illustrate problems with the discussions of race in child placement proceedings before the seminal United States Supreme Court case *Palmore v. Sidoti.*[1]

Disputes between natural parents over the custody of their biracial children have often been decided by matching children with the parent with whom they share the most racialized physical traits. Washington's Supreme Court stated in the 1950 *Ward v. Ward* decision, a custody case between a black father and white mother, that the biracial children were "colored" and would "have a much better opportunity to take their rightful place in society if they [were] brought up among their own people."[2]

The court's assumption that biracial children were de facto "colored" presumes that biracial people can claim only one race. The court assigned those biracial children the race it deemed most appropriate, probably based on appearance.

In 1956, an Illinois county court also awarded custody on the basis of racialized appearance in a dispute between a white mother and a black father, in *Fountaine v. Fountaine*.[3] The judge agreed with plaintiff's petition that the children had "the outstanding characteristics of the Negro race [and that] these children will make a better adjustment to life if allowed to remain identified, reared and educated with the group and basic stock of the plaintiff, their father." However, the judge also noted that if race were not a factor then he would have awarded the mother custody of the children. On review, the Illinois Appellate Court held that "the question of race alone [cannot] outweigh all other considerations and be decisive of the question," and it reversed and remanded the case. However, the Appellate Court never specified how or whether race should factor into the lower court's decision on remand.

Washington's Court of Appeals stepped away from *Ward*'s holding and relied on *Fountaine* in *Tucker v. Tucker*,[4] a 1975 custody dispute between a black father and a white mother. The state court affirmed a lower court decision granting custody of the child to the mother. It stated that while "the court can and should take into consideration all relevant considerations which might properly bear" upon the custody decision, race could not be the decisive factor in a custody battle.

Still, *Tucker*'s discussion of race and its impact is problematic. The court implies that race-matching based on appearances is acceptable in the calculus of determining the best interests of the child, as long as it is not the determinative factor. . . . Although the determinative impact of race had been diluted, judges apparently were still permitted under this analysis to consider the racialized physical characteristics of parents and children in custody decisions.

Racialized appearance remained important in custody determinations in the early 1980s. The New York Supreme Court granted custody to the white mother rather than the black father in the 1981 case *Farmer v. Farmer* but noted that all five experts called in the case agreed that the biracial child would be considered black by society at large and would "endure identity problems, which can be exacerbated in her because of the mixed racial heritage."[5] The court considered race as part of its determination of the best interests of the child but also weighed a number of other factors, including evidence that the child was well cared for by her mother, expert reports claiming that the child would not necessarily suffer maladjustment just because she was raised by her white parent, and a report . . . recommending placement with the mother.

While the court believed race to be only one factor among the many factors weighed in determining the best interests of the child, it spent at least six and a half pages of an eleven-page decision discussing expert testimony on race and the law concerning race in placement decisions. The discussion noted that race is generally not a significant factor in child placement decisions, but it cited a number of decisions in both the child custody and adoption contexts that considered race. Many courts appeared to consider race in placement decisions; few courts, particularly in child custody decisions, were very specific about how they weighed race, perhaps creating a presumption that race was not a significant factor.

The substantial amount of time spent on determining how to consider race both belies claims that it is insignificant and shows the lack of clear statements in case law about its treatment. In the end, the *Farmer* court focused on the mother's ability to help the child develop personally but did not include a consideration of the mother's ability to help the child develop her racial heritage. . . .

Early case law showed a strong proclivity among lower state courts toward placing biracial children with their black fathers rather than with their white mothers. One reason explaining why so many courts overturned traditional presumptions of women as the primary caregivers is that these courts relied on race-matching between the parents and the children to determine custody. Such matching may have occurred because of misguided judicial notions about the best place for a child being among people who "look" like her, unconscious judicial racism, or conscious racism either cloaked in racially neutral terms or not discussed at all.

More recent child placement decisions have begun to grapple with appropriate ways to consider race without violating *Palmore*'s interpretation of the Equal Protection Clause. [See Chapter 62—Ed.]. . . This type of analysis of race in placement decisions needs to be extended to more custody cases in order to place children with the parents who are best equipped to help them form complete personal identities.

IV. Problems with Considering Race in Custody Decisions

While a positive racial identification may be important to a biracial child, one could argue that the law should not step in to try to shape the development of this identification through the consideration of race in custody disputes. The judicial consideration of race in placement decisions may seem to rigidify race by positing that a biracial child's racial identification must be based on biology. Such considerations may also appear to run afoul of the Equal Protection Clause. However, upon examination, neither concern presents a real bar to considering race in custody decisions.

A. Definitional Issues

A consideration of race in custody decisions would use race in a way that is partly biological, in that it would define someone as biracial on the basis of her parents' race. . . . Mandating that courts consider race in custody decisions may reinforce socially created racial categories that should be questioned.

However, in creating a pragmatic test to ensure the protection of biracial children, theory may falter in the face of difficult realities. Custody law needs to address how biracial children reach their fullest potential in a racist society that is not designed to encourage or accept them. Unlike prior legal classifications that have used race in order to divide people and ensure inferior status for some, considering race in custody decisions should work to ensure that people do not feel inferior on the basis of their race. . . . In the end, the importance of protecting the best interest of the child outweighs any reifying effects from having courts seriously consider and, hopefully, examine their presumptions about race.

Some could also argue that considering race in custody disputes is a form of biological predeterminism, forcing biracial people to be bicultural. However, a consideration of race that looked at a parent's ability to teach a biracial child about both of her racial heritages just ensures that biracial children have ample information with which to continually define themselves, and that their parents play an encouraging role in helping them explore all facets of their identities. The state is not stepping in and deciding levels of race consciousness or racial identity for children but is simply saying that children ought not to be limited by parental preconceptions.

. . . If the consideration of race focuses not on defining people but on ensuring that biracial children have the tools with which to define themselves, then it presents a pragmatic approach for determining a child's best interests, while minimizing a court's ability to determine how the child should build an identity.

B. Equal Protection Problems

A consideration of race in child custody decisions that did not assign placements on the basis of race but merely considered which parent would expose the child to both of her racial heritages would not be drawing distinctions between people on the basis of their races. Instead, such an inquiry would ask about a parent's nurturing abilities in relation to the child's racial heritages. As the court would not be distinguishing between people on the basis of race, as in *Palmore* . . . equal protection concerns could be avoided.

Even under strict scrutiny, a consideration of race in child custody decisions need not contravene the Equal Protection Clause. States have a compelling interest in determining the best interests of the child for placement decisions. The United States Supreme Court made this explicit in *Palmore*, when it stated that "[t]he goal of granting custody based on the best interests of the child is indisputably a substantial governmental interest for purposes of the Equal Protection Clause." The importance of appropriate placements for children is also shown by the unusual degree of flexibility granted to judges to make custody decisions.

A consideration of race in custody decisions could also be narrowly drawn to ensure that judges only consider the parents' feelings toward their child's racial identity and their willingness to transmit important information to the child. This would ensure that the focus of the decision remained on the child and on elements in parenting important to the child's emotional development, rather than having an undue focus on the races of the parents.

In light of the importance many studies give to parents helping a biracial child to develop a positive racial identification, there is a strong nexus between the compelling state interest of determining appropriate custody placements for biracial children and the narrowly tailored means of courts considering parental ability to help the child form a strong racial identity. Therefore considering race in custody disputes over biracial children, insofar as the inquiry relates to parental ability to help the child form a positive racial identity, does not contravene the Equal Protection Clause.

NOTES

1. 466 U.S. 429 (1984).
2. 216 P.2d 755, 756 (Wash. 1950).
3. 133 N.E.2d 532 (Ill. App. Ct. 1956).
4. 542 P.2d 789 (Wash. Ct. App. 1975).
5. 109 Misc. 2d 137, 140 (N.Y. Sup. Ct. 1981). . . .

64

Race and Child Placement

The Best Interests Test and the Cost of Discretion

Twila L. Perry

II. The Best Interests Test

In *Palmore v. Sidoti*,[1] following the divorce of a white couple in which custody of their three-year-old daughter was awarded to the wife, the mother began to live with and later married a Black man. The child's father then sued to obtain custody. The lower court ordered the change in custody solely on a belief that the child would be stigmatized if she stayed in a home with her mother and a Black stepfather. The mother appealed. The United States Supreme Court noted that consideration of race, a suspect classification, was subject to strict scrutiny and that the use of race as the basis for governmental action must be justified by a compelling governmental interest and must be necessary to the accomplishment of a legitimate purpose. It went on to find the best interests of the child to be a substantial governmental purpose for purposes of equal protection analysis but found that considering race as the sole basis for the court's decision did not survive strict scrutiny and thus violated the Equal Protection Clause of the Fourteenth Amendment.

Although *Palmore* held that the child's best interests can constitute a compelling state interest that, in the proper circumstances, may withstand an equal protection challenge, the case sheds no light on the really critical question: What is the relationship between race and the child's best interests? It is interesting that, although the Court found the issue presented in the case sufficiently compelling to make a rare venture into the area of child custody, it failed to discuss, mention, or cite even one previous state or federal court decision involving race in child placement.

That *Palmore* failed to elaborate on the relationship between race and the best interests test is not surprising. Although well established in theory, the best interests test remains problematic—not as an ideal but in terms of its capacity to function as a guidepost in the real-world custody cases that are of fundamental importance in the lives of those affected. There certainly is no general agreement as to what a child's best interests are or as to what factors should be examined in seeking to determine it. The standard has long been criticized as being overly vague and subjective. . . .

To those who champion a pure best interests rule, a case-by-case approach provides the court with the necessary flexibility to consider what is most desirable for each child in each case. Under this approach, which embodies a multifactor balancing test, each judge makes a determination as to which considerations are relevant to the child placement issue, and he determines how much weight each factor is to be given.

There is much to suggest that this level of discretion is unwise where race is an issue. Where courts have broad discretion to consider race under the best interests standard, it can easily become the dominant concern, leading courts to minimize or ignore other interests of children about which there is substantial consensus. The multifactor balancing test can become, in effect, dominated by one consideration. Moreover, in each context, the unconfined best interests rule can provide a forum for judges to act upon biased or stereotyped assumptions that are without empirical support. Finally, the way in which race may be considered can often be stigmatizing, violating normative aspirations to racial equality. . . .

A. Custody Modification following Remarriage

Although *Palmore* specifically addressed the context of custody modification, it still left the proper treatment of race in that context unclear. The Supreme Court's holding that "racial prejudice may not be used to remove a child from its mother already determined to be a fit person to have custody" suggests that racial prejudice may not be considered at all in custody modification cases. However, the Court's repeated emphasis on the fact that the lower court premised its decision solely on the factor of race does not clearly exclude consideration of race as one of several factors. *Palmore* also does not make clear whether the decision precludes consideration of any actual injury the child may suffer at the hands of others as a result of racial prejudice or whether a severe reaction by the child herself to the new marriage can be considered. . . .

The one post-*Palmore* case involving race in custody modification suggests that the case does leave room for an argument that, in effect, permits racial prejudice to be considered under the best interests test. In *Holt v. Chenault*,[2] like *Palmore*, following the divorce of a white couple in which custody of their daughter was granted to the mother, the mother married a Black man. Thereafter the father sought to gain custody of the child. At the time the father began the proceedings, the mother was pregnant with a biracial child. The daughter testified that she had been taunted by her schoolmates after her mother's marriage and about her mother's "black baby." She complained to her father about her home situation and stated her intention to leave her mother's home. One day after school, she went to her father's home instead of her mother's. Another time she left her stepfather's mother's home, where she had been left while her mother went to work, and went to her father's workplace.

Despite explicitly finding the mother to be a suitable parent, the trial court granted the custody modification. The findings of fact, as described by the appellate court, included the mother's interracial marriage and "the child's willful reaction to manifestations of racial prejudice, her discontent and her stated intent to run away."

The Supreme Court of Kentucky, citing *Palmore*, wrote what can only be described as a strange and ambiguous decision—but one that is arguably supported by *Palmore*'s endorsement of the best interests test. The court, citing *Palmore*, held that the trial court erred in giving effect to private racial biases involved in the mother's remarriage to a Black man. However, it also held "that the child's emotional reaction to the custodial parent's marital circumstances may enter into deciding what is in the best interests of the child if the reaction is significant and severe and if it does, this is a consideration, whatever the cause." The court then remanded the case to make the child's in camera testimony available to the parents' counsel and directed the court to review the record in full and to "make new findings of fact that do not reflect racial concerns."

At worst, the court's decision appears to be an invitation to the lower court to sanitize the record—to provide another reason to reach the same result it had reached earlier on the basis of racial considerations. At best, it suggests that, despite the Court's pronouncements that decisions should not be made on the basis of racial prejudice, the best interests test leaves room for the spirit of *Palmore* to be circumvented by focusing the analysis on the child's reaction to the parent's remarriage rather than on the prejudices of others.

Should race ever be considered under the best interests test in this context? Since there is often little of real importance to distinguish the parties in custody cases, if race can be considered at all, it can easily become an important consideration, especially where there actually is evidence that the child has been subjected to the prejudices of others.

It is obvious that if race can be considered, it will encourage more custody modification cases to be brought. This presents a problem. Children have an interest in not being the subjects of long and bitter litigations to determine their custody. Many experts have expressed the view that litigated custody disputes can have a negative effect on children, often resulting in tension, uncertainty, and feelings of torn loyalties. The interest of children in stable, uninterrupted relationships is recognized in the law governing custody modification. Thus, although custody decrees are subject to modification, the party seeking modification bears the burden of proof and is usually required to demonstrate that the child's welfare requires the change.

The increased litigation that could result from consideration of race as a factor in the modification context can only be justified if there is a demonstrable relationship between the consideration of race and the child's best interests. But how do we measure the child's best interests in this context? There is no empirical research demonstrating that children are detrimentally affected by growing up with a stepparent of a different race. Should it be presumed that it is so bad for a child to be teased or taunted because his or her home is different that this should be a matter of legal significance? Indeed, some people might argue that the challenge of defending and affirming a life different from the crowd helps develop independence and strength of character. How different is it for a child to be teased about having a Black stepparent than it is to be teased about having freckles, a big nose, or a parent who is particularly obese? Giving vent to a particular judge's subjective judgment that pressure on a child in this situation warrants special treatment presents the danger of perpetuating historical prejudices against interracial families and reduces the question of the significance of race to a matter of mere personal intuition. The same issues are presented where the child herself objects to the remarriage. Courts differ as to when and how children's preferences should be weighed in modification cases. However, modifying custody under the best interests rule on the basis of the child's objections to the race of the new stepparent permits the damaging effects of racism on the child to perpetuate historical biases. Perpetuation of racism is unacceptable whether based on the biases of children or adults.

B. Custody of Biracial Children

The history of racial segregation in this country has also been reflected in cases involving the custody of children of interracial marriages. In this context, some courts automatically assumed it would be proper for the children, who would be defined by the society as Black, to be raised by the Black parent. An example of this perspective may be found in *Ward v. Ward*,[3] in which the court awarded custody of the children of a white [mother] and a Black father to the father, stating, "These unfortunate girls, through no fault of their own, are the victims of a mixed marriage and a broken home. They will have a better opportunity to take their rightful place in society if they are brought up among their own people." In the 1970s, discussion of the issue of race in this context increased in sophistication. Most appellate courts rejected the idea that the racial features of the children should be considered. Instead of the former platitudes about the sufferings or the "proper place" of the biracial child, courts began to consider the testimony of mental health professionals about possible psychological needs of biracial children. Some decisions justified giving at least some consideration to race on the ground that biracial children encounter unique stresses ranging from confusion over self-identity to societal hostility to their biracial ancestry. Courts began to express the view that the custodian's ability to cope with potential issues of identity is important.

The implications of *Palmore* for the context of biracial children, too, are unclear. Here, as in the custody modification context, there is an issue of potential stress on the child due to racial prejudice, because he may appear to be a different race from the adult raising him. However, in the case of the biracial child, the appearance of racial difference and the potential for ostracism was already present in the intact biracial family. Therefore, no steps a court could take can ever completely shield the child from society's prejudices. This analysis would tend to support the view that race should not be considered in this context. However, the situation involving the biracial child is different from the custody modification context because, in addition to the potential for ostracism as a result of the racial prejudices of others, there is the issue of the child's own sense of identity, his feelings about being a mixture of two races in a society in which racial labels are important. Thus it can be argued that race is an issue relevant to the child's best interest that is arguably separable from concerns about the racial prejudice of others. But considering race as a factor under the best interests test in this context gives rise to similar problems present in custody modification cases.

A number of writers have noted the tendency of discretionary rules to encourage litigation over child custody at the time of divorce. To the extent that race may be considered in the court's discretion, it will encourage the parties to litigate the custody issue. Moreover, if race can be considered, it is likely as a practical matter to become the dominant consideration. This may impose hardships on the child that are not justified by a certainty that the ultimate result furthers the child's welfare.

The problem is that in the vast majority of cases that do not involve unfitness of one of the parties, the judge often has little rational basis upon which to prefer one parent to the other. If race can be considered as a factor, the party who feels that he or she has or should have the advantage on this issue (usually the Black parent) is likely to attempt to make it the focus of the case in an attempt to convince the court that there is *some* distinction to be drawn between the parties. This can result in the unhappy scene of parents trading allegations about racism, impaired racial identity, and real, perceived, or invented attitudes of relatives and grandparents about interracial relationships and interracial children. The problem could be compounded if the child is either called to testify in court or subjected to numerous interviews by the parents' attorneys and/or mental health professionals.

Clearly, such a process could be damaging to the child. It focuses attention at a very stressful time on the very issue that the child will have to work out over many years: her racial identity. How heavy the costs to the child might be depends in part on whether or not the child is of sufficient age to understand the nature of the issues being litigated and on the intensity and level of hostility of the parents. However, in general, the conflict between the parents over the factor of race is likely to add to the child's difficulties rather than assist the child in achieving clarity.

Moreover, there are practical and normative problems under the best interests test in this context. Even assuming that the process costs to the child are outweighed by the prospect of a "correct" decision, the kind of evidence gathered in connection with such a decision would involve the commitment of substantial resources by the individuals litigating and the courts. Furthermore, a number of writers have questioned whether the employment of a battery of mental health professionals makes sense in any custody case not involving clear claims of parental unfitness. Even equipped with the findings of such professionals, the judge would still have to make decisions based on factors that are subject to change, such as the racial makeup of the neighborhood the child lives in or the child's relationships with minorities who may serve as guides or role models. Finally, the judge's decision must depend a great deal on subjective value judgments about what kind of racial identity or philosophy should be imparted to the child. Although mental health professionals agree that a positive racial identity is important, there is room for differences of opinion on the question as to what precisely that is. It is difficult to define a particular degree of identification or association with one's own ethnic group as being optimal. In sum, it is questionable whether case-by-case litigation under the best interests standard will ultimately lead to a better decision for the child in light of the emotional and economic costs and the indeterminate value questions.

Finally, there is the troubling matter of racial labeling. The assumption in cases involving children born of Black-white interracial marriages is that the children are Black. This may indeed be the social reality, but it should be questioned whether the best interests rule should affirm an approach that continues racial designations that stem, at least in part, from a rigid historical system of racial identification based on the position that one drop of Black blood was sufficient for removal from the white race. An alternative view could be based on the biological reality that the child is no more one race than the other. Under that view, neither party would have an advantage based on race.

III. A Structured Consideration of Race

The best interests rule traditionally and appropriately starts with a focus on the needs of the child. That orientation should be preserved. Therefore, in determining the approach to race, the first question should be, what are the needs of the children involved? The fact that Black children have needs associated with their racial status has already been discussed. These needs include the need for a healthy racial identity and good self-esteem. However, these children also have other needs, including the need for permanent homes and for continuity in relationships. Finally, children have an interest in avoiding unnecessary litigation that may subject them to torn loyalties and leave their future uncertain.

A. Disputes between Parents

In disputes between natural parents, race should not be considered. This should be so whether the case involves an attempt by the noncustodial parent to modify a custody decree or a dispute between parents of different races over their biracial children.

Obviously, a significant issue in this context is the rights of parents. Even prior to *Palmore*, some courts had held that the removal of a child from its parent on the basis of the parent's choice of a spouse or companion violates the parent's rights of free association and marriage.[4] *Palmore* made it clear that the parent's right to equal protection is implicated in the modification context and that strict scrutiny must be applied. Although not specifically referred to in *Palmore*, parental rights in the context of biracial children warrant a similar analysis. To deprive a parent of custody based on a racial difference between the parent and his or her own child's race would penalize the parent for having chosen to enter into a marriage with a person of a different race. Because the right to equal protection and the right to marry are important rights, they lend solid support to the position that race should not be a factor in interparental custody disputes.

1. Custody Modification following Remarriage

First, . . . eliminating race from consideration decreases the chances of a custody battle likely to threaten the child's stability interests. Second, even where actual as opposed to potential injury to the child is alleged, considering race presents troubling questions of value judgments. There are two kinds of injury that the child might be subjected to: physical and psychological. Teasing and taunting that may result in fighting are common in childhood. It cannot be assumed that fights resulting from the parent's choice of a partner will be any more detrimental than those with their source in other factors. More and more children are growing up in homes that are "different" in some way from the traditional home where there are two heterosexual, biological parents of the same race. Although nontraditional family contexts may be a source of some stress for the children, it is hard to say that this stress is necessarily harmful. Third, the type of distinction the Supreme Court of Kentucky attempted to make in

Holt v. Chenault is a difficult one to justify. It would seem impossible to separate the child's reaction to the prejudices of others from the prejudices that gave rise to the reaction. To consider the negative reaction of a child to a stepparent of a different race where that reaction is the product of hostility of others against interracial marriages is to give legal effect to racial prejudice.

2. Biracial Children

. . . A rule that favors the parent considered by society to be the same race as the child could arguably further two interests: the child's interest in avoiding litigation and her interest in her racial identity. Still, a rule eliminating consideration of race is preferable.

Although the child's interest in avoiding litigation would be served by a rule granting preference to the parent considered the same race as the child, this interest can be equally served by the alternative approach, in which race is not considered. The other issue is whether the child's interest in developing a healthy racial identity would be served by litigation to determine which parent would be most effective with respect to this concern.

[I]n the divorce context, inquiry by the court to determine how the racially different parent will handle racial issues as the child grows older raises difficult problems. First, conditioning a judicial ruling that will determine a parent's continuing relationship with a child on the basis of willingness to structure future personal associations in accordance with the views of the judge, social scientist, or ex-spouse would appear to violate the parent's First Amendment associational rights. Second, as a practical matter, such a condition would be virtually impossible to monitor or enforce. Third, a mother involved in a fight to keep her child would be likely to frame her future intentions in a manner she believes is most likely to further the goal. Fourth, evidence that the mother presently lives an integrated or multiracial lifestyle is not persuasive evidence that such a lifestyle will continue postdivorce because it is hard to determine to what extent the lifestyle was a function of the ongoing interracial marriage. Finally, such an inquiry seems quite unnecessary. It seems likely that a mother with a child whom society considers to be Black is likely to continue to have relationships with other Black people and with mothers of other biracial children. Finally, the marriage of this parent to a person who is Black may reflect a lack of bias and a level of sensitivity to racial issues that would support her ability to deal with the racial needs of the child.

Moreover, if a specific inquiry is made to determine the ability of the mother to handle racial issues concerning the child, it would seem that a similar inquiry would have to be undertaken with respect to the father. The fact that society regards the child as Black does not necessarily eliminate racial identity issues from the child's perspective. The child may feel that regardless of society's definitions, she is in fact a product of the two races, and she may need to reconcile her relationship to each heritage.

It seems overly optimistic to assume that the fact that the parent is Black, in and of itself, assures that the child will develop a healthy racial identity. Indeed, a Black parent of a biracial child may be ambivalent about his own racial identity and therefore may have difficulty in countering the negative messages the child receives from society about being Black. Ultimately, the type of inquiries described above are likely to be difficult, extremely contentious, and not terribly probative in determining which parent should be awarded custody.

Notes

1. 466 U.S. 429 (1984).
2. 722 S.W.2d 897 (Ky. 1987).
3. 36 Wash. 2d 143, 216 P.2d 755 (1950).
4. *Boone v. Boone,* 90 N.M. 466, 468, 565 P.2d 337, 339 (1977); *In re* H., 37 Ohio Misc. 124, 125, 305 N.E.2d 815, 818 (1973).

B.

Transracial Adoption

In this section, Elizabeth Bartholet strongly criticizes race matching in adoption and endorses transracial adoption. Twila Perry outlines the various perspectives on transracial adoption and how they affect one's evaluation of such adoption. Zanita Fenton argues that there are no easy answers to whether race should be considered in placement decisions. Ruth Colker criticizes the transracial adoption debate and emphasizes how mixed race children are forced into a Black/White binary. Finally, Twila Perry offers a feminist analysis of the upswing in the adoption of children from Asia and Latin America by White parents.

Where Do Black Children Belong?
The Politics of Race Matching in Adoption

Elizabeth Bartholet

II. The History

. . . Some state laws . . . prohibited transracial adoption. In the early 1960s, South Carolina's laws provided that *no one* could adopt the child of one white and one black parent.[1]

Judicial opinions in the 1950s and early 1960s reflect some common attitudes of the time. In one case an adoption court denied a black man's petition to adopt his white stepchild, reasoning as follows: "The boy when he grows up might lose the social status of a white man by reason of the fact that by record his father will be a negro. . . ."[2] In another case a transracial adoption was initially denied with this justification: "The good Lord created five races and if he intended to have only one, he would have done so. It was never intended that the races should be mixed."[3] [These cases were reversed on appeal—Ed.]

The 1960s represented a period of relative openness to transracial adoption. Foreign adoptions helped pave the way. In the aftermath of the Korean War, South Korea made many of its abandoned and orphaned children available for adoption. Large numbers of these were mixed race children who had been fathered by black American soldiers stationed in Korea. [See Part 9—Ed.] Adoption agencies and prospective parents looked increasingly to Korea and to Third World countries in a trend that has continued to this day. The children they brought here for adoption, many of whom had identifiably foreign features and dark skin, began to accustom people to the idea of adoptive families that involved a mix of racial and ethnic backgrounds. The civil rights movement in this country brought increasing attention to the plight of the minority children who had languished in the foster care systems over the years. This movement's integrationist ideology made transracial adoption a sympathetic idea to many adoption workers and prospective parents. Transracial adoption also served the needs of the waiting white parents, for whom there were not enough color-matched children available, as well as the interests of the agencies in putting together adoptive families and reducing the foster care population. And so agencies began to place waiting black children with white parents when there were no black parents apparently available. The reported number of transracial placements rose gradually to 733 in

1968, and it more than tripled in the next three years to reach a peak of 2,574 in 1971.[4]

In 1972 this brief era of relative openness to transracial adoption came to an abrupt end. That year an organization called the National Association of Black Social Workers (NABSW) issued a position statement against transracial adoption. It stated:

> Black children should be placed only with Black families whether in foster care or for adoption. Black children belong, physically, psychologically and culturally in Black families in order that they receive the total sense of themselves and develop a sound projection of their future. Human beings are products of their environment and develop their sense of values, attitudes and self concept within their family structures. Black children in white homes are cut off from the healthy development of themselves as Black people.
>
> Our position is based on:
>
> 1. the necessity of self-determination from birth to death, of all Black people.
> 2. the need of our young ones to begin at birth to identify with all Black people in a Black community.
> 3. the philosophy that we need our own to build a strong nation.
>
> . . .
>
> We the participants of the workshop have committed ourselves to go back to our communities and work to end this particular form of genocide.[5]

Others joined in the attack on transracial adoption, arguing with the NABSW that transracial adoption constituted an attack on the black community and that it harmed black children by denying them their black heritage and the survival skills needed for life in a racist society.

The attack on transracial adoption appeared to have an immediate and significant impact. The numbers fell from a peak of 2,574 in 1971, to 1,569 in 1972, to 1,091 in 1973.[6] By 1975, the last year in which these statistics were systematically generated, the number was 831.[7] The influential Child Welfare League, which had in 1968 revised its *Standards for Adoption Service* to encourage consideration of transracial adoption, revised its standards once more in 1973 to re-emphasize the advantages of same-race placements.[8] Adoption agency bureaucrats moved swiftly to accommodate the position taken by the NABSW. . . .

Congress did not pass a law specifically mandating an in-race placement preference for black children or officially proclaiming that black children belong to the black community. But . . . a powerful in-race placement preference has nonetheless been established. Adoption agencies have played a major role in establishing this preference. They have used the massive discretion accorded them by adoption laws to create racial policies that would be difficult for legislators to justify politically, in part because they are of questionable legality given constitutional and legislative guarantees against discrimination based on race. But adoption agencies have operated with the cooperation, and oftentimes the active encouragement, of state and federal legislators and officials responsible for regulating and funding adoption activities, as well as the courts. . . .

III. Current Racial Matching Policies

A. A Picture of the Matching Process at Work

An initial order of business for most adoption agencies is the separation of children and prospective parents into racial classifications and subclassifications. Children in need of homes are typically separated into black and white pools. The children in the black pool are then classified by skin tone—light, medium, dark—and sometimes by nationality, ethnicity, or other cultural characteristics. The prospective parent pool is similarly divided and classified. An attempt is then made to match children in the various "black" categories with their parent counterparts. The goal is to assign the light-skinned black child to light-skinned parents, the Haitian child to Haitian parents, and so on. The white children are matched with white prospective parents.

This matching scheme confronts a major problem in the fact that the numbers of children falling into the black and the white pools do not "fit," proportionally, with the number of prospective parents falling into their own black and white pools. In 1987, 37.1 percent of the children in out-of-home placement were black, as compared with 46.1 percent white.[9] Although no good statistics are available, the general understanding is that a very high percentage of the waiting adoptive parent pool is white. In addition, many whites interested in adopting do not bother to put themselves on the waiting lists because of their understanding that there is such a limited number of children available to them.

The matching policies of today place a high priority on expanding the pool of prospective black adoptive parents so placements can be made without utilizing the waiting white pool. . . . [P]rograms have been created to recruit black parents, subsidies have been provided to encourage them to adopt, and traditional parental screening criteria have been revised.

Nevertheless, the numbers mismatch continues. There are many more black children than there are waiting black families. There is a large pool of waiting white families. In recent years both the number of children in foster care and the proportion that is black have been growing.

Today's matching policies generally forbid the immediate placement of black children available for adoption with waiting white families. These policies . . . tend to preclude such placements, either implicitly or explicitly, for periods ranging from six to eighteen months to several years or longer. In many instances the policies preclude placement altogether.

The matching process surfaces, to a degree, in written rules and documented cases. But it is the unwritten and generally invisible rules that are central to understanding the nature of current policies. Virtually everyone in the system agrees that, all things being equal, the minority child should go to minority parents. . . .

B. The Proverbial Tip of the Iceberg—of Written Rules and Documented Cases

1. Laws, Regulations, and Policy Guidelines Mandating Consideration of Race in the Placement Decision

In recent years, several states have written into law requirements that agencies exercise a same-race preference in placing children in adoptive families. Minnesota and Arkansas have laws specifying a preference for placement with a family of the same racial or ethnic heritage. If a same-race placement is not feasible, the preference shifts to "a family of different racial or ethnic heritage from the child which is knowledgeable and appreciative of the child's racial or ethnic heritage."[10] California law similarly mandates a same-race placement preference, and, in addition, it prohibits placement across racial or ethnic lines for a period of ninety days after a child has been relinquished or declared free for adoption. The law further prohibits such adoption after the ninety-day period "unless it can be documented that a diligent search" for a same-race family has been made, using all appropriate recruitment resources and devices. Only on the basis of such documentation can a child be placed across racial or ethnic lines with a family "where there is evidence of sensitivity to the child's race, ethnicity, and culture."

Other states have regulations or written policies that similarly provide for racial preference in the placement process. Some of these, like the California law, specify mandatory waiting periods during which children must be held in hopes of an in-race placement before a transracial placement can be considered.

The Child Welfare League's current *Standards for Adoption Service*, designed to establish standards for adoption agencies throughout the country, provides: "Children in need of adoption have a right to be placed in a family that reflects their ethnicity or race."[11] The current policy position of the National Committee for Adoption states: "Usually, placement of the child should be with a family of a similar racial or ethnic background."[12]

2. Cases Documenting the Removal of Black Children from White Foster Families to Prevent Transracial Adoption

Numerous cases have surfaced in the media, in congressional hearings, and in litigation involving the removal of black children from white foster families with whom they have lived for long periods, often years. In some cases removal is triggered by the white family's expression of interest in adopting their foster child, and the agency intervenes to move the child to a same-race foster family, which may or may not be interested in adoption. In other cases the agency removes the child simply because a same-race foster family has become available. The white parents have poignant stories to tell. Often they have been given a child in very poor physical or psychological shape, or with serious disabilities, and have nursed the child through hard times. The child has thrived under their care and feels a close attachment. They feel a similar attachment and want to adopt so that the child will be a permanent part of their lives. The agency can offer nothing but a shift to a new foster family as an alternative. Experts testify to the destructive impact that disruption of the only stable relationship the child has known will have. Adoption agencies may or may not be forced to back down in these cases, whether by public pressure or by court order. But either way, these cases reveal something of the power of the racial matching policies operating in the adoption agency world, since there is very general agreement among today's child welfare professionals that stable parent-child relationships should not be disrupted and that appropriate foster families should be given priority consideration for the adoption of children with whom they have formed such relationships. These cases are fought out in the public eye not because they are particularly extreme examples of the racial matching policies at work but because the decision to remove the child and the crucial role race plays in that decision are highly visible.

C. Key Features of the Matching System

1. Holding Policies

Agency policies typically involve holding black children in foster or institutional care for significant periods of time after they are or could be free for adoption if no same-race adoptive family is available. Consideration will not be given during this time to placement with available white families. Sometimes the policies specify a definite time period—three or six or twelve or eighteen months—before a transracial adoption may be considered or after which it must be considered. But even these time-specific policies give no real sense for the length of the holding periods at issue since the time generally starts to run only from the date that a child becomes legally free for adoption. Adoption workers often will not begin the process of freeing a child for adoption until and unless there is a same-race family available. Assuming that an agency does eventually succeed in finding a same-race family for a waiting child, it may be several more years before the child can actually be placed. The court process terminating the biological parents' rights can easily consume two to four years. . . .

Many policies simply require that children be held until active efforts to locate same-race families have proved fruitless or until documentation has been submitted regarding such efforts and the unavailability of a same-race family. Many adoption professionals feel that under these non-time-specific policies black children are held for even longer periods.

It seems likely that the rules officially mandating only a limited in-race preference will often function in a more absolute way. Rules requiring social workers to provide documentation of their minority family recruitment efforts before transracial placements will be permitted place the social worker who contemplates making such a placement in the position of doing additional work and incurring the other costs involved in making an exception to the general rule. Such a social worker also risks invoking the wrath of the NABSW and other vocal critics of transracial adoption. The overburdened and underpaid adoption worker has every incentive to avoid the multiple troubles promised by transracial placement.

Policies amounting to absolute or near-absolute bans on transracial adoption appear common. The NABSW continues to take an absolute stance against transracial adoption: "NABSW steadfastly holds to the position that Black children should not be placed with white parents under any circumstances. . . ."[13] There appear to be many adoption workers who are either sympathetic with the NABSW's position or feel intimidated by NABSW advocates and by others who oppose transracial adoption except in the most limited circumstances.

A sense of the extreme nature of current holding policies is revealed by the stories of some of the transracial adoptions that are allowed to take place. One director of an adoption program for minority children in New York State told me that 99 percent of his agency's placements were in-race placements. He then described one of the few transracial placements he had facilitated. The child had been in the foster care system for eleven years and free for adoption for eight of those years. He was finally placed transracially at the age of thirteen only because of concern that as a result of accumulated bitterness over the years he would be likely to exercise the option he would get at age fourteen to refuse to accept adoption if it was offered. The director, a strong advocate of racial matching, felt that an exception was warranted in these unusual circumstances but noted that he had to do battle with forces within the state and agency bureaucracies in order to implement the transracial placement.

2. Recruitment

There is general agreement among adoption workers that an affirmative effort should be made to recruit black families so that there will be more such families for the available black children, although the resources actually devoted to recruitment vary enormously. There have been some notable efforts to form organizations and adoption agencies under black leadership and to involve black churches and the media in the recruitment attempt. These efforts have had some success in encouraging black families to consider adoption and move through the adoption process. State, regional, and national exchanges of black and other "hard to place" children waiting for adoption have been created both as a means of making their availability more generally known and as a way of recruiting parents not locally available.

There is, of course, no systematic recruitment of white families for waiting black children, since matching policies preclude transracial placement except as a last resort. Nor is there generally any effort to recruit white families even for children for whom there seems little prospect of ever finding black adoptive families. Older black children with very serious mental or physical disabilities constitute a hardcore hard-to-place group. One leader in the world of "special needs" placement told me that she had recently begun to wonder if it would not be appropriate to recruit white as well as black parents, in the interest of finding homes for some of these children, but had run into nothing but opposition from her colleagues.

4. Differential Criteria for Assessing Parental Fitness

Agencies apply significantly different parental screening criteria to prospective black adoptive parents than they do to prospective white adoptive parents in order to increase the prospects for in-race placement. In efforts to increase the number of black prospective parents, agencies reach out to include the kinds of people traditionally excluded from the white parent pool or placed at the bottom of the waiting lists for children—singles, older people in their fifties and sixties, and people living on welfare, Social Security, or similar marginal incomes. Critics of transracial adoption have condemned the traditional screening criteria as discriminatory against the black family, and they feel that agencies have not moved nearly far enough to remove this kind of discrimination. They are quite right that traditional criteria, which emphasize economic stability, marriage, and middle-class American values, do function disproportionately to disqualify blacks. They are also right that agencies have not abandoned their traditional criteria altogether in screening black applicants. Nonetheless, most agencies have either significantly softened or radically departed from their traditional criteria in considering black adoptive applicants.

As a result, the pool of black adoptive parents looks very different in socioeconomic terms from the pool of white parents. Black adoptive parents are significantly older, poorer, and more likely to be single than their white adoptive counterparts. A major study published in 1986 gives some indication of the differences.[14] Fifty percent of minority adoptive families had incomes below $20,000 per year, and 20 percent had incomes below $10,000 per year. By contrast, only 14 percent of nonminority families had incomes below $20,000, and only 2 percent had incomes below $10,000. Forty-five percent of the fathers in the minority families were age forty-five or over, with 14 percent age sixty-one or over. Only 19 percent of the nonminority adoptive fathers were age forty-five or over, and only 2 percent were age sixty-one or over. One study involving a small sample of adoptions reported that one-half of the black single parents involved earned less than $10,000. The former director of one of New York State's major adoption agencies told me agency policies in New York required that "just about anyone" of the minority race be considered eligible as an adoptive parent for minority children.

IV. The Impact of Current Policies

A major issue is the degree to which racial matching policies result in delaying or denying permanent placement for minority children. What we know is that minority children are disproportionately represented in the population of children waiting for adoptive homes; they spend longer waiting than white children; and they are less likely to be eventually placed. Estimates indicate that of the population of children waiting for homes, black children make up over one-third and children of color make up roughly one-half. A recent study found that minority children waited for an average of two years, compared to an average one-year wait for nonminorities.[15] Minority placement rates were 20 percent lower than nonminority placement rates. The minority children were comparable in age with the nonminorities and had other characteristics that, had race not been an issue, should have made it easier to find adoptive placements—they had fewer disabilities and fewer previous placements in foster care. The study concluded that racial status was a more powerful determinant of placement rate than any other factor examined. . . .

The most adamant critics of transracial adoption argue that there are no good figures available on the children waiting for adoption. They say that even if minority children are particularly subject to delays and denial in placement, the solution lies in devoting more resources to the preservation and the reunification of black biological families and to the recruitment of minority families for those children who must be removed from their homes. They argue that with such efforts, black homes could be found for all waiting children. They argue further that whites would not be willing to adopt the minority children who wait, noting that most of the children in foster care are older and that they suffer from a variety of physical and emotional problems.

But the fact is that the resources devoted to the goal of preserving black biological families and to making in-racial adoption work have been limited and are likely to be limited in the foreseeable future. There are and almost certainly will be for some period of time too few black families available for the waiting black children. By contrast, there are many white families eagerly awaiting the opportunity to adopt. Although white adopters, like black adopters, tend to prefer healthy infants, special needs recruitment efforts in recent years have demonstrated that whites as well as blacks are often willing to adopt older children and children with devastating disabilities. . . .

We know that many minority children never receive adoptive homes, and many others spend years waiting in foster care or institutions. We know that while most prospective white adopters prefer to adopt healthy white infants, many are interested in adopting black children and many are interested in adopting older children with serious disabilities. There can be no doubt that the current racial matching regime, by barring and discouraging white parents from transracial adoptions, rather than welcoming them in the agency doors denies adoptive homes to minority children.

The racial matching policies also mean that black children who can be placed in-racially go to families that are as a group significantly different in socioeconomic terms from typical white adoptive families and rate significantly lower according to traditional parental screening criteria. Some are, of course, going to middle-class black couples that look like the classic white adoptive family. But recruitment has never produced enough such couples for the minority children in need. As a result, black children are being placed, on a wholesale basis, with families for whom the limited subsidies available are a necessary precondition for adoption and with families that would be screened out by traditional criteria regarding economic and social stability.

V. The Empirical Studies

[The empirical] studies provide an overwhelming endorsement of transracial adoption. . . . The studies were conducted by a diverse group of researchers that included blacks and whites, critics and supporters of transracial adoption. With astounding uniformity their research shows transracial adoption working well from the viewpoint of the children and the adoptive families involved. The children are doing well in terms of such factors as achievement, adjustment, and self-esteem. They seem fully integrated in their families and communities, yet have developed strong senses of racial identity. They are doing well as compared to minority children adopted in-racially and minority children raised by their biological parents.

VI. The Law

Current racial matching policies are in conflict with the basic law of the land on race discrimination. And they are anomalous. In no other area do state and state-licensed decision makers use race so systematically as the basis for action. In no other area do they promote the use of race so openly. Indeed, in most areas of our community life, race is an absolutely impermissible basis for classification.

The federal constitution, state constitutions, and a mass of federal, state, and local laws prohibit discrimination on the basis of race by public entities. Private entities with significant power over our lives are also generally bound by laws prohibiting discrimination on the basis of race. In the past twenty-five years this body of law has grown so that today there are guarantees against race discrimination not only in housing, employment, and public accommodations but in virtually every area of our community life.

It is true that the anti-discrimination norm has been limited by the principles of respect for privacy and freedom of association. People are permitted to act on the basis of racial preference in choosing their friends and companions and in forming truly private social clubs. Small employers and rooming houses were exempted from the employment and the housing provisions of the 1964 Civil Rights Act partly on the basis of these principles. But the state is not permitted to *insist* that race count as a factor in the ordering of people's most private lives. And so in *Loving v. Virginia*[16] the Supreme Court held it unconstitutional for the state to prohibit interracial marriage, and in *Palmore v. Sidoti*[17] the Court held it unconstitutional for the state to use race as the basis for deciding which of two biological parents should have custody of a child. [See Chapters 9 and 62—Ed.] . . .

The anti-discrimination principle has been interpreted to outlaw almost all race-conscious action by the state and by the agencies that control our community lives. There need be no showing that the action is designed to harm or that it results in harm. Race-conscious action has generally been allowed only where it can be justified on the grounds of compelling necessity, or where it is designed to benefit racial minority groups either by avoiding or preventing discrimination or by remedying its effects, as in the case of affirmative action. But these exceptions have been narrowly defined.

In recent years the Supreme Court has held that for federal law purposes, even "benign" racial classifications are highly suspect and must be limited to narrowly defined situations. In *City of Richmond v. J. A. Croson Company*,[18] the Court held that state and local programs designed to benefit minority groups are subject to the same kind of strict constitutional scrutiny as programs designed to burden such groups. It held further that affirmative action can be justified as constitutional only if shown to be absolutely essential to remedying prior discrimination.

The adoption world is an anomaly in this legal universe in which race-conscious action is deemed highly suspect and generally illegal. In agency adoptions, as we have seen, race-conscious action is one of the major rules of the child allocation game. The fact that race is a recognizable factor in decision making is enough under our general anti-discrimination norm to make out a case of intentional discrimination. Adoption agency policies make race not merely a factor but the overwhelmingly significant factor in the placement process.

The public adoption agencies, as well as many of the private agencies, are governed by legislative and constitutional provisions forbidding race discrimination. The federal Constitution's equal protection clause and the related *Croson* limit on legitimate affirmative action apply to all state and local governmental entities, whether they be adoption agencies, adoption courts, or governmental bodies promulgating legislation, regulations, and other policies governing adoption. Title VI of the 1964 Civil Rights Act[19] bans discrimination by adoption agencies, public and private, that receive federal funds. Accordingly, it applies to virtually all public and many private agencies. Many states have constitutional, statutory, and regulatory provisions that broadly prohibit discrimination by public and private agencies.

But for some reason the anti-discrimination principle is thought to mean something quite different in the adoption area than it means elsewhere. The federal policy guidelines clarifying Title VI's meaning in the context of adoption and foster care are symptomatic of how differently the anti-discrimination norm is understood in this context. The guidelines provide specifically that race can be used as a basis for decision making in foster and adoptive placement as long as it is not used in any absolute or categorical way to prohibit consideration of transracial adoption altogether. They state: "Generally, under Title VI, race, color, or national origin may not be used as a basis for providing benefits or services. However, in placing a child in an adoptive or foster home it may be appropriate to consider race, color, or national origin as one of several factors." The guidelines go on to emphasize that this exception applies only in these contexts: "This policy is based on unique aspects of the relationship between a child and his or her adoptive or foster parents. It should not be construed as applicable to any other situation in the child welfare or human services area covered by Title VI."

Notes

Published originally in 139 University of Pennsylvania Law Review 1163 (1991).

1. *See* S.C. Code Ann. § 10-2585 . . . (repealed 1964).

2. *In re* Adoption of a Minor, 228 F.2d 446, 447 (D.C. Cir. 1955), quoting and reversing unpublished memorandum opinion of District Court of Columbia.

3. This statement is reported in Marriage across the Color Line 67 (C. Larrson, ed., 1965). The case reversing this unreported decision by the Ohio Probate Court is *In re* Baker, 117 Ohio App. 26, 185 N.E.2d 51 (1962).

4. *See* R. Simon and H. Altstein, Transracial Adoption 29–30, 32 (1977). . . .

5. National Association of Black Social Workers, Position Paper (April 1972). . . .

6. *See id.* at 30.

7. *See* R. Simon and H. Altstein, Transracial Adoption: A Follow Up 96 (1981). . . .

8. The 1973 standards provided: "It is preferable to place children in families of their own racial background." Child Welfare League of America, Standards for Adoption Service § 4.5 (1973). The rationale was that "[i]n today's social climate children placed in adoptive families with similar racial characteristics can become more easily integrated into the average family group and community." *Id.*

9. These are APWA [American Public Welfare Association] statistics obtained during my interview with Dr. Toshio Tatara. *See* telephone interview with Dr. Toshio Tatara, director of Research and Demonstration Department, American Public Welfare Association (January 29, 1991). . . .

10. Minn. Stat. Ann. §§ 259.255, 259.28 (West Supp. 1991); Ark. Stat. Ann. § 9-9-102 (1987). . . .

11. Child Welfare League of America, Standards for Adoption Service 34 (1988). . . .

12. National Committee for Adoption, *Statement by the Executive Committee* (August 4, 1984), *reprinted in* National Committee for Adoption, Adoption Factbook 124 (1989).

13. Nat'l Ass'n of Black Social Workers, Inc., Preserving Black Families: Research and Action beyond the Rhetoric 31 (1986). . . .

14. *See* 1 Westat, Inc., Adoptive Services for Waiting Minority and Non-Minority Children H4–14 (Apr. 15, 1986).

15. *See id.*

16. 388 U.S. 1 (1967). . . .

17. 466 U.S. 429 (1984).

18. 488 U.S. 469 (1989).

19. Pub. L. No. 88-352, 78 Stat. 252 (codified as amended at 42 U.S.C. § 2000d [1988]). . . .

66

The Transracial Adoption Controversy
An Analysis of Discourse and Subordination

Twila L. Perry

I. Overview of Transracial Adoption and the Perspectives on Transracial Adoption

B. Colorblind Individualism versus Color and Community Consciousness

In my analysis of the transracial adoption controversy, I have uncovered two competing perspectives, *liberal colorblind individualism* and *color and community consciousness*. Liberal colorblind individualism has three dominant characteristics. The first is a belief that complete eradication of racism in this country can be achieved. The second is the affirmation of colorblindness as an ideal—that race should not be an important factor in evaluating individuals and that a colorblind society should be our ultimate goal. Finally, the perspective of liberal colorblind individualism emphasizes the individual as the primary unit for the analysis of rights and interests. In many ways, this perspective is grounded in traditional notions of American liberalism.

The perspective I call color and community consciousness is far more pessimistic about the eradication of racism. Instead, it views racism as a pervasive and permanent part of the American landscape. This perspective recognizes that race has a profound influence in the lives of individuals—in terms of both the choices they make and the choices they believe they have. In addition, the color and community consciousness perspective values a multicultural society, which requires the continued existence of diverse cultures within our society. Finally, while colorblind individualism views the individual as the significant unit for the analysis of rights and interests, color and community consciousness also emphasizes the rights and interests of the group with which the individual is identified. This ideological difference stems from a strong belief in the interrelationship between the subordination of a group as a whole and the oppression of the individuals within that group.

In thinking about transracial adoption, I have come to associate the perspective of colorblind individualism with white scholars and the perspective of color and community consciousness with minority scholars. However, perspectives on racial issues do not divide clearly along racial lines. Accordingly, I do not suggest that all white scholars agree in whole or in part with colorblind individualism or that all minority scholars agree with the perspective of color and community consciousness. My description of these as perspectives rather than the views of particular racial or ethnic groups is quite intentional.

Various elements of the colorblind individualist perspective may be found in the works of several legal scholars, including Professors Elizabeth Bartholet [see Chapter 65—Ed.], Joan Mahoney,[1] and [others]. . . .

The colorblind individualist approach often minimizes interests it deems unrelated to those of the individual child. . . .

To date, the [National Association of Black Social Workers (NABSW)] has articulated the most vivid expression of the color and community consciousness perspective. [See Chapter 65—Ed.] . . .

C. Sources of the Perspectives: Racial Histories and Racial Narratives

The correlation between an individual's race and her inclination toward either the perspective of colorblind individualism or that of color and community consciousness may be explained by what I call *racial narratives*. Racial narratives represent the mechanism by which people understand the significance of race in contemporary society. These narratives are made up of a combination of factors. One is the actual history of the racial group of which the person is a member. A second is the individual's perception of that history—a perception that may or may not be in accordance with the historical reality. A third factor is the individual's perception of the extent to which race affects people's lives on a day-to-day basis. This perception is based on information from personal experiences, family, friends, relatives, and the media. Black and white Americans have different racial narratives; these narratives shape their perception of racial issues.

Black and white Americans came to this country under radically different conditions. The history of white Americans is, of course, complex and lies beyond the scope of this article. But one important general difference in the experience of whites from that of Blacks is that they did not come as slaves. Instead, they entered a society where they had the opportunity to live their lives as individuals, seeking their fortunes in a new land. As a result, white immigrants were never forced to confront the barrier of racism as Blacks did. Ultimately, most white immigrant groups assimilated into American life, achieving both economic and political power.

The myth that an individual can advance in society as a result of her own personal drive and initiative remains a powerful one in American culture. For many whites, the myth is supported by a present reality in which the power of whites as a group accords a white individual a certain luxury of individualism. As a member of the dominant, privileged group, a white individual's daily experience does not require her to confront the reality of discrimination or to link her personal welfare to the fortunes of an oppressed group. Although most whites are probably aware that their individual advantages are partly the function of group advantage, it is unlikely that whites are continually reminded of the advantages of white skin in the way that Blacks are constantly reminded of the disadvantages of Black skin.

In addition to the theme of individualism, the theme of colorblindness is [] long standing in American ideology. Although, until the Civil Rights Movement of the

1950s and 1960s, segregation on the basis of color was the accepted law of this land, colorblindness had long been expressed as an ideal in both public life and in the law. In the law, the ideal of colorblindness has often been traced to Justice [John Marshall] Harlan's dissent in *Plessy v. Ferguson.*[2] However, a recognizable argument for colorblindness dates back even earlier, to the 1840s, when Blacks in the state of Massachusetts unsuccessfully challenged separate schools for white and Black school children. From at least that time through the passage of the Thirteenth, Fourteenth, and Fifteenth Amendments; the decision of *Brown v. Board of Education;*[3] and the civil rights laws of the 1960s, those who fought racial segregation have argued that the government has no right to classify individuals on the basis of color. The ideal of colorblindness is an important facet of our broader American myth of fairness, opportunity, and individualism. In a colorblind society, race is a nonfactor; it should not play any role in benefiting or hindering individuals, particularly since it provides no indication of a person's ability or character. Under this view, taking race into account would give importance to a factor that should be utterly meaningless.

Although Blacks historically have asserted the ideal of colorblindness as part of their civil rights struggle, in the narrative of most Black people, the ideal of colorblindness is just that—an ideal. It has never been reality. Instead, race is what pervades the history and narrative of Blacks, and the link between the individual and the group has often seemed inescapable.

Research suggests that the relationship between the group and personal identity of Blacks is complex. It is obvious, however, that most Blacks experience their membership in a stigmatized group as a powerful part of their daily experience. It is not surprising, therefore, that among Blacks, the importance of race permeates the analysis of social issues and frequently produces a commonality of position. On issues involving race and racism, Blacks often feel that the welfare of the individual cannot be the only concern. There is a group to protect. That group is the Black community—all Black people of African descent who share a common oppression in this country.

Most Black people view race as a pervasive force in the lives of whites as well—both at conscious and subconscious levels. Race dramatically affects how whites analyze most social issues and, for the most part, determines which interactions whites have and choose to have with Blacks or other persons of color. Yet research indicates that Blacks and whites have very different views about the role of race in American life. Whites as a group see racism as less of a problem and are more optimistic about its eradication. In the view of many Blacks, however, this society is neither colorblind nor is it in the process of becoming so.

Another important part of Blacks' racial narrative is the existence of a close connection between the individual, family, and community. The roots of this connection are in both the African and the African American experience. The experience of Blacks in slavery was an integral part of the development of this communal family and social life. For the enslaved, the nuclear family was not a protected entity. Children, who could at any moment be separated from their parents by death or sale, often were reared by a slave community. As a result of this threat, non-kin slave relationships became imbued with symbolic kinship meanings and functions. [After] slavery, the notion that the extended family encompassed people other than those related by blood or marriage has remained a powerful factor of Black social life. This collectivity contrasts with the social organization of the dominant American culture, which is centered on the nuclear family.

II. Influence of the Perspectives on the Transracial Adoption Controversy

The differing perspectives of colorblind individualism and color and community consciousness shape the transracial adoption controversy in several ways. First, colorblind individualism's focus on the individual accords substantial significance to the right of the individual to make decisions regarding family structure without state interference. In contrast, the color and community consciousness perspective focuses on the struggle of Blacks to make choices to create a meaningful family in light of the oppressive circumstances under which many Black families live. Second, colorblind individualism minimizes the significance of racial differences between parent and child. In contrast, from the perspective of color and community consciousness such racial differences must be recognized and addressed. Third, for colorblind individualists, the interests of the Black community have little relevance to the discussion of transracial adoption; only the immediate best interests of the individual child are important. The perspective of color and community consciousness also focuses on the needs of the individual child but does so within the context of the Black community's legitimate stake in transracial adoption. The color and community consciousness perspective sees the individual Black child as inextricably linked to the Black community and inevitably identified with that community. Finally, to colorblind individualists, cultural genocide is a nonissue because of the small number of children who are transracially adopted. From the perspective of color and community consciousness, cultural genocide—the potential loss of Black culture—is an issue of great practical and symbolic importance. . . .

Notes

Published originally in 21 New York University Review of Law and Social Change 33 (1993).

1. Joan Mahoney, *The Black Baby Doll: Transracial Adoption and Cultural Preservation*, 59 University of Missouri—Kansas City Law Review 487 (1991).

2. 163 U.S. 537, 559 (1896) (Harlan, J., dissenting): "Our Constitution is color-blind, and neither knows nor tolerates classes among citizens." . . .

3. 347 U.S. 483 (1954), declaring segregated schools unconstitutional.

67

In a World Not Their Own
The Adoption of Black Children

Zanita E. Fenton

IV. What History Should Teach Us—Alternatives to Formal Traditions

A. Transracial Adoption—One Issue among Many

Transracial adoption has received a considerable amount of attention in the last two decades. . . .

The literature concerning transracial adoption of Black children constitutes a wealth of information. However, the arguments and central focus of this literature are not on the greater problems facing Black children but on this one controversial issue. In addition, the literature tends to take extreme positions, either advocating or opposing transracial adoption. Advocates of this practice tend to minimize the institutional racism affecting the placement of Black children into Black homes. Opponents of this practice tend to minimize this potential solution for children needing permanent placement. Issues concerning race have never been cut and dried, with one solution or one factor affecting the results. This is also the case with race and adoption—issues cannot be considered in a vacuum.

Transracial adoption should be an integral part of a holistic solution designed to address the problems of the entire system that concerns Black children. Given the current needs of the large number of Black children waiting for adoption, transracial adoption should not be discouraged or prevented. But, given the history of racism in this country and the current social contexts in which racism is still a prevailing part of life for Black people, transracial adoption cannot be viewed as the quick and easy solution to accelerate the placement of Black children in permanent homes. Nor should it be an immediate patchwork solution based on naked statistics that do not address the underlying impetus for those statistics.

The current adoption system needs to accommodate the ethnic diversity of the children and potential parents involved. It does seem easier for a system established by white mainstream culture to look to the white community for solutions rather than dealing with the Black community and Black culture. Culture is easily dismissed when it is minority culture subsumed by the mainstream, rather than in reverse. There are a large number of white parents waiting to adopt a child. But the recruitment of white families to adopt Black children solely for the reason that there is a dearth of white children available would be tantamount to perpetuating the system established to provide babies for childless white couples. This is particularly true when the search for Black families to adopt Black children has not been vigorously pursued.

There is, of course, no excuse for the racist bias, embedded in society and reflected in the system of adoption, that considers the "mixing of the races" and transracial adoption as inappropriate and undesirable. A substantial number of Black children spend unnecessary lengths of time in the foster care system when willing adoptive families are not even considered. If a white family is genuinely interested in adopting a Black child, with all factors being considered, they should be allowed to do so.

As a practical matter, a qualified white couple seeking to adopt a Black child would not have any real difficulties, considering the number of waiting Black children. But realistically, most white people choose not to consider adopting Black children. On the other hand, those white people who do seek to adopt Black children are not typically motivated by a desire to participate in cultural genocide of the Black community. All options for reform, including transracial adoption, that will enable the adoption of more Black children should be explored in a realistic manner.

2. Constitutional Concerns

With the impact that racial issues have on society, race is a *relevant* and *necessary* factor in making placement decisions. The best interests standard requires that all relevant factors be considered. Not that race, or any other factor alone, can be determinative of a placement outcome; but race must be considered as having relevance and potential impact on the life of the child awaiting adoption. Each case should be evaluated individually for the needs of the child. Race should be considered in conjunction with the other factors affecting the placement of a child. Formally excluding race as a factor does not exclude the impact that race has on the adopted child.

Classifications by race are presumptively invalid under the Equal Protection Clause. In the context of adopting Black children, in what sense is equal protection required? If it is equal access to the system for adopting children, on the whole white parents have the most access to the system. Should there be equal access to adopting Black children? Or should equal access be broadly applied to the possibility of adopting a child? If equal access to adopting Black children were required, then equal access to white children would also be required. A proposed system to comply with these concepts would operate on a first-come, first-served basis. All approved prospective parents would be placed on the same list to get the first available child. Given the different needs of every individual concerned, this would not seem to serve the best interests of the child or the concerns of the potential adoptive parents.

All children should have an equal opportunity to be adopted. Unfortunately, it has been shown that Black potential adoptive couples are excluded at least equally as much from adopting Black children as are white couples. The climate of litigation on the issue of transracial adoption has made agencies more reluctant to insist on the virtues of same-race placements, making it easier to place with available white parents than to seek out the Black families that have been historically and systematically excluded. Indeed, Black children lose out on two fronts by the systematic denial of Black parents and by the historical social denial of white parents. It should be recognized that the racial status of these children is a significant reason they are affected in this manner. To ignore race in placement decisions would compound the problem.

The use of race as a factor in adoption placement decisions should be viewed as a benign classification. It has been suggested that this benign classification should not be considered as a form of affirmative action justifying the use. Indeed, affirmative action does not accurately describe this situation. This use of race is not a means of rectifying past discrimination or intended to benefit Black parents as a group. Nor is it a case where remedial efforts discriminate in reverse. The interest here warranting the benign use of race is the state's interest in promoting the well-being of a child by determining her best interests.

All factors, including race, should be considered in an already imprecise determination of the best interests of the child. Although this is not the situation of affirmative action, an analogy to the *Bakke* decision is fully relevant. In the case of *Bakke*, preferential college admissions decisions could not be made in a manner that would preclude the admission of others based on race.[1] However, it was not suggested that a race-blind approach was required. In fact, several of the Justices indicated that a race-blind approach would be inappropriate. The court endorsed the use of race as a *factor* in making admissions decisions, so that each decision is made based on the unique qualifications of the individual. This rationale is congruent with racial preference statutes for adoption placements. Race should not be used in a dispositive manner but as a *factor* that allows each placement decision to be decided individually. To deny consideration of any one factor would be to ignore what may have consequences for the interests the child's well-being.

3. The Realities

To put the option of transracial adoption in perspective, it is unlikely that the wholesale promotion of transracial adoption will solve problems for the vast majority of waiting Black children.

> Much evidence exists that transracial adoption would not reduce the number of children in "temporary" foster care or institutions. "[O]nly 1% or less of white families willing to adopt Black children request children who are most in need of families: children over (8) years of age; sibling groups and emotionally and physically handicapped children." Like most of their Black counterparts, most whites are waiting to adopt want infants, although they will accept toddlers. Across the country, there are waiting lists of Black families who want to adopt pre-school children. To be sure, the [fact that] potential white adoptive parents want pre-school children is indicated by the difficulty and inability adoption agencies have in placing white children who are older or handicapped.[2]

In addition, white couples only marginally qualified (via white middle-class standards) to adopt healthy white infants have adopted Black babies instead. The theory is that white parents who already had children did not need a perfect white baby or that couples only marginally qualified would otherwise not receive a baby. Even if there could be a perfect numbers match between waiting Black children and waiting white families, there are still other considerations.

Race must be considered in order to attain permanence and stability as perceived by the child. Racial issues are still prevalent and affect everyone's life, especially the lives of Black children. The mere fact that there is controversy concerning transracial adoption is a strong indicator of this. Black children, regardless of the race of their adoptive parents, will have to deal with racial issues. The crucial point is making sure that the adoptive family is able to deal with racial issues that may be faced by the adopted child. "Recognizing, understanding, accepting, and learning to cope with racial differences seem critical tasks for the child adopted by racially different parents."[3] Even if transracial adoption were promoted on a more widespread basis, race would still need to be considered, including individual attitudes and motivations of potential parents, environment, and the attitudes of the child.

It is expedient to argue that use of race in placement decisions serves to delay the placement of Black children. However, it is not merely the use of race as a factor that has served to delay and limit the placement of Black children. The biases and attitudes concerning race upon which the system has developed are inherent components of a system that still operates in a manner that ignores the specific needs of Black children and that culturally excludes the Black community from services. Eradication of race from statutes will not automatically eradicate the social biases and prejudices that created the system in the first place.

There would also be a cost for the eradication of race from placement decisions that would have a serious impact on the child. For example, for older children, who may already have an established view of cultural norms, race may be a critical consideration. Also, where there is a shortage of healthy white infants in the current system for adoption, parents desperate for a healthy child may be approved without regard to their racial attitudes or how their attitudes will affect the child. Ignoring race in placement decision[s] would create the possibility of adoption by racist parents who are desperate for a child. Each child has different needs concerning race and racial identity. Potential parents have different experiences and a different understanding of race and racial identity. Therefore, race must be considered for each individual placement decision.

Efforts to recruit white potential-adoptive parents for nonwhite children waiting in foster care must be defined differently than efforts to recruit Black potential-adoptive parents. Because the system is one that was created and operates for the benefit of mainstream white culture, recruitment of white parents for Black children, using media efforts and community organizations, is not needed in the same way that recruitment of Black parents is needed. However, transracial adoption should be presented as an option to white parents seeking to adopt. In this case, attitudes toward race must be considered to determine the ability of the potential parents to meet the needs of the individual child, as in any other adoption placement. The manner in which recruitment of white parents is defined in comparison to the manner in which recruitment for Black parents should reflect the needs created by the established system.

Even though the definition of recruitment of white and Black parents should be different, an extended waiting period before adoption for Black children is not advantageous. If a particular agency has instituted sincere and serious recruitment efforts directed at the Black community for the adoption of the waiting Black children, then it is likely that suitable Black families will be available. If an agency does not make serious efforts to find Black parents, then an extended waiting period serves only to hurt the child. The length of time that Black children wait for adoption is not an argument to stop seeking Black adoptive families; nor is the ongoing search for Black parents a reason to make a child wait longer than necessary in foster care. The question should not be "How long should a child wait?" but "What needs to be done and how much effort should be put into finding suitable parents for Black children?" An answer to the latter question will take care of the former.

Where there are undeniably issues without easy answers, support from the Black community for the families of transracially adopted children is one option. This would enable Black children to be placed in a loving family without delay while still providing for the cultural needs of the child and [would] establish a means with which problems associated with race and racial attitudes may be dealt. This is not something that will just happen. This is an option that will be accomplished when policies become more focused on the specific needs of Black children and more inclusive of the Black community through recruitment efforts. Recruitment efforts can identify more potential adoptive Black parents for the waiting Black children. These efforts can also serve to make transracial adoptions more successful by providing support networks for families of transracially adopted children.

B. The Extended Black Family—The Untapped Resource

The extended Black family provides for adoption agencies additional options that have not been fully explored. Alternatives that include use of the extended family would require early planning and procedures designed to utilize family resources when a child is originally taken from his or her home. Even a minimal inquiry or search for potentially willing, care-providing relatives should be made, including both parents, maternal and paternal grandparents, and aunts and uncles. The extended Black family need not be limited to the narrow concepts of blood relations in traditional family units. Options derived from the broader concepts of the extended family should encompass single parents of both genders, grandparents and older people, fictive kin derived from community networks and friends, and larger community organizations. As society has evolved, so too has the form and function of the extended Black family in order to conform with modern realities. Not only should there be better use of existing extended families but also derivative applications of the extended family as it has been used in history.

Alternatives to "traditional" adoption such as single parent adoption, adoption by grandparents, kinship foster homes, guardianships, open adoptions, should be more utilized. Children can accept parenting from several sources outside the "traditional" concept of family. Especially with the currently high divorce rate, children have been successfully reared by two or more sets of parents and stepparents, by single parents, by grandparents, and other arrangements. These options are consistent with the history and culture of Black families in adoption.

Single-parent adoptions should be an option used more often. More and more, families in the Black and white communities are headed by single parents. This has been a tradition in the Black community. In contrast, single-parent families have been a more recent phenomenon in the white community as a by-product of divorce. "Single-parent families are more common among Blacks than among whites, and, contrary to popular stereotypes, many do very well. Thus it is quite appropriate and in keeping with a part of Black experience for single persons to adopt."[4]

Even though single-parent adopters tend to have incomes lower than two-parent homes, single parents are meeting the needs of an increasing number of special needs placements. Single parents, the majority of whom are women, are more likely than a couple to adopt older children and are more likely to adopt boys. Studies done on single-parent adoption, including Black children placed in single-parent homes, have concluded that "single-parent families were . . . as nurturing and viable as dual-parent families."

Parenting by grandparents and great-grandparents is an option that historically has been utilized in the Black community as a means of child care. Adoption agencies have often discouraged the elderly from adopting children because such families are inconsistent with the "traditional" concept of family. Barring other prohibitive factors, age alone, just like race alone, is not an adequate basis for denying adoption.

Kinship foster care is another example of the extended family relationship that should be promoted. Kinship foster homes have had success in an experiment in New York City. This option is very similar to informal adoption in the Black community. In this program, adult extended relatives within the third degree become the foster family of a minor dependent child whenever possible. These kin foster homes receive the same foster care board rate and options as an unrelated foster family would receive. The kin foster parents who take in the child view that child as already being a part of their family. The relatives consider this placement as permanent, as long as the child will not be returned to the biological parents. They also view formal adoption of the child as unnecessary and as depriving the biological parents of parental rights.

"Relative guardianship," another type of extended family relationship, is an option that would reduce administrative costs, while allowing stipends to continue. Where finances are not a primary consideration, forms of open adoption where the child has at least some knowledge of or contact with the biological parents should be considered. Open adoptions are becoming more acceptable in mainstream society, with varying degrees of openness considered healthy in an adoption. These options are consistent with the history of informal adoption in the Black community, where knowledge of biological parents is emphasized. By these methods, permanency and stability for the child could be accomplished readily and ties to the parents would not have to be severed completely.

The use of community organizations and programs to recruit adoptive homes represents a form of the "surrogate extended family." Given the limitations of the system, particularly in how it is applied to the Black community, community organizations can be a healthy solution. Neighborhood-based organizations help the traditional adoption agency practices with the cultural norms of the community toward which recruitment efforts are made. This process may entail utilizing the resources of organizations already established, such as the NAACP [National Association for the Advancement of Colored People], the Urban League, churches and fraternal organizations, and establishing organizations specifically devoted to the placement of Black children, such as Homes for Black Children or One Church, One Child. There is also an existing network of Black professionals that can be effectively accessed to provide assistance in finding adoptive parents for Black children.

Notes

Published originally in 10 Harvard BlackLetter Law Journal 39 (1993).

1. 438 U.S. 265, 270–71 (1978).

2. James S. Bowen, *Cultural Convergences and Divergences: The Nexus between Putative Afro-American Family Values and the Best Interests of the Child*, 26 Journal of Family Law 491, 506 (1987–1988). . . .

3. Penny R. Johnson et al., *Transracial Adoption and the Development of Black Identity at Age Eight*, 66 Child Welfare 45, 54 (January–February 1987).

4. *See* Dawn Day, The Adoption of Black Children: Counteracting Institutional Discrimination 64 (1979). . . .

68

Bi
Race, Sexual Orientation, Gender, and Disability

Ruth Colker

The National Association of Black Social Workers (NABSW) has strongly influenced our adoption and placement policies through its 1972 position paper, in which it strongly argued against the adoption of black children by white families. [See Chapter 65—Ed.] Although the NABSW may have made an important contribution to our understanding of the best interests of black children seeking family placement, it has also perpetuated stark black-white thinking about society. Its position paper states, "Our society is distinctly black or white and characterized by white racism at every level. We repudiate the fallacious and fantasied reasoning of some that whites adopting Black children will alter that basic character." Unfortunately, in trying to protect the interests of black children, the NABSW ignored the interests of the growing number of mixed race children by assuming that we can easily divide society into black and white categories.

The NABSW position paper has generated extensive discussion on the topic of transracial adoptions. Authors generally debate whether blacks face cultural genocide if black children are made available for adoption by white couples, or whether black children suffer so much from the foster care system that they are better off placed with a white family than allowed to languish in that system. In general, authors seem to recognize the cultural benefits of placing black children with black families but often also recognize the practical difficulties that make such placements difficult.

These authors tend to be concerned about preserving black culture and serving the best interests of black children, but they give little attention to how we define "black." In particular, they ignore that many children available for adoption are mixed race, rather than exclusively white or black. Mixed race children are usually lumped into the category "black" with the assumption that steps need to be taken to preserve their black heritage, without considering whether we are using family law to *create* rather than to preserve cultural heritage.[1] In other words, when we assume that all mixed race children should be treated as if they are black in the context of family placements, we are sending the message that these children should be classified and treated as if they are black.

In one case, *Reisman v. Tennessee Department of Human Services*,[2] the court recognized the "biracial" background of a child and concluded that "bi-racial children shall be placed in foster homes and in adoptive homes with bi-racial families if possible."

But the court never defines exactly what it means by "bi-racial families." Ordinarily, if no adoption takes place and the nuclear family stays intact, a mixed race child is raised by parents of two different races—I will assume white and black for this discussion. Those parents do not have the same racial makeup as the child, who is half white and half black. The only way that child would share the racial makeup of her parents is if the parents were each half white and half black (a possible but not very likely result). In what sense, one must wonder, is it better for a mixed race child to have parents of two different races rather than two parents of the same race? In neither case does the child really fully share her racial heritage with her parents.

The court's use of its term *biracial* also does not seem to appreciate that nearly all blacks and many whites are of mixed race background in the United States. The term *biracial,* as used by the court, seems to be limited to the situation in which a child has a white and a black parent. What happens, one must wonder, when the adoptive child grows up and bears a child? She was a biracial child who grew up in a white household. If she bears a child with a white man, is her child still biracial? What if she bears a child with a black man? Is the child still biracial, or will social convention cause the child to be considered black? The "biracial" category, as used by the court and commentators, seems to reflect only the situation in which a child is exactly 50 percent white and 50 percent black. It is not a term that reflects a spectrum; it simply designates a new point—the middle—on the bipolar racial scale. Ironically, that middle point probably does not even exist in the cases to which it is being applied, because the parent who is labeled "black" probably is the product of a mixed race heritage. Thus, although it might make sense abstractly to recognize the category "biracial" and use that category to find homes for "biracial" children, the category is actually an unworkable one. Nearly all of us are, in fact, multiracial, and it distorts reality further to consider only the child with one white and one black parent to be in a middle category.

These classification questions are challenging because the courts do not define the race of a child in a vacuum. The fact that a court recognizes a child as mixed race will not necessarily cause society to treat the child as mixed race. Society may still choose to treat the child as if she is black. If a court, for example, insists on giving no racial preference to black parents over white parents in the adoption of a mixed race child, and the child is eventually placed with white parents, the child may still face unfavorable treatment by friends, classmates, teachers, employers, and health care workers who consider the child to be black. Some people may therefore argue that we should try to place the mixed race child with a black family so that the child will learn how to deal with a racist society. But such a preferential policy makes the assumption that the best way to learn to deal with society's classification scheme is to adopt it as part of one's self-identity. That presumption is dangerous because it puts the courts and social service agencies in the position of helping to perpetuate an arbitrary classification system. While some people may consider such a racial classification system in the adoption context to be ameliorative, it also helps perpetuate the subordinating "one drop of blood" rule for racial classification. [See Part 2—Ed.] I am therefore suggesting that racial preference policies for adoption of mixed race children do not present exactly the same problems as they do for black children. Classifying a mixed race child as black and thereby preferentially placing her in a black home promotes a racist and subordinating classification system.

In sum, I believe that we get a different perspective on the transracial adoption controversy when we examine it in the context of a multiracial child. First, we see that many of the children whom the courts and social agencies have unreflexively labeled "black" for adoption purposes are in fact multiracial. It is therefore too simplistic to say that these cases raise issues of transracial adoption only when a white couple or individual tries to adopt a multiracial child. Second, we see that our goal should be to respect an individual's full racial heritage, rather than to distort one aspect of it. When courts or social agencies distort one aspect of that racial heritage, they help perpetuate our racist "one drop of blood" rule. Nonetheless, just as we should stop transferring what is considered by some commentators to be good social policy for black children to the context of multiracial children, we should also be careful not to transfer these lessons from cases involving multiracial children to cases involving black children. Our policy of preferring black parents for a black child may be beneficial in terms of preserving racial heritage and even teaching a child how to deal with the racism of our society. My point is simply that stretching that policy to include all multiracial children with a drop of African American blood reinforces racism rather than the best interests of the child. By taking that step, we are helping to construct a bipolar racial model that is disrespectful to the genuine mixed racial heritage of that child. Children should not be the instruments of such social engineering.

Notes

1. *See, e.g., Farmer v. Farmer,* 439 N.Y.S.2d 584 (N.Y. Sup. Ct. 1981); *In re Davis,* 465 A.2d 614 (Pa. 1983); *Ward v. Ward,* 216 P.2d 755 (Wash. 1950).

2. 843 F. Supp. 356 (W.D. Tenn. 1993).

Transracial and International Adoption
Mothers, Hierarchy, Race, and Feminist Legal Theory

Twila L. Perry

III. International Adoption

A. Transracial and International Adoption: A Comparison

To some extent, transracial adoption and the international adoption of children from Latin America and Asia raise different issues. Some of the countries involved in international adoptions, at least in the past, actively supported or promoted such activity. Many of the children adopted are infants whose mothers presumably gave them up knowing that they were to be adopted by Westerners. Indeed, some of these mothers may be pleased that their children will have a chance to have a more economically comfortable life in America than they would have been able to offer in their often impoverished circumstances. Finally, in the United States, the adoption of children from Asia and Latin America may pose fewer social difficulties than the adoption of Black American children. There is, in America, a greater resistance to interracial marriages and interracial families where the nonwhite party is Black rather than Asian or Hispanic. If Asian or Hispanic children are more accepted by white society than are Black children, the "best interests" and/or "survival skills" issues that are so controversial in the transracial adoption of Black children may not seem as controversial with respect to children from these groups.

Still, international adoptions have also been subject to controversy and criticism. It has been argued, for example, that such adoptions run the risk of creating problems of adjustment in older children who must adapt to a new culture and language, and that they sometimes create problems of identity in children who are of a different ethnic group from their parents'. It has also been claimed that the continued practice of intercountry adoption retards the growth of child welfare services in the sending countries. Furthermore, it has been argued that wealthy adopters come to poor countries in the wake of wars, earthquakes, and famines and take many healthy children, leaving behind older and disabled children for institutional care.

Some people in third world countries analogize international adoption to colonial exploitation. Rita Simon and Howard Altstein, who have written extensively on transracial and international adoption, have observed:

> [W]hat the West has generally regarded as charitable, humane—even noble—behavior, developing countries have come to define as imperialistic, self-serving and a return to a form of colonialism in which whites exploit and steal natural resources. In the 1970s and 1980s, children were the natural resources being exploited and out of which developing nations were being cheated.[1]

Moreover, recent incidents in some Latin American countries indicate that not everyone in those countries is favorably disposed toward international adoption. A few years ago, for example, there were rumors in some Central and South American countries that Americans were seeking children for the purpose of using them as household servants or prostitutes or killing them and using them as organ donors for sick children in America. In several instances, the rumors sparked violence against Americans. Such incidents, while not always protests specifically against international adoption, suggest that some people in third world countries suspect that Americans may devalue children who are not white Americans. Such beliefs are likely to lead to critical views of international adoption.

1. The Links of Poverty, Racism, and Patriarchy

There are important links to be drawn between the transracial adoption of Black children in the United States and the adoption of children of color from Asia and Latin America. The factors of racism and economic discrimination that result in large numbers of Black children being separated from their biological parents in this country have counterparts in the international context, where a history of colonialism, neocolonialism, cultural imperialism, and economic exploitation often results in mothers being unable to keep the children to whom they have given birth. Thus, both domestically and internationally, transracial and international adoption often result in a pattern in which there is the transfer of children from the least advantaged women to the most advantaged women. Despite the differences between the specific circumstances of Black women in America and some other third world women, there is a connection in terms of a struggle by both to function as mothers under political and economic conditions that severely challenge their ability to adequately parent their own children. Moreover, many transracial adoptions, international adoptions, and adoptions in which racial and ethnic differences are not a factor, also share another connection—a link to the institution of patriarchy. Because poverty, racism, and patriarchy are often factors when children become available for adoption, consideration of each of them is essential to the development of a feminist approach to adoption.

a. Poverty

Just as poverty is a reason why Black children in America are disproportionately represented among those available for adoption, poverty is often a factor in international adoption. Many women who surrender their children live in dire circumstances where disease, lack of education, and poor housing are part of everyday existence. Although the United States certainly cannot be held solely responsible for these conditions, there are relationships that exist between the United States and some of the countries from which internationally adopted children often come that should be troubling to feminists thinking about international adoption. These relationships have aspects that are economic, political/military, and cultural.

This is the era of the global economy. There is a recent trend for large corporations to shift manufacturing jobs from the United States, where labor costs are high, to poor countries, where labor costs are low. . . .

World markets relocate in search of cheap labor and find a home in countries with unstable (or dependent) political regimes, low levels of unionization, and high unemployment. What is significant about this particular situation is that it is young, third world women who overwhelmingly constitute the labor force.

In recent years, some poor women, particularly in countries in Latin America, have found employment in factories that produce goods for companies in the United States. Unfortunately, the wages for which many of these women work are pitifully low, sometimes as low as forty cents per hour. What are the implications for international adoption of this trend of economic globalization? Clearly the wages these women earn are inadequate. Even if they are the highest wages the women have ever earned, they are not sufficient to lift the women out of poverty, and poverty is clearly a factor in so many children in Latin America being available for adoption by Americans. Indeed, many of the Latin American women who work for American businesses work for companies such as Liz Claiborne, J.C. Penney, and J. Crew, who specifically market their clothing to middle- and upper-middle-class American women.

b. Imperialism, Culture, and International Adoption

A number of countries from which children of color come have a history of colonialism—military and economic domination by Western nations at some point in their histories. Obviously, colonial relationships exist to serve the needs of the colonizing countries; the result is generally exploitation of the people and resources of the country that is dominated. However, colonialism is not simply military and economic—it also has a cultural component. This cultural component often finds expression in the belief that the country that is being militarily and economically subjugated is comprised of an inferior people, and in the eyes of the conqueror, this inferiority justifies the conquest and continued domination. A phenomenon occurs wherein over time, as Edward Said has noted, the dominant group substitutes its own view or representation of the other culture for positive knowledge about it, and the relationship becomes one of "power, of domination, of varying degrees of a complex hegemony. . . ."[2] While the era of actual colonialism may be over in much of the world, the racist and ethnocentric rationales for it linger.

The United States has never formally held colonies in Latin America. Nevertheless, our government has had strong military ties to numerous governments in that area of the world. It has often financed military endeavors favorable to United States interests, and it has developed economic interests and relationships that favor American businesses. The United States has also been a dominant military force in a number of the Asian countries, such as Korea and Vietnam, where many internationally adopted children have been born. The kind of economic and military relationships that the

United States has had with some third world countries can engender the same kind of cultural imperialism that results from more formal colonial relationships.

As troubling as it may be for many to admit, a conception of poor, third world countries as subordinate nations fits very comfortably with the practice of international adoption. This kind of view translates easily into the idea that Western adoptive parents are simply saving unfortunate third world children by bringing them out of primitive, impoverished, and disease-ridden countries into the more affluent life that the West can offer. It permits a discourse that allows Westerners to take the high ground and portray their international adoptions as simple acts of humanitarianism and altruism.

Admittedly, there is a humanitarian aspect to many international adoptions. Obviously, there are children adopted from poor countries who would face a very bleak life or even death in their homelands. However, a feminist analysis of international adoption should go farther than a simple altruism narrative. Indeed, an appropriate question might not be what Westerners are giving to the children of impoverished countries but what they are taking from those countries or from the poor women who live in them. "Taking" might appear to be a harsh word in the context of a situation in which women have voluntarily surrendered their children. However, the "voluntariness" of these surrenders must be examined in light of the economic, social, and political circumstances under which the mothers often live.

c. Patriarchy and Racism

Patriarchy and racism can also be important factors in the availability of children for international adoption, although these phenomena take different forms in different countries. In some countries, patriarchy may be the dominant factor. In Asian countries such as Korea, adoption historically has only been considered as a means to perpetuate family lines in families without a male heir. Because adoption has been unpopular as a general practice, it has been difficult to place children for adoption within the country.

In China, the availability of many baby girls for adoption is also largely a function of patriarchy. The Chinese tradition of favoring male children, combined with the policy limiting families to one child, results in many families choosing to keep a male child and putting female infants in orphanages, or sometimes even putting them to death. Adoption by foreigners has sometimes been a fortunate alternative to these fates. In Vietnam, children fathered by foreigners, often by American soldiers, have not been easily accepted by the society. Where the children have obviously been fathered by Blacks, racial prejudice can compound the factors of foreign blood and birth outside of marriage, placing on these children a triple burden. [See Part 9—Ed.] Simon and Altstein have noted that many West German children who have been adopted by Americans are racially mixed—fathered by Black servicemen stationed in Germany. These children, too, have had difficulty being fully accepted into German society.[3]

Both racism and patriarchy play a role in making children available for adoption in the United States as well. One result of racism in society, and specifically in the child welfare system, is that a disproportionate number of children of color become separated from their parents. Even where white infants, the most sought-after children for adoption, are available, patriarchy is often a factor. Both economics and marital status can be relevant in a woman's decision to give a child up for adoption—a woman who is pregnant and single may feel that the economic future for herself and her child is bleak. As a general matter, unmarried women are economically less well-off than married women, and single mothers are disproportionately poor. The poor economic status of women who are not attached to men as financial providers is a reflection of a patriarchal system that still denies to women the same opportunities it accords to men.

The stigma attached to bearing a child outside of marriage has long been a factor in the availability of babies for adoption. This stigma, too, is largely a function of patriarchy in its quest to control the sexuality and reproductive powers of women. Although the stigma of unwed pregnancy and motherhood is clearly not what it once was, it is likely still a factor in the decisions of some women to give their babies up for adoption.

Finally, racism and patriarchy may operate in tandem in the surrender of some children. A single white woman giving birth to a biracial child may anticipate multiple difficulties. First of all, the child herself is a public announcement that the woman has been involved in a relationship with a Black man. This may result in some social stigma that may devalue the status a white woman would otherwise have on the basis of race. Second, the day-to-day difficulties of raising a child who will be considered to be Black in a racist society may also be daunting. Finally, the stigma of out-of-wedlock birth and the financial difficulties many single mothers face may combine with these other factors to persuade some white birth mothers to surrender their biracial children for adoption.

Notes

Reprinted by permission of the Yale Journal of Law and Feminism, Inc. from the Yale Journal of Law and Feminism, Vol. 10, No. 1, pp. 101–64 (1998).

1. Intercountry Adoption: A Multinational Perspective 93 (Howard Altstein and Rita J. Simon, eds., 1991) [hereafter Intercountry Adoption]. . . .

2. Edward Said, Orientalism 5 (1978).

3. *See* Intercountry Adoption, *supra*, at 4.

C.

The Indian Child Welfare Act

In the United States, an independent body of law governs adoption of Native American children, in large part because of the nation's special relationship with Indian tribes. Lorie Graham discusses the Indian Child Welfare Act, the principal federal law regulating the adoption of Indian children. Christine Metteer studies the law as it has evolved under the act.

"The Past Never Vanishes"

A Contextual Critique of the Existing Indian Family Doctrine

Lorie M. Graham

I. Introduction

Congress passed the [Indian Child Welfare Act (ICWA) in 1978] in response to the massive displacement of Native American children in this country. Prior to the law's passage, one-third of all Native American children were being separated from their families and communities and placed in non-Indian adoptive homes, foster care, and educational institutions by federal, state, and private child welfare authorities. While there were myriad interrelated factors that led up to this Indian child welfare crisis, at its core was the failure of mainstream society to recognize and respect the cultural values and social norms of Native American nations. In a poignant statement to Congress in 1978 on the treatment of American Indian families in this country, Chief Calvin Isaac of the Mississippi Band of Choctaw Indians noted that

> Indian children are removed from the custody of their natural parents by nontribal government authorities who have no basis for intelligently evaluating the cultural and social premises underlying Indian home life and child rearing. Many of the individuals who decide the fate of our children are at best ignorant of our cultural values, and at worst contemptful of the Indian way and convinced that removal, usually to a non-Indian household or institution, can only benefit an Indian child.[1]

This assimilative attitude that Native American children were better off growing up in a non-Indian environment did not surface overnight. Rather, it percolated from centuries of U.S.-sanctioned policies—from boarding schools, to "placing out" programs, to Indian adoption projects—aimed at the erasure of Native American cultures.

The passage of the ICWA marked a reversal in federal Indian policy toward one of self-determination for Native American nations. The law recognized the sovereign authority of tribes to address Indian child welfare issues. Tribal courts were designated as the exclusive forum for certain custody proceedings involving Native American children domiciled or residing on the reservation or a ward of the tribal court, and the preferred forum for proceedings involving nondomiciliary children. Additionally, in state cases involving the termination of parental rights, foster care, and adoption, the law sought to protect the rights of Native American children to be raised and nurtured, whenever feasible, in their families and communities of origin, through the establishment of minimum federal standards and procedural safeguards. The law is limited to Native American children who are members of or eligible for membership in a federally recognized tribe. As one ICWA attorney noted, "the hopeful vision" for the ICWA was a future "in which the states, tribes, and federal government work[ed] together . . . to protect Indian children and to reaffirm the value of Indian family life."[2]

While the law is not flawless, it provides vital protection to Native American children, their families, and tribes. Yet recent studies suggest that one-fifth of all Native American children "are still being placed outside of their natural tribal and family environments."[3] Courts, social welfare agencies, and attorneys who fail to follow the letter and spirit of the law have all contributed to this ongoing crisis. The "Existing Indian Family" doctrine [see Chapter 71—Ed.], a state judicially created exception to the ICWA that has received some recent congressional support, is one such example. While the doctrine varies slightly from state to state, the end results are the same: to cut off a number of Native American children from their extended families and cultural heritages by thwarting the express language and goals of the ICWA and ignoring indigenous views of what constitutes an "Indian family." It is in this way that the doctrine is reminiscent of past U.S. policies. Indeed, these recent challenges to the ICWA cannot be properly evaluated without placing them in the larger historical context of U.S. Indian policy toward American Indian children. The legacies of these policies remain with us today as Native American nations struggle to reconnect with their lost loved ones and maintain a sense of community for their children and their children's children. . . .

III. The Indian Child Welfare Crisis

While self-determination in social welfare and education became an important aim for Native American tribes and organizations during the 1970s, the extent of the Indian child welfare crisis had to be assessed before responsive legislation could be drafted. Toward this end, the Association of American Indian Affairs (AAIA) began to document the number of American Indian children being removed from their homes, as well as the major causes and effects of this dislocation. The results of AAIA's multiyear study were nothing less than shocking.

The AAIA findings were indicative of massive displacement of American Indian children. Conservative estimates indicated that one-third of all American Indian children were being separated from their families and placed in foster care, adoptive homes, or educational institutions. In some individual states the problem was much worse. Minnesota, Montana, South Dakota, and Washington had American Indian placement rates that were five to nineteen times greater than that of the non-Indian rate. In the state of Wisconsin, American Indian children were at risk of being separated from their families at a rate 1,600 times greater than for non-Indian children. Moreover, many of these children were being completely cut off from their communities and heritages. At least 85 percent of the placements were in non-Indian homes and institutions, and a high proportion of those placements were out of state. Federal boarding schools, mission schools, private training schools, and [Bureau of Indian Affairs (BIA)] dormitory programs all contributed to this massive displacement. For instance, in 1971 the BIA school census showed that 34,538 American Indian children lived in its institutional facilities rather than at home. On the Navajo reservation, 20,000 children in grades K–12 were living in boarding schools at the time of the studies. Missing from these statistics were the generations of Native Americans previously disconnected from their families as a result of BIA "relocation" programs, federal "outing" programs, and mission-run "educational" placement programs. Additionally, no study could completely capture the effects of years of national paternalism and attempted assimilation on the psyches of Native Americans. . . .

A. Some Causes

The AAIA studies and legislative hearings revealed how deeply ingrained the assimilative attitudes of the past had become in our society. Social welfare agencies, schools, and the legal system all had a role to play in the crisis. The cultural values and social norms of Native American families—particularly indigenous child-rearing practices—were viewed institutionally as the antithesis of a modern-day "civilized" society. Indeed, in many of the child welfare cases examined, American Indian communities were shocked to learn that the families they regarded as "excellent care-givers" had been judged "unfit" by caseworkers. This disparity in viewpoint was the result of general disdain for American Indian family life. Senator James Abourezk (D.-S.D.) remarked in 1977 that "[p]ublic and private welfare agencies seem to have operated on the premise that most Indian children would really be better off growing up non-Indians."[4]

Cultural misunderstandings and biases were often underlying decisions to separate a child from an Indian home or community. The legislative history to the Indian Child Welfare Act noted that many "[s]ocial workers, untutored in the ways of Indian family life or assuming them to be socially irresponsible, considered leaving the child with persons outside the nuclear family as neglect and thus as grounds for terminating parental rights."[5] In a case involving a Sisseton-Wahpeton Sioux mother, a state welfare department petitioned the court to terminate the rights of the mother to one of her two children on the grounds that she often left him with his sixty-nine-year-old great-grandmother.[6] The social worker interpreted this behavior as evidence that the mother was either incapable or unwilling to care for her child, ignoring the traditional role of the extended family in the rearing of a child. Similarly, cultural misunderstandings within the public school system often led to spurious reports of neglect. The following case history involves a young Indian child attending public school in Oregon in the 1970s:

> The Indian mother of an eight-year-old boy was temporarily unable to care for her son after she broke her leg. She asked her sister to care for her son until she recovered. At school the boy gave his aunt's address as his own. The teacher asked if his mother had moved. He said "no." The teacher then asked with whom he was staying. The boy replied that he was staying with his mother. The teacher became upset and started yelling at

> him. The boy held his ears. The teacher decided the boy was disturbed and made an appointment for him to be tested for schizophrenia. The test could not be administered without the mother's permission. A staff member of the Portland Urban Indian Program, at the request of the school, visited the mother's home to obtain her consent. There the staff member learned that in the culture of the boy's tribe, children are raised by the extended family. In the extended family, children regard both their natural mother and her sisters as mothers because they share maternal responsibilities.[7]

Cultural bias and stereotypes were most evident in cases involving alcohol use. Studies revealed that in areas where rates of problem drinking among Indians and non-Indians were the same, the Indian family was more likely to have their children removed from the home. Moreover, American Indian families were less likely than non-Indian families with alcohol problems to receive supportive services as an alternative to removal of their children. Caseworkers and teachers also misinterpreted the disciplinary practices of Indian families, claiming that American Indian children lacked close parental supervision and strong discipline. Alternative forms of discipline to physical punishment, including teasing, ostracism, peer pressure, and storytelling, were seen as too permissive. Yet, as the legislative history to the ICWA notes, "[w]hat is labeled as 'permissiveness' may often, in fact, simply be a different but effective way of disciplining children. BIA boarding schools are full of children with such spurious 'behavioral problems.'"[8]

Materialism and middle-class notions of what constituted poverty often influenced the removal decision of social welfare agencies. In one 1977 California case, a child was removed from the custody of her aunt by a social worker on the sole ground that "an Indian reservation is an unsuitable environment for a child and that the preadoptive parents were financially able to provide a home and a way of life superior to the one furnished by the natural mother."[9] . . .

American Indian children and their families did not fare any better in court before state judges. The House Committee on Interior and Insular Affairs agreed with advocates of the ICWA that "the abusive actions of social service agencies would be largely nullified if more judges were themselves knowledgeable about Indian life and required a sharper definition of child abuse and neglect."[10] The "best interest of the child" standard utilized in many child custody proceedings was being narrowly interpreted by state courts without recognition of or appreciation for the cultural and familial values of Native American nations. In most cases, judges would merely defer to the opinion of state social workers, placing the burden on the parents to prove that they were capable of caring for their child in accordance with Western notions of childcare. Moreover, extended family members and tribes were rarely, if ever, consulted about the children's welfare. Nor were state courts immune to cultural bias. In a 1979 case involving a Sioux child from the Rosebud reservation, a state court terminated a mother's parental rights on the ground that it would be "detrimental" and "unnatural" to return the child to the mother because of the mother's place of residency on the reservation.[11]

Other court-related causes of removal included procedural irregularities and lack of due process afforded Indian families and tribes. American Indian parents were often not properly notified of court dates and rarely had legal representation or the supporting testimony of expert witnesses on Indian child-rearing practices available to them. In one such case, a child was held in foster care for seven months under a state *ex parte* emergency removal order before a hearing was scheduled. And even then, the mother was notified of the hearing only by publication, despite the fact that she had continuously lived at the same address from which the child had been removed. Advance notification was further complicated by differences in Indian and non-Indian social systems. This problem was succinctly described in the legislative history to the ICWA:

> By sharing the responsibility of child rearing, the extended family tends to strengthen the community's commitment to the child. At the same time, however, it diminishes the possibility that the nuclear family will be able to mobilize itself quickly enough when an outside agency acts to assume custody. Because it is not unusual for Indian children to spend considerable time away with other relatives, there is no immediate realization of what is happening—possibly not until the opportunity for due process has slipped away.[12]

Moreover, although tribes had an obvious interest in these cases, they were often not notified of the proceedings or allowed to intervene. Once again, there was no avenue available for the state courts to be informed of the familial resources available to the children in their own communities. Similarly problematic were the unclear lines of demarcation between state and tribal court jurisdiction over Indian child custody proceedings.

B. Some Effects

The massive displacement of American Indian children has had long-lasting effects on the well-being of Native American children, families, and tribes. One of the most devastating consequences has been the unusually high rate of suicide among American Indian children placed in foster care, adoptive homes, and institutions—a rate twice that of the reservation suicide rate and four times that of the general population. At U.S. congressional hearings on the Indian child welfare crisis, experts testified that Native American children were more likely to face significant social problems in adolescence and adulthood as a result of the displacement. . . .

Other studies have corroborated these findings. Moreover, children raised in boarding schools or other educational institutions knew very little of life in a "family." As parents themselves, they had no patterns to follow in rearing their own children. Many had to learn to live and cope with harsh experiences, such as physical and mental abuse. In addition, they were being educated in systems that devalued their Native cultures, resulting in further alienation from community and loss of self-esteem. High dropout rates and low employment were the norm for many of these students. The large number of American children raised in foster care similarly perpetuated the destruction of the American Indian family. "Stricken by a 'constant sense of not knowing where they will be or how long they'll be there,'" these children found it difficult in adulthood to establish permanent roots.[13] Additionally, because society frowned on their cultures, many American Indians sought to deny their own heritages. This denial caused further distress, often leading to some form of substance abuse. Some of the consequences of the removal process for the individual child were not easily quantifiable, such as the loss of opportunity to learn about one's heritage from one's elders.

Studies did show that when the child was removed from the home without the benefits of proper cultural, political, and social safeguards, it affected the entire kinship community. . . . [S]tudies indicated that removal of a child "effectively destroyed the family as an intact unit . . . exacerbat[ing] the problems of alcoholism, unemployment, and emotional duress among parents." The consistent threat of losing one's child created a sense of hopelessness and powerlessness that made [it] difficult for the adults to function well as parents. Many feared emotional attachment because of the inevitable loss. One psychologist noted that American Indian parents had become so conditioned to the removal process that they would often place their own children in boarding schools as a matter of course.[14] Others would place the children with social service agencies and hospitals, rather than entrusting them to the care of extended family members.

Moreover, since the community's economic and social well-being were built around kinship networks, the destruction of the family unit perpetuated the dire socioeconomic conditions existing on many reservations. The Indian child welfare crisis also chipped away at the cultural heritages of tribes. As Chief Calvin Isaac of the Mississippi Band of Choctaw Indians noted in a 1978 hearing before the Senate:

> Culturally, the chances of Indian survival are significantly reduced if our children, the only means for the transmission of the tribal heritage, are to be raised in non-Indian homes and denied exposure to the ways of their People. Furthermore, these practices seriously undercut the tribes' ability to continue self-governing communities. Probably in no area is it more important that tribal sovereignty be respected than in an area as socially and culturally determinative as family relationships.[15]

C. Congress's Response

. . . In 1978, Congress passed the Indian Child Welfare Act, declaring:

> It is the policy of this Nation to protect the best interests of Indian children and to promote the stability and security of Indian tribes and families by the establishment of minimum Federal standards for the removal of Indian children from their families and the placement of such children in foster or adoptive homes which will reflect the unique values of Indian culture, and by providing for assistance to Indian tribes in the operation of child and family service programs.[16]

The ICWA was designed to achieve a number of interrelated goals. First, the law seeks to reverse the historical policies and practices that led to the massive removal of American Indian children to institutions, foster care, and adoptive homes. The law is an official acknowledgment by the federal government that Indian children are not necessarily "better off" far from the influence of family and community. The law similarly recognizes that an Indian child's best interests may be inextricably connected to that of the tribe. While the law could not dictate a change in the attitudes of social workers, educators, and judges, it could establish minimum standards and procedures for the placement of American Indian children outside the home.

Second, the ICWA seeks to recognize and respect the familial traditions and responsibilities of Native American nations. When viewed in the context of indigenous family and community, the law recognizes the importance of the traditional kinship system and the role of the extended family in the rearing of children. For instance, it recognizes foster care and adoptive placement preferences with extended family members and other tribal members and requires state courts to consider the social and cultural standards of tribes when making placement determinations.

It also seeks to protect the individual rights of Native American children to be raised, whenever feasible, in their families and communities of origin by mandating that families receive culturally appropriate remedial services before a placement occurs. Prior to the law being passed, American Indian families were less likely to receive any supportive services as an alternative to removal of their children, as compared to non-Indian families. Additionally, the Act was designed to be sufficiently flexible to meet the diverse cultural interests and complex social needs of American Indian children. Evidence of this flexibility can be found in the opinions of several state and tribal courts, as well as various tribal and state programs.

Third, it seeks to promote Indian self-determination in the area of child welfare. The doctrine of tribal sovereignty holds that the "powers of Indian tribes are . . . inherent powers of a limited sovereignty which has never been extinguished." The ICWA recognizes the sovereign powers of Native American nations to develop indigenous systems of child welfare. This goal is in line with studies indicating a link between the welfare of Native American children and the extent to which tribes are able to control their own political, social, and economic development. The law reaffirms the jurisdiction of tribal courts over certain child custody proceedings and extends that jurisdiction to children living away from their communities. It ensures that tribes and extended family members will have an opportunity to be heard through notification provisions and the ability to intervene in the proceedings. Finally, it encourages the development and implementation of tribal child welfare services. These provisions recognize the symbiotic relationship between tribe and child, including the child's right to participate in the "fabric of tribal life" and the tribe's right to exist as a distinct political community.

Despite some limitations in the law, there is a general consensus among Native American nations and organizations that the ICWA provides "vital protection to American Indian children, families and tribes." Yet the Act continues to be ignored in many instances. . . .

Notes

1. *Hearings before the Subcomm. on Indian Affairs and Public Lands of the House Comm. on Interior and Insular Affairs*, 95th Cong. 191–92 (1978) [hereafter *1978 Hearings*]. . . .

2. *See* Bruce Davies, *Implementing the Indian Child Welfare Act*, 16 Clearinghouse Review 179, 196 (1982).

3. *See Introduction to* The Indian Child Welfare Act: Unto the Seventh Generation: Conference Proceedings (Troy R. Johnson, ed., 1993).

4. Hon. James Abourezk, *The Role of the Federal Government: A Congressional View, in* The Destruction of American Indian Families 12 (Steven Unger, ed., 1977).

5. *Id.* at 3; H.R. Rep. No. 1386, at 10 (1978), *reprinted in* 1978 U.S.C.C.A.N. 7530 [hereafter House Report)].

6. The Destruction of American Indian Families, *supra*, at 3.

7. *Id.* at 43.

8. House Report, *supra*, at 10. . . .

9. The Destruction of American Indian Families, *supra*, at 3.

10. House Report, *supra*, at 11.

11. On appeal, a Texas court reversed the lower court decision terminating the mother's parental rights, while upholding the part of the order awarding permanent custody to the grandparents. *See Broken Leg v. Butts*, 559 S.W.2d 853 (Tex. Cir. App. 1977). . . .

12. House Report, *supra*, at 11.

13. Russel Lawrence Barsh, *The Indian Child Welfare Act of 1979: A Critical Analysis*, 31 Hastings Law Journal 1287, 1291 (1980). . . .

14. Carolyn Attneave, *The Wasted Strengths of Indian Families, in* The Destruction of American Indian Families, *supra*, at 29, 30.

15. *1978 Hearings*, *supra*, at 193.

16. 25 U.S.C. § 1902 (1994). . . .

71

Pigs in Heaven
A Parable of Native American Adoption under the Indian Child Welfare Act

Christine Metteer

I. Introduction

For eighteen years the Indian Child Welfare Act (ICWA)[] has provided protection against the removal of Indian children from their Indian culture. Such protection is afforded not only to Indian children and Indian parents but also, and of equal importance, to Indian tribes.[] However, a recent California case, *In re Bridget R.*, raised questions concerning both the applicability and constitutionality of the act,[1] and bills have been introduced in both the House and the Senate that would significantly weaken the act.[] The pre-ICWA system of white courts and social workers determining custody of Indian children by considering the best interests of the child, in some instances to the exclusion of any tribal interest in their children,[] is therefore in danger of resurfacing.[] Such a step backward seems unthinkable, given the history of abuses by non-Indian social workers in removing Indian children from their families and tribes in the 1970s and earlier.[] . . .

The spirit behind the act is reflected in Congress's "rising concern" in the 1970s "over the consequences to Indian children, Indian families, and Indian tribes of abusive child welfare practices that resulted in the separation of large numbers of Indian children from their families and tribes through adoption or foster care placement, usually in non-Indian homes."[2] The House report accompanying the act explained that the ICWA "seeks to protect the rights of the Indian child as an Indian and the rights of the Indian community and tribe in retaining its children in its society."[3] Congress's stated intent was to establish "'a Federal policy that, where possible, an Indian child should remain in the Indian community,' and by making sure that Indian child welfare determinations are not based on 'a white, middle-class standard, which, in many cases, forecloses placement with the Indian family.'"[4]

In order to implement these goals, the ICWA puts forward a dual jurisdictional scheme. Section 1911(a) gives a tribe exclusive jurisdiction "over any child custody proceeding involving an Indian child who resides or is domiciled within the reservation of such tribe," with the single exception of "where such jurisdiction is otherwise vested in the State by existing Federal law."[] Section 1911(b) establishes that when an Indian child is not domiciled on the reservation, "the court, in the absence of good cause to the contrary, shall transfer such proceeding to the jurisdiction of the tribe, absent objection by either parent . . . [p]rovided, [t]hat such transfer shall be subject to declination by the tribal court. . . ."[] The U.S. Supreme Court has interpreted § 1911(b) as creating "concurrent but presumptively tribal jurisdiction in the case of children not domiciled on the reservation."[5]

The ICWA also provides substantive provisions to promote its stated goals. These mandate, inter alia, timely notice to the tribe of any involuntary child custody proceeding,[] evidence beyond a reasonable doubt "that the continued custody of the child by the parent or Indian custodian is likely to result in serious emotional or physical damage to the child" before ordering termination of parental rights,[] written and recorded consent of the parent(s) in voluntary termination of parental rights,[] and, absent good cause to the contrary, placing an Indian child according to the following preferences: "with 1) a member of the child's extended family; 2) other members of the Indian child's tribe; or 3) other Indian families."[6]

Despite Congress's stated policies, the Act's jurisdictional and substantive provisions, and the 1989 U.S. Supreme Court decision that found that "Congress perceived the States and their courts as partly responsible for the child separation problem it intended to correct,"[7] state courts have had problems finding the act applicable.[] They have also had problems transferring jurisdiction to tribal courts and following the Act's placement preferences.[] Additionally, non-Indian adoptive parents (and sometimes Indian parents as well) try to defeat the Act's application by invoking "the shibboleth of Euro-American family law when child custody is at issue":[] the "cardinal rule that the best interests of the child are paramount."[8]

In July 1995, the California Second District Court of Appeal invoked this "cardinal rule" by asking parties to address the issue of whether the "best interest of the children is the paramount concern irrespective of the application of the ICWA."[] The court had earlier blocked the lower court's order, under the act, to return the Indian twins to their birth parents.[] That decision left the attorney for the twins "shocked and appalled that the court would subject the twins to this extended judicial torture," [] a result that frequently occurs when the ICWA's provisions are not immediately applied.[]

The controversy in *In re Bridget R.* arose because the Indian father . . . did not reveal his Indian heritage at the time of the adoption. . . .[] However, three months after relinquishing custody of the children, the father and his Pomo tribe challenged the adoption under the ICWA and sought to have the children returned to the birth parents.[] (The twins' mother has subsequently been established as a member of the Yaqui tribe.)[] The adoptive parents refused.[]

The case is problematic on several levels. First, although in *In re a Child of Indian Heritage* a New Jersey superior court upheld a trial court's refusal to set aside an adoption after it learned of the child's Indian heritage when it initially had no reason to know that the child was Indian,[] that case is distinguishable. As one commentator has explained, "The trial court's good faith lack of awareness of the child's Indian status can excuse its failure to give formal notice to the tribe at an earlier stage of the proceeding, but it should not excuse a refusal to permit the tribe to argue for the applicability of the ICWA once the tribe learns about the proposed adoption through other means."[9]

Like the child in *Indian Heritage*, the twin girls in *In re Bridget R.* were relinquished for adoption when their Indian heritage was not acknowledged, and the tribe was therefore not given notice at the time of the initial adoption proceedings. However, the trial court had knowledge of the children's Indian heritage from the beginning, and the Act does not suggest any penalty for a parent's withholding of information about the child's Indian status. The trial judge laid blame for the delay in notice on the attorney handling the adoption. The trial judge reasoned that the attorney "clearly failed in terms of his responsibility to his clients. . . . Had he addressed these issues in the initial interview, we would not all be here today."[] Additionally, "as an officer of the court, the parent's lawyer may have a duty to disclose . . . [and] failure to bring the child's status to the court's attention could be grounds for disciplinary action. . . ."[] In fact, the adoptive parents . . . have filed suit for legal malpractice and breach of fiduciary duty, inter alia, against the attorney handling their adoption.[] The trial court therefore appropriately invalidated the father's consent to the adoption under the ICWA, since the delay in notice to the tribe was not the fault of the Indian parents,[] and ordered the return of the children to their birth parents. The judge found that "[t]he ingredient that was left out in this whole situation was the interests of the tribe."[]

The California court's "attack on the Indian Child Welfare Act"[] [fails to recognize] the history of abuses leading to the enactment of the ICWA and of the provisions of the Act itself, both in letter and spirit. . . .

III. Further Abuses: Problems in Implementing the ICWA

The problems that arise in implementing the [ICWA] can be broken down into two broad categories: (1) determining jurisdiction in Indian children custody proceedings and (2) determining the applicability of the substantive provisions of the act.

A. Jurisdiction

[T]he jurisdictional scheme of the ICWA reflects the fact that "[b]ecause child custody arrangements are heavily laden with cultural and social tradition, the choice of forum as between a state and tribal court can fundamentally affect the outcome of a custody dispute."[] The jurisdictional provisions are therefore "at the heart of the ICWA,"[] reflecting the spirit of the act that "where possible, an Indian child should remain in the Indian community."[10] In fact, "[t]he broad grant of jurisdiction to tribes and the narrowing of state authority were aimed at preventing the . . . evils" set out in § 1901(4)(5) of the act.[]

State courts, however, often wrestle with the spirit of the act in determining jurisdiction, which depends on how the courts choose to define the act's terms. The term most often in question in determining jurisdiction is the "domicile" of the child.[] As might be expected, state courts seeking to retain jurisdiction define the term narrowly to mean the child's physical presence "within the territory set aside for the reservation."[] With such a definition in place, the "heart" of the ICWA, the "broad grant of jurisdiction to the tribes," can easily be set aside, and *individuals* can dictate jurisdiction simply by changing the child's domicile at the time of a custody proceeding.[]

The clear focus of such a definition is on the primacy of the wishes of the parents (rather than on "tribal primacy"),[] who, when wanting "to place their child for adoption . . . typically argue for an interpretation of the rules of domicile that permits state court jurisdiction."[] Despite the fact that such a definition's "receptivity . . . to [the] non-Indian placement of an Indian child is precisely one of the evils at which the ICWA was aimed,"[] no less than three U.S. Supreme Court justices have embraced the view that

> allowing the tribe to defeat the parents' deliberate choice of jurisdiction would be conducive neither to the best interests of the child nor to the stability and security of Indian tribes and families. . . . "By allowing the Indian parents to 'choose' the forum that will decide whether to sever the parent-child relationship, Congress promotes the security of Indian families by allowing the Indian parents to defend in the court system that most reflects the parents' familial standards." . . . [N]o purpose of the ICWA is served by closing the State Courthouse door to them.[11]

Such a definition of domicile, however, defeats the clear intent Congress embodied in § 1911 by removing the tribe as the preferred forum, and similarly defeats the spirit of the act, which is to protect the interests of the tribe in determining "who will have the care and custody of its children."[] As the court in *[In re] Halloway* found, "to permit [parents] to change . . . domicile as part of a scheme to facilitate . . . adoption by non-Indians . . . weakens considerably the tribe's ability to assert its interest in its children . . . which is distinct from but on a parity with the interest of the parents."[12] The majority in *Holyfield* agreed and held that "the law of domicile Congress used in the ICWA cannot be one that permits individual reservation-domiciled tribal members to defeat the tribe's exclusive jurisdiction by the simple expedient of giving birth and placing the child for adoption off the reservation."[13] Such a definition, in the Supreme Court's opinion, "would, to a large extent, nullify the purpose the ICWA was intended to accomplish."[] The Supreme Court therefore found that Congress intended a uniform definition of the term *domicile,* not subject to individual state law's interpretations.[]

The Supreme Court's broad construction of the term *domicile* for purposes of determining jurisdiction under § 1911 caused the *Holyfield* case to be heralded as "good news for proponents of a broad reading of the Act."[14] While some state courts have indeed found that "*Holyfield* also carries the clear message that [the ICWA] would be read liberally, perhaps creatively, to protect the rights of the tribe even against the clearly expressed wishes of the parents . . . ,"[15] others have refused to read *Holyfield* expansively, limiting the case to its own facts and narrow issue.[16] And although *Holyfield* called for a uniform definition of key terms of the Act, state courts' individual definitions of another provision of the Act's jurisdictional scheme, "good cause" not to transfer proceedings to the tribal court,[] has also plagued the liberal application of the act as envisioned by Congress.

Under § 1911(b), any proceeding involving an Indian child not domiciled on the reservation must be transferred to the jurisdiction of the tribe, with three exceptions: (1) objection of either parent, (2) declination of the tribe to accept jurisdiction, or (3) good cause to the contrary.[] The first two exceptions are objectively verifiable and pose no definitional problems. However, determining good cause not to transfer is subjective. The Bureau of Indian Affairs [BIA] has issued guidelines for determining good cause not to transfer, but although they must be accorded great weight in construing the ICWA, they are not controlling.[]

Since "there is no federally-defined 'best interest of the Indian child' standard," state courts, defying the spirit of the act and the BIA Guidelines, have had a "tendency to answer prematurely the substantive question of the case without first determining whether they have jurisdiction" to do so.[] In determining who has jurisdiction to determine where an Indian child should be placed by considering the best interests of the child, courts have inappropriately merged the two issues into one.[] The problem underlying this approach is that "[s]tate courts can convincingly enumerate the many good reasons why the child should remain where he is. Invariably, however, the courts neglect to demonstrate how it is in the child's best interest to deny his tribe's court the right to adjudicate the matter."[]

In the wake of *Holyfield*, however, one court has demanded uniform definition of the Act's "good cause" not to transfer provision and found that such a provision must not be "interpreted by individual state law."[17] Following the BIA Guidelines, the court reasoned that "considerations involving the best interests of the child are relevant not to determine jurisdiction, but to ascertain placement."[] The court based such reasoning on Congress's expressed "preference for the tribal court to determine these [child custody] matters regardless of any psychological impact upon the child."[] The court held, therefore, that "any psychological effects the transfer may have . . . are not factors which should be considered when deciding jurisdiction."[]

Such a decision is in direct keeping with the Act's "broad grant of jurisdiction to tribes"[] to determine the placement of their children. It reflects courts' understanding of Congress's and the Supreme Court's mandate that the ICWA is "a means of protecting not only the interests of individual Indian children and families, but also of the tribes themselves."[] This mandate is reflected in an approach to jurisdiction which acknowledges "that [although] a state court may take jurisdiction [this] does not necessarily mean that it should do so, as the court should consider the rights of the child, the rights of the tribe[] . . . and should balance the interests of the state and the tribe." . . .

B. Substantive Applicability

In addition to thwarting the spirit of the ICWA to protect tribal primacy in determining the placement of their children by refusing to grant exclusive jurisdiction under § 1911(a) or transferring jurisdiction under § 1911(b), state courts have also skirted Congress's intent to keep Indian families together, or at least to keep Indian children within their tribe, as provided by the Act's substantive provisions. The most flagrant violation of the spirit of the Act is the so-called existing Indian family exception.[]

The stated policy of the act is to "protect the best interests of Indian children and to promote the stability and security of Indian tribes and families by the establishment of minimum Federal standards for the removal of Indian children from their families. . . ."[18] Additionally, the Supreme Court has found that "[t]he numerous prerogatives accorded the tribes through the ICWA's substantive provisions . . . must . . . be seen as a means of protecting not only the interests of individual Indian children and families, but also of the tribes themselves." However, state courts have carved out an exception and refused to apply the Act if they determine that the Indian child was not taken from an existing Indian family.[19]

Using this exception the courts have disregarded Congress's warning, codified in § 1901, that the state courts "often fail[] to recognize the essential tribal relations of Indian people and the cultural and social standards prevailing in Indian communities and families."[20] The court in *Claymore v. Serr*, for example, stated that it would not apply the Act if the child was not taken from an existing Indian family and then proceeded to define "family" according to the cultural and social standards of white society:

> The circuit court implies that the definition should be restricted to the nuclear family or parents and offspring and should not include a broader or extended family. We believe that the references made in the Act to an "Indian family" suggest [that] definition of family. The narrow[] definition is also implicated by the Act's reference to all other relatives as "extended family members."
>
> *Black's Law Dictionary*, Fifth Edition, states that the definition of "family" . . . [m]ost commonly . . . refers to a group of persons consisting of parents and children, immediate kindred, constituting the fundamental societal unit in civilized society. . . . We believe this primary definition is controlling in this case.[21]

The court therefore found that the Act did not apply to an illegitimate child of an Indian father and a non-Indian mother who had never resided with the father or in any other Indian family.[]

The problem with the existing Indian family exception is that it first calls into question both what it means to be an Indian child and an Indian family and then applies the definition of white "civilized society" to answer these questions. By its own terms the act applies to the Indian child on the basis of his or her tribal membership or eligibility and the tribal membership of the biological parent.[] However, raising the first question, the courts, instead of relying on the Act's definition of an Indian child,

> have fashioned . . . levels of "Indian-ness" to try to manipulate their use of the existing Indian family exception . . . [which] becomes a second litmus test for "Indian-ness" [including] such notions as: 1) ties to the tribe, 2) Indian cultural setting, and 3) length of time in an Indian home—effectively adding a new requirement or redefining an "Indian child."[22]

The courts tend to define "Indian-ness" by evaluating whether the child lives in an "actual Indian dwelling,"[] apparently thinking of a teepee, hogan, or pueblo. However, "[l]imiting the Act's applicability solely to situations where nonfamily entities physically remove Indian children from actual Indian dwellings deprecates the very links—parental, tribal, and cultural—the Act is designed to preserve."[23]

Despite a broad reading of *Holyfield* that allowed the North Dakota Supreme Court to find its use of the existing Indian family exception in *Claymore* "incorrect . . . fail[ing] to recognize the legitimate concerns of the tribe that are protected under the Act,"[] the California court in *In re Bridget R.* similarly considered "Indian-ness" in determining the Act's applicability. The court found that "it does not follow from *Holyfield* that ICWA should apply when neither the child *nor either natural parent* has ever resided or been domiciled on a reservation or maintained any significant social, cultural, or political relationship with an Indian tribe."[] The court then remanded the case so that that factual determination could be made, but not before prolonged reasoning showing that in the appellate court's opinion, "the events and circumstances leading up to the relinquishment of the twins strongly suggests that no such relationship exists."[]

The twins' Indian family, however, "is bitter over having to prove how Indian" they are.[] The birth parents argue that "questions about their lineage and commitment to their culture are insulting and should be left to Native Americans themselves."[24] The twins' former attorney likens such determination of "Indian-ness" to "trying to determine who is a good Catholic or a good Jew. The function of the government is not to assess those things."[] The twins' grandmother explains, "It's not how many activities you go to . . . it's something you feel."[] The Indian father's tribe agrees that "it only takes one gene, one piece to make them [Indian]. . . . We don't want to lose a single one of our children. They are our heart and soul."[]

. . . The ICWA was enacted to prevent the breakup of Indian families "by the removal, often unwarranted, of their children from them"[25] and to recognize "the essential tribal relations of Indian people and the cultural and social standards prevailing in Indian communities and families."[26] According to Indian definition, the larger family is broken up anytime a child is removed from the tribe of which it is eligible to be a member. Therefore, the judicially created existing Indian family exception is in direct violation of the spirit, and quite probably the letter, of the law.

Notes

Published originally in 28 Arizona State Law Journal 589 (1996). Copyright © 1996 by Christine Metteer. Reprinted with permission.

In this excerpt, "[]" denotes where a footnote was omitted; the author requested the specific designation of omitted footnotes.

1. *In re Bridget R.*, 49 Cal. Rptr. 507, 536 (Ct. App. 1996).
2. *Mississippi Band of Choctaw Indians v. Holyfield,* 490 U.S. 30, 32 (1989).
3. H.R. Rep. No. 1386, 95th Cong., 2d Sess. 23 (1978) [hereafter House Report].
4. *Id.* at 24.
5. *Holyfield*, 490 U.S. at 36.
6. 25 U.S.C. § 1915(a) (1994).
7. *Holyfield*, 490 U.S. at 30.
8. *In re C.W.*, 479 N.W.2d 105, 114 (Neb. 1992). . . .

9. Joan H. Hollinger, *Beyond the Best Interests of the Tribe: The Indian Child Welfare Act and the Adoption of Indian Children*, 66 University of Detroit Law Review 451, 474 (1989).

10. *Holyfield*, 490 U.S. at 37.

11. *Id.* at 60–61, 63 (Stevens, J., dissenting).

12. *In re Halloway,* 732 P.2d 962, 969 (Utah 1986).

13. *Holyfield*, 490 U.S. at 53.

14. Roger A. Tellinghuisen, *The Indian Child Welfare Act of 1978: A Practical Guide with [Limited] Commentary*, 34 South Dakota Law Review 660, 662 (1989).

15. *In re Baade,* 462 N.W.2d 485, 489–90 (S.D. 1990); Tellinghuisen, *supra*, at 666.

16. *See, e.g., In re S.C.,* 833 P.2d 1249, 1254 (Okla. 1992), declining to extend *Holyfield* and apply the Act to an Indian father who had never had custody of or regular contact with a child several years of age; *In re Infant Boy Crews,* 825 P.2d 305, 310 (Wash. 1992), finding *Holyfield* inapplicable "when an Indian child is not being removed from an Indian cultural setting."

17. *In re Armell,* 550 N.E.2d 1060, 1066 (Ill. App. Ct. 1990).

18. 25 U.S.C. § 1902 (1994).

19. *See, e.g., In re Adoption of Baby Boy L.,* 643 P.2d 168 (Kan. 1982), finding that no Indian family existed when the child was the illegitimate son of a non-Indian mother and a five-eighths Kiowa Indian father; *Claymore v. Serr,* 405 N.W.2d 650, 651 (S.D. 1987), finding that no Indian family existed when the child was the illegitimate daughter of a non-Indian mother and a father who was an enrolled member of the Cheyenne River Sioux. . . .

20. 25 U.S.C. § 1901(5) (1994).

21. 405 N.W.2d 650, 653–54 (S.D. 1987) (citations omitted).

22. Toni H. Davis, *The Existing Indian Family Exception to the Indian Child Welfare Act*, 69 North Dakota Law Review 465, 489 (1993).

23. *In re Crystal K.,* 276 Cal. Rptr. 619 (Ct. App. 1990).

24. James Rainey, *Court Blocks Return of Adopted Twin Girls,* Los Angeles Times, July 7, 1995, at B4.

25. 25 U.S.C. § 1901(4) (1994).

26. 25 U.S.C. § 1901(5) (1994).

Review Questions

1. Should the race of a parent be a factor in a child custody decision of a mixed race child? Does it matter which parent the child physically resembles?
2. Should the law encourage or discourage transracial adoptions?
3. Is the Indian Child Welfare Act and its efforts to regulate the adoption of Indian children by non-Indians a sensible compromise?
4. Would you adopt a child of a race different from your own? Explain your response.
5. Classroom Exercise: Half of the class should defend Professor Bartholet's colorblind position on transracial adoption, and the other half should challenge it.

Suggested Readings

Anita L. Allen, *The Black Surrogate Mother*, 8 Harvard BlackLetter Journal 17 (1991).

Barbara Ann Atwood, *Fighting over Indian Children: The Uses and Abuses of Jurisdictional Ambiguity*, 36 UCLA Law Review 1051 (1989).

———, *Identity and Assimilation: Changing Definitions of Tribal Power over Children*, 83 Minnesota Law Review 927 (1999).

Anjana Bahl, *Color-Coordinated Families: Race Matching in Adoption in the United States and Britain*, 28 Loyola University Chicago Law Journal 41 (1996).

R. Richard Banks, *The Color of Desire: Fulfilling Adoptive Parents' Racial Preferences through Discriminatory State Action*, 107 Yale Law Journal 875 (1998).

Russel Lawrence Barsh, *The Indian Child Welfare Act of 1978: A Critical Analysis*, 31 Hastings Law Journal 1287 (1980).

Elizabeth Bartholet, Family Bonds: Adoption and the Politics of Parenting (1993).

———, *Private Race Preferences in Family Formation*, 107 Yale Law Journal 2351 (1998).

Katharine T. Bartlett, *Comparing Race and Sex Discrimination in Custody Cases*, 28 Hofstra Law Review 877 (2000).

Eileen M. Blackwood, *Race as a Factor in Custody and Adoption Disputes:* Palmore v. Sidoti, 71 Cornell Law Review 209 (1985).

Suzanne Brannen Campbell, *Taking Race Out of the Equation: Transracial Adoption in 2000*, 53 Southern Methodist University Law Review 1599 (2000).

Richard R. Carlson, *Transnational Adoption of Children*, 23 Tulsa Law Journal 317 (1988).

Nancy E. Dowd, *A Feminist Analysis of Adoption*, 107 Harvard Law Review 913 (1994).

Heidi W. Durrow, *Mothering across the Color Line: White Women, "Black" Babies*, 7 Yale Journal of Law and Feminism 227 (1995).

Kim Forde-Mazrui, *Black Identity and Child Placement: The Best Interests of Black and Biracial Children*, 92 Michigan Law Review 925 (1994).

Carol R. Goforth, *"What Is She?" How Race Matters and Why It Shouldn't*, 46 DePaul Law Review 1 (1996).

Susan J. Grossman, *A Child of a Different Color: Race as a Factor in Adoption and Custody Proceedings*, 17 Buffalo Law Review 303 (1968).

Cynthia G. Hawkins-Leon, *The Indian Child Welfare Act and the African American Tribe: Facing the Adoption Crisis*, 36 Brandeis Journal of Family Law 201 (1997–1998).

Gilbert A. Holmes, *The Extended Family System in the Black Community: A Child-Centered Model for Adoption Policy*, 68 Temple Law Review 1649 (1995).

Joan Heifetz Hollinger, *Beyond the Best Interests of the Tribe: The Indian Child Welfare Act and the Adoption of Indian Children*, 66 University of Detroit Law Review 451 (1989).

Margaret Howard, *Transracial Adoption: Analysis of the Best Interests Standard*, 59 Notre Dame Law Review 503 (1984).

Ruth-Arlene W. Howe, *Redefining the Transracial Adoption Controversy*, 2 Duke Journal of Gender Law and Policy 131 (1995).

Julie C. Lythcott-Haims, *Where Do Mixed Babies Belong? Racial Classification in America and Its Implications for Transracial Adoption*, 29 Harvard Civil Rights–Civil Liberties Law Review 531 (1994).

Joan Mahoney, *The Black Baby Doll: Transracial Adoption and Cultural Preservation*, 59 UMKC Law Review 487 (1991).

Angela T. McCormick, *Transracial Adoption: A Critical View of the Courts' Present Standards*, 28 Journal of Family Law 303 (1989–1990).

Christine M. Metteer, *A Law unto Itself: The Indian Child Welfare Act as Inapplicable and Inappropriate to the Transracial/Race-Matching Adoption Controversy*, 38 Brandeis Law Journal 47 (1999–2000).

Rachel F. Moran, Interracial Intimacy: The Regulation of Race and Romance (2001).

Shari O'Brien, *Race in Adoption Proceedings: The Pernicious Factor*, 21 Tulsa Law Journal 485 (1986).

Sandra Lee Patton, Birthmarks: Transracial Adoption in Contemporary America (2000).

D. Michael Reilly, *Constitutional Law: Race as a Factor in Interracial Adoptions*, 32 Catholic University Law Review 1022 (1983).

Dorothy Roberts, *The Genetic Tie*, 62 University of Chicago Law Review 209 (1995).

Jennifer L. Rosato, *"A Color of Their Own": Multiracial Children and the Family*, 36 Brandeis Journal of Family Law 41 (1997–1998).

Sandra C. Ruffin, *Postmodernism, Spirit Healing, and the Proposed Amendments to the Indian Child Welfare Act*, 30 Pacific McGeorge Law Review 1221 (1999).

Sharon E. Rush, *"If Black Is So Special, Then Why Isn't It in the Rainbow?"* 26 Connecticut Law Review 1195 (1994).

———, Loving across the Color Line: A White Adoptive Mother Learns about Race (2000).

———, *Sharing Space: Why Racial Goodwill Isn't Enough*, 32 Connecticut Law Review 1 (2000).

Rita James Simon and Howard Altstein, Transracial Adoption (1977).

Jacinda T. Townsend, *Reclaiming Self-Determination: A Call for Intraracial Adoption*, 2 Duke Journal of Gender Law and Policy 173 (1995).

Michelle Van Leeuwen, *The Politics of Adoptions across Borders: Whose Interests Are Served? (A Look at the Emerging Market of Infants from China)*, 8 Pacific Rim Law and Policy Journal 189 (1999).

Peter K. Wahl, *Little Power to Help Brenda? A Defense of the Indian Child Welfare Act and Its Continued Implementation in Minnesota*, 26 William Mitchell Law Review 811 (2000).

Barbara Bennett Woodhouse, *"Are You My Mother?" Conceptualizing Children's Identity Rights in Transracial Adoptions*, 2 Duke Journal of Gender Law and Policy 107 (1995).

Myriam Zreczny, *Race-Conscious Child Placement: Deviating from a Policy against Racial Classifications*, 69 Chicago-Kent Law Review 1121 (1994).

Part IX

The Immigration and Naturalization Laws

Part 9 discusses mixed race peoples and their treatment under the U.S. immigration laws. The immigration and naturalization laws have a long history of racial exclusions. In fact, being a "free White person" was a naturalization requirement for much of U.S. history. (See generally Ian F. Haney López, *White by Law: The Legal Construction of Race* [1996].) During this period, a mixed race person found herself classified as "not White" and therefore ineligible for naturalization.

Laws designed to exclude Chinese immigrants flourished from the 1880s until 1965.(See generally Lucy E. Salyer, *Laws Harsh as Tigers: Chinese Immigrants and the Shaping of Modern Immigration Law* [1995].) For purposes of the immigration and naturalization laws, Congress and the courts classified mixed race immigrants as non-White and ineligible for naturalization. (See Immigration and Nationality Act of 1952, 66 Stat. 163, 177 § 202[b][6] [1952] [repealed], stating that the "Asian-Pacific" quota applied to an "immigrant born outside the Asia-Pacific triangle who is attributable by *as much as one-half of his ancestry to peoples indigenous*" to Asian countries [emphasis added]; *Wagio Kong Tjauw Wong v. Esperdy,* 214 F. Supp. 264 [S.D.N.Y. 1963] [applying section]; see also *Hitai v. INS,* 343 F.2d 466 [2d Cir. 1965], *cert. denied,* 382 U.S. 816 [1965], applying immigration law to treat alien born of Japanese parents in Brazil as subject to the Japanese quota).

The U.S. naturalization laws at one time discouraged interracial relationships. Early in the twentieth century, the law stripped a U.S. citizen woman of her citizenship if she married an immigrant ineligible to naturalize (i.e., a non-White). Similarly, in modern times, illegitimate children of a U.S. citizen and a noncitizen possess different immigration rights depending on the gender of the parent who, as a citizen, sponsors their immigration to the United States. (See *Nguyen v. INS,* 533 U.S. 53 [2001], rejecting the challenge that the law violated Equal Protection Clause.) This results in disparate impacts on mixed race children, because U.S. military men, often serving in the developing world, find it more difficult to bring "illegitimate" children, generally of mixed ancestry, born in other countries to the United States. The United States has recognized certain legal obligations toward Amerasian children, many of whom suffer from severe discrimination and ostracization in their native land.

In Part 9, Dudley McGovney in a 1934 article discusses the cases addressing whether mixed race immigrants were "White" for naturalization purposes. Kevin

Johnson considers how U.S. citizen women were stripped of their citizenship if they married immigrants ineligible for naturalization. Robin Levi outlines the hardships faced by Amerasian children, a group that grew with U.S. military involvement in Asia, and how the law responded. Finally, Kif Augustine-Adams analyzes the gender and racial impacts of modern citizenship laws.

Naturalization of the Mixed-Blood

A Dictum

Dudley O. McGovney

In [an] opinion of the Supreme Court of the United States,[1] prepared by Mr. Justice [Benjamin] Cardozo, appears this *dictum*:

> The privilege of naturalization is denied to all who are not White (unless the applicants are of African nativity or African descent); and men are not white if the strain of colored blood in them is a half or a quarter, or, not improbably, even less, the governing test always (United States v. Bhagat Singh Thind, [261 U.S. 204 (1923)], being that of common understanding. Dean v. Com., 4 Grat. (45 Va.) 541; Gentry v. McMinnis, 3 Dana (Ky.) 382; In re Camille (C.C.) 6 F. 256; In re Young (D.C.) 198 F. 715, 717; In re Lampitoe (D.C.) 232 F. 382; In re Alverto (D.C.) 198 F. 688; In re Knight (D.C.) 171 F. 299; 2 Kent Comm. (12th Ed.) 73, note. *Cf.* The decisions in the days of slavery. Gentry v. McMinnis, 3 Dana (Ky.) 382; Morrison v. White, 16 La. Ann. 100, 102; see Scott v. Raub, 88 Va. 721, 727–729, 14 S.E. 178.

The point actually decided in the case was the invalidity under the due process of law clause of the Fourteenth Amendment of a procedural provision of the Alien Land Law of California. The result reached needed no bolstering by obiter refinements about the possible meaning of "White persons" or "persons of African descent" in the naturalization law. . . .

. . . The *dictum* concerns itself with the meaning of "White persons" and "aliens of African nativity" and "persons of African descent" in our naturalization statute. The last two phrases are commonly taken to mean alien negroes. The statute in form says that the provisions for naturalization "apply" to these two descriptions of persons. It has always been construed as declaring these only to be eligible to naturalization. Who are eligible within these terms is the question. Or, who are White persons and who are negroes within the meaning and benefit of the naturalization law? Few of the decided cases have dealt with persons of mixed blood, the problem here. They have been concerned with the question whether Chinese, Japanese, Hindus, Syrians, Malays, American Indians, and so forth, as racial stocks, are of the White or negro races. In most of the cases the alien applying for naturalization was in fact, or [was] assumed to be, of the full blood of the racial stock discussed. This is true of the only cases on the subject that have gone to the Supreme Court. In *Ozawa v. United States*[2] a question certified

by the circuit court of appeals was "Is one who is of the Japanese race and born in Japan eligible to citizenship under the naturalization laws?"
The Court said:

> Beginning with the decision of Circuit Judge Sawyer, in *Re Ah Yup* (1878) 5 Sawy. 155, the Federal and state courts, in an almost unbroken line, have held that the words "White person" were meant to indicate only a person of what is popularly known as the Caucasian race. . . . The appellant . . . is clearly of a race which is not Caucasian. . . .

In *United States v. Bhagat Singh Thind*[3] a question certified by the lower court was "Is a high caste Hindu of full Indian blood" eligible? The whole opinion is summed up with fidelity in a single quotation:

> What we now hold is that the words "free white persons" are words of common speech, to be interpreted in accordance with the understanding of the common man, synonymous with the word "Caucasian" only as that word is popularly understood. As so understood and used, whatever may be the speculation of the ethnologist, it does not include the body of people to whom the appellee belongs.

In both cases Justice [George] Sutherland, for the Court, said the test was a racial one and laid down the test of common understanding to determine what races are regarded as White.

The Court did not have before it a person who was half Hindu and half English. The rule of that decision would be applicable to the case of a person half English and half Hindu only to determine that half his blood came from a race whose whole-bloods are ineligible. There is nothing in the opinion or in any other opinion of the Supreme Court prior to Justice Cardozo's *dictum* that suggests that the Court has ever considered the problem of a person whose parentage is partly of an eligible race and partly of an ineligible race.

Not a single one of the five other naturalization cases cited, decisions of the lower federal courts, supports the *dictum* beyond the point that one in whom blood of the favored races does not preponderate over the blood of the unfavored is ineligible; they all are cases holding ineligible persons whose blood is only half or less derived from the White race. There are no reported cases holding against one who has only a quarter or less of the blood of ineligible races. There are no cases that have discussed such conditions. It might be supposed that there are other *dicta* or that some court in a naturalization case had pursued a line of reasoning that would support the *dictum,* but even this is not true with a possible exception, *Young*'s case, soon to be stated. The test suggested by the words "or, not improbably, even less" seems to include the test used in social relations in many parts of the United States whereby a person who has the least visible trace of negro ancestry is regarded as not White. [See Part 2 for a discussion of the "one drop" rule—Ed.] The only cases cited by Justice Cardozo in which a test of a quarter or less has been applied are cases applying it to questions quite remote from naturalization. . . .

[The article proceeds to summarize lower court naturalization decisions.—Ed.]

Camille[4] was foreign-born, of a White father and Canadian Indian mother. The court applied the Caucasian race test to American Indians as a racial stock, concluding that they are not White persons, and asked, "What is the status in this respect of the petitioner, who is a person of one-half Indian blood?" The court refers to a rule applied in Louisiana, "the colonial *code noir* of France," and "in Carolina," that if the proportion of African blood did not exceed one-eighth, the person was deemed White; and to the rule in Ohio that a person nearer White than black or red was a "White" person. Without choosing between these rules the court said of Camille: "As a matter of fact, he is as much an Indian as a White person, and might be classed with the one race as properly as the other. Strictly speaking, he belongs to neither." The conclusion was that Camille "is not a 'White person' . . . within any rule that has ever been promulgated on the subject."

This seems to be the earliest case of a mixed-blood under the naturalization law. The statute does not say pure White. Judge Deady saw the inapplicability of logic. Camille was as much White as he was Indian. He might be classed with the one race as properly as with the other. "Strictly speaking," he was neither. Obviously a rule of strict speaking is inappropriate. Under it an alien who is half White and half negro would be ineligible, though a full-blood of either race is eligible. Some test must be arrived at that is consistent with the function of the limitation. The actual decision in *Camille*'s case is consistent with the view that a mere predominance of eligible blood is sufficient.

Young[5] was half German, half Japanese. The court applied the test of common understanding in determining, "whether we consider the Japanese as of the Mongolian race, or the Malay race, they are not included in what are commonly understood as 'white persons,'" which, the court said, includes all Europeans and the Caucasians around the Mediterranean Sea. The court also said that "it cannot be said that one who is half white and half brown or yellow is a white person, as commonly understood."[6] The court does not clarify its thought as to common understanding. It immediately refers without discrimination to the Louisiana test of one-eighth and the Virginia and Kentucky test of one-quarter, used in those States to determine who have the disabilities of free negroes [such as being subject to the segregation laws—Ed.], and the Ohio test of predominance of the White blood determining who were eligible to vote as White persons. The actual decision is consistent with the predominance test.

Knight's[7] father was English and his mother was half Chinese and half Japanese. The court said, "[N]o case to which the attention of the court has been drawn seems to specifically determine what percentage of Mongolian blood will exclude the applicant from classification as a 'white person'" and rested its decision, against the applicant, upon *Camille*'s case. That case, the court said, "is based upon a number of decisions in Ohio." The court seems to suppose that the court in *Camille*'s case applied the Ohio test, that unless the White blood preponderated the applicant was ineligible.

Alverto[8] was, "ethnologically speaking, one-fourth of the white or Caucasian race and three-fourths of the brown or Malay race." The court referred to *Camille*'s and *Knight*'s cases and held Alverto ineligible. Obviously, if the half White is ineligible, the one-fourth White is also. There is no statement of doctrine or test in the opinion.

The only naturalization case remaining of those cited by Justice Cardozo is *Lampitoe*'s.[9] Lampitoe also was one-fourth white and three-fourths Malay. Judge Learned Hand in a six-line opinion said that the case fell exactly within the decision in *Alverto*'s case and added:

> There may be some doubt about such cases as *In re* Camille (C.C.) 6 Fed. 256, or *In re* Knight, 177 Fed. 299; but where the Malay blood predominates it would be a perversion of language to say that the descendant is a "white person." Certainly any white ancestor, no matter how remote, does not make all his descendants white.

This doubt expressed as to cases holding half White insufficient manifests a clear opinion that a predominance of White blood is sufficient.

The only authorities Justice Cardozo cites for the proposition that a quarter or even less of the blood of the disfavored race disqualifies are early cases in Southern courts determining what degree of negro blood was, according to the law of the state, sufficient to subject a person to the disabilities of negroes, or mulattoes, or colored persons. None of these cases adopt a test of less than one-eighth.

Notes

1. *Morrison v. People of California,* 54 Sup. Ct. 281 (January 8, 1934).
2. 260 U.S. 178 . . . (1922).
3. 261 U.S. 204 (1923).
4. *In re Camille,* 6 Fed. 256 (C.C.D. Ore. 1880).
5. *In re Young,* 198 Fed. 715 (W.D. Wash. 1912).
6. *Id.* at 716–17.
7. *In re Knight,* 171 Fed. 299 (E.D.N.Y. 1909).
8. *In re Alverto,* 198 Fed. 688 (E.D. Pa 1912).
9. *In re Lampitoe,* 232 Fed. 382 (S.D.N.Y. 1916).

73

Racial Restrictions on Naturalization

The Recurring Intersection of Race and Gender in Immigration and Citizenship Law

Kevin R. Johnson

. . . Consistent with the notion of coverture [the concept that a women possessed no separate legal identity from that of her husband—Ed.], women for a time were ineligible for naturalization if they married a foreigner ineligible for citizenship. A 1907 law was even more extreme, stripping American women of citizenship when they married aliens ineligible for citizenship.[1] Because the most immutable bar to citizenship was race-based, these gender-linked laws penalized White women (who were citizens or would be eligible for citizenship) married to non-White noncitizens. Moreover, non-White immigrant women who married U.S. citizens were barred at one time from becoming citizens because of their race.[2]

Like the race-based naturalization requirements, the gender classifications in the citizenship laws jar modern sensibilities. They enforced a perceived social order that discouraged interracial marriages. [See Part 1—Ed.] Women citizens or lawful permanent residents stood to lose much by transcending racial boundaries. These laws contrasted starkly with the long history of laws affording male citizens the opportunity to secure the immigration (though perhaps not citizenship) of their wives—White or not—to the United States.

The Supreme Court refused to disturb the blatant gender discrimination in the citizenship laws. In the landmark case of *MacKenzie v. Hare*,[3] the Court upheld Congress's authority, as an inherent power of sovereignty, to expatriate a female U.S. citizen who married a foreign national. Despite the harsh treatment of women citizens under the law upheld by the Court, this case is frequently recalled more for the extraordinary power given to Congress in allowing for expatriation than for the impact on women who bucked the racial line.

Notes

1. [*See* Act of March 3, 1931, ch. 442, § 4, 46 Stat. 1511; Act of March 2, 1907, ch. 2534, § 3, 34 Stat. 1228—Ed.]

2. *See, e.g., Chang Chan v. Nagle,* 268 U.S. 346, 351–53 (1925), reviewing various immigration laws to this effect; *Kelly v. Owen,* 74 U.S. 496, 498 (1896), stating that only "free white women" could become citizens by marrying U.S. citizens.

3. 239 U.S. 299 (1915).

74

Legacies of War

The United States' Obligation toward Amerasians

Robin S. Levi

II. U.S. Military Involvement in Asia

[This section details U.S. military in Vietnam, South Korea, and the Philippines in the post–World War II period.—Ed.]

III. The U.S. Government's Attitude toward Relationships with Asian Women

A. Vietnam

In contrast to the popular perception held in Vietnam and the United States (and reinforced by *Miss Saigon*), most Amerasian children came from long-term relationships between servicemen and Vietnamese women who were not bargirls. These women usually worked around military bases as launderers, hotel clerks, or menial laborers in other occupations.

Soldiers in Vietnam frequently felt the need to find solace in women and liquor. The U.S. military encouraged this behavior with a tacit "bread and circuses" attitude. The government encouraged "R & R" as a way to escape from the rigors of jungle warfare. But while the military flew married men to meet their wives in Hawaii, it sent single men to other exotic cities. Unmarried servicemen were sent to Asian locales, which led them to believe the U.S. government expected them to conduct their "R & R" with Asian women.

The U.S. military also facilitated the use of local prostitutes. For example, after monthly trips to town resulted in chaos, Marine commanders at Danan decided to restrict their men's sexual activity to areas surrounding the base. Military brothels could be found within the perimeter of at least three U.S. base camps. The military brothels were set up by military commanders and were under the direct operational control of a brigade commander with the rank of colonel. Further, the military periodically checked the health of the prostitutes to curtail the spread of sexually transmitted diseases. The military also regulated prices. If women requested more than a certain price, the military would declare their brothel off-limits.

The U.S. Army officially disapproved of U.S. servicemen living with Vietnamese women, and at times the military police sanctioned soldiers. But unofficially, the U.S. Army allowed many of these living situations (which the soldiers called "liv[ing] on the economy with a national") to continue in order to preserve the soldiers' morale.

Once a serviceman completed his tour of duty, the military's disapproval of his relationship with a Vietnamese woman resurfaced. It was incredibly difficult for servicemen to maneuver through the U.S. bureaucracy to bring their children, girlfriends, or wives back to the United States. Some servicemen tried for many years to get their children out of Vietnam, while others gave up before they left. Some were so busy preparing to end their "year abroad" that they forgot to try to return with those who had been their families there. Some men did not care, and some did not know that they had children. Regardless of what stood in the serviceman's way (government, bureaucracy, confusion, or indifference), the result remained the same: tens of thousands of children left in Vietnam after 1975, rejected by Vietnamese society and dreaming of their unknown father and his land.

B. South Korea and the Philippines

The relationships in South Korea and the Philippines are fairly similar to those that existed in Vietnam. In South Korea the troops are now on one-year tours similar to those soldiers had in Vietnam and the Philippines. Most of the men come through for short stays while their ships are repaired. About eighteen thousand registered women work in the bar or club areas near U.S. bases in South Korea. Registered women have identification cards and are the only ones allowed to work in the clubs. In order to get an ID card, a woman must have a chest X ray and blood test every six months and an AIDS test every three months. In addition, the women are tested every week for sexually transmitted diseases [STDs]. The Korean police conduct spot checks to ensure that all women have proper ID cards; women without cards can receive jail sentences of up to twelve months. Furthermore, the clubs themselves are checked for cleanliness and STD rates among the women.

The bases in the Philippines had a similar system of registering sex workers. Fifteen thousand to seventeen thousand sex workers were employed around Subic Bay, approximately nine thousand of whom were registered. As in South Korea, unregistered sex workers could be jailed. The U.S. military provided medicine and technical assistance to the clinics. Here, as in South Korea, the military deemed a club "off-limits" for U.S. servicemen if too many women tested positive for sexually transmitted diseases. Most of the U.S. servicemen did not take responsibility for the children born from their relationships, whether short- or long-term, with sex workers. Furthermore, the U.S. government failed to instruct its servicemen regarding possible parental responsibility. Instead, the government focused on teaching servicemen to avoid venereal disease.

IV. The Lives of Amerasians

A. Amerasians in Vietnam

Vietnam does not accept Amerasians either legally or socially and subjects them to mistreatment that leads to severe emotional trauma. Because nationality, race, and personal identity derive from the father in Vietnamese society, the Vietnamese government considers Amerasians U.S. nationals. In Vietnam the father registers the birth in the family registry, claims paternity, registers the child for school, and procures employment for the child. Without a father to perform these essential functions (at times a stepfather has assisted the Amerasian), a child in Vietnam will have difficulty becoming a functioning part of Vietnamese society. Amerasians are told they are not Vietnamese, although the person who is supposed to give them their identity is not present. The fact that Vietnamese social and legal institutions make it difficult for Amerasians to establish an identity intensifies the identity crisis that mixed race children inherently face.

Vietnam has a Confucian, patriarchal family system, where a person's identity is derived more from the family group, including both the living members and ancestors, than from the individual self. Therefore, an Amerasian child lacks not only a father but also a father's family and ancestors. A child in Vietnam without a supporting familial group is seen as something less than a full person, which increases the Amerasians' lack of identity.

Another factor that contributes to discrimination against Amerasians in Vietnam is homogeneity. Mixed racial ancestry is easily noticed, and Vietnamese society considers people with mixed ancestry as contributing to "racial impurity in the nation." An official from Ho Chi Minh City's Department of Social Welfare stated, "Our society does not need these bad elements."[1]

The final factor contributing to the ostracism of Vietnamese Amerasians is that they are living reminders of the foreign occupation of Vietnam. For some of them, even their names, given by their families, *My Lai* (American half-breed) or *My Phuong* (Vietnamese American), are insults. Vietnamese society faults Amerasians' mothers for consorting with the enemy and considers the mothers prostitutes. Amerasians are considered the children of the enemy: "It was not unusual for an Amerasian child to be singled out by a teacher or a police officer as the offspring of the enemy who had bombed the village."[2] Because communist education emphasizes the evils of the United States, it is very difficult for Amerasians to attend school. Students are taunted in school and by the public and are sometimes told to go back to their "country." Many Amerasians quickly drop out of school; thus a large number of them are illiterate. Amerasian children's identity crises are often intensified by the fact that many mothers destroyed all mementos of their relationships with their children's fathers so that the government would not send them to reeducation camps as punishment for fraternizing with the enemy.

Regardless of the destruction of documentary evidence linking Amerasians to their American fathers, their non-Asian features frequently betray the children's mixed heritage. Some mothers try to disguise the children's American features by putting shoe polish in their hair and powder on their skin. The Amerasians who have experienced the greatest discrimination and whose identities have been the most difficult to hide are the children of African American servicemen. One example is the story of a young black Amerasian: "Vinh Doan came to expect rejection. His father was a black serviceman whom he never met. His Vietnamese mother spent years telling him he was ugly because he looked like his father, then gave him to a neighbor when he was seven years old."[3] Black Amerasians are lowest in the hierarchy of Vietnamese society due to the traditional prejudice against dark skin found in all Asian societies, as well as racial prejudice brought by the European and American presence.

Although the Vietnamese government officially denies discriminating against Amerasians, it prevents many mothers from participating in certain government programs. Mothers of Amerasians are often rejected by their families due to the humiliation the mother has caused the family. A significant percentage of mothers, refusing to live under these conditions, give up their children for adoption, sell their children for their potential value as a ticket to the United States, or simply abandon them. Many Amerasians have ended up in orphanages. Since Vietnamese orphanages are often run badly and have severe overcrowding problems, most Amerasian children have ended up on the streets, and many have turned to prostitution.

B. Amerasians in South Korea

South Korea is also a homogenous and Confucian nation with a strict class hierarchy. A more dramatic disparity between the upper and lower classes exists there than in Vietnam, and it is very difficult to be successful unless one attends one of the top universities, which are expensive and exclusive. As in Vietnam, the father is the cornerstone of family life and the conduit to public life. Without a father, it is impossible to carry out the traditional responsibilities of ancestor worship. While the religious importance of ancestor worship has decreased with modernization, some symbolic value remains, and the Amerasian who is not able to conduct ancestor worship naturally will be viewed as "different." In recent years, nationalism and cultural pride, along with economic clout, have increased in South Korea. Koreans equate citizenship with their homogenous racial ancestry. Thus, Amerasians remain only marginal members of Korea's society, because without fathers they are prevented from fully participating in Korean culture and religion.

Official discrimination against Amerasians is formally outlawed in South Korea, but covert discrimination continues. The most egregious example is that Amerasians are not allowed to serve in the Korean military. In a nation that considers itself consistently on the brink of war, exclusion from military service serves as a serious obstacle to being accepted by the society and obtaining a good job. Further, most Amerasians cannot afford to go to the better universities. The cumulative effect of not having fathers, military service capability, education credentials, and economic power relegates Amerasians to the lower classes of Korean society.

The degree to which Korean Amerasians encounter discrimination depends on the race of the father. If the father was black, racial discrimination is more blatant. If the father was white, the Amerasian child has a better chance of adoption by society. Nonetheless, all Amerasians are taunted for their American-looking features and are immediately branded as children of imperialists and prostitutes.

Although it should be acknowledged that the U.S. and South Korean governments have taken some financial responsibility for the few registered Amerasians in South Korea, Korean Amerasians have lives similar to Vietnamese Amerasians, filled with poverty, discrimination, and solitude. It is unlikely that financial support from the United States or South Korea will continue once the U.S. military leaves.

C. Amerasians in the Philippines

Filipino Amerasians were excluded from previous Amerasian immigration laws because of the perception that Filipino Amerasians did not experience discrimination at significant levels. This perception could have been generated by the belief that the Philippines support a very diverse population and therefore mixed race children would be easily accepted. Indeed, Amerasians are capable of being accepted and succeeding in the Filipino society; for example, the mayor of Olongapo, Richard Gordon, is a white Amerasian. Some white Amerasians have become big performing stars in the Philippines, prized for their light skin.

Nevertheless, Filipinos consider themselves a homogenous population, despite their history of intermarriages over the centuries. They also have a strong belief in kinship relations. Because most Filipino Amerasians are interracial children from single-parent households, they are left at a disadvantage with regard to both of these traditions.

The most significant obstacle to Filipino Amerasians is that they are often judged by the circumstances of their birth. Amerasians from certain parts of the Philippines are immediately assumed to be the children of prostitutes and U.S. servicemen, and they are treated as such. Therefore, even though in the past Amerasians have been functioning members of society, Amerasians with U.S. servicemen for fathers are not so lucky. Further, because most are born into a life of poverty next to the bases, many end up working in the bar system that facilitated their birth. Others are sold by their mothers or abandoned. Amerasians in the Philippines experience discrimination and hardship remarkably similar to that experienced by the Amerasians discussed above. Most struggle to survive in the bar scene near the base.

Since the U.S. military withdrew, these children have become subject to increased anti-American sentiment. The closing of the bases also removed the main source of health services and income for the Amerasians and their mothers. Like Vietnamese Amerasians, Filipino Amerasians are now the remaining traces of U.S. intervention in the Philippines. Any residual resentment against the U.S. presence in the Philippines can easily be vented against Filipino Amerasians. They are without resources and discriminated against in a country that is itself poor.

VI. The U.S. Government's Treatment of Amerasians

A. Amerasians under U.S. Immigration Law

A child born in the United States can elect U.S. citizenship regardless of the nationality of her parents. Attaining citizenship is more difficult when the child is born outside the United States. A child born outside the United States to married parents can be a U.S. citizen if one parent is a U.S. citizen who has fulfilled certain age and residency requirements. However, children born out of wedlock, like most Amerasian children, face significantly more stringent citizenship requirements. [See Chapter 75—Ed.] This factor has made it unlikely that more than a small percentage of Amerasians could receive U.S. citizenship through their parents.

Amerasian children are in the lowest preference category for emigration to the United States because they are usually unable to prove officially that they are related to any U.S. citizen. Rarely can they find U.S. citizens to sponsor them.

B. Statutes Assisting Amerasians

1. Orderly Departure Program

The first U.S. effort to help Amerasians began inadvertently, after the government became concerned with the plight of the boat people fleeing Vietnam. The media attention given to the Vietnamese refugees in rickety boats on unsafe seas, and their subsequent unpleasant treatment by unwelcoming Southeast Asian countries, led the U.S. government in 1979 to develop the Orderly Departure Program (ODP) under the auspices of the United Nations.[4] The United Nations designed the ODP to give people a safe method of exit from Vietnam. Vietnam agreed to grant exit visas, and the UN High Commissioner for Refugees (UNHCR) agreed to be the processor. . . .

Under the ODP, Vietnamese Amerasians are in a better position to immigrate to the United States than they were under the conventional immigration regulations. Amerasians must fill out applications to participate in the ODP, but the U.S. government no longer requires supporting documents from them. Further, President [Ronald] Reagan accorded priority status to Amerasians by including them in one of three categories of refugees given priority for orderly departure.

Nevertheless, the ODP as it relates to Amerasians has several problems. First, since the United States government and Vietnam do not have diplomatic relations, the United States has been hampered by not having a processing office in Ho Chi Minh City. Moreover, Amerasians often do not have the knowledge necessary to successfully apply. Many of them, living in the streets, may not even have heard about the ODP. Second, because the ODP classifies recipients as refugees, the Vietnamese government does not think Amerasians should be included; it considers them U.S. citizens. Thus their exclusion from official services, according to the Vietnamese government, does not constitute discrimination.

2. The Refugee Act of 1980

The 1980 Refugee Act, implementing the 1951 [United Nations] Convention Relating to the Status of Refugees and its updated Protocol,[5] did little to help Amerasians. The Refugee Act characterized a refugee as a person fleeing a country "because of persecution or a well-founded fear of persecution on account of race, religion, nationality, [or] membership in a particular social group." . . . However, the U.S. government did not direct this legislation specifically at Amerasians, and it has several proof requirements and forms. The act is likely to benefit mainly the more educated Asians who are able to fulfill the specific requirements and successfully complete the forms and interviews. . . . In the case of South Korea and the Philippines, the U.S. government tends to be unwilling to grant Amerasians refugee status, as they are from countries with governments friendly to the United States. Therefore, the Refugee Act is rarely used by Amerasians.

3. 1982 Amerasian Amendments

The United States' next effort to assist Amerasians was the enactment of the 1982 Amerasian Amendments.[6] These amendments were the result of a concerted effort by some legislators—who saw the Amerasians as the United States' responsibility—to help those children. The amendments cover Amerasian children from Korea, Vietnam, Laos, Cambodia, and Thailand. They put qualified children into the highest preference category for immigration. In order to qualify, children must petition the Attorney General and give [his or] her reason to believe that they were fathered by a U.S. citizen and were born between 1950 and October 22, 1982. The physical appearance of the Amerasian is to be considered, along with documentary proof. By expanding coverage to Amerasians in some nations, the amendments have helped the non-Vietnamese Amerasians who did not benefit under the ODP. Also, the amendments expand eligibility to those born as late as 1982, taking account of the fact that not all Amerasians are born during military conflicts.

Several problems remain. First, the amendments still force Amerasians to emigrate alone, often leaving loved ones behind. In addition, although Amerasians from several countries can take advantage of the amendments, the strict provisions of the amendments and the lack of diplomatic relations between the United States and Vietnam combine to make it particularly difficult for Vietnamese Amerasians to qualify. Moreover, the amendments do not cover the many Amerasians in the Philippines, and the 1982 cutoff date eliminates Amerasians who were subsequently born in Asia. Finally, the financial sponsor requirements are difficult to fulfill and defy the obligation of the United States to take responsibility for Amerasians.

4. 1984 Amerasian Initiative

President Reagan attempted to ameliorate some of the damaging effects of the 1982 amendments on Vietnamese Amerasians through the 1984 Amerasian Initiative. In contrast to earlier policy, the Initiative allows Vietnamese Amerasians using the ODP to emigrate with qualifying family members. This provision has encouraged more Amerasians to emigrate, because they need not leave their families behind. It has also increased their chances of building successful lives in the United States, because they will have familial support with them.

Unfortunately, the U.S. government offended Vietnam by claiming that the Vietnamese government was using the ODP to facilitate emigration of ethnic Chinese rather than Vietnamese Amerasians, and that as a result the quotas set by the Initiative for Vietnamese Amerasians remained unfilled. Vietnam claimed that the United States was trying to make the Vietnamese government the "bad guy." As a result, Vietnam suspended the ODP program to the United States in 1986 but resurrected it eighteen months later after a sharp increase in the number of people trying to escape Vietnam by boat. Thus the Initiative suffered from both poor United States–Vietnam relations and its limited scope.

VII. The Homecoming Act

The most recent and comprehensive legislation concerning Amerasians is the Indochinese Refugee Resettlement and Protection Act of 1987 (Homecoming Act).[7] The purpose of the Homecoming Act was to fulfill the United States' legal and moral obligations to Vietnamese Amerasians. . . .

The Homecoming Act, enacted in March 1988, stated that all Amerasian children born in Vietnam between January 1, 1962, and January 1, 1976, could emigrate to the United States, accompanied by either immediate family, guardians, or a spouse. The act set a deadline of two years for all Amerasians to arrive in the United States and exempted them from immigration quotas. Congress included the two-year deadline to speed the processing of Amerasian immigrants, because processing under the ODP had been so slow. The State Department claimed that the deadline was too stringent to allow for adequate processing of all Amerasians. Nonetheless, comparing the speed of processing under the Homecoming Act with the speed under previous acts shows that the deadline did accelerate processing.

In 1990, Congress indefinitely extended the deadline for allowing Amerasians into the United States and removed the provision that had forced them to choose between spouse and family for immediate immigration. The act's original budget and timetable were based on an estimate of twelve thousand to fourteen thousand Amerasians remaining in Vietnam, but this estimate was later revised to forty thousand. Finally, the act did not characterize Amerasians as refugees, which appeased the Vietnamese government.

After Congress passed the Homecoming Act, [its two Congressional co-sponsors—Ed.] traveled to Vietnam to reach an agreement with Vietnamese Foreign Minister Nguyen Co Thach. The agreement stated that the Vietnamese government would allow the Amerasians to emigrate to the United States. This new spirit of cooperation stems from Vietnam's desire for the U.S. government to end its trade embargo, as Vietnam is willing to make the necessary efforts to improve its relationship with the United States. Vietnam has also tried to assist the U.S. government in processing Amerasians by transporting them from outlying areas to Ho Chi Minh City and by increasing the number of carriers that are permitted to fly emigrants out of Vietnam.

B. Problems Faced by Amerasians in the United States: Squawking like a Chicken

. . . In Asia, most Amerasians lived in the street, frequently surviving through criminal means and having little education and limited familial support. As a result of their background and lack of identity, Amerasian immigrants are at higher risk for problems such as drug use, crime, and suicide than previous Indochinese immigrants.

Although many other refugee groups have similar problems, these problems are more acute among Amerasians. One important reason is that upon arrival in the United States, Amerasians are, on average, eighteen years old, much older and less adaptable than French Eurasians who emigrated to France. Amerasians in the United States have a saying: "I was born like a duck but lived with the chickens. Now I live with the ducks but I squawk like a chicken."

Many Amerasians thought that once they arrived in the United States they would find their fathers and their identities. They also thought that they would be welcomed by their fathers, like lost children finally finding their way home. In short, Amerasians hoped to find the answers to all their problems in the United States. . . .

The Amerasian dream least likely to be fulfilled is that of finding one's American father in the United States. Very few Amerasians have clear identifying information about their fathers; most just have names and hometowns. The U.S. government has led Amerasians to believe that it will help them contact their fathers and give the fathers the option of caring for their children. But due to a combination of domestic privacy laws and government inactivity, that help has not materialized.

As a result of the Freedom of Information Act and a British case concerning children fathered by U.S. soldiers in Great Britain, the U.S. government must allow limited access to records about U.S. servicemen. Other organizations, such as the Red Cross, the Amerasian Registry, and the Buck Foundation, use that information to assist Amerasians searching for their fathers. However, this information is frequently too limited to be useful. Even if Amerasians do find their fathers, often the fathers do not want them or the reunions otherwise fail to work out. Amerasians find such rejections devastating because they expected their fathers to help them find their identities and fill the role Vietnamese fathers play. Although there have been some success stories, many workers at volunteer agencies do not think they make up for the countless other rejections. In fact, some mothers have tried to prevent their children from even beginning the search for their fathers.

The presence of racism in the United States also surprises Amerasians, especially black Amerasians. Further, the Vietnamese community that rejected them in Vietnam continues to reject them in the United States, although the rejection is less severe. As one unemployed Amerasian said, "[I]f the discrimination in Vietnam was 100, the discrimination here is about 50." Many examples exist of Amerasians trying to talk with Vietnamese people in Vietnamese and being snubbed. These rejections increase the Amerasians' sense of alienation; even though they are in the United States, the old problem of discrimination continues to plague them.

Another problem that many Vietnamese Amerasians face is not having attended school in Vietnam. Many stopped attending school as a result of taunts from their schoolmates and teachers. Most are illiterate in Vietnamese and unaccustomed to school, which makes it difficult for them to learn in the United States. Further, as a result of their Vietnamese illiteracy, it is very difficult for them to learn to read and write English. . . .

The street is an environment with which most Amerasians are familiar. [M]any survived by living on the street; they robbed, prostituted themselves, and participated in other illegal activities. In Asia, they supported themselves on the street without any help from the government. When Amerasians in the United States begin having problems in school, finding jobs, or living on welfare, some of them revert to the familiar methods of street survival. This leaves Amerasians at a high risk for becoming criminals and suffering the consequences of criminal activity.

All of the problems discussed above are easily noticed and measured. Less quantifiable, but just as serious, is the general feeling of depression and alienation that affects many Amerasians, leaving them at high risk for suicide. Unfortunately, not nearly enough counselors are available to talk with them about their emotional problems. . . .

VIII. Conclusion and Recommendations

The problems facing Amerasians are daunting but not insurmountable. The settlement of Vietnamese Amerasians in the United States has been fairly effective and can provide guidance for programs to assist other groups of Amerasians. The federal government and volunteer organizations have worked as partners and have shown that the government, when willing, can rectify its wrongs. Based on its international obligations, however, the United States still has a long way to go in helping Amerasians.

Notes

Published originally in 29 Stanford Journal of International Law 459 (1993). Reprinted with the permission of the Stanford Journal of International Law.

1. Marilyn T. Trautfield, Note, *America's Responsibility to Amerasian Children: Too Little Too Late*, 10 Brooklyn Journal of International Law 55, 61 (1984).

2. *See* Anne Keegan, *Children of Vietnam Find Few Fathers at U.S. Doors*, Chicago Tribune, May 13, 1987, at C1.

3. Lisa Belkin, *Children of Two Lands in Search of Home*, New York Times, May 19, 1988, at A20. . . .

4. *See* Marykim DeMonaco, Note, *Disorderly Departure: An Analysis of the United States Policy toward Amerasian Immigration*, 15 Brooklyn Journal of International Law 641, 653–57 (1989).

5. [United Nations] Convention Relating to Status of Refugees, July 28, 1951, 189 U.N.T.S.

137; [United Nations] Protocol Relating to the Status of Refugees, *entered into force*, January 31, 1967, 19 U.S.T. 6223.

6. 8 U.S.C. § 1154 (1988).

7. Indochinese Refugee Resettlement and Protection Act, Pub. L. No. 100-202, 101 Stat. 1329–40 (1987).

75

Gendered States

A Comparative Construction of Citizenship and Nation

Kif Augustine-Adams

I. Introduction

The differential regulation of mothers and fathers in the transmission of citizenship to their children profoundly impacts who we are as citizens and as nations, both in the conceptual, imagined form of court opinions and in the practical, corporeal form of population. Here, I critique and challenge the continued impact of gender on citizenship through an analysis of legal rules that construct a discriminatory and exclusive nation by differentially regulating the ability of mothers and fathers, married and unmarried, to transmit citizenship to their children. In the past twenty-five years, the courts of numerous nations, including the United States, have decided cases contesting *jus sanguinis* citizenship rules that differentiate between mothers and fathers in the transmission of citizenship to their children. [In a footnote, the author explains:

> Most countries use either *jus solis* or *jus sanguinis*, or a combination of the two rules, to determine citizenship. *Jus solis* citizenship is granted to persons born within the territory of the state. *Jus sanguinis* citizenship is granted to persons based on lineage. The United States relies primarily on *jus solis*, granting citizenship to virtually all children born here, including those of tourists, visiting students, and undocumented persons. *See* Const. Amend. XIV, § 1; 8 U.S.C. § 1401(a) (1994). With certain limitations, the United States also grants citizenship to the children of citizens born abroad. *See* 8 U.S.C. § 1401(c)–(h). . . .]

Most basically, each court and country faced a fundamental question: whether and under what circumstances its citizens, embodied individually as mothers and fathers, could reproduce not only children, but citizens as well, and thus produce the nation itself.

II. *Differential Treatment of Men and Women Upheld*

A. *Miller v. Albright,* Supreme Court of the United States, 1998

1. Unmarried Women Birth Citizens; Unmarried Men Leave behind Children

In 1970, Lorelyn Penero Miller was born in the Philippines to a Filipina mother and a U.S. serviceman father. Because her parents were not married, her birth certificate left blank the father's name and nationality, stating that her birth was illegitimate.[1] When, as an adult, Ms. Miller petitioned to be registered as a U.S. citizen, the U.S. State Department denied her application, stating that under the Immigration and Nationality Act (INA), Ms. Miller did not qualify as a U.S. citizen. First, Ms. Miller could not receive U.S. citizenship *jus solis* because she had been born outside the territory of the United States. Second, Ms. Miller could not receive U.S. citizenship *jus sanguinis* from her mother because her mother was not a U.S. citizen. Third, under applicable U.S. law, Ms. Miller could not receive citizenship *jus sanguinis* from her U.S. citizen father because she was born out of wedlock and her father had not obtained an official paternity decree identifying himself as Ms. Miller's father before she reached the age of majority. If the gender of Ms. Miller's U.S. citizen parent had been female, she would have automatically received U.S. citizenship upon her birth. Under provisions of the Immigration and Nationality Act (INA), codified at 8 U.S.C. section 1409, where a citizen mother meets very generous U.S. residency requirements prior to her child's birth, she automatically bestows her U.S. citizenship on her children born abroad and out of wedlock. On the contrary, U.S. citizen fathers do not.

On Ms. Miller's challenge to the discriminatory provisions of the INA, the United States Supreme Court granted certiorari to answer whether the distinction in section 1409 "between 'illegitimate' children of United States citizen mothers and 'illegitimate' children of United States citizen fathers" violated the equal protection provisions of the Fifth Amendment of the U.S. Constitution.[2] The Court found that no Fifth Amendment violation existed in section 1409's requirement that unmarried U.S. fathers, but not unmarried U.S. mothers, obtain an official decree of parentage before the child reaches the age of majority, leaving Ms. Miller without U.S. citizenship.

The judgment of the Court was expressed in three different opinions, yet there was no specific holding on the merits. Thus, for a variety of reasons, the Court let stand a rule that deeply genders U.S. citizenship. . . . [In 2001 a bare majority of the Supreme Court upheld the gender discrimination in section 1409, over a vigorous dissent by Justice Sandra Day O'Connor. See *Nguyen v. INS,* 533 U.S. 53 (2001)—Ed.]

2. Justice Stevens's Opinion and Section 1409

a. An Essentialized Approach to Gender.

Justice [John Paul] Stevens's opinion announcing the judgment of the Court most clearly genders citizenship in the United States, as he naturalizes the mother-child relationship to justify excluding the children of unmarried U.S. men from citizenship.

Most succinctly, he states: "The biological differences between single men and single women provide a relevant basis for differing rules governing their ability to confer citizenship on children born in foreign lands." Even as he naturalizes biological difference, however, Stevens cannot escape the connection between biology and social constructs. He proposes that biological differences matter for single men and women, not for all men and women. It is not clear that Stevens would have made the same statement regarding married individuals, namely, that the biological differences between married men and married women provide a relevant basis for differing rules governing their ability to confer citizenship on children born in foreign lands. If Stevens did propose that biological difference mattered for married men and women, which way would biology cut—for or against citizenship for the children of married U.S. women born abroad? Only since 1994 have children born abroad to U.S. citizen mothers, regardless of the date of their birth and their mothers' marital status, been able to claim U.S. citizenship. Likewise, would biology cut for or against citizenship for children born abroad to married U.S. men? A strong version of the biological arguments Justice Stevens makes in *Miller* supports differentiating between men and women, whether married or single, in the transmission of citizenship to their children born abroad.

Essential to Justice Stevens's opinion and section 1409 is a differential construction of women as mothers and men as fathers. For an unmarried U.S. citizen man to confer citizenship on his child born abroad, section 1409(a) requires, in addition to the father's term of residency in the United States, that

> (1) a blood relationship between the person and the father is established by clear and convincing evidence,
> (2) the father had the nationality of the United States at the time of the person's birth,
> (3) the father (unless deceased) has agreed in writing to provide financial support for the person until the person reaches the age of 18 years, and
> (4) while the person is under the age of 18 years—
> (A) the person is legitimated under the law of the person's residence or domicile,
> (B) the father acknowledges paternity of the person in writing under oath, or
> (C) the paternity of the person is established by adjudication of a competent court.

In contrast, for an unmarried U.S. citizen woman to transmit citizenship to her child born abroad, section 1409(c) provides that

> . . . a person born, after December 23, 1952, outside the United States and out-of-wedlock shall be held to have acquired at birth the nationality status of his mother, if the mother had the nationality of the United States at the time of such person's birth, and if the mother had previously been physically present in the United States or one of its outlying possessions for a continuous period of one year.

Thus, under the law, an unmarried mother's biological connection to her child is socially meaningful to the nation and creates a citizen, whereas an unmarried father's biological connection to his child is not socially meaningful and does not confer citizenship.

b. Legal Fatherhood, Natural Motherhood.

Men are not fathers in the relevant sense for U.S. citizenship until, as Justice Stevens states, "either the father or his child takes certain affirmative steps to create or confirm their relationship." Tellingly, Stevens's notion that a father has to "create" or "confirm" a relationship with his child through affirmative, legally identified steps implies the lack of any relationship, or at least any relevant relationship, despite the fact that the word "father" is, by definition, relational. Moreover, biological paternity was unquestioned in *Miller*. Thus, under the law upheld by Stevens, the biological and natural process of siring a child does not make a man a father; rather, fatherhood exists as a legally created construct. Men do not—indeed cannot—become fathers until they comply with the legal indicators of fatherhood, despite their biological connection with a child. Unmarried men choose to become fathers, in the legally relevant sense, after siring a child by fulfilling the formal requirements of U.S. citizenship law. The biological tie of fatherhood is not sufficient; what creates a father is a man's choice to economically support a child and confer legitimacy. In contrast, an unmarried mother's biological connection to her child is legally determinative. Under the law, she transmits citizenship to her child at birth and thus embodies the nation. Under this reasoning, fatherhood is legal and a matter of choice, whereas motherhood is natural and a matter of biology.

c. Ambiguous Paternity, Obvious Maternity.

Similarly, using the biological differences between men and women to justify differential regulation in the transmission of citizenship, Justice Stevens states that the blood relationship between a mother and her child "is immediately obvious" and "is typically established by hospital records and birth certificates." In fact, the blood relationship between a particular mother and child is "immediately obvious" only at one moment: birth. As recent discoveries of baby-switching at hospitals remind us, however, the blood relationship between a specific mother and a specific child is not immediately and clearly obvious at other moments even shortly after birth.

Similarly, the degree to which hospital records and birth certificates "typically establish" the blood relationship between a mother and a child is culturally dependent and may not be as reliable for establishing the required blood relationship as Stevens suggests, even in the United States. Birth certificates are notoriously easy to forge or obtain fraudulently. . . . Whether a mother is a U.S. citizen or not, registering a child's birth in many parts of the world is a tentative rather than conclusive venture. The point is simply that maternity, like paternity, involves questions of proof that are subject to many of the same concerns and criticisms that both Justice Stevens and section 1409 assume apply only to paternity. Maternity is only potentially, not necessarily, easier to prove than paternity. The statute and Justice Stevens's opinion rest primarily on the assumption that the mother-child relationship is naturally determined, inseverable, and always obvious, while the father-child relationship is socially determined, severable, and rarely clear.

e. Biology Determines Social Ties.
The differential construction of the mother-child relationship and the father-child relationship, in Justice Stevens's view, acceptably constructs the U.S. nation by excluding children born abroad to unmarried fathers unless certain postbirth criteria are met. In Stevens's words, "Congress obviously has a powerful interest in fostering ties with the child's citizen parent and the United States during his or her formative years." The nation is thus marked not just with biological ties but also with social ties, those social ties that Stevens believes unmarried men do not and perhaps cannot provide. Because of biology, unmarried citizen fathers cannot be counted on to foster the relevant social ties with their children; ". . . due to the normal interval of nine months between conception and birth, the unmarried father may not even know that his child exists, and the child may not know the father's identity." Consequently, children born abroad to unmarried U.S. citizen men cannot embody the U.S. nation at birth. In contrast, in Stevens's view, because of biology, unmarried citizen mothers foster the relevant social ties with their children born abroad:

> When a child is born out of wedlock outside of the United States, the citizen mother, unlike the citizen father, certainly knows of her child's existence and typically will have custody of the child immediately after the birth. Such a child thus has the opportunity to develop ties with its citizen mother at an early age, and may even grow up in the United States if the mother returns.

3. Discriminatory Impact of Current Rule

In practice, the rule that includes the children of unmarried citizen women born abroad but not the children of unmarried citizen men born abroad races and genders U.S. citizenship and the U.S. nation in an exclusive and discriminatory manner. First, the law races current citizenship as it largely excludes children of color from the United States. Second, the law genders citizenship by tying citizenship to reproduction in ways that reinforce women as sexually responsible mothers and men as sexually irresponsible philanderers.

a. Exclusion of Children of Color.
In imagining the U.S. nation, Stevens suggests that Congress was especially concerned about U.S. servicemen abroad when it differentiated between the children born abroad and out of wedlock to U.S. men and women:

> Congress had legitimate concerns about a class of children born abroad out of wedlock to alien mothers and to American servicemen who would not necessarily know about, or be known by, their children. It was surely reasonable when the INA was enacted in 1952, and remains equally reasonable today, for Congress to condition the award of citizenship to such children on an act that demonstrates, at a minimum, the possibility that those who become citizens will develop ties with this country—a requirement that performs a meaningful purpose for citizen fathers but normally would be superfluous for citizen mothers.

The exclusion of U.S. servicemen's children born abroad and out of wedlock results in a distinct physical embodiment of the nation. Under the current citizenship rule, the U.S. citizen population is whiter than it would be under a rule that granted U.S. citizenship at birth to both the children of unmarried U.S. citizen women and unmarried U.S. citizen men. As Justice Stevens notes, the overwhelming majority of U.S. service people abroad are and have been men. Over the past few decades, these U.S. servicemen have left behind children in countries with populations of color: Vietnam, the Philippines, Japan, Korea, and other Southeast Asian countries. [See the discussion of Amerasian children in Chapter 74—Ed.] Moreover, minorities of color are represented in the U.S. military at a greater percentage than in the U.S. population generally. Thus the children excluded under the current rule are most often children of color, through their mother, their father, or both. The practical impact of the rule excluding from the United States children born abroad to unmarried U.S. men is a raced citizenry, a nation without the children of color that belong to its unmarried fathers abroad.

b. Reinforcement of Male Citizens as Sexually Irresponsible and Female Citizens as Sexually Responsible.

As he expresses it, Stevens's concern about the children of U.S. servicemen abroad confirms men as sexually irresponsible and women as sexually responsible. U.S. women are citizen mothers when they procreate abroad because their biology supposedly allows them to transmit American values to their children. U.S. servicemen, however, despite the fact that they are engaged in military duty, a distinctive marker of male citizenship, do not count as citizens when they procreate abroad. Under the current rule, U.S. men abroad construct the nation as soldiers, but male U.S. soldiers are constrained in producing the nation as fathers. On the other hand, U.S. citizen women are largely constrained in constructing the nation as soldiers at home or abroad, as they produce the nation primarily as mothers.

The assumption behind the differential social ties that biology supposedly allows women but not men to create is that women naturally take responsibility for their sexual choices (i.e., becoming caring parents) while men do not. What Justice Stevens's opinion fails to recognize is how the INA itself reinforces women's responsibility and men's lack of responsibility for their children. Section 1409 dictates that women are automatically responsible for their children at birth, while men are not. Certainly, some will argue that the INA actually encourages rather than discourages unmarried men in taking responsibility for their children by requiring public acknowledgment of the relationship. The INA does require men to pay enough attention to know a child exists, to commit to supporting a child financially, and to acknowledge under oath a relationship with the child before she reaches eighteen. These very statutory requirements that create a father for citizenship purposes also allow a man and the nation to permanently evade responsibility for a child by failing to fulfill them. If he does not meet the relevant requirements by the time the child turns eighteen, a father's relationship is meaningless for citizenship purposes. The INA encourages the potentially differential social ties that exclude the children of unmarried U.S. men born abroad by communicating to men that their decisions to engage in sexual conduct abroad are not significant, in and of themselves, even if they sire a child. Section 1409 excludes children from the national community despite biological connections with U.S. citizen men, rather than including such children and thus making U.S. citizen men, and the nation to which they belong, responsible for their sexual conduct. Stevens's naturalization of the mother-child relationship as the basis for excluding children born abroad to unmarried citizen fathers thus results in an exclusive, discriminatory nation and citizenship.

Notes

Published originally in 41 Virginia Journal of International Law 93 (2000).

1. 523 U.S. 420, 424–25 (1998).
2. *Id.* at 428.

Review Questions

1. Given the existence of the "one drop" rule, see Part II, isn't it logical that the immigration and naturalization laws tended to classify mixed race immigrants as non-white?
2. How do the immigration laws discriminate against mixed race children of color? Are the disparate racial impacts intentional?
3. Is the United States doing enough for Amerasian children?
4. Would you marry an immigrant of color? Explain.

Suggested Readings

Candice Lewis Bredbenner, A Nationality of Her Own: Women, Marriage, and the Law of Citizenship (1998).

Kitty Calavita, *The Paradoxes of Race, Class, Identity, and "Passing": Enforcing the Chinese Exclusion Acts,* 25 Law and Social Inquiry 1 (2000).

Kristin Collins, *When Fathers' Rights Are Mothers' Duties: The Failure of Equal Protection in* Miller v. Albright, 109 Yale Law Journal 1669 (2000).

George W. Gold, *The Racial Prerequisite in the Naturalization Law,* 15 Boston University Law Review 462 (1935).

Charles Gordon, *The Racial Barrier to American Citizenship,* 93 University of Pennsylvania Law Review 237 (1945).

Bonnie Kae Grover, *Aren't These Our Children? Vietnamese Amerasian Resettlement and Restitution,* 2 Virginia Journal of Social Policy and the Law 247 (1995).

Linda Kelly, *Republican Mothers, Bastards' Fathers and Good Victims: Discarding Citizens and Equal Protection through the Failures of Legal Images,* 51 Hastings Law Journal 557 (2000).

Elizabeth Kolby, *Moral Responsibility to Filipino Amerasians: Potential Immigration and Child Support Alternatives,* 2 Asian Law Journal 61 (1995).

Ian F. Haney López, White by Law: The Legal Construction of Race (1996).

Ronald Low, *No Child Should Be without Love and Protection: The Legal Problems of Amerasians,* 26 Howard Law Journal 1527 (1983).

Charles J. McClain, *Tortuous Path, Elusive Goal: The Asian Quest for American Citizenship,* 2 Asian Law Journal 33 (1995).

Maria B. Montes, *U.S. Recognition of Its Obligation to Filipino Amerasian Children under International Law,* 46 Hastings Law Journal 1621 (1995).

Ranjana Natarajan, *Amerasians and Gender-Based Equal Protection under U.S. Citizenship Law,* 30 Columbia Human Rights Law Review 123 (1998).

John Tehranian, *Performing Whiteness: Naturalization Litigation and the Construction of Racial Identity in America,* 109 Yale Law Journal 817 (2000).

John Hayakawa Torok, *Reconstruction and Racial Nativism: Chinese Immigrants and the Debates on the Thirteenth, Fourteenth, and Fifteenth Amendments and Civil Rights Laws,* 3 Asian Law Journal 55 (1996).

Anthony Tran and Allan M. Tow, *America, Your Children Are Left Behind,* 13 Journal of Paralegal Education and Practice 115 (1997).

Part X

Racial Mixture Outside the United States

Part 10 provides a look at how mixed race peoples have been treated under the laws of different countries, including those with a history of slavery. (See generally Orlando Patterson, *Slavery and Social Death: A Comparative Study* [1982].) Racial hierarchies in South Africa and Latin America offer insights into legal classifications of mixed race peoples. Some nations have more willingly recognized racial fluidity than the United States, while others embrace intricate racial classification schemes. Socially constructed notions of racial difference, however, have remained important in most countries.

The varying classification of mixed race people in different nations is concisely described at a personal level by Professor Adrien Wing:

> [I]n the United States, I am considered a member of the Black race. Both of my parents and both sets of my grandparents are African Americans. But in South Africa, my light skin tone, nose, and hair cause me to be regarded as a Coloured or mixed race person, because I am far too light-skinned to be considered Black. When I appear publicly in South Africa with my boyfriend, who is a dark-skinned Black American, we are viewed as an interracial couple. In contrast, I am considered white in Brazil because there, only the darkest people of relatively unmixed African descent are considered Black.
>
> These examples also illustrate the importance of an identity based on color. Because of my skin tone, I have been called Latina, Indian, Arab, mulatto, and biracial. Within the Black American community, my coloring has historically led to a privileged position, because I am something known as "high yellow." Lighter skinned Blacks have received benefits dating back to slavery, often because they were the master's illegitimate progeny. They may have become "house niggers" instead of field hands. They remain overrepresented in the numbers of Blacks who have attended college and attained professional status. (Adrien Katherine Wing, *Violence and State Accountability: Critical Race Feminism,* 1 Georgetown Journal of Gender and the Law 95, 99 [1999].)

Importantly, racial mixture has not necessarily led to racial harmony in other nations. For example, in Peru (and for that matter much of Latin America) subordinated indigenous people see power concentrated in the mestizo population. (See Marisol de la Cadena, *Indigenous Mestizos: The Politics of Race and Culture in Cuzco, Peru, 1919–1991* [2000].) Similar claims have been made in modern Mexico, with the 1994 Zapatista rebellion by indigenous peoples in the state of Chiapas serving as a sharp reminder of the conflicts surrounding racial subordination in that country despite racial mixture. Part 9 included readings on discrimination against mixed race people in certain Asian nations. In Canada, European settlement in the west, where established indigenous communities lived, resulted in "[m]iscegenation [that] produced a new native people who emerged as a distinctive group" (J. R. Miller, *Skyscrapers Hide the Heavens: A History of Indian-White Relations in Canada* 124 [1989]). Known as métis, these racially mixed inhabitants long have suffered discrimination and receive specific protections under the Canadian Constitution. (See *id.* at 239–40.)

In Part 10, Estelle Lau tells the amazing story of how Whiteness and its privileges could be purchased in colonial Venezuela. Robert Cottrol compares the experience of persons of Afro-Latina/o ancestry in the Americas, focusing particularly on Colombia and Venezuela. Martha Menchaca discusses the racial caste system existing in Mexico at the time of the Mexican-American War and its transformation after the U.S. conquest of the Southwest in 1848. In two selections, Christopher Ford describes the complex racial classification schemes—with mixed race "coloreds" in the middle—in South Africa, both before and after the demise of apartheid. Charles Lawrence analyzes how multiracial political coalitions, including the "colored" population, contributed to the end of apartheid.

76

Can Money Whiten?

Exploring Race Practice in Colonial Venezuela and Its Implications for Contemporary Race Discourse

Estelle T. Lau

I. The Contradiction of Race in Eighteenth-Century Venezuela

A. Racial Stratification in Colonial Venezuela

The social composition of late-eighteenth-century colonial Venezuela reflected two centuries of Spanish conquest and slavery. The Spanish immigrated to an area originally populated by scattered Indian tribes and introduced Africans—both free and slave—to the colony at the onset of their conquest. Despite formal anti-miscegenation laws and other legal barriers, the general population largely disregarded any efforts to limit the sexual interaction of these groups. Indeed, "racial and cultural mixing affected the inhabitants of Venezuela more than almost any other American society."[1] Thus, in 1810, approximately 780,000 people lived in Venezuela; 25 percent were White, 15 percent were African, 15 percent were Indian, and approximately 45 percent were multiracial. These rough numbers, however, conceal the diversity of formally recognized racial groups. Members of Venezuelan society identified and labeled race in an exact manner based on an individual's precise ancestry. The following list illustrates the general disregard for anti-miscegenation laws and the specificity of biologically determined racial categories used to label members of a complex, racially mixed population:

1. *blancos* (Whites): persons of Spanish descent
2. *negros* (Blacks): persons of African descent
3. *indios* (Indians): persons indigenous to the region
4. *mestizos*: children of *blancos* and *indios*

The following groups were generally known as *pardos*:

5. *mulatos*: children of *negros* and *blancos*
6. *zambos*: children of *indios* and *negros*
7. *zambos prietos*: children of *negros* and *zambos*
8. *tercerones*: children of *mulatos* and *blancos*

9. *cuarterones*: children of *tercerones* and *blancos*
10. *quinterones*: children of *cuarterones* and *blancos*
11. *salto-atras*: children who were "darker" than their mothers.[2]

Following these biologically determined racial categories, colonial Spanish society distributed social and material goods according to a rigorously enforced hierarchy. Indeed, complex rules established the rights and obligations of the various social groups and stratified this increasingly mixed society according to race.

The colonial practice of racial classification flowed directly from Spanish doctrines developed in the fifteenth century to distinguish and stratify persons based on family lineage. The doctrines of *Limpieza de Sangre* (Cleanliness of Blood) and *Nobleza de Sangre* (Nobility of Blood) were the most well established mechanisms to prove and measure descendence. The doctrine of *Limpieza de Sangre* stratified society according to an individual's direct legitimate descent to White ancestors of the Christian faith. It presupposed that only persons who could demonstrate their *cleanliness* or *purity of blood*, as shown by the length of their Christian ancestry, could enter "`honorable´ occupations," such as the clergy, medicine, law, or public office. Similarly, *Nobleza de Sangre* further stratified society based on nobility. The unique social function of members who were granted nobility of blood, or *hidalguía*, to serve the community in its military or as leaders further separated these individuals from the general population.

Because all persons in the Spanish Empire, including colonial Venezuela, were measured in terms of their purity and nobility of blood, the specific racial categories drew from these practices. But Spain modified the application of the doctrines as systems of stratification within the colonial context. In addition to recognizing the "cleanliness of blood" of *blancos* in the colonies, Spain awarded all persons deemed *blancos*—from whatever social class—*Nobleza de Sangre*. Accordingly, those most proximate to *blancos*, whose faith, skin color, and ancestry most closely approximated these Spanish ideals, were at the top of the social ladder and accorded all material and social benefits; those closer to *negros*, who exclusively formed the slave class, found their economic and social opportunities increasingly restricted.

Blancos formed the elite class in colonial Venezuela. Some commentators have noted a separation of *blancos* into two groups: those born in Spain and those born in Venezuela who could trace their ancestry directly to Spain.[3] Persons in this second group were known as *criollo*, or Creole, meaning literally of Spanish descent though native born. The relatively smaller group of Spanish-born *blancos* arrived in Venezuela as royal bureaucrats and clergymen, enjoying the greatest prestige. Nevertheless, *criollos* shared much of the same prestige since they owned land and dominated local politics.

At the opposite end of the social spectrum, *negros* as slaves primarily lived as field hands in the coastal valleys and agricultural regions. Although slaves were never a large part of the overall population of Venezuela, they could be found in every part of colonial Venezuela, including the urban areas, where they provided service as servants, coachmen, or stevedores. In addition, as the *blanco* population disdained all types of manual labor, they taught artisanal skills to their slaves, including mechanics, building techniques, carpentry, and others.

Slaves were not only valued for the work they were forced to perform; they were also markers of status and luxury within *blanco* Venezuelan society:

> Upper-class women of the Caracas elite, for example, would parade to and from Mass on Sundays accompanied by all their slave entourage, the well-dressed servants carrying a pillow, missal, and other such accouterments as their mistresses' morning excursion to church required. Status, of course, could be determined by the number and dress of the Black slaves accompanying the women on display.[4]

Manumission practices throughout the Spanish Empire fostered a movement toward freedom that benefited Venezuelan slaves. The Crown made numerous means of manumission available, but most common were various forms of self-purchase upon payment (or promise of future payment) and unconditional release by the slaveholder. Procedures became increasingly institutionalized and slaveholders promoted manumission by allowing slaves to set aside a portion of their work product as payment toward their manumission.

Freed *negros* or *pardos* entered Spanish society with significantly better status than slaves but still inferior to that of *blancos*, *mestizos*, or *indios*. Throughout the Spanish Empire,

> [v]isible African pigmentation or features saddled the free person of color with the presumption of illegitimacy and inferiority. The former charge was frequently true, and, along with the shadow of slave origin, led colonial authorities and the public to brand the free colored as vile, treacherous, lazy, prone to drunkenness, and, in general, infamous and immoral by his very nature.[5]

Because of the negative characteristics (illegitimacy and moral inferiority) attributed to free *negros* and *pardos*, attitudes toward them vacillated between "contempt and fear."[6] Extensive legislation restricted the movement of free *negros* and *pardos* and differentiated them as separate from and inferior to other free persons. From prohibitions against carrying firearms to sumptuary laws restricting the rights of free *negros* and *pardos* to wear certain types of clothing or use certain luxury items, Spanish legislation attempted to prevent the assimilation—both material and social—of this evergrowing group. Thus the legal structure bolstered and enhanced the customs that separated *blancos* from free *negros* or *pardos* in their daily social interaction.

Despite prejudice within this biologically determined hierarchy, at least a portion of the *pardo* population attempted to circumvent or ignore their legal disabilities and improve their economic and social lot. While *pardos* could not enter certain professions zealously protected by *blancos,* such as medicine, the clergy, or law, they could practice artisanal crafts or work as laborers, shopkeepers, and even plantation overseers. Many *pardos* were able to accumulate personal wealth, facilitating somewhat their acceptance by *blanco* society. As they gained more wealth, *pardos* bought additional education and religious training for themselves or their children, thereby further assimilating into Spanish society and rising in the social hierarchy.

B. Buying Whiteness: *The Gracias al Sacar*

The systematic application of the race-based exemptions of the *Gracias al Sacar* continued in Venezuela for approximately fifteen years, from 1795 to 1810. It can be traced to the *Real Cédula de Gracias al Sacar de 10 de Febrero de 1795* (Royal Decree of 1795), which added exemptions from the qualities of *pardo* and *quinterón* for the fixed price of 500 and 800 *reales* respectively, to the list of licenses, privileges, and exemptions previously available from the Crown.[7] Moreover, the Royal Decree of 1795 allowed the purchase of the feudal title of *Don* for 1,000 *reales*.[8] The combination of these new exemptions under the Royal Decree of 1795 allowed for the possible elevation of a *pardo* from the lower social classes to nobility. The Crown specifically added these exemptions to serve the colonial clientele. Seventy-one categories of exemptions provided opportunities available upon payment of the appropriate fees, ranging from the privilege of founding an entailed estate to a license for a woman to own and run a store "as a young man."

In 1801, to raise additional revenues by increasing fees, the Crown repeated almost verbatim the text of the Royal Decree of 1795 in the *Real Cédula de 3 de Agosto de 1801 de "Gracias al Sacar"* (Royal Decree of 1801).[9] . . . The fee for a racial exemption increased from 500 to 700 *reales* in the case of *pardos* and from 800 to 1,100 *reales* for *quinterones*. The Crown made no other substantive changes in the exemptions, or *Gracias*, available.

This schedule remained in effect throughout the wars of independence in Spanish America. By 1810, however, the *Gracias al Sacar* no longer had practical application in Venezuela. Agitation on the Iberian Peninsula, caused by Napoleon's 1808 invasion of Spain, led to the issuance of another order by the King in 1810 that temporarily suspended the distribution of *Gracias al Sacar*. Because of the growing movement within Venezuela toward independence and the later enfranchisement by the revolutionary government of all free persons—regardless of racial origin—as full citizens, the promulgation of *Gracias al Sacar* never resumed.

II. Toward Progressivity and Entrenchment

Although the *Gracias al Sacar* were a race practice during the late eighteenth and early nineteenth century in colonial Venezuela, it is possible to tease out some propositions that can be applied to other examples of racial negotiation, including contemporary examples in the United States. First, the history of the *Gracias al Sacar* demonstrates that the apparent rigidity of racial categories masks negotiated reality. Second, the *Gracias al Sacar* show that individual negotiation for advantage both sustains and undermines racial hierarchy. Third, they suggest that racial negotiation is always constrained by history and structure.

The *Gracias al Sacar* expose the fact that the apparent rigidity of racial categories masks negotiated reality. Despite the apparent fixity and closure of racial categories in colonial Venezuela, the *Gracias al Sacar* simultaneously were material and ideological arenas of negotiation. Within these arenas, groups and individuals exchanged wealth and contested meanings. The Crown sought to use the *Gracias al Sacar* to leverage support and funds during a particularly vulnerable period. *Pardos* sought to improve their social situation within Venezuelan society through the purchase of concrete goods such as entrance into the university or the right to enter the priesthood. *Blancos* sought to preserve their privilege and social status by resisting the *Gracias al Sacar*. Moreover, as the *Gracias al Sacar* served in the material struggles, so too they served in a constitutive capacity, revealing contradictory ideas about individual merit and equality.

The relationship between the material and ideological negotiations was not straightforward. A "win" in one arena did not necessarily carry with it a "win" in the other. An individual *pardo* received dispensation from his racial category and became a *blanco*. But to successfully petition often necessitated the rejection of his heritage and a contention that his original classification was erroneous. Thus, as in this instance, a material gain did not carry with it an ideological victory.

Likewise, the long-term effects of these negotiations do not follow naturally. The movement from *pardo* up to *blanco* may have reinforced the stratification of Venezuelan society. Alternatively, the recitation of personal genealogy needed to gain entry to *blanco* status may have created more levels of racial hierarchy. Not only did the racial categories conceal the vigorous negotiation of their implementation, but they concealed the variety of outcomes possible.

The *Gracias al Sacar* also demonstrate that individual negotiation for advantage both sustains and undermines collective racial hierarchy. Individuals used the *Gracias al Sacar* to seek personal gain and status. They mobilized their resources, instrumentally maneuvering within the social structure for their personal benefit. What is not clear, however, are the collective, systemic, or institutional consequences of these personally motivated strategies for self-advancement. At times, individual gains may have helped group advancement. At others, they may have hindered it. For example, it is likely that as individuals attained education and wealth, they and others like them might have become more assimilated into Spanish culture. However, individual acceptance would also make it easier to justify the subordination of others who were less assimilated. Thus individual achievement could serve to eliminate the possibility of social advancement for other members of the group. Moreover, as the analysis has shown, the acceptance of individual *pardos* made the exclusion of *negros* more acceptable, reinforcing the racial hierarchy. Thus a gain for one social group may have precipitated a loss for others.

Notes

1. Winthrop Wright, Café con Leche: Race, Class, and National Image in Venezuela 21 (1990).

2. *See generally* Robert M. Levine, Race and Ethnic Relations in Latin America and the Caribbean: An Historical Dictionary and Bibliography (1980), defining racial categories and

terms; Magnus Mörner, Race Mixture in the History of Latin America (1967), discussing racial categories in Latin America. . . .

3. *See* Edwin Lieuwen, Venezuela 25–26 (1961). . . .

4. Frederick P. Bowser, *Colonial Spanish America, in* Neither Slave nor Free: The Freedman of African Descent in the Slave Societies of the New World 50 (David W. Cohen and Jack P. Greene, eds., 1972).

5. *Id.* at 38–39 (citations omitted).

6. *Id.* at 39.

7. Real Cédula de Gracias al Sacar de 10 de Febrero de 1795 *in* Santos Rodolfo Cortes, El régimen de "Las gracias al sacar" en Venezuela durante el período hispanico 58–64 (1978). . . .

8. *Id.* at 63.

9. Real Cédula de 3 de Agosto de 1801 de "Gracias al Sacar," *in* 2 Cortes, *supra,* at 161.

The Long, Lingering Shadow

Law, Liberalism, and Cultures of Racial Hierarchy and Identity in the Americas

Robert J. Cottrol

III. Afro-Americans: A Hemispheric Perspective

A. Historical Overview

The black experience in the United States is actually a fairly small part of a much larger history of the forced transportation and settlement of Africans in the New World and the histories of their Afro-American and non-Afro-American descendants. Our best information indicates that less than 6 percent of Africans brought to the Americas settled in what became the United States. The experiences of Portugal, Spain, and later Latin America with African and Afro-American slavery were of a far longer duration than that of British North America, later the United States. African slavery would begin in metropolitan Spain and Portugal early in the fifteenth century, before Columbus's voyage to the New World. Latin American slavery would formally end nearly five hundred years later in Brazil in 1888, a generation after Appomattox and the passage of the Thirteenth Amendment. Over 4 million African captives were brought to Brazil alone. The giant Lusophonic colony and nation received the largest number of Africans from the transatlantic slave trade, more than seven times the 560,000 Africans that are estimated to have come to what would become the United States. The Spanish-speaking regions of the Western Hemisphere received 1,662,400 African captives. The sugar plantation economies of the Americas were the biggest magnet for the African slave trade. Northeastern Brazil and the Caribbean received the largest number of Africans brought during the nearly four centuries of the transatlantic slave trade, and the British and French Caribbean colonies combined received more than 3 million Africans. The pull of the sugar plantation economy was so strong that Cuba is estimated to have imported over 780,000 African slaves between 1790 and 1867 alone, nearly 140 percent of the total number of Africans brought to the United States between the seventeenth century and the end of the Civil War.

From the beginning, the Portuguese and Spanish experiences with slavery differed from the experience in British North America. Very few Portuguese or Spanish settlers came to the Americas. In most American territories the small, predominantly male

Portuguese and Spanish settler populations uneasily ruled over large Indian populations. For a number of political and religious reasons, both the Portuguese and Spanish governments decided that although Indians would be subject to various forced labor regimes, they would not be formally enslaved. Legal slave status would be reserved for Africans and their descendants. This, of course, added further to the anxieties of Portuguese and Spanish colonists as a growing population of African slaves were brought to the Americas to labor on the plantations and mines of the New World. Asserting and maintaining control over the majority of the population, which was neither Spanish nor Portuguese, was a major preoccupation of the Iberian settlers in a way that dwarfed similar concerns of the British settlers of North America.

If Portuguese and Spanish settlers came to the Americas with somewhat greater fears concerning their slave populations, they also arrived with a tool that their English counterparts initially lacked—an already well developed body of slave law and law concerning free persons of African descent. Portuguese and Spanish slave codes derived from the slave law of ancient Rome. Spain received Roman law in the thirteenth century during the reign of Alfonso X, the Wise. Roman law, including the Roman law of slavery, was codified into Spanish law in *Las Siete Partidas*.

In Latin America, Roman doctrine was modified in light of Spanish Christianity. Roman law, for example, was extremely harsh against potential slave rebellions. If a slave killed his master, Roman law specified that all the slaves in the household were to be put to death. The law prescribed that this was to be accomplished before the reading of the deceased master's will so that no slave in the household could be freed and hence be ineligible for execution. Spanish law confined punishment in such cases to the slaves actually responsible for the killing.

Spanish and Portuguese law was concerned with far more than simply establishing a disciplinary code for slaves, as important as that was. The law was also concerned with the assignment and preservation of status. It specified how a slave might be set free, preserving much of the Roman law doctrine on this topic. Portuguese and Spanish law, especially municipal ordinances, sought to control the behavior of slaves and free blacks who lived and worked in cities such as Lisbon and Madrid or who toiled on the sugar plantations in the Azores and Cape Verde Islands. There were even ordinances in Lisbon, Madrid, and the other cities of Portugal and Spain that strangely anticipated the Jim Crow regulations of the U.S. South in the early twentieth century. There existed laws forbidding free Negroes from wearing clothing above their station or carrying swords, and other kinds of status regulations.

Portuguese and Spanish laws regulating slaves and free people of color were adapted to meet immediate needs. Both nations, even before Colombus's voyages of exploration, were in a process of expanding from a system of domestic slavery, where slaves were employed to expand the household labor force, to a system of what some historians have termed "industrial slavery," where slaves would supply the principal labor force for an expanding export economy built around plantation agriculture or mining. The development of sugar plantation agriculture in the Azores and in the Canary and Cape Verde Islands made slavery more important to the economies of Portugal and Spain. It also brought significant numbers of Africans into both nations, making questions of race and status more critical.

Although the slave laws of Portugal and Spain were concerned with the immediate question of governing the growing African populations of the two nations, there is one way that the law of slavery made an enduring contribution to the culture of race relations in Latin America: the laws of Spain and Portugal reflected a stringent concern with group classification. This concern would increase with the Spanish and Portuguese settlement of what would become Latin America. Spanish and Portuguese settlers in the Americas, aware of their minority status, sought to maintain rigid separations among the different African, Indian, and mixed peoples that they ruled. This was to be accomplished through codification, the development of a highly precise system of racial classification through law. Spanish lawmakers were particularly artful at this, importing racial categories developed in Spain and adding to them classifications developed in the New World. Mexican anthropologist Gonzalo Aguirre Beltrán reported on one such scheme employed in eighteenth-century Mexico.[1] The codified categories indicated the designation and status of individuals according to the race and color of an individual's parents. The offspring of a

1. Spaniard with an Indian woman is a Mestizo;
2. Mestizo woman with a Spaniard is a Castizo;
3. Castizo man with a Spanish woman is a Spaniard;
4. Spaniard man with a Black woman is a Mulatto;
5. Mulatto woman with a Spaniard is a Morisco;
6. Morisco man with a Spanish woman is a Chino;
7. Chino man with an Indian woman is a Step Backward;
8. A Step Backward man with a Mulatto woman is a Wolf;
9. A Wolf man with a Chino woman is a Gibaro;
10. A Gibaro man with a Mulatto woman is a Leper;
11. A Leper man with a Black woman is a Cambujo (very dark);
12. A Cambujo man with an Indian woman is a Zambaigo;
13. A Zambaigo man with a Wolf woman is a Calpa Mulatto;
14. A Calpa Mulatto man with a Cambujo woman is a Stay in the Air;
15. A Stay in the Air man with a Mulatto woman is an I Don't Understand Thee; and
16. An I Don't Understand Thee man with an Indian woman is a Step Backward.

This and other similarly meticulous classification schemes were developed in part to strengthen Portuguese and Spanish rule in the Americas. Spanish colonial law in particular attempted to group the different racial categories into different castes with differing sets of legal privileges. This was done as part of a divide-and-rule strategy. Spanish and Portuguese colonial administrators were particularly concerned with preventing the subject peoples in their American colonies, the African, Indian, and mixed race populations, from making common cause. Their idea was that a strictly codified caste system—the Spanish actually used the word *casta,* or caste—would foster a strict separation of the differing groups, facilitating Spanish or Portuguese rule.

The legal attempt to make fine racial distinctions had an ironic consequence. Far from strengthening the boundaries between the different subordinate groups, the multiplicity of racial classifications actually contributed to a culture of racial mobility and what, to North American eyes, appears to be a culture of racial ambiguity in Latin American societies. It would become possible to improve one's racial standing with the improvement of one's social standing. If being white meant that one was at the top of the social pyramid, while being black meant that one was at the bottom, these were not legally immutable characteristics. The successful individual, the military captain, the person who struck it rich in the gold fields, those whom fortune smiled upon, could aspire to be white. In some cases, legal recognition of one's "whiteness" could actually be purchased. [See Chapter 76—Ed.] Even if whiteness might be beyond an individual's grasp, a free person of African descent might aspire to be recognized as a Mulatto, a Morisco, or some other mixed category.

Racial mobility, of course, can only exist where there is a clear notion of racial hierarchy or stratification. Firm notions of the proper place and status of the three races existed in Spanish and Portuguese thought. Whites were deemed superior. Indians, as a group, were seen as nobler than Africans. As might be expected, this picture became more complicated when cultural issues and racial mixtures came into play. As Africans, and more particularly their Afro-American descendants, adapted to the Portuguese and Spanish cultures, they became part of Latin American colonial societies. Because Africans were enslaved, more of them were likely to adopt the principal features of the Portuguese and Spanish cultures, particularly language and religion, than [were the] Indians, many of whom were effectively beyond the control of their nominal European masters. This helped to create a system of racial stratification, a pyramid if you will, that persists to the present day in most Latin American nations. Whites generally have a superior status. People of Indian racial background whose cultural practices are mainly of Portuguese or Spanish derivation—Portuguese or Spanish is their first language, Catholicism is largely unmixed with indigenous religious practices—would be next on the social ladder. Mestizos, people of mixed indigenous and white background, would have a higher rating than those of largely Indian background. At the bottom of the social pyramid would be Afro-Americans, with mulattoes occupying a higher social status than blacks. Indians who retain indigenous cultural patterns—and in most nations Indians are defined culturally, not racially—are frequently viewed as being outside the society's social structure, frequently with devastating results. It was in this hierarchical framework that law in colonial Latin America provided a formal legitimization to the notion of racial mobility.

B. Race and Contemporary Afro-Latins: The Elusive Problem

Slavery has left a mixed legacy to the American hemisphere. There are visible Afro-American populations throughout the hemisphere. Every nation in the Americas numbers among its citizens descendants of African slaves, most who are classified as black or mulatto, and some who are numbered among the white or mestizo populations of their nations. Here, just as in our previous discussion with slave importation, it might be useful to attempt to contrast the size of the black population of the United States with the Afro-American population in the hemisphere as a whole. This is a somewhat difficult task. While the records of slave-trading companies, combined with tax records, have given demographic historians a reasonably accurate portrait of the size of the slave trade and the destinations of the African captives who came to the Americas, the data are much less firm on contemporary Afro-American populations.

The first problem is one of definition. Who should we count as Afro-Brazilian, Afro-Mexican, or Afro-Colombian? To North Americans, that seems like an incredibly easy question. We are accustomed to viewing anybody with traceable African ancestry as black. Surely, even conceding to Latin Americans that blacks and mulattos are distinct groups and that our notion of hypodescent is carrying things a bit far, we should be able to determine if there is a proximate black ancestor, perhaps drawing the line at grandparents or great-grandparents, and thus decide if an individual might fall into an Afro-American category. This should not be too difficult. It is. Concepts that either developed or intensified during slavery, views of black inferiority, and notions of racial mobility complicate the task of determining who should be included in the Afro-American population of Latin America. If U.S. history and culture dictated that anyone with traceable African ancestry was to be included in the black population, circumstances during slavery and after emancipation in Latin America dictated almost exactly the opposite—people of mixed background or even people largely of African ancestry above a certain social standing were to be counted as something other than black.

There is yet another level of complexity that must be added to the question of who should be counted as an Afro-American within the Latin American context. After a while, the North American researcher begins to get the hang of things. There is a strong distinction between blacks and mulattoes. There are individuals with admitted black ancestors who regarded themselves, and are regarded by others, as white or mestizo. Racial mobility is possible—you need not remain a member of the racial group into which you were born. Just as you get used to these ideas, certain facts throw a curveball or two your way. If it is true that phenotype and social position determine race—and not remote ancestry, as has been the case in the United States—why is the tragic mulatto story a genre in Latin American as well as North American fiction? Or why does one occasionally encounter individuals who are phenotypically white or Indian who nonetheless identify themselves as Afro-Colombians or Afro-Mexicans? These seeming counterexamples tend to make the North American student of race even less surefooted when traversing the difficult terrain of race and status in Latin America.

In some cases African ancestry is denied altogether, even when it is apparent. The population of the Dominican Republic, for example, is predominantly of African descent. Only a minority of the population is phenotypically white, and a majority of that group probably has some African ancestry. Despite this, it has been customary among some Dominicans, until relatively recently, to define themselves as Indians or descendants of Indians and not as Afro-Dominicans. Blacks have frequently used the term *Indio Oscuro*, or Dark Indian, while mulattos have tended to use the term *Indio Claro*, or Light Indian. This tendency has in part reflected the traditional higher status for people of Indian descent in Latin America, as well as the fact that Haitians have traditionally been seen as the "other" in Dominican society.

All of this makes determining the size and scope of the Afro-American population in the Western Hemisphere a somewhat difficult undertaking. This task is made yet more difficult because, with the exception of Brazil, most of the nations of Latin America have not kept systematic records of their African-descended populations in national censuses. . . .

By any estimate the Afro-American population of Latin America is substantial. In some countries, including Brazil, Colombia, Cuba, the Dominican Republic, and Venezuela, people of visible African descent make up one-third or more of the population. In other nations, Mexico and Peru, for example, there are substantial Afro-American populations, but their presence tends to be overshadowed by the large indigenous populations and the tensions between the white and mestizo populations and those who retain an indigenous culture. In a number of Latin American nations, the Afro-American population is quite small, and there has been a tendency to claim that they have disappeared altogether. This has been true, to varying degrees, of Argentina, Chile, and Uruguay in the twentieth century. In some countries the Afro-American population is largely an immigrant population, particularly in many Central American nations, where there has been large English-speaking Afro-Caribbean immigration in the twentieth century. In a number of nations this has added an overlay of cultural conflict . . . to their racial conflict.

Despite significant variations in the different nations, certain common patterns with respect to race and discrimination regularly appear in the historical and social science literature discussing Afro-Americans in Latin America. Racial hierarchy, a social pyramid with blacks on the bottom and whites on top; the idea of relative fluidity in racial classifications; and the concept of racial mobility have all been reasonably well explored in the recent social science literature. A generation or two ago, historians and social scientists, partly influenced by the contrast with the Jim Crow United States, were likely to describe racial interactions in Latin America in terms of the concept of "racial democracy," attributing the different conditions under which blacks and whites lived to class differences, not racial discrimination. Today there is a much greater willingness in the literature to recognize the extent of Latin American racial discrimination in such areas as employment, public accommodations, receipt of government services, and even . . . public stereotyping and racial insult. There are efforts in some Latin American countries to strengthen anti-discrimination laws. There is also a debate over how much might be learned from the U.S. experience in this area.

Note

Robert J. Cottrol, *The Long Lingering Shadow: Law, Liberalism, and Cultures of Racial Hierarchy and Identity in the Americas*, originally published in 76 Tulane Law Review 11–79 (2001). Reprinted with the permission of the Tulane Law Review Association, which holds the copyright.

1. *See* Gonzalo Aguirre Beltrán, La Población Negra de Mexico: Estudio Etnohistórico 176–77 (1946).

78

Chicano Indianism

A Historical Account of Racial Repression in the United States

Martha Menchaca

Conflicting Racial Laws in the Conquered Territories

In 1848, with the end of the Mexican-American War, the United States politically disenfranchised all Indians of the Southwest by rescinding Mexico's racial laws in the newly conquered territories. Since 1812, Mexico had given Indians the right to claim citizenship and full political rights. . . . Mexico also no longer practiced a legally based racial caste system. Thus new racial restriction policies instituted in the conquered territories came to threaten the civil rights of the Mexicans because under U.S. laws, Indians and "half-breeds" were not considered citizens. . . .

The eradication of Mexico's racial caste system had begun in the late 1700s when the Spanish crown resolved that generations of miscegenation had thoroughly blurred racial distinctions. . . . In 1812, the legal basis of the racial ranking order was finally abolished. The racial caste system, which for two centuries had distinguished individuals on the basis of race, became nonfunctional for political and social purposes. Its gradual breakdown resulted from the growth of the mestizo population and the political power obtained by upper-class mestizos. By the turn of the nineteenth century, the mestizos had become the majority and were heavily represented in the upper classes.

Before the breakdown of the racial caste system, Mexico's population had been divided among Spaniards, *castas,* and Indians. . . . Distinguishing the population on the basis of parental origin had been an adequate legal method of according economic privilege and social prestige to the Spaniards. The Spaniards included both *peninsulares,* individuals who had been born in Spain and were of full European descent, and *criollos,* who were also of full European descent but had been born in the New World. As miscegenation increased among the Spanish elite, the criollo category eventually came to be redefined. The *castas* were mestizos and other persons of mixed blood. The Indian category included only people of full indigenous descent.

Of the various racial groups, the Spaniards enjoyed the highest social prestige and were accorded the most extensive legal and economic privileges. The legal system did not make distinctions between *peninsulares* and *criollos.* Nevertheless, the Spanish crown instituted policies requiring that high-level positions in the government and the Catholic Church be assigned to *peninsulares* . . . , on the rationale that only *peninsulares* were fervently loyal to the Spanish crown. . . .

The social and economic mobility of the rest of the population was seriously limited by the legal statuses ascribed to their ancestral groups. In theory, Indians were economically more privileged than mestizos because they held title to large parcels of communal land protected by the Spanish crown and the Catholic Church. . . . However, regardless of their landed property, the Indians were accorded little social prestige in Mexican society and were legally confined to subservient social and economic roles regulated by the Spanish elite. Most Indians were placed in *encomiendas* and *repartimientos* (Indian communities where land and labor were controlled by Spanish missionaries or government officials), Indian pueblos, or haciendas and were held in a perpetual state of tutelage. The mestizos enjoyed a higher social prestige than the Indians but were considered inferior to the Spaniards. They were also often ostracized by the Indians and the Spaniards, and they did not enjoy certain legal privileges accorded to those groups. For example, most mestizos were barred by royal decree from obtaining high- and mid-level positions in the royal and ecclesiastical governments. . . . Moreover, the Spanish crown did not reserve land for the mestizos as it did for the Indians. For the most part, the only economic recourse most mestizos had was to enter the labor market or migrate toward Mexico's northern and southern frontiers. Each migrant who was the head of a household was awarded 150 acres and exempted from taxation for a period of approximately ten years. . . . After 1680, mestizos were occasionally allowed to become parish priests in Mexico's frontier settlements or in sparsely populated areas.

By the late 1700s, the rigid racial order had relaxed owing to changes in the interracial sexual and cohabitation practices of the Spanish elite. . . . It had become common for upper-class Spanish males to take mestizo or Indian women as concubines and afterward legitimate their offspring. In such cases the racial status of the child became *criollo* and not mestizo. These *criollos* had the racial status of Spaniards but were not accorded the corresponding legal privileges. They were barred from positions reserved for the Spaniards of full European descent, and they suffered certain sanctions for marrying peninsular women. By the early 1800s, large numbers of *criollos,* mestizos, and Indians were becoming increasingly defiant of bounded social roles and were trespassing their borders with deliberate speed. *Criollos* attempted to pass for *peninsulares* in order to obtain more social privileges. Indians often passed for mestizos in order to obtain wage labor in the urban centers; mestizos passed for Indians as a means of acquiring the land titles of the Indians . . . ; and mestizos who had amassed great fortunes tried to improve their social standing by passing for *criollos.* [See Part 3 on "Passing"—Ed.] The blurring of the racial distinctions made it difficult for the Spanish crown to enforce the laws and the prescribed social norms, in particular because the majority of the population was indistinguishably mestizo.

The final blow to the racial order came about through the political defection of the masses. By the early 1800s, movements to liberate Mexico from Spanish colonial rule had erupted throughout the country, and as a consequence the Spanish crown attempted to avert revolutionary action by instituting the 1812 Spanish Constitution of Cadiz. The new constitution legally abolished the *casta* system and the racial laws. Theoretically, the constitution conferred on Spaniards, mestizos, and Indians the same political rights regardless of racial origin. The laws of Cadiz, however, were unable to avert the national independence movements. In 1821, the masses won the Mexican War for Independence and instituted a provisional constitution (the Plan de Iguala) reaffirming the racial philosophy of the Constitution of Cadiz. After the War of Independence, race could no longer be legally used to prevent Indians and mestizos from exercising citizenship rights. For example, it became common for mestizos and full-blooded Indians to be elected to the presidency. All subsequent Mexican constitutions ratified the spirit and language of the Constitution of Cadiz.

In northern Mexico, the frontier experienced the same legislative changes as the interior. Indians were considered Mexican citizens and were accorded full political rights. In New Mexico, southern Arizona, and California the acculturated Indians and the secularized mission Indians actively exercised those rights. . . . In New Mexico, numerous Pueblo Indians were elected to town and county political offices, and in California, acculturated American Indians often held high-ranking posts in the military. . . . Of course, the new laws had limited effects on the majority of the American Indians, because Mexico held title to territories inhabited by unconquered indigenous populations. The majority of the Shoshone, Navajo, Apache, and Comanche Indians had not been conquered by the Mexican state. And the new legislation did not eradicate the Mexican elites' attitudes of racial and economic superiority toward the American Indians and mestizos.

When Mexico ceded its northern territory to the United States, then, it had already abolished all racial restrictions on citizenship. The Indians had theoretically been incorporated as Mexican citizens. In practice, of course, this legislation had not abolished racial prejudice and discrimination in Mexico, and the Indians continued to be stigmatized as uneducated people. However, the mestizo racial category had taken on a new social meaning. Because most of the population was mestizo, being mestizo had become a source of pride rather than a stigma. The European race continued to hold high social prestige in Mexico, but the masses no longer considered it the only prestigious racial group. . . . In the legal domain, race could no longer be used as a civil rights barrier.

The racial policies of the United States, however, were less liberal than Mexico's. The United States at that time conferred full citizenship rights on "free whites" only. Thus the states' constitutional right to deny Indians U.S. citizenship introduced the ideological and legal foundation for limiting the Mexican people's political rights. Moreover, government officials often used the Mexicans' indigenous heritage to undermine the civil rights language of the Treaty of Guadalupe Hidalgo. [This treaty ended the U.S.–Mexican War in 1848.—Ed.] . . .

Regardless of the treaty, however, the U.S. government refused to ratify the racial equality laws of Mexico. When the annexed southwestern territories joined the Union, their state constitutions did not extend to American Indians the political rights guaranteed by the Treaty of Guadalupe Hidalgo and the Mexican constitution. And soon after the enactment of the treaty, controversy arose over the citizenship status of the Mexicans. The exclusionary Indian citizenship laws, endorsed by the southwestern legislators, became the legal basis for limiting the political rights of the Mexicans. . . .

Ironically, the political privileges that the Spanish and Mexican governments had previously given people in the Southwest were abolished by the U.S. racial laws. The

Mexican mestizos and Indians entered a new racial caste-like order in which their civil rights were limited. Given the nature of the U.S. racial system and its laws, the conquered Mexican population learned that it was politically expedient to assert their Spanish ancestry; otherwise, they were susceptible to being treated as American Indians. . . . At the same time, as this historical blueprint suggests, it became politically expedient for American Indians to pass for Mexican mestizos if they wished to escape the full impact of the discriminatory Indian legislation. . . .

The Denial of Citizenship for American and Mexican Indians

After ratification of the Treaty of Guadalupe Hidalgo, government representatives of the annexed region began to pass new racial-restriction citizenship laws. . . . Most American Indians were prohibited from obtaining citizenship, and the anti-Indian legislation adversely affected the Mexicans of partial or full Indian descent. Unless a Mexican was predominantly white, he or she was subject to racial harassment. . . . Those classified as Mexican Indians were not entitled to exercise full political rights or even basic civil rights: they were not allowed to vote, practice law, marry Anglo-American women, or run for political offices such as district judge. . . . They were also subject to severe human rights infringements, such as being placed in debt peonage and being forced to live on reservations.

After the annexation of Mexico's northern frontier, the southwestern territories and states enacted ruthless, discriminatory Indian legislation. The Anglo-American legislators were able to enforce the laws with the help of the U.S. military and the Anglo-American settlers. It became common policy to place American Indians on reservations, drive them out of the Southwest, or exterminate them. . . . By the late 1870s, the process of displacing Indians from their fertile southwestern land was practically complete. Thousands of Indians had been exterminated and the remainder placed on reservations. In Texas, indeed, this had been achieved as early as 1852. . . . The Anglo Americans' blatant disregard for the Indians' right to life became an alarming warning to the Mexicans. If Mexicans were to have more political rights than Indians, they could not be identified as Mexican Indians.

Of the annexed regions, California and Arizona enacted the most discriminatory Indian legislation, clearly and strongly professing that all Indians, regardless of territorial origin, were to be denied citizenship. To a large extent, California's and Arizona's exclusionary racial laws reflected the Anglo-American political brokers' interest in limiting the rights of the Mexicans and preventing them from having any governmental power. Both states passed laws to disenfranchise Mexicans of Indian descent and to allow only white Mexicans full political rights.

Administering Identity

The Determination of "Race" in Race-Conscious Law

Christopher A. Ford

South Africa's system of apartheid was built upon a statutory system of race classification that tied every aspect of social and economic life, and even "national" affiliation, to individual classifications. In its philosophical scope, the apartheid scheme went far beyond the segregationist aspirations of the Jim Crow South, encompassing also an ideal of complete political and territorial separation. In the full flowering of what the governing Afrikaner-dominated National Party termed (without conscious irony) a system of "separate development" and "separate freedoms," it was argued that the individual development of the various racial "nations" of South Africa would in time produce a patchwork quilt of sovereign states living alongside each other in relationships of economic interconnectedness but political independence. Ultimately, "South Africa" itself would be a purely White state, surrounded by distinct "national" or "tribal" homelands confederally allied to it. This sweeping articulation of a "separate but equal" doctrine of absolute partition rationalized the apartheid state's all-embracing system of racial segregation and discrimination—from the everyday matters of public amenities to the wholesale demarcation of impoverished and discontinuous quasi-colonial "homelands" (or "Bantustans"), such as Bophuthatswana, KwaNdebele, KwaZulu, and Transkei, which were reserved for South Africa's tribal "nations" (Twsana, Ndebele, Zulu, Xhosa, etc.).

The backbone of the apartheid state was a system of universal population registration, which wrote into law the classification of individuals into discrete groups. Under section 5 of the Population Registration Act of 1950:

> (1) Every person whose name is included in the [census] register shall be classified by the Director [of the Census] as a white person, a coloured person or a native, as the case may be, and every coloured person and every native whose name is so included shall be classified by the Director according to the ethnic or other group to which he belongs.
>
> (2) The Governor-General may by proclamation . . . prescribe and define the ethnic or other groups into which coloured persons and natives shall be classified in terms of sub-section (1), and may in like manner amend or withdraw any such proclamation.

The original text of the act defined South Africa's racial groups as follows:

(iii) "coloured person" means a person who is not a white person or a native; . . .

(x) "native" means a person who in fact is or is generally accepted as a member of any aboriginal race or tribe of Africa; . . .

(xv) "white person" means a person who in appearance obviously is, or who is generally accepted as a white person, but does not include a person who, although in appearance obviously a white person, is generally accepted as a coloured person.[1]

The operation of this classification system can perhaps best be seen in the procedures provided for racial "reclassification." Benefit-allocation was strongly tied to racial classification—for example, residential areas were segregated under the Group Areas Act, intergroup marriages were prohibited by the Prohibition of Mixed Marriages Act, intergroup sex was banned by section 16 of the Immorality Act, and public facilities were segregated by the Reservation of Separate Amenities Act.[2] In such a system it was not uncommon for many individuals to wish to challenge the classification they had been assigned. For example, a "coloured person" could enjoy greater benefits if he could be reclassified as a "white person."

By choosing a classification scheme based on an "in appearance obviously is, or who is generally accepted as" standard, the architects of apartheid were shrewd enough to avoid any scientific definition of race or ethnicity. In essence, the government had the power to classify and reclassify individuals at will. Section 5 of the Population Registration Act provided:

> If at any time it appears to the Director that the classification of a person in terms of sub-section (1) is incorrect, he may . . . after giving notice to that person . . . specifying in which respect the classification is incorrect, and affording such person . . . an opportunity of being heard, alter the classification of that person in the register.[3]

Reclassifications at an individual's own request were more complicated. Applicants would be deemed members of a racial group only if other designated members of that group accepted them as members, as determined by a panel of "experts" commissioned for the occasion. Section 11 of the act regulated challenges to individual classification orders:

(1) Any person who considers himself aggrieved by his classification by the Director in terms of section five and any person who has any objection to the classification of any other person in terms of the said section, may at any time object in writing to the Director against that classification.

(2) Every such objection shall be lodged in duplicate and shall be accompanied by an affidavit in duplicate setting forth fully the grounds upon which the objection is made, and if the objection relates to the classification of a person other than the objector, a copy of the objection and the affidavit shall be transmitted by the Director to the person to whose classification the objection relates.

(3) Every objection received . . . shall be referred by [the Director] . . . to a board . . . constituted for the purpose by the Minister. . . .

(5) . . . [T]he Director and every objector and every person in regard to whose classification the objection has been made, shall be entitled to appear before the board concerned . . . to cross-examine witnesses and to adduce such evidence as may be relevant to the matter before the board. . . .

(7) The decision of a board shall be final and binding upon all persons including the Director: Provided that any person who considers himself aggrieved by a decision of a board in regard to his own classification may . . . appeal against that decision . . . to the provincial or local division of the Supreme Court of South Africa. . . .[4]

Under section 11, one could even challenge the racial classification of *another* person, making it possible for a concerned citizen to have a suspect neighbor "expelled" from his racial category.

The standards such boards employed revolved around not whether an applicant for reclassification was socially acceptable to the members of the group to which he or she had asked to be admitted but rather whether the racial group members felt the applicant actually to be a member of that racial group. In other words, it would be legally irrelevant for reclassification purposes that White citizens were willing to welcome a Colored applicant into their hitherto White-reserved neighborhood. Reclassification would be permissible only if they were willing to swear that the applicant was in fact not Colored at all but really White. One opposition parliamentarian described the process as follows:

> One must have photographs taken—colour pictures; front and side views—on the basis of which somebody can judge whether one can pass as White. One has to appear before a committee of officials who will then listen to one's pronunciation of English or Afrikaans or whatever other language in order to judge whether one will fit in. . . . One has to obtain opinions from other people in one's community . . . as to whether one is acceptable to Whites *as a White.*
>
> . . . [One must obtain opinions that one is] acceptable in a White community *as a White person.*[5]

Such was the race-classification scheme of apartheid.

The South Africans thus took "intuitive appraisal" tests to a relatively high level of formality, establishing an extensive judicial and bureaucratic system for the allocation and reallocation of racial identity. There, summary bureaucratic authority to allocate racial identity was the rule, but formal procedures were provided for individuals to challenge the classifications thus made. For a society that took its racism and its legal formality seriously, there was scarcely any way to avoid building such an elaborate classificatory edifice. The centrality of racial identity in South Africa to the allocation of even the most basic necessities of everyday life—let alone those precious civic commodities of citizenship, voting power, nationhood, and civil and political rights—demanded nothing less.

Notes

1. An Act to Make Provision for the Compilation of a Register of the Population of the Union; For the Issue of Identity Cards to Persons Whose Names Are Included in the Register; and For Matters Incidental Thereto, No. 30, § 1(iii), (x), (xv), § 5 (1950) (South Africa) [hereinafter Population Registration Act].
2. Illustrated History of South Africa 375–77 (Dougie Oakes, ed., 1988).
3. Population Registration Act, *supra*, at § 5(3).
4. *Id.* at § 11.
5. 2 Parl. Deb. (Hansard), House of Assembly 4435–36 (1988) (statement of S. S. van der Merwe) (emphasis added).

80

Race, Multiculturalism, and the Jurisprudence of Transformation

Charles R. Lawrence III

In June 1955, the Congress of the People was convened in Kliptown, South Africa, a village on "a scrap of veld a few miles southwest of Johannesburg." The Congress, conceived and organized by a multiracial coalition of black, white, Indian, and Colored organizations, was a convention that united all of the oppressed and all of the progressive forces in South Africa to issue a clarion call for change and to create a set of principles that would be the foundation of a new South Africa.

President Nelson Mandela recalls the meeting of the Congress in his autobiography:

> More than three thousand delegates braved police intimidation to assemble and approve the final document. They came by car, bus, truck, and foot. Although the overwhelming number of delegates were black, there were more than three hundred Indians, two hundred Coloureds, and one hundred whites. . . .
>
> . . . . The platform was a rainbow of colors: white delegates from the COD [Congress of Democrats], Indians from the SAIC [South African Indian Congress], Coloured representatives from SACPO [South African Coloured People's Organization] all sat in front of a replica of a four-spoked wheel representing the four organizations in the Congress Alliance. . . .
>
> . . . . There were dozens of songs and speeches. Meals were served. The atmosphere was both serious and festive. On the afternoon of the first day, the charter was read aloud, section by section, to the people in English, Sesotho, and Xhosa. After each section, the crowd shouted its approval with cries of "Afrika!" and "Mayibuye!"[1]

The Congress of the People stands as a landmark in the history of South Africa's freedom struggle, and the Freedom Charter became a blueprint for that struggle. It remains the foundational document for South African progressives in their continuing effort to realize the full fruits of their revolution.

I. Liberal Theory and Transformative Theory: Two Views on the Project of Equality

[T]he history of the Congress of the People . . . is a story of a multicultural coalition and . . . it is a story of freedom fighters who understood that the primary and fundamental goal of a struggle for human dignity and equality must be the complete transformation of a society founded on dehumanization and the maintenance of inequality. The members of the Congress knew that apartheid imprisoned every woman and man. Blacks, whites, Asians, biracials, multiracials, Zulus, Xhosas, Sothos: All were dehumanized by the ideology and institutions of white supremacy. None of them would be free until all were free. None could claim an individual right to equal treatment, to a job or a university education, in a world defined by fundamental inequality.

The drafters of the Freedom Charter, and those who continue the freedom struggle as newly enfranchised South African citizens, understood and understand that apartheid cannot be ended by pronouncement. It must be dismantled. . . .

If the drafters of the Freedom Charter were asked how best to address the problem of interminority group conflict, I think their approach would be very different from one that views protection of the individual as the primary task of the project of equality. Their first question might be "In what different, complex, and interrelated ways is the experience of each group related to the maintenance of white supremacy?" This is not an easy question to answer. . . . But it is very different from asking whether one group has been more disadvantaged or more victimized than another, or whether one group's disadvantage is "intractable" and another's is not, or whether individual members of one group are more like one another, in disadvantage suffered, cultural affinity, or political outlook, than individual members of another group. It is a different question because its ultimate concern is with righting a wrong done to us all and not with compensating individuals or the groups they compose. This kind of question seeks out the interrelatedness and intersection of our injuries. It is not just blacks who are injured by stereotypes about blacks but Latinos and Asians and even whites.

The drafters of the Freedom Charter might well ask whether, in a particular instance, a race-based admissions policy or a separate dorm for blacks advances the struggle against apartheid. But that question is necessarily answered in context. It requires a concrete response to specifically felt forms of domination. For example, since its inception in 1912, the ANC [African National Congress] has steadfastly pursued a policy of nonracialism, but prior to 1965, only Africans were admitted as members. There was a felt need for an organization for Africans that had the chief goal of achieving African unity and full political rights. This was not a case of "separatists . . . circling the wagons around their own race" or "reject[ing] the possibility of interracial understanding." It did not inhibit the ANC's close cooperation with progressive whites, Coloreds, and Indians or their active participation in multiracial coalitions. Nor did it prevent them from later opening the organization's membership to non-Africans. . . .

II. Building Coalitions and Working at Home: Fighting White Supremacy within Racially Subordinated Communities

A. How White Supremacy Turns Us against Ourselves and Each Other

Because South Africa's racial hierarchy was made explicit and codified, it provides the clearest example of how white supremacy divides and conquers the racially subordinated. The Population and Registration Act and the Group Areas Act formed the cornerstones of apartheid. The Populations and Registration Act authorized the government to officially classify all South Africans according to race. Under the Group Areas Act, each racial group could own land, occupy premises, and do business only in its own separate area. While all three nonwhite groups were deprived of political and social rights, apartheid created clear status distinctions between the groups, giving Asians some privileges denied to Coloreds, who in turn were more privileged than Africans. President Mandela describes how the South African prisons not only separated political detainees by color but also served them different meals according to their place in the racial hierarchy. White prisoners received white sugar and white bread with their meals. Indian and Colored prisoners were given brown sugar and bread, and African prisoners received neither bread nor sugar.

My students from South Africa tell me that shortly before the first free national elections in their country, the National Party, the ruling party during the apartheid regime, distributed a comic book throughout Miller's Plain, a large segregated subdivision in Cape Town populated entirely by South Africans designated under apartheid as "coloured." The housing in the subdivision is modest and significantly poorer than most white neighborhoods in Cape Town, but it is a significant step up from the townships where Africans have been forced to live. The residents of Miller's Plain are mostly the working poor. Many of them hold jobs that were reserved for Coloreds under apartheid.

The National Party's campaign comic book depicted a typical Miller's Plain Colored family: a mother, a father, three children, and a dog. Each strip told a tale of how, if elected, Mandela and the ANC would allow the Africans to take everything the Colored family had worked so hard to get. The depictions in the comic of both Coloreds and Africans employed blatantly racist stereotypes. In one strip, an unkempt African rings the doorbell. The mother goes to the door and asks what he wants. "I've come to look at the house that Mandela is giving me after the elections," he says. The Cape Town province was the only province the National Party carried in the elections. Colored voters overwhelmingly supported the National Party. . . .

Note

1. Nelson Mandela, A Long Walk to Freedom 150–51 (1994). . . .

81

Challenges and Dilemmas of Racial and Ethnic Identity in American and Post-Apartheid South African Affirmative Action

Christopher A. Ford

I. Affirmative Action in South Africa

With the ANC's [African National Congress's] victory in the April 1994 elections and Nelson Mandela's inauguration as South Africa's first non-White president on May 10, 1994, the former apartheid state moved into a new era. . . .

C. Affirmative Action in South African Practice

Despite its ambitious campaign rhetoric about increasing opportunities for non-Whites (and women), the ANC-dominated government has proven somewhat cautious about undertaking affirmative action programs—in large part for fear of the economic and political problems that might result from alienating White civil servants (who still run much of the machinery of government) and business leaders (who still dominate the economy). Though, as we shall see, affirmative action programs in both the private and public sectors continue apace, and the topic remains highly controversial.

1. The Public Sector

The job security of South Africa's 1.2 million-strong Afrikaner-dominated civil service was a subject of great sensitivity during the multiparty talks that produced the interim constitution. Ultimately, the ANC was willing to promise to protect the jobs of the apartheid-era civil servants. Non-Whites are being brought into the government bureaucracy to replace Whites who retire or resign, but although early retirement is encouraged and many new positions (fillable by non-Whites) have been created, few, if any, Whites have yet been actually laid off.

The Mandela government's relatively cautious and conciliatory approach to public-sector affirmative action has, in fact, apparently proven quite frustrating to many ANC supporters who had hoped quickly to be given government employment after the 1994 elections. After Mandela's inauguration, for instance, some 2 million job applications reportedly flooded in for the eleven thousand civil service openings then available.

The government's reluctance simply to fire White workers, however, should not be mistaken for any ambivalence about policies that Americans would recognize as "affirmative action." As the above account should suggest, public-sector hiring by the Mandela government has focused almost exclusively on the hiring and promotion of non-Whites, particularly Africans. Indeed, at least some of the country's numerous state-owned institutions have adopted dramatic, virtually "non-Whites-only" hiring policies. South African Airways (SAA), the national park service, and the state rail company, Transnet, for example, have all announced that no White can be hired without formal approval from their chairmen. Accordingly, the non-White proportion of the civil service has been steadily increasing, even to the point of prompting protest demonstrations in Johannesburg by White public-sector workers.

Interestingly, perhaps the most dramatic immediate increases in non-White public-sector employment in South Africa have occurred in the security services, particularly in the South African National Defense Force (SANDF). While the South African Police (SAP) force is facing an affirmative action–related shakeup—with dozens of new national and regional police commissioners being appointed in order to make the organization more racially representative—the most tumultuous changes have occurred in the South African Army.

The ANC has shown itself steadfastly committed to affirmative action in South Africa's public sector. Indeed, it has clearly been the Mandela government's intention that the public bureaucracies should set an example for the private sector in the creation of opportunities for non-Whites in both hiring and promotion. For the most part, the private sector seems to be working hard to keep up.

2. The Private Sector

If it is the aim of private-sector affirmative action programs to begin to overcome the dramatic racial disparities in South Africa, they certainly have their work cut out for them. By some accounts, Whites, just 13 percent of the population, hold 80 percent of the professional positions in South Africa and 93 percent of management positions in private business. For their part, Africans occupy only 1 percent of top executive positions and less than 3 percent of managerial jobs. Making matters worse, the country's economic problems have resulted in the overall loss of some four hundred thousand jobs since 1990, increasing the sting of South Africa's nearly 50 percent African unemployment and making it very difficult for businesses to make much progress in providing opportunities to non-Whites, at least in the short term.

Businesses in South Africa pursue affirmative action programs for a number of reasons. To some extent, there are significant economic incentives to reach out to non-Whites. According to forecasts by South Africa's Absa Bank, the minority White community is increasingly unable to provide the numbers of skilled managerial personnel the economy needs. It is also, however, widely believed in the business community that if the private sector fails to make progress on its own, through the "voluntary" adoption of aggressive affirmative action programs, the Mandela government will step in to compel them. Although, at the time of this writing, "no law yet requires set-asides, racial preferences or other affirmative action programs familiar to Americans," the government has set up an office in the Labour Ministry to "monitor" affirmative action progress. More directly, state organizations such as the Gauteng Tender Board—which approves some $1 billion in annual infrastructural projects in South Africa's new Gauteng Province—have been steering governmental contracts to private firms on the basis of those firms' adoption of affirmative action programs.

Accordingly, various sources have reported that between 59 percent and 94 percent of South African companies have undertaken some variety of affirmative action program. Not all sectors of the economy have responded with equal alacrity, and it is not clear that South Africa will meet the ambitious affirmative action goals propounded by groups such as the Black Management Forum, but change is unquestionably in the air.

In an economy long officially segregated by race and in which non-Whites, and especially Africans, were deliberately and systematically denied access to more than the most rudimentary education and job training, the scramble to adopt affirmative action hiring and promotion goals has been greatly hampered by shortages of qualified candidates. Adult literacy in South Africa is approximately 73 percent, but as many as 80 percent of Africans are said to be unable to read beyond the fifth-grade level. Reports indicate, for example, that there were only thirty black engineers in South Africa and thirty-one black pharmacists. In 1994 a study found only sixty-five black chartered accountants and fewer than twenty black architects.[1] Even if they exaggerate shortages—perhaps by somewhat undercounting Africans who acquired technical and professional educations abroad during the apartheid years—such figures are alarming. Less than 7 percent of South African Ph.D. holders are African, and most Africans who received higher educations during the apartheid era did so in areas such as law and teaching rather than in the fields most in demand in today's affirmative action regime: business, finance, engineering, and the sciences. The paucity of non-Whites with the education, training, and job experience needed in higher managerial positions has produced "feverish" bidding wars among private employers for a relative handful of highly skilled non-White employees, but it bodes ill for hopes of significant immediate progress in integrating the middle and upper ranks of private industry.

II. Group Identity: Commodification and Competition

A. Identity Politics in Post-Apartheid South Africa

After decades of formal racial classifications, on the basis of which were distributed some of South Africa's most fundamental social goods—employment, land, housing, education, and public services—it is probably to be expected that White, Colored, Indian, and "tribal" African identities retain some salience in South African political life. . . .

1. Affirmative Action and "Colored" Identity

a. White South Africa's "Colored Project."

The various White-run governments of South Africa have spent the better part of the last century and a half trying, quite deliberately, to cultivate a sense of a separate "Colored" identity among that country's mixed race population. This policy began in the nineteenth century, before South African independence from Britain and during a period when the British Colonial Office was "increasingly committed to a strategy of 'divide and rule.'"[2] It acquired a special significance at the turn of the century, however, as the term *Colored*—once applied broadly to non-Europeans, as in traditional American practice—was gradually "reconstituted" to mean mixed race South Africans, in contradistinction to "full-blooded" Whites and Africans.

In the 1920s, various legislative enactments helped create barriers both between this new stratum of "Coloreds" and Africans and between Coloreds and the dominant White population. With the advent of formal residential segregation and "influx control" measures designed to prevent the migration of Africans to urban areas in search of employment, Coloreds were exempted from the tightest restrictions. At the same time, laws were passed to legitimate White closed-shop rules that cut off Coloreds from avenues of economic advancement available to White workers.

The most aggressive governmental attempts to cultivate a distinct Colored identity, however, materialized in the era of full-blown apartheid after the Afrikaner-dominated [Nationalist Party (NP)] won power in 1948. The Nationalists, whose political strength depended on fierce appeals to White Afrikaner solidarity, were eager both to foster Colored identity vis-à-vis Africans and to distinguish themselves sharply from Coloreds—who, despite their somewhat darker skin, nonetheless spoke Afrikaans as their first language and shared the Dutch Reformed faith and much of their culture with their paler Afrikaner brethren. "Recognising that identification is firmly rooted in material experience, the NP set about restructuring the social, political and economic world inhabited by the people they defined as Coloureds."[3] Thus did the apartheid state acquire its rigid three-tiered system of racial classification: Whites on top, Africans on the bottom, and Coloreds and Indian South Africans—in equivalent but legally separate positions—in the middle.

In the Western Cape region, home to most of the country's Colored population, those positions not falling under White "job reservation" rules were subjected to a "Coloured Preference Policy," which allowed the Colored working class to monopolize them and "deepen[ed] the conservatism of Colored workers whilst simultaneously increasing the distance between Coloured and African workers." Most dramatically—after flirting with the idea of establishing a Colored "homeland" analogous to those assigned to South Africa's various African "tribes"—the government in 1984 established a "tricameral" constitutional scheme, whereby Coloreds and Indians would participate in a system of "power sharing" with Whites. For a few years in the 1980s, therefore, South Africa had three parallel parliaments: the all-White "House of Assembly," the Indian "House of Delegates," and the Colored "House of Representatives." Each house of parliament had jurisdiction over a selection of "own affairs" in South Africa's system of segregated housing, education, and public services, while the cooperation of all three was (in theory) required for decisions pertaining to "general affairs" of national importance such as justice, transport, defense, and foreign affairs.

b. The Collapse of the "Colored Project."

It is, paradoxically, both the failure and the success of this century-old project that may speak to us most ominously of the dilemmas of identity politics in an era of affirmative action. Until the abdication of the apartheid regime in the early 1990s, it was generally believed that the National Party's program of cultivating a separate Colored identity had failed. Part of the government's problems with encouraging Colored self-identity among mixed race South Africans stemmed from dramatic class divisions within the Colored community, which undercut feelings of collective solidarity. But the principal obstacle to Colored identity in late-apartheid South Africa was the common enemy faced by *all* non-White South Africans: the apartheid regime itself.

In the upwelling of popular protest, anti-government demonstrations, and work and school boycotts across South Africa that accompanied and grew out of the Soweto riots of 1976, Coloreds (especially Colored youths) allied themselves closely with Africans. This radicalization continued in the early 1980s, as from April 1980 there occurred "virtually a total boycott of Coloured educational establishments" in collaboration with similar African stay-aways. Despite decades of governmental efforts to divide the two groups, this protest activity "indicated a rejection of the distinction between African and Coloured people." Coloreds also largely boycotted the 1984 referendum establishing the "tricameral" constitution by refusing to register to vote—and did so to such effect that a candidate for the Colored house of parliament in one constituency, for example, won the seat with only 118 votes.

Whatever success the apartheid state might otherwise have had in cultivating a sense of Colored separateness, it was overwhelmed by the intensity of anti-government feeling among South Africans of all hues. The Coloured Preference Policy in the Western Cape was finally abandoned in the 1980s, in part because it had failed in its principal object. The long-awaited collapse of the policy led one scholar to conclude that "[p]olitical resistance to the National Party [had overcome] many of the divisions which the National Party set out to create between African and Coloured people in the Western Cape."

c. The Resurrection of Colored Identity

But where the party of apartheid failed to realize its dreams of cementing a separate "Colored" identity upon the mixed race South Africans of the Western Cape, the ANC seems to be succeeding. Many Coloreds today feel threatened by the ANC government. They fear African antagonism after Africans' years of suffering the indignities of third-class citizenship (as compared to Coloreds' second-class status), and they worry that the ANC's eagerness to divert development-aid resources to impoverished African communities will leave nothing for Coloreds. And, it should be noted, they are concerned that the ANC's affirmative action agenda will pass them by for not being "black enough."

In September 1994, for example, a crowd of Colored citizens made headlines by rioting against the new ANC government. Coloreds have also organized rent boycotts protesting government plans to adopt (lower) flat-rate rents and service charges exclusively in African townships. Furthermore, since the April 1994 elections, "there has been a proliferation of coloured groups fighting for anything from the emancipation of coloureds, resistance to affirmative action in favor of the majority blacks, to a homeland for mixed-race people."[4] Some of these groups are comparatively innocuous, such as the South Western Joint Civics Organization, which complains of government neglect of Colored residential areas and condemns affirmative action as "affirmative discrimination." Others, however, are positively alarming, none perhaps more so than the "Coloured Resistance Movement"—*Kleurling Weerstandbeweging*, or KWB—which models itself after Eugene Terreblanche's notorious neo-Nazi "Afrikaner Resistance Movement," or AWB. The KWB advocates a Colored "homeland" analogous to those to which the NP once tried to confine South Africa's various African "tribes." Its leader, Mervyn Ross, teaches that Africans are colonizers just like Whites and warns darkly that "the brown people have to defend their own against intruders."

The NP has lost no time in taking advantage of Colored worries about ANC "Africanism," eagerly taking up an unaccustomed role as champion of Colored interests against a government it depicts as devoting itself exclusively to African concerns. Campaigning on what was almost, in effect, a *swart gevaar* (black peril) platform lifted from its own segregationist past, the NP won power in the Western Cape's provincial assembly in the April 1994 elections, largely on the strength of Colored bloc voting, by winning more than 53 percent of the total. Even as the NP's leader, President F. W. de Klerk, stepped down from office in Pretoria in favor of the ANC's Nelson Mandela, a former NP minister of law and order stepped into office as governor of the Western Cape—at the head of a White and Colored voting bloc antagonistic to the ANC.

The Mandela government, not surprisingly, is quite concerned about such developments. President Mandela himself professes to have been almost personally wounded by Colored antagonism: "It hurts me very much that having acquired freedom for all South Africans—where for the first time Africans, coloureds, Indians and whites can be the masters of their own future—the actions of certain groups in the coloured community are causing their own marginalization."[5] As these comments suggest, however, the ANC may be quite prepared to countenance such Colored "marginalization," making mixed race anxieties self-fulfilling and miring post-apartheid politics in a new area of racial conflict and division.

It is thus one of the bizarre and uncomfortable ironies of South African politics that the ANC's ambitious affirmative action program is in this sense helping the present government complete the NP's great apartheid project of cultivating a separate "Colored" identity among South Africa's mixed race population.

Notes

Originally published in 43 UCLA Law Review 1953 (1996).

1. Figures compiled from Bob Drogin, *Ending Apartheid at Work*, Los Angeles Times, August 14, 1995, at A10; *The Darkening of White South Africa*, The Economist, May 20, 1995, at S18. . . .

2. Ian Goldin, Making Race: The Politics and Economics of Coloured Identity in South Africa 236 (1987). . . .

3. *Id.* at 79.

4. Rich Mkhondo, *Mixed-Race South Africans Say Freedom Struggle Just Begun,* Reuters, September 15, 1995, *available in* LEXIS, Nexis Library, Reuters File.

5. *Id.*

Review Questions

1. How have the United States' classifications for mixed race people been similar to, and different from, those employed in other countries?
2. What lessons can the United States learn from the racial classifications employed in other countries?
3. Does Part 10's comparative look at the legal treatment of racial mixture around the world support the notion that "race" is a social construction?
4. Would you prefer to be a mixed race person in the United States or in some other country? Explain.

Suggested Readings

Afrocuba: An Anthology of Cuban Writing on Race, Politics and Culture (Pedro Perez Sarduy and Jean Stubbs, eds., 1993).

Frederick P. Bowser, *Colonial Spanish America, in* Neither Slave nor Free: The Freedman of African Descent in the Slave Societies of the New World 50 (David W. Cohen and Jack P. Greene, eds., 1972).

John Clytus, Black Man in Red Cuba (1970).

Mark Christian, Multiracial Identity: An International Perspective (2000).

Marisol de la Cadena, Indigenous Mestizos: The Politics of Race and Culture in Cuzco, Peru, 1919–1991 (2000).

Alejandro de la Fuente, *Race, Ideology, and Culture in Cuba: Recent Scholarship*, 35 Latin America Research Review 199 (2000).

Azra Daniel Francis, Growing Up Brown in White Apartheid South Africa with the Spotted Tongue (1998).

Ian Goldin, Making Race: The Politics and Economics of Coloured Identity in South Africa (1987).

Tanya K. Hernández, *An Exploration of the Efficacy of Class-Based Approaches to Racial Justice: The Cuban Context*, 33 University of California Davis Law Review 1135 (2000).

A. Leon Higginbotham Jr., *Racism in American and South African Courts: Similarities and Differences,* 65 New York University Law Review 479 (1990).

———, *Seeking Pluralism in Judicial Systems: The American Experience and the South African Challenge,* 42 Duke Law Journal 1028 (1993).

A. Leon Higginbotham Jr., F. Michael Higginbotham, and S. Sandile Ngcobo, *De Jure Housing Segregation in the United States and South Africa: The Difficult Pursuit for Racial Justice,* 1990 University of Illinois Law Review 763 (1990).

Now That We Are Free: Coloured Communities in a Democratic South Africa (Wilmot James, Daria Caliguire, and Kerry Cullinan, eds., 1996).

Thomas G. Krattenmaker, *Race Relations Law in a Reformed South Africa,* 10 Harvard BlackLetter Journal 117 (1993).

Lundy R. Langston, *Affirmative Action, A Look at South Africa and the United States: A Question of Pigmentation or Leveling the Playing Field?* 13 American University International Law Review 333 (1997).

Robert M. Levine, Race and Ethnic Relations in Latin America and the Caribbean: An Historical Dictionary and Bibliography (1980).

Nelson Mandela, A Long Walk to Freedom (1994).

J. R. Miller, Skyscrapers Hide the Heavens: A History of Indian-White Relations in Canada (1989).

Minority Rights Group, The Position of Blacks in Brazilian and Cuban Society (Anani Dzidzienyo and Lourdes Casal, eds., 1979).

Carlos Moore, Castro, The Blacks, and Africa (1988).

Magnus Mörner, Race Mixture in the History of Latin America (1967).

Orlando Patterson, Slavery and Social Death: A Comparative Study (1982).

Julissa Reynoso, *Race, Censuses, and Attempts at Racial Democracy*, 39 Columbia Journal of Transnational Law 533 (2001).

Mona Rosendahl, Inside the Revolution (1997).
Allister Sparks, The Mind of South Africa (1990).
Jon Michael Spencer, The New Colored People: The Mixed-Race Movement in America (1997).

Part XI

A Mixed Race Society

The End of Racism?

Part 11 discusses the possible impacts of increasing intermarriage and greater numbers of mixed race people in the United States. Since the invalidation of the anti-miscegenation laws (see Part 1), combined with the elimination of racial quotas in the immigration laws in 1965 (see Gabriel J. Chin, *The Civil Rights Revolution Comes to Immigration Law: A New Look at the Immigration and Nationality Act of 1965*, 75 North Carolina Law Review 273 [1996]), racial mixture has greatly increased. The racial mixtures also have increased in their diversity.

Black-White marriages have become more common over the last fifty years. Latina/o, Asian, and White intermarriage rates are significantly higher, all increasing substantially over the last few decades. Biracial couples report growing social acceptance of their relationships. (See Darryl Fears and Claudia Dean, *Biracial Couples Report Tolerance*, Washington Post, July 5, 2001, at A1; *but see* Part 1, noting some modern resistance to interracial relationships.)

The 2000 Census (see Part 4) gave the nation a glimpse into the size and character of the multiracial population in the United States. Over the coming decades, we unquestionably will see growth in the number of multiracial people.

A cautionary note is in order. Black-White intermarriage, while increasing, remains relatively rare, with same-race marriages persisting. (See Rachel F. Moran, *Interracial Intimacy: The Regulation of Race and Romance* 101–25 [2001].) Does this suggest that

TABLE 1
Projected Marriages to Other Groups, 1995 to 2050, by Population Group and Generation (Percent)

Population Group	Overall Total (1995)	Generation			
		1st	2nd	3rd	4th+
White	8	10	9	8	8
Black	10	14	12	10	10
Hispanic	30	8	32	57	57
Asian	20	13	34	54	54
American Indian	40	20	30	40	50

Source: Barry Edmonston and Jeffrey S. Passel, *How Immigration and Intermarriage Affect the Racial and Ethnic Composition of the U.S. Population, in* Immigration and Opportunity: Race, Ethnicity, and Employment in the United States 373, 389 (Frank D. Bean and Stephanie Bell Rose, eds., 1999).

racism against African Americans in U.S. society is greater than that against other groups?

One wonders what the changing demographics of racial mixture in the United States will mean for the future of civil rights in the United States. A few optimistic commentators envision the decline of racism. Others are more circumspect, especially given the long history of deep racial division in this country. For a pessimistic prognosis, consider the following:

> . . . [H]istory (in the United States and throughout the world) suggests that racism will not die a quick or easy death. This nation has a long history of racial classification and discrimination, even when, as in the case of nineteenth-century Irish and Eastern European immigrants, "racial" differences are subtle or non-existent. Rather than the demise of racism, the increase of multiracial people may result in new forms of racial subordination. Society will construct new races, perhaps based on lightness or darkness of skin color, language, culture, or religion. The bloody war in Bosnia in the 1990s . . . offers a chilling possibility. (Kevin R. Johnson, *How Did You Get to Be Mexican? A White/Brown Man's Search for Identity* 179 [1999].)

The following excerpts offer alternative visions of the impacts of multiracialism in the United States. In a controversial article, Jim Chen sees the "Creole Republic" as the cure to racism and criticizes Critical Race Theorists for allegedly opposing interracial relationships. Suggesting more tempered optimism, James Gordon opines that the first Justice Harlan's racial sensibilities were shaped positively—as reflected in his opinions as a Justice on the U.S. Supreme Court—by the fact that he had a half-Black brother. Garrett Epps and Peter Kwan look skeptically at the claim that multiracial people will ameliorate the nation's racial ills. Finally, David Hollinger studies the impact of the multiracial population on the civil rights paradigm in the United States.

Unloving

Jim Chen

II. The Creole Republic

As a matter of first legal principles and of ultimate societal aspirations, I regard the United States of America as the Creole Republic. Whether attained by blood, soil, or toil, American citizenship has uniform privileges and immunities. This land not only bled mightily as expiation for its original sin of institutionalizing slavery; it had the foresight to establish a single, undiluted class of citizenship. Despite suffering comparable or even greater violence, other nations are still struggling with ethnic problems summarized by phrases such as "*echt deutsch*" [see T. S. Eliot, *The Waste Land, in* The Waste Land and Other Poems 29 (1922): "*Bin gar keine Russin, stamm' aus Litauen, echt deutsch*" ("I ain't Russian—I'm from Lithuania, a real German")—Ed.] and traceable to constitutional provisions linking citizenship to ethnic origin. Admittedly, naturalized American citizens are ineligible to be President, but that peculiar distinction is based on immigrant status rather than race or ethnicity. The key point is that the quality of America's legal mercy is not strained according to the ethnic origins of individual citizens. Now that the tragic era in which American law denied citizenship to certain immigrants has ended [see Part 9—Ed.], we Americans have achieved the minimal, formal prerequisites for egalitarian colorblindness.

Before I go further, one word on nomenclature: Just as a soufflé in a Vieux Carré bistro cannot survive a brisk breeze, the delicate elegance of the word "American," the verbal emblem of the Creole Republic's common political culture, cannot survive dilution. Every term such as "African American," "Italian American," or "Swedish American" detracts from the true significance of the slogan *e pluribus unum* ["Out of many, one"—Ed.]. . . . [T]he term "Asian American" is misleading at best and self-defeating at worst. There is no uniform Asian culture, as anyone with the slightest sense of history knows. In fact, the latest ethnological and linguistic research suggests that northeast Asians such as Japanese and Koreans have more in common, genetically and linguistically, with Europeans than with southeast Asians such as Chinese and Thai. The tenuous connections that do bind the diverse inhabitants of South and East Asia do not travel well over the Pacific. . . .

With each passing American generation, integration nudges social reality closer toward legal utopia. Despite legal and physical barriers, people of different races and ethnicities will mix their cultural traditions over time. If ever a manifest destiny gripped this nation, this continent, this hemisphere, it was the fate that made America the world's biological and sociological clearinghouse. Five centuries of tempestuous interaction between the Old and New Worlds have spawned countless instances of cross-fertilization, both in ecological and in human terms.

Consider the humble yet profound project of eating. Mao Zedong asserted that "[a] revolution is not a dinner party." A deeper untruth may not exist in the Great Helmsman's vast collection of fallacies and lies. A reliable food source is the first and arguably the most indispensable element of human civilization, which begins with the production of means to satisfy the human need for sustenance. Even in a society rich enough to take agriculture for granted and to wield food exports as a foreign policy weapon, individuals and families treat mealtime as the paramount moment of thanksgiving, the most frequent occasion at which they acknowledge their God.

America's creolization of the world's palate and population can be measured at the dinner table. It is an astonishing import/export trade. Maize and potato harvests—mountains of plants once found only in the Americas—feed masses in Europe, Asia, and Africa. Conversely, the American tongue drips with the nutritional contributions of diverse immigrant groups: yam, goober, pretzel, lefse, tempura, bok choi, salsa, and the same noodles known in America by two names, lo mein and spaghetti. *Lax,* once the native Germanic word for salmon, died out in England sometime after the Norman invasion, only to be reborn in America as *lox,* a Yiddish loanword for a salmon delicacy. The Creole melting pot heats a uniquely American dish of gumbo, each ingredient discernible but irrevocably flavored by all the others. Just as "the American accent, the multiplicity of sound bearing the history of our nation,"[1] communicates the linguistic diversity of the Creole, the American cornucopia yields the culinary harvest of our mutual Creole history.

In short, we Americans have "mixed people as though they were of no more consequence than the swill [we have] slopped together for [our] pigs."[2] The rest of the world should be so fortunate.

Cross-breeding in the Creole fashion is not confined to the garden and to the kitchen. It also extends to the bedroom. Sexuality, like water and money, seeks its own level. Of course, unlike plant or animal reproduction, human sexuality transcends mere biology. But the sociological factors intertwined within the funny thing called love are no more stable than the biological influences on human, animal, and plant reproduction. If anything, arbitrariness in social structuring renders the sociological element even more chaotic. Within the population that so many Americans consider monolithically "black," subtle gradations of color (and corresponding differences in perceived social status) can provoke employment discrimination actionable under Title VII [of the Civil Rights Act of 1964].[3] Shades of blackness have inspired cultural introspection, both scholarly and popular. [See Part 6—Ed.]

Needless to say, the nontoxic colors of American "Creola" do not belong exclusively to Africa or, for that matter, to Europe, Asia, or the Americas. Every segment of the American population that is temporarily and arbitrarily identified by some ethnic designation traces its origins to multiple and diverse genetic pools. Rather than treat this Creole heritage as the shameful vestige of slavery and a racist past, America ought to celebrate it. Whatever else it might honor, multicultural America must surely venerate the "half-breed" survivors who endured and eventually conquered racism. By living, eating, and reproducing in each other's presence, the people of America have kept forging in their neighborhoods the same mongrel race that their farmers and cooks long ago created in crops and foods.

Intermarriage and its handmaiden, interbreeding, are running riot in America. Within two decades—roughly the span of a single human generation—the number of interracial marriages in the United States has grown from 310,000 to 1.1 million.[4] The incidence of mixed race births has multiplied twenty-six times as quickly as that of any other group. A full decade ago, the number of known mixed race children in America reached 1 million. The exogamy-fueled, predominantly European melting pot of early twentieth-century America reached such searing temperatures that popular discourse today rarely draws legally significant distinctions between "white" ethnic groups. Efforts at affirmative action favoring Italian Americans—by most accounts a traditionally disadvantaged European ethnic group—have drawn sharp criticism on the grounds that the sons and daughters of Italy in America are white, racially indistinguishable from the dominant Anglo-Saxon ruling class.

Moreover, ethnic blending in America now includes ethnicities commonly lumped into the nonwhite, presumably isolated groups within the "people of color" coalition. "[E]xogamy rates for Mexican Americans have long been at least as high as those for European immigrant groups earlier this century."[5] One Asian American group—those of Japanese descent—has intermarried into the general American population so rapidly that 65 percent have spouses without Japanese heritage. Since 1981 the number of babies born to one Japanese American and one white parent has exceeded the number born to two Japanese American parents.[6] That Japanese Americans should lead this trend comes as no surprise. This group boasts one of the highest levels of economic and educational achievement of any ethnic group in America, white or nonwhite, and access to wealth and higher education breaks down social barriers to intermarriage.

Through the intensity and virtual involuntariness of the bonds created by marriage or parenthood, family relationships hold the key to the resolution of racial conflicts. Nearly four centuries of positive lawmaking by the United States and its predecessor sovereigns have contributed less toward overcoming racial tensions at the person-to-person level, *at the level that counts,* than discrete acts of family-building across racial lines. All the law and legalism that the positive state can spew can scarcely match the power of "an explosion of joy or a miracle like love, . . . [t]he deep commitment of a loving couple, [or] the birth of a baby" to spark "the building of communities not based on color but based on conscience."[7]

No less genuine an American by virtue of naturalization than a compatriot born to putatively white parents on American soil, I claim and enjoy full citizenship in our Creole Republic. Perhaps only a full appreciation of the dynamic origins and continued evolution of the Creole Republic enables an immigrant, from Asia or elsewhere, to cast his or her eyes forward toward a future and a hope in America rather than backward toward a lost ancestral land. The broad seas separating the United States from Africa, Asia, and Europe function like the waters of Styx and Lethos, inducing forgetfulness as immigrants cross into the new country. But it is no death that awaits in America. The Creole Republic promises new life. That new life is assuredly different from the one left behind. Perhaps, just perhaps, that new life is and will remain unattainable for those who refuse to risk losing the old.

IV. Love Means Never Having to Say We're Different

. . . Would some racialists, if forced to make a yes or no decision, reject *Loving* [*v. Virginia*][8] outright? [See Part 1—Ed.] [Professor Chen intimates that Critical Race Theorists, who focus on the law's impact on racial minorities, are "racialists" who advocate separation of the races.—Ed.] Perhaps. Deep down, racialism resists exogamy. The fundamentalist vision of race dictates as much. Unless races in America remain static, unless the boundaries separating black, brown, red, white, and yellow in America remain fixed, the creationistic narrative of white oppressors and colored victims will collapse. Interracial marriage and adoption—the inevitable products of color-blind family formation—pose the ultimate, unanswerable threat to the intellectual, political, and financial security of professors who preach racial fundamentalism. In a truly Creole Republic, with freedom of family formation across all racial lines, racial fundamentalism would carry little weight, as any person's abuse of members of other races will likely redound to the detriment of a family member. Might the careers of race-conscious legal scholars become the new battle lines of the debate over intermarriage as a symbolic skirmish in a grander race- and wealth-based class struggle?

Accepting the premises underlying the racial fundamentalists' opposition to transracial adoption dictates a rejection of *Loving.* Both the absolutist argument against transracial adoption and the milder argument favoring same-race placement whenever feasible rest on the same assumptions. [See Part 8—Ed.] In a predominantly white society, a nonwhite child presumably cannot develop a healthy racial identity unless he or she is raised by parents of the same race. The corollary to this assumption prescribes ethnic matching between parent and child so that a nonwhite child can learn how to defend himself or herself against domineering whites in a racist society. Contrary to the very notion of adoption, which holds out hope that love between parent and child will grow despite the absence of biological kinship, proponents of race-matching in child placement have glorified and legitimated the primitive instinct that a child must physically resemble his or her parents. Race-matching thus serves as an impregnable Siegfried line against the white hordes who would suppress nonwhite cultures by stealing nonwhite children.

These premises are profoundly flawed. In a Creole Republic where men and women more and more frequently marry across racial lines, it is astonishing that the entire debate over transracial adoptions has divided the world of aspiring parents into rigid "white" and "nonwhite" compartments. How would a social worker, a devout racial fundamentalist, respond to a petition by a racially mixed couple—white husband, black wife—to adopt an orphaned black child? Treat the couple as white on the theory that an authentically black woman would never have married a white man? Oppose the petition on the grounds that the husband would be unable to prepare the black child for survival among white racists? If that rationale prevails, would the wife improve her chances of success on the petition by divorcing her white husband? Contrary to almost every established tenet of family law, racial fundamentalism ordains an affirmative answer. The right race is a necessary condition for adoption. "Love," by contrast, "is . . . not enough."

Race-matching fully collides with *Loving* and the Creole creed when one considers that intermarried couples might reproduce biologically. Under a rigidly fundamentalist view of race, the biological child of a mixed-race couple is a member of the darker race. If the couple divorces and a dispute over child custody arises, the logic underlying race-matching in adoptions dictates awarding custody to the darker parent. As a member of a socially oppressed race, the biracial child needs a parent who can help him or her cope with white racism. If this factor can justify awarding custody over a biracial child to black foster parents instead of white biological grandparents, it should a fortiori prove decisive in custody disputes between a white parent and a nonwhite parent. And it has, for white and nonwhite parents alike. Just as one court concluded that white children would "be better reared with members of their own race,"[9] another reasoned that the biracial daughters of a black father and a white mother would "have a better opportunity to take their rightful place in society if they [were] brought up" in the black father's home, raised "among their own people."[10] Even when the racially mismatched parent prevails, he or she must overcome a judicial presumption that the lighter parent will be less able to help the child "endure identity problems" arising from a "mixed racial heritage."

One might have thought the Supreme Court in *Palmore v. Sidoti*[11] [see Part 8—Ed.] had put an end to the use of race in custody proceedings by barring consideration of societal hostility toward a parent's remarriage to a person of a different race. Later cases, however, have conferred the narrowest of readings on *Palmore*; courts in fact may and do consider race under the guise of protecting the child's emotional reaction to a particular racial setting.[12] The rigid view of race that racial fundamentalism endorses readily converts that distinction into a preference or even a full-blown requirement for matching the races of parents and children. This legal trend bodes nothing but ill for biracial children, the citizens whose yearning to breathe free will most likely smash strict racial categorization in the Creole Republic. As excruciating as custody disputes are for children, a biracial child bears an inordinately painful burden when heartless parents, courts, and social workers inject racial issues into disputes over family formation and reformation.

Policies favoring race-matching in adoption and child custody inexorably erode the rationale underlying *Loving v. Virginia*. Marriage is frequently the first step in family building: When you choose a spouse, you presumably are also choosing a second parent for your children, whether acquired by biological reproduction or by adoption. If, as a nonwhite, you want to love your future children, you can't choose a white spouse. Those children will belong to your race, not your spouse's. Should death or divorce part the two of you, you run the risk that racially hostile white folks will control your children. Even in the absence of marital failure, your white spouse will be unfit to transmit *your* culture to a child who will have inherited your ethnic heritage alone. In fact, unless you wish to risk casting your child entirely outside your own ethnic heritage, you simply can't marry outside your own race. The biological offspring of an Asian American and a black will owe blood-borne cultural allegiance to Africa, not Asia. *Loving* thus gives you the technical freedom to miscengenate, but allegiance to the one true racial faith counsels a wise decision to marry within your race. When you outgrow the impulsive affairs of your youth, you'll stop looking for mates in those exotic "other" races.

Racial fundamentalism therefore displays an undeniable core of animosity toward all forms of interracial family formation, whether by intermarriage, cross-breeding, or transracial adoption. Here lies the theory's heart of darkness. In return for a "precious trickle of ivory" from the racialist legal establishment, racial fundamentalists manipulate their purported constituents as though nonwhites were so many "dusty niggers with splay feet," unable to think, dream, live, and love outside the law's paternalistic embrace.[13]

It is no answer to argue that white supremacists also abhor miscegenation and that oppressed nonwhite scholars are accordingly entitled to wield any countervailing weapon at hand. No less than the notions of white supremacy that inspired anti-miscegenation laws in the first place, the fundamentalists' hostility to transracial marriage and adoption stems from a grotesque desire "'to preserve . . . racial integrity . . .' and to prevent the 'corruption of blood,' 'a mongrel breed of citizens'; and 'the obliteration of racial pride.'"[14] Like the Southern whites who massively resisted integration, the new racialists are fretting over the prospect that "little black boys would be sitting next to little white girls . . . and the next thing would be intermarriage and worse." At a logical extreme, by opposing romantic perforations of an implicit color bar, racial fundamentalism emasculates "deviant" nonwhite men after the fashion of a violent white supremacist who shouts, "Now you'll let white women alone, even in hell."

Nor is it defensible to complain that white-dominated social opprobrium awaits families of mixed race. Courts have rejected this lame excuse in disputes over child custody, employment discrimination, housing discrimination, and desegregation of public facilities. I defy racial fundamentalists to defend an attitude that does not suffer interracial families to form.

No defense will succeed unless it forswears color-consciousness in family formation. The aptly named struggle of *Loving v. Virginia* shows not only where the battle lines are drawn but also why there can be no apology for the losing side. By denying the truth of one Latin proverb, *amor omnia vincit* (love conquers all), racial fundamentalism proves another: *sic semper tyrannis* (thus always with tyrants). Suffocating love, marriage, and childrearing—arguably the most fundamental impulses involving a person besides the self—in the name of racial solidarity is one of the most grotesque forms of tyranny imaginable. It is also self-defeating. "[U]ntil individuals can be dissuaded from accepting as normal the choice of intimates by race, race will always divide."[15] By enforcing a norm of racial purity in family formation, a fundamentalist approach to race and racism will never bridge racial divides in America.

Notes

1. Mari J. Matsuda, *Voices of America: Accent, Antidiscrimination Law, and a Jurisprudence for the Last Reconstruction*, 100 Yale Law Journal 1329, 1407 (1991).
2. O. E. Rölvaag, Peder Victorious 138–39 (Nora O. Solum and O. E. Rölvaag, trans., 1929).
3. *See Walker v. Secretary of Treasury*, 713 F. Supp. 403 (N.D. Ga. 1989). . . .
4. Jill Smolowe, *Intermarried . . . With Children*, Time (special issue), Fall 1993, at 64.
5. Peter Skerry, *Not Much Cooking: Why the Voting Rights Act Is Not Empowering Mexican Americans*, Brookings Review, Summer 1993, at 42, 43. *See generally* Peter Skerry, Mexican Americans: The Ambivalent Minority (1993).
6. *See* Smolowe, *supra*, at 64.
7. Syl Jones, *In Matters of Love, Why Should Color Matter So Much to So Many?* Minneapolis Star-Tribune, March 4, 1994, at 21A.
8. 388 U.S. 1 (1967).
9. *Boone v. Boone*, 565 P.2d 337, 338 (N.M. 1977). . . .
10. *Ward v. Ward*, 216 P.2d 755, 756 (Wash. 1950).
11. 466 U.S. 429 (1984).
12. *See, e.g.*, *Holt v. Chenault*, 722 S.W.2d 897, 898 (Ky. 1987).
13. Joseph Conrad, Heart of Darkness 83–84 (1902; reprint 1950).
14. *Loving*, 388 U.S. at 7. . . .
15. Note, *Racial Steering in the Romantic Marketplace*, 107 Harvard Law Review 877, 894 (1994).

83

Did the First Justice Harlan Have a Black Brother?

James W. Gordon

On September 18, 1848, James Harlan, father of future Supreme Court Justice John Marshall Harlan, appeared in the Franklin County Court for the purpose of freeing his mulatto slave, Robert Harlan. This appearance formalized Robert's free status and exposed a remarkable link between this talented mulatto and his prominent lawyer-politician sponsor.

This event would have little historical significance but for the fact that Robert Harlan was no ordinary slave. Born in 1816 and raised in James Harlan's household, blue-eyed, light-skinned Robert Harlan had been treated by James Harlan more like a member of the family than like a slave. Robert was given an informal education and unusual opportunities to make money and to travel. While still a slave in the 1840s, he was permitted sufficient freedom to have his own businesses, first in Harrodsburg, Kentucky, and then later in Lexington, Kentucky. More remarkably still, he was permitted to hold himself out to the community as a free man of color at least as early as 1840, not only with James Harlan's knowledge but apparently with his consent. After making a fortune in California during the Gold Rush, Robert moved to Cincinnati in 1850 and invested his money in real estate and a photography business. In the years that followed, he became a member of the Northern black elite, and, in the period after 1870, established himself as one of the most important black Republican leaders in Ohio.

Although a humane master, James Harlan's treatment of Robert was paradoxical. James's tax records show that he bought and sold slaves throughout his life. The slave census of 1850 lists fourteen slaves in James Harlan's household, ranging in age from three months to seventy years. The census for 1860 lists twelve slaves ranging in age from one to fifty-three years. James neither routinely educated nor often emancipated his slaves, although his ambivalence about the "peculiar institution" was well enough known to become a political liability in Kentucky, a state that was firmly committed to the preservation of slavery.

What about Robert Harlan was so special as to lead to such exceptional treatment by James? In the view of one scholar, the peculiarity of James Harlan's relationship with Robert Harlan is easily explained. Robert Harlan, he asserts, was James Harlan's son.[1] If true, this means that another of James's sons, the first Justice John Marshall Harlan, had a black half-brother.

When James emancipated Robert, John Harlan was fifteen years old. Thereafter, James and Robert continued to have contacts. After James's death in 1863, John and Robert remained in touch. Robert was an anomalous feature of John's childhood in slaveholding Kentucky and remained a part of this perception of blacks as an adult.

John deeply loved and respected his father, James. He lived in his father's house until after his own marriage. James taught John law and politics. In both arenas, father and son were partners and seem to have confided freely in one another. James remained the most important influence in John's life until the older man died in 1863, when John was thirty years old.

James Harlan's ambivalent but generally negative feelings about slavery surely influenced John's views on the subject. But even more important, James's peculiar relationship with Robert during John's youth and the ongoing contacts between James, John, and Robert after Robert's emancipation must have affected John's attitudes toward blacks. Robert was smart and ambitious but lived his life in the twilight between two worlds, one black, the other white. He was never completely at home in either. Robert's lifelong experience of the significance of the color line became, vicariously, a part of John's experience. Robert was also a continuing example of something John Harlan could not later, as a Supreme Court Justice, bring himself to deny—the humanity of blacks and the profound unfairness of their treatment by a racist America.

Given his connection to Robert, Justice John Harlan's progressive views on race, views that he repeatedly articulated in his famous dissents as an Associate Justice of the United States Supreme Court, become more comprehensible. Indeed, it is reasonable to assume that we will never understand fully the sources of Justice Harlan's advanced views on race until we better understand his relationship with the black man who might have been his half-brother. Justice Harlan argued repeatedly that the Civil War Amendments had given black Americans the same civil rights as whites:

> [T]here cannot be, in this republic, any class of human beings in practical subjection to another class, with power in the latter to dole out to the former just such privileges as they may choose to grant. The supreme law of the land has decreed that no authority shall be exercised in this country upon the basis of discrimination, in respect of civil rights, against [free men] and citizens because of their race, color, or previous condition of servitude.[2]

Harlan further denied that blacks constituted

> a class which may still be discriminated against, even in respect of rights of a character so necessary and supreme, that, deprived of their enjoyment in common with others, a [free man] is not only branded as one inferior and infected, but, in the competitions of life, is robbed of some of the most essential means of existence.

In *Plessy v. Ferguson*,[3] Harlan, standing alone against the rest of the Court, again dissented:

> In respect of civil rights, common to all citizens the Constitution of the United States does not . . . permit any public authority to know the race of those entitled to be protected in the enjoyment of such rights. . . . I deny that any legislative body or judicial

> tribunal may have regard to the race of citizens when the civil rights of those citizens are involved.

Elsewhere in the same opinion, in words that have since become famous, Harlan wrote:

> [I]n view of the Constitution, in the eye of the law, there is in this country no superior, dominant, ruling class of citizens. There is no caste here. Our Constitution is color-blind, and neither knows nor tolerates classes among citizens. In respect of civil rights, all citizens are equal before the law.

If Robert and John were brothers, a provocative dimension for contemplation is opened. The careers of these two talented, ambitious men offer us parallel examples of life on different sides of the color line in nineteenth-century America. They grew up in the same household and, if brothers, carried many of the same genes. Each was given every opportunity that his status and skin color permitted. Each succeeded to a remarkable extent, again within the limits imposed on him by the society in which they both lived. Each man was shaped by his own perceptions of these limits and by their reality. In the end, John Harlan climbed as high as his society permitted *any man*. Robert Harlan climbed as high as his society permitted *any black man*. Although in the end Robert did not rise as high as did John, his achievements were, upon reflection, equally impressive and worthy of exploration.

One year before Robert Harlan's death, John Harlan wrote in dissent in *Plessy v. Ferguson*, "The destinies of the two races, in this country, are indissolubly linked together, and the interests of both require that the common government of all shall not permit the seeds of race hate to be planted under the sanction of law." I wonder whether, when John Harlan penned these words, he reflected on their truth in his own life. His life, his father's life, and Robert's life had indeed been "indissolubly linked together." That link, like the country's, was forged in slavery and continued into an ambiguous twilight of freedom. Drawing upon his own experience for inspiration, John Harlan wrote of a color-blind future and, by writing about it, began the process of creating it. In a way, the writing of these words was John Marshall Harlan's greatest achievement.

Notes

1. This connection was made by Dr. Paul McStallworth in his brief biographical entry on "Robert James Harlan" in the Dictionary of American Negro Biography. Dictionary of American Negro Biography 287–88 (Rayford W. Logan and Michael R. Winston, eds., 1983). Dr. McStallworth's conclusion appears to rest primarily upon a biographical article about Robert Harlan, that was published in a Cincinnati newspaper thirty-seven years after Robert's death. *See Brief Biography of Colonel Robert Harlan*, Cincinnati Union, December 13, 1934. . . .

2. *Civil Rights Cases*, 109 U.S. 3, 62 (1883) (Harlan, J., dissenting).

3. 163 U.S. 537, 554–55, 559 (1896) (Harlan, J., dissenting).

84

What's *Loving* Got to Do with It?

Garrett Epps

As far as I can reconstruct Professor [Jim] Chen's reasoning, it seems to be that (1) intermarriage of the races offers hope for a cessation of racial hostility and oppression; (2) intermarriage is in fact the *only* such hope, but it is such a powerful hope that the vision of future generations living together in a harmonious racial blend negates the validity and even the existence of concrete examples of racism directed at living individuals today; (3) those who question the sovereign power of intermarriage to alleviate all racial wrongs are "racial fundamentalists" who believe that race is a fixed, essential quality and seek to force others to adhere to their vision; (4) anyone who imagines a future in which his or her children are *not* married to a person of another race must implicitly oppose such marriage. . . .

The logic is at best elusive. For even if we assume that every person of color will take it as a moral duty to find a person of another race, marry that person, and raised mixed race families, the prospect of the happy future those children will create does not, in itself, negate the reality of mistreatment of people of color who have had the misfortune or bad taste *not* to be born of cross-racial marriages—mistreatment that is taking place not in a notional future but today. . . .

. . . Is the onrush of intermarriage that Professor Chen perceives sufficient to transform American society into a racial paradise without any need for education or structural change? . . . I have carefully read *Loving* [*v. Virginia*].[1] . . . [See Part 1—Ed.]

The statute that was used to void the Lovings' marriage and to hound them out of Virginia did not proscribe miscegenation as such; it simply rendered void all marriages between a "white person" and a "colored person." In other words, "colored persons"—be they African American, Native American, Asian American, Chicano(a)/Latino(a), or any admixture thereof—could marry each other as they would; the white race for whose protection the statute was designed would take no notice. A "white person" was defined to mean "such person as has no trace whatever of any blood other than Caucasian; but persons who have one-sixteenth or less of the blood of the American Indian and have no other non-Caucasic blood shall be deemed to be white persons." This seems at first a curious circumlocution; but the drafters of the statute apparently wrote it because [of] "the desire of all to recognize as an integral and honored part of the white race the descendants of John Rolfe and Pocahontas."[2]

This exception casts an interesting light on Professor Chen's thesis. Pocahontas, the daughter of Chief Powhatan, must stand (contemporary depictions of her as a multicultural heroine . . . notwithstanding) as the quintessential assimilationist. At the age of eighteen, she was abducted from her family and taken as a hostage by the English settlers at Jamestown. The colonists originally hoped to use Pocahontas as a lever with which to blackmail Powhatan into giving them back captured English prisoners and weapons and granting them favorable peace terms and "also a great quantitie of Corne." But . . . Pocahontas found that her father was unwilling to bargain for her freedom. Powhatan left her in the care of her captors, Sir Thomas Gates and Sir Thomas Dale, "the two highest ranking colonists in Virginia."

> Gates and Dale soon realized that if Pocahontas was to be used as pawn in their political chess game with the Indians, the abduction in itself was not going to produce checkmate. Several other moves would have to be made. . . . Thus, while they waited hopefully for some positive response from Chief Powhatan, they attended more or less deliberately to the transformation of Pocahontas into a "model Indian princess." Pocahontas was placed in the care of the Reverend Alexander Whitaker, who took her to his farm near Henrico. His women parishioners taught her to wear English dress, and he undertook the Pygmalion-like role of molding the young savage into an English lady. No longer was she permitted to offer sacrifices to Ahone at mealtime or repeat traditional Powhatan chants to the god. . . . Finally, in the spring of 1614, Whitaker reviewed her in the catechism, received her renunciation of paganism, heard her confession of faith in Jesus Christ, and through the sacrament of baptism renamed her Rebecca and welcomed her into the fellowship of the Church of England.[3]

The Englishman John Rolfe married the new Christian, even though, he admitted, her "education hath bin rude, her manners barbarous, her generation accursed, and her nutriture so discrepant in all things from myself."[4] Further, Rolfe was aware of the biblical and civil prohibitions against marrying "strange wives." However, Pocahontas's captors gave permission because the marriage would be "justification for attempting once again to press Chief Powhatan for a peaceful settlement of hostilities." Pocahontas herself agreed to marry Rolfe because of her pain at her father's indifference to her captivity. King James of England sought to prosecute Rolfe for high treason for the marriage, but his wrath subsided when the Privy Council assured him that Rebecca's issue would not be heirs to England's holdings in Virginia. Rolfe and his Rebecca were married on April 5, 1614. The next year, Rebecca Rolfe bore John Rolfe a son, Thomas Rolfe. In 1616 the Virginia Company prevailed upon her to come to England to help raise money for the colony. But once in England, her health quickly deteriorated, and in 1617 she died and was buried at Gravesend as "Rebecca Rolfe."

The life and death of this model princess is a painful story—of dual disinheritance and misunderstanding, of apostasy, exploitation, alienation, exile, and lonely, premature death; its legacy is the odd phenomenon of aristocratic Virginia segregationists who proudly (and often falsely) claimed her as an ancestor—who claimed proudly to be "white," in other words, only by an act of legislative grace.

What does the Pocahontas proviso prove? Nothing definitively. But to me it suggests that to hope that mere intermarriage can dismantle an oppressive scheme of domination is, at best, naive. The wishful thought behind it is that if my children, or their children, can simply look different from me, then those who hate me because of how I look will be transformed from enemies into brothers and friends.

Notes

Published originally in 81 Iowa Law Review 1489 (1996).

1. 388 U.S. 1 (1967).
2. *See id.* at 5 n.4. . . .
3. Grace Steele Woodard, Pocahontas 156 (1969). . . .
4. *Id.* at 158–59 (footnotes omitted). . . .

85

Unconvincing

Peter Kwan

. . . [I]t is far from clear that there exists a necessary relationship between racial hatred at individual levels and at societal levels, with the diminution of one necessitating the diminution of the other. As [Jim] Chen himself acknowledged [see Chapter 82—Ed.], "intermarriage and its handmaiden, interbreeding, are running riot in America," yet . . . it is difficult to claim that racial hatred is plummeting in American society as a result.

If Chen's Creole Republicanism contains the prescriptive element I suggest, then it follows that those who do not engage in interbreeding are not doing what one should to realize Chen's racial utopia. Fortunately, nonbreeders such as myself and others need not worry that nonsubscription to Chen's Creole Republicanism implies that we are not pulling our weight for racial harmony. . . .

[Another] problem with Chen's Creole Republicanism is his total reliance on faith that the creation of multiracial, or racially blended families will change racial beliefs and attitudes. As I have noted above, Chen writes that "[t]hrough the intensity and virtual involuntariness of the bonds created by marriage or parenthood, family relationships hold the key to the resolution of racial conflicts." However, as this quotation suggests, his notion of the family turns out to be rather restricted. It is a notion of the family as rooted in the institutions of marriage and parenthood. This is consistent with Chen's emphasis on interbreeding throughout his article. Chen's emphasis and reliance on marriage in turn privilege the position of men over women and heterosexual love and relationships over homosexual love and relationships. Protected by law and custom, marriage is an institution that has perpetuated and continues to preserve the subordinated position of women in a patriarchal society. Moreover, the heterosexist assumptions of marriage hardly need elaboration. Should anyone require evidence that marriage is regarded as a heterosexist domain, one need only recall the rhetoric supporting recent state and federal legislative initiatives drafted to preempt the possibility of having to recognize same-sex marriages from Hawaii. Like the military, conservatives of all stripes are taking up arms politically to "defend" marriage for heterosexuals. Quite beyond his discussion of marriage, Chen's discussion of family and interbreeding also contains heterosexist assumptions. Nowhere in his article does he discuss or mention lesbian and gay families, nor lesbian and gay parents.

In a way, one hopes that Chen's Creole Republic theory is right. For if the true path to racial harmony lies with integration, assimilation, interracial marriage and interracial breeding, then on that basis one can make a case in favor of interracial lesbian and gay marriages as well. The fairly obvious reasoning would go something like this: if the true path to racial harmony lies with interracial marriages, then by maximizing the chances and the number of such marriages occurring in a society, one would also maximize the chances of attaining racial harmony in that society. Thus, if a society prohibits interracial lesbian or gay marriages, or discourages them by denying legal recognition to interracial lesbian or gay marriages, these laws should be reversed or eliminated as barriers to racial harmony or as a form of state-mandated affirmative action policy. In addition, the state should fully recognize the interracial children of lesbian couples as children of a family consisting of two lesbian parents (particularly if it is an interracial lesbian couple) and even provide assistance and encouragement to lesbians (whether single or not) to be inseminated by sperm from a sperm donor of a different race. Gay men or lesbians who want to adopt across racial categories should also be given similar assistance and encouragement.

Naturally, one can argue that social prejudices against gay and lesbian marriages and family formations may be stronger than the desire to achieve interracial harmony; therefore, the urge to attain interracial harmony should not be a sufficient reason for the recognition of lesbian and gay marriages. But this, I submit, is not self-evidently so. It is not at all clear that as rational moral beings, one must *a priori* be more against gays and lesbians than racists. If one is convinced by Chen's Creole creed, then for those who abhor racism more than homosexuality, what I suggested in the previous paragraph may, *in conjunction with* the Creole creed, not sound so outrageous. Moreover, for those who are *equally* against gays and lesbians as they are against racists, then at the very least the acceptance or rejection of the measures described in the previous paragraph must be carefully and thoughtfully weighed against and considered in light of other factors, rather than rejected out of hand.

Alas, this world may not currently be ready for Chen's legal utopia. The reason for this is not surprising. The proper response to racism lies not in the institution of marriage alone, nor does it rely on procreation. The paths to "racial healing," as Harlon Dalton has so vividly written, lie with compassion, understanding, empathy, trust, patience, self-sacrifice, humility, and struggle.[1] These may be found when two people decide to marry or to create a baby. They may not. These attributes may also be found in other places—in friendship, in love between lesbian and gay couples who cannot marry, between heterosexual couples who choose not to or cannot bear children, in religion and within religious institutions, between the stranger and the Good Samaritan; or in the relationship between teacher and pupil.

Note

Published originally in 81 Iowa Law Review 1557 (1996).

1. Harlon L. Dalton, Racial Healing 96–101 (1995).

86

Postethnic America
Beyond Multiculturalism

David A. Hollinger

The most potent threat to the ethno-racial pentagon is probably the increase in avowed double minorities and multiple minorities. People whose descent is divided between African American and one or more of the other non-Euro-American blocs represent a special challenge. . . . The phenomenon of the double minority is not new. But persons of mixed African American and either indigenous or Latino descent were traditionally classified as belonging to any one or another of these three blocs, depending on the immediate social environment. The "one drop" rule [see Part 2—Ed.] was sometimes quietly compromised when non-Euro-American people were involved. But this compromise has become less quiet in the wake of two developments.

First, the greater pride taken in indigenous and Latino as well as African American descent in recent years has made more compelling the claims of each descent on any individual who happens to be heir to more than one of them. If the affirmation of a white heritage has traditionally risked bringing upon anyone of partially African American descent the charge of denying solidarity with black people and "wanting to be white," this difficulty diminishes with double minorities. The difficulty is not altogether absent in the case of affirmation of Latino descent, but now that Latinos, whether white or not, are in possession of their own race-equivalent bloc in the pentagon, the problem is smaller. Nor does the difficulty raised by "wanting to be white" loom large in the affirmation of safely nonwhite indigenous descent.

Second, there has recently emerged for the first time on a demographically significant scale a new kind of double minority: Asian African. The mixed race individuals who lobby the most adamantly for a new census category to accommodate them are often Asian African Americans. [See Part 4—Ed.]

If the "one drop" rule ever falls, it is mostly likely to do so under the specific pressure brought upon it by double and multiple minorities, who may then create an atmosphere in which this rule can weaken elsewhere, even where it now serves to separate the Euro-American and the African American segments of the pentagon. Even now, this strongest of all ethno-racial barriers is being chipped away as individuals of white and African American mixture are heard more frequently in public hearings trying to defy the "one drop" rule.

While the demand to add mixed race to the federal census can be construed as merely an effort to turn the pentagon into a hexagon, the logic of mixed race actually threatens to destroy the whole structure. A concern for the political cohesion of the African American bloc, in particular, has led a number of scholars and activists to resist this innovation. "Instead of draining the established categories of their influence," a writer for the *New Yorker* recently found some African American intellectuals in the process of concluding, "it would be better to eliminate racial categories altogether."[1] The various blocs of the pentagon are literally filled with mixed race people. Although this fact is noted the most often in regard to the African American bloc . . . , it is also visible in the indigenous bloc, where it has reached the point of a statistical apocalypse.

Tribal governments, which are legally empowered to decide who shall be counted as a member of any given tribe, apply radically divergent standards. [See Part 2—Ed.] At least one tribal government will enroll "those with 1/256 Indian blood heritage," reports Terry Wilson, while other tribal governments demand "one-half quantum from the *mother's* heritage," and still others follow an old practice of the U.S. government, classifying as Indian anyone with one-quarter indigenous ancestry.[2] In the meantime, no individual needs to obtain tribal authorization to self-identify on a census form as a member of the American Indian race. Thousands of Americans who had never before declared themselves to be indigenous peoples have done so in recent censuses in response, presumably, to the promise of entitlements and to the cultural reality of more positive public attitudes toward Indians. The number of Americans who identified themselves as American Indians on federal census forms increased by 259 percent between 1960 and 1990.[3]

No industrialized nation has so large a percentage of its population in prison as does the United States. And no such nation is producing so many mixed race people. These two facts about the United States are not directly related. Yet they bear mention together because of the antithetical implications these two realities have for a postethnic America. The extraordinary increase in marriage and reproduction across the lines of the ethno-racial pentagon presents a fundamental challenge to the authority of descent-defined categories. A critical mass of acknowledged mixed race people heightens the credibility of an ideal according to which individuals decide how tightly or loosely they wish to affiliate with one or more communities of descent. These Americans help move the society in a postethnic direction. In the meantime, the imprisoning of more and more of the population is an emblem for a complex of social and economic conditions that obstruct postethnicity and feed the suspicion that the United States is in the process of squandering whatever opportunity it may now have to become more postethnic.

Mixed race people are a powerful symbol for an opportunity long said to distinguish American society from that of most societies in Europe and Asia: the making of new affiliations. If this willingness to forge new communities and new cultural combinations has often been limited by racism, this willingness is nonetheless a common theme in American folklore, popular ideology, and law. Legal scholar Robert Post has pointed out that an important "function of law" according to much of American constitutional adjudication "is to protect the capacity of individuals to form new and different groups."[4] By contrast, British courts are more likely to assume that the law's function in relation to cultural diversity is rather to "protect the integrity of established and stable groups" within "a stable and established social fabric."[5] Mixed race people are performing a historic role at the present moment: they are reanimating a traditional American emphasis on the freedom of individual affiliation, and they are confronting the American nation with its own continued reluctance to apply this principle to ethno-racial affiliations.

Notes

Published originally in David A. Hollinger, Postethnic America: Beyond Multiculturalism 43–46, 165–66 (1995).

1. Lawrence Wright, *One Drop of Blood,* New Yorker, July 25, 1994, at 54–55.
2. Terry Wilson, *Blood Quantum: Native American Mixed Bloods, in* Racially Mixed People in America 121 (Maria P. P. Root, ed., 1992).
3. Wright, *supra*, at 53.
4. Robert Post, *Cultural Heterogeneity and the Law: Pornography, Blasphemy, and the First Amendment,* 76 California Law Review 320 (1988).
5. *Id.*

Review Questions

1. Will intermarriage and the increase in the number of mixed race people make the United States a more racially tolerant nation?
2. Is racial discrimination in the United States likely to subside over time with the growth of the mixed race population?
3. Is Professor Chen correct to see multiracialism as the answer to the racial woes of the United States?
4. In your experience, do mixed race people generally have a better understanding of racism and races than other people?

Suggested Readings

Keith Aoki, *The Scholarship of Reconstruction and the Politics of Backlash*, 81 Iowa Law Review 1467 (1996).

Margaret Chon, *Chon on Chen on Chang*, 81 Iowa Law Review 1535 (1996).

Harlon L. Dalton, Racial Healing (1995).

Dinesh D'Souza, The End of Racism: Principles for a Multiracial Society (1995).

Neil Gotanda, *Chen the Chosen: Reflections on Unloving*, 81 Iowa Law Review 1585 (1996).

Frederick Dennis Greene, *The Resurrection of Gunga Din*, 81 Iowa Law Review 1521 (1996).

Natsu Saito Jenga, *Unconscious: The "Just Say No" Response to Racism*, 81 Iowa Law Review 1503 (1996).

Fumitaka Matsuoka, The Color of Faith: Building Community in a Multiracial Society (1998).

J. Harvie Wilkinson III, *The Law of Civil Rights and the Dangers of Separatism in Multicultural America*, 47 Stanford Law Review 993 (1995).

Alfred C. Yen, *Unhelpful*, 81 Iowa Law Review 1573 (1996).

Part XII

Future Mixed Race Legal Studies

Part 12 sketches thoughts on the future of mixed race scholarship and the law. Emerging bodies of scholarly inquiry, including Critical Race Theory and other approaches, analyze the salience of race to law in the United States. (See, e.g., *Crossroads, Directions, and a New Critical Race Theory* [Francisco Valdes, Jerome McCristal Culp, and Angela P. Harris, eds., forthcoming 2002]; Richard Delgado and Jean Stefancic, *Critical Race Theory: An Introduction* [2001].) Critical Latina/o theory and burgeoning Asian American critical scholarship have moved the study of civil rights beyond a Black/White focus. (See, e.g., Juan F. Perea et al., *Race and Races: Cases and Resources for a Diverse America* [2000]; Richard Delgado and Jean Stefancic, *The Latino/a Condition: A Critical Reader* [1998]; Timothy Davis, Kevin R. Johnson, and George A. Martínez, *Readings on Race, Civil Rights, and the Law: A Multiracial Approach* [2001]; Robert S. Chang, *Disoriented: Asian Americans, Law, and the Nation-State* [2000].) Indeed, even a Critical White Studies, which interrogates "White" identity, has emerged. (See *Critical White Studies: Looking behind the Mirror* [Richard Delgado and Jean Stefancic, eds., 1997].) Is a critical mixed race studies on the horizon?

In this last chapter, Jean Stefancic outlines possible directions of emerging critical mixed race scholarship. It is literally the case that this chapter in many ways is yet to be written.

87

Multiracialism
A Bibliographic Essay and Critique

Jean Stefancic

I. Critical Multiracial Studies: Early Writing and Themes

Critical Multiracial Studies began in earnest in the years following the U.S. Supreme Court decision in *Loving v. Virginia,*[1] which struck down anti-miscegenation statutes in nearly one-half of the states. (See Part 1—Ed.) . . . With *Loving* and the loosening of immigration restrictions, both occurring in the mid-1960s, multiracialism came to the fore on the national scene. The number of interracial couples and children grew rapidly; scholarship addressing the legal status of multiracialism and multiracial people followed suit.

II. Major Themes and Writers

[The author reviews the major themes in the existing literature, including interracial relationships and marriage, racial identity, racial formation, Census categories and other categorizations, essentialism and intersectionality, transracial adoption and child custody, and the emergence of a multiracial society.—Ed.]

III. Future Directions

What issues lie ahead for critical scholars of multiracialism? . . . U.S. society has been slow to address these issues. Certainly, we will see more work dealing with dissolution or refinement of racial categories. We will also see discussions of the problems of multiracial persons (marriage, job discrimination, child custody) as well as their macrosocial correlates—voting power, representation, and political clout. As globalization of markets and industries proceeds, the role of multiracial (and multilingual) persons may become more prominent. Will multinational corporations co-opt diversity in the search for greater profits? As the number of mixed race persons increases, the possibilities of "passing for white" [see Part 3—Ed.] will be open to more and more persons. But as whites become a numerical minority and as power shifts to nonwhite groups, will this option begin to seem less attractive? Or, as sometimes happens today, will whites attempt to "pass" in the other direction?

What role will multiracial people play in the new society? At first, their number will be smaller than that of either whites or persons clearly nonwhite. Will embattled whites attempt to capture and manipulate them to do their bidding, as in the former South Africa, in an effort to resist the transfer of power? [See Part 10—Ed.] If so, will multiracials accept the offer? If whites succeed in remaining "the fairest of them all," multiracials may find that role tempting, but a decentering of white beauty and privilege is equally possible.

The concrete challenges posed by the numerical growth of multiracial people may prompt a wide-ranging reconsideration of the way in which legal categories and terms allocate power, authority, and other social goods. If so, Critical Multiracial Studies may prove to be the most subversive yet constructive branch of critical thought of all.

Note

1. 388 U.S. 1 (1967).

Review Questions

1. What is the future of mixed race scholarship? As racial mixture increases in complexity and frequency, will race and civil rights scholarship become more sophisticated?
2. Will, as Jean Stefancic states, "Critical Multiracial Studies . . . prove to be the most subversive yet constructive branch of critical thought of all"?
3. What would critical multiracial studies look like in terms of analysis of race, races, and civil rights? (See Lewis R. Gordon, *Critical "Mixed Race,"* 1 Social Identities 381 [1995], for consideration of this question.)
4. Do you think that mixed race issues are any different from those generally faced by minorities?

Suggested Readings

Timothy Davis, Kevin R. Johnson, and George A. Martínez, A Reader on Race, Civil Rights, and the Law: A Multiracial Approach (2001).

Critical White Studies: Looking behind the Mirror (Richard Delgado and Jean Stefancic, eds., 1997).

Lewis R. Gordon, *Critical "Mixed Race,"* 1 Social Identities 381 (1995).

Trina Grillo, *Anti-Essentialism and Intersectionality: Tools to Dismantle the Master's House,* 10 Berkeley Women's Law Journal 16 (1995).

Rachel F. Moran, Interracial Intimacy: The Regulation of Race and Romance (2001).

Juan F. Perea, Richard Delgado, Angela P. Harris, and Stephanie M. Wildman, Race and Races: Cases and Resources for a Diverse America (2000).

Author Index

Subject Index

About the Editor

Kevin R. Johnson is Associate Dean for Academic Affairs and Professor of Law and Chicana/o Studies at the University of California at Davis. He is the author of numerous articles and books on race, civil rights, and the law, including *How Did You Get to Be Mexican? A White/Brown Man's Search for Identity* (1999) and, with Timothy Davis and George A. Martínez, *A Reader on Race, Civil Rights, and the Law* (2001).